FOURTH EDITION

LEADERSHIP
Research Findings, Practice, and Skills

ANDREW J. DUBRIN
Rochester Institute of Technology

HOUGHTON MIFFLIN COMPANY
New York   Boston

To Camila

V. P., Editor-in-Chief: George Hoffman
Associate Sponsoring Editor: Susan M. Kahn
Editorial Associate: James R. Dimock
Project Editor: Claudine Bellanton
Editorial Assistant: Rachel B. Zanders
Production/Design Coordinator: Carol Merrigan
Manufacturing Manager: Florence Cadran
Marketing Manager: Steven Mikels

Cover photo: © Ernest Manewal/AlaskaStock.com

Printed in the U.S.A.

Library of Congress Control Number: 2002109431

ISBN: 0-618-30596-3

56789-MP-07 06 05

BRIEF CONTENTS

CHAPTER 2
Traits, Motives, and Characteristics of Leaders   31

CHAPTER 3
Charismatic and Transformational Leadership   62

CHAPTER 4
Leadership Behaviors, Attitudes, and Styles   94

CHAPTER 5
Contingency and Situational Leadership   133

CHAPTER 8
Influence Tactics of Leaders   230

CHAPTER 9
Developing Teamwork   258

CHAPTER 10
Motivation and Coaching Skills   289

CHAPTER 11
Creativity, Innovation, and Leadership   324

Welcome to the Fourth Edition of *Leadership: Research Findings, Practice, and Skills.* The new edition of this text is a thorough update of the Third Edition that has been used widely in both graduate and undergraduate courses in leadership.

Leadership has long been a key topic in several disciplines. In recent years, however, teaching and research about leadership have surged, with many students majoring in leadership. Many scholars and executives alike are convinced that effective leadership is required to meet most organizational challenges. More so than previously, business organizations recognize that leadership transcends senior executives. As a result, they require people with appropriate leadership skills to inspire and influence others in small teams, task forces, and units at all organizational levels.

Without effective leadership at all levels in private and public organizations, it is difficult to sustain profitability, productivity, and good customer service. In dozens of different ways, researchers and teachers have demonstrated that leadership does make a difference. Many curricula in business schools and other fields therefore now emphasize the development of leadership skills.

With the recent exposures of the dark side of business leadership, such as CEOs finding ways to create fortunes for themselves at the expense of employees and stockholders, more attention than ever is being paid to the values and personal characteristics of leaders. Toward that end, this text continues its emphasis on the qualities of effective leaders, and also adds an entire chapter on leadership ethics and social responsibilities.

PURPOSE OF THE TEXT

The purpose of this text is implied by its title—*Leadership: Research Findings, Practice, and Skills,* Fourth Edition. It is designed for undergraduate and graduate courses in leadership that give attention to research findings about leadership, leadership practice, and skill development. The text best fits courses in leadership that emphasize application and skill building. *Leadership* is also designed to fit courses in management development that emphasize the leadership aspect of management. In addition, it can serve as a supplement to organizational behavior or management courses that emphasize leadership.

The student who masters this text will acquire an overview of the voluminous leadership literature that is based both on research and experience. Information in this text is not restricted to research studies and syntheses of research and theories. It also includes the opinions of practitioners, consultants, and authors who base their conclusions on observations rather than empirical research.

What the text is *not* also helps define its nature and scope. This book does not attempt to duplicate the scope and purpose of a leadership handbook by integrating theory and research from several thousand studies. At the other extreme, it is not an evangelical approach to leadership espousing one leadership technique. I have attempted to find a midpoint between a massive synthesis of the literature and a trade book promoting a current leadership fad. *Leadership: Research Findings, Practice, and Skills,* Fourth Edition is designed to be a mixture of scholarly integrity, examples of effective leadership in action, and skill development.

It is important to note that this book is not intended to duplicate or substitute for an organizational behavior text. Because almost all organizational behavior texts are survey texts, they will mention many of the topics covered here. My approach, however, is to emphasize skill development and prescription rather than to duplicate basic descriptions of concepts and theories. I have tried to minimize overlap by emphasizing the leadership aspects of any concept presented here that might also be found in an organizational behavior or management text. Often when overlap of a topic exists, the presentation here focuses more on skill development than on a review of theory and research. For example, the section on motivation emphasizes how to apply basic explanations of motivation such as expectancy theory.

One area of intentional overlap with organizational behavior and management texts does exist: a review of all basic leadership theories. In such instances, however, I emphasize skill development and ideas for leadership practice stemming from these older theories.

FEATURES OF THE BOOK

To accomplish its purpose, this text incorporates many features into each chapter in addition to summarizing and synthesizing relevant information about leadership:

- **Chapter outlines** giving the reader a quick overview of the topics covered
- **Learning objectives** to help focus the reader's attention on major outcomes
- Boldfaced **key terms,** listed at the end of the chapter and defined in a **glossary** at the back of the text

- Real-life and hypothetical **examples** throughout the text
- **Leader in Action** inserts describing the leadership practices, behaviors, and personal attributes of real-life leaders
- **Self-assessment quizzes** relating to both skills and personal characteristics
- **Skill development** and **application exercises,** including role plays, to emphasize the activities and skills of effective leaders
- End-of-chapter **summaries** that integrate all key topics and concepts
- End-of-chapter **Guidelines for Action and Skill Development,** giving additional suggestions for improving leadership skill and practice
- **Discussion questions** and **activities** suited for individual or group analysis
- Two **Leadership Case Problems** per chapter, which illustrate the major theme of the chapter and contain questions for individual or group analysis
- **Internet Skill-Building Exercises** that reinforce the Internet as another source of useful information about leadership. Where possible, the student is directed toward an interactive exercise

FRAMEWORK OF THE TEXT

The text is a blend of description, skill development, insight development, and prescription. Chapter 1 describes the meaning, importance, and nature of leadership, including leadership roles. Chapter 2 identifies personal attributes associated with effective leaders, a subject that has experienced renewed importance in recent years. Charismatic and transformational leadership, an extension of understanding the personal attributes of leadership, is the subject of Chapter 3.

Chapter 4 surveys behaviors and practices associated with effective leadership in a variety of situations and describes leadership styles. Chapter 5 extends the study of styles by describing the contingency and situational aspects of leadership. Chapter 6 focuses on leadership ethics and social responsibility. Chapter 7 describes how leaders use power and politics. Chapter 8 extends this topic by analyzing the tactics leaders use to influence people. Chapter 9 describes how leaders foster teamwork and empower team members.

The next five chapters deal with specific leadership skills: motivating and coaching skills (Chapter 10), which constitute the basis of many leadership positions; creativity and innovation (Chapter 11); communication (including nonverbal and cross-cultural communication) and conflict resolution skills (Chapter 12); vision and strategy creation and knowledge management (Chapter 13); and effective leadership in international and culturally diverse settings (Chapter 14).

Chapter 15 concludes the book with an overview of approaches to leadership development and learning. In addition, there is a discussion of leadership succession and the importance of followership as part of effective leadership.

CHANGES IN THE FOURTH EDITION

The Fourth Edition of *Leadership: Research Findings, Practice, and Skills* is a thorough update of the Third Edition, along with a refocusing of several chapters. Some of the changes in this edition reflect the recent leadership information I felt should be included in the new edition. Many changes, though, reflect suggestions made by adopters and reviewers. For example, one reviewer suggested that I present information about crisis leadership. Another major change is the devotion of Chapter 6 to leadership ethics and social responsibility. To make way for the new material, I consolidated information about behaviors, attitudes, and styles into Chapter 4. Also, I have reduced coverage of classic explanations of leadership, such as Fiedler's theory and the Leadership Grid, that receive less attention today. A comprehensive list of changes appears in the "Transition Guide" at the beginning of the *Instructor's Resource Manual*. The following list highlights the changes to the Fourth Edition:

Changes Throughout the Text

- New, often interactive, web exercises at the end of each chapter
- Additional information on applying skill-building exercises and self-assessment quizzes, and explanations of their relevance
- New critical-thinking questions in the Leader in Action boxes
- Fourteen new chapter introductions
- Fourteen new Leader in Action boxes
- Twenty-five new cases and two updated cases from the Third Edition
- More emphasis on leaders of less well-known firms, middle managers in larger firms, and small-business owners
- New examples throughout
- Several new Guidelines for Action and Skill Development
- Several new Self-Assessment Quizzes
- More explicit emphasis on the development of interpersonal skills for leadership

Yet another important change is the more explicit emphasis on interpersonal skills. Aside from the cognitive aspects of leadership, such as strategic and creative thinking, leadership generally emphasizes interpersonal skills. We make frequent mention of the term *interpersonal skills* throughout the text to highlight its importance. The following five text examples demonstrate the importance of interpersonal skills to leadership:

- Chapter 2 describes the general personality traits associated with leadership effectiveness: self-confidence, humility, enthusiasm, trustworthiness, extroversion, assertiveness, emotional stability, and sense of humor and warmth. All of these traits contribute to interpersonal skill.

- Leadership Self-Assessment Quiz 3-1, The Emotional Expressiveness Scale, focuses on the vital interpersonal skill of effectively expressing feelings in the workplace.

- The Leader in Action box in Chapter 3 describes how Janine Bay of Ford Motor Company uses her interpersonal skills to achieve important work objectives.

- The Guidelines for Action and Skill Development in Chapter 6 give pointers on the interpersonal skill of relationship building.

- Leadership Skill-Building Exercise 7-1, Conducting an Empowerment Session, gives suggestions on several interpersonal skills such as encouraging self-leadership.

- The section "Using Recognition to Motivate Others," presented in Chapter 10, deals with the essential interpersonal skill of recognizing the accomplishments of group members.

Content Changes within Chapters

Chapter 3 presents a new set of company visions. Chapter 4 presents research comparing the job performance of male and female managers. Chapter 5 contains a current version of Victor Vroom's normative decision model and information on leadership during a crisis. Chapter 6 presents a table on the unethical and illegal behavior of seven well-known executives. Chapter 9 includes sections on group emotional intelligence, selecting team-oriented members, and using technology that enhances teamwork.

Chapter 10 describes the relevance of unrealistic goals for certain complex, high-level tasks, new evidence on the contribution of behavior modification to employee motivation, and ethical problems in the practice of executive coaching. Chapter 11 now includes a discussion of innovation, a separate description of the componential theory of individual creativity, and current business examples of thinking outside the box. In addition, sections are devoted to systematically collecting fresh ideas, engaging in playful physical activities to stimulate the mind, and adopting leadership practices than enhance innovation.

Chapter 12 contains new information on the steps necessary for successful persuasion, using anecdotes to communicate meaning, and the six basic principles of persuasion. The chapter also offers suggestions for enhancing cross-cultural communication through attention to individual differences in appearance and resolving conflict by searching for the value in the differences between the two sides. Chapter 13 examines the strategies of growth through acquisition and "peoplepalooza" (competitive advantage through hiring talented people).

Chapter 14 features empirical research from the United States Postal Service on the advantages of having a culturally diverse workforce, and discusses work orientation/leisure orientation as a cultural value. Also new are the coverage of

German managers' distinctive leadership style and insight into human motivation as a global leadership skill.

Chapter 15 includes information about the CEO Academy where new chief executives profit from the experiences of seasoned CEOs, examines shadowing as a way of gaining experience, and updates the key characteristics of a leadership development program. Also new is the discussion of the personal growth approach to development espoused by the Institute for Women's Leadership and the leadership pipeline model of succession and development. A final section examines the question, "Who will be the new top business leaders?" (The answer, of course, is some of the readers of this book, provided that they are qualified.)

SUPPLEMENTS

Several supplements that facilitate teaching accompany this edition.

Instructor's Resource Manual with Test Bank.   This manual features chapter outlines and lecture notes, possible answers to discussion questions and case questions, and comments on exercises in the text. The test bank portion includes 25 multiple-choice and 25 true/false questions for each chapter. The instructor's manual also describes how to use Computer-Assisted Scenario Analysis (CASA). Especially designed for helping students develop a contingency point of view, CASA is a user-friendly technique that can be used with any word processing software. It allows the student to insert a new scenario into the case and then re-answer the questions based on the new scenario. CASA helps to develop an awareness of contingency factors in making leadership decisions, as well as creative thinking. A brief version of CASA was published in the October 1992 issue of *The Journal of Management Education*. It also features an updated list of leadership-related web sites.

HMTesting.   This computerized version of the *Test Bank* allows instructors to select, edit, and add questions, or generate randomly selected questions to produce a test master for easy duplication. Online Testing and Gradebook functions allow instructors to adminster tests via their local area network or the World Wide Web, set up classes, record grades from tests or assignments, analyze grades, and compile class and individual statistics. This program can be used on both PCs and Macintosh computers.

Transparencies.   A set of nearly 70 transparencies offers visual teaching assistance to the instructor. Figures, tables, diagrams, and illustrations from the text are included.

Videos.   The video package focuses on important leadership and teamwork skills and concepts found throughout the text. A Video Guide with segment overviews and discussion questions is included.

Web Site.   The fourth edition of *Leadership* offers a web site. The **student site** contains new ACE Self-Tests, chapter links to companies highlighted in the text, and a Resource Center with links to professional organizations and other sites related to leadership. The password-protected **instructor site** provides electronic lecture notes from the *Instructor's Resource Manual* and PowerPoint® slides for downloading. These slides include summaries of key concepts, concise text, art, and other supplementary information to create a total presentation package.

ACKNOWLEDGMENTS

Any project as complex as this one requires a team of dedicated and talented people to see that it achieves its goals. First, I thank the many effective leaders whom I have observed in action for improving my understanding of leadership. Second, I thank the following professors who offered suggestions for improving this and previous editions:

Steven Barry
University of Colorado–Boulder

John Bigelow
Boise State University

Felipe Chia
Harrisburg Area Community College

Emily J. Creighton
University of New Hampshire

Justin Frimmer
Jacksonville University

Barry Gold
Pace University

George B. Graen
University of Cincinnati

Stephen G. Green
Purdue University

James R. Harris
North Carolina Agricultural and Technical State University

Paul Harris
Lee College

Nell Hartley
Robert Morris College

Winston Hill
California State University–Chico

Avis L. Johnson
University of Akron

Marvin Karlins
University of South Florida

David Lee
University of Dayton

Brian McNatt
University of Georgia

Ralph Mullin
Central Missouri State University

Linda L. Neider
University of Miami

Rhonda S. Palladi
Georgia State University

Joseph Petrick
Wright State University

Judy Quinn
Kutztown University

Clint Relyea
Arkansas State University

Robert Scherer
Wright State University

Marianne Sebok
Community College of Southern Nevada

Randall G. Sleeth
Virginia Commonwealth University

Ahmad Tootoonchi
Frostburg State University

John Warner
University of New Mexico

David Van Fleet
Arizona State University West

The editorial and production team at Houghton Mifflin also receives my gratitude. By name they are George Hoffman, Susan Kahn, Jim Dimock, Claudine Bellanton, and Rachel Zanders. Writing without loved ones would be a lonely task. My thanks therefore also go to my family members—Drew, Douglas and Gizella, Melanie, Rosie, Clare, and Camila.

A.J.D.

Andrew J. DuBrin is a Professor of Management in the College of Business at the Rochester Institute of Technology, where he teaches courses and conducts research in leadership, organizational behavior, and career management. He also served as department chairman and team leader in previous years. He received his Ph.D. in Industrial Psychology from Michigan State University.

DuBrin has business experience in human resource management, and consults with organizations and individuals. His specialties include leadership, influence tactics, and career development. DuBrin is an established author of both textbooks and trade books, and also contributes to professional journals, magazines, newspapers, and online shows. He has written textbooks on organizational behavior, management, and human relations. His trade books cover many topics including charisma, team play, coaching and mentoring, office politics, and self-discipline.

The Nature and Importance of Leadership

CHAPTER 1

In Tom Freston's world, the beat goes on—an endless, pulsing, driving rhythm that carries him and everyone who works for him along, like participants in the ultimate dance marathon, all facing the same challenge: Keep up or face elimination.

Mr. Freston's company, MTV Networks, is built around catering to the young, an audience with capricious tastes. Perhaps more than any other media company in the world, MTV Networks aims to take viewers from cradle (or just barely out of it) to grave (or the equivalent by commercial television standards, where viewers succumb to irrelevance at the age of 50).

As Tom sums it up, "In the youth market, nothing lasts forever." Except apparently, Tom Freston himself. Mr. Freston, 56, has been the chief executive of MTV Networks since 1987. His run has been so consistently successful that Mr. Freston faces industry speculation that he might be tapped for even larger media jobs, such as the number 2 spot at Viacom Inc., the parent company of MTV Networks. Freston, who says he continues to like his current job too much to leave it, has been at the youth appeal game for so long that many current viewers of his channels were not even born when he began running MTV.

Mr. Freston generally has a reputation for self-effacement, and he spreads the credit for the success of his company to the senior executives under him, many of whom have been with him for most of his run. But his own boss, Mel Karmazin, the president of Viacom, pinpoints the credit for the consistency of the company's success on Freston. When so many channels are doing well, Mr. Karmazin said, "it can't be a coincidence. It has to be because of the leadership." In a recent year, MTV Networks took in about 13 percent of Viacom's revenue.

Mr. Freston's leadership is distinctive for its sixties counterculture flavor, certainly fitting for the corporate culture of a company founded on the popularity of rock music. At a meeting of international MTV channels held in a museum in the South Beach area of Miami, Mr. Freston burnished his laid-back credentials by dressing in khaki shorts, a white T-shirt, and sandals to take in presentations from MTV operations in places like India, Italy, England, and Russia.[1]

The characterization of Tom Freston touches on many leadership topics to be covered in this book. Among these topics are that imaginative leadership can make a difference in an organization's success, that a successful leader works well with his or her team, and that leaders adapt to the situation. Our introductory chapter begins with an explanation of what leadership is and is not. We then examine how leaders make a difference, the various roles they play, and the major satisfactions and frustrations they experience. The chapter concludes with an explanation of how reading this book and doing the various quizzes and exercises will enhance your own leadership skills.

THE MEANING OF LEADERSHIP

By keeping his company's entertainment offerings fresh and alive, Tom Freston exerted leadership. He made a difference in company performance. His pleasant style of leadership combined with his intelligent business decisions influenced his executive team to remain with him for a long time in a volatile industry.

You will read about many other effective organizational leaders throughout this text. The common characteristic of these leaders is their ability to inspire and stimulate others to achieve worthwhile goals. The people who can accomplish these important deeds practice leadership. Compatible with the theme of this text, **leadership** is the ability to inspire confidence and support among the people who are needed to achieve organizational goals.[2]

About 40,000 research articles, magazine articles, and books have been written about leadership. As a consequence, leadership has been defined in many ways. Several other representative definitions of leadership are as follows:

- Interpersonal influence, directed through communication toward goal attainment
- The influential increment over and above mechanical compliance with directions and orders
- An act that causes others to act or respond in a shared direction
- The art of influencing people by persuasion or example to follow a line of action
- The principal dynamic force that motivates and coordinates the organization in the accomplishment of its objectives[3]
- A willingness to take the blame (as defined by legendary football quarterback Joe Montana)[4]

A major point about leadership is that it is not found only among people in high-level positions. Leadership is needed at all levels in an organization and can be practiced to some extent even by a person not assigned to a formal leadership position. For example, working as a junior accountant, a person might take the initiative to suggest to management that they need to be more careful about what they classify as a true sale. An extreme example of the importance of workers exercising leadership is Roadway Express, Inc. After implementing a program of employee involvement in productivity improvement, Roadway management concluded that to compete in an industry in which net profit margins are less than 5 percent in a good year, every one of its 28,000 employees must be a leader.[5]

The ability to lead others effectively is a rare quality. It becomes even more rare at the highest levels in an organization because the complexity of such positions requires a vast range of leadership skills. One manifestation of this problem is that firms in search of new leadership seek out a select group of brand-name executives.[6] Another manifestation of this problem is that companies now emphasize leadership training and development to create a new supply of leaders throughout the firm.

Leadership as a Partnership

The current understanding of leadership is that it is a long-term relationship, or partnership, between leaders and group members. According to Peter Block, in a

partnership the leader and the group members are connected in such a way that the power between them is approximately balanced. Block also describes partnership as the opposite of parenting (in which one person—the parent—takes responsibility for the welfare of the other—the child). Partnership occurs when control shifts from the leader to the group member, in a move away from authoritarianism and toward shared decision making.[7] Four things are necessary for a valid partnership to exist:

1. *Exchange of purpose.* In a partnership, every worker at every level is responsible for defining vision and values. Through dialogue with people at many levels, the leader helps articulate a widely accepted vision.

2. *A right to say no.* The belief that people who express a contrary opinion will be punished runs contrary to a partnership. Rather, a person can lose an argument but never a voice.

3. *Joint accountability.* In a partnership, each person is responsible for outcomes and the current situation. In practice, this means that each person takes personal accountability for the success and failure of the organizational unit.

4. *Absolute honesty.* In a partnership, not telling the truth to one another is an act of betrayal. When power is distributed, people are more likely to tell the truth because they feel less vulnerable.[8]

Block's conception of leadership as a partnership is an ideal to strive toward. Empowerment and team building—two major topics in this book—support the idea of a partnership.

Looking at leadership as a partnership is also important because it is linked to an optimistic view of group members, referred to as **stewardship theory.** This theory depicts group members (or followers) as being collectivists, pro-organizational, and trustworthy.[9] A collectivist is a person who is more concerned about the welfare of the group than about his or her personal welfare. Have you met many collectivists in the workplace?

Leadership Versus Management

To understand leadership, it is important to grasp the difference between leadership and management. We get a clue from the standard conceptualization of the functions of management: planning, organizing, directing (or leading), and controlling. Leading is a major part of a manager's job, yet a manager must also plan, organize, and control.

Broadly speaking, leadership deals with the interpersonal aspects of a manager's job, whereas planning, organizing, and controlling deal with the administrative aspects. Leadership deals with change, inspiration, motivation, and influence. Table 1-1 presents a stereotype of the differences between management and leadership. As is the case with most stereotypes, the differences tend to be exaggerated.

According to John P. Kotter, a prominent leadership theorist, managers must know how to *lead* as well as manage. Without being led as well as managed, or-

TABLE 1-1 Leaders Versus Managers

Leader	Manager
Visionary	Rational
Passionate	Business-like
Creative	Persistent
Inspiring	Tough-minded
Innovative	Analytical
Courageous	Structured
Imaginative	Deliberative
Experimental	Authoritative
Independent	Stabilizing
Shares knowledge	Centralizes knowledge
Trusting	Guarded
Warm and radiant	Cool and reserved
Expresses humility	Rarely admits to being wrong
Initiator	Implementer
Acts as coach, consultant, teacher	Acts as a boss
Does the right things	Does things right

Source: Genevieve Capowski, "Anatomy of a Leader: Where Are the Leaders of Tomorrow?" Management Review, *March 1994, p. 12; David Fagiano, "Managers Versus Leaders: A Corporate Fable,"* Management Review, *November 1997, p. 5; Keki R. Bhote,* The Ultimate Six Sigma *(New York: AMACOM, 2002).*

ganizations face the threat of extinction. Following are several key distinctions between management and leadership:

- Management is more formal and scientific than leadership. It relies on universal skills such as planning, budgeting, and controlling. Management is an explicit set of tools and techniques, based on reasoning and testing, that can be used in a variety of situations.

- Leadership, in contrast to management, involves having a vision of what the organization can become and mobilizing people to accomplish it.

- Leadership requires eliciting cooperation and teamwork from a large network of people and keeping the key people in that network motivated, using every manner of persuasion.

- Leadership produces change, often to a dramatic degree, such as by spearheading the launch of a new product or opening a new market for an old product. Management is more likely to produce a degree of predictability and order.

- Top-level leaders are likely to transform their organizations, whereas top-level managers just manage (or maintain) organizations.
- A leader creates a vision (lofty goal) to direct the organization. In contrast, the key function of the manager is to implement the vision. The manager and his or her team thus choose the means to achieve the end that the leader formulates.[10]

If these views are taken to their extreme, the leader is an inspirational figure and the manager is a stodgy bureaucrat mired in the status quo. But we must be careful not to downplay the importance of management. Effective leaders have to be good managers themselves, or be supported by effective managers. A germane example is the inspirational entrepreneur who is so preoccupied with motivating employees and captivating customers that internal administration is neglected. As a result, costs skyrocket beyond income, and such matters as funding the employee pension plan and paying bills and taxes on time are overlooked. In short, the difference between leadership and management is one of emphasis. Effective leaders also manage, and effective managers also lead.

The Impact of Leadership on Organizational Performance

An assumption underlying the study of leadership is that leaders affect organizational performance. Boards of directors —the highest-level executives of an organization—make the same assumption. A frequent antidote to major organizational problems is to replace the leader in the hope that the newly appointed leader will reverse performance problems. An example of this assumption in action took place in 2002 with Qwest Communications International Inc., the telephone and telecommunications company. The company had been facing a financial crisis and a federal accounting probe, so the board forced CEO Joseph Nacchio to resign. Qwest employees clapped enthusiastically when Nacchio's replacement, Richard C. Notebaert, was introduced at a meeting. Notebaert had been the CEO of Tellabs, Inc., a manufacturer of network equipment. Investors responded to this change with a buying surge that increased the battered company stock by 20 percent.[11]

Here we will review some of the evidence and opinion, pro and con, about the ability of leaders to affect organizational performance. The Leader-in-Action profile provides a positive example of the importance of effective leadership.

Research and Opinion: Leadership Does Make a Difference

The belief that leaders actually influence organizational performance and morale is so plausible that there is not an abundance of research and opinion that deals with this issue. (Nor do we have loads of studies demonstrating that sleeping reduces fatigue.) Here we look at a sample of the existing research and opinion.

Leader in Action

Martha Stewart of Martha Stewart Living Omnimedia, Inc.

"Martha Stewart" is a well-known brand name, a synonym for gracious living, a famous entrepreneur, and a business leader. As founder and CEO of Martha Stewart Living Omnimedia, Inc., Stewart has a succinct company mission: "We are the leading authority for the home" (*BusinessWeek*, January 8, 2001, p. 72). More than a year after going public in 1999, her company expanded its reach well beyond the garden and kitchen, including television specials. One of the company's most successful efforts was the introduction of Martha Stewart Everyday Kitchen, a housewares line for Kmart Corporation that includes 700 products from cookware to cutlery.

Investors strongly approve of Stewart's ability to get the most out of her content. Stewart has learned to stretch information over several media. Material from a special Halloween issue of her magazine reappeared on her TV show, web site, and syndicated column. "That strategy allows her not to be dependent on one medium," says a financial analyst. "It should be a model for other companies" (*BusinessWeek*, January 8, 2001, p. 72).

Meanwhile, Stewart is continuing to develop more magazine and TV specials. She shows no signs of slowing as she cooks, plants, and goes Alaskan dog sledding her way to being a media mogul. In her early sixties, Stewart strives relentlessly to expand her empire.

The Early Years. Stewart grew up the second of six children in an entrepreneurial household. Children were expected to earn their own pin money, so she organized neighborhood parties beginning at age 10. She modeled clothes as a teenager and attended Barnard College with a major in art history. After graduation she found a job as a Wall Street stockbroker. Stewart says, "We did a lot of research on a few companies. Then we would take those investment ideas and sell the hell out of them. I learned really what made a good company, what made a good investment, and what made a lot of money" (*BusinessWeek*, March 25, 2002, p. 56). Later, while staying home to raise her daughter, she launched a successful catering business.

The Business Model. Martha Stewart Living has eight core content areas that feed all the business segments of the company. The company's success hinges on leveraging good ideas, using the company research, and spreading that knowledge across as many different platforms as possible. An example of this synergy in action is taking information, converting it into a magazine article, and then converting it to a television program, or taking it to *CBS This Morning* and modifying and expanding the information. The magazine article might explain how to plant a tree, but the TV show might explain how to harvest the fruits from that tree—all based on the same research.

The Martha Stewart Impact on the Brand. Stewart was asked whether she thinks the brand transcends the person, and how her visibility influences the brand. She replied, "I don't know exactly. I'm still alive and well and vivacious and energetic. I think that my role model is Walt Disney. There are very few brands that were really started by a person, with a person's name that have survived as nicely as that. Estée Lauder has certainly survived beautifully despite Mrs. Lauder's absence from the business for about the last 15 years. I would like to engender that same kind of spirit and the same kind of high quality" (*BusinessWeek*, March 25, 2002, p. 60).

Stewart's Personal Style and Interpersonal Approach. Asked about the number 1 attribute that put her where she is today, Stewart replied, "I would like to think it's curiosity, it's energy, it's wanting to learn something new every day" (*BusinessWeek*, March 25, 2002, p. 60). Many people who have worked closely with Stewart think that her obsession for details about every facet of the business—including the quality of a coffee pot—contributes to her success as a businessperson. Fans of Stewart believe that her forceful personality inspires them, and her closest team members are handsomely compensated.

Some workers perceive Stewart's striving for perfection as an overcontrolling, smothering style of management. Other associates accuse Stewart of being a workaholic who expects the same dedication from everyone. Christopher Byron, a Stewart biographer, quotes insiders as saying that she is prone to berating and hurling obscenities at her employees.

Although Stewart works long and hard, she leaves some time for a celebrity lifestyle and for managing her investments. Among her friends is the highly social Samuel Waksal, CEO of the biotechnology firm ImClone Systems Incorporated. Waksal was arrested on charges of attempted insider trading, including tipping off family members that the Federal Drug Administration (FDA) had refused to review ImClone's application for the cancer treatment drug Erbitux. Several family members and Stewart sold about 178,440 shares of ImClone stock shortly after Waksal informed them of the FDA decision. Stewart sold all her 3,928 shares, but she claimed that her broker had standing instructions to sell ImClone if it fell below $60. Stewart was then placed in the awkward position of having to defend herself against charges of insider trading. Despite the distraction, Stewart maintained her active day-by-day presence at Martha Stewart Living.

At one point it appeared that Martha Stewart might serve prison time for insider trading, obstruction of justice, and fraud. Because of the scandal, Stewart gave up her prestigious seat on the board of the New York Stock Exchange. However, her business empire held up relatively well except for a plunge in the stock price. Even if Stewart were barred from being CEO of Martha Stewart Living Omnimedia, Inc., she would still be able to play a creative role in the company.

John Small, who launched the web site SaveMartha.com in July 2002, says that Stewart's fans have banded together online to form Kmart shopping parties and to purchase Martha Stewart Living stock as well as "Save Martha" T-shirts.

QUESTIONS

1. Does Martha Stewart appear to be more of a leader or more of a manager? Or a good combination of both?

2. Explain whether or not you would like to work for Martha Stewart.

SOURCE: *"Martha Stewart Thriving,"* BusinessWeek, *March 25, 2002, pp. 56, 60; Diane Brady, "Behind the Martha Mystique," review of Christopher Bryon,* Martha Inc.: The Incredible Story of Martha Stewart Living Omnimedia *(New York: Wiley, 2002), in* BusinessWeek, *April 22, 2002, p. 22; "The Top 25 Managers,"* BusinessWeek, *January 8, 2001, p. 72; Jerry Markon, "Stewart, Broker Differ on ImClone Sale,"* Wall Street Journal, *June 17, 2002, p. A3; Julie Creswell, "Will Martha Walk?"* Fortune, *November 25, 2002, pp. 121–124.*

A team of researchers investigated the impact of transactional (routine) and charismatic (inspirational) leadership on financial performance.[12] The researchers analyzed 210 surveys completed by senior managers from 131 *Fortune* 500 firms. Transactional and charismatic leadership styles were measured with a leadership questionnaire. Each participant was asked to think about the CEO of his or her company and rate that individual on the leadership scale. Participants also completed a questionnaire that measured *perceived environmental uncertainty* because an uncertain environment often makes having a strong leader more important. Organizational performance was measured as net profit margin (NPM), computed as net income divided by net sales. The performance data were gathered from public information about the companies.

The results of the study disclosed that (1) transactional leadership was not significantly related to performance, (2) charismatic leadership showed a slight positive relationship with performance, and (3) when the environment is uncertain, charismatic leadership is more strongly related to performance. The idea that a charismatic leader can influence the financial performance of a firm during uncertain times is supported by the experience of J.C. Penney Company, Inc. The retailing industry has faced a turbulent environment for many years. In 2001, J.C. Penney brought in Allen Questrom, an experienced and charismatic retail executive, to help revitalize the retail chain. Questrom quickly spearheaded efforts to close poorly performing stores, redecorate existing stores, enhance the merchandise, and centralize merchandise buying to bring about consistency in store offerings. Within one year, the venerable retail chain had regained market share and had become more profitable.[13]

Psychoanalyst Michael Maccoby conducted in-depth interviews with business executives twenty-five years ago. He concluded that organizations required a higher level of leadership than ever before to survive and prosper. Among the challenges Maccoby saw confronting organizations were increasing competition, technological advances, changing governmental regulations, and changing worker attitudes. These observations are relevant because they persist today.[14]

In addition to tangible evidence that leadership makes a difference, the perception of these differences is also meaningful. An understanding of these perceptions derives from **attribution theory,** the process of attributing causality to events. Gary Yukl explains that organizations are complex social systems of patterned interactions among people. In their efforts to understand (and simplify) organizational events, people interpret these events in simple human terms. One especially strong and prevalent explanation of organizational events is to attribute causality to leaders. They are viewed as heroes and heroines who determine the fates of their organizations.[15] The extraordinary success of Southwest Airlines Co. during the 1990s is thus attributed to Herb Kelleher, its flamboyant chief executive. Kelleher initiated no-frills, low-cost air service and built Southwest into a highly profitable airline. If we accept the logic of attribution theory in a positive way, most organizational successes are attributed to heroic leaders.

Research and Opinion: Formal Leadership Does Not Make a Difference

Leadership has a smaller impact on organizational outcomes than do forces in the situation, according to the antileadership argument. To personalize this perspective, imagine yourself appointed as the manager of a group of highly skilled investment bankers. How well your group performs could be attributed as much to their talent and to economic conditions as to your leadership. The three major arguments against the importance of leadership are substitutes for leadership, leadership irrelevance, and complexity theory.

Substitutes for Leadership.   At times competent leadership is not necessary, and incompetent leadership can be counterbalanced by certain factors in the work situation. Under these circumstances, leadership itself is of little consequence to the performance and satisfaction of team members. According to this viewpoint, many organizations have **substitutes for leadership.** Such substitutes are factors in the work environment that provide guidance and incentives to perform, making the leader's role almost superfluous.[16] Figure 1-1 shows four leadership substitutes: closely knit teams, intrinsic satisfaction, computer technology, and professional norms.

Closely knit teams of highly trained individuals.   When members of a cohesive, highly trained group are focused on a goal, they may require almost no leadership to accomplish their task. Several researchers have studied air traffic controllers who direct traffic into San Francisco, and pilots who land jet fighters on a nuclear aircraft carrier. With such groups, directive (decisive and task-oriented) leadership is seemingly unimportant. When danger is the highest, these groups rely more on each other than on a leader.

Intrinsic satisfaction.   Employees who are engaged in work they find strongly self-motivating, or intrinsically satisfying, require a minimum of leadership. Part of the reason is that the task itself grabs the worker's attention and energy. The worker may require a minimum of leadership as long as the task is proceeding smoothly. Many information technology firms provide a minimum of leadership and management to computer professionals, who may be totally absorbed in work such as creating software to link various parts of the organization together.

Computer technology.   Some companies today use computer-aided monitoring and computer networking to take over many of the supervisor's leadership functions. The computer provides productivity and quality data, and directions for certain tasks are entered into the information system. Even error detection and goal setting are incorporated into some interaction systems. Instead of asking a supervisor for assistance, some employees use the computer network to ask for assistance from other workers. (We could argue here that the computer is being used to control rather than to lead workers.)

FIGURE 1-1   Substitutes for Leadership

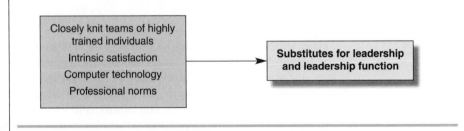

Professional norms.   Workers who incorporate strong professional norms often require a minimum of supervision and leadership. A group of certified professional accountants may not need visionary leadership to inspire them to do an honest job of auditing the books of a client or advising against tax fraud.

Although the leadership substitute concept has some merit, it reflects naiveté about the role of organizational leadership. Bass notes that self-management by groups and individuals requires delegation by a higher authority. In addition, higher-ranking managers provide guidance, encouragement, and support.[17]

A recent research study suggests that the theory of substitutes for leadership may be flawed and that leadership does indeed have an impact on group effectiveness. A team of researchers conducted a study of 49 organizations with at least 50 employees and two levels of management. The sample consisted of 940 employees and 156 leaders. Measures of substitutes for leadership were similar to the information presented above, such as "I am a member of a professional group whose standards and values guide me in my work." In short, the study suggested that "leadership matters." The likeability of the leader and whether the leader provides rewards for good performance were found to be the major correlates of performance.[18]

Leader Irrelevance.   According to the theorizing of Jeffrey Pfeffer, leadership is irrelevant to most organizational outcomes. Rather, it is the situation that must be carefully analyzed. Pfeffer argues that factors outside the leader's control have a larger impact on business outcomes than do leadership actions.[19] During the early 1990s the trend toward many people working at home created a surge in demand for personal computers and related telecommunications equipment. The sales boom in this electronic equipment could be better attributed to an outside force than to inspirational leadership within computer companies.

Another aspect of the leader irrelevance argument is that high-level leaders have unilateral control over only a few resources. Furthermore, the leader's control of these resources is limited by obligations to stakeholders like consumers and stockholders. Finally, firms tend to choose new organizational leaders whose values are compatible with those of the firm. The leaders therefore act in ways similar to previous leaders.

Jim Collins, who has extensively researched how companies endure and how they shift from average to superior performance, also doubts the relevance of leadership. According to his earlier research, corporate leaders are slaves of much larger organizational forces. Collins makes the analogy of children holding a pair of ribbons inside a coach and imagining they are driving the horse. It is not the leader's personality that makes a difference; more important is the organization's personality. A specific example given is that Jack Welch was the product rather than the producer of GE's success during his long reign.[20]

The leader irrelevance argument would have greater practical value if it were recast as a *leader constraint theory*, which would hold that leaders are constrained in what they can do, but still have plenty of room to influence others.

Complexity Theory.   Similar to the pessimistic outlook of leader irrelevance is the perspective of *complexity theory*, which holds that organizations are complex systems that cannot be explained by the usual rules of nature. Leaders and managers can do little to alter the course of the complex organizational system. The same view holds that a company's fate is determined by forces outside the leader/manager's control. Managers cannot predict which business strategies or product mixes will survive. The best they can hope for is to scramble or innovate in order to adapt to outside forces. Ultimately all companies will die, but at different times, because it is the system, not leadership and management, that dominates.[21]

LEADERSHIP ROLES

Another way to gain an understanding of leadership is to examine the various roles carried out by leaders. A *role* in this context is an expected set of activities or behaviors stemming from one's job. Leadership roles are a subset of the managerial roles studied by Henry Mintzberg and others.[22] Before reading ahead to the summary of leadership roles, you are invited to complete Leadership Self-Assessment Quiz 1-1.

Leading is a complex activity, so it is not surprising that Mintzberg and other researchers identified nine roles that can be classified as part of the leadership function of management.

1. *Figurehead.* Leaders, particularly high-ranking managers, spend some part of their time engaging in ceremonial activities, or acting as a figurehead. Four specific behaviors fit the figurehead role of a leader:
   a. entertaining clients or customers as an official representative of the organization
   b. making oneself available to outsiders as a representative of the organization
   c. serving as an official representative of the organization at gatherings outside the organization
   d. escorting official visitors

2. *Spokesperson.* When a manager acts as a spokesperson, the emphasis is on answering letters or inquiries and formally reporting to individuals and groups outside the manager's direct organizational unit. As a spokesperson, the managerial leader keeps five groups of people informed about the unit's activities, plans, capabilities, and possibilities (vision):
   a. upper-level management
   b. clients or customers
   c. other important outsiders such as labor unions
   d. professional colleagues
   e. the general public

   Dealing with outside groups and the general public is usually the responsibility of top-level managers.

Readiness for the Leadership Role

INSTRUCTIONS   Indicate the extent to which you agree with each of the following statements, using the following scale: 1, disagree strongly; 2, disagree; 3, neutral; 4, agree; 5, agree strongly.

1.	It is enjoyable having people count on me for ideas and suggestions.	1 2 3 4 5
2.	It would be accurate to say that I have inspired other people.	1 2 3 4 5
3.	It's a good practice to ask people provocative questions about their work.	1 2 3 4 5
4.	It's easy for me to compliment others.	1 2 3 4 5
5.	I like to cheer people up even when my own spirits are down.	1 2 3 4 5
6.	What my team accomplishes is more important than my personal glory.	1 2 3 4 5
7.	Many people imitate my ideas.	1 2 3 4 5
8.	Building team spirit is important to me.	1 2 3 4 5
9.	I would enjoy coaching other members of the team.	1 2 3 4 5
10.	It is important to me to recognize others for their accomplishments.	1 2 3 4 5
11.	I would enjoy entertaining visitors to my firm even if it interfered with my completing a report.	1 2 3 4 5
12.	It would be fun for me to represent my team at gatherings outside our department.	1 2 3 4 5
13.	The problems of my teammates are my problems too.	1 2 3 4 5
14.	Resolving conflict is an activity I enjoy.	1 2 3 4 5
15.	I would cooperate with another unit in the organization even if I disagreed with the position taken by its members.	1 2 3 4 5
16.	I am an idea generator on the job.	1 2 3 4 5
17.	It's fun for me to bargain whenever I have the opportunity.	1 2 3 4 5
18.	Team members listen to me when I speak.	1 2 3 4 5

19. People have asked me to assume the leadership of an   1 2 3 4 5
activity several times in my life.

20. I've always been a convincing person.   1 2 3 4 5

Total score: _____

SCORING AND INTERPRETATION   Calculate your total score by adding the numbers circled. A tentative interpretation of the scoring is as follows:

- 90–100   high readiness for the leadership role
- 60–89   moderate readiness for the leadership role
- 40–59   some uneasiness with the leadership role
- 39 or less   low readiness for the leadership role

If you are already a successful leader and you scored low on this questionnaire, ignore your score. If you scored surprisingly low and you are not yet a leader, or are currently performing poorly as a leader, study the statements carefully. Consider changing your attitude or your behavior so that you can legitimately answer more of the statements with a 4 or a 5. Studying the rest of this text will give you additional insights that may be helpful in your development as a leader.

3. *Negotiator.* Part of almost any manager's job description is trying to make deals with others for needed resources. Researchers have identified three specific negotiating activities:
   a. bargaining with superiors for funds, facilities, equipment, or other forms of support
   b. bargaining with other units in the organization for the use of staff, facilities, equipment, or other forms of support
   c. bargaining with suppliers and vendors for services, schedules, and delivery times

4. *Coach and motivator.* An effective leader takes the time to coach and motivate team members. This role includes four specific behaviors:
   a. informally recognizing team members' achievements
   b. providing team members with feedback concerning ineffective performance
   c. ensuring that team members are informed of steps that can improve their performance
   d. implementing rewards and punishments to encourage and sustain good performance

5. *Team builder.* A key aspect of a leader's role is to build an effective team. Activities contributing to this role include:
   a. ensuring that team members are recognized for their accomplishments, such as through letters of appreciation
   b. initiating activities that contribute to group morale, such as giving parties and sponsoring sports teams
   c. holding periodic staff meetings to encourage team members to talk about their accomplishments, problems, and concerns

6. *Team player.* Related to the team-builder role is that of the team player. Three behaviors of team players are:
   a. displaying appropriate personal conduct
   b. cooperating with other units in the organization
   c. displaying loyalty to superiors by supporting their plans and decisions fully

7. *Technical problem solver.* It is particularly important for supervisors and middle managers to help team members solve technical problems. Two activities contributing to this role are:
   a. serving as a technical expert or adviser
   b. performing individual contributor tasks on a regular basis, such as making sales calls or repairing machinery

8. *Entrepreneur.* Although not self-employed, managers who work in large organizations have some responsibility for suggesting innovative ideas or furthering the business aspects of the firm. Three entrepreneurial leadership role activities are:
   a. reading trade publications and professional journals to keep up with what is happening in the industry and profession
   b. talking with customers or others in the organization to keep aware of changing needs and requirements
   c. getting involved in situations outside the unit that could suggest ways of improving the unit's performance, such as visiting other firms, attending professional meetings or trade shows, and participating in educational programs

9. *Strategic planner.* Top-level managers engage in strategic planning, usually assisted by input from others throughout the organization. Carrying out the strategic-planner role enables the manager to practice strategic leadership. Specific activities involved in this role include:
   a. setting a vision and direction for the organization
   b. helping the firm deal with the external environment
   c. helping develop organizational policies

A common thread in the leadership roles of a manager is that the managerial leader in some way inspires or influences others. An analysis in the *Harvard Business Review* concluded that the most basic role for corporate leaders is to release the human spirit that makes initiative, creativity, and entrepreneurship possible.[23] An important practical implication is that managers at every level can exercise leadership. For example, a team leader can make an important contribution to the firm's thrust for quality by explaining to team members how to minimize duplications in a mailing list. Leadership Skill-Building Exercise 1-1 provides additional insights into the various leadership roles.

Up to this point we have described the meaning of leadership, how leadership affects organizational performance, and the many activities carried out by leaders. You have had an opportunity to explore your attitudes toward occupying the leadership role. We now further personalize information about leadership.

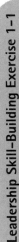

Leadership Skill-Building Exercise 1–1

Identifying Leadership Roles

Three months into his job at J.C. Penney Company, Inc., Allen Questrom delivers a spiel and he's sticking to it. It's the Questrom way: dole out the broad vision and repeat it until everyone gets it right. He is giving J.C. Penney employees two to five years to turn the ship around. He doesn't plan to do it alone. He's not taking any guarantees, but he's comfortable being captain.

"A business isn't run by one person. It's run by teams," said J.C. Penney's chairman and chief executive officer during an interview at the company's Plano, Texas, headquarters. "My job is to set the objectives and get people to understand them and execute them." He's asking employees who are helping to rebuild the J.C. Penney organization to rethink everything. A major challenge Questrom faces is that some critics think that J.C. Penney's fashions are tired, and its prices are too high.

Questrom joined J.C. Penney in September from Barneys New York but is best known for his long tenure at Federated Department Stores, Inc. He brought that company out of bankruptcy and acquired the Macy's and Broadway chains, which gave Federated a strong market share up and down both coasts. The veteran retailer has been charming employees, customers, and creditors for years. Particularly impressive has been his ability to turn around prestigious stores that have fallen on hard times. In addition to Federated, Questrom helped revive Neiman Marcus and Barneys.

Questrom says he believes in the J.C. Penney brand and he is trying to get back to J.C. Penney's roots as the department store of choice for middle-income Americans. (J.C. Penney also owns the Eckerd drugstore chain.) But he's not sentimental, and he's not wedded to ideas that haven't worked. In November 2000, J.C. Penney reported its first loss from operations in the history of the company. The retailer, which is almost 100 years old, is being called a dinosaur. Questrom has this to say about the task he faces:

"I spend time thinking about getting this company in order. What difference does it make if it's 100 or 10 or 20? What's meaningful to me is whether our stores are current. I would like this company to be successful on its 100th anniversary. I've only been here a few months, and I see a very loyal but an unhappy group of people."

Questrom says the only way to boost morale is to start making money again. Profit will take care of the stock price as well. J.C. Penney's market value has declined to about $3 billion from a peak of $20 billion two years ago. Since the mid-1990s, the retailer has lost customers to discount chains such as Target and Wal-Mart and to moderate-priced retailers, including Kohl's and Old Navy, as they have expanded nationwide. Becoming profitable is going to be painful because it means change, Questrom says. To offer competitive prices to shoppers, the company needs a more competitive cost structure, which means cutting costs.

Questrom says J.C. Penney's department stores must have the right assortment of merchandise at competitive prices. The only way to do that is to centralize the buying decisions. Headquarters picks and delivers the merchandise, and store personnel focus on running the stores. J.C. Penney fell behind its competitors when it didn't centralize sooner, Questrom says. It is no longer efficient to have 1,150 stores each making that many decisions about merchandise. It's slow, expensive, and confusing to the customers. It also prevents the company from developing a national message.

Questrom says that some of the immediacy of having vendors knocking on your door every day was lost when the company moved to Dallas from New York in 1988. "We have to be aware of what's happening in the fashion world and bring that to middle America at great values." He's considering adding offices in New York and Los Angeles to put J.C. Penney merchandisers closer to the biggest concentration of vendors.

One of Questrom's first moves was to close 44 of J.C. Penney's 1,000 stores and lay off some 5,000 staff, taking a restructuring charge of $275 million. "We're looking at the entire organization and looking at getting rid of things we wouldn't have if we were just starting out as a new company." Another part of Questrom's turnaround plan is to recruit outsiders to key positions, to help enliven the J.C. Penney corporate culture. He is also remodeling stores to make them less cluttered and better lit. Questrom looks forward to the challenge of helping revive J.C. Penney. He says, "I've been involved most of my life in turnaround situations. I look at this as another mountain to climb."

Retail analysts think that the biggest challenge at J.C. Penney is to redefine what the brand is about. Questrom emphasizes that the company caters to the broad middle market, where the bulk of consumers are. J.C. Penney's national presence, along with a good catalog and online business, are also assets. Analysts at Morningstar.com were particularly harsh about the problems facing J.C. Penney and Questrom: "The company's problems are nothing short of humongous, and include an inefficient supply chain, outdated apparel offerings, a stodgy brand name, and a money-losing drugstore operation."

Department stores haven't been viewed as a growth business in the retail industry. But even they can operate in a very profitable way, Questrom says. "Federated and May [Department Stores] can grow earnings 12 percent to 15 percent a year, which is a lot more money than the Amazon.com's can do."

SKILL DEVELOPMENT   Jot down all the leadership roles you perceived in the case history just presented. Specify the activity and the role it reflects. Refer to the nine leadership roles described previously. You might also want to visit www.jcpenney.com to see how well the store is doing. Go beyond the advertising to search the page for investor information.

SOURCE: *"Penney's Chief Ready to Rebuild,"* Knight Ridder, *January 2, 2001; Stephanie Anderson, "Can an Outsider Fix J.C. Penney?"* BusinessWeek, *February 12, 2001, pp. 56–58;* www.jcpenney.com; http://news/Wire/O,12302837,00.ht.

THE SATISFACTIONS AND FRUSTRATIONS OF BEING A LEADER

The term *leader* has a positive connotation for most people. To be called a leader is generally better than to be called a follower or a subordinate. (Note that the term *follower* has virtually disappeared in organizations, and the term *subordinate* has fallen out of favor. The preferred term for a person who reports to a leader or manager is *team member, group member,* or *associate.* Researchers, however, continue to use the terms *subordinate* and *follower* for technical purposes.) Yet being a leader, such as a team leader, vice president, or COO (chief operating officer) does not always bring personal satisfaction. Some leadership jobs are more fun than others, such as being the leader of a successful group with cheerful team members.

Because most of you are contemplating becoming a leader or moving further into a leadership role, it is worthwhile to examine some of the potential satisfactions and frustrations many people find in being an organizational leader.

Satisfactions of Leaders

The type of satisfactions that you might obtain from being a formal leader depends on your particular leadership position. Factors such as the amount of money you are paid and the type of people in your group influence your satisfaction. There are seven sources of satisfaction that leaders often experience.

1. *A feeling of power and prestige.* Being a leader automatically grants you some power. Prestige is forthcoming because many people think highly of people who are leaders. In many organizations, top-level leaders are addressed as Mr., Mrs., or Ms., whereas lower-ranking people are referred to by their surnames.

2. *A chance to help others grow and develop.* A leader works directly with people, often teaching them job skills, serving as a mentor, and listening to personal problems. Part of a leader's job is to help other people become managers and leaders. A leader often feels as much of a "people helper" as does a human resources manager or a counselor.

3. *High income.* Leaders, in general, receive higher pay than team members, and executive leaders in major business corporations typically earn several million dollars per year. A handful of business executives receive compensation of over $100 million per year. If money is an important motivator or satisfier, being a leader has a built-in satisfaction. In some situations a team leader earns virtually the same amount of money as other team members. Occupying a leadership position, however, is a starting point on the path to high-paying leadership positions.

4. *Respect and status.* A leader frequently receives respect from group members. He or she also enjoys a higher status than people who are not occupy-

ing a leadership role. Status accompanies being appointed to a leadership position on or off the job. When an individual's personal qualifications match the position, his or her status is even higher.

5. *Good opportunities for advancement.* Once you become a leader, your advancement opportunities increase. Obtaining a leadership position is a vital first step for career advancement in many organizations. Staff or individual contributor positions help broaden a person's professional experience, but most executives rise through a managerial path.

6. *A feeling of "being in on" things.* A side benefit of being a leader is that you receive more inside information. For instance, as a manager you are invited to attend management meetings. In those meetings you are given information not passed along to individual contributors. One such tidbit might be plans for expansion or downsizing.

7. *An opportunity to control money and other resources.* A leader is often in the position of helping to prepare a department budget and authorize expenses. Even though you cannot spend this money personally, knowing that your judgment on financial matters is trusted does provide some satisfaction. Many leaders in both private and public organizations control annual budgets of several million dollars.

Dissatisfactions and Frustrations of Leaders

About one out of ten people in the work force is classified as a supervisor, administrator, or manager. Not every one of these people is a true leader. Yet the problems these people experience often stem from the leadership portions of their job. Many individual contributors refuse to accept a leadership role because of the frustrations they have seen leaders endure. The frustrations experienced by a wide range of people in leadership roles revolve around the problems described next.

1. *Too much uncompensated overtime.* People in leadership jobs are usually expected to work longer hours than other employees. Such unpaid hours are called *casual overtime.* People in organizational leadership positions typically spend about fifty-five hours per week working. During peak periods of peak demands, this figure can surge to eighty hours per week.

2. *Too many "headaches."* It would take several pages to list all the potential problems leaders face. Being a leader is a good way to discover the validity of Murphy's law: "If anything can go wrong, it will." A leader is subject to a batch of problems involving people and things. Many people find that a leadership position is a source of stress, and many managers experience burnout.

3. *Not enough authority to carry out responsibility.* People in managerial positions complain repeatedly that they are held responsible for things over which they have little control. As a leader, you might be expected to work with an ill-performing team member, yet you lack the power to fire him or her. Or you might be expected to produce high-quality service with too small a staff and no authority to become fully staffed.

4. *Loneliness.* As Secretary of State and former five-star general Colin Powell says, "Command is lonely." The higher you rise as a leader, the lonelier you will be in a certain sense. Leadership limits the number of people in whom you can confide. It is awkward to confide negative feelings about your employer to a team member. It is equally awkward to complain about one group member to another. Some people in leadership positions feel lonely because they miss being "one of the gang."

5. *Too many problems involving people.* A major frustration facing a leader is the number of human resources problems requiring action. The lower your leadership position, the more such problems you face. For example, the office supervisor spends more time dealing with problem employees than does the chief information officer.

6. *Too much organizational politics.* People at all levels of an organization, from the office assistant to the chairperson of the board, must be aware of political factors. Yet you can avoid politics more easily as an individual contributor than you can as a leader. As a leader you have to engage in political byplay from three directions: below, sideways, and upward. Political tactics such as forming alliances and coalitions are a necessary part of a leader's role. Another troublesome aspect of organizational politics is that there are

---

TABLE 1–2   The Nine Dilemmas Leaders Face

Broad-based leadership versus high-visibility leadership. Should the leader share leadership responsibilities widely, or be a highly visible charismatic leader?

Independence versus dependence. Should the organizational units work competitively against one another, or should they cooperate highly in a team mode?

Long term versus short term. Should the leader invest in projects with a long-term payout at the expense of actions that bring immediate results and profits?

Creativity versus discipline. Should imaginative thinking be encouraged at the expense of disciplined activities such as meeting budgets and deadlines?

Trust versus change. To maintain a high level of trust, it is important for the leader not to make too many changes, yet change is necessary to move the organization forward.

Bureaucracy busting versus economies of scale. If the leader decentralizes, there is less hierarchy, yet the organization may lose out on the cost savings possible from manufacturing or purchasing on a large scale.

Productivity versus people. To attain high productivity, it may be necessary to push people to a point where their health and personal lives are disrupted.

Leadership versus managerial and technical capability. The people-and-vision skills that produce good leadership are quite different from the managerial and technical skills required for efficient operations.

Revenue growth versus cost containment. Organizational growth requires free spending, but an organization must still control costs.

Source: Assembled and adapted from information in Thomas A. Stewart, "The Nine Dilemmas Leaders Face," Fortune, March 18, 1996, pp. 112–113.

people lurking to take you out of the game, particularly if you are changing the status quo. These enemies within might attack you directly in an attempt to shift the issue to your character and style and avoid discussing the changes you are attempting to implement. Or, your superiors might divert you from your goals by keeping you overwhelmed with the details of your change effort.[24] Furthermore, backstabbers may agree with you in person but badmouth you to others.

7. *The pursuit of conflicting goals.* A major challenge leaders face is to navigate among conflicting goals. The central theme of these dilemmas is attempting to grant others the authority to act independently, yet still getting them aligned or pulling together for a common purpose. As identified by a group of senior bank executives, these dilemmas are listed in Table 1-2.[25] Many of the topics relating to these conflicting goals are discussed at later points in the text.

A FRAMEWORK FOR UNDERSTANDING LEADERSHIP

Many different theories and explanations of leadership have been developed because of the interest in leadership as a practice and as a research topic. Several attempts have been made to integrate the large number of leadership theories into one comprehensive framework.[26] The framework presented here focuses on the major sets of variables that influence leadership effectiveness. The basic assumption underlying the framework can be expressed in terms of a simple formula with a profound meaning:

$$L = f(l, gm, s)$$

The formula means that the leadership process is a function of the leader, group members (or followers), and other situational variables.[27] In other words, leadership does not exist in the abstract but takes into account factors related to the leader, the person or persons being led, and a variety of forces in the environment. A charismatic and visionary leader might be just what a troubled organization needs to help it achieve world-class success. Yet a group of part-time telemarketers might need a more direct and focused type of leader to help them when their telephone calls mostly meet with abrupt rejection from the people solicited.

The model presented in Figure 1-2 extends this situational perspective.[28] According to this model, leadership can best be understood by examining its key variables: leader characteristics and traits, leader behavior and style, group member characteristics, and the internal and external environment. At the right side of the framework, **leadership effectiveness** refers to attaining desirable outcomes such as productivity, quality, and satisfaction in a given situation. Whether or not the leader is effective depends on the four sets of variables in the box.

Beginning at the top of the circle, *leader characteristics and traits* refers to the inner qualities, such as self-confidence and problem-solving ability, that help a

FIGURE 1-2   A Framework for Understanding Leadership

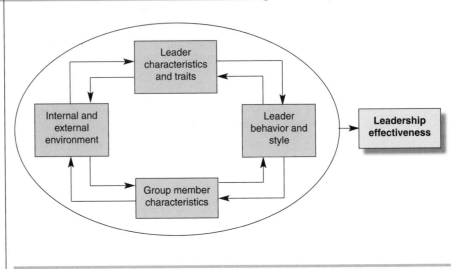

Source: *Managing Today! by Stephen P. Robbins, © 1997. Reprinted by permission of Prentice-Hall Inc. Upper Saddle River, N.J.*

leader function effectively in many situations. *Leader behavior and style* refers to the activities engaged in by the leader, including his or her characteristic approach, that relate to his or her effectiveness. A leader who frequently coaches group members and practices participative leadership, for example, might be effective in many circumstances.

Group member characteristics refers to attributes of the group members that could have a bearing on how effective the leadership attempt will be. Intelligent and well-motivated group members, for example, help the leader do an outstanding job. The *internal and external environment* also influences leadership effectiveness. A leader in a culturally diverse environment, for example, will need to have multicultural skills to be effective. All of the topics in this text fit somewhere into this model, and the fit will be more obvious at some places than at others. Table 1-3 outlines how the elements of the leadership model line up with chapters in the text.

The arrows connecting the four sets of variables in the model suggest a reciprocal influence among them. Some of these linkages are stronger than others. The most pronounced linkage is that a leader's characteristics and traits will typically influence the leader's style. If a given individual is extroverted, warm, and caring, it will be natural for him or her to adopt a people-oriented leadership style. Another linkage is that the group members' characteristics might influence the leader's style. If the members are capable and self-sufficient, the leader is likely to choose a leadership style that grants freedom to the group. It will be easier for the leader to empower these people. A final linkage is that the internal and external environment can influence or mediate the leader's traits to some extent. In an environment in which creativity and risk taking are fostered, leaders are more likely to give expression to their tendencies toward creative problem solving and risk taking.

Relationship Between Chapter Topics and the Framework for
TABLE 1–3   Understanding Leadership

Component of the Model	Relevant Chapter or Chapters
Leader characteristics and traits	Chapter 2, "Traits, Motives, and Characteristics of Leaders"
	Chapter 3, "Charismatic and Transformational Leadership"
	Chapter 6, "Leadership Ethics and Social Responsibility"
	Chapter 11, "Creativity, Innovation, and Leadership"
	Chapter 12, "Communication and Conflict Resolution Skills"
Leader behavior and style	Chapter 4, "Leadership Behaviors, Attitudes and Styles"
	Chapter 6, "Leadership Ethics and Social Responsibility"
	Chapter 8, "Influence Tactics of Leaders"
	Chapter 9, "Developing Teamwork"
Group member characteristics	Chapter 5, "Contingency and Situational Leadership"
	Chapter 10, "Motivation and Coaching Skills"
Internal and external environment	Chapter 13, "Strategic Leadership and Knowledge Management"
	Chapter 14, "International and Culturally Diverse Aspects of Leadership"
	Chapter 7, "Power, Politics, and Leadership"
	Chapter 15, "Leadership Development, Succession, and Followership"

SKILL DEVELOPMENT IN LEADERSHIP

Leadership skills are in high demand. A survey indicated that executives seeking candidates for management jobs listed leadership skills as the top attributes they wanted. Forty-seven percent of the executives surveyed listed leadership first, followed by communication skills at 35 percent.[29] Although students of leadership will find this information encouraging, developing leadership skills is more complex than developing a structured skill such as sending photos over the Internet. Nevertheless, you can develop leadership skills by studying this text, which follows a general learning model:

1. *Conceptual knowledge and behavioral guidelines.* Each chapter in this text presents useful information about leadership, including a section titled "Guidelines for Action and Skill Development."

2. *Conceptual information demonstrated by examples and brief descriptions of leaders in action.* Much can be learned by reading about how effective (or ineffective) leaders operate.

3. *Experiential exercises.* The text provides an opportunity for practice and personalization through cases, role plays, and self-assessment quizzes.

Self-quizzes are emphasized here because they are an effective method of helping you personalize the information, thereby linking conceptual information to yourself. For example, you will read about the importance of assertiveness in leadership and also complete an assertiveness quiz.

4. *Feedback on skill utilization, or performance, from others.* Feedback exercises appear at several places in the text. Implementing some of the skills outside of the classroom will provide additional opportunities for feedback.

5. *Practice in natural settings.* As just implied, skill development requires active practice. A given skill has to be practiced many times in natural settings before it becomes integrated comfortably into a leader's mode of operation. A basic principle of learning is that practice is necessary to develop and improve skills.[30] Suppose, for example, that you read about giving advice in the form of questions, as described in Chapter 10. If you practice this skill at least six times in live settings, you will probably have acquired an important new skill for coaching others.

SUMMARY

Leadership is the ability to inspire confidence in and support among the people who are needed to achieve organizational goals. Leading is a major part of a manager's job, but a manager also plans, organizes, and controls. Leadership is said to deal with change, inspiration, motivation, and influence. In contrast, management deals more with maintaining equilibrium and the status quo. An important current development is to regard leadership as a long-term relationship, or partnership, between leaders and group members.

Some research evidence supports the widely accepted view that the leader affects organizational performance. It is also observed that many people attribute organizational performance to leadership actions. The concept of substitutes for leadership argues that factors in the work environment make the leader's role almost superfluous. Among these factors are closely knit teams of highly trained workers, intrinsic satisfaction with work, computer technology, and professional norms. Another antileadership argument is that the leader is irrelevant in most organizational outcomes because the situation is more important. Part of the leadership irrelevance argument is that

the leader has unilateral control over only a few resources. Another part is that new leaders are chosen whose values are compatible with those of the firm.

Complexity theory argues that leaders and managers can do little to alter the course of the complex organizational system. The system, rather than the leader, dictates that all companies ultimately die.

Examining the roles carried out by leaders contributes to an understanding of the leadership function. Nine such leadership roles are the figurehead, spokesperson, negotiator, coach and motivator, team builder, team player, technical problem solver, entrepreneur, and strategic planner. An important implication of these roles is that managers at every level can exert leadership.

A leadership position is often a source of satisfaction to its holder, stemming from such factors as power, prestige, the opportunity to help others, high income, and the opportunity to control resources. At other times being a leader carries with it a number of frustrations, such as insufficient authority, having to deal with human problems, and too much organizational politics. The leader also faces many dilemmas centering around the theme of granting organizational members independence versus getting them aligned.

The framework for understanding leadership presented here is based on the idea that the leadership process is a function of the leader, group members, and other situational variables. According to the model, leadership can best be understood by examining its key variables: leader characteristics and traits, leader behavior and style, group member characteristics, and the internal and external environment. Leadership effectiveness is dependent on all four sets of variables.

Leadership skills can be developed by following a general learning model. Its components include acquiring conceptual knowledge, reading examples, doing experiential exercises, obtaining feedback, and practicing in natural settings.

KEY TERMS

Leadership

Partnership

Stewardship theory

Attribution theory

Substitutes for leadership

Leadership effectiveness

 ## GUIDELINES FOR ACTION AND SKILL DEVELOPMENT

Vast amounts of information have been gathered about leaders and leadership, and many different leadership theories have been developed. Many leadership research findings and theories are confusing and contradictory. Nevertheless, from this thicket of information emerge many useful leadership concepts and techniques to guide you toward becoming a more effective leader.

As you work toward leadership effectiveness, first be familiar with the approaches to leadership described in this text. Then choose the formulation that seems best to fit the leadership situation you face. For example, if you are leading a team, review the information about team leadership. Typically an effective leader needs to combine several leadership approaches to meet the demands of a given situation. For instance, a leader might need to combine creative problem solving and emotional support to members to help the team rebound from a crisis.

DISCUSSION QUESTIONS AND ACTIVITIES

1. What would be several practical problems stemming from the idea that the leader creates a vision, whereas the manager implements it?

2. In recent years, there have been dozens of financial scandals involving business executives (such as the problems at Enron and Global Crossing). What impact has this information had on your interest in becoming, or remaining, a leader in a business setting?

3. Give an example of how you have exerted leadership on or off the job in a situation in which you did not have a formal leadership

position. Explain why you describe your activity as leadership.

4. What would a boss of yours have to do to demonstrate that he or she is an effective leader and an effective manager?

5. Identify a business or sports leader who you think is highly effective. Present your observations to the class.

6. Based on an informal survey, many people who were voted "the most likely to succeed" in their high school yearbooks became leaders later on in their career. How can you explain this finding?

7. Martha Stewart is an inspiration to millions of people, yet at the same time she is criticized by many for her strong ambition and her con-

trolling, perfectionist tendencies. She is even the subject of many jokes. What does this contradictory information tell you about the nature of leadership?

8. After reading this chapter, do you believe that a person who is not a "born leader" still has a good chance of becoming an effective leader? Explain.

9. Top-level leaders of major business corporations receive some of the highest compensation packages in the work force. Why are business leaders paid so much?

10. Which of the nine leadership roles do you think you are the most suited for at this stage in your career? Explain your reasoning.

Leadership Case Problem A

Big Jeff Immelt Faces the Future at GE

In September 2001, Jeffrey R. Immelt replaced the legendary Jack Welch as the chairman and CEO at General Electric Company. With confidence, he asserted, "Believe it or not, I know operationally how to do this job" (*Time*, September 10, 2001, p. 42). Immelt was convinced that company insiders were ready to accept the transition because he had established an excellent reputation in his previous leadership assignments with GE. Immelt had 20 years of experience with the company, most recently as president and CEO of GE Medical Systems. His formal education includes an M.B.A. from Harvard. At Dartmouth College Immelt pushed himself to achieve. He was a double major in applied math and economics, president of his fraternity, and offensive tackle for the football team.

Company outsiders believed that Immelt faced enormous challenges as he faced the future. Above all, it is difficult to succeed a powerful leader like Jack Welch. In addition, Immelt took over the reins at the beginning of a bear stock market and a global economic slowdown intensified by the attacks of September 11. Furthermore, a proposed GE merger with Honeywell had just fallen through, and the Environmental Protection Agency was forcing GE to fix the problems created by dumping PCBs into the Hudson River.

Immediately after winning the top spot over two other highly acclaimed executives, Immelt began a campaign to make his presence felt as the new head of GE. He crisscrossed the globe to meet with employees, key customers, suppliers, and investors. "I've used the time to transfer relationships (from Welch to himself)," he said. "It's got to be done retail, face to face, and you've got to keep doing it" (*Time*, p. 44).

Major Tasks Facing Immelt. On day two in his new position, terrorists attacked the World Trade Center. Two GE employees were killed, the GE insurance business took a $600 million hit, and the aircraft operations slowed down immediately. Furthermore, a period of distrust in the financial integrity of major business corporations had begun.

Immelt's first strategic initiative was to hasten GE's transformation from a low-profit-margin manufacturer to a more lucrative service company that sells problem-solving capability even more than durable goods. Although GE already earns 70 percent of its revenues from services, much of this revenue stems from the giant GE Capital subsidiary. An example of services would be that GE maintains the aircraft engines it sells. GE management has even toyed with the idea of getting out of the highly competitive household appliance business. Immelt wants to hasten the pace of innovation at GE. Some analysts believe that the huge size of GE (300,000 employees with $130 billion annual sales) makes substantial growth difficult. Immelt, who perceives GE as a collection of smaller companies with ample room for growth, disagrees. "I don't feel burdened by size. A great idea at GE is worth a billion dollars, not a million" (*Time,* p. 44).

GE did not escape the careful scrutiny that outside financial analysts and regulatory agencies gave many business firms in 2002. Although GE was at the top of *Fortune*'s Most Admired Companies for five consecutive years, some analysts believed that Welch used creative accounting practices to report 10 percent earnings growth for many years. Thus Immelt was forced into the position of explaining to outsiders that he is not an earnings cheat. It has been GE practice for years to find ways to report smooth earnings growth. If, for example, earnings spiked too high in one quarter, the company would look for a way to take a big charge to reduce those earnings. Another concern about the growth in GE earnings is that much of the revenue growth comes from purchasing other companies and from cheap debt.

Immelt says he wants to use the power of digitization to reduce administrative costs. About 40 percent of the company is now administration, finance, and backroom functions, and he wants to reduce that by 75 percent. Immelt hopes to also reduce costs by expanding the use of online auctions to purchase parts and supplies. Another initiative has been to acquire more companies. Immelt explains that the low stock prices in 2002 made it easier to purchase other companies because they cost less to acquire—what he describes as a strategy of playing offense.

Immelt's Personal Style and Interpersonal Approach. Welch was known for an explosive temper, whereas Immelt is more likely to tease employees than to scold them to get his point across. An Immelt colleague explained that if you missed your financial targets, he wouldn't berate you, but you would leave a meeting with him feeling that you had let him down. Immelt perceives himself as being a tough-minded leader/manager, but not mean. Friends and colleagues note that Immelt is intense and competitive. He has a passion for new ideas and is willing to wield the ax for a poor-performing business unit.

Immelt contends that he went from being a boy to a man during a brief stint at GE Appliances. In the late 1980s, he had to manage a massive, ugly recall of more than a million refrigerator compressors. In the process, he evolved from a quiet leader to a vocal one. To help elevate morale, Immelt would on occasion climb up on a forklift truck on the shop floor and give a rousing speech. Several times he put on a GE service uniform, got in a truck, and went on house calls with the repair technicians to fix the compressor problem. The stress took its toll in the form of overeating, and Immelt ballooned to 280 pounds (his height is 6 feet 5 inches). Immelt has since lost 60 pounds, but his weight still increases during periods of intense stress. He typically works seven days a week, and he sleeps for five hours a night. "I think about the company all the time," he says, "and I don't need much sleep" (*BusinessWeek*, January 28, 2002, p. 102).

Immelt believes strongly that dealing with adversity helps develop managerial and leadership skills. GE uses low-margin businesses like appliances to train managers because the appliance business is always in a recession. Immelt contends that you learn unbelievable management skills in struggling businesses.

Asked by a reporter what kept him up at night, Immelt responded, "It's always an integrity issue of some kind. With 300,000 people, you always worry that somebody doesn't get it. We can survive bad markets. What you can't live through is anybody who takes from the company or does something wrong in the community" (*Business-Week*, January 28, 2002, p. 104).

Immelt has an enormous ego to fit his accomplishments. However, he is able to laugh at himself. He says, "I know how serious the job is. Still, I've always found humor a great way to keep things in context."

QUESTIONS

1. What leadership challenges does Immelt face?

2. What can Immelt and the rest of the executive team do to convince financial analysts that GE is truthful about its earnings?

3. Which leadership roles does Immelt appear to be emphasizing?

SOURCE: *Diane Brady, "The Education of Jeff Immelt,"* BusinessWeek, *April 29, 2002, pp. 80–87; "A Talk with GE's Jeff Immelt,"* BusinessWeek, *January 28, 2002, pp. 102–104; Justin Fox, "What's So Great About GE?"* Fortune, *March 4, 2002, pp. 64–67; "The Man Who Would Be Welch,"* BusinessWeek, *December 11, 2000, pp. 94–97; Daniel Eisenberg, "Jack Who?"* Time, *September 10, 2001, pp. 42–44, 53.*

Leadership Case Problem B

Jen Lee Wants the Fast Track

At age 25, Jen Lee already had impressive leadership experience. She was the head of her Girl Scout troop at age 11, the president of the Asian Student Association in high school, and the captain of her soccer team in both high school and college. She also organized a food drive for homeless people in her hometown for three consecutive summers. So Lee believed that these experiences, in addition to her formal education, were preparing her to be a corporate leader. At college Lee majored in information systems and business administration.

Lee's first position in industry was a business analyst at a medium-size consulting firm that helped clients implement large-scale systems such as enterprise software. She explained to her team leader at the outset that she wanted to be placed on a management track rather than a technical track because she aspired to becoming a corporate executive. Lee's team leader explained, "Jen, I know you are in a hurry to get ahead. Lots of capable people are looking to climb the ladder. But you first have to build your career by proving that you are an outstanding analyst."

Lee thought, "It looks like the company may need a little convincing that I'm leadership material, so I'm going to dig in and perform like a star." And Lee did dig in, much to the pleasure of her clients, her team leader, and her coworkers. Her first few performance appraisals were outstanding, yet the company was still not ready to promote Jen to a team leader position. Lee's team leader explained, "Bob [the team leader's manager] and I both agree that you are doing an outstanding job, but promotions are hard to come by in our company these days. The company is shrinking more than expanding, so talks about promotion are a little futile right now."

Lee decided that it would take a long time to be promoted to team leader or manager in her present company, so she began to quietly look for a new position in her field. Her job hunt proceeded more swiftly than she anticipated. Through a sports club contact, Lee was granted a job interview with a partner in a larger consulting firm offering similar services. After a series of four interviews, Lee was hired as a senior business analyst performing work on a system similar to the one she had been working with for two years. During her interviews, Lee emphasized her goal of occupying a leadership position as soon as the company believed that she was ready for such a role. Her first client assignment was helping a team of consultants install a state income tax call center.

After a one-month-long orientation and training program, Lee was performing billable work at her new employer. At the outset, she reminded her new manager and team leader that she preferred the managerial route to remaining in a technical position. After six months of hard work, Lee looked forward to her first formal performance evaluation. Her team leader informed her that her performance was better than average, but short of

outstanding. Lee asked for an explanation of why her performance was not considered outstanding. She informed her team leader and manager, "I need an outstanding rating to help me achieve my goal of becoming a leader in our company."

The manager replied, "Our performance evaluations are based on your contribution to the company. We care much less about writing performance evaluations to help a senior business analyst reach her career goals. Besides, Jen, you've made your point enough about wanting to be a leader in our firm. Let your performance speak for itself."

That evening, Jen met with her fiancé, Kenneth, to discuss her dilemma. "The problem, Ken, is that they don't get it. I'm leadership material, and they don't see it yet. I'm performing well and letting my intentions be known, but my strategy isn't working. The company is missing out on a golden opportunity by not putting me on a fast leadership track. I have to convince them of their error in judgment."

Kenneth, a human resource specialist, replied, "I'm listening to you, and I want to give you good advice. Let me be objective here despite the fact that I love you. What have you done lately to prove to the company that you are leadership material?"

QUESTIONS

1. Who has the problem here? Jen or the consulting firm in question?

2. What advice can you offer Jen to help her increase her chances of occupying a formal leadership position in the company?

3. What is your evaluation of the advice Ken offered Jen?

INTERNET SKILL-BUILDING EXERCISE

Apply the chapter concepts! Visit the Web and complete this Internet skill-building exercise to learn more about current leadership topics and trends.

The New Face of Leadership

Fast Company has compiled stories about whom it considers the "best of the best" leaders. Steven Miller, a high-level executive at Royal Dutch/Shell, received this designation because of his commitment to participative decision making. Miller has also spearheaded workplace diversity at Royal Dutch/Shell and has attempted to change the face of leadership at the company. Visit **www.fastcompany.com/miller47**. After reading the article, explain what Miller means by "changing the face of leadership," and give several examples of his approach.

Leadership Skill-Building Exercise 1-2

What It Takes to Be a Leader

Becoming a leader or further developing your leadership skills is a lengthy, complex, yet rewarding process. Peter Drucker, a management and leadership guru for about 60 years, contends that if you possess the qualities described below you are a true leader. These "qualities" are essentially behaviors and attitudes that you can develop.

- Leaders start projects by asking, "What has to be done? instead of "What do *I* need?"
- Leaders next ask, "What do I have to do to make a real contribution?" The best answer suits the leader's strengths and the needs of the project.
- Leaders continually ask, "What are my organization's purposes and objectives?" and "What qualifies as acceptable performance and adds to the bottom line?"
- Leaders don't want clones of themselves as employees. They never ask, "Do I dislike this employee?" But they won't tolerate poor performance.
- Leaders aren't threatened by others who have strengths they lack.

When faced with your next leadership assignment, whether on the job or off the job, implement at least one of these ideas. For example, you might choose as a team member someone you think is smarter and better qualified than you.

SOURCE: *Reprinted in* Communications Briefings, *Volume 20, Number 1 (distributed 2002). The* Briefings *source is Peter Drucker, cited in* Forbes ASAP, *Forbes Inc., 60 5th Avenue, New York, NY 10011.*

Traits, Motives, and Characteristics of Leaders

CHAPTER 2

Pattye Moore rolls into a Sonic Drive-In for enough cherry limeades, cream pie shakes, and child-cheese coneys to quiet a carload of third-grade soccer players. To the carhop, she looks like an average mom. But Moore is the new president of the $2 billion fast-food chain, the largest drive-in restaurant brand in America. If the service is bad, she's likely to walk into the kitchen and ask what the problem is. "That doesn't happen often, though," she says, sitting at a red metal picnic table in her office. Moore would much rather visit drive-ins than sit behind her desk at corporate headquarters in Oklahoma City.

Moore eats at Sonic with her daughters three or four times a week. She spends about half her working hours visiting store owners. "We really get a lot of our ideas that way," she says. "We just go out and ask them what they're fixing for themselves. We encourage our employees to play with their food. Our concept is fun. Our food is fun. It's hard to be very serious when you're selling cherry limeades and strawberry cheesecake shakes."

Moore moved up quickly in the company. She came to Sonic Corp. in 1992 as vice president of marketing after handling the company's account at a Tulsa advertising agency. By 2000, Moore, age 44, was executive vice president. She was promoted to president in January 2002, second in command only to the chairman and CEO.

Moore says she stays energized because she likes meeting people and developing new strategies. "It probably sounds kind of corny, but what makes me tick is I love what I do. I love Sonic, and so while it's hard to go on trips and leave my family, it's easy to continue to be motivated, because I like my job and I like the people I work with."

"Our vision is to become America's most-loved restaurant brand," Moore says. "That's a pretty bold vision. That's not necessarily being the biggest or being everywhere. That means being the best."[1]

The vignette just presented describes someone with enthusiasm for her job, one of the leadership traits discussed in this chapter. Traits are important because, when managers are evaluated by others in terms of their leadership effectiveness, their traits and personal characteristics are scrutinized. Instead of focusing only on the results the leader achieves, those making the evaluation assign considerable weight to the leader's attributes, such as adhering to high standards. Many people believe intuitively that personal characteristics strongly determine leadership effectiveness.

The belief that certain personal characteristics and skills contribute to leadership effectiveness in many situations is the **universal theory of leadership.** According to this theory, certain leadership traits are universally important—that is, they apply in all situations. This and the following chapter concentrate on the personal characteristics aspect of the universal theory; Chapter 4 describes the behaviors and skills that are part of the universal theory. Recognize, however, that personal characteristics are closely associated with leadership skills and behaviors. For example, creative thinking ability (a characteristic) helps a leader formulate an exciting vision (leadership behavior).

Characteristics associated with leadership can be classified into three broad categories: personality traits, motives, and cognitive factors. These categories of behavior serve as helpful guides but are not definitive. A convincing argument can often be made that an aspect of leadership placed in one category could be placed in another. Nevertheless, no matter how personal characteristics are classified, they point toward the conclusion that effective leaders are made of the *right stuff.* Published research about the trait (*great person*) approach first appeared at the turn of the century; it continues today. A full listing of every personal characteristic ever found to be associated with leadership would take several hundred pages. Therefore, included here are the major and most consistently found characteristics related to leadership effectiveness.

PERSONALITY TRAITS OF EFFECTIVE LEADERS

Observations by managers and human resource specialists, as well as dozens of research studies, indicate that leaders have certain personality traits.[2] These characteristics contribute to leadership effectiveness in many situations as long as the leader's style fits the situation reasonably well. For example, an executive might perform admirably as a leader in several different high-technology companies with different organizational cultures. However, his intellectual style might make him a poor fit with production workers. Leaders' personality traits can be divided into two groups: general personality traits, such as self-confidence and trustworthiness, and task-related traits, such as an internal locus of control.

General Personality Traits

We define a general personality trait as a trait that is observable both within and outside the context of work. That is, the same general traits are related to success and satisfaction in both work and personal life. Figure 2-1 lists the general personality traits that contribute to successful leadership.

FIGURE 2–1   General Personality Traits of Effective Leaders

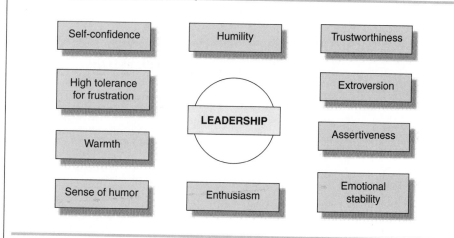

Self-Confidence.   In virtually every leadership setting, it is important for the leader to be realistically self-confident. A leader who is self-assured without being bombastic or overbearing instills self-confidence in team members. A self-confident team leader of a group facing a seemingly impossible deadline might tell the group, "We are understaffed and overworked, but I know we can get this project done on time. I've been through tough demands like this before. If we work like a true team, we can pull it off."

Self-confidence was among the first leadership traits researchers identified. In addition to being self-confident, the leader must project that self-confidence to the group. He or she may do so by using unequivocal wording, maintaining good posture, and making appropriate gestures such as pointing an index finger outward.

Self-confidence is not only a personality trait. It also refers to a behavior and an interpersonal skill that a person exhibits in a number of situations. It is akin to being cool under pressure. We can conclude that a person is a self-confident leader when he or she maintains composure when dealing with a crisis such as managing a large product recall. The interpersonal skill comes in being able to keep others calm during turmoil.

Humility.   Although self-confidence is a key leadership trait, so is humility, or being humble at the right times. Part of humility is admitting that you don't know everything and can't do everything, and admitting your mistakes to team members and outsiders. A leader, upon receiving a compliment for an accomplishment, may explain that the group deserves the credit. The case for humility as a leadership trait is made strongly by Stephen G. Harrison, the president of a consulting firm, in his comment about how the definition of great leadership has changed: "Great leadership is manifested or articulated by people who know how to understate it. There is leadership value in humility, the leadership that comes from putting people in the limelight, not yourself. Great leadership comes from entirely unexpected places. It's understatement, it's dignity, it's service, it's selflessness."[3]

Research by Jim Collins on what makes companies endure and dramatically improve their performance supports the importance of humility. He uses the term *Level 5 Leader* to describe the most accomplished leaders, who are modest yet determined to accomplish their objectives.[4] Leadership Case Problem A at the end of this chapter describes Reuben Mark, a remarkably successful business leader who is noted for his humility.

Trustworthiness.   Evidence and opinion that being trustworthy and/or honest contributes to leadership effectiveness continue to mount.[5] The importance of trust has worked its way into everyday discussions about leadership and managerial effectiveness. An effective leader/manager is supposed to *walk the talk,* thereby showing a consistency between deeds (walking) and words (talk). In this context, **trust** is defined as a person's confidence in another individual's intentions and motives, and in the sincerity of that individual's word.[6] Leaders must be trustworthy, and they must also trust group members. Given that so many people distrust business leaders, as well as political leaders, gaining and maintaining trust is a substantial challenge. The following trust builders are worthy of a prospective leader's attention and implementation:[7]

- Make your behavior consistent with your intentions. Practice what you preach and set the example. Let others know of your intentions and invite feedback on how well you are achieving them.
- When your organization or organizational unit encounters a problem, move into a problem-solving mode instead of looking to blame others for what went wrong.
- Honor confidences. One incident of passing along confidential information results in a permanent loss of trust by the person whose confidence was violated.
- Maintain a high level of integrity. Build a reputation for doing what you think is morally right in spite of the political consequences.
- Tell the truth. It is much easier to be consistent when you do not have to keep patching up your story to conform to an earlier lie.
- Conduct yourself in the way you ask others to conduct themselves. If you urge others to treat work associates fairly, practice fairness yourself.
- Make trust pay in terms of receiving rewards. Trust needs to be seen as a way of gaining advantage. During difficult times, leaders must make the effort to be perceived as trustworthy. For example, when business results are not as good as anticipated, managers should not create false pictures of financial health to the public.

It takes a leader a long time to build trust, yet one brief incident of untrustworthy behavior can permanently destroy it. Leaders are usually allowed a fair share of honest mistakes. In contrast, dishonest mistakes quickly erode leadership effectiveness.

Substantial research indicates that a leader being perceived as trustworthy leads to positive outcomes for the organization. Kurt T. Dirks and Donald L. Ferrin examined the findings and implications of the research that has been conducted during the last four decades about trust in leadership. The review involved 106 studies and 27,103 individuals. The meta-analysis (quantitative synthesis of studies) emphasized supervisory leadership based on the importance of trust in day-to-day interactions with group members. Trusting a leader was more highly associated with a variety of work attitudes of group members. The highest specific relationships with trust were as follows:[8]

- Job satisfaction ($r = .51$)
- Organizational commitment ($r = .49$)
- Turnover intentions ($r = -.40$) (If you trust your leader, you are less likely to intend to leave.)
- Belief in information provided by the leader ($r = .35$)
- Commitment to decisions ($r = .24$)
- Satisfaction with the leader ($r = .73$)
- LMX ($r = .69$) (LMX refers to favorable exchanges with the leader)

The relationship of trust to job performance was statistically significant but quite low ($r = .16$). One reason the relationship might be weak is that many people perform well for a leader they distrust out of fear of being fired or bad-listed.

Leadership Self-Assessment Quiz 2-1 gives you the opportunity to examine your own tendencies toward trustworthiness.

Extroversion.   Extroversion has been recognized for its contribution to leadership effectiveness because it is helpful for leaders to be gregarious and outgoing in most situations. Also, extroverts are more likely to want to assume a leadership role and participate in group activities. Even though it is logical to think that extroversion is related to leadership, many effective leaders are laid-back and even introverted. Michael Dell, the famous founder of Dell Computer Corp., is a reserved individual, sometimes referred to as having a vanilla personality.

Assertiveness.   Letting others know where you stand contributes to leadership effectiveness. **Assertiveness** refers to being forthright in expressing demands, opinions, feelings, and attitudes. Being assertive helps leaders perform many tasks and achieve goals. Among them are confronting group members about their mistakes, demanding higher performance, setting high expectations, and making legitimate demands on higher management. An assertive director of her company's cellular telephone service unit said to her staff, "Our cell service is the worst in the industry. We have to improve."

To be assertive differs substantially from being aggressive or passive. An assertive leader/manager makes explicit remarks without turning them into bullying threats.[9] Aggressive people express their demands in an overly pushy, obnoxious, and abrasive manner; passive people suppress their own ideas, attitudes, feelings, and thoughts as if they were likely to be perceived as controversial. As a result of being passive, a person might not be recommended for large salary increases, good assignments, and promotions.

To determine how assertive you are, do Leadership Self-Assessment Quiz 2-2 on pages 39–41.

Emotional Stability.   Anyone who has ever worked for an unstable boss will attest to the importance of emotional stability as a leadership trait. **Emotional stability** refers to the ability to control emotions to the point that one's emotional responses are appropriate to the occasion. Emotions associated with low emotional stability include anxiety, depression, anger, embarrassment, and worry.

Emotional stability is an important leadership trait because group members expect and need consistency in the way they are treated. A sales manager had this to say about her boss, the vice president of marketing: "It was difficult to know whether to bring problems to Larry's attention. Some days he would compliment me for taking customer problems seriously. Other times he would rant and rave about the ineffectiveness of the sales department. We all worry about having our performance appraised on one of Larry's crazy days." In contrast is Ken Chenault, the highly regarded CEO of American Express Company. Although an assertive and demanding leader, he is known for his even temper when facing substantial challenges as well as during calm situations.

Leadership Self-Assessment Quiz 2–1

Behaviors and Attitudes of a Trustworthy Leader

INSTRUCTIONS   Listed below are behaviors and attitudes of leaders who are generally trusted by their group members and other constituents. After you read each characteristic, check to the right whether this is a behavior or attitude that you appear to have developed already, or whether it does not fit you at present.

		Fits Me	Does Not Fit Me
1.	Tells people he or she is going to do something, and then always follow through and gets it done		
2.	Is described by others as being reliable		
3.	Is good at keeping secrets and confidences		
4.	Tells the truth consistently		
5.	Minimizes telling people what they want to hear		
6.	Is described by others as "walking the talk"		
7.	Delivers consistent messages to others in terms of matching words and deeds		
8.	Does what he or she expects others to do		
9.	Minimizes hypocrisy by not engaging in activities he or she tells others are wrong		
10.	Readily accepts feedback on behavior from others		
11.	Maintains eye contact with people when talking to them		
12.	Appears relaxed and confident when explaining his or her side of a story		
13.	Individualizes compliments to others rather than saying something like "You look great" to a large number of people		
14.	Doesn't expect lavish perks for himself or herself while expecting others to go on an austerity diet		
15.	Does not tell others a crisis is pending (when it isn't) just to gain their cooperation		
16.	Collaborates with others to make creative decisions		

17. Communicates information to people at all organizational levels   _____   _____

18. Readily shares financial information with others   _____   _____

19. Listens to people and then acts on many of their suggestions   _____   _____

20. Generally engages in predictable behavior   _____   _____

SCORING AND INTERPRETATION   These statements are mostly for self-reflection, so no specific scoring key exists. However, the more of the above statements that fit you, the more trustworthy you are—assuming you are answering truthfully. The usefulness of this self-quiz increases if somebody who knows you well answers it for you to supplement your self-perceptions. Your ability and willingness to carry out some of the behaviors specified in this quiz could have an enormous impact on your career because so many business leaders in recent years have not been perceived as trustworthy. Being trustworthy is therefore a career asset.

One study found that executive leaders who are emotionally unstable and lack composure are more likely to handle pressure poorly and give in to moodiness, outbursts of anger, and inconsistent behavior. Such inconsistency undermines their relationships with group members, peers, and superiors. In contrast, effective leaders are generally calm, confident, and predictable during a crisis.[10]

Enthusiasm.   In almost all leadership situations, it is desirable for the leader to be enthusiastic. Group members tend to respond positively to enthusiasm, partly because enthusiasm may be perceived as a reward for constructive behavior. Enthusiasm is also a desirable leadership trait because it helps build good relationships with team members. A leader can express enthusiasm both verbally ("Great job"; "I love it") and nonverbally (making a "high five" gesture). An executive newsletter made an enthusiastic comment about enthusiasm as a leadership trait:

> People look to you for [enthusiasm] to inspire them. It is the greatest tool for motivating others and for getting things done. As a leader, you have to get out in front of your people. Even the most enthusiastic employee is loath to show more of it than his or her boss. If you don't project a gung-ho attitude, everybody else will hold back.[11]

Sense of Humor.   Whether humor is a trait or a behavior, the effective use of humor is an important part of the leader's role. Humor adds to the approachability and people-orientation of a leader. Claudia Kennedy was a three-star army general and the army's senior intelligence official, thereby occupying a key leadership position. During an interview for a magazine article, she mentioned that although she had no regrets, her demanding career had not allowed for having a husband and children. The reporter commented, "You could still get married." Kennedy retorted, "Well certainly—put my phone number in this article."[12]

Leadership Self-Assessment Quiz 2-2

The Assertiveness Scale

INSTRUCTIONS Indicate whether each of the following statements is mostly true or mostly false as it applies to you. If in doubt about your reaction to a particular statement, think of how you would *generally* respond.

		Mostly True	Mostly False
1.	It is extremely difficult for me to turn down a sales representative when he or she is a nice person.		
2.	I express criticism freely.		
3.	If another person is being very unfair, I bring it to that person's attention.		
4.	Work is no place to let your feelings show.		
5.	It's no use asking for favors; people get what they deserve.		
6.	Business is not the place for tact; say what you think.		
7.	If a person looks as if he or she is in a hurry, I let that person in front of me in a supermarket line.		
8.	A weakness of mine is that I'm too nice a person.		
9.	If my restaurant bill is even 50 cents more than it should be, I demand that the mistake be corrected.		
10.	If the mood strikes me, I will laugh out loud in public.		
11.	People would describe me as too outspoken.		
12.	I am quite willing to have the store take back a piece of furniture that was scratched upon delivery.		
13.	I dread having to express anger toward a coworker.		
14.	People often say that I'm too reserved and emotionally controlled.		
15.	I have told friends and work associates exactly what it is about their behavior that irritates or displeases me.		
16.	I fight for my rights down to the last detail.		
17.	I have no misgivings about returning an overcoat to the store if it doesn't fit me right.		

18. After I have an argument with a person, I try to avoid _____ _____
    him or her.

19. I insist that my spouse (or roommate or partner) do _____ _____
    his or her fair share of undesirable chores.

20. It is difficult for me to look directly at another person _____ _____
    when the two of us are in disagreement.

21. I have cried among friends more than once. _____ _____

22. If someone near me at a movie keeps up a conversa- _____ _____
    tion with another person, I ask him or her to stop.

23. I am able to turn down social engagements with peo- _____ _____
    ple I do not particularly care for.

24. It is in poor taste to express what you really feel about _____ _____
    another individual.

25. I sometimes show my anger by swearing at or belit- _____ _____
    tling another person.

26. I am reluctant to speak up at a meeting. _____ _____

27. I find it relatively easy to ask friends for small favors _____ _____
    such as giving me a ride to work while my car is
    being repaired.

28. If another person is talking very loudly in a restaurant _____ _____
    and it bothers me, I inform that person.

29. I often finish other people's sentences for them. _____ _____

30. It is relatively easy for me to express love and affec- _____ _____
    tion toward another person.

SCORING KEY

1. Mostly false	11. Mostly true	21. Mostly true
2. Mostly true	12. Mostly true	22. Mostly true
3. Mostly true	13. Mostly false	23. Mostly true
4. Mostly false	14. Mostly false	24. Mostly true
5. Mostly false	15. Mostly true	25. Mostly true
6. Mostly true	16. Mostly true	26. Mostly false
7. Mostly false	17. Mostly true	27. Mostly true
8. Mostly false	18. Mostly false	28. Mostly true
9. Mostly true	19. Mostly true	29. Mostly true
10. Mostly true	20. Mostly false	30. Mostly true

SCORING AND INTERPRETATION   Score +1 for each of your answers that agrees
with the scoring key.

- 0–15   Nonassertive
- 16–24   Assertive
- 25+   Aggressive

Do this exercise again about thirty days from now to give yourself some indication of the stability of your answers. You might also discuss your answers with a close friend to determine if that person has a similar perception of your assertiveness.

A score in the nonassertive range could suggest that you need to develop your assertiveness and self-confidence and become less shy to enhance those aspects of your leadership that involve face-to-face interaction with people. To help verify the accuracy of this score, ask a present or former boss whether he or she agrees that you are nonassertive.

Laughter and humor serve such functions in the workplace as relieving tension and boredom and defusing hostility. Because humor helps the leader dissolve tension and defuse conflict, it helps him or her exert power over the group. Self-effacing humor is the choice of comedians and organizational leaders alike. By being self-effacing, the leader makes a point without insulting or slighting anybody. Instead of criticizing a staff member for being too technical, the leader might say, "Wait, I need your help. Please explain how this new product works in terms that even I can understand." Notice that General Kennedy's comments were slightly self-effacing by implying that she needed to have her phone number widely disseminated in order to obtain dates.

Leadership Skill-Building Exercise 2-1 provides you with an opportunity to use humor effectively.

Warmth.   Being a warm person and projecting that warmth contribute to leadership effectiveness in several ways. First, warmth helps establish rapport with group members. Second, the projection of warmth is a key component of charisma. Third, warmth is a trait that helps provide emotional support to group members. Giving such support is an important leadership behavior. Fourth, in the words of Kogan Page, "Warmth comes with the territory. Cold fish don't make good leaders because they turn people off."[13]

High Tolerance for Frustration.   Two researchers content-analyzed televised interviews of thirty business executives. Most of the executives showed **high tolerance for frustration,** or the ability to cope with the blocking of goal attainment.[14] This trait is important because a leader encounters many frustrations. For example, a manager might invest a year in developing a strategic plan and then be informed that top management does not want the plan implemented.

Task-Related Personality Traits

Certain personality traits of effective leaders are closely associated with task accomplishment, even though they still seem to fall more accurately in the trait

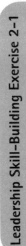

A Sense of Humor on the Job

One person plays the role of the company president, who has scheduled a staff meeting. The president's task is to inform employees that the seventh top manager in the last year has just resigned. You want to make effective use of humor to relieve some of the tension and worry. Make a couple of humorous introductory comments. Five other people should play the roles of the remaining staff members. Make effective use of humor yourself in response to the president's comments.

category rather than the behavior category. The task-related traits described here are outlined in Figure 2-2.

Passion for the Work and the People. A dominant characteristic of effective leaders is their passion for their work and to some extent for the people who help them accomplish the work. The passion goes beyond enthusiasm and often expresses itself as an obsession for achieving company goals. Many leaders begin their workday at 6 A.M. and return to their homes at 7 P.M. After dinner they retreat to their home offices to conduct business for about two more hours. Information technology, such as personal digital assistants and cell phones, feed the passion for work, making it possible to be in touch with the office even during golf or a family picnic.

Passion for their work is especially evident in entrepreneurial leaders, no matter what size and type of business. A given business, such as refurbishing engines might appear mundane to outsiders. The leader of such a business, however, is willing to talk for hours about tearing down old engines and about the wonderful people who help do the job. Jeff Bezos, the founder of Amazon.com and one of the world's best-known entrepreneurs, exemplifies passion for work. Asked if running Amazon was as much fun as it used to be, he replied:

> The truth is yes. Sure I like being the poster child instead of the *piñata* a little bit more. But I'm a change junkie. I love the rate of change. I love the intellectual challenge of what we're doing. I love the people I work with. It's not like me against the world. We've got a big team of people. It's fun.[15]

Being passionate about the nature of the business can be a major success factor in its survival. Randy Komisar, a strategy consultant to many dot-com business firms, argues that the purpose of business cannot be simply to make lots of

FIGURE 2–2   Task–Related Personality Traits of Leaders

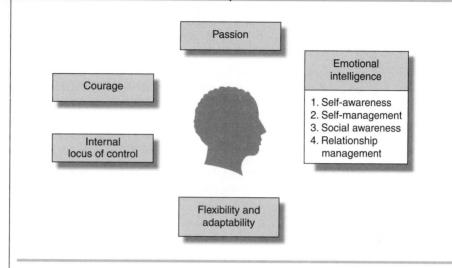

money. He says that too many business startups lack a deep foundation in values and are managed by a drive for success, not by passion. "Drive pushes you toward an objective, and you can deny part of yourself by sheer will to achieve a goal," Komisar explains. "Passion irresistibly pulls you toward the need to express yourself and has to come from within and be nurtured." A problem with drive alone is that the end justifies the means.[16]

Emotional Intelligence.   Leadership researchers and experienced workers have long known that how well a person manages his or her emotions and those of others influences leadership effectiveness. For example, recognizing anger in yourself and others, and being able to empathize with people, can help you be more effective at exerting influence. In recent years, many different aspects of emotions, motives, and personality that help determine interpersonal effectiveness and leadership skill have been placed under one comprehensive label. **Emotional intelligence** refers to qualities such as understanding one's feelings, empathy for others, and the regulation of emotions to enhance living. This type of intelligence generally has to do with the ability to connect with people and understand their emotions. Many of the topics in this chapter (such as warmth) and throughout the text (such as political skill) can be considered related to emotional intelligence.

Based on research in dozens of companies, Daniel Goleman discovered that the most effective leaders are alike in one essential way: they all have a high degree of emotional intelligence. General intelligence (or IQ) and technical skills are considered threshold capabilities for success in executive positions. Yet, according to Goleman, without a high degree of emotional intelligence, a person can have excellent training, superior analytical skills, and loads of innovative suggestions, but he or she still will not make a great leader. His analysis also revealed that emotional intelligence played an increasingly important role in high-level management positions, where differences in technical skills are of negligible importance. Furthermore, when star performers were compared with average ones in senior leadership positions, differences in emotional intelligence were more pronounced than differences in cognitive abilities.[17]

Four key factors in emotional intelligence are described next, along with a brief explanation of how each factor links to leadership effectiveness. The components of emotional intelligence have gone through several versions, and the version presented here is tied closely to leadership and interpersonal skills. The leader who scores high in emotional intelligence is described as *resonant*.[18]

1. *Self-awareness*. The ability to understand your own emotions is the most essential of the four emotional intelligence competencies. Having high self-awareness allows people to know their strengths and limitations and have high self-esteem. Resonant leaders use self-awareness to accurately measure their own moods, and they intuitively understand how their moods affect others. (Effective leaders seek feedback to see how well their actions are received by others. A leader with good self-awareness would recognize such factors as whether he or she was liked or was exerting the right amount of pressure on people.)

2. *Self-management*. This is the ability to control one's emotions and act with honesty and integrity in a consistent and adaptable manner. The right degree of self-management helps prevent a person from throwing temper tantrums when activities do not go as planned. Resonant leaders do not let their occasional bad moods ruin their day. If they cannot overcome the bad mood, they let work associates know of the problem and how long it might last. (A leader with high self-management would not suddenly decide to fire a group member because of one difference of opinion.)

3. *Social awareness*. This includes having empathy for others and having intuition about organizational problems. Socially aware leaders go beyond sensing the emotions of others by showing that they care. In addition, they accurately size up political forces in the office. (A team leader with social awareness, or empathy, would be able to assess whether a team member had enough enthusiasm for a project to assign him to that project. A CEO who had empathy for a labor union's demands might be able to negotiate successfully with the head of the labor union to avoid a costly strike.)

4. *Relationship management*. This includes the interpersonal skills of being able to communicate clearly and convincingly, disarm conflicts, and build strong personal bonds. Resonant leaders use relationship management skills to spread their enthusiasm and solve disagreements, often with kindness and humor. (A leader with good relationship management skills would not burn bridges and would continue to enlarge his or her network of people to win support when support is needed. A leader/manager with good relationship management skills is more likely to be invited by headhunters to explore new career opportunities.)

Many of the leaders described in this text have high emotional intelligence. The accompanying Leader in Action section describes a middle manager with a high degree of empathy, a key component of social awareness. In contrast, many leaders and managers have low emotional intelligence, a weakness that often keeps them from achieving their full potential. Jeffrey Skilling, the CEO of Enron Corporation and a central figure in the company's financial scandals, is a notable example. Skilling would often become verbally abusive toward team members, particularly if he disagreed with their opinion. Sherron Watkins, a key whistle-blower in the exposé of financial manipulations, chose to express her concerns anonymously rather than receive a tongue lashing by Skilling.[19]

Research on emotional intelligence and leadership has recently focused on the importance of the leader's mood in influencing performance. Daniel Goleman, Richard Boyatzis, and Annie McKee believe that the leader's mood and his or her associated behaviors greatly influence bottom-line performance. One reason is that moods are contagious. A cranky and ruthless leader creates a toxic organization of underachievers (who perform at less than their potential). In contrast, an upbeat and inspirational leader breeds followers who can surmounnt most challenges. Thus mood finally affects profit and loss. The implication for leaders is that they have to develop emotional intelligence regarding their moods. It is also helpful to develop a sense of humor, because lightheartedness is the most contagious of moods.[20]

Flexibility and Adaptability. A leader is someone who facilitates change. It therefore follows that a leader must be flexible enough to cope with such changes as technological advances, downsizings, a shifting customer base, and a changing work force. **Flexibility,** or the ability to adjust to different situations, has long been recognized as an important leadership characteristic. Leaders who are flexible are able to adjust to the demands of changing conditions, much as anti-lock brakes enable an automobile to adjust to changes in road conditions. Without the underlying trait of flexibility, a person could be an effective leader in only one or two situations. The public utility industry exemplifies a field in which situation adaptability is particularly important because top executives are required to provide leadership for both the regulated and nonregulated units within their organization.

Internal Locus of Control. People with an **internal locus of control** believe that they are the prime mover behind events. Thus, an internal locus of control helps a leader in the role of a take-charge person because the leader believes fundamentally in his or her innate capacity to take charge. An internal locus of control is closely related to self-confidence. A strong internal locus facilitates self-confidence because the person perceives that he or she can control circumstances enough to perform well.

Supervisory leaders with an internal locus of control are favored by group members.[21] One reason is that an "internal" person is perceived as more powerful than an "external" person because he or she takes responsibility for events. The leader with an internal locus of control would emphasize that he or she can

Leader in Action

Boris Slogar of the Ohio Department of Taxation

When Boris Slogar enters a room, people notice. He's 6 feet 5 inches tall and powerfully built. He has a trimmed black beard peppered with gray that ages him beyond his 36 years. His stride suggests someone who likes to lead. Slogar also has an imposing title: deputy tax commissioner and chief of staff for the Ohio Department of Taxation. His job puts him in a top position in one of the biggest agencies in the Ohio state government.

If he wanted to, Slogar could wield his authority in nasty ways. But he doesn't. In fact, Slogar is a classic nice guy. The story of email comes to mind. It all started when Slogar's boss told him to contact employees who would be eligible for retirement within two years. For understandable planning purposes, the agency wanted to get a handle on what people intended to do once they could retire. Several hundred people qualified, so Slogar decided to send them an email asking about their plans.

Many managers would see this as a straightforward solicitation of information. They'd pound out a memo, send it off, and be done. But Slogar realized that such a letter could raise questions, suspicions, and fears about management intentions and job security. He proceeded to think, rethink, and agonize. He put himself in the shoes of those several hundred people who'd be receiving the email. He thought about his days at the Ohio Department of Natural Resources, where he had worked as an engineer in dam safety, and what it was like to get coolly upsetting emails from senior managers.

The next morning, Slogar sat at his computer. He labored over a first draft, searching for the right words. He wrote, read, reread, and revised. As he worked, he tried to imagine himself on the receiving end. "I kept asking, 'What would I want to read that wouldn't offend me?'"

Slogar circulated the draft to a few close associates for their feedback. Then he leaned over his keyboard and carefully made some revisions. "I didn't want to spill my heart out and go too far," he recalls, "but I didn't want to sound iron-fisted either. I figured, if I can write this as sincerely and respectfully as I'd say it in person, maybe some of the goodwill will come through."

The final product came to 500 words. Here's an excerpt:

> Keep in mind that this should be not construed as a nudge to move you along and out of the door. You've given years of service to this department and to the state of Ohio. I believe we can all agree that it would be nearly impossible to replace your experience, skill, and abilities. With proper planning, however, we can pass along your knowledge about systems and processes. Taking these steps will help to ensure that our customers will not experience a large drop-off in service. We need your help.

Slogar spent twice as much time as one would expect for the email writing. But the extra hours paid off. About 95 percent of the recipients wrote back with the requested information. The others responded after a reminder. Only one person expressed deep concerns. Most important, the email never sparked rumors or fears. People took Slogar at his word.

QUESTIONS

1. In what way did Boris Slogar demonstrate empathy?

2. How would you rate Slogar's emotional intelligence?

SOURCE: *Tom Terez, "Remember, They're* Human Re-sources,"*Workforce, January 2002, pp. 22–24. Copyright © 2002 Crain Communications, Inc. Reproduced with permission of Crain Communications, Inc. in the format Textbook via Copyright Clearence Center.*

change unfavorable conditions, as did Allen Questrom of J.C. Penney (Chapter 1). You may recall that he also encouraged the managers reporting to him to take responsibility for their own problems.

Leadership Skill-Building Exercise 2-2 provides you an opportunity to begin strengthening your internal locus of control. Considerable further work would be required to shift from an external to an internal locus of control.

Courage.   Leaders need courage to face the challenges of taking prudent risks and taking initiative in general. They must also face up to responsibility and be willing to put their reputations on the line. It takes courage for a leader to suggest a new undertaking because if the undertaking fails, the leader is often seen as having failed. It also takes courage to take a stand that could backfire. Managers at Home Depot once put pressure on several of their major suppliers *not* to sell over the Internet because by so doing the suppliers would be competing with Home Depot. For example, a customer might purchase a lawnmower over the Internet rather than visiting the retailer. Such a decision could have created much unfavorable press if leadership at Home Depot had been too heavy-handed. The more faith people place in the power of leaders to cause events, the more strongly they blame leaders when outcomes are unfavorable.

LEADERSHIP MOTIVES

Effective leaders, as opposed to nonleaders and less effective leaders, have frequently been distinguished by their motives and needs. In general, leaders have an intense desire to occupy a position of responsibility for others and to control them. Figure 2-3 outlines four specific leadership motives or needs. All four motives can be considered task-related.

The Power Motive

Effective leaders have a strong need to control resources. Leaders with high power motives have three dominant characteristics: (1) They act with vigor and determination to exert their power; (2) they invest much time in thinking about ways to alter the behavior and thinking of others; and (3) they care about their personal standing with those around them.[22] The power motive is important because it means that the leader is interested in influencing others. Without power, it is much more difficult to influence others. Power is not necessarily good or evil; it can be used for the sake of the power holder (personalized power motive) or for helping others (socialized power motive).[23]

Personalized Power Motive.   Leaders with a personalized power motive seek power mostly to further their own interests. They crave the trappings of power, such as status symbols, luxury, and money. In recent years, some leaders have taken up power boating, or racing powerful, high-speed boats. When asked how

Developing an Internal Locus of Control

A person's locus of control is usually a deeply ingrained thinking pattern that develops over a period of many years. Nevertheless, you can begin developing a stronger internal locus of control by analyzing past successes and failures to determine how much influence you had on the outcome of these events. By repeatedly analyzing the relative contribution of internal versus external factors in shaping events, you may learn to feel more in charge of key events in your life. The events listed below are a good starting point.

1. A contest or athletic event that you either won or made a good showing in

What were the factors within your control that led to you winning or making a good showing?

_____

_____

_____

What were the factors beyond your control that led to your winning or making a good showing? _____

_____

_____

2. A course in which you received a poor grade

What were the factors within your control that led to this poor grade?

_____

_____

_____

What were the factors beyond your control that led to this poor grade?

_____

_____

_____

3. A group project to which you were assigned that worked out poorly

What were the factors within your control that led to this poor result?

_____

_____

_____

What were the factors beyond your control that led to this poor result?

_____

_____

_____

After you have prepared your individual analysis, you may find it helpful to discuss your observations in small groups. Focus on how people could have profited from a stronger internal locus of control in the situations analyzed.

FIGURE 2–3   Leadership Motives

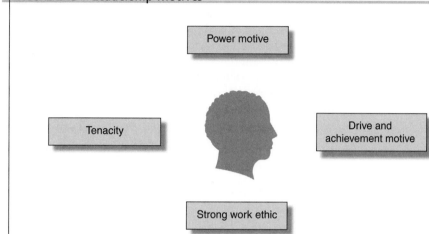

he liked his power-boating experience, an entrepreneurial leader replied, "It's fun, but the start-up costs are about $350,000."

Donald Trump® is seen as a leader with a strong personalized power motive because of his love of the trappings of power. Even the name *Donald Trump* is registered, and is supposed to be written with the "registered" symbol upon first mention. He has a penchant for naming yachts, hotels, and office buildings after himself. Trump's drive for power is intertwined with his immodesty and lack of humility. In 2000, when Trump was making tentative plans to run for the president of the United States, he explained to a reporter while flying on his private jet:

> If I feel I could win—*win*—then I'd run. I think I have a good chance. Hey, I've got my name on half of the major buildings in New York. I went to the Wharton School of Finance, which is the No. 1 school. I'm intelligent. Some people would say I'm very, very, intelligent. I've written three No. 1 bestsellers. You know I am the highest-paid speaker in the country?[24]

Despite Trump's elevated personalized power motive, he does not fit all three characteristics stated above. Trump gives his financial managers considerable latitude in managing his enterprises. In contrast to Trump, some leaders with strong personalized power motives typically enjoy dominating others. Their need for dominance can lead to submissive subordinates who are frequently sycophants and yes-persons.

Socialized Power Motive.   Leaders with a socialized power motive use power primarily to achieve organizational goals or a vision. In this context, the term *socialized* means that the leader uses power primarily to help others. As a result, he or she is likely to provide more effective leadership. Leaders with socialized power motives, in contrast to leaders with personalized power motives, tend to be more emotionally mature. Also, they exercise power more for the benefit of the entire organization and are less likely to manipulate others through the use of power. Leaders with socialized power motives are less defensive and more willing to accept expert advice. Finally, they have longer-range perspectives.[25]

It is important not to draw a rigid line between leaders with personalized power motives and those with socialized power motives. The distinction between doing good for others and doing good for oneself is often made on the basis of very subjective criteria. A case in point is H. Ross Perot, the highly successful business founder, social activist, and two-time candidate for U.S. president. Perot supporters attest to his genuine desire to create a good life for others and to serve them. His detractors, however, regard Perot as a leader obsessed with power and self-importance.

Drive and Achievement Motive

Leaders are known for their strong effort in achieving work goals. The importance of strong motivation for leadership is well accepted. **Drive** refers to a propensity to put forth high energy into achieving goals and to a persistence in applying that energy. Drive also includes **achievement motivation**—finding joy in accomplishment for its own sake. Entrepreneurs and high-level corporate managers usually have strong achievement motivations. A person with a strong achievement motivation has a consistent desire to:

1. Achieve through one's own efforts and take responsibility for success or failure
2. Take moderate risks that can be handled through one's own efforts
3. Receive feedback on level of performance
4. Introduce novel, innovative, or creative solutions
5. Plan and set goals[26]

Strong Work Ethic

Effective leaders typically have a strong **work ethic,** a firm belief in the dignity of work. People with a strong work ethic are well motivated because they value hard work. Most leaders need this quality because they have a heavy workload. A strong work ethic helps the organizational leader believe that the group task is worthwhile. For example, the outside world might not think that the production of specialty soft drinks (such as high-caffeine cola) and bottled spring water is important. Yet the founder of one such company said that he delights in the pleasure his company brings to so many people. He also added, "A lot of IT [information technology] specialists wouldn't be nearly as productive without getting energized by our cola."

Tenacity

A final observation about the motivational characteristics of organizational leaders is that they are *tenacious.* Leaders are better at overcoming obstacles than are nonleaders. Tenacity multiplies in importance for organizational leaders because it takes so long to implement a new program or consummate a business deal such as acquiring another company. Being tenacious is also essential for growing a business. Pat Croce, owner of the Philadelphia 76ers basketball team and the Sports Physical Therapists chain, exemplifies a tenacious empire builder. He rose from poverty and obscurity to become a well-known entrepreneur, and much of his success has been attributed to dogged determination, a willingness to work hard, and a positive attitude.[27]

A study of 150 leaders conducted by Warren Bennis reinforces the link between leadership effectiveness and tenacity. All interviewees embodied a strongly developed sense of purpose and a willful determination to achieve what they wanted. "Without that," said Bennis, "organizations and individuals are not powerful. The central ingredient of power is purpose."[28]

COGNITIVE FACTORS AND LEADERSHIP

Mental ability as well as personality is important for leadership success. To inspire people, bring about constructive change, and solve problems creatively, leaders need to be mentally sharp. Another mental requirement is the ability to sort out essential information from the less essential, and then store the most important in memory. Problem-solving and intellectual skills are referred to collectively as **cognitive factors.** The term *cognition* refers to the mental process or faculty by which knowledge is gathered. Our discussion of cognitive factors focuses on five factors closely related to cognitive intelligence, as shown in Figure 2-4. The descriptor *cognitive* is somewhat necessary to differentiate traditional mental ability from emotional intelligence.

Knowledge of the Business or Group Task

Intellectual ability is closely related to having knowledge of the business or the key task the group is performing. An effective leader has to be technically competent in

FIGURE 2-4   Cognitive Factors and Leadership

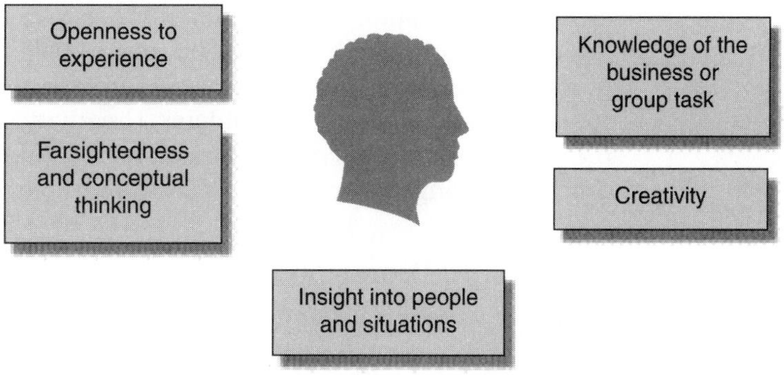

some discipline, particularly when leading a group of specialists. It is difficult for the leader to establish rapport with group members when he or she does not know what they are doing and when the group does not respect the leader's technical skills.

A representative example of the relevance of knowledge of the business for corporate leadership took place when Xerox Corporation chose Lawrence A. Zimmerman as their new chief financial officer in 2002. Zimmerman was a long-time IBM Corporation executive with experience in restructuring troubled operations. Xerox chairman and chief executive officer said in a statement, "Larry has a proven track record as an effective financial executive with balanced experience in global operations, strategic planning, accounting, and internal controls."[29] Zimmerman, who retired from IBM after thirty-one years of service, also had strong interpersonal skills.

The importance of knowledge of the business is increasingly being recognized as an attribute of executive leadership. Leaders at every level are expected to bring forth useful ideas for carrying out the mission of the organization or organizational unit. A recent analysis of CEO leadership concluded that one of the basic ways in which top executives lead is through the **expertise approach.** Executives who lead by using this approach think that the leader's most important responsibility is providing an area of expertise that will be a source of competitive advantage. Such CEOs devote most of their time to continually improving their expertise through such means as studying new technological research, analyzing competitors' products, and conferring with customers and engineers.[30]

Knowledge of the business or the group task is particularly important when developing strategy and formulating mission statements. Chapter 13 deals with strategy formulation at length.

Creativity

Many effective leaders are creative in the sense that they arrive at imaginative and original solutions to complex problems. Creative ability lies on a continuum, with some leaders being more creative than others. At one end of the creative continuum are business leaders who think of innovative products and services. One example is Steve Jobs of Apple Computer, Inc. and Pixar Animation Studios. Jobs has contributed creative product ideas to both firms. At the middle of the creativity continuum are leaders who explore imaginative—but not break-through—solutions to business problems. At the low end of the creativity continuum are leaders who inspire group members to push forward with standard solutions to organizational problems. Creativity is such an important aspect of the leader's role in the modern organization that the development of creative problem-solving skills receives separate attention in Chapter 11.

Insight into People and Situations

Another important cognitive trait of leaders is **insight,** a depth of understanding that requires considerable intuition and common sense. Intuition is often the mental process used to provide the understanding of a problem. Insight helps speed along decision making. Lawrence Weinbach, chairman, president, and CEO of Unisys, puts it this way: "If we want to be leaders, we're going to have to make decisions with maybe 75 percent of the facts. If you wait for 95 percent, you are going to be a follower."[31]

Insight into people and situations involving people is an essential characteristic of managerial leaders because it helps them make the best use of both their own and others' talents. For example, it helps them make wise choices in selecting people for key assignments. Insight also enables managers to do a better job of training and developing team members because they can wisely assess the members' strengths and weaknesses. Another major advantage of being insightful is that the leader can size up a situation and adapt his or her leadership approach accordingly. For instance, in a crisis situation, group members welcome directive and decisive leadership. Being able to read people helps the manager provide this leadership.

Insight helps one perceive trends in the environment. Leaders must be able to process many different types of information and use their perceptions to predict the direction of environmental forces. According to Manfred F. R. Kets De Vries, leaders are effective in searching out and structuring the kind of information they need. They can make sense of a complex environment and then use the data for problem solving.[32] For example, many human resource managers size up the environment to identify factors that will attract talented professionals to their firm during a labor shortage. Among the key factors are opportunity for continuous learning, flexible work schedules, and stock options. A more traditional approach might emphasize high starting salaries and opportunity for promotion.

You can gauge your insight by charting the accuracy of your hunches and predictions about people and business situations. For example, size up a new coworker or manager as best you can. Record your observations and test them against how that person performs or behaves many months later. The feedback from this type of exercise helps sharpen your insights.

Farsightedness and Conceptual Thinking

To develop visions and corporate strategy, a leader needs **farsightedness,** the ability to understand the long-range implications of actions and policies. A farsighted leader recognizes that hiring talented workers today will give the firm a long-range competitive advantage. A more shortsighted view would be to hire less talented workers to satisfy immediate employment needs. The farsighted leader/manager is not oblivious to short-range needs but would devise an intermediate solution, such as hiring temporary workers until people with the right talent were ultimately found.

Conceptual thinking refers to the ability to see the overall perspective, and it makes farsightedness possible. A conceptual thinker is also a *systems thinker* because he or she understands how the external environment influences the organization and how different parts of the organization influence each other. A good conceptual thinker recognizes how his or her organizational unit contributes to the firm or how the firm meshes with the outside world.

Being farsighted benefits the leadership of basic businesses as well as of high-technology firms. Two twin brothers, Norman Leenhouts and Nelson Leenhouts, started a real estate business fifty years ago that is now called Home Properties. Today their total properties are valued at $2.5 billion and include 40,000 apartments in twelve states and more than 1 million square feet of commercial space. The Leenhouts have been able to see the possibilities in properties that others might consider undesirable. Their basic concept is to buy older, mostly brick complexes with deteriorating kitchens and bathrooms. Home Properties then fixes up the kitchens and bathrooms, raises the rents, and turns a profit.[33]

Openness to Experience

Yet another important cognitive characteristic of leaders is their openness to experience, or their positive orientation toward learning. People who have a great deal of openness to experience have well-developed intellects. Traits commonly associated with this dimension of the intellect include being imaginative, cultured, curious, original, broad-minded, intelligent, and artistically sensitive.

To help personalize the information about key leadership traits presented so far, do Leadership Skill-Building Exercise 2-3.

THE INFLUENCE OF HEREDITY AND ENVIRONMENT ON LEADERSHIP

Does heredity or environment contribute more to leadership effectiveness? Are leaders born or made? Do you have to have the right stuff to be a leader? Many people ponder these issues now that the study of leadership is more in vogue than ever. The most sensible answer is that the traits, motives, and characteristics required for leadership effectiveness are caused by a combination of heredity and environment. Personality traits and mental ability traits are based on certain inherited predispositions and aptitudes that require the right opportunity to develop. Mental ability is a good example. We inherit a basic capacity that sets an outer limit to how much mental horsepower we will have. Yet people need the right opportunity to develop their mental ability so that they can behave brightly enough to be chosen for a leadership position.

The physical factor of energy also sheds light on the nature-versus-nurture issue. Some people are born with a biological propensity for being more energetic than others. Yet unless that energy is properly channeled, it will not help a person become an effective leader.

The nature-versus-nurture issue also surfaces in relation to the leadership characteristic of creativity and innovation. Important genetic contributors to imaginative thinking include brain power and emotional expressiveness. Yet these traits require the right environment to flourish. Such an environment would include encouragement from others and ample opportunity to experiment with ideas.

Group Feedback on Leadership Traits

Your instructor will organize the class into groups of about seven people. A volunteer sits in the middle of each group. Each group member looks directly at the person in the "hot seat" and tells him or her what leadership trait, characteristic, or motives he or she seems to possess. It will help if the feedback providers offer a few words of explanation for their observations. For example, a participant who is told that he or she has self-confidence might also be told, "I notice how confidently you have told the class about your success on the job." The group next moves on to the second person, and so forth. (We assume that you have had some opportunity to observe your classmates prior to this exercise.)

Each member thus receives positive feedback about leadership traits and characteristics from all the other members in the group. After all members have had their turn at receiving feedback, discuss as a group the value of the exercise.

Research about emotional intelligence reinforces the statements made so far about leadership being a combination of inherited and learned factors. The outermost areas of the brain, known as the neocortex, govern analytical thinking and technical skill, which are associated with cognitive or traditional intelligence. The innermost areas of the brain govern emotions, such as the rage one feels when being criticized by a customer. Emotional intelligence originates in the neurotransmitters of the limbic system of the brain, which governs feelings, impulses, and drives.

A person therefore has genes that influence the emotional intelligence necessary for leadership. However, experience is important for emotional intelligence because it increases with age,[34] and a person usually becomes better at managing relationships the more practice he or she has. As one turnaround manager said, "I've restructured five different companies, and I've learned to do it without completely destroying morale."

The case histories of six sets of brothers highlight the complexity of sorting out the influences of heredity versus environment on leadership. All twelve achieved the title of president or higher at companies of at least 100 employees or $10 million in annual revenues. For example, the Leiwekes became CEOs of hockey teams. Tod is the president of the Minnesota Wild, and Tim is the president of the Los Angeles Kings. The reporter who gathered these case histories presented them as evidence of "CEO DNA."[35] Whether or not the author was totally serious, the implication is that heredity was the primary determinant of the similar successes of all these brothers. However, these brothers also had quite similar environments: same parents, primary and secondary school study in the same neighborhood, similar education, similar learned values, and so forth.

THE STRENGTHS AND LIMITATIONS OF THE TRAIT APPROACH

A compelling argument for the trait approach is that the evidence is convincing that leaders possess personal characteristics that differ from those of nonleaders. Based on their review of the type of research reported in this chapter, Kirkpatrick and Locke concluded: "Leaders do not have to be great men or women by being intellectual geniuses or omniscient prophets to succeed. But they do need to have the 'right stuff' and this stuff is not equally present in all people."[36] The current emphasis on emotional intelligence and ethical conduct, which are really traits and behaviors, reinforces the importance of the trait approach.

Understanding the traits of effective leaders serves as an important guide to leadership selection. If we are confident that honesty and integrity, and creativity and imagination are essential leadership traits, then we can concentrate on selecting leaders with those characteristics. Another important strength of the trait approach to leadership is that it can help people prepare for leadership responsibility and all of the issues that accompany it. A person might seek experiences that enable him or her to develop vital characteristics such as self-confidence, good problem-solving ability, and assertiveness.

A limitation to the trait approach is that it does not tell us which traits are absolutely needed in which leadership situations. We also do not know how much of a trait, characteristic, or motive is the right amount. For example, some leaders get into ethical and legal trouble because they allow their ambition to cross the borderline into greed and gluttony. In addition, too much focus on the trait approach can breed an elitist conception of leadership. People who are not outstanding on key leadership traits and characteristics might be discouraged from seeking leadership positions.

Peter Drucker, a key figure in the modern management movement, is skeptical about studying the qualities of leaders. He believes that a leader cannot be categorized by a particular personality type, style, or set of traits. Instead, a leader should be understood in terms of his or her constituents, results, example setting, and responsibilities. A leader must look in the mirror, and ask if the image is the kind of person the leader wants to be. (Without realizing it, Drucker in this instance is probably alluding to the leader's traits and values!)[37]

A balanced perspective on the trait approach is that certain traits, motives, and characteristics increase the probability that a leader will be effective. Yet they do not guarantee effectiveness, and the leadership situation often influences which traits will be the most important.[38]

SUMMARY

A universal theory of leadership contends that certain personal characteristics and skills contribute to leadership effectiveness in many situations. The trait approach to leadership studies the traits, motives, and other characteristics of leaders. General personality traits associated with effective leadership include (1) self-confidence, (2) humility, (3) trustworthiness, (4) extroversion, (5) assertiveness, (6) emotional stability, (7) enthusiasm, (8) sense of humor, (9) warmth, and (10) high tolerance for frustration.

Some personality traits of effective leaders are closely associated with task accomplishment. Among them are (1) passion for the work and the people, (2) emotional intelligence, (3) flexibility and adaptability, (4) internal locus of control, and (5) courage. Emotional intelligence is composed of four traits: self-awareness, self-management, social awareness, and relationship management.

Certain motives and needs associated with leadership effectiveness are closely related to task accomplishment. Among them are (1) the power motive, (2) drive and achievement motivation, (3) a strong work ethic, and (4) tenacity.

Cognitive factors, including mental ability, are also important for leadership success. Intellectual ability is closely related to the leadership requirement of possessing knowledge of the business or group task, and to being technically competent. Creativity is another important cognitive skill for leaders, but effective leaders vary widely in their creative contributions. Insight into people and situations, including the ability to make effective judgments about business opportunities, also contributes to leadership effectiveness. Farsightedness and conceptual thinking help leaders to understand the long-range implications of actions and policies, and to take an overall perspective. Being open to experience is yet another cognitive characteristic associated with effective leaders.

The issue of whether leaders are born or bred frequently surfaces. A sensible answer is that the traits, motives, and characteristics required for leadership effectiveness are a combination of heredity and environment.

The trait approach to leadership is supported by many studies showing that leaders are different from nonleaders, and effective leaders are different from less effective leaders. Nevertheless, the trait approach does not tell us which traits are most important in which situations, or the amount of the trait required.

KEY TERMS

Universal theory of leadership

Trust

Assertiveness

Emotional stability

High tolerance for frustration

Emotional intelligence

Flexibility

Internal locus of control

Drive

Achievement motivation

Work ethic

Cognitive factors

Expertise approach

Insight

Farsightedness

✔ GUIDELINES FOR ACTION AND SKILL DEVELOPMENT

Considering that emotional intelligence is so important for leadership success, many organizations sponsor emotional intelligence training for managers. One way to get started on improving emotional intelligence would be to attend such a training program. However, like all forms of training, emotional intelligence training must be followed up with consistent and determined practice. A realistic starting point in improving your emotional intelligence is to work with one of its four components at a time, such as the empathy aspect of social awareness.

Begin by obtaining as much feedback as you can from people who know you. Ask them if they think you understand their emotional reactions, and how well they think you understand them. It is helpful to ask someone from another culture or someone who has a severe disability how well you communicate with him or her. (A higher level of empathy is required to communicate well with somebody much different from yourself.) If you have external or internal customers, ask them how well you appear to understand their position.

If you find any area of deficiency, work on that deficiency steadily. For example, perhaps you are not perceived as taking the time to understand a point of view quite different from your own. Attempt to understand other points of view. Suppose you believe strongly that money is the most important motivator for practically everybody. Speak to a person with a different opinion and listen carefully until you understand that person's perspective.

A few months later, obtain more feedback about your ability to empathize. If you are making progress, continue to practice. Then, repeat these steps for another facet of emotional intelligence. As a result you will have developed another valuable interpersonal skill.

DISCUSSION QUESTIONS AND ACTIVITIES

1. How much faith do voters place in the trait theory of leadership when they elect public officials?

2. Suppose a college student graduates with a major for which he or she lacks enthusiasm. What might this person do about becoming a passionate leader?

3. What would a manager to whom you report have to do to convince you that he or she has high self-confidence?

4. What would a manager to whom you report have to do to convince you that he or she has humility?

5. Describe any leader or manager, whom you know personally or have watched on television, who is unenthusiastic. What effect did the lack of enthusiasm have on group members?

6. Why is emotional intelligence considered more important than technical skill at high-level leadership positions?

7. A CEO made the following comment about leadership and intelligence: "Sometimes a less than top IQ is an advantage because that person doesn't see all the problems. He or she sees the big problem and gets on and gets it solved. But the extremely bright person can see so many problems that he or she never gets around to solving any of them." What is your reaction to his comment?

8. A disproportionate number of people who received an M.B.A. at Harvard Business School are top executives in *Fortune* 500 business firms. How does this fact fit into the evidence about the roles of heredity and environment in creating leaders?

9. Visualize the least effective leader you know. Identify the traits, motives, and personal characteristics in which that person might be deficient.

10. Many people who disagree with the trait approach to leadership nevertheless still conduct interviews when hiring a person for a leadership position. Why is conducting such interviews inconsistent with their attitude toward the trait approach?

Leadership Case Problem A

What Leadership Characteristics Does Reuben Mark Possess?

Many high-profile CEOs have changed positions in recent years, but not Reuben Mark. He has been the top executive at Colgate-Palmolive Company since 1984. Mark has worked his way successfully through previous business slumps, so it did not surprise outside analysts that he was able to keep the company on track during the economic slowdown in the first two years of the new century.

Business Accomplishments. A key factor in Mark's favor has been his relentless focus on developing new products and getting them into markets around the world at high speed. In 2000, Colgate earned 38 percent of its revenues from products launched in the past five years. Four years earlier, 27 percent of revenues were derived from relatively new products. In the last quarter of 2001, Colgate-Palmolive had earnings growth of 7.6 percent, in comparison to losses at its major competitors.

It would be difficult for most people on Wall Street, or Main Street, to believe that during a recent seventeen-year period Colgate-Palmolive has quietly outperformed legendary GE, not to mention Coke, IBM, and the benchmark S&P 500. Even as rival consumer goods giants Procter & Gamble and Gillette have stumbled badly, Colgate has risen steadily.

Despite these accomplishments, Mark has been unwilling to bask in the glory so many other CEOs savor. He even refused to cooperate in a *Fortune* story about his accomplishments, explaining that he would prefer that the spotlight be on Colgate's 38,000 employees.

Leadership continuity has been a key factor in Colgate's success. While Procter & Gamble has burned through four CEOs in ten years, Mark and Colgate president Bill Shanahan have run a tight ship, with few defections and a consistent habit of delivering the numbers. Financial analyst Andrew Shore said about Colgate, "It grabbed the brass ring a long time ago" (*Fortune*, April 16, 2001, p. 180).

The clearest evidence of management's success is the company's margins. Since Mark became CEO, Colgate's gross profit margin has risen from 39.4 percent to 54.4 percent. Analysts attribute the gains to a culture that is continually looking to improve efficiency by sweating the small stuff. For example, a simple redesign of Mennen deodorant's packing saved a few cents on each unit.

"The senior management of Colgate isn't just talking strategy at 60,000 feet, they are deeply involved in the details," says Mike Dolan, the CEO of Colgate's only advertising agency (*Fortune*, p. 180). Dolan recently spent two solid days behind closed doors with Mark, Shanahan, and other Colgate executives reviewing the company's global advertising. They were all business, with cell phones and laptops turned off. Says Dolan, "Reuben Mark is very smart, very demanding, and very, very, funny" (*Fortune*, p. 180).

Personal Life and Community Involvement. Mark avoids media interviews because he does not like to draw too much attention to himself. He is happier filling the role of the CEO devoted to his employees. One summer day he was spotted cheering for the Colgate softball team in New York's Riverside Park. In the past, he and his wife Arlene have spent many Saturdays tutoring kids in Manhattan as part of the "I Have a Dream" foundation. At Mark's urging, Colgate has become involved: The company financed the rebuilding of a school in Harlem. Mark rarely talks about community activities.

Born in blue-collar Jersey City, New Jersey, Mark attended Middlebury College and later earned an M.B.A. from Harvard Business

School. He and his family live in the fashionable New York suburb of Greenwich, Connecticut.

QUESTIONS

1. Which leadership traits, characteristics, and motives does Mark (and his executive team) appear to possess? Support your answer with specific statements in the case history.

2. Which traits, motives, and characteristics do you perceive to be Mark's strongest?

3. What suggestions can you offer Reuben Mark to improve as a leader or to improve the company?

SOURCE: *Nelson D. Schwartz, "Colgate Cleans Up,"* Fortune, *April 16, 2001, pp. 179–180; "The Top 25 Managers: Reuben Mark, Colgate-Palmolive,"* Business-Week, *January 14, 2002, p. 65.*

Leadership Case Problem B

The Urban Improvement Guys

Larry Glazer admits his latest project is a bit of an experiment. Along with partner Harold Samloff, Glazer is in the middle of rehabbing the long-vacant Michael-Sterns building on North Clinton Avenue in Rochester, New York. They plan to turn it into a mix of office spaces and loft apartments.

It's a project that's a bit out of character for Glazer and Samloff's Buckingham Properties. "We're gambling a bit," Glazer says. "If it works we might try it again." That willingness to branch out into different areas has turned Buckingham Properties into one of Rochester's top developers. Buckingham has made its name by piecing together assemblages of properties—first residential, then industrial, Glazer likes to say.

Now Glazer, 56, and Samloff, 65, have turned their attention to an eclectic mix of properties in the Inner Loop, a highway around the downtown area. They are hoping to find a profit in the growing demand for fashionable office space. They say they have a firm commitment to improving life in the city. "We've always said that just like urban blight spreads, urban improvement spreads too."

Glazer and Samloff credit an even division of labor with helping them succeed. Glazer's title is chief executive officer; Samloff is chief operating officer. Samloff tackles management issues while Glazer pores over new prospects for the company. The staff members they have assembled have allowed Glazer and Samloff to focus more on the strategic future of the company than on the day-to-day intricacies of managing properties. "When we started out, we were doing everything," Glazer says. But the two still keep close tabs on their holdings. "We're tire-kickers," Samloff says. "We like to visit our projects on a regular basis."

The partnership is more than thirty years old. Glazer and Samloff met each other in 1970 during a Sunday morning tennis game organized by some friends. Samloff decided to ask Glazer if he wanted to partner on a rental property. Soon they were buying more houses together. At the time, Samloff was a full-time attorney and Glazer was working in the printing industry. Gradually, the real estate venture became a full-time job.

They continued to expand their holdings, buying houses and stores in the city not far from downtown. Then an opportunity to renovate an old industrial site presented itself—and Samloff and Glazer found they liked managing industrial properties. "We never really did have a game plan," Samloff says. "We just reviewed opportunities as they came to us."

The Michael-Sterns building was formerly a men's clothing plant that closed in 1977. Buckingham will spend about $6.5 million on renovation; but that price tag isn't so bad considering the company bought the building from the city for $10,000.

One of the tenants in the building is the Catholic Family Center. Carolyn Portanova, the CEO of the center, says that she has great admiration for her new landlords. She says the project could be a catalyst for rehabilitating the whole neighborhood. "There's an energy there when you work with someone who has a vision about what something can be." Another tenant says he appreciates the fact that the Buckingham partners strike a deal and stick by it.

Both Glazer and Samloff enjoy the hands-on nature of their work and are also active in the community. The two men are now looking to the future. Both admit they are looking at life for their company after they leave. "We've got a business plan that we think should be continued," Samloff says. "We take something and say, this is pretty raw, but is there a gem in this ore we can extract?"

QUESTIONS

1. Explain whether or not Glazer and Samloff qualify as leaders.

2. In what ways do the traits and characteristics of Glazer and Samloff complement each other?

3. What evidence do you find that Glazer and Samloff are farsighted?

4. What cognitive skills are reflected in the leadership of Buckingham Properties?

SOURCE: *David Tyler, "Buckingham to Broadway," Rochester, New York, Democrat and Chronicle, April 11, 2002, pp. 1E, 8E; personal interview with Harold Samloff, June 21, 2002.*

INTERNET SKILL–BUILDING EXERCISE

Measuring Your Emotional Intelligence

Apply the chapter concepts! Visit the Web and complete this Internet skill-building exercise to learn more about current leadership topics and trends.

Go to **www.eqhelp.com/saelfimp2.htm**, and choose one of two alternatives. (1) Obtain a scientific measurement of your emotional intelligence for about the price of a fully loaded pizza or fancy T-shirt. (Choose the option for the Simmons EQ Insights.) Compare your score on the test with your self-evaluation of your emotional intelligence. (2) For free, rate yourself on the thirteen key areas of emotional intelligence mentioned in the web site. Which of these areas are closely related to the traits, motives, and characteristics of leaders presented in this chapter?

Charismatic and Transformational Leadership

CHAPTER 3

Andrea Jung waits in the wings of the Thomas & Mack Center in Las Vegas to address the biggest crowd she has ever faced. Jung couldn't be more cool and composed. In her red floor-length ball gown with spaghetti straps and white shoes with sharp-pointed toes, Jung, at 41, looks more like a movie star than the CEO of a $5.3 billion company, Avon Products, Inc. As she strides onto the stage, she is met by an explosion of applause from some 13,000 mostly 40- and 50-something Avon women reps who have traveled to Las Vegas from all across the U.S. to see Avon's new product lines, listen to live entertainers, and do aerobics.

The contrast is striking: the svelte, fashionable, Ivy League–educated, New York fast-tracker preaching to mostly Middle America moms and grandmas whose fashion tastes lean toward slacks for dressy occasions and sweat suits and sneakers for the rest of the convention.

Still, with a mike in her hand and giant TV screens in the background projecting her image, Jung has no problem firing up the crowd. "Avon is first and foremost about you," she proclaims. "I stand here before you and promise you that that will never change." Jung vows that Avon Products, Inc. can be as big in the women's beauty business as Walt Disney Co. is in the entertainment business. Later in the presentation Jung describes her business strategy for selling Avon products through the Internet and retail stores, door-to-door, and at house parties.

"We will change the future of women around the world!" she exclaims. And as the audience rises to a standing ovation, Jung wraps up with the most amazing declaration of all: "I love you all."[1]

Andrea Jung exemplifies leaders who are so warm, engaging, and passionate about people and products that their constituents eagerly accept their leadership. Such leaders are said to be charismatic. The same leaders are described as transformational when they facilitate major changes in organizations and get people to transcend their personal interests for the good of the organization. The study of charismatic and transformational leadership is an extension of the trait theory, and has resurfaced as an important way of understanding leadership.

In this chapter we examine the meaning and effects of charismatic leadership, the characteristics of charismatic leaders, how such leaders form visions, and how one develops charisma. We also describe the closely related and overlapping subject of transformational leadership. Finally, we look at the dark side of charismatic leadership.

THE MEANINGS OF CHARISMA

Charisma, like leadership itself, has been defined in various ways. Nevertheless, there is enough consistency among these definitions to make charisma a useful concept in understanding and practicing leadership. To begin, *charisma* is a Greek word meaning divinely inspired gift. In the study of leadership, **charisma** is

TABLE 3-1   Definitions of Charisma and Charismatic Leadership

1. A certain quality of an individual personality by virtue of which he or she is set apart from ordinary people and treated as endowed with supernatural, superhuman, or at least specifically exceptional powers or qualities (sexist language changed)

2. A devotion to the specific and exceptional sanctity, heroism, or exemplary character of an individual person, and of the normative patterns revealed or ordained by that person

3. Endowment with the gift of divine grace

4. The process of influencing major changes in the attitudes and assumptions of organization members, and building commitment for the organization's objectives

5. Leadership that has a magnetic effect on people

6. In combination with individualized consideration, intellectual stimulation, and inspirational leadership, a component of transformational leadership

Source: (1) Max Weber, The Theory of Social and Economic Organization *(New York: The Free Press, 1947), p. 358. (Original work published in 1924.); (2) Max Weber, cited in S. N. Eisenstadt,* Max Weber: On Charisma and Institution Building *(Chicago: University of Chicago Press, 1968); (3) Bernard M. Bass, "Evolving Perspectives on Charismatic Leadership," in* Charismatic Leaders, *eds. Jay A. Conger, Rabindra N. Kanungo, et al. (San Francisco: Jossey-Bass, 1988), p. 40; (4) Gary A. Yukl,* Leadership in Organizations, *3rd ed. (Upper Saddle River, N.J.: Prentice Hall, 1994), p. 207; (5) James M. Kouzes and Barry Z. Posner,* The Leadership Challenge: How to Get Extraordinary Things Done in Organizations *(San Francisco: Jossey-Bass, 1987), p. 123; (6) Bernard M. Bass, cited in Kenneth E. Clark and Miriam B. Clark (eds.),* Measures of Leadership, *A Center for Creative Leadership Book (West Orange, N.J.: Leadership Library of America, 1990).*

a special quality of leaders whose purposes, powers, and extraordinary determination differentiate them from others.[2] Table 3-1 presents a sampling of additional definitions of charisma, all of which reflect different subtleties of charisma.

The various definitions of charisma have a unifying theme. Charisma is a positive and compelling quality of a person that makes many others want to be led by him or her. The term *many others* is chosen carefully. Few leaders are perceived as charismatic by *all* their constituents. A case in point is Bill Gates, the chairman and cofounder of Microsoft Corporation, whose name surfaces frequently in discussions of charisma. Despite his wide appeal, many people consider Gates to be brash, outspoken, too all-controlling, and obsessed with demolishing the competition—hardly characteristics of an inspiring leader.

Given that charisma is based on perceptions, an important element of charismatic leadership involves the *attributions* made by group members about the characteristics of leaders and the results they achieve. According to attribution theory, if people perceive a leader to have a certain characteristic, such as being a visionary, the leader will more likely be perceived as charismatic. Attributions of charisma are important because they lead to other behavioral outcomes, such as commitment to the leaders, self-sacrifice, and high performance.

A recent study of attributions and charisma found that the network a person belongs to influences the attributions. The subjects in the study were police workers who rated the director of a police organization, and students in an introductory business course who rated the charisma of their professors. Network members influenced to some extent whether the study participants perceived their leader or professor to be charismatic. Perceptions of charisma were the closest among friends within networks.[3] What about you? Are your perceptions of the charisma of your professors influenced by the opinions of your network members?

Charisma: A Relationship Between the Leader and Group Members

A key dimension of charismatic leadership is that it involves a relationship or interaction between the leader and the people being led. (The same, of course, holds true for all types of leadership.) Furthermore, the people accepting the leadership must attribute charismatic qualities to the leader. John Gardner believes that charisma applies to leader-constituent relationships in which the leader has an exceptional gift for inspiration and nonrational communication. At the same time the constituent's response is characterized by awe, reverence, devotion, or emotional dependence.[4] The late Sam Walton, founder of Wal-Mart Stores, had this type of relationship with many of his employees. Walton's most avid supporters believed he was an inspired executive to whom they could trust their careers.

Charismatic leaders work deliberately at cultivating the relationship with group members through impression management. In other words, they take steps to create a favorable, successful impression. Charismatic leaders recognize that the perceptions of constituents determine whether they function as charismatics. Following are two of the many propositions (or conclusions and interpretations) offered by William L. Gardner and Bruce J. Avolio to explain how charismatic leaders use impression management:[5]

1. Charismatic leaders, to a greater extent than noncharismatic leaders, value and pursue an interrelated set of images—trustworthy, credible, morally worthy, innovative, esteemed, and powerful. Constructing and maintaining these images in the minds of followers is essential for the leader's charismatic image.

2. Charismatic leaders, to a greater extent than noncharismatic leaders, use the assertive impression management strategies of exemplification and promotion to secure and maintain desired identity images of their selves, vision, and organization.

An implication of the impression management analysis of charismatic leaders is that they are skillful actors in presenting a charismatic face to the world. And the behaviors and attitudes of these leaders go well beyond superficial aspects of impression management, such as wearing fashionable clothing or speaking well.

Charismatic leadership is possible under certain conditions. The beliefs of the constituents must be similar to those of the leader, and unquestioning acceptance of and affection for the leader must exist. The group members must willingly obey the leader, and they must be emotionally involved both in the mission of the charismatic leader and in their own goals. Finally, the constituents must have a strong desire to identify with the leader.[6]

The Effects of Charisma

Robert J. House developed a theory of charismatic leadership that defines charisma in terms of its effects. A charismatic leader, according to House, is any person who brings about certain outcomes to an unusually high degree. Charismatic leadership has taken place when extraordinary levels of devotion, identification, and emulation are aroused in group members. The nine charismatic effects are as follows:[7]

1. Group members' trust in the correctness of the leader's beliefs
2. Similarity of group members' beliefs to those of the leader
3. Unquestioning acceptance of the leader
4. Affection for the leader
5. Willing obedience to the leader
6. Identification with and emulation of the leader
7. Emotional involvement of the group members or constituents in the mission
8. Heightened goals of the group members
9. Feeling on the part of group members that they will be able to accomplish, or contribute to, the accomplishment of the mission

Jane A. Halpert factor-analyzed (statistically clustered) these nine hypothesized outcomes into three groups or dimensions, as outlined in Figure 3-1.[8] The first six effects refer to the power exerted by the leader. Three of them (similarity of beliefs, affection for the leader, identification with and emulation of the leader) are related to referent power. **Referent power** is the ability to influence others that stems from the leader's desirable traits and characteristics. Three other effects

FIGURE 3-1   Halpert's Dimensions of Charisma

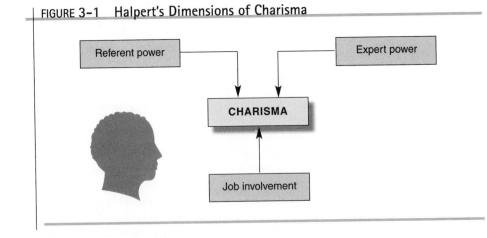

(group member trust, unquestioning acceptance, and willing obedience) are related to expert power. **Expert power** is the ability to influence others because of one's specialized knowledge, skills, or abilities.

The last three effects are perceptions related to the task or mission. Halpert noted also that the job-related effects (emotional involvement, heightened goals, and perceived ability to contribute) are concerned with *job involvement.* As a result, charismatic leaders will encourage group members to be job involved. An empirical study provides more evidence of the relationship between charismatic leadership and job satisfaction. (Job involvement is a key component of satisfaction.) Using a sample of state government employees, the researchers found that managers who rated their own managers as high on charisma tended to have high satisfaction with supervision. Working for a charismatic leader also enhanced commitment to the organization.[9]

In summary, the nine charismatic effects in House's theory can be reduced to three dimensions: referent power, expert power, and job involvement. Such information is useful for the aspiring charismatic leader. To be charismatic, one must exercise referent power and expert power and must get people involved in their jobs.

TYPES OF CHARISMATIC LEADERS

The everyday use of the term *charisma* suggests that it is a straightforward and readily understood trait. As already explained, however, charisma has different meanings and dimensions. As a result, charismatic leaders can be categorized into five types: socialized charismatics, personalized charismatics, office-holder charismatics, personal charismatics, and divine charismatics.[10]

Following the distinction made for the power motive, some charismatic leaders use their power for the good of others. A **socialized charismatic** is a leader who restrains the use of power in order to benefit others. This type of leader also attempts to develop a value congruence between himself or herself and constituents. The socialized charismatic formulates and pursues goals that fulfill the needs of group members and provide intellectual stimulation to them. Followers of socialized charismatics are autonomous, empowered, and responsible.

A second type of charismatic leader is the **personalized charismatic.** Such individuals exercise few restraints on their use of power so they may best serve their own interests. Personalized charismatics impose self-serving goals on constituents, and they offer consideration and support to group members only when it facilitates their own goals. Followers of personalized charismatics are typically obedient, submissive, and dependent.

Another type of charismatic leader is the *office-holder charismatic.* For this type of leader, charismatic leadership is more a property of the office occupied than of his or her personal characteristics. The chief executive officer of General

Electric, for example, might have considerable luster but would lose much of it immediately after leaving office. By occupying a valuable role, office-holder charismatics attain high status. Office-holder charisma is thus a byproduct of being placed in a key position.

In contrast to office-holder charismatics, *personal* (not *personalized*) charismatics gain very high esteem through the extent to which others have faith in them as people. A personal charismatic exerts influence whether he or she occupies a low- or high-status position because he or she has the right traits, characteristics, and behaviors. Secretary of State Colin H. Powell would qualify in the eyes of many as a personal charismatic. After retiring from his position as the top-ranking U.S. army general, Powell was deluged with offers to serve on corporate boards and to make speaking appearances. He was eventually appointed as secretary of state in the George W. Bush administration.

A historically important type of charismatic leader is the *divine charismatic*. Originally, charismatic leadership was a theological concept: A divine charismatic is someone endowed with a gift of divine grace. In 1924 Max Weber defined a charismatic leader as a mystical, narcissistic, and personally magnetic savior who would arise to lead people through a crisis. When Steven Jobs helped lead Apple Computer back to profitability and acclaim in the late 1990s, many company employees and Apple Computer fans reacted to him as if he were a divine charismatic. At stockholder meetings, some stockholders screeched and cheered as if Jobs were a famous rock star.

The Leader in Action box describes a charismatic executive. After reading the excerpt, categorize this leader into one of the five types just described.

CHARACTERISTICS OF CHARISMATIC LEADERS

The outstanding characteristic of charismatic leaders is that they are charismatic! In addition, they have other distinguishing characteristics. Many of these characteristics also apply to transformational leaders because charisma is a key component of transformational leadership. A **transformational leader** is one who brings about positive, major changes in an organization. Many charismatic leaders, however, are not transformational. Although they inspire people, they may not bring about major organizational changes. As we look at the characteristics of charismatic leaders,[11] you will note that many of these characteristics apply to leaders in general.

Charismatic leaders are *visionary* because they offer an exciting image of where the organization is headed and how to get there. A vision is more than a forecast; it describes an ideal version of the future of an entire organization or an organizational unit. The next section provides additional information about vision in leadership, including guidelines on how to develop a vision. Chapter 13, in discussing the leadership aspects of business strategy, also contains information about formulating visions.

Leader in Action

John Chambers of Cisco Systems, Upbeat Leader and Salesman

John T. Chambers, the CEO of Cisco Systems, Inc., has been referred to as "Mr. Internet." His impact on the Internet has been compared to the impact of Bill Gates on the personal computer. Chambers envisions a new world network that will blend the technology of the Internet with high-speed optical fibers, cable, and wireless systems to carry voice and data everywhere.

The Cisco Business. Cisco was for a time the fastest-growing computer company in history. The company builds products to network the Internet. Cisco provides a broad range of products for transporting data, voice, and video within buildings and throughout the world. It has 38,000 employees and about $16 billion in annual revenues. Cisco frequently purchases companies that offer products or services that provide a promising new technology or the opportunity to expand market share in a particular niche.

During the Internet boom, everything Cisco did seemed bigger, faster, and better. Its sales and earnings growth were at the top of the industry. The company was a leader in selling equipment over the Internet, as it hurried to meet a demand for Internet equipment that seemed insatiable. For 43 consecutive quarters Cisco met or beat Wall Street's expectations for higher earnings. For one brief moment, Cisco had the highest total stock value of any company.

Chambers's Personal Style and Leadership. Chambers, a former manager at both IBM and Wang, talks flamboyantly about Cisco, with statements like "We want to create the greatest company in history" and "We want to change the world" (*Fortune*, May 15, 2000, p. 118). Even during a severe business downturn several years ago, Chambers insisted that Cisco could still change the world and increase revenues by more than

30 percent annually. "There is a confidence that if we execute right, we have a higher probability of winning now than ever before. I believe that the best years are in front of us" (*BusinessWeek*, January 21, 2002, p. 55).

In his upbeat, rat-a-tat style, Chambers continues with his stump speech to investors and business analysts. He contends that the company's customer focus, culture of empowerment, skills in acquiring companies, and dominant market share allow it to overcome hurdles. "Let's not kid ourselves," he says. "This market is coming to us. It is going to consolidate. Who in this industry is better at consolidation than Cisco? And who by the way, has the assets that Cisco does?" (*BusinessWeek*, January 21, 2002, p. 57). Chambers thinks he can reach his stretch growth targets by taking greater market share from rivals and conquering new markets.

Despite his optimism, Chambers does not dismiss the negative impact of the downturn of the Internet economy. He likens the slump to a 100-year flood. "It's something you don't expect to see in your lifetime. We never built models to anticipate something of this magnitude" (*Fast Company*, July 2001, p. 102). Chambers stays attuned to employee thoughts and feelings through periodic meetings in the company auditorium.

Chambers prefers managing and leading in a growth environment than during a downturn. The decision to lay off 8,500 employees in March 2001 was difficult for him. A long-time colleague said, "He's almost too nice to kick the asses that needed to be kicked" (*BusinessWeek*, January 21, 2002, p. 61).

Chambers says that everybody likes periods of growth, but that you have to deal with the world the way it is, not the way you wish it to be. He believes that you develop character during difficult times. This is when you have to help the whole team learn, especially the newer managers, who have not dealt with adversity. "You have to listen very carefully, be as sure as possible that you've got the issues right, set the direction—and get your whole team pulling in that direction. Then it's all about leadership. You keep people very calm, very focused, and yet with a sense of urgency, because this is the chance to really gain market share" (*Fast Company*, July 2001, p. 102).

Chambers believes that in the midst of difficult times you need a willingness to take risk. It is important to listen closely to customers and look for signs that something they want is not yet on the market, and then respond.

Chambers avoids allowing managers to build up ever-larger empires because he believes that such growth prevents a more focused approach to customers. A smaller sales group must pay more attention to each customer. He believes that the small-unit approach works best if people are empowered. "If your style is top-down and centralized, you'll get very consistent performance, but you'll also limit growth" (*Fast Company*, July 2001, p. 108).

Controversy About Cisco. Although the Cisco business performance has been widely acclaimed, some analysts believe that some of Cisco's impressive results can be attributed to an exaggerated statement of its true earnings. Nevertheless, the company's accounting practices have been regarded as aggressive but not illegal. One example would be to frantically ship as much product as possible the last night of a fiscal quarter to count the merchandise as "sold."

The success of Cisco and Chambers's rise as a New Economy visionary might have been due to a fascination with technology stocks, a massive Internet buildup, and an era that looked aside at creative accounting practices. A senior technology analyst said that Cisco most likely will not be able to repeat its early successes. One concern is that many Cisco customers went bankrupt and put much of their Cisco equipment for sale at clearance prices. Although Cisco brags about having a sophisticated inventory planning system, it was caught with excess inventory during the dot-com downturn.

QUESTIONS

1. What evidence does this case history present that Chambers is charismatic?

2. How would you describe Chambers's communication style?

3. What do you like (or dislike) about Chambers's approach to leadership and management?

SOURCE: *John A. Byrne and Ben Elgin, "Cisco Behind the Hype,"* BusinessWeek, *January 21, 2002, pp. 54–61; George Anders, "John Chambers After the Deluge,"* Fast Company, *July 2001, pp. 100–111; Andy Serwer, "There's Something About Cisco,"* Fortune, *May 15, 2000, pp. 114–138; "John Chambers, President and CEO, Cisco Systems,"* PeopleTalk Online Magazine, *"Profile—Cisco Systems, Inc.," March–May 2000, www.peopletalkonline.com/en/new/peopletalk/ mar2000/ceo/;http://biz.yahoo.com/p/c/csco.html.*

Charismatic leaders have *masterful communication skills.* To inspire people, the charismatic leader uses colorful language and exciting metaphors and analogies. (More about the communication skills of charismatic leaders is presented later in this chapter.) Another key characteristic is the *ability to inspire trust.* Constituents believe so strongly in the integrity of charismatic leaders that they will risk their careers to pursue the chief's vision. Charismatic leaders are *able to make group mem-*

bers feel capable. One technique for helping group members feel more capable is to enable them to achieve success on relatively easy projects. The leader then praises the group members and gives them more demanding assignments.

An *energy and action orientation* characterizes charismatic leaders. Like entrepreneurs, most charismatic leaders are energetic and serve as role models for getting things done on time. *Emotional expressiveness and warmth* are also notable. A key characteristic of charismatic leaders is the ability to express feelings openly. A bank vice president claims that much of the charisma people attribute to her can be explained simply: "I'm up front about expressing positive feelings. I praise people, I hug them, and I cheer if necessary. I also express my negative feelings, but to a lesser extent." Nonverbal emotional expressiveness, such as warm gestures and frequent (nonsexual) touching of group members, is also characteristic of charismatic leaders.

Since emotional expressiveness is such an important part of being and becoming charismatic, you are invited to take Leadership Self-Assessment Quiz 3-1. It will help you think about a practical way of developing charismatic appeal.

Charismatic leaders *romanticize risk.* They enjoy risk so much that they feel empty in its absence. Jim Barksdale, now a venture capitalist for online startup companies and former CEO of Netscape, says that the fear of failure is what increases your heart rate. As great opportunists, charismatic people yearn to accomplish activities others have never done before. Risk taking adds to a person's charisma because others admire such courage. In addition to treasuring risk, charismatic leaders use *unconventional strategies* to achieve success. The charismatic leader inspires others by formulating unusual strategies to achieve important goals. Anita Roddick, the founder of the worldwide chain of cosmetic stores called The Body Shop, accomplishes her goals unconventionally. She travels around the world into native villages, searching out natural beauty products that in the manufacturing process do not harm the environment or animals.

Charismatic leaders often have a *self-promoting personality.* They frequently toot their own horn and allow others to know how important they are. Richard Branson, the colorful chairman of the Virgin Group, has relied on self-promotion to build his empire, a collection of about 200 companies with the Virgin trademark. Among his antics have been to fly around the world in a balloon and to slide down the side of a silver ball attached to a New York City building.

Another characteristic observed in many charismatic leaders is that they challenge, prod, and poke. They test your courage and your self-confidence by asking questions like "Do your employees really need you?"

A final strategy for becoming more charismatic is really an amalgam of the ideas already introduced. Being *dramatic and unique* in significant, positive ways is a major contributor to charisma. Being dramatic and unique stems from a combination of factors such as being energetic, promoting yourself, romanticizing risk, and being emotionally expressive. Andrea Jung, the executive described at the outset of this chapter, is dramatic and unique in the sense that she expresses love for all the Avon ladies.

The Emotional Expressiveness Scale

INSTRUCTIONS   Indicate how well each of the following statements describes you by circling the best answer: very inaccurately (VI); inaccurately (I); neutral (N); accurately (A); very accurately (VA).

		VI	I	N	A	VA
1.	While watching a movie there are times when I will shout in laughter or approval.	1	2	3	4	5
2.	During a group meeting, I have occasionally shouted my approval with a statement such as "Yes" or "Fantastic."	1	2	3	4	5
3.	During a group meeting, I have occasionally expressed disapproval by shouting an expression such as "absolutely not" or "horrible."	1	2	3	4	5
4.	Several times, while attending a meeting, someone has said to me, "You look bored."	5	4	3	2	1
5.	Several times while attending a social gathering, someone has said to me, "You look bored."	5	4	3	2	1
6.	Many times at social gatherings or business meetings, people have asked me, "Are you falling asleep?"	5	4	3	2	1
7.	I thank people profusely when they do me a favor.	1	2	3	4	5
8.	It is not unusual for me to cry at an event such as a wedding, graduation ceremony, or engagement party.	1	2	3	4	5
9.	Reading about or watching news events, such as an airplane crash, brings tears to my eyes.	1	2	3	4	5
10.	When I was younger, I got into more than my share of physical fights or shouting matches.	1	2	3	4	5
11.	I dread having to express anger toward a coworker.	1	2	3	4	5
12.	I have cried among friends more than once.	1	2	3	4	5
13.	Other people have told me that I am affectionate.	1	2	3	4	5
14.	Other people have told me that I am cold and distant.	5	4	3	2	1
15.	I get so excited watching a sporting event that my voice is hoarse the next day.	1	2	3	4	5
16.	It is difficult for me to express love toward another person.	5	4	3	2	1

17.	Even when alone, I will sometimes shout in joy or anguish.	1 2 3 4 5
18.	Many people have complimented me on my smile.	1 2 3 4 5
19.	People who know me well can easily tell what I am feeling by the expression on my face.	1 2 3 4 5
20.	More than once, people have said to me, "I don't know how to read you."	5 4 3 2 1

SCORING AND INTERPRETATION   Add the numbers you circle, and use the following as a guide to your level of emotionality with respect to being charismatic and dynamic.

- 90–100   Your level of emotionality could be interfering with your charisma. Many others interpret your behavior as being out of control.
- 70–89   Your level of emotionality is about right for a charismatic individual. You are emotionally expressive, yet your level of emotional expression is not so intense as to be bothersome.
- 20–69   Your level of emotionality is probably too low to enhance your charisma. To become more charismatic and dynamic, you must work hard at expressing your feelings.

If you believe that the emotional expressiveness aspect of charisma is a trait and behavior out of your reach or inclination, direct your efforts toward self-development of other traits and behaviors associated with charisma. For example, work on developing visions and taking risks.

THE VISION COMPONENT OF CHARISMATIC LEADERSHIP

A major buzzword in leadership and management is **vision,** the ability to imagine different and better conditions and ways to achieve them. A vision is a lofty, long-term goal. An effective leader is supposed to have a vision, whereas an ineffective leader either lacks a vision or has an unclear one. Creating a vision is one of the major tasks of top management. A vision is also considered an important part of strategy implementation. Implementing the vision (or ensuring that the vision is executed) is part of the leader's role. This is true despite the opinion that the leader creates the vision and the manager implements it. Jürgen Schrempp, the chairman of DaimlerChrysler, believes strongly that the leader must also help execute his or her vision. He observes: "The chief should not be the one who just sort of guides the board on vision and strategy. You should also know what you are talking about. I go to the factories and we have debates on how cars should look five years from now."[12]

Visions have become so popular that some companies have them reproduced on wallet-size plastic cards, key rings, and coffee mugs. Several sample vision statements are as follows:

Avon Products, Inc.: The ultimate relationship marketer of products and services for women.

Microsoft Corporation: To give people the power to do anything they want, anywhere they want, and on any device, whether it's on a PC or on a web phone.

Vietnam Airlines: The strategic vision for Vietnam Airlines in the next 10 to 20 years is to become one of the best airlines in the region, to operate efficiently, and to become even better at meeting the increasing requirements of the society for air transportation.

Tommy Hilfiger Corporation: Be whatever our customers want us to be.

The idea of a vision is closely linked to charisma. Charismatic leaders inspire others with their vision. A vision uplifts and attracts others. Scott McNealy, the CEO of Sun Microsystems, exemplifies a charismatic leader who has inspired company insiders and outsiders with his compelling visions. In recent years he has been promoting his vision that "the network is the computer." The vision refers to the idea that his web-focused Java language is the platform on which to build a new generation of inexpensive, single-purpose network appliances. These include TV set-top boxes and cell phones. Another component of the same vision is "to create a combination of services and products that lets companies do pretty much everything a company does—but on the Web."[13]

Although many vision statements appear as if they could be formulated in fifteen minutes, managers invest considerable time in their preparation and often use many sources of data. To create a vision, obtain as much information from as many of the following sources as necessary:

- Your own intuition about developments in your field, the market you serve, demographic trends in your region, and the preferences of your constituents.

- The work of futurists (specialists in making predictions about the future) as it relates to your type of work.

- A group discussion of what it takes to delight the people your group serves.

- Annual reports, management books, and business magazines to uncover the type of vision statements formulated by others.

- Group members and friends; speak to them individually and collectively to learn of their hopes and dreams for the future.

- For a vision for an organizational unit, the organization's vision. You might get some ideas for matching your unit's vision with that of the organization.

Leadership Skill-Building Exercise 3-1 gives you an opportunity to practice vision formulation. Keep in mind that a critic of vision statements once said that it is often difficult to tell the difference between a vision and a hallucination.

Leadership Skill-Building Exercise 3–1

Formulating a Vision

Along with your teammates, assume the role of the top management group of an organization or organizational unit that is in need of revitalization. Your revitalization tactic is to create a vision for the organization. Express the vision in not more than twenty-five words. Use the guidelines for developing a vision described in the text. Come to an agreement quickly on the organization or large organizational unit that needs a vision. Or choose one of the following:

- The manufacturer of an electric-powered automobile
- A sausage manufacturer
- A waste disposal company
- The human resources department of a large company
- A manufacturer of watches retailing for $25,000

The Communication Style of Charismatic Leaders

Charismatic and transformational leaders communicate their visions, goals, and directives in a colorful, imaginative, and expressive manner. In addition, they communicate openly with group members and create a comfortable communication climate. To set agendas that represent the interests of their constituents, charismatic leaders regularly solicit constituents' viewpoints on critical issues. They encourage two-way communication with team members while still promoting a sense of confidence.[14] Here we describe two related aspects of the communication style of charismatic leaders: management by inspiration and management by anecdote.

Management by Inspiration

According to Jay A. Conger, the era of managing by dictate is being replaced by an era of managing by inspiration. An important way to inspire others is to articulate a highly emotional message. Roger Enrico, the long-time dynamic CEO of PepsiCo, Inc., directed a leadership development program for selected company managers. At the outset of the program, he knocked participants off balance by telling them that "nobody in this room can look at the company's problems and blame the turkeys at the top. You're now one of them."[15] Conger has observed two major rhetorical techniques of inspirational leaders: the use of metaphors and analogies, and the ability to gear language to different audiences.[16]

Using Metaphors and Analogies. A well-chosen analogy or metaphor appeals to the intellect, to imagination, and to values. The charismatic Mary Kay Ash, founder of the cosmetics company Mary Kay Inc., made frequent use of metaphors during her career. To inspire her associates to higher performance, she often said: "You see, a bee shouldn't be able to fly; its body is too heavy for its wings. But the bumblebee doesn't know that and it flies very well." Mary Kay explains the message of the bumblebee metaphor in these terms: "Women come to us not knowing they can fly. Finally, with help and encouragement, they find their wings—and then they fly very well indeed."[17]

Gearing Language to Different Audiences.   Metaphors and analogies are inspiring, but effective leaders must also choose the level of language to suit the audience. The challenge of choosing the right level of language is significant because constituents vary widely in verbal sophistication. One day, for example, a CEO might be attempting to inspire a group of Wall Street financial analysts, and the next day she or he might be attempting to inspire first-level employees to keep working hard despite limited salary increases.

Conger has observed that an executive's ability to speak on a colloquial level helps create appeal. A person with the high status of an executive is expected to use an elevated language style. When the person unexpectedly uses the everyday language of an operative employee, it may create a special positive response.

Management by Anecdote

Another significant aspect of the communication style of charismatic and transformational leaders is that they make extensive use of memorable anecdotes to get messages across. **Management by anecdote** is the technique of inspiring and instructing team members by telling fascinating stories. The technique is a major contributor to building a strong company culture. David Armstrong, an executive at Armstrong International, uses the following anecdote to reinforce the importance of listening to customers:

> Bill, our sales manager, wanted to add an obsolete feature to our company's new fish finder. We thought he was crazy. Bill knew that we preferred only to offer high-end, advanced products in order to hold on to our market share. The "flasher mode" he wanted to add to our fish finders was outdated, since it only told the fishers that fish were nearby—while our new computerized models would also indicate the fish's location and size.
>
> Who on earth would want the old-fashioned fish finder? Our customers, as it turned out. Many of them were old-time fishermen and didn't feel comfortable with the newfangled model, which confused them. They wanted the kind of machine they were used to.
>
> Nobody agreed with Bill at first, but eventually he got his way. We put the "flasher" back on the fish finder. Customers are still calling us to tell us how much they like this feature. We've sold a lot more units, because we listened to the market.[18]

After Armstrong tells this story, he explains the lessons illustrated by the story. One is, "Listen, listen, listen to your salespeople and your customers. Get direct

Leadership Skill-Building Exercise 3-2

Charismatic Leadership by Anecdote

INSTRUCTIONS   Gather in a small problem-solving group to develop an inspiring anecdote about something that actually happened, or might have happened, at a present or former employer. Here are some guidelines:

1.   Make up a list of core values the firm holds dear, such as quality, service, or innovation.

2.   Think of an incident in which an employee strikingly lived up to (or violated) one of these values. Write it up as a story with a moral.

3.   Share your stories with other members of the class, and discuss whether this exercise could make a contribution to leadership development.

SOURCE: *From "Management by Anecdote,"* SUCCESS, *December 1992, p. 35. Copyright © 1992 SUCCESS Publishing Inc. Reprinted by permission.*

feedback and don't second-guess them." Another is, "Ask yourself if this feature is necessary. Technology is not an end in itself." The third lesson is that classic products can outsell new products. Experts told the Coca-Cola Company to change its formula, but Coca-Cola drinkers didn't agree.[19]

To get started developing the skill of management by anecdote, do Leadership Skill-Building Exercise 3-2.

THE DEVELOPMENT OF CHARISMA

By developing some of the traits, characteristics, and behaviors of charismatic people, a person can increase his or her charisma. Several of the charismatic characteristics described earlier in the chapter are capable of development. For example, most people can enhance their communication skills, become more emotionally expressive, take more risks, and become more self-promoting. In this section we examine several behaviors of charismatic people that can be developed through practice and self-discipline.

Create Visions for Others.   Being able to create visions for others will be a major factor in your being perceived as charismatic. A vision uplifts and attracts others. To form a vision, use the guidelines presented previously in the chapter. The visionary person looks beyond the immediate future to create an image of what the organization or unit thereof is capable of becoming. A vision is designed to close the discrepancy between present and ideal conditions. The vision thus sees beyond present realities.

Another characteristic of an effective vision formulated by the leader is that it connects with the goals and dreams of constituents.[20] The leader of a group manufacturing fuel cells for electric cars might listen to the team members talk about their desires to help reduce pollution in the atmosphere. This dream might translate into the vision statement as a "desire to save the planet" or "reduce global warming."

Be Enthusiastic, Optimistic, and Energetic.   A major behavior pattern of charismatic people is their combination of enthusiasm, optimism, and high energy. Without a high level of all three characteristics, a person is unlikely to be perceived as charismatic by many people. A remarkable quality of charismatic people is that they maintain high enthusiasm, optimism, and energy throughout their entire workday and beyond. Elevating your energy level takes considerable work, but here are a few feasible suggestions:

1. Get ample rest at night, and sneak in a fifteen-minute nap during the day when possible. If you have a dinner meeting where you want to shine, take a shower and nap before the meeting.
2. Exercise every day for at least 10 minutes, including walking. No excuses allowed, such as being too busy or too tired, or the weather being a handicap.
3. Switch to a healthy, energy-enhancing diet.
4. Keep chopping away at your To Do list so you do not have unfinished tasks on your mind, draining your energy.

An action orientation contributes to being enthusiastic, optimistic, and energetic. "Let's do it" is the battle cry of the charismatic person. An action orientation also means that the charismatic person prefers not to agonize over dozens of facts and nuances before making a decision.

Be Sensibly Persistent.   Closely related to the high energy level of charismatics is their almost-never-accept-no attitude. I emphasize the word *almost* because outstanding leaders and individual contributors know when to cut their losses. If an idea or a product will not work, the sensible charismatic absorbs the loss and moves in another, more profitable direction. An executive at a telecommunications company said, "A test of executive material in our company is whether the middle manager has the guts to kill a failed project. Some managers become so ego-involved in a product they sponsored, they fight to keep it alive long after it should have died. They twist and distort financial information to prove that there is still life left in their pet product. A person with executive potential knows when to fold his or her tent."

Remember Names of People.   A consistent behavior of charismatic leaders, as well as other successful people, is remembering the names of people with whom they have infrequent contact. (Sorry, no charisma credits for remembering the name of everyday work associates.) The personal interest charismatic leaders take in their work associates contributes to their ability to remember the names of so many people. Pat Croce, the owner of the Philadelphia 76ers, exemplifies a charismatic leader with an exceptional ability to remember names. He greets the 500-plus men and women who work at the 76ers' arena on game night with an easy familiarity, and he calls people by their first names. Adding to his charisma, Croce waves, makes high-five gestures, and shakes hands as he circles the arena.[21]

Many systems and gimmicks are available for remembering names, such as making an association between the person's name and a visual image. For example, if you meet a woman named Betsy Applewhite visualize her with an apple (or a white personal computer) on her head. The best system of name-retention remains to listen carefully to the name, repeat it immediately, and study the person's face.

Make an Impressive Appearance.   By creating a polished appearance, a person can make slight gains in projecting a charismatic image. If exquisite clothing and good looks alone made a person a charismatic leader, those impressive-looking store associates in upscale department stores would all be charismatic leaders. Ralph Lauren, the most successful fashion designer in American history,[22] is a leader who has enhanced his charisma through his impeccable physical appearance. Given that he is in the fashion business, a "Ralph Lauren-like" appearance is important for his personal image as well as to help build a brand image.

In attempting to enhance your charisma through appearance, it is necessary to analyze your work environment to assess what type of appearance is impressive. Ralph Lauren, with his exquisite suits, cuff links, and pocket handkerchief, would create a negative image at a Silicon Valley firm. His carefully cultivated appearance would detract from his charisma. (Of course, Lauren could enhance his charisma by wearing clothing from his sporty Polo line.)

Be Candid.   Charismatic people, especially effective leaders, are remarkably candid with people. Although not insensitive, the charismatic person is typically explicit in giving his or her assessment of a situation, whether the assessment is positive or negative. Charismatic people speak directly rather than indirectly, so that people know where they stand. Instead of asking a worker, "Are you terribly busy this afternoon?" the charismatic leader will ask, "I need your help this afternoon. Are you available?"

Display an In-Your-Face Attitude.   The preferred route to being perceived as charismatic is to be a positive, warm, and humanistic person. Yet some people earn their reputation for charisma based on toughness and nastiness. An in-your-face attitude may bring you some devoted supporters, although it will also bring you many detractors. The tough attitude is attractive to people who themselves would like to be mean and aggressive.

TRANSFORMATIONAL LEADERSHIP

The focus on transformational leadership is on what the leader accomplishes, rather than on the leader's personal characteristics and his or her relationship with group members. As mentioned previously, the transformational leader helps bring about major, positive changes. To explain further, the transformational leader moves group members beyond their self-interests for the good of the group, organization, or society. In contrast, the transactional leader focuses on more routine transactions with an emphasis on rewarding group members for meeting standards (contingent reinforcement). Extensive research by Bernard M. Bass indicates that the transformational-versus-transactional distinction has been observed in a wide variety of organizations and cultures.[23]

So who is a transformational leader? An extreme example is Dale Fuller, the president and CEO of Inprise, a software company specializing in developer tools. When Fuller took on the assignment of rescuing Borland Software Corporation (the company name in 1999), the reactions of his friends ranged from disbelief to horror. Said Fuller, "My friends all said the same thing: 'You're going to go in there and start performing CPR on a corpse.' They were right. The company wasn't on the ropes, it was *hanging* by a rope. It wasn't even still twitching."[24] (Notice the communication style of a charismatic leader.) Fuller crafted a plan for short-term emergency measures such as drastic cost cutting, and a longer-term plan that focused on Internet applications. He also manipulated Microsoft into paying Inprise $100 million for the rights to use its patented technology in Microsoft products. Fuller and his team worked fourteen hours every day for nine months, and they developed sophisticated new products focusing on the company's strengths. Within one year the firm was profitable.

How Transformations Take Place

Leaders often encounter the need to transform organizations from low performance to acceptable performance, or from acceptable performance to high performance. At other times, a leader is expected to move a firm from a crisis mode to high ground, as with Dale Fuller, just mentioned. To accomplish these lofty purposes, the transformational leader attempts to overhaul the organizational culture or subculture. His or her task can be as immense as the process of organizational change. To focus our discussion specifically on the leader's role, we look at several ways in which transformations take place.[25] (See Figure 3-2.)

1. *Raising people's awareness.* The transformational leader makes group members aware of the importance and values of certain rewards and how to achieve them. He or she might point to the pride workers would experience should the firm become number 1 in its field. At the same time, the leader should point to the financial rewards accompanying such success.

2. *Helping people look beyond self-interest.* The transformational leader helps group members look to "the big picture" for the sake of the team and the

FIGURE 3-2   How Transformations Take Place

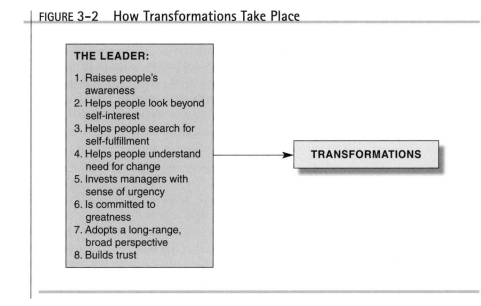

THE LEADER:

1. Raises people's awareness
2. Helps people look beyond self-interest
3. Helps people search for self-fulfillment
4. Helps people understand need for change
5. Invests managers with sense of urgency
6. Is committed to greatness
7. Adopts a long-range, broad perspective
8. Builds trust

→ **TRANSFORMATIONS**

organization. The executive vice president of a bank told her staff members, "I know most of you dislike doing your own support work. Yet if we hire enough staff to make life more convenient for you, we'll be losing money. Then the government might force us to be taken over by a larger bank. Who knows how many management jobs would then have to be cut."

3. *Helping people search for self-fulfillment.* The transformational leader helps people go beyond a focus on minor satisfactions to a quest for self-fulfillment. The leader might explain, "I know that making sure you take every vacation day owed you is important. Yet if we get this proposal out on time, we might land a contract that will make us the envy of the industry." (Being the envy of the industry satisfies the need for self-fulfillment.)

4. *Helping people understand the need for change.* The transformational leader must help group members understand the need for change both emotionally and intellectually. The problem is that change involves dislocation and discomfort. An effective transformational leader recognizes this emotional component to resisting change and deals with it openly. Organizational change is much like a life transition. Endings must be successfully worked through before new beginnings are possible. People must become unhooked from their pasts.

Dealing with the emotional conflicts of large numbers of staffers is obviously an immense task. One approach taken by successful leaders is to conduct discussion groups, in which managers and workers are free to discuss their feelings about the changes. This approach has been used quite effectively when firms are downsized. Many of the "survivors" feel guilty that they are still employed while many competent coworkers have lost their jobs. Clearly, conducting these sessions requires considerable listening skill on the manager's part.

5. *Investing managers with a sense of urgency.* To create the transformation, the leader assembles a critical mass of managers and imbues in them the urgency of change. The managers must also share the top leader's vision of what is both necessary and achievable. To sell this vision of an improved organization, the transformational leader must capitalize on available opportunities.

6. *Committing to greatness.* Peter Koestenbaum argues that business can be an opportunity for individual and organizational greatness. By adopting this greatness attitude, leaders can ennoble human nature and strengthen societies. Greatness encompasses striving for business effectiveness such as profits and high stock value, as well as impeccable ethics. An emphasis on ethical leadership instills a desire for customer service and quality and fosters feelings of proprietorship and involvement.[26] (A commitment to greatness is, of course, important for all leaders, not just those who are charismatic.)

7. *Adopting a long-range perspective and at the same time observing organizational issues from a broad rather than a narrow perspective.* Such thinking on the part of the transformational leader encourages many group members to do likewise. Unless many people think with a future orientation, and broadly, an organization cannot be transformed.[27]

8. *Building trust.* Another useful process for transforming a firm is to build trust between leaders and group members, particularly because distrust and suspicion are rampant during a company revival. Executive Carlos Ghosn found that building trust was an essential ingredient of his turnaround efforts at Nissan Motors in Japan several years ago. One component of building trust was to impose transparency on the entire organization. In this way everyone knew what everyone else was doing.[28]

Attributes of Transformational Leaders

Transformational leaders possess the personal characteristics of other effective leaders, especially charismatic leaders. In addition, a compilation of studies suggests seven qualities that are particularly helpful in enabling leaders to bring about transformations.[29] Above all, transformational leaders are *charismatic.* Two key personality factors enhancing their charisma are agreeableness and extroversion, which combine to enhance their interpersonal relationships.[30] Unless they are the brutal slash-and-burn type of turnaround manager, transformational leaders have the respect, confidence, and loyalty of group members.

Charismatic, transformational leaders create a *vision.* By communicating a vision, they convey a set of values that guide and motivate employees. Although transformational leaders are often heavily concerned with organizational survival, they also take the time to *encourage the personal development of their staff.*

Dale Fuller, the transformational leader mentioned above, gave a clear direction to his staff about focusing on Net products. As a result, the staff developed by concentrating on products that the company badly wanted. Transformational leaders also give *supportive leadership* through such means as giving positive feedback to group members and recognizing individual achievements.

Transformational leaders practice *empowerment* by involving team members in decision making, as do most effective leaders and managers. John Chambers of Cisco, who is somewhat of a transformational leader, regards empowerment as the distinguishing feature of his leadership. *Innovative thinking* helps transformational leaders achieve their goals, such as developing ways to raise cash and cut costs quickly. Transformational leaders encourage their staff to think innovatively and give them challenging assignments. As with other effective leaders and managers, they also *lead by example*. During a period of cost-cutting, for example, a transformational leader might fly business coach and eat in the company cafeteria (instead of having gourmet food catered to his or her office).

A new line of thinking about transformational leadership suggests that some characteristics may be more important for maximum performance than for typical performance. The study involved an East Asian military sample of new leaders who were rated by several observers. Analysis of the data indicated that maximum performance was associated with openness to experience and extroversion. Being emotionally stable was more important for typical performance.[31]

The description of the characteristics of transformational leaders is a useful stopping point for a disclaimer that applies to many aspects of the study of leaders. Not every leader classified as transformational will have the seven characteristics just described. For example, some transformational leaders are brusque with people rather than agreeable. Furthermore, it is not always easy to determine whether a given leader can be accurately described as transformational.

The Impact of Transformational and Charismatic Leadership on Performance

Although the present discussion deals primarily with transformational leadership, it would be artificial to separate its impact on performance from that of charismatic leadership. An important reason is that charismatic leadership, as already discussed, is a component of transformational leadership. A concern some scholars have about transformational leadership is that it sounds too mystical and "soft." Fortunately, several empirical studies have been conducted on the effects of charismatic and transformational leadership in work settings. We review two of them here.

Business Unit Performance. As part of a larger study, Jane M. Howell and Bruce J. Avolio investigated the relationship of transformational leadership to business unit performance.[32] The sample included seventy-eight managers from the highest four levels of management in a large Canadian financial institution. At the time of the study, the firm was facing a turbulent external environment because of increased competition. A modification of the MLQ Charismatic Leadership Scale was developed to measure three aspects of transformational leadership: charisma, intellectual stimulation, and individual consideration. (A similar version of the MLQ appears in Manager Assessment Quiz 3-2.) The measure of business unit performance represented the degree to which the manager reached goals for the year, calculated in terms of the percentage of goals met. Each goal was measured against criteria for expected, superior, and outstanding performance.

Data analysis revealed that leaders who displayed more individualized consideration, intellectual stimulation, and charisma positively contributed to business unit performance. Leaders who used the techniques of management by exception and contingent rewards (positive reinforcement) were less likely to increase unit performance. The authors concluded that the more positive contribution to business unit performance came from behaviors associated with transformational leadership.

Charismatic Leader Behavior in Military Units.   A study of charismatic leadership behavior was conducted with fifty field companies in the Israel Defense Forces. Four factors were used to measure charisma: (1) showing supportive behavior toward soldiers; (2) displaying exemplary behavior such as showing energy and activity, courage, and self-confidence; (3) emphasizing ideological convictions, including connecting the unit's mission and tasks to broad values; and (4) emphasizing collective identity, or producing a distinctive collective identity for the group.

The researchers hypothesized that the more a leader engages in three of the charismatic behaviors just mentioned (emphasizing ideology, emphasizing collective identity, and displaying exemplary behavior), the higher the performance appraisal of the leader by his or her superior. Analysis of the data indicated that the performance appraisal by a leader's superior was positively and strongly related to two of the charismatic behaviors, an ideological emphasis and exemplary behavior.[33] In brief, two specific aspects of charismatic behavior by leaders were related to higher performance as perceived by their superiors. As a leader, it pays to emphasize ideology and be a positive role model.

CONCERNS ABOUT CHARISMATIC LEADERSHIP

Up to this point, an optimistic picture has been painted of both the concept of charisma and charismatic leaders. For the sake of fairness and scientific integrity, contrary points of view must also be presented. The topic of charismatic leadership has been challenged from two major standpoints: the validity of the concept, and the misdeeds of charismatic leaders.

Challenges to the Validity of Charismatic Leadership

Some leadership researchers doubt that charisma can be accurately defined and measured. Conducting research about charisma is akin to conducting research about high quality: You know it when you see it, but it is difficult to define in

Manager Assessment Quiz 3–2

The MLQ Charismatic Leadership Scale

INSTRUCTIONS   Rate your current manager, or any other manager you remember well, on the items below. Use the following 5-point scale: 0 (not at all), 1 (once in a while), 2 (sometimes), 3 (fairly often), and 4 (frequently).

1.	Makes me feel good to be around him or her.	0 1 2 3 4
2.	Commands respect from everyone.	0 1 2 3 4
3.	Is a model for me to follow.	0 1 2 3 4
4.	In my mind, he or she is a symbol of success and accomplishment.	0 1 2 3 4
5.	I am ready to trust his or her capacity and judgment to overcome any obstacle.	0 1 2 3 4
6.	Is an inspiration to us.	0 1 2 3 4
7.	Makes me proud to be associated with him or her.	0 1 2 3 4
8.	Has a special gift for seeing what is really important for me to consider.	0 1 2 3 4
9.	Increases my optimism for the future.	0 1 2 3 4
10.	Inspires my loyalty to the organization.	0 1 2 3 4
11.	I have complete faith in him or her.	0 1 2 3 4
12.	Excites us with his or her visions of what we may be able to accomplish if we work together.	0 1 2 3 4
13.	Encourages me to express my ideas and opinions.	0 1 2 3 4
14.	Encourages understanding of points of view of other members.	0 1 2 3 4
15.	Gives me a sense of overall purpose.	0 1 2 3 4
16.	Has a sense of mission that he or she transmits to me.	0 1 2 3 4
17.	Makes everyone around him or her enthusiastic about assignments.	0 1 2 3 4

SCORING AND INTERPRETATION

- 0–17   Your manager has below-average charisma.
- 18–36   Your manager has about average charisma.
- 37–50   Your manager has above-average charisma.
- 51–68   Your manager is highly charismatic.

SOURCE: *Adapted with permission of The Free Press, a Division of Simon & Schuster, Inc., from* Leadership and Performance Beyond Expectations *by Bernard M. Bass. Copyright © 1985 by The Free Press.*

operational terms. Furthermore, even when one leader is deemed to be charismatic, he or she has many detractors. According to the concept of **leadership polarity,** leaders are often either revered or vastly unpopular. People rarely feel neutral about them. Bill Gates is a prime example of leadership polarity. Thousands of people are almost mesmerized by Gates, but thousands of other people dislike him intensely (or are envious). By the year 2000 about 200 web sites had accumulated of the nature "*www.ihatebillgates.com*" (a generic site not directing the reader to a specific site). Martha Stewart is another popular leader who experiences leadership polarity. Many of her fans are mesmerized by her personality and accomplishments. Many of her detractors detest her (perhaps based on envy) and were gleeful when Stewart was accused of insider trading in 2002.

Another problem with the concept of charisma is that it may not be necessary for leadership effectiveness. Warren Bennis and Burt Nanus have observed that very few leaders can accurately be described as charismatic. The organizational leaders the two researchers studied were "short and tall, articulate and inarticulate, dressed for success and dressed for failure, and there was virtually nothing in terms of physical appearance, personality, or style that set them apart from followers."

Based on these observations, Bennis and Nanus hypothesized that instead of charisma resulting in effective leadership, the reverse may be true. People who are outstanding leaders are granted charisma (perceived as charismatic) by their constituents as a result of their success.[34]

The Dark Side of Charismatic Leadership

Some people believe that charismatic leadership can be exercised for evil purposes. This argument was introduced previously in relation to personalized charismatic leaders. Years ago, Robert Tucker warned about the dark side of charisma, particularly with respect to political leaders:

> The magical message which mesmerizes the unthinking (and which can often be supplied by skilled phrase makers) promises that things will become not just better but perfect. Charismatic leaders are experts at promising Utopia. Since perfection is the end, often the most heinous actions can be tolerated as seemingly necessary means to that end.[35]

More recently it has been observed that some charismatic leaders are unethical and lead their organizations toward illegal and immoral ends. People are willing to follow the charismatic leader down a quasi-legal path because of his or her referent power.[36] Garry Winnick, the former chairman of Global Crossing Ltd., is a recent symbol of how gluttonous and destructive a charismatic leader can be. Winnick, a former junk bond broker, charmed thousands with his affable personality. He purchased several Rolls Royce automobiles as gifts for social friends and work associates. On the way to leading Global Crossing toward bankruptcy, he sold about $730 million of his own company stock. His work space was a replica of the White House Oval Office. While thousands of workers were being laid off, Winnick was building the most expensive private residence in the world for himself and his family. With renovations, the property in Bel Air, California, was valued at about $90 million.

Another way of framing the issues of the dark side of charisma is that some charismatic and transformational leaders neglect their social responsibility. A charismatic leader's ability to influence constituents multiplies the importance of his or her having a strong sense of social responsibility (described in Chapter 6). For example, a CEO who invests substantial personal time in helping community groups will inspire workers throughout the firm to do the same. Leaders who are not particularly charismatic also have an obligation to behave in socially responsible ways, thus serving as positive models.

SUMMARY

Charisma is a special quality of leaders whose purposes, powers, and extraordinary determination differentiate them from others. It is also a positive and compelling quality of a person that makes many others want to be led by that person. An important element of charismatic leadership involves the attributions made by group members about the characteristics of leaders and the results they achieve. Social network members often influence a person's attributions of charisma. The relationship between group members and the leader is important because of these attributions. Charismatic leaders frequently manage their impressions to cultivate relationships with group members.

Charismatic leadership can be understood in terms of its effects, such as group members' trust in the correctness of the leader's beliefs. One study showed that the effects of charismatic leadership can be organized into three dimensions: referent power, expert power, and job involvement. Charismatic leadership enhances job satisfaction.

Charismatic leaders can be subdivided into five types: socialized, personalized (self-interested), office-holder, personal (outstanding characteristics), and divine. Charismatic leaders have characteristics that set them apart from noncharismatic leaders. Charismatic leaders have a vision, masterful communication skills, the ability to inspire trust, and are able to make group members feel capable. They also have an energy and action orientation, are emotionally expressive and warm, romanticize risk, use unconventional strategies, have a self-promoting personality, and emphasize being dramatic and unique.

The idea of vision is closely linked to charisma because charismatic leaders inspire others with their vision, and a vision uplifts and attracts others. In formulating a vision, it is helpful to gather information from a variety of sources, including intuition, futurists, and group members.

Charismatic and transformational leaders communicate their visions, goals, and directives in a colorful, imaginative, and expressive manner. Communication effectiveness allows for management by inspiration. One communication technique to inspire others is through metaphors, analogies, and organizational stories. Another is gearing language to different audiences. Charismatic and transformational leaders also extensively use memorable anecdotes to get messages across.

A person can increase his or her charisma by developing some of the traits, characteristics, and behaviors of charismatic people. The suggestions presented here include creating visions for others; being enthusiastic, optimistic, and energetic; being sensibly persistent; remembering names of people; making an impressive appearance; being candid; and displaying an in-your-face attitude.

To bring about change, the transformational leader attempts to overhaul the organizational culture or subculture. The specific change techniques include raising people's awareness of the importance of certain rewards and getting people to look beyond their self-interests for the sake of the team and the organization. Transformational leaders help people search for self-fulfillment and understand the need for change, and they invest managers with a sense of urgency. The transformational leader also commits to greatness, adopts a long-range perspective, and builds trust.

Transformational leaders have characteristics similar to those of other effective leaders. In addition, they are charismatic, create a vision, encourage personal development of the staff, and give supportive leadership. Emphasis is also placed on empowerment, innovative thinking, and leading by example.

Empirical research indicates that leaders who display more individualized consideration, intellectual stimulation, and charisma (transformational leaders) have high business unit performance. A study conducted in military units indicated that performance appraisals by leaders' superiors were positively related to the specific charismatic behaviors of ideological emphasis and exemplary behavior. One concern about charismatic and transformational leadership is that the concept is murky. Many noncharismatic leaders are effective. Another concern is that some charismatic leaders are unethical and devious, suggesting that being charismatic does not necessarily help the organization. By behaving in a socially responsible manner, charismatic leaders can avoid abusing their influence over others.

KEY TERMS

Charisma

Referent power

Expert power

Socialized charismatic

Personalized charismatic

Transformational leader

Vision

Management by anecdote

Leadership polarity

GUIDELINES FOR ACTION AND SKILL DEVELOPMENT

Roger Dawson offers suggestions to help a person act in a charismatic manner, thus creating charismatic appeal. All of them relate to well-accepted interpersonal skill techniques.

1. **Be sure to treat everyone you meet as the most important person you will meet that day.** For example, when at a company meeting, shake the hand of every person you meet.

2. **Multiply the effectiveness of your handshake.** Shake firmly without creating pain, and make enough eye contact to notice the color of the other person's eyes. When you take that much trouble, you project care and

concern. Think a positive thought about the person whose hand you shake.

3. **Give sincere compliments.** Most people thrive on flattery, particularly when it is plausible. Attempt to compliment only those behaviors, thoughts, and attitudes you genuinely believe merit praise. At times you may have to dig to find something praiseworthy, but it will be a good investment of your time.

4. **Thank people frequently, especially your own group members.** Thanking others is still so infrequently practiced that it gives you a charismatic edge.

5. **Smile frequently, even if you are not in a happy mood.** A warm smile seems to indicate a confident, caring person, which contributes to a perception of charisma. A smile generally says, "I like you. I trust you. I'm glad we're together."

6. **Maintain a childlike fascination for your world.** Express enthusiasm for and interest in the thoughts, actions, plans, dreams, and material objects of other people. Your enthusiasm directed toward others will engender enthusiasm in you.[37]

DISCUSSION QUESTIONS AND ACTIVITIES

1. Identify a business, government, education, or sports leader whom you perceive to be charismatic. Explain the basis for your judgment.

2. Identify a well-known leader who is *not* charismatic. Explain what other qualities might have helped this leader succeed.

3. Steven Jobs of Apple Computer, Inc. and many fashion designers wear the same outfit most of the time, even for press interviews and trade shows or fashion shows. The outfit consists of a long-sleeve or short-sleeve T-shirt and blue jeans without a belt. How does this costume affect their projection of charisma?

4. Describe how a person might write email messages to give an impression of being charismatic.

5. Aside from contributing to leadership effectiveness, for what other types of jobs might charisma be an asset?

6. Explain why the presence of a charismatic leader tends to enhance the job satisfaction of group members.

7. What opportunities might a first-level supervisor or team leader have to be a transformational leader?

8. In what way is a *transactional* leader functioning more as a manager than a leader?

9. A concern has been expressed that leaders who are charismatic are often incompetent. They simply get placed into key positions because they create such a good impression. What do you think of this argument?

10. Design a research study or survey to determine if you are perceived as being charismatic. Be prepared to share your observations with other class members.

Leadership Case Problem A

Pat Russo Wants to Rescue Lucent

Lucent Technologies designs, builds, and delivers a wide range of public and private networks, communication systems and software, data networking systems, business telephone systems, and microelectronic components. Bell Laboratories is the research and development component of the company (www.lucent.com). Lucent was spun off from AT&T in 1996 and showed excellent progress in sales, profits, and stock price for four years. Then the company was hard hit by the tumbling Internet industry, starting in 2000.

Russo Brought In for the Turnaround. Patricia Russo was recruited back to Lucent as its new chief executive to complete a complex turnaround started by predecessor Henry Schacht. Russo had previously spent nine months as the president and chief operating officer at Eastman Kodak Company. She held a variety of managerial positions at Lucent between 1992 and 2001. When she returned to Lucent, Russo said, "This is a job that I feel like I've been preparing for all my life" (Associated Press, June 10, 2002).

Russo is considered so competitive that colleagues have asked her to avoid sports on company retreats. "They actually asked her to stop playing golf and tennis because she would win every time," said a former AT&T manager who has known Russo for fifteen years.

But Russo needs considerable drive as she attempts to restore confidence within Lucent Technology's drastically smaller work force and among its biggest customers, the giant communication service providers. "My focus is that we both survive and thrive, and they are sequential," Russo, age 49, says. "It's my intent that as we come through this industry downturn we emerge stronger, leaner, more competitive and a more customer-focused company than we've ever been" (Associated Press, June 10, 2002).

Russo took over as Lucent's CEO just fourteen months into a restructuring that had seen the company's work force slashed from about 120,000 to 56,000 through retirement buyouts, asset sales, spinoffs, and some 20,000 layoffs. Many employees still felt uneasy because at that point 6,000 more layoffs were being planned. Starting in 2000, Lucent had repeatedly missed earnings targets. During the fall the company had to reduce previously reported revenues by $125 million for sales booked prematurely.

Before Russo returned, Lucent also faced other major problems. The company was focusing on a technology for increasing the capacity of fiber-optic communications networks while rival Nortel Networks was pushing another technology that was more in demand by customers. Around the same time, Lucent financed big equipment purchases by Internet-based companies that collapsed without paying the loans.

Schacht said that Russo was an excellent fit for the position because she knew Lucent's business well and had previously turned around AT&T's Business Communications Systems division. She had reduced costs, improved products, earned the trust of customers, and restored profits. Furthermore, she strengthened her leadership skills during her brief time as president of Kodak. "She hit the ground without any break in stride," Schacht said. "It's early days, but so far, so good" (Associated Press, June 10, 2002).

Russo's assignment at Lucent is considered one of the toughest corporate repair jobs in America. Lucent has a glamorous history, yet it is a high-profile flameout and has credibility problems with Wall Street and millions of disappointed shareholders. To add to the challenge, most of Lucent's major phone company and telecommunications customers are plagued with profitability struggles of their own, as well as investor distrust.

Russo strode calmly into the storm. In her first quarter as CEO, Lucent cut its loss to about $400 million from $3.7 billion a year earlier, sharply improved its gross margin, returned to a positive cash flow, and increased revenues slightly while competitors' sales were falling. Yet the company's costs are still high for its sales volume.

Russo's Leadership and Management Approach. Russo is intense but reserved, unlike many of the flamboyant leaders that boards turn to when the company needs a quick fix. Her posture is flawless, and she chooses her words with precision. During informal meetings with customers and chats with employees, she loosens up a bit and appears more amiable.

Her taste of power as head of the AT&T business communications unit triggered her thinking about wanting to lead a major corporation. "It was my first real job where I was in charge, and I had control of all the levers," Russo says. "I realized I liked it. I liked the relationship between choosing and planning, and seeing what worked and why" (Fortune, April 15, 2002, p. 128).

Russo continues to drive down costs and aims to reach break-even after the second quarter of her tenure. She is expanding Lucent's small board of directors and has brought in new executives. A financial analyst who called Lucent's stock "toxic waste" a few years ago is recommending the stock again. He says that Russo is a strong manager whose executives "will walk through walls for her." "My concern about Pat is whether she has the outside world perspective and the creativity to grow the company," the analyst says (Associated Press, June 10, 2002).

Current and former colleagues and industry analysts say Russo is a consensus builder who inspires loyalty from both managers and rank-and-file workers. Joe McCabe, a colleague at AT&T, describes her as a decisive but approachable leader who takes time to get input from colleagues and low-level managers. When Russo became president of the struggling business phone systems unit in 1995, she had to lay off thousands of workers to restore profitability. By year's end the unit was back on track. By keeping the staff informed about what to expect, she prevented a victim mentality from developing. "She'll tell it like it is," McCabe says. "That builds loyalty, and that builds morale" (Associated Press, June 10, 2002).

As Russo looks toward the revitalization of Lucent, her basic plan seems to be to continue along the track that her predecessor Henry Schacht had established: sell more equipment to the world's largest wireless and wired telecommunications companies. To accomplish this goal, Russo will emphasize improving customer relations with the big telecom companies. She notes, "Nobody is going to give anything to us. We have to earn their business each and every day, in everything that we do" (Fortune, April 15, 2002, p. 130).

"Pat has the opportunity to earn her way into the business hall of fame," says Jim Citrin, the executive recruiter who placed her at Kodak. "She'll have to execute spectacularly—and the strategy has to be right" (Fortune, April 15, 2002, p. 128). By autumn 2002, Russo was still struggling to implement her strategy. Lucent Technologies announced that it would lay off an additional 10,000 workers because revenues continued to plunge and losses continued to mount. The executive team said that job cuts and other restructuring moves, such as an inventory write-down, were needed for Lucent to lower its break-even point.

QUESTIONS

1. In what ways might Russo be classified as a transformational leader?

2. Based on the evidence presented, how would you rate Russo's charisma?

3. What suggestions might you offer Patricia Russo to help accelerate the turnaround at Lucent?

4. How ethical was Russo in leaving Lucent, taking a top job at Kodak, and then returning to Lucent in nine months?

SOURCE: Linda A. Johnson, "CEO's Drive Spurs Lucent Rebound," The Associated Press, June 10, 2002; Stephanie N. Mehta, "Pat Russo's Lucent Vision," Fortune, April 15, 2002, pp. 126–130; "Lucent Tech to Lop Off 10,000 More Workers," Associated Press, October 12, 2002.

Leadership Case Problem B

Charismatically Challenged Chad

Twenty-seven-year-old Chad McAllister worked as a merchandising specialist for ValuMart, one of the largest international retail chains. Based in the United States, ValuMart also has a strong presence in Canada, Europe, Japan, and Hong Kong. Chad began his employment with ValuMart as an assistant store manager, and two years later he was invited into the training program for merchandising specialists.

Chad performed well as a merchandising trainee in the soft-goods line. His specialty areas included men's, women's, and children's clothing, linens and bedding, men's and women's jewelry, and home decorations. For several years in a row, Chad received performance evaluation ratings of above average or outstanding. Among the write-in comments made by his supervisors were "diligent worker," "knows the tricks of merchandising," "good flair for buying the right products at the right price," and "fits right into the team."

Despite the positive performance appraisals supported with positive comments, Chad had a gnawing discontent about his career at ValuMart. Although he had five years of good performance, he was still not invited to become a member of the "ValuTrackers," a group of merchandising and operations specialists who are regarded as being on the fast track to becoming future ValuMart leaders. The leaders hold high-level positions such as head merchandiser, regional vice president, and store manager.

Several times when Chad inquired as to why he was not invited to join the ValuTrackers, he was told that he was not quite ready to be included in this elite group. He was also told to not be discouraged because the company still valued his contribution.

One day Chad thought to himself, "I'm headed toward age 30, and I want a great future in the retail business now." So he convinced his boss, the merchandising supervisor (Evan Tyler), to set up a career conference with three people: Chad, his boss, and his boss's boss (Heather Bridges), the area merchandising manager. He let Evan know in advance that he wanted to talk about his potential for promotion.

Evan started the meeting by saying, "Chad, perhaps you can tell Heather and me again why you requested this meeting."

Chad responded, "Thanks for asking, Evan. As I mentioned before, I'm wondering what you think is wrong with me. I receive a lot of positive feedback about my performance, but I'm not a ValuTracker. Also, you seem to change the subject when I talk about wanting to become a merchandising supervisor, and eventually a merchandising executive. What am I doing wrong?"

Heather responded, "Evan and I frequently talk about the performance and potential of all our merchandising specialists. You're a good performer, Chad, but you lack that little spark that makes a person a leader. You go about your job efficiently and quietly, but that's not enough. We want future leaders of ValuMart to make an impact."

Evan added, "I go along with Heather's comments. Another point, Chad, is that you rarely take the initiative to suggest ideas. I was a little shocked by your request for a three-way career interview because it's one of the few initiatives you have taken. You're generally pretty laid back."

"Then what do I have to do to convince you two that I should be a ValuTracker?" asked Chad.

Heather replied, "Start acting more like a leader. Be more charismatic." Evan nodded in agreement.

QUESTIONS

1. What career advice can you offer Chad McAllister?

2. What might Chad do to develop more charisma?

3. What is your opinion of the fairness of the ValuTracker program?

INTERNET SKILL–BUILDING EXERCISE

Charisma Tips from the Net

Apply the chapter concepts! Visit the Web and complete this Internet skill-building exercise to learn more about current leadership topics and trends.

A section in this chapter offered suggestions for becoming more charismatic. Search the Internet for additional suggestions and compare them to the suggestions in the text. A good starting point is www.PowerPointers.com. Be alert to contradictions, and offer a possible explanation for each contradiction. You might want to classify the suggestions into two categories: those dealing with the inner person, and those dealing with more superficial aspects of behavior. A suggestion of more depth would be to become a visionary, and a suggestion of less depth would be to wear eye-catching clothing.

Leadership Behaviors, Attitudes, and Styles

CHAPTER 4

Sam Walton made a deal with Wal-Mart employees, expressed in these terms: "If you're good to people, and fair with them, and demanding of them, they will eventually decide that you're on their side." Walton died in 1992, but the language of that deal still peppers the dialogue of Wal-Mart executives and the company's official literature. A quote that runs, in large type, across the top of a page in Wal-Mart's associate handbook is typical: "The undeniable cornerstone of Wal-Mart's success can be traced back to our strong belief in the dignity of each individual."

Or, listen to Wal-Mart spokesman Jay Allen: "If we didn't practice respect for the individual, didn't operate in an open-door environment, we would not be living up to the expectations that our associates have of us." Coleman Petersen, the head of human resources at Wal-Mart Stores, Inc., made a similar point: "The higher up in the organization you go, the more of a servant you need to become because of the respect and expectations that Wal-Mart associates have of you as a leader."[1]

The brief statements just made by leaders at Wal-Mart illustrate the importance of relationship-oriented behaviors and attitudes—including being a servant to group members—for achieving success as a leader. The chapter describes a number of key behaviors and attitudes that help a manager's function as a leader. We also describe the closely related topic of leadership styles.

Frequent reference is made in this chapter, and at other places in the text, to leadership effectiveness. A working definition of an **effective leader** is one who helps group members attain productivity, quality, and satisfaction.

THE CLASSIC DIMENSIONS OF INITIATING STRUCTURE AND CONSIDERATION

Studies conducted at Ohio State University in the 1950s identified 1,800 specific examples of leadership behavior that were reduced to 150 questionnaire items on leadership functions.[2] The functions are also referred to as *dimensions of leadership behavior*. This research became the foundation for most of future research about leadership behavior, attitudes, and styles. The researchers asked team members to describe their supervisors by responding to the questionnaires. Leaders were also asked to rate themselves on leadership dimensions.

Two leadership dimensions accounted for 85 percent of the descriptions of leadership behavior: "initiating structure" and "consideration." **Initiating structure** means organizing and defining relationships in the group by engaging in such activities as assigning specific tasks, specifying procedures to be followed, scheduling work, and clarifying expectations for team members. A team leader who helped group members establish realistic goals would be engaged in initiating structure. Other concepts that refer to the same idea include *production emphasis*, *task orientation,* and *task motivation.* The task-related leadership behaviors and attitudes described later in this chapter are specific aspects of initiating structure.

Leaders who score high on this dimension define the relationship between themselves and their staff members, as well as the role that they expect each staff member to assume. Such leaders also endeavor to establish well-defined channels of communication and ways of getting the job done. Five self-assessment items measuring initiating structure are as follows:

1. Try out your own new ideas in the work group.
2. Encourage the slow-working people in the group to work harder.
3. Emphasize meeting deadlines.
4. Meet with the group at regularly scheduled times.
5. See to it that people in the work group are working up to capacity.

Consideration is the degree to which the leader creates an environment of emotional support, warmth, friendliness, and trust. The leader creates this environment by being friendly and approachable, looking out for the personal welfare of the group, keeping the group abreast of new developments, and doing small favors for the group.

Leaders who score high on the consideration factor typically are friendly, are trustful, earn respect, and have a warm relationship with team members. Leaders with low scores on the consideration factor typically are authoritarian and impersonal in their relationships with group members. Five questionnaire items measuring the consideration factor are as follows:

1. Do personal favors for people in the work group.
2. Treat all people in the work group as your equal.
3. Be willing to make changes.
4. Back up what people under you do.
5. Do little things to make it pleasant to be a member of the staff.

The relationship-oriented behaviors described later in this chapter are specific aspects of consideration. Another key example of consideration is *making connections* with people. Julia Stewart, president of the Applebee's division of Applebee's International, Inc., believes that making connections is one of her most essential leadership functions. She spends about five minutes every day checking in with each of the nine managers who directly report to her. They talk about such social topics as where they ate over the weekend (even if it wasn't Applebee's). Stewart says that leaders cannot afford *not* to take time to chitchat. "I worry about the bosses who are in the crisis mode 80 or 90 percent of the time. By spending the first couple of minutes each day with the employees, I have more of an understanding of what makes them tick."[3]

An important output of the research on initiating structure and consideration was a categorization of leaders with respect to how much emphasis they place on the two dimensions. As implied by Figure 4-1, the two dimensions are not mutually exclusive. A leader can achieve high or low status on both dimensions.

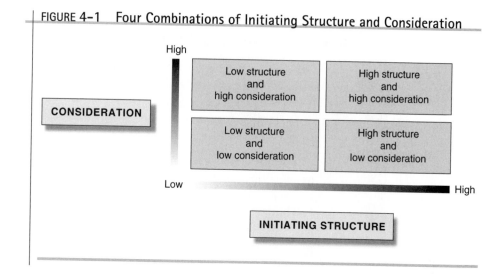

FIGURE 4–1   Four Combinations of Initiating Structure and Consideration

For example, an effective leader might contribute to high productivity and yet still place considerable emphasis on warm human relationships. The four-cell grid of Figure 4-1 is a key component of several approaches to describing leadership style. We return to this topic later in this chapter and in Chapter 5.

TASK-RELATED ATTITUDES AND BEHAVIORS

The task-related versus relationship-related classification remains a useful framework for understanding leadership attitudes, behaviors, and practices. This section identifies and describes task-related attitudes and behaviors that are characteristic of effective leaders, as outlined in Table 4-1. *Task-related* in this context means that the behavior, attitude, or skill focuses more on the task to be performed than on the interpersonal aspect of leadership. Before reading further, do Leadership Self-Assessment Quiz 4-1.

TABLE 4–1   Task-Related Leadership Attitudes and Behaviors

1. Adaptability to the situation
2. Direction setting
3. High performance standards
4. Risk taking and a bias for action
5. Hands-on guidance and feedback
6. Stability of performance
7. Ability to ask tough questions

Leadership Self-Assessment Quiz 4–1

How Effective Are You as a Leader?

INSTRUCTIONS   Circle the number on the 1–5 scale that best indicates how you really feel. If you are not now a manager, project how you would react if you were a manager.

1. I'll wait until things settle down. **1 2 3 4 5** I really like change.

2. Most of my staff meetings are about internal procedures and budgeting. **1 2 3 4 5** I spend much of my time talking to and about customers.

3. If there's a way, I'll find it. **1 2 3 4 5** Top management should make the first move.

4. I'll wait for orders from above. **1 2 3 4 5** Let's get it done right now.

5. I seek responsibility beyond my job description. **1 2 3 4 5** I fulfill my job description.

6. How can I enhance revenue? Add value? **1 2 3 4 5** I'll stay within my budget plan.

7. My people should "challenge the system." **1 2 3 4 5** I carefully review subordinates' work.

8. If I haven't been told *yes*, I can't do it. **1 2 3 4 5** If I haven't been told *no*, I can do it.

9. I'll take responsibility for my failures. **1 2 3 4 5** I usually make excuses for my failures.

10. I won't take risks because I may fail. **1 2 3 4 5** I'll take my risks although I may fail.

11. We've got to do things faster. **1 2 3 4 5** We can't turn things around that fast.

12. I want to know what other departments are doing and what their needs are. **1 2 3 4 5** I protect my own department.

13. I talk mainly to those people who are formally linked to me. **1 2 3 4 5** I'll go beyond the organization chart to share information and resources.

14. Leave my people and me alone and let us get our job done.	**1 2 3 4 5**	I'll cross department lines to get the job done.
15. I trust only a few people within the firm.	**1 2 3 4 5**	I volunteer to share ideas and resources with people in other departments.

SCORING AND INTERPRETATION   Measure your effectiveness as a managerial leader as follows: For questions 1, 2, 4, 8, 10, 13, 14, and 15, simply add up the scores. For questions 3, 5, 6, 7, 9, 11, and 12, flip the scale so that a response score of 1 becomes 5, 2 becomes 4, 4 becomes 2, and 5 becomes 1. A total score of 60 means you have the mindset of an effective manager. If you scored below 45, you have some work to do.

SKILL DEVELOPMENT   As with the other self-quizzes in this text, you can squeeze more value out of the quiz by thinking of each item as a potential nugget of wisdom you might be able to apply now or in the future. For example, statement 10 about risk taking could be a reminder that risk taking is an effective leadership behavior.

SOURCE: *Adapted from Oren Harari and Linda Mukai, "A New Decade Demands a New Breed of Manager,"* Management Review, *August 1990, p. 23. Copyright© Oren Harari. Reprinted with permission.*

1. *Adaptability to the situation.* Effective leaders adapt to the situation. Adaptability reflects the contingency viewpoint: A tactic is chosen based on the unique circumstances at hand. A leader who is responsible for psychologically immature group members would find it necessary to supervise them closely. If the group members were mature and self-reliant, the leader would use less supervision. The adaptive leader also selects an organization structure that is best suited to the demands of the situation, such as choosing between a brainstorming group and a committee.

2. *Direction setting.* Given that a major responsibility of leadership is to produce change, the leader must set the direction of that change. Direction setting is part of creating a vision and a component of strategy. The strategy describes a feasible way of achieving the vision. One of the most dramatic examples of direction setting took place at IBM Corporation in 1993 when Louis Gerstner, the new chairman and CEO at the time, pointed the company in a new direction. Instead of emphasizing the manufacture and sale of hardware, the new IBM concentrated on selling services and software.

3. *High performance standards.* Effective leaders consistently hold group members to high standards of performance. When performance is measured against these high standards, productivity is likely to increase, since

people tend to live up to the expectations of their superiors. This is called the **Pygmalion effect,** and it works in a subtle, almost unconscious way. When a managerial leader believes that a group member will succeed, the manager communicates this belief without realizing it. Conversely, when a leader expects a group member to fail, that person will not disappoint the manager. The manager's expectation of success or failure becomes a self-fulfilling prophecy because the perceptions contribute to success or failure.

Charles F. Knight of Emerson Electric Co., a well-respected business leader, is among a handful of CEOs who have been at the helm for decades. He is known for maintaining high standards. Says a company officer, "He's tough as hell and he's demanding, but it's always about business and never personal."[4]

4. *Risk taking and a bias for action.* A bias for action rather than contemplation has been identified as a characteristic of a successful organization.[5] Combined with sensible risk taking, it is also an important leadership behavior. To bring about constructive change, the leader must take risks and be willing to implement those risky decisions. A bias for action is a desire to execute a plan, rather than a tendency to create visions without following through on them. Larry Bossidy, who held high-level positions at GE and Allied Signal, has this to say about the importance of execution: "I'm an impatient person, and I get more satisfaction from seeing things get done than I do about philosophizing or building sand castles. Many people regard execution as detail work that's beneath the dignity of a business leader. That's wrong. It's a leader's most important job."[6]

5. *Hands-on guidance and feedback.* You will recall that technical competence and knowledge of the business are important leadership characteristics. They enable the leader to provide group members with hands-on guidance about how to accomplish important work. The leader who provides such guidance helps the group accomplish important tasks; at the same time, group members learn important skills. Too much guidance of this nature, however, can be a symptom of poor delegation and micromanagement (managing too closely).

Closely related to guidance is giving frequent feedback on performance. The leader can rarely influence the actions of group members without appropriate performance feedback. This feedback tells group members how well they are doing so that they can take corrective action if needed. It also serves as a reinforcer that prompts group members to continue favorable activities. Leadership Skill-Building Exercise 4-1 provides practice in developing feedback skills.

6. *Stability of performance.* Effective leaders are steady performers, even under heavy workloads and uncertain conditions. Remaining steady under conditions of uncertainty contributes to effectiveness because it helps team members cope with the situation. When the leader remains calm, group members are reassured that things will work out. Stability also helps the managerial

Leadership Skill-Building Exercise 4–1

Feedback Skills

After small groups have completed an assignment such as answering the case questions or discussion questions, hold a performance feedback session. Also use observations you have made in previous problem-solving activities as the basis for your feedback. Each group member provides some feedback to each other member about how well he or she thinks the other person performed. Use only volunteers, because this type of feedback may be uncomfortable and disturbing to some individuals. Students not receiving the feedback can serve as observers and later present their feedback on what took place during the exercise. To increase the probability of benefiting from this experience, feedback recipients must listen actively. Refer to the section in Chapter 10 on coaching skills and techniques for more information on feedback and active listening.

A convenient way to do this exercise is for everyone to sit in a circle. Choose one feedback recipient to begin. Going clockwise around the circle, each group member gives that person feedback. After all people have spoken, the feedback recipient gives his or her reactions. The person to the left of the first recipient is the next one to get feedback.

After everyone has had a turn receiving performance feedback, hold a general discussion. Be sure to discuss three key issues:

1. How helpful was the feedback?

2. What was the relative effectiveness of positive versus negative feedback?

3. Were some group members better than others in giving feedback?

leader appear professional and cool under pressure. Many business leaders displayed enormous stability of performance after the September 11, 2001 attacks on the World Trade Center. Among the many heroes and heroines emerging from the crisis were leaders at Morgan Stanley, the World Trade Center's largest tenant. The firm was fully operational forty-eight hours after the tragedy. As Morgan Stanley leaders assured workers that the company would survive, employees were routed to backup facilities in New Jersey and Brooklyn.[7]

7. *Ability to ask tough questions.* There are many times when leaders can be effective by asking tough questions rather than providing answers. A **tough question** is one that makes a person or group stop and think about why they are doing or not doing something. (A tough question might also be considered the *right* question.) In this way, group members are forced to think about the effectiveness of their activities. They might ask themselves, "Why didn't I think of that? It seems so obvious." Asking questions

is important because quite often group members may have the solutions to difficult problems facing the organization.[8]

Here is an example of a tough question: The division general manager says to the marketing manager, "The sales forecast you made for the next four years assumes that teenagers will continue to purchase jeans at the same rate. Suppose jeans suddenly fall out of fashion with teenagers? Why do you depend so heavily on one product? What can you do to prevent a crisis?"

Now that you have studied various components of task-oriented attitudes and behaviors, do Leadership Self-Assessment Quiz 4-2. It will further sensitize you to the task activities of leaders and managers.

RELATIONSHIP-ORIENTED ATTITUDES AND BEHAVIORS

Leadership involves influencing people, so it follows that many effective leadership attitudes, behaviors, and practices deal with interpersonal relationships and are the basis for effective interpersonal skills. Randy Komisar, known as a "virtual CEO" because he helps launch startup technology firms, presents a strong case for building interpersonal relationships. Asked how he sweeps into companies and manages employees effectively, Komisar replied: "I rely on relationship power, not traditional position power that comes from my title. I find that building relationships with people and inspiring them are the key to my leadership. That's how I think any manager becomes a leader."[9]

Table 4-2 lists the seven relationship-oriented attitudes and behaviors that we will discuss next. (Most other parts of this book describe the interpersonal skill aspects of leadership.)

Aligning and Mobilizing People.   Getting people pulling in the same direction and working together smoothly is a major interpersonal challenge. To get people pulling together, it is necessary to speak to many people. The target population

---

TABLE 4-2   Relationship-Oriented Attitudes and Behaviors

1. Aligning and mobilizing people
2. Concert building
3. Creating inspiration and visibility
4. Satisfying higher-level needs
5. Giving emotional support and encouragement
6. Promoting principles and values
7. Being a servant leader

Task–Oriented Attitudes and Behaviors

Leadership Self-Assessment Quiz 4–2

INSTRUCTIONS Indicate whether you mostly agree or mostly disagree with the following statements. Relate the statements to any work situation, including sports, community activities, and school activities, in which you have been responsible for the work of others. If a work situation does not come to mind, imagine how you would act or think.

	Mostly Agree	Mostly Disagree
1. I keep close tabs on productivity figures and interpret them to the group.	___	___
2. I send frequent email messages to group members, giving them information about work procedures.	___	___
3. I clearly specify the quality goals our group needs to achieve.	___	___
4. I maintain clear-cut standards of performance.	___	___
5. When I conduct a meeting, the participants can count on a clear-cut agenda.	___	___
6. I feel good about my workweek only if our team has met or exceeded its productivity goals.	___	___
7. People shouldn't be spending time with computers in the office unless the computers are actually increasing productivity.	___	___
8. I freely criticize work that does not meet standards.	___	___
9. I spend at least 20 percent of my workweek either planning myself or helping team members with their planning.	___	___
10. I spend a good deal of time solving technical or business problems myself, or helping group members do the same.	___	___

INTERPRETATION If you responded "mostly agree" to eight, nine, or ten of the above statements, you have a strong task orientation. If you responded "mostly disagree" to four or more of the statements, you have below-average task-oriented behaviors and attitudes.

SKILL DEVELOPMENT A task orientation is important because it can lead directly to goal attainment and productivity. Nevertheless, a task orientation must be balanced with a strong people orientation and interpersonal skills for maximum effectiveness.

can involve many different stakeholders. Among them are managers and team leaders, higher-ups, peers, and workers in other parts of the organization, as well as suppliers, government officials, and customers. Anyone who can implement the vision and strategies or who can block implementation must be aligned.[10] Once aligned, organizational members can pull together toward a higher purpose.

Whereas alignment of people takes place at almost a spiritual level, mobilization is more involved with getting the group working together smoothly. Mobilizing people is getting individuals with different ideas, skills, and values to carry out the work of the group. Two mobilizing behaviors of the leader are (a) communicating expectations clearly and (b) demonstrating care for team members.

Concert Building.   The leader's role of **concert building** involves both aligning and mobilizing in a manner similar to an orchestra leader. The concert builder's goal is to produce a system that is self-evaluating, self-correcting, self-renewing, and ongoing. David S. Brown describes concert-building leadership in these terms:

> The system can be thought of as a large modern orchestra with a number of professionals playing quite different instruments and performing separate— and often very difficult—tasks. Each instrumentalist, like so many in large organizations, is indeed a specialist in a particular field whose work must be integrated with the work of others to make up a whole.[11]

Henry Mintzberg has updated the analogy of the leader as concert builder. He believes that the way an orchestra conductor leads may serve as a good model for managers in a wide range of businesses. The conductor does a lot of hands-on work, while at the same time inspiring the musicians. The musicians, much like highly skilled professionals in organizations, are highly trained and competent yet need to be infused with energy from time to time.[12] Becoming an organizational concert builder requires many of the skills and insights described throughout this book. Building teamwork, as described in Chapter 9, is particularly relevant.

Creating Inspiration and Visibility.   As described in the discussion of charismatic and transformational leadership, inspiring others is an essential leadership practice. Surveys and focus groups have identified five inspiring practices:

1. Promoting the development of people's talents
2. Recognizing the contribution of others
3. Enabling others to feel like leaders
4. Stimulating others' thinking
5. Building enthusiasm about projects and assignments[13]

Another part of being inspirational is being visible and available, because human contact and connections reinforce inspiration. Former General Electric CEO Jack Welch had this to say about what chief business executives should do: "They have to be visible to their employees, communities, and investors. They have to be candid and they have to be open. They can't be canceling meetings because they're unsure of the economy or this or that or the next thing."[14]

Becoming inspired is an emotional process that is triggered by a variety of behaviors on the part of the leader. The next few sections describe some of the things leaders try to achieve with group members.

Satisfying Higher–Level Needs.

To inspire people, effective leaders motivate people by satisfying higher-level needs, such as needs for achievement, a sense of belonging, recognition, self-esteem, and a feeling of control over one's life. A strictly managerial—rather than leadership—approach would be to push people in the right direction through control mechanisms.[15] An example would be suspending people who did not achieve work quotas. Although this managerial approach might work in the short range, the workers would not be inspired.

Many leaders in organizations express an awareness of the importance of need satisfaction for building good relationships with workers. Dick DeVos, the chief executive of Amway Corp., the multilevel seller of personal and home products, sees need satisfaction as being part of having a genuine regard for workers. He notes:

> My father [the company founder] always looked at his job as being that of a cheerleader, and the more I have been here, the more I appreciate his observation. If the person who ultimately delivers the Amway product doesn't get the job done right because of some need that I have neglected, then I have failed as a CEO. If that person has needs, I have to have compassion enough to recognize and respond to them.[16]

Giving Emotional Support and Encouragement.

Supportive behavior toward team members usually increases leadership effectiveness. A supportive leader gives frequent encouragement and praise. One of the many work-related ways of encouraging people is to allow them to participate in decision making. Emotional support generally improves morale and sometimes improves productivity. In the long term, emotional support and encouragement may bolster a person's self-esteem.[17] Being emotionally supportive comes naturally to the leader who has empathy for people and who is a warm person.

Promoting Principles and Values.

A major part of a top leader's role is to help promote values and principles that contribute to the welfare of individuals and organizations. The promotion of values and principles can be classified as relationship-oriented because it deals directly with the emotions and attitudes of people, and indirectly with the task. Steven Covey, who is widely quoted for his uplifting messages, advises that an organization's mission statement must be for all good causes.[18] Leaders who believe in these good causes will then espouse principles and values that lead people toward good deeds in the workplace. Almost every leader or manager—even the most devious—claims to harbor values and principles that promote human welfare and the general good. Yet not all leaders and managers actually implement such values and principles.

To encourage managers and all other employees to conduct their work affairs at a high moral level, many companies put their values in written form. Ted Waitt, the founder of Gateway Inc., the direct seller of computers, observed that at one point his company was growing too rapidly. He felt that the culture was changing too rapidly and that company values were no longer ingrained. So he wrote down a series of values that he believed were of critical importance to Gateway's success. Most employees can now recite the list of values in the order Waitt proposed: respect, caring, teamwork, common sense, aggressiveness, honesty, efficiency, and fun. "These values provide our boundaries along the path to prosperity," Waitt wrote.[19]

Leadership Skill-Building Exercise 4-2 gives you an opportunity to think through your work-related values so that you can better provide moral leadership to others. Providing moral leadership begins with understanding one's own values.

Being a Servant Leader.   As mentioned in the chapter opener, servant leadership is considered essential at higher levels at Wal-Mart. A **servant leader** serves constituents by working on their behalf to help them achieve their goals, not the leader's own goals. The idea behind servant leadership, as formulated by Robert K. Greenleaf, is that leadership derives naturally from a commitment to service.[20] Serving others, including employees, customers, and community, is the primary motivation for the servant leader. A servant leader is therefore a moral leader. Servant leadership has been accomplished when group members become wiser, healthier, and more autonomous. Key aspects of servant leadership are described next.[21]

1. *Place service before self-interest.* A servant leader is more concerned with helping others than with acquiring power, prestige, financial reward, and status. The servant leader seeks to do what is morally right, even if it is not financially rewarding. He or she is conscious of the needs of others and is driven by a desire to satisfy them. (You will recall that wanting to satisfy the needs of others is a basic relationship behavior.)

2. *Listen first to express confidence in others.* The servant leader emphasizes listening in order to get to know the concerns, requirements, and problems of group members. Instead of attempting to impose his or her will on others, the servant leader listens carefully to understand what course of action will help others accomplish their goals. After understanding others, the best course of action can be chosen. Through listening, for example, a servant leader might learn that the group is more concerned about team spirit and harmony than striving for companywide recognition. The leader would then concentrate more on building teamwork than searching for ways to increase the visibility of the team.

3. *Inspire trust by being trustworthy.* Being trustworthy is a foundation behavior of the servant leader, so he or she is scrupulously honest with others, gives up control, and focuses on the well-being of others. The servant leader, however, does not have to work hard at being trustworthy because people who aspire to become such leaders are already quite moral.

4. *Focus on what is feasible to accomplish.* Even though the servant leader is idealistic, he or she recognizes that one individual cannot accomplish

Leadership Skill-Building Exercise 4-2

Clarifying Your Work Values

INSTRUCTIONS   To provide effective value leadership, it is essential that you first understand your own values with respect to dealing with others. Rank from 1 to 12 the importance of the following values to you as a person. The most important value on the list receives a rank of 1; the least important, a rank of 12. Use the space next to "Other" if we have left out an important value in your life.

____ Having respect for the dignity of others

____ Ensuring that others have interesting work to perform

____ Earning the trust of others

____ Earning the respect of others

____ Impressing others with how well my group performs

____ Giving others proper credit for their work

____ Inspiring continuous learning on the part of each member in our group, myself included

____ Holding myself and others accountable for delivering on commitments

____ Helping others grow and develop

____ Inspiring others to achieve high productivity and quality

____ Developing the reputation of being a trustworthy person

____ Other

1. Compare your ranking of these values with that of the person next to you, and discuss.

2. Perhaps your class, assisted by your instructor, might arrive at a class average on each of these values. How does your ranking compare to the class ranking?

3. Look back at your own ranking. Does your ranking surprise you?

4. Are there any surprises in the class ranking? Which values did you think would be highest and lowest?

Clarifying your values for leadership is far more than a pleasant exercise. Many business leaders have fallen into disgrace and brought their companies into bankruptcy because of values that are unacceptable to employees, stockholders, outside investigators, and the legal system. For example, a CEO who valued "developing the reputation of being a trustworthy person," would not borrow $400 million from the company while paying thousands of employees close to the minimum wage.

everything. So the leader listens carefully to the array of problems facing group members and then concentrates on a few. The servant leader thus systematically neglects certain problems. A labor union official might carefully listen to all the concerns and complaints of the constituents and then proceed to work on the most pressing issue.

5. *Lend a hand.* A servant leader looks for opportunities to play the Good Samaritan. On Lawrence Weinbach's first day as CEO of Unisys Corp., he opened the door for an employee carrying a desktop computer and picked up a piece of paper she dropped.

6. *Provide tools.* Encourage group members to tell you what they need to perform their jobs better. When giving an assignment, ask, "Do you have all the necessary tools and resources to get this done?"

The accompanying Leader in Action box describes a manager who exhibits a variety of leadership attitudes and behaviors, including effective interpersonal skills.

360-DEGREE FEEDBACK FOR FINE-TUNING A LEADERSHIP APPROACH

In the majority of large organizations, leaders not only provide feedback to group members, they also receive feedback that gives them insight into the efficacy of their attitudes and behaviors. The feedback is systematically derived from a full sampling of parties who interact with the leader. In particular, **360-degree feedback** is a formal evaluation of superiors based on input from people who work for and with them, sometimes including customers and suppliers. It is also referred to as multisource feedback or multirater feedback. The process is also called 360-degree survey, because the input stems from a survey of a handful of people.

Three hundred and sixty–degree feedback is more frequently used for leadership and management development than for performance evaluation. Particularly when used for development, 360-degree feedback includes self-evaluation. When self-evaluation is included, the individual completes the same form that all others used to describe his or her behavior. The feedback is communicated to the leader (as well as others receiving 360-degree feedback) and interpreted with the assistance of a human resources professional or an external consultant.

The data from the survey can be used to help leaders fine-tune their attitudes and behavior. For example, if all the interested parties gave the leader low ratings on "empathy toward others," the leader might be prompted to improve his or her ability to empathize. Action plans for improving empathy would include reading about empathy, attending a seminar, and simply making a conscious attempt to empathize when involved with a conflict of opinion with another person.

According to Robert Hoffman, a major reason for using 360-degree feedback is that it can detect barriers to success.[22] Feedback sometimes indicates that a leader perceived as a hurdle by those working with or for him or her is stalling

Leader in Action

Janine Bay of Ford Focuses on Interpersonal Skills

In the twenty-five years since she joined Ford Motor Company, Janine Bay has climbed the ladder to become director of vehicle personalization for the automotive consumers services group. From her company headquarters in Dearborn, Michigan, she manages 177 employees, including 70 in Europe and 12 in Asia. Her noteworthy accomplishments were the subject of an interview with *Executive Leadership*.

EL: How did you earn so many promotions?

Bay: I had an executive coach a while back who helped me. Usually, a coach might interview you and then focus on what you need to change or what you don't do quite right. But my coach forced me to focus on what I did well and why my strengths were important to Ford Motor Co.

EL: What are your strengths?

Bay: My coach found I had strong people skills, I was fairly entrepreneurial, and I was fairly innovative. Twenty years ago, these skills wouldn't have been as important at Ford. Now they are. Once you know your strong suits, you can seek out jobs that capitalize on them. Play to your strengths and you'll get promotions.

EL: It's great that you're an innovator. But how do you turn your ideas into action?

Bay: You need to walk a fine line between edge and arrogance. If you're too arrogant, you'll step on people. But if you don't have enough edge to believe in your ideas and stick with them, you won't get very far.

EL: You've led the Ford Mustang team. How did that high-profile job advance your career?

Bay: I learned how to manage diverse opinions. I took a great class on collaborative decision making in 1994. I realized that if you don't see things the same as someone else, both of you should write down how you see things, how you think the other person sees things, and why there's a difference. Then share what you've written.

EL: How does that help?

Bay: Writing it down forces you to think less emotionally. It desensitizes you to the situation. And it clarifies issues that you need to address. In fact, writing down how you feel about a big decision also works when evaluating career opportunities.

QUESTIONS

1. Which relationship behaviors does Janine Bay think are important for leadership?

2. Which task behaviors does Janine Bay think are important for leadership?

SOURCE: *"A Drive to Succeed: Janine Bay Blazes Her Own Path,"* Executive Leadership, *June 2001, p. 3. Reprinted with permission from* Executive Leadership, *Copyright © 2001 The National Institute of Business Management, McLean, VA (800) 543-2055, www. exec-leadership.com.*

organizational or unit growth. Success can be limited by such restricted behaviors as inflexibility, hostility, refusing to give information, lack of initiative, and inappropriate leadership style.

This 360-degree feedback is also a key component of *Benchmarks,* a widely used leadership training program developed by the Center for Creative Leadership. The leader and a good sampling of work associates complete a lengthy questionnaire about dozens of specific behaviors. (It easily takes 2 hours to respond to all the questions.) Self-ratings are then compared to ratings by others. Assume that a leader rates himself in the 90th percentile on "Putting people at ease: Displays warmth and a good sense of humor." If others rated him at the 15th percentile on this dimension, the leader is probably not as good at putting workers at ease as he or she thinks. An example of a 360-degree feedback form (not from *Benchmarks*) is shown in Figure 4-2.

The example just cited hints at the importance of professionally trained counselors being involved in 360-degree feedback. Some people feel emotionally crushed when they find a wide discrepancy between their self-perception on an interpersonal skill dimension and the perception of others. A middle manager involved in a 360-degree evaluation prided herself on how well she was liked by others. The feedback that emerged, however, depicted her as intimidating, hostile, and manipulative. Upon receiving the feedback, the woman went into a rage (proving the feedback true!) and then into despondency. Professional counseling can sometimes help a person benefit from critical feedback and place it in perspective.

Approaches to implementing 360-degree feedback for performance evaluation and development continue to emerge. One variation of the method is to build a 360-degree feedback system accessed via the Internet and the company's intranet. The Internet systems reduce some of the burdensome amount of paper

FIGURE 4-2   A 360-Degree Feedback Chart

Manager evaluated: *Bob Germane*

Ratings *(10 is highest)*

Behavior or Attitude	Self Rating	Average Group Rating	Gap
1. Gives right amount of structure	9	7.5	-1.5
2. Considerate of people	10	6.2	-3.8
3. Sets a direction	9	3.9	-5.1
4. Sets high standards	7	9.0	+2.0
5. Gives frequent feedback	10	6.3	-3.7
6. Gets people pulling together	9	5.1	-3.9
7. Inspires people	10	2.8	-7.2
8. Gives emotional support	8	3.7	-4.3
9. Is a helpful coach	10	4.5	-5.5
10. Encourages people to be self-reliant	6	9.4	+3.4

NOTE: A negative gap means you rate yourself higher on the behavior or attitude than does your group. A positive gap means the group rates you higher than you rate yourself.

involved in most 360-degree feedback systems, yet the participants must still fill out electronic forms. One such system, LEAPS (Leading Empowered, Active People Survey), enables people to evaluate one person in about 20 minutes and to send the finished appraisal via email.[23] An engineering group within Otis Elevator Co. used this system successfully to develop leaders by combining the feedback with coaching.

For best results, it is extremely important that 360-degree surveys reflect those behaviors and attitudes that the organization values most highly. Care should also be taken that the dimensions measured reflect important aspects of leadership functioning.

Despite the widespread use and apparent validity of 360-degree surveys, the results are sometimes disappointing. A review of over 600 studies of 360-degree feedback found that only one-third reported performance improvements. Another one-third reported performance decreases, and one-third reported no impact on performance.[24] Following are some suggestions for making better use of 360-degree surveys.[25]

- Focus on business goals and strategy. Feedback should provide leaders and managers with insight into the skills they need to help the organization meet its goals.

- Ensure that the feedback dimensions reflect important aspects of leadership functioning.

- Train workers in giving and receiving feedback. Providing constructive feedback takes coaching, training, and practice. One study showed that negative feedback received from a 360-degree survey is perceived as less useful than positive feedback.[26]

- Create an action plan for improvement for each leader based on the feedback. For example, a leader rated low on interpersonal skills might benefit from training in emotional intelligence.

LEADERSHIP STYLES

A leader's combination of attitudes and behaviors leads to a certain regularity and predictability in dealing with group members. **Leadership style** is the relatively consistent pattern of behavior that characterizes a leader. The study of leadership style is an extension of understanding leadership behaviors and attitudes. Most classifications of leadership style are based on the dimensions of initiating structure and consideration. Phrases such as "he's a real command-and-control-type," and "she's a consensus leader" have become commonplace.

Here we describe the participative leadership style, the autocratic leadership style, the Leadership Grid®, the entrepreneurial leadership style, gender differences in leadership style, and choosing the best style. Chapter 5 continues the exploration of leadership styles by presenting several contingency leadership theories.

Participative Leadership

Sharing decision making with group members and working with them side by side has become the generally accepted leadership approach in the modern organization. **Participative leaders** share decision making with group members. Participative leadership encompasses so many behaviors that it can be divided into three subtypes: consultative, consensus, and democratic.

Consultative leaders confer with group members before making a decision. However, they retain the final authority to make decisions. **Consensus leaders** strive for consensus. They encourage group discussion about an issue and then make a decision that reflects general agreement and that will be supported by group members. All workers who will be involved in the consequences of a decision have an opportunity to provide input. A decision is not considered final until it appears that all parties involved will at least support the decision. **Democratic leaders** confer final authority on the group. They function as collectors of group opinion and take a vote before making a decision.

The participative style has also been referred to as *trickle-up leadership* because the leader accepts suggestions for managing the operation from group members. Welcoming ideas from below is considered crucial because as technology evolves and organizations decentralize, front-line workers have more independence and responsibility. These workers are closer to the market, closer to seeing how the product is used, and closer to many human resource problems. Front-line knowledge can provide useful input to leader for such purposes as developing marketing strategy and retaining employees.[27]

In recent years Bill Gates (his official title at Microsoft Corporation is chief software architect, not chairman and CEO) has intensified his trickle-up style. By 2002 he was devoting most of his time to communing with the information technology specialists who build Microsoft products. He collects input so he can understand how new products can be woven into industry standard products.[28]

The participative style encompasses the teamwork approach. Predominant behaviors of participative leaders include coaching team members, negotiating their demands, and collaborating with others. This style is well suited to managing competent people who are eager to assume responsibility. Such people want to get involved in making decisions and giving feedback to management. Since the majority of graduates from business and professional programs expect to be involved in decision making, participative leadership works well with the new breed of managers and professionals.

Participative leadership does have some problems. It often results in extensive and time-consuming team meetings and committee work. Sometimes participative leadership is carried to extremes. Team members are consulted about trivial things that management could easily handle independently. Another problem is that many managers still believe that sharing decision making with members reduces their power.

In contrast to participative leaders are **autocratic leaders** who retain most of the authority. They make decisions confidently, assume that group members will comply, and are not overly concerned with group members' attitudes toward a decision. Autocratic leaders are considered task-oriented because they place heavy emphasis on getting tasks accomplished. Typical autocratic behaviors include telling people what to do, asserting themselves, and serving as a model for team members. A positive example of a famous business leader who was usually autocratic is Louis Gerstner of IBM. A highly decisive and intelligent person, he would move quickly on major decisions without receiving much input from others.

Part of your skill development as a leader involves gaining insight into your own leadership style or potential style. To this end, take Leadership Self-Assessment Quiz 4-3.

Leadership Grid® Styles

A classic method of classifying leadership styles suggests that the best way to achieve effective leadership is to integrate the task and relationship orientations. The **Leadership Grid®** is a framework for simultaneously specifying concern for the production and people dimensions of leadership. Grid leadership styles are based on the extent of a person's concern for production and people.[29]

Concern for production, rated on the horizontal axis, includes such matters as results (including high quality), the bottom line, performance, profits, and mission. Concern for people, rated on the vertical axis, is reflected in such matters as showing support for team members, getting results based on trust and respect, and worrying about employees' job security. Each concern is rated on a 1–9 scale. The benchmark styles on the Leadership Grid are as follows:

Authority-Compliance (9,1). The authority-compliance style is characterized by a maximum concern for production combined with a minimum concern for people. A leader with this orientation concentrates on maximizing production by exercising power and authority and by dictating to people.

Country Club Management (1,9). The "country club" style shows a minimum concern for production and a maximum concern for people. Primary attention is placed on good feelings among team members and coworkers, even at the expense of achieving results.

Impoverished Management (1,1). The impoverished management style shows a minimum concern for both production and people. Such a leader does only the minimum required to remain a member of the firm. (According to the current definition of leadership, this type of manager does not qualify as a leader.)

Middle-of-the-Road Management (5,5). In the center is the 5,5 orientation. Leaders with this middle-of-the-road style do their job but avoid making waves and conform to the status quo.

Team Management (9,9). The team management style integrates concern for production and people. It is a goal-directed team approach that seeks to gain optimum results through participation, involvement, and commitment.

Managers generally have one dominant leadership style and a backup style. Leaders tend to use the backup style when the dominant style does not achieve

Leadership Self-Assessment Quiz 4-3

What Style of Leader Are You or Would You Be?

INSTRUCTIONS   Answer the following questions, keeping in mind what you have done, or think you would do, in the scenarios and attitudes described.

	Mostly True	Mostly False
1. I am more likely to take care of a high-impact assignment myself than turn it over to a group member.	——	——
2. I would prefer the analytical aspects of a manager's job rather than working directly with group members.	——	——
3. An important part of my approach to managing a group is to keep the members informed almost daily of any information that could affect their work.	——	——
4. It's a good idea to give two people in the group the same problem, and then choose what appears to be the best solution.	——	——
5. It makes good sense for the leader or manager to stay somewhat aloof from the group, so you can make a tough decision when necessary.	——	——
6. I look for opportunities to obtain group input before making a decision, even on straightforward issues.	——	——
7. I would reverse a decision if several of the group members presented evidence that I was wrong.	——	——
8. Differences of opinion in the work group are healthy.	——	——
9. I think that activities to build team spirit, like the team fixing up a poor family's house on a Saturday, are an excellent investment of time.	——	——
10. If my group were hiring a new member, I would like the person to be interviewed by the entire group.	——	——
11. An effective team leader today uses email for about 98 percent of communication with team members.	——	——
12. Some of the best ideas are likely to come from the group members rather than the manager.	——	——
13. If our group were going to have a banquet, I would get input from each member on what type of food should be served.	——	——

14. I have never seen a statue of a committee in a museum or park, so why bother making decisions by a committee if you want to be recognized?   ____ ____

15. I dislike it intensely when a group member challenges my position on an issue.   ____ ____

16. I typically explain to group members how (what method) they should use to accomplish an assigned task.   ____ ____

17. If I were out of the office for a week, most of the important work in the department would get accomplished anyway.   ____ ____

18. Delegation of important tasks is something that would be (or is) very difficult for me.   ____ ____

19. When a group member comes to me with a problem, I tend to jump right in with a proposed solution.   ____ ____

20. When a group member comes to me with a problem, I typically ask that person something like, "What alternative solutions have you thought of so far?"   ____ ____

SCORING AND INTERPRETATION   The answers for a participative leader are as follows:

1. Mostly False	**8.** Mostly True	**15.** Mostly False
2. Mostly False	**9.** Mostly True	**16.** Mostly False
3. Mostly True	**10.** Mostly True	**17.** Mostly True
4. Mostly False	**11.** Mostly False	**18.** Mostly False
5. Mostly False	**12.** Mostly True	**19.** Mostly False
6. Mostly True	**13.** Mostly True	**20.** Mostly True
7. Mostly True	**14.** Mostly False	

If your score is 15 or higher, you are most likely (or would be) a participative leader. If your score is 5 or lower, you are most likely (or would be) an authoritarian leader.

SKILL DEVELOPMENT   The quiz you just completed is also an opportunity for skill development. Review the twenty questions and look for implied suggestions for engaging in participative leadership. For example, question 20 suggests that you encourage group members to work through their own solutions to problems. If your goal is to become an authoritarian leader, the questions can also serve as useful guidelines. For example, question 19 suggests that an authoritarian leader looks first to solve problems for group members.

the desired results. For instance, you might use the 9,9 approach, only to find that most team members are unenthusiastic about implementing a total quality program. It might then be necessary to shift to a 9,1 approach.

The creators of the Grid argue strongly for the value of team management (9,9). They present evidence that the team management orientation usually results in improved performance, low absenteeism and turnover, and high employee satisfaction. A synthesis of a number of studies indicates that effective leaders score highly on concern for both people and production. The researchers who analyzed the studies caution, however, that one should investigate each leadership situation before prescribing the best leadership style.[30] Similarly, the Leadership Grid does not dictate that the manager mechanically use one style in trying to lead very different groups. Instead, he or she should use principles of human behavior to size up the situation.

Entrepreneurial Leadership

Many entrepreneurs use a similar leadership style that stems from their personality characteristics and circumstances. Although there are different types of entrepreneurs, in general an entrepreneur is a person who founds and operates an innovative business. Not all business owners, including franchise operators, are therefore entrepreneurial leaders. The general picture that emerges of an entrepreneur is a task-oriented and charismatic person. Entrepreneurs drive themselves and others relentlessly, yet their personalities inspire others.

This entrepreneurial leadership style often incorporates the behaviors described in the following paragraphs.[31] However, authorities disagree about whether an entrepreneurial personality exists.

1. *Strong achievement drive and sensible risk taking.* Entrepreneurs have stronger achievement motives than most leaders (see Chapter 2). Building a business is an excellent vehicle for accomplishment and risk taking. To accomplish what they think needs to be accomplished, entrepreneurs are willing to work extraordinary hours, with 12-hour days, seven days a week not being unusual. Naveen Jain is the 40-year-old chairman of InfoSpace, Inc., a company that sells packaged information to web sites. Last seen he was still working 120 hours per week to build his business.[32] Because entrepreneurs take sensible risks, many do not perceive themselves as being risk takers—just as many tightrope walkers believe they are not taking risks because they are in control. Some entrepreneurs are so flexible they will take risks at both ends of the continuum. For example, Charles Schwab founded his brokerage business as a discount company that avoided giving advice to help keep brokerage fees low. During the business downturn of 2001, Schwab took the opposite tack: his firm began giving investment advice to clients via software online.[33] Leadership Self-Assessment Quiz 4-4 gives you the opportunity to think about your risk-taking tendencies.

2. *High degree of enthusiasm and creativity.* Entrepreneurs are highly enthusiastic, partially because they are so excited about their achievements. As

What Is Your Propensity for Taking Risks?

INSTRUCTIONS   Indicate how well each of the following statements reflects your attitudes or behavior, using this scale: very inaccurately (VI); inaccurately (I); moderately well (MW); accurately (A); very accurately (VA).

		VI	I	MW	A	VA
1.	If I had a serious illness, I would purchase generic instead of brand-name drugs.	1	2	3	4	5
2.	I invest (or would invest) much more money in bonds or CDs (certificates of deposit) than in stocks.	1	2	3	4	5
3.	The thought of starting my own business appeals to me.	1	2	3	4	5
4.	I am (or was) willing to go on blind dates frequently.	1	2	3	4	5
5.	My career advice to young people is to pursue a well-established occupation with a high demand for newcomers to the field.	1	2	3	4	5
6.	I would be willing to relocate to a city where I had no family or friends.	1	2	3	4	5
7.	During the last few years, I have taken up a new sport, dance, or foreign language on my own.	1	2	3	4	5
8.	My preference is to have at least 90 percent of my compensation based on guaranteed salary.	1	2	3	4	5
9.	From time to time I buy jewelry, clothing, or food from street vendors.	1	2	3	4	5
10.	The idea of piloting my own single-engine plane over the ocean appeals to me.	1	2	3	4	5

Total score _____

SCORING AND INTERPRETATION   Obtain your score by adding the numbers you have circled.

- 46–50 You are a heavy risk taker, bordering on reckless at times. You are most likely not assessing risk carefully enough before proceeding.

- 38–45 You probably are a sensible risk taker and an adventuresome person in a way that enhances your leadership appeal to others.

- 5–37 You have a propensity to avoid risks. Your conservatism in this regard could detract from an entrepreneurial leadership style.

Risk taking is important for leadership because both charismatic and entrepreneurial leaders are noted for their risk taking. In addition, it is difficult to bring about change (a vital leadership function) if you are averse to taking risks.

Entrepreneur magazine puts it, "Something about being an entrepreneur is, for them, a five-star, butt-kicking, rocket-boosting blast."[34] Entrepreneurs' enthusiasm, in turn, makes them persuasive. As a result, they are often perceived as charismatic. Some entrepreneurs are so emotional that they are regarded as eccentric.

3. *Tendency to act quickly when opportunity arises.* Entrepreneurs are noted for seizing upon opportunity. When a deal is on the horizon, they push themselves and those around them extra hard. As the founder of an information systems firm told his staff after receiving an important inquiry, "Cancel all your weekend plans. We work until this proposal is completed to my satisfaction and that of our prospect."

4. *Constant hurry combined with impatience.* Entrepreneurs are always in a hurry. While engaged in one meeting, their minds typically begin to focus on the next meeting. Their flurry of activity rubs off on group members and those around them. Entrepreneurs often adopt a simple dress style in order to save time, and they typically allow little slack time between appointments. John Schnatter, the founder of Papa John's International pizza chain, is a well-known entrepreneur with an impatient, brusque approach to people. Five executives, including the company president, quit in a two-year period, in part because of Schnatter's brusque management style.[35]

5. *Visionary perspective.* Entrepreneurs, at their best, are visionaries. As with other types of effective leaders, they see opportunities others fail to observe. Specifically, they have the ability to identify a problem and arrive at a solution. Ted Turner of CNN is a legendary example of an entrepreneurial visionary. Turner picked up on a trend that people wanted—an all-news cable channel that they could access anytime. Not only is CNN, including Headline News, a commercial success, but it has revolutionized the way people get their news all over the globe.

6. *Dislike of hierarchy and bureaucracy.* Entrepreneurs are not ideally suited by temperament to working within the mainstream of a bureaucracy. Many successful entrepreneurs are people who were frustrated by the constraints of a bureaucratic system. The implication for leadership style is that entrepreneurs deemphasize rules and regulations when managing people.

7. *Preference for dealing with external customers.* One of the reasons why entrepreneurs and intrapreneurs have difficulty with bureaucracy is that they focus their energies on products, services, and customers, rather than on employees. Some entrepreneurs are gracious to customers and money lenders but brusque with company insiders. A blind spot many entrepreneurs have is that they cannot understand why their employees do not share their passion for work and customer focus. As a result, they may be brusque with employees who do not share their dedication to the firm.

8. *Eye on the future.* Entrepreneurs have the pronounced characteristic of thinking about future deals and business opportunities even before a

Entrepreneurial Leadership

An important part of the entrepreneurial role is to convince others of the merit of your idea so that they will invest in your company or lend you money. Two students play the role of a team of entrepreneurs who have a new product or service and want to launch a business. (The two entrepreneurs choose the product or service.) About five other students play the role of a group of venture capitalists or bankers listening to the presentation to decide whether to invest or lend money. The entrepreneurs will communicate excitement and commitment about their product, along with a good business plan. (You might want to quickly review the material about persuasive communication in Chapter 12.) The students who are not participating will evaluate how well the two entrepreneurs displayed aspects of the entrepreneurial leadership style.

current business is running smoothly. "Where is my next deal coming from?" is the mantra of the true entrepreneur. Even after accumulating great wealth from a present business activity, the entrepreneurial leader looks toward future opportunities. A good example is Richard Branson of the Virgin Group. His empire contains about 200 companies with the Virgin label, yet he continues to look for the next company to start or acquire.

To practice one aspect of entrepreneurial leadership, do Leadership Skill-Building Exercise 4-3.

Gender Differences in Leadership Style

Controversy over whether men and women have different leadership styles continues. Several researchers and observers argue that women have certain acquired traits and behaviors that suit them for relations-oriented leadership. Consequently, women leaders frequently exhibit a cooperative, empowering style that includes nurturing team members. According to this same perspective, men are inclined toward a command-and-control, militaristic leadership style. Women find participative management more natural than do men because they feel more comfortable interacting with people. Furthermore, it is argued that women's natural sensitivity to people gives them an edge over men in encouraging group members to participate in decision making. Here we look briefly at some of the evidence and reasoning showing that gender differences do and do not exist between the leadership styles of today's organizational leaders.

A significant side issue here is that the terms *sex* and *gender* arouse controversy for both scientific and political reasons. As the term is used by many researchers, *gender* refers to perceptions about the differences among males and females. An example would be believing that women managers tend to be better listeners than their male peers. Sex differences, however, refer to actual (objective and quantitative) differences, such as the fact that the mean height of men exceeds that of women. Despite these observations, the terms *gender* and *sex* are still used interchangeably in general usage and to some extent in scholarly writings.

The Argument for Male–Female Differences in Leadership Style.

In an article that stimulated considerable debate, Judy Rosener concluded that men and women do tend toward opposite styles. Based on self-reports, she found that men tended toward a command-and-control style. In contrast, women tended toward a transformational style, relying heavily on interpersonal skills.[36]

Bernard M. Bass has found some specific male-female differences in leadership style. Data collected from subordinates suggest that women are less likely to practice management-by-exception (intervening only when something goes wrong). Yet women and men appear to use contingent recognition with equal frequency. Even when the women leaders studied do practice management-by-exception, they typically temper criticism with positive feedback. Bass also found that women leaders are slightly more likely to be described as charismatic. In a survey of sixty-nine world-class leaders (nine women included), women scored higher on the transformation factor than did men.[37]

Another perspective on gender differences is that women entrepreneurs are more likely than their male counterparts to perceive their business as a family. As corporate managers, women tend to place greater emphasis on forming caring, nurturing relationships with employees. Women are also more likely than men to praise group members. And when an employee falls short of expectations, women are more likely to buffer criticism by finding something praiseworthy.[38]

One question relating to gender differences is whether men or women are more effective as leaders. A group of researchers at management consulting firms studied performance evaluations of executives based on ratings from superiors, peers, and subordinates. The intent of these studies was not to search for gender differences in leadership effectiveness but to study patterns in performance evaluations. Of the 425 executives evaluated, each by approximately twenty-five people, women leaders achieved higher ratings on forty-two of the fifty-two skills measured. Most of the gender differences were small. The data from 27 studies showed that the performances of men and women executives on the following dimensions were as follows:

- Motivating others (women scored higher in 5 studies)
- Fostering communication (women scored higher in 4 studies)
- Producing high-quality work (women scored higher in 5 studies)
- Strategic planning (men scored higher in 2 studies and women scored higher in 2 other studies)

- Listening to others (women scored higher in 5 studies)
- Analyzing issues (men scored higher in 2 studies and women scored higher in 2 other studies)[39]

Many different interpretations were offered for these small but consistent differences in performance evaluations between men and women executives. One argument is that women who hold executive positions have to be outstanding workers to get the job and thus tend to receive higher evaluations than their male counterparts, who might not have to be so outstanding.

Despite the many ways in which research suggests that women leaders might have the edge, some opinion suggests that men are more likely to have *executive presence*, or "it." Executive presence is much like the aspects of charisma described in Chapter 3. As explained by Michele Conlin:

> Executive presence refers to that ability to take hold of a room by making a polished entrance, immediately shaking people's hands, and forging quick, personal connections instead of defaulting to robotic formalism and shrinking into a chair. When leaders with executive presence speak, people listen—because the talk is filled with conviction instead of equivocation.[40]

Fundamental differences in the biological and psychological makeup of men and women have also been used as evidence that the two sexes are likely to manifest different leadership styles. One such set of differences has been uncovered by brain researchers Raquel Gur and Ruben Gur.[41] They found that women may be far more sensitive to emotional cues and verbal nuances than men. Women leaders would therefore be more suited to responding to the feelings of group members and understanding what they really mean by certain statements. Gender differences in communication also are reflected in leadership style. Above all, women are more likely to use spoken communication for building relationships and giving emotional support than are men.[42] Men focus more on disseminating information and demonstrating competence. Women are therefore more likely to choose a relationship-oriented leadership style.

The Argument Against Gender Differences in Leadership Style.   Based on a literature review, Jan Grant concluded that there are apparently few, if any, personality or behavioral differences between men and women managers. Also, as women move up the corporate ladder, their identification with the male model of managerial success becomes important; they consequently reject even the few managerial feminine traits they may have earlier endorsed.[43] Studies reviewed by Bass (other than his own research) indicate no consistent pattern of male-female differences in leadership style.[44]

To what extent the stereotypes of men and women leaders are true is difficult to judge. Even if male and female differences in leadership style do exist, they must be placed in proper perspective. Both men and women leaders differ among themselves in leadership style. Plenty of male leaders are relationship-oriented, and plenty of women practice command and control (the extreme task orientation). Many women believe that women managers can be more hostile and vindictive than men managers.

A more important issue is how to capitalize on both male and female leadership tendencies. Connie Glaser believes that the best approach to leadership takes advantage of the positive traits of both men and women. She sees a new management style that blends the male and female sides:

> While the female may impart that sense of nurturing, the sensitivity to individual and family needs, that's offset by certain traits that the male brings to the table. The ability to make decisions quickly, the sense of humor, the risk-taking—those are qualities that traditionally have been associated with the male style of management.[45]

Selecting the Best Leadership Style

An underlying theme of our discussion of leadership styles, and the next chapter, is that there is no one best or most effective leadership style. A recent study with 3,000 executives revealed that leaders who get the best results do not rely on one style. Instead, they use several different styles in one week, such as by being autocratic in some situations and democratic in others.[46] Another consideration is the culture in which the leadership takes place. For example, an effective leadership style for most German workers would be a high performance (task) orientation and a modest amount of compassion (consideration).[47] More will be said about cultural differences in Chapter 14. Thirty years ago pioneering researcher Ralph Stogdill made a statement about selecting a leadership style that still holds today: "The most effective leaders appear to exhibit a degree of versatility and flexibility that enables them to adapt their behavior to the changing and contradictory demands made on them."[48]

Table 4-3 presents useful information for choosing between the participative and autocratic styles, depending on the needs of the group members and other forces in the situation. The most successful leaders typically find the right blend of task and relationship orientations.

Leadership Self-Assessment Quiz 4-5 provides an opportunity to think about your own willingness to adapt to circumstances as a leader. By developing such flexibility, you increase your chances of becoming an effective leader—one who achieves high productivity, quality, and satisfaction. Finally, before moving on to the end-of-chapter activities, do Leadership Skill-Building Exercise 4-4.

TABLE 4–3   Choosing a Leadership Style to Fit the Situation

Consider Being Participative Under These Conditions:

Leader/manager	Has limited power and limited authority to use it
	Needs input from valuable employees
	Risks rejection of his or her authority
	Has few existing time pressures
	Has limited sanctions that he or she can exert
Group members	Expect to have some control over methods used
	Have predominantly middle-class values
	Possess relatively scarce skills
	Like the system, but not authority
Work situation	Encourages consensus building
	Is characterized by overall organizational objectives
	Involves shared responsibility for control
	Has some time pressures
	Consists of gradual changes or regularly spaced changes
	Occasionally involves actual or potential hazards
	Values teamwork skills

Consider Being Autocratic Under These Conditions:

Leader/manager	Has lots of power and limited restraints on its use
	Has a way of saving matters in an emergency
	Has some unique knowledge useful to the group
	Is firmly entrenched in his or her position
Group members	Are dependent on the leader
	Are rarely asked for an opinion
	Are readily replaced by other workers
	Recognize emergencies
	Are autocrats themselves
	Have little need for independence
Work situation	Requires a clear direction
	Requires a new vision because of changes
	Is characterized by strong controls
	Is marked by low profit margins or tight cost controls
	Includes physical dangers
	Requires low-level skills from workers
	Requires that changes be made frequently and quickly

Source: Personnel *by* Rendero, Thomasine. *Copyright 1981 by* American Management Association (J). *Reproduced with permission of* American Management Association (J) *in the format Textbook via Copyright Clearance Center. Updated with information from Daniel Goleman, "Leadership That Gets Results,"* Harvard Business Review, *March–April 2000, pp. 82, 83.*

How Flexible Are You?

INSTRUCTIONS   To succeed as a managerial leader, a person needs a flexible style: an ability to be open to others and a willingness to listen. Where do you stand on being flexible? Test yourself by answering "often," "sometimes," or "rarely" to the following questions.

_____ **1.** Do you tend to seek out only those people who agree with your analysis of issues?

_____ **2.** Do you ignore most of the advice from coworkers about process improvements?

_____ **3.** Do your team members go along with what you say just to avoid an argument?

_____ **4.** Have people referred to you as "rigid" or "close-minded" on several occasions?

_____ **5.** When presented with a new method, do you immediately look for a flaw?

_____ **6.** Do you make up your mind early on with respect to an issue, and then hold firmly to your opinion?

_____ **7.** When people disagree with you, do you tend to belittle them or become argumentative?

_____ **8.** Do you often feel you are the only person in the group who really understands the problem?

CHECK YOUR SCORE   If you answered "rarely" to seven or eight questions, you are unusually adaptable. If you answered "sometimes" to at least five questions, you are on the right track, but more flexibility would benefit your leadership. If you answered "often" to more than four questions, you have a long way to go to improve your flexibility and adaptability. You are also brutally honest about your faults, which could be an asset.

Leadership Skill-Building Exercise 4-4

Contrasting Leadership Styles

One student plays the role of a new associate working for a financial services firm that sells life insurance and other investments. The associate has completed a six-week training program and is now working full-time. Four weeks have passed, and the associate still has not made a sale. The associate's boss is going to meet with him or her today to discuss progress. Another student plays the role of a task-oriented leader. The two people participate in the review session.

Before playing (or assuming) the role of the associate or the boss, think for a few minutes how you would behave if you were placed in that role in real life. Empathize with the frustrated associate or the task-oriented leader. A good role player is both a script writer and an actor.

Another two students repeat the same scenario except that this time the manager is a strongly relationship-oriented leader. Two more pairs of students then have their turn at acting out the task-oriented and relationship-oriented performance reviews. Another variation of this role play is for one person to play the roles of both the task-oriented and the relationship-oriented boss. Other class members observe and provide feedback on the effectiveness of the two styles of leadership.

SUMMARY

Effective leadership requires the right behaviors, skills, and attitudes, as emphasized in the classic Ohio State University studies. Two major dimensions of leadership behavior were identified: initiating structure and consideration. Initiating structure is the degree to which the leader organizes and defines relationships in the group by such activities as assigning tasks and specifying procedures. Consideration is the degree to which the leader creates an environment of emotional support, warmth, friendliness, and trust. Making connections with people is a current aspect of consideration.

Many task-related attitudes and behaviors of effective leaders have been identified. Among them are (1) adaptability to the situation, (2) direction setting, (3) high performance standards, (4) risk taking and a bias for action, (5) hands-on guidance and feedback, (6) stability of performance, and (7) ability to ask tough questions.

Many relationship-oriented attitudes and behaviors of leaders have also been identified. Among them are (1) aligning and mobilizing people, (2) concert building, (3) creating inspiration and visibility, (4) satisfying higher-level needs, (5) giving emotional support and encouragement, (6) promoting principles and values, and (7) being a servant leader.

Servant leaders are committed to serving others rather than achieving their own goals. Aspects of servant leadership include placing service before self-interest, listening to others, inspiring trust by being trustworthy, focusing on what is feasible to accomplish, lending a hand, and providing tools.

Many leaders today are receiving extensive feedback on their behaviors and attitudes in the form of 360-degree feedback, whereby people who work for or with the leader provide feedback on the leader's performance. Such feedback is helpful in detecting barriers to success, especially when the feedback relates to business goals and strategy and to important aspects of leadership, when training is provided in giving and receiving feedback, and when action plans are developed.

Understanding the concept of leadership style is an extension of understanding leadership attitudes and behavior. Participative leaders share decision making with group members. The participative style can be subdivided into consultative, consensus, and democratic leadership. The participative style is well suited to managing competent people who are eager to assume responsibility. Yet the process can be time consuming, and some managers perceive it to be a threat to their power. Autocratic leaders retain most of the authority for themselves. The Leadership Grid classifies leaders according to their concern for both production (task accomplishment) and people.

Another important style of leader is the entrepreneur. The entrepreneurial style stems from the leader's personal characteristics and the circumstances of self-employment. It includes a strong achievement drive and sensible risk taking; a high degree of enthusiasm and creativity; acting quickly on opportunities; hurriedness and impatience; a visionary perspective; a dislike of hierarchy and bureaucracy; a preference for dealing with external customer; and an eye on the future.

Male-female differences in leadership style have been observed. Women have a tendency toward relationship-oriented leadership, whereas men tend toward command and control. Some people argue, however, that male-female differences in leadership are inconsistent and not significant.

Rather than searching for the one best style of leadership, managers are advised to diagnose the situation and then choose an appropriate leadership style to match. To be effective, a leader must be able to adapt his or her style to the circumstances.

KEY TERMS

Effective leader

Initiating structure

Consideration

Pygmalion effect

Tough question

Concert building

Servant leader

360-degree feedback

Leadership style

Participative leaders

Consultative leaders

Consensus leaders

Democratic leaders

Autocratic leaders

Leadership Grid®

✔ GUIDELINES FOR ACTION AND SKILL DEVELOPMENT

Most leadership style classifications are based on the directive (task-oriented) dimension versus the nondirective (relationship-oriented) dimension. In deciding which of these two styles is best, consider the following questions:

1. **What is the structure of your organization and the nature of your work?** You might decide, for example, that stricter control is necessary for some types of work, such as dealing with proprietary information.

2. **Which style suits you best?** Your personality, values, and beliefs influence how readily you can turn over responsibility to others.

3. **Which style suits your boss and organization?** For example, a boss who is highly directive may perceive you as weak if you are too nondirective.

4. **How readily will you be able to change your style if good results are not forthcoming?**

Morale can suffer if you grant too much latitude today and have to tighten control in the future.

5. **Is there high potential for conflict in the work unit?** A directive leadership style can trigger conflict with independent, strong-willed people. A more nondirective style allows for more freedom of discussion, which defuses conflict.[49]

DISCUSSION QUESTIONS AND ACTIVITIES

1. How is initiating structure related to planning, organizing, and controlling?

2. Give an example of a high consideration behavior that a supervisor of yours showed on your behalf. What was your reaction to his or her behavior?

3. Why is direction setting still an important leadership behavior in an era of empowerment?

4. Ask an experienced leader how he or she gives emotional support to team members. Be prepared to discuss your findings in class.

5. In what ways might a *personalized charismatic leader* have quite different motives than a servant leader?

6. How might a manager use email to help carry out both task-oriented and relationship-oriented behaviors?

7. How would you characterize the leadership style of your favorite executive, athletic coach, or television character who plays a boss?

8. Why is the consensus leadership style widely recommended for providing leadership to Generation X and Generation Y workers?

9. Find a printed or Internet article on a business entrepreneur (or think of one from personal experience). How well does that person fit the entrepreneurial leadership style?

10. What are the practical implications of knowing that men and women typically have different leadership styles?

Leadership Case Problem A

The Confusing 360-Degree Feedback

Calvin Haskins, age 33, is the information systems manager for National Auto Supply Inc., a major supplier to auto parts and supply stores. National is a distributor whose customers include several of the larger chains of auto supply stores, as well as hundreds of smaller, independent stores. The company thus works as an intermediary between manufacturers and retailers. Founded in 1952, National has prospered even during business recessions.

CEO Troy Wentworth explains that National does particularly well during downturns in the economy because people are likely to hold on to their vehicles longer, making the purchase of auto parts and tires more necessary. Also, during the downturn more people purchase used vehicles, which require more replacement parts than do newer cars.

During the last several years, ecommerce has created new challenges for National Auto Supply. Company managers and professionals are working hard to develop a business model that will enable National as a distributor to prosper during the age of ecommerce. One challenge they face is that many auto parts manufacturers are selling directly to auto parts stores over the Internet. National Auto Supply sells over the Web selectively because it does not want to alienate its customers, the auto supply stores, by going directly to consumers.

Wentworth has been acutely aware that National is undergoing a major transition in adapting to ecommerce, and that many employees are confused and worried about the transition. Although he talks confidently to employees, stockholders, and research analysts about the future of the company, Wentworth has some concerns about National's ability to survive. In discussing the challenges with a management consultant, he said: "I guess the right term is *disintermediarization*. Some intermediaries, or distributors, are vanishing in the era of the Net. On the other hand, other distributors are prospering better than ever. I'm not sure yet which group we will fall into."

One action Wentworth took to help support the company during the transition was to look toward strengthening its leadership and management. Based on articles he had read in management magazines and on discussions with

his consultant, Wentworth thought that a good starting point would be to conduct 360-degree surveys for the entire management team, including himself. He noted, "We're big enough men and women here to find out what our internal and external customers think of us. If we are making any major errors in dealing with people, we need to know about it in a hurry. National will not survive this industry shakeout without all our leaders performing at their best."

National Auto Supply hired one of the leading firms in the field to conduct 360-degree surveys for seven key people. Contributors to the survey included the other managers in the company, a large group of employees, a handful of major customers, and self-evaluations. Five people receiving the feedback thought the activity was beneficial, in that it would help them fine-tune their approach to leading and managing workers. The finance vice president said the activity was a total waste of time. He noted, "My wife and children have been telling me the same thing for years. Why pay a consultant to gather that type of information when I can get it for free at home? Besides, my job is to manage the company's financial resources, not run a happiness camp."

Calvin Haskins had a different problem, saying that he wanted to improve as a leader and a manager, but that the feedback was pulling him in different directions. He had one feedback session with Nancy Gonzalez, the organizational psychologist who conducted the 360-degree survey for National. Still confused as to what changes he should make, Haskins had another session planned with Gonzalez.

Haskins explained his dilemma in these terms: "I'm getting feedback that is contradictory and confusing. I realize that high-tech professionals do not all have the same personality and needs, but the feedback still has me baffled. This chart is a little wacky [referring to the feed-

EXHIBIT 1 A 360-Degree Feedback Chart for Calvin Haskins, Manager of Information Systems, National Auto Supply, Inc.

Manager evaluated: *Calvin Haskins*

Ratings *(10 is highest)*

Behavior or Attitude	Self Rating	Average Group Rating	Gap
1. Gives right amount of structure	9	4.5	-4.5
2. Considerate of people	6	6.2	+0.2
3. Sets a direction	10	3.9	-6.1
4. Sets high standards	7	9.0	+2.0
5. Gives frequent feedback	10	8.1	-1.9
6. Gets people pulling together	9	7.1	-2.9
7. Inspires people	7	9.2	+2.2
8. Gives emotional support	8	7.7	-0.3
9. Is a helpful coach	10	4.5	-5.5
10. Encourages people to be self-reliant	6	8.4	+2.4

NOTE: A negative gap means you rate yourself higher on the behavior or attitude than does your group. A positive gap means the group rates you higher than you rate yourself.

back form shown in Exhibit 1]. It looks like I'm not giving the right amount of structure, and I'm not doing a good job of setting direction. Yet I have good ratings for setting high standards and inspiring people. Also, I give enough feedback, but I'm not a very good coach. Are they talking about the same person?

"The written comments that I received in addition to the ratings also leave me puzzled as to what improvements I should make. Here's a sampling of them:

- Gets too bogged down in technology at times to do a good job as a leader.
- Tends to leave me on my own too much without giving me enough direction.
- Can be a real micromanager.
- Calvin is a little heavy-handed in his feedback.
- I appreciate Calvin's candid feedback.
- Forgets sometimes that we are humans, not information technology machines.
- Should be the next CEO of National.
- Maybe Calvin should consider a career switch. Management is definitely not his field.

"As I analyze this feedback," said Haskins, "I'm concerned that I might make changes in my leadership approach that would decrease rather than increase my effectiveness."

QUESTIONS

1. What changes in leadership attitudes and behaviors do you think Haskins should make?

2. How might you explain the differences of opinion that Haskins found in the written feedback and in the ratings shown in Exhibit 1?

3. In which leadership behavior described in this chapter might Haskins particularly need improvement?

NOTE: *The names of the company and leaders have been changed to protect client confidentiality.*

Leadership Case Problem B

Getting Northstar in the Winning Mode

Northstar Marketing is bidding for an important marketing contract with New Hope Industries, a Christian record company that has exclusive contracts with three internationally known singers, several bands, and ten new artists. The contract with New Hope would enable Northstar to do all of the record company's promotional activities.

Kim, the division manager of Northstar, is responsible for the preparation of the final bid to be submitted in three months to the executive team at New Hope. One of Kim's direct reports is David, the acting marketing manager who has been working with the company for twelve years. He supervises two marketers, including Robert and Sarah. Robert has been working for the company for ten years. In the past he has coordinated several projects successfully. His primary focus is getting the job done as quickly as possible, and he monitors progress in daily meetings. Sarah has been working for the company for six years. She is a valuable employee because of her ability to motivate the other marketers, researchers, and administrative assistants. Sarah is also perceived as a strong team player.

Division Meeting. During a division meeting, Kim says, "Good morning, ladies and gentlemen. I would like to thank you for being so punctual. Before we get down to business, I would like to thank each of you for all your hard work last month on the American Cancer Society's Relay for Life. It was a splendid success thanks to all of your promotional efforts.

"This morning I would like to discuss the upcoming bidding process for the contract with New Hope. This project is a wonderful opportunity for Northstar to branch out into the Christian music industry. This contract is important to our company because it could help us achieve a long-term goal of diversifying our client base. Our prestige would soar, along with our profits.

"To ensure our success, I am looking for collaboration. David has named Robert as the project coordinator. Robert will check in with David as often as necessary. I would like to form three teams to handle bids for the promotional needs of concerts, albums, and special events. Creativity is of the utmost importance. Do not be afraid to pursue wild ideas. Remember, there are no bad ideas in this company.

"I know that this contract is different from those we are used to working with. However, I have total confidence in your ability to produce a competitive bid for this work and to complete the project on time. Because we will be pressed for time and undoubtedly will be working many late nights in the upcoming months, management is offering bonuses to everyone involved in the bidding if we win the contract.

"What questions can I answer at this time? [Kim answers a few questions.] Keep in mind also that you are invited to come by my office or drop a note in the suggestion box located in the break room if you have any questions, comments, or concerns as the project progresses. Don't forget to sign up for the training retreat by next week."

David's Office. During a meeting with David, Robert discusses his plans for the next three months so the bid will be ready in time. He tells David that he has asked Sarah to assist him in managing the project. David doesn't seem to be interested. After Robert has finished talking, David says, "Whatever you do will be fine. I know that you are capable, or else Kim and I would not have chosen you to head this job. We don't need to meet as long as you give me weekly progress reports. I will send you emails with any suggestions I have.

"I don't care what you have to do or how much overtime you have to put in, but I do want this completed well, and a week before our internal deadline. If something happens and our contract bid is not a success, there will be serious consequences. Don't forget that the company meetings for employee promotions begin in four months. That's all for now."

David gets up to walk Robert out of his office. As he closes the door he says, "Remember, if you need any help, my door is always open."

Robert's Office. Sarah greets Robert and asks how she can help him. Robert thanks Sarah for coming and describes his meeting with David. He adds, "I know how effective you are with the other workers in this company, so I am going to ask your help to motivate them. Here are some preliminary ideas I have about who should be on which teams and some areas they can brainstorm. I need to establish some workable deadlines. I know that I have a tendency to think only about getting the project completed, and not enough about the people involved. So I want you to help me be more sensitive."

"I would love to," responded Sarah. "I have a special interest in this because I love Christian music. Aimee Grade is one of my favorite singers. Almost everyone I have talked to feels the same way. Some people have shown interest in specific areas. I know that Michael really wants to work on the special events, and Rebecca would love to promote the new albums.

"To motivate workers we can play some of the artist's music in the break room. I think that D. C. Reden, one of New Hope's most popular alternative bands, is having a concert here in Atlanta next month. Maybe we could send some interested employees to the concert and have them do some research while they are at the concert."

Robert says, "That's a wonderful suggestion. I'll run it by David tomorrow. Do you have the time to work on team assignments now, or do you want to set a meeting for tomorrow?"

"I'll talk to everyone today and we can meet tomorrow at three, if that fits your schedule," replies Sarah.

"Three o'clock sounds great. Thank you for your cooperation. I think that with your help everything will run smoothly," says Robert.

QUESTIONS

1. Which person best demonstrated effective leadership? Explain the reason for your answer.

2. Which person least demonstrated effective leadership? Explain the reason for your answer.

3. Where on the Leadership Grid would you place Kim, David, Robert, and Sarah? Explain the basis for your answer.

SOURCE: *Adapted slightly from case and questions contributed by Amy-Catherine Aring and Leanne C. McGrath, University of South Carolina Aiken, 1999.*

INTERNET SKILL–BUILDING EXERCISE

Identifying Leadership Behaviors and Attitudes

Apply the chapter concepts! Visit the Web and complete this Internet skill-building exercise to learn more about current leadership topics and trends.

Select a business or sports leader of interest to you. If you cannot think of a leader offhand, visit web sites of a company or athletic team that might interest you. For example, if you have been a fan of Kellogg Corp. products for a long time, search the Kellogg web site to identify a key company executive. Search the site for any clues to the executive's leadership behaviors and attitudes, as perhaps revealed in statements about employee relations or management philosophy. For example, an executive might make a statement about where the company is headed in the next five years, thereby indicating *direction setting*. You will probably not get enough information on the company web site, so plug your leader's name into a search engine to find two articles about him or her.

After you have gathered your case history information, identify at least four separate leadership behaviors and attitudes practiced by the leader in question. You will have to make inferences because a leader will rarely say, "Here are my leadership behaviors and attitudes."

Contingency and Situational Leadership

CHAPTER 5

133

Several years ago, Roger Cary called a "code orange" in the hospital he runs in Zion, Illinois. A code orange means a major disaster—for the cancer treatment center it meant that a single-engine plane had collided with the fifth floor.

The incident caused about $8 million worth of damage and $20 million in lost business. And while no patients were injured, the hospital's staff was devastated. It was up to Cary, the hospital's CEO, to meet both employee and patient needs. He believes that the most important thing he did during the crisis was to remain on the front lines and in touch with the staff. "I rolled up my sleeves and worked with the employees," he says. "I was there for every shift, encouraging everybody to hang in there."

Because Cary emphasized teamwork, staffers took on different tasks to ensure things moved smoothly. "We set up an employee call center because a lot of families were calling to see if their relatives were okay," he said. "We also had a patient information center—our patients come from all over the country and from foreign countries as well. We had to create a media communications center so that press inquiries wouldn't clog lines specified for employees or patients."

Within 20 minutes all patients had been transferred to area hospitals. Insurance covered the damage, which ended employees' fears of losing their jobs. The next few days were spent cleaning up. "The tragedy helped employees bond as a team and a hospital. It wasn't just the housekeeping department cleaning up: everybody worked, including myself," Cary says. "We all had to walk the extra mile."

The hospital accepted outpatients one week after the crash and was fully reopened for business within a year. "It took someone to stand tall and assure our employees we would work through this difficult time," Cary says. "On the upside, I really know the people that work here very well now."[1]

The incident about managing a near-catastrophe at a hospital illustrates an increasingly important leadership task: leading people through a crisis. Leadership of this type is a special case of the general subject of this chapter—adjusting one's approach based on factors in the situation. Cary emphasized emotional support and hands-on leadership to get the hospital through the crisis created by an airplane colliding with the building. Contingency and situational leadership further expands the study of leadership styles by adding more specific guidelines about which style to use under which circumstance.

In this chapter we present an overview of the situational perspective on leadership. We then summarize the five best-known contingency theories of leadership: Fiedler's contingency theory, path-goal theory, the situational leadership model, the normative decision model, and cognitive resource theory. We also describe a contingency model that applies mostly to CEOs. In addition, we describe crisis leadership, because leading others through a crisis has become a frequent challenge in recent years.

SITUATIONAL INFLUENCES ON EFFECTIVE LEADERSHIP BEHAVIOR

As mentioned in relation to leadership attitudes and behavior and leadership styles, the situation can influence which leadership behavior or style a leader emphasizes. The essence of a **contingency approach to leadership** is that leaders are most effective when they make their behavior contingent upon situational forces, including group member characteristics. Both the internal and the external environment have a significant impact on leader effectiveness. For example, the quality of the work force and the competitiveness of the environment could influence which behaviors the leader emphasizes. A manager who supervises competent employees might be able to practice consensus readily. And a manager who faces a competitive environment might find it easier to align people to pursue a new vision.

Research comparing entrepreneurial leaders with those from large corporations illustrates situational influences on leadership. One of the research questions asked was whether CEOs from different corporate environments have different attributes, skills, and abilities. A sample of thirty-five *Fortune* 500 (large-company) CEOs and thirty-five *Inc.* (small-company) CEOs was assessed on a psychological assessment battery of nine different inventories. The battery evaluates higher-level personnel ranging from supervisors and nonmanagerial professionals to presidents and CEOs.

The profiles of the large-company and small-company CEOs were then compared. Many significant differences between the two groups were found. The skills of small-company CEOs appeared to be centered primarily on production. For example, *Inc.* CEOs significantly exceeded *Fortune* 500 CEOs in developing and implementing technical ideas. Small-company CEOs were significantly stronger in coping with difficulties and emergencies and in handling outside contacts. The researchers explained that the environment of the entrepreneurs requires them to perform tasks that their *Fortune* 500 counterparts delegate to others.

The large-company CEOs had a significantly better developed subset of interpersonal skills. They scored higher than their small-company counterparts on communications, developing group cooperation and teamwork, developing employee potential, and supervisory practices. The large-company CEOs also scored better on leadership and group participation.[2]

FIEDLER'S CONTINGENCY THEORY OF LEADERSHIP EFFECTIVENESS

Fred E. Fiedler developed a widely researched and quoted contingency model that holds that the best style of leadership is determined by the situation in which the leader is working.[3] Here we examine how the style and situation are evaluated, the overall findings of the theory, and how leaders can modify situations to their advantage.

Measuring Leadership Style: The Least Preferred Coworker (LPC) Scale

Fiedler's theory classifies a manager's leadership style as relationship-motivated or task-motivated. According to Fiedler, leadership style is a relatively permanent aspect of behavior and thus difficult to modify. He reasons that once leaders understand their particular leadership style, they should work in situations that match their style. Similarly, the organization should help managers match leadership styles and situations.

The least preferred coworker (LPC) scale measures the degree to which a leader describes favorably or unfavorably his or her least preferred coworker—that is, an employee with whom he or she could work the least well. A leader who describes the least preferred coworker in relatively favorable terms tends to be relationship-motivated. In contrast, a person who describes this coworker in an unfavorable manner tends to be task-motivated. You can use this scale to measure your leadership style by doing Leadership Self-Assessment Quiz 5-1.

Measuring the Leadership Situation

Fiedler's contingency theory classifies situations as high, moderate, and low control. The more control exercised by the leader, the more favorable the situation is for him or her. The control classifications are determined by rating the situation on its three dimensions, as follows: (1) *Leader-member relations* measure how well the group and the leader get along; (2) *task structure* measures how clearly the procedures, goals, and evaluation of the job are defined; and (3) *position power* measures the leader's authority to hire, fire, discipline, and grant salary increases to group members.

Leader-member relations contribute as much to situation favorability as do task structure and position power combined. The leader therefore has the most control in a situation in which his or her relationships with members are the best.

Overall Findings

The key points of Fiedler's contingency theory are summarized and simplified in Figure 5-1 (page 139). The original theory is much more complex. Leadership effectiveness depends on matching leaders to situations in which they can exercise more control. The theory states that task-motivated leaders perform the best in situations of both high control and low control. Relationship-motivated leaders perform the best in situations of moderate control. Task-motivated leaders perform better in situations that are highly favorable for exercising control because they do not have to be concerned with the task. Instead, they can work

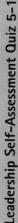

The Least Preferred Coworker (LPC) Scale for Measuring Leadership Style

Throughout your life you will have worked in many groups with a wide variety of different people—on your job, in social groups, in religious organizations, in volunteer groups, on athletic teams, and in many other situations. Some of your coworkers may have been very easy to work with in attaining the group's goals, while others were less so.

Think of all the people with whom you have ever worked, and then think of the person with whom you could work *least well*. He or she may be someone with whom you work now or someone with whom you have worked in the past. This does not have to be the person you liked least well, but should be the person with whom you had the most difficulty getting a job done, the *one* individual with whom you could work *least well*.

Describe this person on the scale that follows by placing an "X" in the appropriate space. Look at the words at both ends of the line before you mark your "X." *There are no right or wrong answers.* Work rapidly: Your first answer is likely to be the best. Do not omit any items, and mark each item only once.

Now describe the person with whom you can work least well.

Scoring

	8	7	6	5	4	3	2	1		
Pleasant	__	__	__	__	__	__	__	__	Unpleasant	_____
Friendly	__	__	__	__	__	__	__	__	Unfriendly	_____
	8	7	6	5	4	3	2	1		

	1	2	3	4	5	6	7	8		
Rejecting	__	__	__	__	__	__	__	__	Accepting	_____
Tense	__	__	__	__	__	__	__	__	Relaxed	_____
Distant	__	__	__	__	__	__	__	__	Close	_____
Cold	__	__	__	__	__	__	__	__	Warm	_____

	8	7	6	5	4	3	2	1		
Supportive	__	__	__	__	__	__	__	__	Hostile	_____

	1	2	3	4	5	6	7	8		
Boring	__	__	__	__	__	__	__	__	Interesting	_____
Quarrelsome	__	__	__	__	__	__	__	__	Harmonious	_____
Gloomy	__	__	__	__	__	__	__	__	Cheerful	_____

Open									Guarded	_____
	8	7	6	5	4	3	2	1		
Backbiting									Loyal	_____
	1	2	3	4	5	6	7	8		
Untrustworthy									Trustworthy	_____
	1	2	3	4	5	6	7	8		
Considerate									Inconsiderate	_____
	8	7	6	5	4	3	2	1		
Nasty									Nice	_____
	1	2	3	4	5	6	7	8		
Agreeable									Disagreeable	_____
	8	7	6	5	4	3	2	1		
Insincere									Sincere	_____
	1	2	3	4	5	6	7	8		
Kind									Unkind	_____
	8	7	6	5	4	3	2	1		

Total _____

SCORING AND INTERPRETATION   To calculate your score, add the numbers in the right column. If you scored 64 or higher, you are a high LPC leader, meaning that you are relationship-motivated. If you scored 57 or lower, you are a low LPC leader, meaning that you are task-motivated. A score of 58 to 63 places you in the intermediate range, making you a socioindependent leader. Compare your score to your score in Leadership Self-Assessment Quiz 4-1.

In attempting to make sense of your score, recognize that the LPC scale is but one measure of leadership style and that the approach to measurement is indirect. The leadership style measure presented in Self-Assessment Quiz 4-1 is more direct. To repeat, the general idea of the LPC approach is that if you have a positive, charitable attitude toward people you had a difficult time working with, you are probably relationship-oriented. In contrast, if you took a dim view of people who gave you a hard time, you are probably task-oriented. The message here is that a relationship-oriented leader should be able to work well with a variety of personalities.

SOURCE: *Adapted from* Improving Leadership Effectiveness *by Fred E. Fiedler, Martin M. Chemers, and Linda Mahar, Copyright © 1976 by John Wiley & Sons. Reprinted by permission of the authors.*

on relationships. In moderately favorable situations, the relationship-motivated leader works well because he or she can work on relationships and not get involved in overmanaging.

In very-low-control situations, the task-motivated leader is able to structure and make sense out of confusion, whereas the relationship-motivated leader wants to give emotional support to group members or call a meeting.

FIGURE 5-1   Summary of Findings from Fiedler's Contingency Theory

Task-motivated leaders perform best when they have the most control (highly favorable). *High*	Relationship-motivated leaders perform best when they have moderate control (moderately favorable). *Moderate*	Task-motivated leaders perform best when they have low control (highly unfavorable). *Low*

← **AMOUNT OF SITUATIONAL CONTROL BY LEADER** →

a. Leader-member relations are good. b. Task is well structured. c. Leader has high position power.	Both favorable and unfavorable factors are present.	a. Leader-member relations are poor. b. Task is poorly structured. c. Leader has low position power.

Making the Situation More Favorable for the Leader

A practical implication of the contingency theory is that leaders should modify situations to best match their leadership style, thereby enhancing their chances of being effective. Imagine the scenario of leaders who are task-motivated who decide that they need to exercise more control over the situation to achieve higher productivity in their work units. To increase control over the situation, they can do one or more of the following:

- Improve leader-member relations through such means as displaying an interest in the personal welfare of group members, having meals with them, actively listening to their concerns, telling anecdotes, and in general being a "nice person."

- Increase task structure by engaging in behaviors related to initiating structure, such as being more specific about expectations, providing deadlines, showing samples of acceptable work, and providing written instructions.

- Exercise more position power by requesting more formal authority from higher management. For example, the leader might let it be known that he or she has the authority to grant bonuses and make strong recommendations for promotion.

Now imagine a scenario in which a relationship-motivated leader wanted to create a situation of moderate favorability so that his or her interests in being needed by the group could be satisfied. The leader might give the group tasks of low structure and deemphasize his or her position power.

Evaluation of Fiedler's Contingency Theory

A major contribution of Fiedler's work is that it has prompted others to conduct studies about the contingency nature of leadership. Fiedler's theory has been one of the most widely researched theories in industrial psychology, and at one time it was used extensively as the basis for leadership training programs. The model has also alerted leaders to the importance of sizing up the situation to gain control. Despite its potential advantages, however, the contingency theory is too complicated to have much of an impact on most leaders. A major problem centers on matching the situation to the leader. In most situations, the amount of control the leader exercises varies from time to time. For example, if a relationship-motivated leader were to find the situation becoming too favorable for exercising control, it is doubtful that he or she would be transferred to a less favorable situation or attempt to make the situation less favorable.

THE PATH-GOAL THEORY OF LEADERSHIP EFFECTIVENESS

The **path-goal theory** of leadership effectiveness, as developed by Robert House, specifies what the leader must do to achieve high productivity and morale in a given situation. In general, a leader attempts to clarify the path to a goal for a group member so that he or she receives personal payoffs. At the same time, job satisfaction and performance increase.[4] Like the expectancy theory of motivation, on which it is based, path-goal theory is complex and has several versions. Its key features are summarized in Figure 5-2.

The major proposition of path-goal theory is that the manager should choose a leadership style that takes into account the characteristics of the group members and the demands of the task. Two key aspects of this theory will be discussed: matching the leadership style to the situation, and steps the leader can take to influence performance and satisfaction.

Matching the Leadership Style to the Situation

Path-goal theory emphasizes that the leader should choose among four different leadership styles to achieve optimum results in a given situation. Two important sets of contingency factors are the type of subordinates and the type of work they perform. The type of subordinates is determined by how much control they think they have over the environment (locus of control) and by how well they think they can do the assigned task.

Environmental contingency factors consist of factors that are not within the control of group members but that influence satisfaction and task accomplishment. Three broad classifications of contingency factors in the environment are (1) the group members' tasks, (2) the authority system within the organization, and (3) the work group.

To use path-goal theory, the leader must first assess the relevant variables in the environment. Second, she or he selects the one of the four styles listed next that fits those contingency factors best.

FIGURE 5–2   The Path–Goal Theory of Leadership

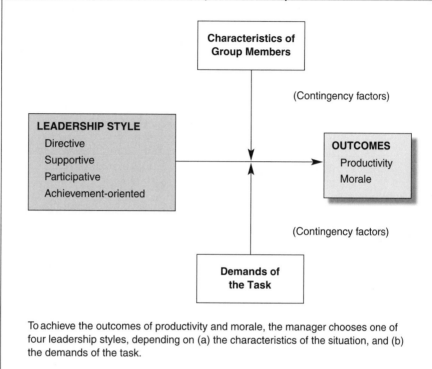

To achieve the outcomes of productivity and morale, the manager chooses one of four leadership styles, depending on (a) the characteristics of the situation, and (b) the demands of the task.

1. *Directive style.* The leader who is directive (similar to task-motivated) emphasizes formal activities such as planning, organizing, and controlling. When the task is unclear, the directive style improves morale.

2. *Supportive style.* The leader who is supportive (similar to relationship-motivated) displays concern for group members' well-being and creates an emotionally supportive climate. He or she enhances morale when group members work on dissatisfying, stressful, or frustrating tasks. Group members who are unsure of themselves prefer the supportive leadership style.

3. *Participative style.* The leader who is participative consults with group members to gather their suggestions, and then takes these suggestions seriously when making a decision. The participative leader is best suited for improving the morale of well-motivated employees who perform nonrepetitive tasks.

4. *Achievement-oriented style.* The leader who is achievement-oriented sets challenging goals, pushes for work improvement, and sets high expectations for team members. Group members are also expected to assume responsibility. The achievement-oriented leadership style works well with achievement-oriented team members, and also with those working on ambiguous and nonrepetitive tasks.

Although not specified in path-goal theory, a leader can sometimes successfully combine more than one of the four styles. The accompanying Leader in Action vignette features a leader who brought a company to profitability by removing a frustrating barrier to reaching goals. He also fit the situation by having the political skill necessary to deal with the complex bureaucracy of the FDA (Food and Drug Administration).

How the Leader Influences Performance

In addition to recommending the leadership style to fit the situation, the path-goal theory offers other suggestions to leaders. Most of them relate to motivation and satisfaction, including the following:

1. Recognize or activate group members' needs over which the leader has control.

2. Increase the personal payoffs to team members for attaining work goals. The leader might give high-performing employees additional recognition.

3. Make the paths to payoffs (rewards) easier by coaching and providing direction. For instance, a manager might help a team member be selected for a high-level project.

4. Help group members clarify their expectations of how effort will lead to good performance, and how performance will lead to a reward. The leader might say, "Anyone who has gone through this training in the past came away knowing how to implement an ISO 9000 (quality standards) program. And most people who learn how to meet these standards wind up getting a good raise."

5. Reduce frustrating barriers to reaching goals. For example, the leader might hire a temporary worker to help a group member catch up on paperwork and electronic mail.

6. Increase opportunities for personal satisfaction if the group member performs effectively. The "if" is important because it reflects contingent behavior on the leader's part.

7. Be careful not to irritate people by giving them instructions on things they already can do well.

8. To obtain high performance and satisfaction, the leader must provide structure if it is missing, and must also supply rewards contingent upon adequate performance. To accomplish this, leaders must clarify the desirability of goals for the group members.[5]

As a leader, you can derive specific benefit from path-goal theory by applying these eight methods of influencing performance. Chemers points out that although research interest in path-goal theory has waned in recent years, the basic tenets of the theory are on target. Any comprehensive theory of leadership must include the idea that the leader's actions have a major impact on the

Leader in Action

Lee Erlichman Applies CPR to Cardiac Telecom

Cardiac Telecom Corporation of Greensburg, Pennsylvania, a manufacturer of medical devices, needed to find a chief executive who could steer it through a regulatory maze. The company had developed a home-based, real-time surveillance system. A recovering heart patient wears a wireless, 11-ounce heart monitor at home that relays data to paramedics at the Cardiac Telecom office. Back in 1989, the company's officials expected the Food and Drug Administration (FDA) to approve the device in ninety days.

Actual lapsed time? Eight years.

During that time the company had five chief executives. "They were all good people," says Mel Pirchesky, a local venture capitalist who backed the company, "just not the right fit." None could get FDA approval.

The first was an engineer who lacked business experience. He quit. Going to the opposite extreme, the company then hired a marketing person who was weak on technology. He was fired. Next, working through a headhunter, they hired a veteran of a large company, who was rattled by the extreme demands of a startup. Following him was the inventor of the device, who decided it wasn't the role for him. Finally, a board member, an experienced health care professional, took the post, but he died unexpectedly a few months later.

Meanwhile, perfunctory FDA filings bounced around, never getting to the heart of the issues, says Mr. Pirchesky. The agency approved the device for hospitals, but not for home use—the company's business model.

The Solution. Then the company tapped Lee Erlichman, a former chief executive of a small software company. He understood execution. Most importantly, he understood that in a regu-

lated business the care and feeding of regulators must come first.

Erlichman abandoned the previous FDA filings. He started from scratch, launching new clinical trials to address FDA issues that the company had never satisfied. It was really costly and time-consuming, but ultimately successful. "We needed to make the FDA part of the solution instead of the problem," Mr. Erlichman said. Soon the company was marginally profitable.

But the firm found itself in another regulatory morass—Medicare. Cardiac Telecom had partnered with a company that encountered a billing problem with Medicare. Once again, Mr. Erlichman went full bore at regulators whose inaction threatened to unplug the company.

After Medicare's Pennsylvania medical director viewed the operation live, reimbursement resumed. It took six months—an eternity in an angel-financed startup, and Mr. Erlichman worked without pay. An "angel" is essentially a person who gives financial support to a new venture, despite the risk. Today, Cardiac Telecom is back on track and has just added two sales positions to its fifteen employees.

The Lesson. Pick the CEO who can solve the biggest problem. "In a startup, it's like a horse race," says Mr. Pirchesky, the investor. "It's all about the jockey."

QUESTIONS

1. What does the story about Cardiac Telecom have to do with leadership?

2. What interpersonal skill was particularly effective in helping Erlichman get the job done?

3. What does this story tell about the cognitive aspects of leadership?

motivation and satisfaction of group members.[6] Despite path-goal theory's potential contributions, however, it contains so many nuances and complexities that it has attracted little interest from managers.

THE HERSEY–BLANCHARD SITUATIONAL LEADERSHIP® MODEL

The two contingency approaches to leadership presented so far take into account collectively the task, the authority of the leader, and the nature of the subordinates. Another explanation of contingency leadership places its primary emphasis on the characteristics of group members. The **situational leadership model** of Paul Hersey and Kenneth H. Blanchard explains how to match the leadership style to the readiness of the group members. The term *model* rather than *theory* is deliberately chosen because situational leadership does not attempt to explain why things happen (as a theory would). Instead, the situational leadership model offers some procedures that can be repeated.[7]

Before delving further into the situational leadership model, do Leadership Self-Assessment Quiz 5-2. It will help alert you to the specific behaviors involved in regarding the characteristics of group members as key contingency variables in choosing the most effective leadership style.

Basics of the Model

Leadership style in the situational model is classified according to the relative amount of task and relationship behavior the leader engages in. The differentiation is akin to structure initiation versus consideration. **Task behavior** is the extent to which the leader spells out the duties and responsibilities of an individual or group. It includes giving directions and setting goals. **Relationship behavior** is the extent to which the leader engages in two-way or multiway communication. It includes such activities as listening, providing encouragement, and coaching. As Figure 5-3 shows, the situational model places combinations of task and relationship behaviors into four quadrants. Each quadrant calls for a different leadership style.

> *Style 1—High task and low relationship.* The "telling" style is very directive because the leader produces a lot of input but a minimum amount of relationship behavior. An autocratic leader would fit here.

> *Style 2—High task and high relationship.* The "selling" style is also very directive, but in a more persuasive, guiding manner. The leader provides considerable input about task accomplishment but also emphasizes human relations.

Leadership Self-Assessment Quiz 5–2

Measuring Your Situational Perspective

INSTRUCTIONS   Indicate how well you agree with the following statements, using the following scale: DS = disagree strongly; D = disagree; N = neutral; A = agree; AS = agree strongly. Circle the most accurate answer.

1. Workers need to be carefully trained before you can place high expectations on them.   **DS D N A AS**

2. The more knowledgeable the worker, the less he or she needs a clear statement of objectives.   **DS D N A AS**

3. "Hand holding" is an ineffective leadership technique for anxious group members.   **DS D N A AS**

4. The same well-delivered pep talk will usually appeal to workers at all levels.   **DS D N A AS**

5. As a manager, I would invest the least amount of time supervising the most competent workers.   **DS D N A AS**

6. It is best not to put much effort into supervising unenthusiastic staff members.   **DS D N A AS**

7. An effective leader delegates equal kinds and amounts of work to group members.   **DS D N A AS**

8. Even the most effective workers need frequent reassurance and emotional support.   **DS D N A AS**

9. If I noticed that a group member seemed insecure and anxious, I would give him or her extra-clear instructions and guidelines.   **DS D N A AS**

10. Many competent workers get to the point where they require relatively little leadership and supervision.   **DS D N A AS**

Total score: _____

SCORING AND INTERPRETATION
1. DS = 1, D = 2, N = 3, A = 4, AS = 5
2. DS = 1, D = 2, N = 3, A = 4, AS = 5
3. DS = 5, D = 4, N = 3, A = 2, AS = 1
4. DS = 5, D = 4, N = 3, A = 2, AS = 1
5. DS = 1, D = 2, N = 3, A = 4, AS = 5
6. DS = 5, D = 4, N = 3, A = 2, AS = 1
7. DS = 5, D = 4, N = 3, A = 2, AS = 1
8. DS = 5, D = 4, N = 3, A = 2, AS = 1
9. DS = 1, D = 2, N = 3, A = 4, AS = 5
10. DS = 1, D = 2, N = 3, A = 4, AS = 5

- 45–50 points   You have (or would have) a strong situational perspective as a leader and manager.
- 30–44 points   You have (or would have) an average situational perspective as a leader and manager.
- 10–29 points   You rarely take (or would take) a situational perspective as a leader and manager.

SKILL DEVELOPMENT   For the vast majority of leadership and management assignments it pays to sharpen your situational perspective. If you scored lower than you want, sharpen your insights into situations by asking yourself, "What are the key factors in this situation that will influence my effectiveness as a leader/manager?" Study both the people and the task in the situation.

FIGURE 5-3   Situational Leadership Model

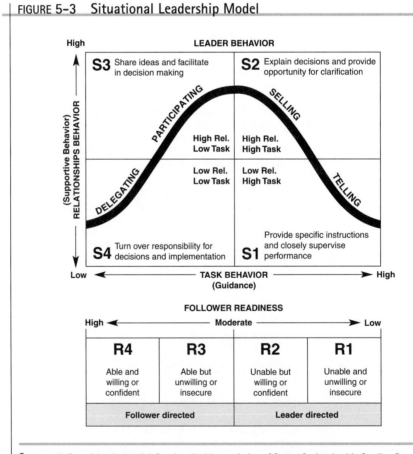

Style 3—High relationship and low task. In the "participating" leadership style, there is less direction and more collaboration between leader and group members. The consultative and consensus subtypes of participative leader generally fit into this quadrant.

Style 4—Low relationship and low task. In the "delegating" leadership style, the leader delegates responsibility for a task to a group member and is simply kept informed of progress. If carried to an extreme, this style would be classified as free-rein.

The situational leadership model states that there is no one best way to influence group members. The most effective leadership style depends on the readiness level of group members. **Readiness** in situational leadership is defined as the extent to which a group member has the ability and willingness or confidence to accomplish a specific task. The concept of readiness is therefore not a characteristic, trait, or motive—it relates to a specific task.

Readiness has two components, ability and willingness. *Ability* is the knowledge, experience, and skill an individual or group brings to a particular task or activity. *Willingness* is the extent to which an individual or group has the confidence, commitment, and motivation to accomplish a specific task.

The key point of situational leadership theory is that as group member readiness increases, a leader should rely more on relationship behavior and less on task behavior. When a group member becomes very ready, a minimum of task or relationship behavior is required of the leader. Guidelines for the leader, outlined in Figure 5-3, can be summarized as follows:

Situation R1—Low readiness. When followers are unable, unwilling, or insecure, the leader should emphasize task-oriented behavior and be very directive and autocratic, using a *telling* style.

Situation R2—Moderate readiness. When group members are unable but willing or confident, the leader should focus on being more relationship-oriented, using a *selling* style.

Situation R3—Moderate-to-high readiness. Group members are able but unwilling or insecure, so the leader needs to provide a high degree of relationship-oriented behavior but a low degree of task behavior, thus engaging in a *participating* style.

Situation R4—High readiness. When followers are able, willing, or confident, they are self-sufficient and competent. Thus the leader can grant them considerable autonomy, using a *delegating* style.

Evaluation of the Situational Model

The situational model represents a consensus of thinking about leadership behavior in relation to group members: competent people require less specific direction than do less competent people. The model is also useful because it builds on other explanations of leadership that emphasize the role of task and relationship behaviors. As a result, it has proved to be useful as the basis for leadership training. The situational model also corroborates common sense and is therefore intuitively appealing. You can benefit from this model by attempting to diagnose the readiness of group members before choosing the right leadership style.

Nevertheless, the model presents categories and guidelines so precisely that it gives the impression of infallibility. In reality, leadership situations are less clear-cut than the four quadrants suggest. Also, the prescriptions for leadership will work only some of the time. For example, many supervisors use a telling style with unable and unwilling or insecure team members (R1) and still achieve poor results. Research evidence for the situational model has been mixed. A major concern is that there are few leadership situations in which a high-task, high-relationship orientation does not produce the best results.[8]

Leadership Skill-Building Exercise 5-1 provides you with the opportunity to practice implementing the situational leadership model. The same exercise also supports other contingency and situational models.

THE NORMATIVE DECISION MODEL

Another contingency viewpoint is that leaders must choose a style that elicits the correct degree of group participation when making decisions. Since many of a leader's interactions with group members involve decision making, this perspective is sensible. The **normative decision model** views leadership as a decision-making process in which the leader examines certain factors within the situation to determine which decision-making style will be the most effective. Here we present the latest version of the model that Victor Vroom and his associates have been evolving for over thirty years, based on research with over 100,000 managers.[9]

Decision-Making Styles

The normative model (formerly known as the leader-participation model) identifies five decision-making styles, each reflecting a different degree of participation by group members.

1. *Decide.* The leader makes the decision alone and either announces or sells it to the group. The leader might use expertise in collecting information from the group or from others who appear to have information relevant to the problem.

2. *Consult (Individually).* The leader presents the problem to the group members individually, gathers their suggestions, and then makes the decision.

3. *Consult (Group).* The leader presents the problem to group members in a meeting, gathers their suggestions, and then makes the decision.

4. *Facilitate.* The leader presents the problem, then acts as a facilitator, defining the problem to be solved and the boundaries in which the decision

Leadership Skill-Building Exercise 5-1

Applying the Situational Leadership Model

One student plays the role of a team leader whose team is given the responsibility of improving customer service at a consumer electronics megastore. Before jumping into this task, the team leader decides to use the situational leadership model. Today you are going to meet with three group members individually to estimate their *readiness* to perform the customer-service-improvement task. You will want to estimate both the *ability* and the *willingness* of team members to perform the task. Three different people will play the role of group members whose readiness is being assessed. After the brief interviews (about five minutes) are conducted, the team leader will announce which leadership style he or she intends to use with each of the people interviewed. Class members not directly involved in the role play will offer feedback on how well readiness was assessed.

must be made. The leader wants concurrence and avoids having his or her ideas receive more weight based on position power.

5. *Delegate.* The leader permits the group to make the decision within prescribed limits. Although the leader does not directly intervene in the group's deliberations unless explicitly asked, he or she works behind the scenes, providing resources and encouragement.

Contingency Factors and Application of the Model

The leader diagnoses the situation in terms of seven variables, or contingency factors, that contribute to selecting the most appropriate decision-making style. Based on answers to those variables, the leader or manager follows the path through decision matrices to choose one of five decision-making styles. The model includes two versions: one when time is critical and one when a more important consideration is developing group members' decision-making capabilities. When development of group members receives high priority, the leader or manager relies more on the group to make a decision even if the process is time-consuming.

Figure 5-4 depicts the matrix for time-driven group problems, a situation in which a decision must be reached rapidly. The situational factors, or problem variables, are listed at the top of the matrix. Specifying these factors makes the model a contingency approach. The decision-making style chosen depends on these factors, which are defined as follows:

Decision Significance: The significance of the decision to the success of the project or organization

Importance of Commitment: The importance of team members' commitment to the decision

FIGURE 5-4   The Time-Driven Model for Choosing a Decision-Making Style

Instructions: The matrix operates like a funnel. You start at the left with a specific decision problem in mind. The column headings denote situational factors which may or may not be present in that problem. You progress by selecting High or Low (H or L) for each relevant situational factor. Proceed down from the funnel, judging only those situational factors for which a judgment is called for, until you reach the recommended process.

Decision Significance	Importance of Commitment	Leader Expertise	Likelihood of Commitment	Group Support	Group Expertise	Team Competence	
H	H	H	H	-	-	-	Decide
H	H	H	L	H	H	H	Delegate
H	H	H	L	H	H	L	Consult (Group)
H	H	H	L	H	L	-	Consult (Group)
H	H	H	L	L	-	-	Consult (Group)
H	H	L	H	H	H	H	Facilitate
H	H	L	H	H	H	L	Consult (Individually)
H	H	L	H	H	L	-	Consult (Individually)
H	H	L	H	L	-	-	Consult (Individually)
H	H	L	L	H	H	H	Facilitate
H	H	L	L	H	H	L	Consult (Group)
H	H	L	L	H	L	-	Consult (Group)
H	H	L	L	L	-	-	Consult (Group)
H	L	H	-	-	-	-	Decide
H	L	L	-	H	H	H	Facilitate
H	L	L	-	H	H	L	Consult (Individually)
H	L	L	-	H	L	-	Consult (Individually)
H	L	L	-	L	-	-	Consult (Individually)
L	H	-	H	-	-	-	Decide
L	H	-	L	-	-	H	Delegate
L	H	-	L	-	-	L	Facilitate
L	L	-	-	-	-	-	Decide

Note: The left-hand side of the matrix is labeled vertically "PROBLEM STATEMENT".

Source: Victor H. Vroom's Time-Driven Model, reproduced from A Model of Leadership Style, Copyright 1998. Reprinted by permission of the author.

Leader Expertise: Your knowledge or expertise in relation to the problem

Likelihood of Commitment: The likelihood that the team will commit itself to a decision you might make on your own

Group Support: The degree to which the team supports the organization's objectives at stake in the problem

Group Expertise: Team members' knowledge or expertise in relation to the problem

Team Competence: The ability of the team members to work together in solving problems

Accurate answers to these seven situational factors can be challenging to obtain. The leader may have to rely heavily on intuition and also minimize distorted thinking, such as believing he or she has some expertise when in fact it might be lacking.

To use the model, the decision maker begins at the left side of the matrix, at "Problem Statement." At the top of the matrix are the seven situational factors, each of which may be present (H for high) or absent (L for low) in that problem. You begin by ascertaining if the decision is significant. If so, you select H and answer the second question, concerning the importance of gaining group commitment. If you continue the process without crossing any horizontal line on the matrix, you will arrive at one of the five recommended decision styles. Sometimes a conclusive determination can be made based on two factors, such as L, L. Others require three (such as L, H, H), four (such as H, H, H, H), or as many as seven factors (such as H, H, L, L, H, H, H).

Different people giving different answers to the situational factors will arrive at different conclusions about the recommended decision style in the situation. The leader needs sufficient information to answer each of seven questions accurately. To help you apply the model, Leadership Skill-Building Exercise 5-2 presents a scenario developed by Vroom.

The normative model provides a valuable service to practicing managers and leaders. It prompts them to ask questions about contingency variables in decision-making situations. It has been found that for previous versions of the model, managers who follow its procedures are likely to increase their decision-making effectiveness. Furthermore, managers who make decisions consistent with the model (again, based on previous versions) are more likely to be perceived as effective managers.[10] These same good results are probable for Vroom's new model because it incorporates most of the concepts in the previous models but is easier to follow. As with other contingency approaches, however, the model does not deal with the charismatic and inspiration aspects of leadership.

When the leader concludes that group decision making is appropriate, morale will often be elevated. Lois Juliber, a Colgate-Palmolive executive, implemented a program of encouraging people throughout the organization to make decisions. She noted, "All of a sudden, people got the sense that they could really make a decision, and no one was going to second-guess them. And for morale, it was just fantastic. Second-guessing is the absolute paralyzer of an organization, and not what you do in a turnaround when you need speed."[11]

Applying the Time–Driven Model

The exercise presented here can be done individually or in small groups.

The bank examiners have just left, having insisted that many of your commercial real estate loans be written off, which will deplete your already low capital. Along with the many other banks in your region, your bank is in serious danger of being closed by the regulators. As the financial problems surfaced, many of the top executives left to pursue other interests, but fortunately you were able to replace them with three highly competent younger managers. Although they had no prior acquaintance with one another, each is a product of a fine training program with one of the money center banks, in which they rotated through positions in all of the banking functions.

Your extensive experience in the industry leads you to the inevitable conclusion that the only hope is a two-pronged approach involving the reduction of all but the most critical expenses and the sale of assets to other banks. The task must be accomplished quickly because further deterioration of the quality of the loan portfolio could result in a negative capital position and force regulators to close the bank.

The strategy is clear to you, but you have many details that will need to be worked out. You believe that you know what information will be needed to get the bank on a course for future prosperity. You are fortunate in having three young executives to help you. Although they have had little or no experience in working together, you know that each is dedicated to the survival of the bank. Like you, they know what needs to be done and how to do it.

The suggested path is found on page 505 in the references to Chapter 5.

COGNITIVE RESOURCE THEORY: HOW INTELLIGENCE, EXPERIENCE, AND STRESS INFLUENCE LEADERSHIP

Another contingency theory describes how a leader's intelligence and experience can influence performance when the stress level of the people is considered. The general thrust of **cognitive resource theory** is that stress plays a key role in determining how a leader's intelligence is related to group performance.[12] The theory, as developed by Fiedler and his colleagues, also explains how directive behavior is tied in with intelligence. Several of the many predictions made by cognitive resource theory are as follows:

1. Because experienced leaders have a larger variety of behaviors to fall back on, leaders with greater experience but lower intelligence are likely to have higher-performing groups under high-stress conditions. The veteran leader/manager has acquired the necessary skills and knowledge to guide

the group through a difficult situation, such as dealing with a competitive threat. Under low-stress conditions, leader experience is less relevant.

2. Because experience leads to habitual behavior patterns, highly experienced leaders will often use old solutions to problems when creativity is necessary. Leaders with high intelligence are more valuable than experienced leaders when innovation is needed and stress levels are low. The highly intelligent leader relies on intellectual ability to analyze the problem and find an optimal solution. (Leader experience helps under high-stress conditions but is not a significant factor when stress levels are low.)

3. If a leader is experiencing stress, his or her intellectual abilities will be diverted from the task at hand. As a result, measures of leader intelligence and competence will not correlate with group performance when the leader is stressed.

4. The intellectual abilities of directive leaders will correlate more highly with group performance than will the intellectual abilities of nondirective leaders. This is true because the directive leader provides more ideas and suggestions to the group.[13] The nondirective leader is more likely to urge the group member to be more self-reliant.

5. A leader's intellectual abilities will be related to group performance to the degree that the task requires the use of intellectual ability.[14] Cognitive resource theory assumes that intelligent leaders devise better plans for doing the work than less intelligent leaders, especially when the plan is complex. (Do you think this finding merits a Nobel Prize?)

The cognitive resource theory is useful in that it highlights how intelligence, experience, and stress can influence both leader and group performance. However, the theory also neglects the utility of a combination of an experienced *and* intelligent leader in low-stress and high-stress situations. In reality, leaders who are both intelligent and experienced will perform the best in most situations.

CONTINGENCY LEADERSHIP IN THE EXECUTIVE SUITE

An investigation of how top-level executives lead their organizations provides additional insight into contingency leadership.[15] The approach these leaders take lies on the borderline between style and strategy. We include the information here under contingency leadership because each approach is chosen based on an analysis of the requirements of the situation. A leadership approach is defined as a coherent, explicit style of management, not a personal style. However, the style of management centers on leadership behaviors.

Charles M. Farkas, Philippe De Backer, and Suzy Wetlaufer interviewed 163 top executives on six continents to learn how these leaders delivered consistently extraordinary results. They scrutinized 12,000 pages of interview transcripts to reach their conclusions. Five distinct approaches were revealed by the interview analysis: strategic, human assets, expertise, box, and change agent. The overriding conclusion from the study is that successful CEOs assess their companies' needs, then adapt their leadership style to fit the particular situation. Here we will summarize each approach, including its associated contingency factors and leadership behaviors. Table 5-1 provides an outline of the approaches and accompanying contingency factors.

The *strategic approach* is a systematic, dispassionate, and structured analysis of a company's strengths and weaknesses and of its mission. CEOs using this approach perceive their major contribution as creating, testing, and designing the implementation of a long-term business strategy. Much of their workday is devoted to activities intended to analyze their organization's current situation and most advantageous business position in the future. CEOs using this approach devote about 80 percent of their time to external factors such as customers, competitors, technological advances, and market trends.

An example of a successful use of the strategic approach is Michael Dell of Dell Computer. Dell logs on to the Internet each day to track information and opinions about market trends and reactions to his company's products and those of competitors. Day-to-day operation of the business is delegated extensively to trusted subordinates.

CEOs should use the strategic approach in unstable environments where the volume and pace of change are high. Significant complexity in terms of technology, geography, or functions is another contingency factor calling for the strategic approach. For example, the CEO of Coca-Cola uses a strategic approach because the company has 32,000 employees in approximately 200 countries worldwide. The strategic approach is often chosen by CEOs who must frequently make decisions of enormous consequence.

TABLE 5-1   Contingency Factors for Five Approaches to CEO Leadership

CEO Leadership Approach	Contingency Factors
Strategic (create, test, and design long-term strategy)	Unstable environment, high rate of change, complexity.
Human assets (add value through hiring, retention, and development programs)	Business units are better positioned than headquarters to make strategy.
Expertise (design and implement programs around specific expertise such as technology)	Certain expertise can be source of significant competitive advantage.
Box (add value through controls that set boundaries for employee performance)	Presence of government examiners who insist on strict controls to protect consumer and company.
Change agent (create an environment of continual reinvention)	Company wants to remain a leader in the field, and status quo is unacceptable.

Source: From Charles M. Farkas and Suzy Wetlaufer, "The Ways Chief Executive Officers Lead," Harvard Business Review, May–June 1996, pp.110–122; Farkas and Philippe De Backer, Maximum Leadership: The World's Leading CEOs Share Their Five Strategies for Success (New York: Henry Holt, 1996).

In the *human assets approach,* the CEO and the corporate staff add value to the organization through hiring, retention, and development programs. CEOs using this approach believe that strategy formulation belongs in the business units. These CEOs believe that their most important job is to impart selected values, behaviors, and attitudes by managing the growth and development of individuals. To implement this approach, these executives travel extensively and spend most of their time in human resource activities such as recruiting, performance evaluation, and career planning. An important goal of the human assets approach is to develop business unit managers to the point at which they act and make decisions the way the CEO would. The human assets CEO believes that good employees should do things the *company way.* Herb Kelleher, the former CEO of Southwest Airlines, said, "We hire great attitudes, and we'll teach them any functionality they need."[16]

The human assets approach is most frequently used when a company has such far-flung operations that managers in the business units are better equipped to formulate strategy than people in the corporate group. Consistency in running the geographically remote businesses is achieved by the CEO's imparting corporate values to employees worldwide. Consistency in values is also enhanced when the CEO is involved in hiring key people. Another contingency factor favoring the human assets approach is if key executives strongly believe that the company values and standards of behavior are necessary for the success of the business.

Executives who use the *expertise approach* believe that the CEO's key responsibility is selecting and disseminating throughout the organization an area of expertise that will give the firm a competitive advantage. The majority of their working time is devoted to activities that foster the cultivation and continual improvement of this expertise. Among these activities are studying new technological research, analyzing competitors' products, and meeting with engineers and customers. Areas of expertise include marketing, manufacturing, technology, and distribution. Organizational members who have good technical expertise and share it across organizational units are rewarded. A key contingency factor for favoring the expertise approach is if a certain expertise can give the firm a significant competitive advantage. The CEO of Cardiac Telecom featured in the Leader in Action vignette used the expertise approach to deal with FDA officials.

A *box approach* occurs when the corporate group adds value by creating, communicating, and overseeing an explicit set of controls. The controls can take a variety of forms, including financial measures, rules, procedures, and values that define boundaries for the performance of all employees. The purpose of these controls is to ensure uniform and predictable experiences for employees and customers, and to lower risk. CEOs who use the box approach devote much of their workdays to attending to deviations from standard, such as quarterly results that are below forecast. They also devote time to rewarding employees whose behavior and performance match the control standards.

The key contingency factor favoring the box approach is a regulated environment such as banking or nuclear power plants in which the government insists on strict controls to protect employees and customers. The purpose of the controls is to strive for consistency. Claude Bébéar, the president of AXA Advisors, LLC, an international insurance company, has invented a language of words and symbols to enhance uniform behavior among the company's 50,000 employees in twelve countries. For example, employees are encouraged to use "TNT action" to express the rapid implementation of decisions.

CEOs who use the *change agent approach* believe that their most critical role is to create an environment of continual reinvention, even if such an emphasis on change creates short-term disturbances such as anxiety, confusion, and poorer financial results. Change agent CEOs spend up to 75 percent of their time using speeches, meetings, and other forms of communication to motivate members to embrace change. They meet regularly with a variety of stakeholders to beat the drums for change. Change agent executives regularly visit factories, create and answer email, and attend company picnics. (It's a good thing these CEOs have a strong internal staff to run the business!) Employees who embrace change receive the biggest rewards. At the investment bank Goldman, Sachs, a talented young banker was promoted to partner two years ahead of his class because he was willing to accept an assignment in Asia. At the time, few U.S. employees were willing to work abroad.

The change agent approach appears to be triggered when the CEO believes that the status quo will lead to the company's undoing, such as when a software development company is content with its current lineup of products. The contingency factor is not obvious, such as a troubled organization needing change; rather, the CEO has the vision to recognize that trouble lies ahead unless changes are made now.

The five leadership approaches just described are not mutually exclusive, and sometimes a CEO will emphasize more than one approach. For example, the change agent approach might be needed to implement a radical business strategy. Yet in the most effectively run organizations, the CEO usually has a dominant approach or style that serves as a compass and rudder for all corporate decisions. In general, emphasizing one of these approaches, at least for a period in a firm's history, can help a CEO to lead with clarity, consistency, and commitment.

LEADERSHIP DURING A CRISIS

Among the potential crises facing organizations are a drastic revenue decline, pending bankruptcy, homicide in the workplace, scandalous or criminal behavior by executives, floods, earthquakes, bombings, and terrorist attacks. Leading during a crisis can be regarded as contingency leadership because the situation demands that the leader emphasize certain behaviors, attitudes, and traits. **Crisis leadership** is the process of leading group members through a sudden and largely unanticipated, intensely negative, and emotionally draining circumstance. Here we describe six leadership attributes and behaviors associated with successfully leading an organization or organizational unit through a crisis.

Be Decisive. The best-accepted principle of crisis leadership is that the leader should take decisive action to remedy the situation. After the plan is formulated, it should be widely communicated to help reassure group members that something concrete is being done about the predicament. After their physical facilities were destroyed at the World Trade Center attack of 9/11, several leaders announced the next day that their firms would move to nearby backup locations. Communicating plans helps reduce uncertainty about what is happening to the firm and the people in it. A leader who takes highly visible action to deal with a crisis is likely to be viewed as competent.[17]

Lead with Compassion. Displaying compassion with the concerns, anxieties, and frustrations of group members is a key interpersonal skill for crisis leadership. The type of compassionate leadership that brings about organizational healing involves taking some form of public action that eases pain and that inspires others to act as well. Compassionate leadership involves two related sets of actions. The first is to create an environment in which affected workers can freely discuss how they feel, such as a group meeting to talk about the crisis or disaster. The second is to create an environment in which those workers who experience or witness pain can find a method to alleviate their own suffering and that of others. The leader might establish a special fund to help the families of workers who were victims of the disaster, or give workers the opportunity to receive grief counseling.

The two-pronged approach to leading with compassion is illustrated by TJX president and CEO Edmund English, who lost seven employees aboard one of the airplanes that struck the World Trade Center. He assembled his staff members together shortly after the attacks to confirm the names of the victims, encouraging his workers to express their feelings. English called in grief counselors that same day and charted a plane to fly in victims' relatives from Europe and Canada to company headquarters in Massachusetts.[18] As another example, after the attacks of September 11 major companies in New York and other U.S. cities hired Crisis Management International (CMI), a firm that delivers crisis counseling in the workplace. Although CMI has only nine full-time employees, it has a network of 1,402 therapists and psychologists, all trained by CMI in "critical-incident stress debriefing." Counselors met with traumatized employees in both individual and group settings.[19]

Reestablish the Usual Work Routine. Although it may appear callous and counterintuitive, an effective way of helping people deal with a workplace crisis is to encourage them to return to their regular work. It is important for workers to first express their feelings about the crisis before refocusing on work, but once they have, returning to work helps ground people in reality and restores purpose to their lives. Randall Marshall, director of trauma studies for the New York State Office of Mental Health, said after 9/11, "A healthy response to this type of situation is to get back into a routine."[20]

Avoid a Circle-the-Wagons Mentality.   One of the worst ways to lead a group through a crisis is to strongly defend yourself against your critics or deny wrong-doing. The same denial approach is referred to as maintaining a bunker mentality, or stonewalling the problem. Instead of cooperating with other stakeholders involved in the crisis, the leader takes a defensive posture. A case in point is Yoichiro Kaizaki, the former chairman of Bridgestone Corporation (the Japanese owner of Firestone tires). Rather than act promptly to control the damage when the news of the faulty Firestone tires on Ford Explorers first surfaced, he refused to face critics until the controversy was raging. His stubborn behavior appears to have worsened the publicity for Firestone and Bridgestone.[21]

Display Optimism.   Pessimists abound in every crisis, so optimism by the leader can help energize group members to overcome the bad times. The effective crisis leader draws action plans that give people hope for a better future. John Chambers of Cisco has been successful in leading his company through difficult times, in part by continuously reinforcing the idea that the Internet has a glorious future. Barbara Baker Clark contends that the role of a leader during a crisis is to encourage hopefulness. She states,

> I'm not saying that you have to plaster a stupid grin on your face even if the bottom line is tanking or people are dying in battle. I am saying don't wallow in pessimism. Believe it or not, it matters to your employees that you remain reasonably optimistic. It will reduce anxiety and keep everyone motivated. That's the power of leadership.[22]

Be a Transformational Leader.   During times of large and enduring crisis, transformational leadership may be the intervention of choice. The transformational leader can often lead the organization out of its present misery. You may recall the case problem at the end of Chapter 3 about Patricia Russo being recruited to lead Lucent out of the crisis it faced several years ago. Transformational leadership is likely to benefit the troubled organization both in dealing with the immediate crisis and in performing better in the long run.

SUMMARY

Theories of contingency and situational leadership build further upon the study of leadership style by adding more specific guidelines about which style to use under which circumstances. Leaders are most effective when they make their behavior contingent upon situational forces, including group member characteristics. One study suggested that entrepreneurial leaders are faced with an environment that prompts them to emphasize production-oriented behaviors. In contrast, large-company CEOs work in an environment more conducive to emphasizing interpersonal behaviors and skills.

Fiedler's contingency theory states that the best style of leadership is determined by the situation in which the leader is working. Style, in Fiedler's theory, is measured by the least preferred coworker (LPC) scale. If you have a reasonably positive attitude toward your least preferred coworker, you are relationship-motivated. You are task-motivated if your attitude is negative. Situational control, or favorability, is measured by a combination of the quality of leader-member relations, the degree of task structure, and the leader's position power.

The key proposition of Fiedler's theory is that in situations of high control or low control, leaders with a task-motivated style are the most effective. In a situation of moderate control, a relationship-motivated style works best. Leaders can improve situational control by modifying leader-member relations, task structure, and position power.

The path-goal theory of leadership effectiveness specifies what the leader must do to achieve high productivity and morale in a given situation. Effective leaders clarify the paths to attaining goals, help group members progress along these paths, and remove barriers to goal attainment. Leaders must choose a style that best fits the two sets of contingency factors—the characteristics of the subordinates and the tasks. The four styles in path-goal theory are directive, supportive, participative, and achievement-oriented.

The situational leadership model (developed by Hersey and Blanchard) explains how to match leadership style to the readiness of group members. The model classifies leadership style according to the relative amounts of task and relationship behavior the leader engages in. The four styles are different combinations of task and relationship behavior, both rated as high versus low. *Readiness* refers both to ability and to willingness to accomplish a specific task. As group member readiness increases, a leader should rely more on relationship behavior and less on task behavior. When a group member becomes very ready, however, minimum task or relationship behavior is required.

The normative decision model explains that leadership is a decision-making process. A leader examines certain contingency factors in the situation to determine which decision-making style will be the most effective in either a time-driven or developmental situation. The model defines five decision-making styles: two individual and three group. By answering a series of seven diagnostic questions in a matrix, the manager follows the path to a recommended decision style.

Cognitive resource theory describes how a leader's intelligence and experience can influence performance under conditions of stress. A major prediction of the theory is that leaders with high intelligence are more valuable than experienced leaders when innovation is needed and stress levels are low. The highly intelligent leader relies on intellectual ability to analyze the problem and find an optimal solution. Also, the intellectual abilities of directive leaders will correlate more highly with group performance than will the intellectual abilities of nondirective leaders.

CEOs who are successful assess their companies' needs, then adapt their leadership style to fit the particular situation. The five approaches or styles are strategy, human assets, expertise, box (emphasis on controls), and change agent. Each of these approaches is emphasized under different circumstances; for example, the human assets approach is used when business units are better positioned than headquarters to make strategy.

Leading others through a crisis can be considered a form of contingency leadership because the leader adapts his or her style to the situation. In a crisis, leaders should (a) be decisive, (b) lead with compassion, (c) reestablish the usual work routine, (d) avoid a circle-the-wagons mentality, (e) display optimism, and (f) be a transformational leader.

KEY TERMS

Contingency approach to leadership
Path-goal theory
Situational leadership model
Task behavior
Relationship behavior

Readiness
Normative decision model
Cognitive resource theory
Crisis leadership

 GUIDELINES FOR ACTION AND SKILL DEVELOPMENT

1. To apply contingency and situational theory, a leader typically has to achieve the right balance between a task and a relationship orientation. Unless there is strong evidence to the contrary, the leader should strive to emphasize both tasks and relationships.

2. Consider four factors as a shortcut to deciding whether a decision is best made by a group. The stronger the need for *buy-in* or *commitment*, the more important is group participation. When a *creative solution* is important, group input is valuable because varied viewpoints ordinarily enhance creativity. When *time is scarce*, it is better for the leader to make the decision. When a decision is needed that *reflects the bigger picture*, the leader will often be in the best position to make the decision.

3. An effective way to develop your leadership skills is to look for opportunities to exert a small amount of helpful leadership rather than wait for opportunities to accomplish extraordinary deeds. The "little leadership" might involve such behaviors as mentoring a struggling team member, coaching somebody about how to use a new high-tech device, or making a suggestion about improving a product. In the words of Michael E. McGill and John W. Slocum, Jr., "For those who want to stand atop the dugout, dance with the elephants, fly with the buffaloes, soar with eagles, or perform other mystical and heroic acts of large leadership, our little leadership may seem all too managerial, too modest, and too mundane."[23] Nevertheless, many situations call for a modest amount of leadership.

DISCUSSION QUESTIONS AND ACTIVITIES

1. Ed Whitacre, an executive at SBC Communications Inc., said that sometimes he is a strategic manager and at other times a hands-on manager. In what way does his comment reflect the contingency approach to leadership?

2. In what ways do contingency theories go beyond stating that the best leadership approach depends on the situation?

3. How would a manager know which variables in a given situation should influence which approach to leadership he or she should take?

4. What difference in leadership approach have you noticed between top-level managers and first-level supervisors?

5. Which of the four path-goal styles do you think would be the best for managing a professional football or professional soccer team? Justify your answer.

6. According to the situational model of leadership, which style is likely to be the most effective for leading a strongly motivated group of ecommerce specialists?

7. Suppose a company has been rocked with financial scandal, and a new CEO is brought in from the outside. Which of the five approaches to contingency leadership in the executive suite should this new CEO implement? Explain your reasoning.

8. Why might a transformational leader be helpful in a crisis?

9. Identify a business leader whose organization is facing a crisis today. Explain why you consider his or her situation to be a crisis.

10. Show the normative decision model to an experienced leader. Obtain his or her opinion on its practicality, and be ready to discuss your findings in class.

Leadership Case Problem A

Hector Alvarez, the Multifaceted Team Leader

Hector Alvarez is the team leader for fleet operations of Belasco Inc., an American tire and battery manufacturer. His major responsibility is to manage the company's fleet of trucks and the team members that deliver tires to distributors and large customers. Top-level management recognizes that timely delivery of tires and batteries is a major success factor for its business. One of the major challenges Belasco faces is that distributors and retailers want to minimize inventory on their premises. The problem becomes particularly acute after the first winter snowstorm in the north, which creates a spike in demand for snow tires.

Alvarez Reflects on His Job. When asked about the major demands of his position as team leader, Alvarez responded: "Managing a truck fleet is a much more demanding job than most people think. My team members and I deal with a gaggle of problems every day. Our trucks have to be in good shape. We have to deliver the right products to the customers on time when they need it. We work on very short lead times. If we don't do our job right, the company doesn't get paid. So the efforts of manufacturing and marketing go down the drain.

"I just mentioned some of the business challenges. Yet I think the people challenges can be even greater. You get a wide range of personalities in the tire-and-battery industry. Some of the people working on our team are the dirty-fingernail types who can be crude and rude toward each other. Then you get some of the business-grad types who are dead serious about their careers and who want to grab as much responsibility as they can. Sometimes they are a little unrealistic in what they want to do. One Boston University grad we hired wants to develop a new business model for Belasco that would enable us to bypass distributors by selling over the Net."

Alvarez in Action. One Friday morning Ashley Cohen (the Boston University graduate) met with

Alvarez to discuss some ideas she had been working on at night and on the weekends. She said she had been developing a new business model that would enable Belasco to compete successfully in the twenty-first century. Cohen said that by shifting most of the company business to ecommerce Belasco could vaporize the distributors, allowing the company to enjoy greater profit margins. She wanted the company to support a pilot project.

Alvarez thought for a moment, then told Cohen, "What you are saying makes a lot of sense. The general idea that we should be doing more business over the Net sounds plausible. We are already getting a lot of our orders by computer. As the team leader, I applaud your efforts. We need some advanced thinking here. For now, I can authorize you to work on this project every Friday afternoon. I will try to arrange a meeting for you with top management. I would like to attend also.

"Maybe top management will grant you the funds to develop your project further. I want to encourage you, Ashley, but I have to work within the limits of my authority."

Cohen left her meeting with Alvarez feeling excited and elated. She told him, "This is really great. I appreciate your confidence in me, and I know I can make this team proud by coming up with a business model that will prove useful for the company."

The following Monday morning, Alvarez was touring the garage so he could get a first-hand look at operations. Mary, a truck dispatcher, rushed up to him in tears, and said, "Please, let's get outside right away. We've got to talk."

Alvarez suggested that the two walk over to the benches by the gas pumps. "What's bothering you?" he asked Mary as they sat down.

"It's Bill, my creep of a supervisor. For the fifth consecutive day he has grabbed my buttocks and asked me to go out for a drink with him after work. I was polite the first time he grabbed me, but the next few times I told him to never touch me again.

"It's not just me either. Bill has been hitting on Jill, the new office assistant, something terrible."

Alvarez told Mary he would investigate the problem immediately. Within ten minutes he visited with Jill, asking her if Bill had in any way made her feel uncomfortable or conducted himself inappropriately. Jill explained that Bill hugged her at least once a day, and had asked her for a date three times.

"Worst of all," said Jill, "he knows I'm a respectable married woman."

Soon after his meeting with Jill, Alvarez located Bill and told him to drop what he was doing and follow him to his office. With a stern look on his face and an angry tone in his voice, Alvarez said to Bill, "I have heard two complaints about you this morning that could very well be sexual harassment. As a supervisor, you know that Belasco has zero tolerance for sexual harassment. What do you have to say for yourself?"

Fidgeting, Bill responded, "Hector, please don't be so trigger happy. These days you wink at a lady, and she cries sexual harassment. A guy can't even act natural these days."

"That's a pathetic defense," said Hector. "Go home right now. You are suspended with pay pending a complete investigation. If you are guilty of sexual harassment, I will recommend that you be fired. From my standpoint, you will have no second chance."

"Okay," said Bill, "I'll leave right now, but you are not giving me a fair chance to tell my side of the story."

Leadership Case Problem B

Excite@Home Goes Down the Tubes

In April 2001, Patti Hart was appointed chairman and CEO of Excite@Home. The company operated the Excite site and provided broadband Net connections over cable TV networks. Bleeding rivers of cash, the portal that once rivaled Yahoo! was sliding toward a sad ending. "The cash position of the company is paramount," said Hart. "I need to investigate all of the alternatives" (*BusinessWeek*, May 14, 2001, p. 96).

Excite@Home was in desperate financial condition. For the year 2000 it had revenues of $616 million and lost $7.4 billion, including a large-scale writedown of assets it acquired that became useless. The company was burning cash so fast that it needed to raise about $80 million to survive for another forty days. It needed to raise at least $75 million by the end of June 2001.

Hart's Qualifications and Tactics. The headhunter who placed Hart said that she was an incredible find and almost a perfect fit for the job at Excite@Home. Hart had built a positive reputation at Sprint Corporation, having risen to the head of the core long-distance business. In June 1999, she left to run upstart Telocity Inc., which provided broadband connections over telephone lines. But by December 2000, Telocity had begun to floun-

der, and Hart negotiated a deal to sell the company to Hughes Electronics Corporation, which provides broadband Net connections through a subsidiary.

Hart's broadband experience seemed promising for her job at Excite. "People who know me say this is such an obvious fit for you," said Hart (*BusinessWeek*, May 14, 2001, p. 98). Still, she was cautious about taking the job because of the rough experience at Telocity. As a source close to Hart said, "Patti can't afford to be on the wrong side of another one" (*BusinessWeek*, May 14, 2001, p. 98). When Hart ultimately agreed to sell Telocity to Hughes, it was for $2.15 a share, 82 percent less than the initial price of the stock. A cable executive said that Hart did as well for her investors as anybody could have.

Hart set up a deal to be well paid even if Excite@Home were sold or went under. She received a signing bonus of $1 million spread over eighteen months, and she would also receive one year's salary and a bonus, even if the company failed.

Then, after being informed about Excite's dire financial straits, Hart toughened her negotiations with the company's board. She insisted that she be given the authority to sell or shut Excite and also that she be given the chairmanship, said one source. "I think Patti didn't want any confusion about who was in charge of the company," said an outside financial analyst (*BusinessWeek*, May 14, 2001, p. 98). Hart's version of what happened is different. She says she had detailed conversations with Excite@Home's board about how much freedom she would have to sell off certain assets, but she did not insist that chairman George Bell resign. Nevertheless, Bell did resign at the suggestion of a board member.

When Hart researched Excite's public filings, it appeared that although the company was losing money, it had enough cash in reserve to keep running for a while. Hart also took comfort in the backing of AT&T, Excite's controlling shareholder. She described her strategy for saving the company in these terms: "I will look for opportunities that will help us deliver a superior service, address the current cash situation, and drive towards profitability. I plan to provide clarity and focus for the company and executive on our substantial market opportunity. My operational expertise will provide the foundation to nurture the wealth of talent at the company, taking us to the next level of service with the goal of becoming profitable. [Service problems had developed because the company's networks often became overloaded, and quality deteriorated.]

"I'm a broadband believer, and today, we're just at the beginning of the game. Broadband has and will continue to change the way we work and live—it is the future of communications and entertainment" (www. internetnews.com).

Troubles Continue. A stable line of business for Excite@Home appeared to be installing broadband connections for AT&T and other cable operators. The @Home piece of the business had become the largest provider of broadband connections in the United States with 3.2 million subscribers. One contingency plan in case Excite@Home ran out of cash was to fold its opera-

tions into AT&T or divide them up among several cable companies. Hart was determined to not let that happen. "We're leaders in an industry that everybody believes in," she said (*BusinessWeek*, May 14, 2001, p. 98).

Nevertheless, Hart set up a tentative deal to sell parts of Excite's network to AT&T to raise the cash it needed. That would have only solved the company's cash woes for one year, however, and selling the Excite portal also would be a difficult task because the demand for Net portals had fallen considerably.

Excite@Home continued to struggle financially. Hart explained that online ads had continued to plunge, that other companies planning to lease Excite@Home's office space had disappeared, and that suppliers were demanding cash up front.

In August 2001, Hart made a last-ditch effort to save the company by setting up a videoconference with top executives from AT&T. She told AT&T's CEO, Excite@Home board member C. Michael Armstrong, and other AT&T officials that @Home had $100 million less in cash than her team had told her to expect several weeks earlier. Despite her emotional plea, however, Armstrong refused to advance any cash; AT&T had already lost $3.5 billion on its investment in Excite@Home. So, after filing for bankruptcy protection in September 2001, Excite@Home auctioned off its few remaining assets. A bankruptcy judge in San Francisco allowed it to shut off service to 850,000 AT&T customers. Investors were left with virtually nothing. The stock was selling for 3 cents versus a high of $94, and bondholders would be receiving about 10 cents on the dollar.

Today when you visit www.excite.com and search for Excite@Home, you are informed, "Since Excite@Home has filed for bankruptcy and is no longer accepting new customers, DIRECTTV DSL is the best opinion for high-speed, broadband Internet access."

QUESTIONS

1. What crisis was Patti Hart facing?

2. What else might Hart have done from a leadership standpoint to rescue Excite@Home?

3. Which business strategies might have salvaged Excite@Home?

SOURCE: *Peter Elstrom, "If Anyone Can Save Excite . . ."* Business Week, *May 14, 2001, pp. 96, 98; Elstrom, "Excite@Home: A Saga of Tears, Greed, and Ego,"* BusinessWeek, *December 17, 2001, pp. 94–99; Thor Olavsrud, "Excite@Home Names Hart Chairman, CEO,"* www.internetnews.com, *April 23, 2001.*

INTERNET SKILL–BUILDING EXERCISE

Apply the Chapter Concepts! Visit the Web and complete this Internet skill-building exercise to learn more about current leadership topics and trends.

Listen to Experts About Crisis Management

How would you like to *listen* to 13 leading management scholars and consultants speak about managing in a crisis? The participants include three of the best-known management gurus: Ken Blanchard, Tom Peters, and Steven Covey. To do this assignment you will need Windows Media Player, which is available as a free download. Visit **www.masie.com/perspectives**, and follow the instructions. You will be able to choose from among 14 different, leading thinkers, each making a five-minute presentation about crisis management. Listen to at least five of these contributors. Write down at least six points you have learned from this Internet audio experience.

1. How does this crisis management advice compare to what you learned in this chapter?

2. Which of these ideas are you the most likely to use next time you face a crisis?

Leadership Ethics and Social Responsibility

CHAPTER 6

166

One month before she died, Detroit businesswoman Marilyn Malin asked the family to bedeck the funeral home in children's coats instead of flowers so that students attending Samuel Gompers Elementary School in Detroit would stay warm in winter. Malin was the president of Staff Solutions Inc., a temporary staffing agency.

"Marilyn's generosity will live on in our hearts and in the educational programs she enriched," said Gompers principal Gale Lewis at a memorial tree-planting ceremony. With Malin's help, the school received more than $20,000 in donations in addition to state and national recognition. The funds helped purchase high-tech equipment and send high achievers to science camp in the spring. The funds were also used to pave a running track near the playground for students, teachers, and families residing in the community.

"Marilyn overheard one student telling a teacher that his brother couldn't come to school that day because they shared a coat and it was too cold for the other to venture out," Lewis said. "The next day she returned with 14 new coats and vowed to return with more."

Members of the National Association of Women Business Owners (NAWBO) collected 150 coats within days of Malin's death from pancreatic cancer. They expected to reach a goal of 350 coats, 1 for every student, within five months after starting the collection. Malin, the president of NAWBO for one year, first encountered the Gompers school while visiting the members of her Leadership Detroit group.

Lewis said that business-educational partnerships are increasing throughout the Detroit schools to augment traditional funding. Malin led the Friends of Gompers school-funding campaign. "With private-sector support we could buy new rugs and drapes for our auditorium—money that wasn't available in the budget," Lewis said. "Kids are very aware of a learning atmosphere. If the rugs look raggedy and worn, the kids figure their education is raggedy. If everything looks fresh, the children are inspired to learn."[1]

Marilyn Malin and her co-contributors exemplify the type of generosity, thoughtfulness, ethical behavior, and social consciousness shown by many business leaders. However, the "good side" of business leaders rarely receives as much publicity as the "bad side." In this chapter we examine leadership ethics and social responsibility from several major perspectives: principles of ethical and moral leadership, an ethical decision-making guide, examples of ethical violations, examples of social responsibility, how leaders develop an ethical and socially responsible culture, and the link between business ethics and organizational performance.

PRINCIPLES OF ETHICAL AND MORAL LEADERSHIP

Enough attention has been paid to what leaders at all levels *should* do that some principles of ethical and moral leadership have emerged. Since terms dealing with the ideal behavior of leaders are used so loosely, it is helpful to define what these terms have generally come to mean in the business community. **Ethics** is the study of moral obligations, or of separating right from wrong. *Ethics* can also be a plural noun meaning the accepted guidelines of behavior for groups or institutions.[2] In this sense it means much the same as **morals**, which are an individual's determination of what is right or wrong; morals are influenced by a person's values. Values are tied closely to ethics because ethics become the vehicle for converting values into action. If a leader values fairness, he or she will evaluate group members on the basis of their performance, not personal friendships. And a moral leader will practice good ethics.

In this section we present a sampling of ethical and moral behaviors, all centering on the idea that a leader should do the *right* thing, as perceived by a consensus of *reasonable* people. Note that all of these terms can be challenged, and they cannot be pinned down with great precision. We will also present a brief explanation of why the ethical and moral behavior of leaders differs so widely. Before studying these principles, take Leadership Self-Assessment Quiz 6-1 to think through your work-related ethics and morality.

Five Ethical Leadership Behaviors

Be Honest and Trustworthy and Have Integrity in Dealing with Others.   As described in Chapter 2, trustworthiness contributes to leadership effectiveness. A perception that high-ranking business leaders were untrustworthy contributed to the spectacular decline in stock prices during the 2000–2002 period. An ethical leader is honest (tells the truth), and trustworthy (constituents accept his or her word). In other words, he or she has integrity. According to Thomas E. Becker, this quality goes beyond honesty and conscientiousness. **Integrity** refers to loyalty to rational principles; it means practicing what one preaches regardless of emotional or social pressure.[3] For example, a leader with integrity would believe that employees should be treated fairly, and the pressure to cut costs would not prompt him or her to renege on a commitment to reimburse an employee for relocation expenses. As another example, a leader who preached cultural diversity would assemble a diverse team of his or her own.

Pay Attention to All Stakeholders.   An ethical and moral leader strives to treat fairly all interested parties affected by his or her decision. To do otherwise creates winners and losers after many decisions are made. The widely held belief that a CEO's primary responsibility is to maximize shareholder wealth conflicts with the principle of paying attention to all stakeholders. A team of management scholars observes: "We used to recognize corporations as both economic and social institutions—as organizations that were designed to serve a balanced set of stakeholders, not just the narrow interests of the shareholder."[4] A leader interested in maximizing shareholder wealth might attempt to cut costs and increase profits in such ways as (a) laying off valuable employees to reduce payroll costs, (b) overstating profits to impress investors, (c) overcharging customers, (d) siphoning

The Leader Integrity Scale

INSTRUCTIONS   Circle the numbers to indicate how well each item describes your current attitudes and behavior or how you would behave in a group situation. Response choices: 1 = not at all; 2 = somewhat; 3 = very much; 4 = exactly.

1. I use other people's mistakes to attack them personally.   1 2 3 4

2. I always get even.   1 2 3 4

3. As a leader, I would give special favors to my favorite employees.   1 2 3 4

4. I lie to group members if it fits my purposes.   1 2 3 4

5. I would let a group member take the blame to protect myself.   1 2 3 4

6. I would deliberately fuel conflict among group members.   1 2 3 4

7. People who know me well consider me to be evil.   1 2 3 4

8. I would use a performance appraisal to criticize an individual as a person.   1 2 3 4

9. I hold grudges against people.   1 2 3 4

10. I would allow coworkers to be blamed for my mistakes.   1 2 3 4

11. I would falsify records to help my work situation.   1 2 3 4

12. My morals are low.   1 2 3 4

13. I would make fun of someone's mistakes rather than coach the person on how to do the job better.   1 2 3 4

14. I would exaggerate someone's mistakes to make him or her look bad to my superiors.   1 2 3 4

15. I am vindictive.   1 2 3 4

16. I would blame a group member for my mistakes.   1 2 3 4

17. I would avoid coaching an employee so that he or she could fail.   1 2 3 4

18. A person's ethnic group influences how I treat him or her.   1 2 3 4

19. I would deliberately distort what another person said to make me look good.   1 2 3 4

20.	I would deliberately make employees angry with each other.	1 2 3 4
21.	I am a hypocrite.	1 2 3 4
22.	I would limit the training opportunities of others to prevent them from advancing.	1 2 3 4
23.	I would blackmail an employee if I thought I could get away with it.	1 2 3 4
24.	I enjoy turning down the requests of group members.	1 2 3 4
25.	If an employee were to get on my bad side, I would make trouble for him or her.	1 2 3 4
26.	I would take credit for the ideas of others.	1 2 3 4
27.	I would steal from the organization.	1 2 3 4
28.	I would engage in sabotage against the organization just to get even.	1 2 3 4
29.	I would fire a person I didn't like if I could get away with it.	1 2 3 4
30.	I would do things that violate organizational policy, and then expect employees to cover for me.	1 2 3 4

SCORING AND INTERPRETATION   Add up the responses on all 30 items. The interpretation of what the score represents is given below. In interpreting your score, recognize that people tend to overrate themselves on ethical behavior because it is painful to admit to being devious and unethical.

- 30–35 very ethical — If you scored in this range, your self-image is that you are very trustworthy and highly principled. If your answers are accurate, it could mean that your high ethics could be an asset to you as a leader.

- 36–61 moderately ethical — Scores in this range mean that your impression is that you sometimes engage in slightly unethical behavior. You might strive to be more consistently ethical.

- 62–120 very unethical — This range describes leaders who may be perceived as doing things that are dishonest, unfair, and unprincipled. Although many unethical leaders are successful for a while, your unethical attitudes and behavior could be career-limiting factors. It is time to reflect on your values and start taking corrective action. Studying ethics can also help.

SOURCE: *Adapted from S. B. Craig and S. B. Gustafson, "Perceived Leader Integrity Scale: An Instrument for Assessing Employee Perceptions of Leader Integrity,"* Leadership Quarterly, *vol. 9 (2), 1998, pp. 143–144.*

money from the employee pension fund, and (e) reducing health benefits for retirees. Although the aforementioned may be standard practice, they all violate the rights of stakeholders.

Build Community.   A corollary of taking into account the needs of all stakeholders is that the leader helps people achieve a common goal. Peter G. Northouse explains that leaders need to take into account their own and followers' purposes and search for goals that are compatible to all.[5] When many people work toward the same constructive goal, they build a community. The business leader who worked with many people to help poor schoolchildren is an ideal example of someone who builds community.

Respect the Individual.   Respecting individuals is a principle of ethical and moral leadership that incorporates other aspects of morality. If you tell the truth, you respect others well enough to be honest. If you keep promises, you also show respect. And if you treat others fairly, you show respect.[6] Showing respect for the individual also means that you recognize that everybody has some inner worth and should be treated with courtesy and kindness. An office supervisor demonstrated respect for the individual in front of his department when he asked a custodian who entered the office: "What can we do in this department to make your job easier?"

Accomplish Silent Victories.   According to the case history research of Joseph L. Badaracco, Jr., modesty and restraint are largely responsible for the achievements of the most effective moral leaders in business. The ethical and moral leader works silently, and somewhat behind the scenes, to accomplish moral victories regularly. Instead of being perceived as a hero or heroine, the moral leader quietly works on an ethical agenda. Quite often he or she will work out a compromise to ensure that a decision in process will have an ethical outcome.[7]

A case in point is the middle manager at a telecommunications company whose senior managers decided to outsource the manufacture of a product line to China. As a result the small U.S. community was to lose about 200 jobs. The middle manager lobbied for months for the company to establish its new call center in the same town, thereby enabling about 65 of the workers to continue employment with the company.

Factors Contributing to Ethical Differences

There are many reasons for differences in ethics and morality among leaders. One is the leader's *level of greed, gluttony, and avarice.* Many people seek to maximize personal returns, even at the expense of others. A representative example is the CEO of a consulting firm who announced that all partners would receive a 7 percent salary increase the following year, yet salaries for all others would remain fixed. Federal Reserve chairman (and economist) Alan Greenspan commented publicly on the problem of executive greed. He said that "an infectious greed" had contaminated the business community in the late 1990s, as one executive after another manipulated earnings or resorted to fraudulent accounting to capitalize on soaring stock prices.[8]

Another key contributor to a leader's ethics and morality is his or her *level of moral development*.[9] Some leaders are morally advanced, while others are morally challenged—a condition that often develops early in life. People progress through three developmental levels in their moral reasoning. At the *preconventional level,* a person is concerned primarily with receiving external rewards and avoiding punishments. A leader at this level of development might falsify earnings statements for the primary purpose of gaining a large bonus. At the *conventional level,* people learn to conform to the expectations of good behavior as defined by key people in their environment and societal norms. A leader at this level might be moral enough just to look good, such as being fair with salary increases and encouraging contributions to the United Way campaign. At the *postconventional level* people are guided by an internalized set of universal principles that may even transcend the laws of a particular society. A leader at the postconventional level of moral behavior would be concerned with doing the most good for the most people, whether or not such behavior brought him or her recognition and fortune. The servant leader described in Chapter 4 would be at this advanced level of moral development.

A third factor contributing to unethical and immoral leadership behavior is the *situation,* particularly the organizational culture.[10] If leaders at the top of the organization take imprudent, quasi-legal risks, other leaders throughout the firm might be prompted to behave similarly. The risk-taking culture at Enron Corporation is said to have contributed to leaders through the firm engaging in questionable financial transactions such as creating false profit statements.

GUIDELINES FOR EVALUATING THE ETHICS OF A DECISION

Several guidelines, or ethical screens, have been developed to help the leader or other influence agent decide whether a given act is ethical or unethical. The Center for Business Ethics at Bentley College has developed six questions to evaluate the ethics of a specific decision:[11]

- *Is it right?* This question is based on the deontological theory of ethics that there are certainly universally accepted guiding principles of rightness and wrongness, such as "thou shall not steal."

- *Is it fair?* This question is based on the deontological theory of justice that certain actions are inherently just or unjust. For example, it is unjust to fire a high-performing employee to make room for a less competent person who is a relative by marriage.

- *Who gets hurt?* This question is based on the utilitarian notion of attempting to do the greatest good for the greatest number of people.

- *Would you be comfortable if the details of your decision or actions were made public in the media or through email?* This question is based on the universalist principle of disclosure.

- *What would you tell your child, sibling, or young relative to do?* This question is based on the deontological principle of reversibility, which evaluates the ethics of a decision by reversing the decision maker.

- *How does it smell?* This question is based on a person's intuition and common sense. For example, counting as a sale a product inquiry over the Internet would "smell" bad to a sensible person.

The question of ethics arises when a person conducts a job search. The job seeker might want to size up the ethical climate established by company leaders. The wave of corporate scandals taking place a few years ago prompted more job seekers to examine prospective employers' ethical standards and practices. They pored over company message boards looking for employees' evaluation of management, checked financial histories, and sought meetings with present and past employees.[12] Table 6-1 presents a list of ethics-related questions the job seeker might ask before joining a firm. In this way the prospective leader would have a chance of finding an ethical and moral climate compatible with his or her values.

Leaders regularly face the necessity of running a contemplated decision through an ethics test. Leadership Skill-Building Exercise 6-1 provides an opportunity to think through the ethics of a decision facing a telecom firm.

TABLE 6-1   A Job Seeker's Ethics Audit

Some probing questions to ask about a prospective employer:

- Is there a formal code of ethics? How widely is it distributed? Is it reinforced in other formal ways such as through decision-making systems?

- Are workers at all levels trained in ethical decision making? Are they also encouraged to take responsibility for their behavior or to question authority when asked to do something they consider wrong?

- Do employees have formal channels available to make their concerns known confidentially? Is there a formal committee high in the organization that considers ethical issues?

- Is misconduct disciplined swiftly and justly within the organization?

- Is integrity emphasized to new employees?

- How are senior managers perceived by subordinates in terms of their integrity? How do such leaders serve as models for ethics-related behavior?

Source: Linda K. Treviño, Chair of the Department of Management and Organization, Smeal College of Business, Pennsylvania State University (As reprinted in Kris Maher, "Wanted: Ethical Employer," The Wall Street Journal, July 9, 2002, p. B1).

Dialing for Dollars

Imagine that you and several other classmates are Lucent Technologies executives and that you are reviewing the following case history related to your consumer sales group:

> Roberta Sweetow, 67, keeps the hulking black rotary telephone, the one she has had in her possession since 1964, on her nightstand, in case her husband Herb, 74, receives an early-morning call to substitute-teach in a Skokie, Illinois, high school. Sweetow purchased the phone for $9 last year, after finally noticing a charge buried in her bill every three months: $18 to lease a telephone. "I realized I've paid over $1,000 for a phone I hardly use," she says. "Who in the world rents a telephone?"
>
> Lawyers representing approximately 44 million customers in a $10 billion class action lawsuit believe that many consumers still use rotary phones. The suit is filed against AT&T, which administered the post–Ma Bell leasing program from 1984 to 1996, and Lucent, its consumer products spinoff. Lucent administers the rotary-phone leasing program today. The suit alleges that after the Bell breakup, AT&T failed to adequately inform customers of their options to lease, purchase, or return their old telephones.
>
> Customers who took no action continued to be charged for renting the phones, a fee recorded on their bill in vague line items like TRAD ROT DSK MISC (traditional desktop rotary). Several former AT&T Lucent employees contend that the companies pressured them to keep leasing. At the time these facts were collected, some 860,000 households still leased nearly 1 million rotary phones.

Your assignment as part of the Lucent team is to first decide whether leasing rotary phones is ethical by running the decision through the ethical decision-making guide presented in this chapter. Second, decide what plans Lucent should make for the program, including a variety of options such as cease the leasing, begin a marketing campaign to sell more rotary phones, or sell the phones to the remaining customers. Keep in mind that Lucent needs all the revenue it can find because the turnaround is not yet complete.

This exercise is important because it helps program your mind to examine the ethics of a contemplated decision. In the current climate, many companies are seeking to promote into leadership positions at any level those individuals with a track record of making ethical decisions.

SOURCE: *Based on Sean Gregory, "How'd You Like to Rent This Baby?"* Time, *July 8, 2002, p. 18.*

A SAMPLING OF UNETHICAL LEADERSHIP BEHAVIORS

We have been alluding to unethical behavior in this and previous chapters. Here we present a sampling of unethical behaviors from the past and present. A statement often made is that about 95 percent of business leaders are ethical, and that the 5 percent of bad apples (mostly senior executives) get all the publicity. Even if only 5 percent of business leaders have been unethical, their impact has been enormous. Unethical behavior has brought companies into bankruptcy, led to the layoffs of thousands of workers, diminished trust in stock investments, and discouraged many talented young people from embarking upon a business career.

Table 6-2 presents a sampling of unethical, immoral, and often illegal behaviors engaged in by business leaders whose acts have been publicly reported. Thousands of other unethical acts go unreported, such as a business owner placing a family member, friend, or lover on the payroll at an inflated salary for work of limited value to the firm.

TABLE 6-2   Examples of Unethical Behavior by Leaders

Executive and Company	Charges or Complaints	Defenses Against the Charges	Current Status of Executive and Company
Kenneth Lay, former chairman and CEO of Enron	Company executives under investigation for creating and approving outside partnerships that kept millions of dollars in losses off of Enron's books. Enron sold phony assets to these partnerships at high prices to create bogus income. Lay unloaded $100 million in company stock before price tumbled.	Lay said he was not fully informed of the executive-run partnerships. Asserted Fifth Amendment right not to testify before Congress.	Lay resigned and told Congress of his profound sadness about what happened to the company. Enron declared bankruptcy in 2002.
Joseph R. Nacchio, former chairman and CEO of Qwest Communication	Company may not have properly accounted for about $1.4 billion in sales of fiber-optic capacity. Nacchio is also accused of cashing out on more than $300 million of his personal holdings.	Qwest's attorney said that company accounting was reasonable. Nacchio said his stock sales were part of a board-approved plan to justify his holdings.	Nacchio resigned under pressure in June 2002. New top management is selling off assets and downsizing to survive. Justice Department has launched criminal investigation into Qwest's accounting practices.

(continued)

TABLE 6-2   Examples of Unethical Behavior by Leaders (cont.)

Executive and Company	Charges or Complaints	Defenses Against the Charges	Current Status of Executive and Company
Bernard Ebbers of WorldCom	Investigators are looking into whether he was aware of the $3.8 billion classified as capital expenses rather than operating costs. Later investigation revealed that WorldCom executives misclassified about $9 billion in expenses. Ebbers is being asked to explain why the company lent him $408 million to cover margin calls on loans secured by company stock. May still owe banks and brokerage firms about $1 billion, borrowed using WorldCom stock as collateral. Company is also accused of overcharging customers by up to 10 percent.	Ebbers said he was not directly involved in the accounting error. Has sold a boat and a few other possessions to help pay back the money.	Ebbers was forced out by the board. WorldCom stock was almost worthless in 2002. Company laid off thousands of workers to reduce costs. Is negotiating with potential buyers.
L. Dennis Kozlowski, former CEO of Tyco International	Accused of failing to pay more than $1 million in sales taxes on artwork by shipping it to an office in another state. Company is probing whether he used company funds for real estate and other expenses. Apparently borrowed hundreds of millions from Tyco, then secretly found a way to forgive these loans. Is accused of padding earnings growth of acquisitions by making them prepay expenses and forgo new revenue.	Entered a plea of not guilty on avoiding sales tax.	Kozlowski resigned to "pursue other interests." Tyco is still functioning. The SEC found no wrongdoing in earnings manipulations. As SEC investigation continued, Tyco faced criminal charges.

(continued)

TABLE 6-2   Examples of Unethical Behavior by Leaders (cont.)

Executive and Company	Charges or Complaints	Defenses Against the Charges	Current Status of Executive and Company
Joseph Beradino, former CEO of Andersen Worldwide	Company found guilty of criminal obstruction of justice in Enron case. Also accused of covering up poor accounting practices at several other major clients.	Andersen will appeal the verdict. Beradino admitted that document shredding took place under his watch.	Beradino resigned. Company was barred from auditing books of public companies, and soon went out of business.
Gary Winnick, former CEO and chairman of Global Crossing	Company boosted profits by swapping network capacity with another carrier. Global booked the sales revenue immediately yet spread costs over time. Winnick sold more than $735 million in stock just before company downfall.	Winnick has said nothing about dumping stock. Work continued on his $95 million home in California while firm struggled through bankruptcy proceedings.	Winnick has left the company and is not charged with a crime. Company is bankrupt and listening to offers to sell its fiber-optic network. Pension plans of thousands of employees are left with worthless stock. Winnick later offered to distribute $25 million of personal funds to help former employees left with pensions of no value.
Charles Keating, former (1989) CEO and chairman of Lincoln Savings and Loan	Convicted of fraudulently marketing junk bonds and making phony deals. Federal government paid $3.4 billion to rescue failed Savings and Loan.	Keating professed his innocence and defended his business practices.	Sentenced to 12.5 years in jail, he served only 5 (good prisoner). Lincoln ordered out of business.
Kim Tae Gou, former Daewoo Motor chairman	Kim and other Daewoo executives charged with financial fraud. For example, to book profits at a failed Ukraine factory, Daewoo Motor received fully built Korean cars, tore them down, and reassembled them at the Ukraine plant. Sales were booked as if they were produced by the plant. Manipulation valued at $3.6 billion.	Kim and seven of his top executives are reserving their comments for court.	Daewoo Motor declared bankruptcy in 2000 but is still operating. General Motors is still negotiating to buy the company.

Source: "High Profiles in Hot Water, "The Wall Street Journal, June 28, 2002, p. B1; Julie Rawe, "Heroes to Heels,"Time, June 17, 2002, p. 48; Clifton Leaf, "Enough Is Enough,"Fortune, March 18, 2002 p. 64; Moon Ihlwan, "Kim's Fall from Grace,"BusinessWeek, February 19, 2001, p. 51.

LEADERSHIP AND SOCIAL RESPONSIBILITY

One way of being ethical and moral is to guide the firm, or a unit within, toward doing good deeds. **Social responsibility** is having obligations to society beyond the company's economic obligations to owners or stockholders and also beyond those prescribed by law or contract. Both ethics and social responsibility relate to the goodness or morality of organizations, but social responsibility relates to an organization's impact on society and goes beyond doing what is ethical.[13] To behave in a socially responsible way, leaders must be aware of how their actions influence the environment.

Social responsibility is a vast topic, often the subject of a course or an entire book. Our focus here is on several illustrative actions leaders take to enhance social responsibility: creating a pleasant work environment, helping to preserve the outside environment, being involved in politics, and engaging in philanthropy. The accompanying Leader in Action vignette describes a CEO who regards social responsibility as a major aspect of her leadership.

Creating a Pleasant Workplace

A social responsibility initiative that directly affects people's well-being is to create a comfortable, pleasant, and intellectually stimulating work environment. Because many people invest about one-third of their time in work, a pleasant work environment increases the chances that their life will be enriched. Also, career-oriented people derive much of their meaning and satisfaction from their career.

Robert Levering and Milton Moskowitz in cooperation with *Fortune* have institutionalized the idea of being a "best company to work for." Employers nominate themselves, and two-thirds of the score is based on how randomly selected employees respond to the Great Place to Work Trust Index, a survey measuring organizational culture. An evaluation of the Institute's Culture Audit by staff members at the Great Place to Work Institute determines the rest of the score. The focus is on employee satisfaction, yet those firms that fall into the "the 100 best companies to work for" are also typically profitable. Among the perks offered by these companies are flexible working hours, on-site day care, concierge services like dry-cleaning pickup, domestic-partner benefits to same-sex couples, and fully paid sabbaticals. Following are the three most highly rated companies:[14]

> *Edward Jones, St. Louis:* Stockbroker with small-town values grabs the number 1 spot. No layoffs, despite a difficult year, and bonuses came a week early to help brokers hurt by trading decline. Employees praise ethics: 97 percent say management is honest.

> *Container Store, Dallas:* Workers at this retailer of boxes and shipping material remain enthusiastic about good pay (salespeople average $36,256), great benefits (1,900 percent match for 401[k] up to 4 percent of pay), and respect (94 percent surveyed feel they make a difference).

Leader in Action

Laura Scher, CEO of Working Assets, Does Good Work

Results matter to Laura Scher, the chair and CEO of Working Assets, based in San Francisco. However, these results pertain to much more than the bottom line. Her business plan includes a cleaner environment, shelter for the homeless, and access to education for the nation's poor. So fifteen years ago, the new Harvard MBA co-founded with Michael Kieschnick a business committed to social change.

Today, Working Assets, which provides long-distance calling plans, credit cards, and Internet service, rakes in $140 million in annual revenue and donates a generous cut to a revolving list of about sixty nonprofits. It has given away more than $20 million so far. How is Scher putting her money where her morals are?

"We are successful because we've always had a vision of what we wanted to do. Even if others said we had to change to succeed, we just stuck to 'This is a company working for social change and this is what our customers want us to be.'

"It's important that everything we do is consistent with our mission. We're a values-oriented business—that drives our product development, our corporate culture, and our management decisions. For example, we use 100 percent post-consumer recycled paper for our phone bills. A woman in our office spent six months searching for paper that could go through the printers that we used. In addition, we plant trees based on our paper usage.

"I believe strongly in leading by example, personally and professionally. On my 9-year-old daughter's birthday, we had a cooking party and afterward took the dishes to a homeless shelter. Even a fun party can be turned into a way to give back."

Scher says that her role model was her mother, who worked when Scher was growing up and served on nonprofit boards and the League of Women Voters. Her mother was an economics professor at a time when being a full-time working mother was not so common.

QUESTIONS

1. Visit workingassets.com to see how well the company is doing today.

2. How can a company with only $140 million in annual revenue justify giving away $20 million to charity?

SOURCE: *Adapted from Kathleen Jacobs, "Laura Scher," in "The Top 500 Women-Owned Businesses,"* Working Woman, *June 2000, p. 79; www.workingassets.com.*

SAS Institute, Cary, North Carolina: Superlative child care centers for a $250 monthly fee and a huge fitness center used by nearly 80 percent of employees are just a few perks at this software developer. A health center offers free annual mammograms and lab tests.

The employee programs that qualify a company as a best place to work focus on employee benefits. However, the leaders of these companies also emphasize stimulating work.

Guarding the Environment

Socially responsible leaders influence others to preserve the external environment through a variety of actions that go beyond mandatory environmental controls such as managing toxic waste. For example, automotive industry executives compete with one another to establish fuel-efficient vehicles (even among high-gas consumption vehicles such as SUVs). And many companies sponsor team-building events in which participants build a playground or refurbish an old house in a declining neighborhood.

Brenda L. Flannery and Douglas R. May studied individual and situational factors associated with corporate leaders making ethical (or socially responsible) environmental decisions. The group studied was executives in the metal finishing business. The research task was for the executives to put themselves in the shoes of environmental engineers in wastewater treatment scenarios. The various scenarios described consequences to both human and nonhuman victims. For example, an overflow of wastewater might cause cancer in people and kill fish. Managers' treatment of wastewater was found to depend on three factors, according to the respondents:

1. *Attitudes toward wastewater treatment.* If managers believe strongly in treating wastewater, they will plan to do a careful job of taking care of hazardous wastewater.

2. *Assessment of support from others.* If managers believe key people will support their efforts, they are more likely to take corrective action against hazardous wastewater.

3. *Perception of financial costs.* Being green depends to some extent on how much green money it takes.[15] Sometimes ethics gives way to the bottom line.

The study also found that the magnitude of the consequences moderated (or influenced) the managers' attitudes toward dealing with the environment. The more serious the potential negative consequences, the more likely it is that the leader will take decisive action to protect the environment. (Would you have guessed this outcome without the benefit of a lengthy research study?)

Being Involved in Political Causes

Social responsibility can be shown by a leader who becomes involved in a political cause that benefits people, such as advocating against unjust child labor. Involvement in a political cause for the welfare of society is not the same as donating money to a political party in the hopes of receiving favorable legislation, a common practice among some business leaders. It is doing something for the good of *others.* An example of a business leader exerting influence to help a political cause for others is M. Farooqu Kathwari, the chairman and CEO of Ethan Allen Inc.

Kathwari, a Muslim who left Kashmir over thirty-five years ago and who is now an American citizen, is attempting to bring peace to his native country. Kathwari's 19-year-old son was killed in combat in 1992 when he joined the nearby

Afghanistan battle against Russia. Kashmir has also had a great deal of civil strife. In 1996, Kathwari, once a student activist in Kashmir, assembled a group of predominantly American politicians, academics, and former diplomats to suggest ways to reduce this strife. He said, "I wanted to try to save parents from the agony of losing a child." After September 11, Kathwari placed a full-page notice in the *Washington Post* and *New York Times* asking America's leaders to continue fostering unity among people of all faiths.[16]

Engaging in Philanthropy

A standard organizational leadership approach to social responsibility is to donate money to charity and various causes. Most charities are heavily dependent on corporate support, including those that collect through payroll deductions, such as United Way. Colleges, universities, and career schools also benefit from corporate donations. In 2000 alone, Microsoft "chief architect" Bill Gates gave $5 billion to a variety of charities, aside from whatever money Microsoft donated.

A recent development in philanthropy is for corporate leaders to demand a good return on investment for their donated money. Many corporate donors want their charitable investments to benefit the end consumer, and not get lost in red tape and overhead. The new breed of philanthropist studies each charitable cause like a potential business investment, seeking maximum return in terms of social impact. The philanthropist might seek follow-up data, for example, on how many children were taught to read, or by what percent new cases of AIDS declined. A case in point is Jim Barksdale, the former Netscape CEO. He donated $100 million to the University of Mississippi for a program to help students from K to grade 3 learn to read. Barksdale believed that because the child literacy rate in Mississippi was below average, the potential rate of social return on his investment was high.[17]

The new breed of philanthropist is sometimes actively involved in the cause receiving the funding. A case in point is John R. Alm, the president of Coca-Cola Enterprises Inc. He provides ongoing, intensive support to at-risk youths living in inner city Los Angeles, from middle school through college. Alm's immediate efforts are supported by a broader plan for helping the young people, and he devotes a large portion of his discretionary time to implementing the plan.[18]

INITIATIVES FOR ACHIEVING AN ETHICAL AND SOCIALLY RESPONSIBLE ORGANIZATION

The initiatives described in the preceding section are designed specifically to enhance social responsibility. Here we look at five other initiatives that executive leadership can take to help create an ethical and socially responsible culture: (1) leading by example, (2) establishing written codes of ethical conduct, (3) developing formal mechanisms for dealing with ethical problems, (4) accepting whistleblowers, and (5) providing for training in ethics.

Leading by Example.   A high-powered approach to enhancing ethics and social responsibility is for corporate leaders to behave in such a manner themselves. If people throughout the firm believe that behaving ethically is "in" and behaving unethically is "out," ethical behavior will prevail. A curious instance of unethical leadership by example took place at Oracle Corporation under the leadership of flamboyant CEO Larry Ellison. The Oracle chief hired private investigators to peruse the dumpsters of groups defending his rival Microsoft in its antitrust case. Ellison defended his actions, noting that his investigators had uncovered evidence that Microsoft was secretly funding "front groups" to manipulate public opinion in its favor. Ellison insisted that his dumpster diving was a "civic duty" against Bill Gates, a "convicted monopolist."[19] Stunts like this by senior management encourage questionable ethical behavior throughout the organization. Of note, many Oracle customers have complained that the company's contracts and billing practices are less than customer-friendly.

Establishing Written Codes of Ethical Conduct.   Many organizations use written codes of conduct as guidelines for ethical and socially responsible behavior. Such guidelines continue to grow in importance because workers in self-managing teams have less leadership than previously. Some general aspects of these codes require people to conduct themselves with integrity and candor. The code of conduct for several stock brokerage firms emphasizes placing the welfare of clients above earning commissions for investments. A written code of conduct is more likely to influence behavior when it is referred to frequently by both formal and informal leaders throughout the firm.

Developing Formal Mechanisms for Dealing with Ethical Problems.   Forty-five percent of companies with 500 or more employees have ethics programs of various types. Large organizations frequently establish ethics committees to help ensure ethical and socially responsible behavior. Committee members include a top management representative plus other managers throughout the organization. An ethics and social responsibility specialist from the human resources department might also join the group. The committee establishes policies about ethics and social responsibility, and may conduct an ethical audit of the firm's activities. In addition, committee members might review complaints about ethical problems.

Top-level leadership participation in these formal mechanisms gives them more clout. The aerospace firm Lockheed Martin Corporation is a major federal contractor, so the company has to keep tight watch over potential ethical violations. As a result, highly placed leaders in the company participate in the company ethics compliance program.[20]

Accepting Whistleblowers.   A **whistleblower** is an employee who discloses organizational wrongdoing to parties who can take action. It was a whistleblower who began the process of exposing the scandalous financial practices at Enron Corp., such as hiding losses. Sherron Watkins, a vice president, wrote a one-page anonymous letter exposing unsound, if not dishonest, financial reporting: Enron had booked profits for two entities that had no assets. She dropped the letter off at company headquarters the next day.[21]

Whistleblowers are often ostracized and humiliated by the companies they hope to improve. For example, they may receive no further promotions or poor performance evaluations. More than half the time, the pleas of whistleblowers are ignored. So it is important for leaders at all levels to create a comfortable climate for legitimate whistleblowing. The leader needs the interpersonal skill to sort out the difference between a troublemaker and a true whistleblower. Careful investigation is required.

Providing for Training in Ethics and Social Responsibility. Many companies train managerial workers in ethics. Forms of training include messages about ethics and social responsibility from company leadership, classes on ethics at colleges, and exercises in ethics. These training programs reinforce the idea that ethically and socially responsible behavior is both morally right and good for business. Much of the content of this chapter reflects the type of information communicated in such programs. Leadership Skill-Building Exercise 6-2 gives you the opportunity to engage in a small amount of ethics training.

Ethical Behavior and Organizational Performance

Recent evidence suggests that high ethics and social responsibility are related to good financial performance. According to the International Business Ethics Institute, socially responsible behavior does enhance profits. The overall financial performance of the 2001 list of the 100 Best Firms was significantly better than that of the remaining companies in the S&P 500, according to the research of Elizabeth Murphy and Curtis C. Verschoor. The study took into account measures of responsibility reflecting quality service to seven stakeholder groups: community, minorities, women, employees, environment, foreign stakeholders, and customers.[22]

The relationship between social responsibility and profits can also work in two directions. More profitable firms can better afford to invest in social responsibility initiatives, and these initiatives can in turn lead to more profits. Sandra A. Waddock and Samuel B. Graves conducted a large-scale study that supports the two-way conclusion. The researchers analyzed the relationship between corporate social performance and corporate financial performance for 469 firms, spanning thirteen industries, for a two-year period. Many different measures of social and financial performance were used. An example of social performance would be helping to redevelop a poor community.

Dealing with Defining Moments

The toughest ethical choices for many people occur when they have to choose between two rights. The result is a defining moment, because we are challenged to think in a deeper way by choosing between two or more ideals. Working individually or in teams, deal with the two following defining moments. Explain why these scenarios could require choosing between two rights, and explain the reasoning behind your decisions.

1. You are the manager of a department in a business firm that assigns each department a fixed amount of money for salary increases each year. An average-performing member of the department asks you in advance for an above-average increase. He explains that his mother has developed multiple sclerosis and requires the services of a paid helper from time to time. You are concerned that if you give this man an above-average increase, somebody else in the department will have to receive a below-average increase.

2. You are the team leader of a group of packaging scientists at a large consumer products company. Two years ago top management decided that any employee who is late more than 10 percent of the time over the course of a year should be fired. At about the same time, top management began incorporating a measure of *diversity success* into managers' performance appraisals. Managers who hired and retained targeted groups would receive a high rating on *diversity success*. Poor hiring and retention of targeted groups would result in a low performance rating. It is now mid-December, and Tim, the only employee over age 60, has been late 11 percent of the time. Several former employees have recently charged your company with age discrimination. Firing Tim will enable you to comply with the lateness policy, yet at the same time your diversity performance will suffer. Also, top management does not want to deal with any more employment discrimination suits.

Getting started dealing with defining moments is useful practice because so many leadership issues are in the gray zone—neither completely right nor completely wrong. Part of dealing with defining moments is therefore to be able to do some soul searching.

Researchers found that levels of corporate social performance were influenced by prior financial success. The results suggest that financial success creates enough money left over to invest in corporate social performance. The study also found that good corporate social performance contributes to improved financial performance as measured by return on assets and return on sales. Waddock and Graves concluded that the relationship between social and financial performance may be a **virtuous circle,** meaning that corporate social performance and corporate financial performance feed and reinforce each other.[23]

Being ethical also helps avoid the costs of paying huge fines for being unethical, including charges of discrimination and class action lawsuits because of improper financial reporting. Because many firms have been fined for unethical and illegal activities, it is almost unfair to select one as an example. However, the $180 million in fines that Texaco Inc. paid for discriminating against people of color illustrates the gravity of the problem. Since then Texaco has striven to become a model equal employment opportunity company.

Being accused of unethical and illegal behavior can also result in a sudden dropoff in customers and clients, as well as extreme difficulty in obtaining new customers and clients. When Arthur Andersen was accused of shoddy auditing practices in relation to Enron, clients exited in droves. (However, prior large-scale accusations against Andersen did not have the same dramatic effect.) Telemarketers for telecommunications firms involved in major financial scandals met with much more resistance than usual when soliciting new business. As one irate consumer said, "Why should I shift my long-distance business to you? You laid off my neighbor and thousands of other employees, and you don't even pay your bills."

In short, a leader who is successful at establishing a climate of high ethics and social responsibility can earn and save the company a lot of money.

SUMMARY

Principles of ethical and moral leadership all center on the idea that a leader should do the right thing, as perceived by a consensus of reasonable people. Key principles of ethical and moral leadership are as follows: (a) be honest and trustworthy and have integrity in dealing with others, (b) pay attention to all stakeholders, (c) build community, (d) respect the individual, and (e) accomplish silent victories. Differences in ethics and morality can be traced to three factors: (a) the leader's level of greed, gluttony, and avarice, (b) the leader's level of moral development (preconventional, conventional, and postconventional), and (c) situational influences.

Before reaching a decision about an issue that is not obviously ethical or blatantly unethical, a leader or manager should seek answers to the following questions: Is it right? Is it fair? Who gets hurt? Would you be comfortable if the decision were exposed? What would you tell your child, sibling, or young relative to do? How does it smell? Before joining a company, a job seeker should search for answers to ethics-related questions, such as "Is there a formal code of ethics?"

Unethical behavior has brought companies into bankruptcy, led to layoffs of thousands of workers, diminished trust in stock investments, and discouraged many talented young people from embarking upon a business career. Table 6-2 presents examples of unethical behavior by business leaders.

Another way a leader can be ethical and moral is to spearhead the firm, or a unit within, toward doing good deeds—toward being socially responsible. Among the many possible socially responsible acts are (a) creating a pleasant workplace, (b) guarding the environment, (c) being involved in political causes, and (d) engaging in philanthropy.

Initiatives for achieving an ethical and socially responsible organization include (a) leading by example, (b) establishing written codes of conduct, (c) developing formal mechanisms for dealing with ethical problems, (d) accepting whistleblowers, and (e) providing training in ethics.

High ethics and social responsibility are related to good financial performance, according to research evidence and opinion. Also, more profitable firms have the funds to invest in good social programs. Being ethical helps avoid big fines for being unethical, and ethical organizations attract more employees.

KEY TERMS

Ethics   Social responsibility
Morals   Whistleblower
Integrity   Virtuous circle

GUIDELINES FOR ACTION AND SKILL DEVELOPMENT

Behaving ethically is also an effective interpersonal skill. If you develop close relationships with people, you are more likely to be ethical in your dealings with them. A provocative explanation of the causes of unethical behavior emphasizes the strength of relationships among people.[24] Assume that two people have close ties to each other—they may have worked together for a long time or have known each other both on and off the job. As a consequence they are likely to behave ethically toward one another on the job. In contrast, if a weak relationship exists between two people, either party is more likely to treat the other badly. In the work environment, the people involved may be your work associates, your contacts, or your internal and external customers.

DISCUSSION QUESTIONS AND ACTIVITIES

1. If the president of the United States, George W. Bush, engaged in questionable ethical behavior while he was an energy company executive, why should you worry about being ethical?

2. The majority of business executives accused of unethical behavior have studied ethics either as a subject in a business course or as an entire course. So what do you think went wrong?

3. Companies that make and sell alcoholic or tobacco products are an easy target for individuals demanding social responsibility. Should leaders of companies that produce fattening food that can lead to cardiac problems and obesity also be targeted for being socially irresponsible?

4. Practically every job candidate describes himself or herself as being "honest and trustworthy". What steps can a company take to increase the chances of hiring leaders who really are honest and trustworthy—and therefore ethical?

5. An increasing number of critics are demanding that no executive should receive a total compensation of $100 million or more in one year. What is your position on the ethics of a business leader receiving so much compensation?

6. Teenagers from poor neighborhoods purchase a disproportionate number of basketball-style shoes costing over $125 a pair. In your opinion, are companies that target their athletic-shoe advertising to these teenagers being socially responsible? Explain your answer.

7. What is the explanation for the fact that many profitable business corporations are also socially responsible?

8. Based on what you have read, heard, or seen, at which level (or levels) in the organization are highly ethical leaders the most likely to be found?

9. How can consumers use the Internet to help control the ethical behavior of business leaders?

10. In what ways are many retail customers quite unethical?

Leadership Case Problem A

Fast-Talking Fastow of Enron

At age 40, Andrew Fastow was at the center of one of the most scandalous bankruptcies in U.S. history. He was removed from his post as chief financial officer at Enron Corp. amid controversy over off-balance-sheet business partnerships that he managed and in which he invested. The partnerships were described as *off-balance-sheet* because they transferred debts off the balance-sheet of Enron and onto smaller business entities.

People who worked with Fastow agreed that he always appeared to be highly self-confident. That same self-confidence led to an arrogance that contributed to Enron's financial collapse. As a trusted lieutenant of his CEO, Fastow created the increasingly complex and unusual off-balance-sheet financing that fueled the growth of Enron. He was also the major player in selling the deals to banks and institutional investors—sometimes using veiled threats and at other times sweet talk. A high-ranking insider said that Fastow had a dual personality. "He could be charming but could also be irrationally mean" (*BusinessWeek*, February 4, 2002, p. 40).

Fastow quickly became one of the primary targets in the search for the guilty parties in Enron's demise. He dreamed up the LJM partnerships that triggered the controversy over the accounting methods used at the company. ("LJM" stands for the first initials of the first names of Fastow's wife and children.) Fastow's lawyers emphasize that Enron top management and the board approved the LJM partnerships. Furthermore, they say that another executive who did not report to Fastow was responsible for approving the accounting methods used for the deals. Yet some other former and present Enron executives believe that Fastow may have hidden some aspects of the partnerships from the managers to whom he reported.

Fastow and a few of his close associates profited mightily from the off-balance-sheet deals. He and at least six others involved in his financial manipulations, all with jobs or spouses at Enron, made a minimum of $42 million on investments totaling $161,000. Some of these profits came literally overnight. Fastow earned about $30 million from his stakes in the Enron partnerships. While this small group was earning millions, the partnerships Fastow created were collapsing in value.

Many colleagues and bankers who knew Fastow saw him as one of the villains in the Enron saga. Insiders saw him as sometimes emotionally explosive and vindictive, determined to be promoted by pleasing CEO Jeffrey K. Skilling. That meant assembling financial entities that enabled Enron to expand its business without adding too much debt to the balance sheet or jeopardizing its credit rating.

To build his new home in the exclusive River Oaks section of Houston, Fastow hired the same architect Skilling had employed. Some at Enron even believed that Fastow named his first son, Jeffrey, after Skilling—a contention denied by Fastow's wife. However, another company insider said about Fastow, "He wanted to make Jeff happy" (*BusinessWeek*, February 4, 2002, p. 41).

According to colleagues, the aggressive Skilling was in favor of Fastow's screaming, table-pounding approach to winning his way. Fastow's belittling of group members also made him worthy of promotion in Skilling's eyes. One Enron executive said that Fastow was fond of making people look stupid in front of an audience. Some former coworkers said that he frequently remembered personal slights or grudges when it came time for performance reviews. The evaluation system at Enron allowed top-level managers to offer their evaluations of anyone, even those who did not report to them. Said one colleague, "Andy was such a cutthroat bastard that he could use disagreement or criticism against you in the performance review committee" (*BusinessWeek*, February 25, 2002, p. 120).

Fastow's aggressiveness fit in with Skilling's plan to transform Enron into a fast-growth, technology-oriented trading company. The company would make money by acting as a broker between sellers and buyers of energy. Fastow joined Enron's finance group in 1990. He and Skilling quickly became partners in the effort to reshape Enron, and Skilling relied on Fastow to help develop the financing that would stimulate the growth of his empire.

At first, the off-balance-sheet financings that Fastow and his group created were not particularly risky. Early deals were backed by payments from oil and gas producers. Before long, however, Enron began using its growing clout to include in the deals a hodge-podge of assets, some of questionable quality. Many bankers went along with the questionable deals because they didn't want to miss out on getting a piece of Enron's business. Fastow controlled some $80 to $100 million in annual fees for a wide variety of banking and investment bank services.

Fastow could also turn on the charm to win favor from bankers. He delivered flowers to the house of one banker after his son's baptism. A spokesman for Fastow denies that he ever threatened bankers to get them into Enron deals.

Andy Fastow's legal problems mounted, and he was indicted on seventy-eight federal counts claiming that he masterminded a scheme to artificially inflate Enron's profits. The charges included fraud, money laundering, conspiracy, and obstruction of justice. If convicted, Fastow could face several hundred years in prison and millions of dollars in fines. Also, Deputy Attorney General Larry Thompson, head of a corporate fraud task force, said federal officials "will use every appropriate measure to recover the ill-gotten gains of these corporate schemers" (The Associated Press).

Some observers place some of the blame for the type of deals Fastow made on a company atmosphere with an unrelenting emphasis on earnings growth and individual initiative. Eventually this push led to unethical corner cutting. Also, too much leeway was granted to young, inexperienced managers without the necessary controls to decrease the chances of failure.

Outside the office, Fastow was a different personality. He was a major benefactor to the city's art museums, a fundraiser for the local Holocaust Museum, and a cofounder of a synagogue.

"The Andy Fastow I know is one of the most thoughtful and generous people in Houston," says an attorney and close friend of Fastow (*BusinessWeek*, February 4, 2002, p. 41). High school chums recall Fastow as popular and well liked, though extremely ambitious.

QUESTIONS

1. Which specific behaviors of Fastow would you perceive as unethical?

2. Does the fact that Fastow has not yet been charged with a crime influence your evalua-tion of his ethics? (During congressional in-quiries, under legal counsel he chose to re-main silent.) Explain your reasoning.

3. In what ways was Fastow socially responsible?

4. How would you rate Fastow's emotional in-telligence?

SOURCE: *Wendy Zellner, "The Man Behind the Deal Ma-chine,"* BusinessWeek, *February 4, 2002, pp. 40-41; Bethany McLean, "Monster Mess,"* Fortune, *February 4, 2002, p. 96; John A. Byrne, "The Environment Was Ripe for Abuse,"* BusinessWeek, *February 25, 2002, pp. 118-120; Bill Saporito, "Speak No Evil,"* Time, *February 18, 2002.*

Leadership Case Problem B

Bad Credit? No Credit? College Student? Providian Loves You.

For more than ten years Providian Financial Corporation outdistanced the competition un-der the leadership of math whiz Chairman Shailesh J. Mehta. By using every medium from cable TV to the Internet to troll for business from students and other consumers, Providian be-came the nation's fifth-biggest credit card com-pany. But soon its fortunes took a downturn.

Nature of the Business. The company pioneered the business of issuing credit cards to risky or *subprime* customers. Lenders like Providian seek out customers with either spotty credit his-tories or no credit histories at all—typically low-income people—and often charge them exorbitant rates and fees to compensate for the possibility of a loan default. The business strat-egy dates back to the 1930s. Personal finance companies were built on subprime loans made during the Depression. After credit cards be-came a part of American life and companies learned how to use demographics to target po-tential borrowers, the business began to flour-ish. By 2002, the number of subprime credit card accounts in the entire industry surged to 26.8 million.

Providian's expertise was in segmenting people based on financial behavior. The com-pany created a system that made it possible to find the "ideal" credit card customer: a person who cared more about low minimum monthly payments than high interest rates and who would pile up debt but rarely default. Mehta was one of the people who helped develop its trade-secret mathematical model for finding the ideal customer. His PhD research dealt with credit card risk. "We found the best of the bad," said a former executive (*Fortune*, March 4, 2002, p. 144).

At first Providian had the subprime credit card market to itself. It charged some customers an application fee, in addition to an annual fee, for a card with a limit between $300 and $500. Interest rates often reached 24 percent. A marketing technique was to send checks to potential customers. When the check was cashed, interest fees would be immediately charged to the customer. Prospects who declined to cash the check did not receive credit cards because they did not fit the profile of a person who embraced debt. In one promotion, after targeted customers accepted a "no annual fee" credit card, Providian charged them a mandatory $156 "credit protection fee."

Company Decline and Exit of Mehta. By November 2001, Providian's fortunes began to decline. When earnings began to slow down, the company attempted to compensate by generating more and more subprime customers. To find them, Providian lowered its standards and handed out credit cards to people whom its mathematical models would have rejected in the past.

Credit card issuers in general have experienced difficult times recently as bankruptcies have risen and debts have mounted. Yet Providian is more troubled than most of its competitors because its charge-offs for noncollectable loans climbed from 7.6 percent of assets to 10.3 percent in one year, and are approaching 12 percent. For most companies, noncollectable loans are below 5.5 percent.

Mehta complained that consumer spending has been below expectations. However, Providian has been troubled for a while. One concern is that Providian's hard sell to high-risk customers at times has been hucksterism. In 2000, Providian paid $300 million to settle charges by the comptroller of the currency and the San Francisco district attorney that it had misled and deceived consumers with less than candid marketing. Investigators said that the company's telemarketers refused to specify promised "great savings" on interest rates and failed to spell out extra charges on "no annual fee" cards (*BusinessWeek*, November 5, 2001, p. 96). Providian settled without admitting or denying the charges.

When Wall Street analysts learned about the mounting problems, Providian's share price plunged. The company then revised its practices for writing off bad accounts, delaying the impact of the customer bankruptcies for up to thirty days. To keep earnings growth looking good, Providian management deferred about $30 million in credit losses to another quarter without informing Wall Street. The analysts were angry, and Providian lost its credibility with investors.

As the company started to nose-dive, Mehta and his number 2 executive began liquidating their personal stock. Shortly thereafter, lawyers began filing class action suits against the company and its top executives for fraudulently misleading investors and having used insider knowledge to sell their stock at inflated prices.

When consumer protection advocates criticized Providian, Mehta said his company was providing a valuable service in offering credit to customers whom other banks refused to serve. Yet as pressures continued to mount, Mehta resigned and stayed on until a successor was appointed.

In 2001, Providian pulled in its horns. In March, it stopped running television ads with 800 numbers to call to apply for credit cards. The company also phased down a TV campaign to reach a web site that offered cards with rates as high as 27.99 percent.

Mehta's Better Days. While Providian was growing rapidly, Mehta profited substantially. In October 2000, his stockholdings in the company were worth more than $300 million. He lived with his family in a 17,000-square-foot house that was a replica of the White House. Says a former Providian board member: "He was more motivated by money than anyone I've ever met" (*Fortune*, March 4, 2002, p. 144). As long as the company stock continued to climb, Wall Street cheered Mehta on.

The Future? Joseph Saunders, the new CEO and chairman, is now focusing Providian on the middle market, a notch higher than subprime. Although this market has a lower default rate, the competition is intense. As a stopgap measure, Saunders has sold off some of Providian's best loans to another financial company, and he

has also attained other funding for a relief fund of about $11 billion.

QUESTIONS

1. In what ways has Providian been unethical and socially irresponsible?

2. What argument can you present that Providian has been socially responsible?

3. What could company leadership have done to guide Providian in a better direction?

SOURCE: *Suzanne Koudski, "Sleazy Credit,"* Fortune, *March 4, 2002, pp. 143–147; Joseph Weber, "Let the Bidding Begin for Providian,"* BusinessWeek, *November 5, 2001, p. 96.*

INTERNET SKILL–BUILDING EXERCISE

Career Consequences of Unethical Leadership Behavior

Apply the chapter concepts! Visit the Web and complete this Internet skill-building exercise to learn more about current leadership topics and trends.

In this chapter and at other places in the text, you have read about business executives accused of unethical, illegal, or socially irresponsible behavior. An important issue is to understand the career consequences to these individuals stemming from their misbehavior. Use the Internet to learn of the present status of four executives whose unethical behavior has been cited in this text. Verify their present status, looking for potential consequences such as (a) new employment in a corporation, (b) self-employment, (b) loss of employment, (c) working as a consultant, (e) elected as a public official, or (e) incarceration. Based on your findings, draw a conclusion about the career consequences of unethical leadership behavior.

Some executives, or former executives, you might want to track down are Gary Winnick, Andrew Fastow, Martha Stewart, Bernard Ebbers, Kenneth Lay, Jeffrey Skilling, and Mark Schwartz (formerly of Kmart).

Power, Politics, and Leadership

CHAPTER 7

Airbus S.A.S., the consortium of European aerospace companies based in Toulouse, France, has too often resembled the proverbial horse designed by a committee. But Noël Foregard has taken a big stride toward transforming this industrial camel into a swift-winged Pegasus. With his diplomatic and managerial skills, Airbus has pulled even with archrival Boeing to command half the global market for commercial aircraft.

Much of Foregard's on-the-job training for the Airbus position came during eleven years at Lagardère Group, a French conglomerate with interests ranging from publishing to missiles. There he learned how to forge joint ventures between traditionally secretive European and U.S. defense companies. Says a former Lagardère colleague: "He appears low-key, but he can be very tough, and when he has set a goal, nothing can distract him from it. He has an impressive ability to set priorities, to focus on his goals, and then set up a very strong team to achieve these goals."

With his keen political sensitivities, Foregard has also defused cross-border rivalries at Airbus, allotting construction projects so that all nations feel they have been treated equitably. Foregard also faces the challenge of dealing with Boeing complaints to the White House that Airbus gets unfair trade subsidies in the form of low-interest loans from European governments. Defusing that issue will be just another test for the high-flying industrial diplomat.[1]

Noël Foregard exercises enormous power. In addition to being a keen business strategist, Foregard is also skillful at organizational politics. He is diplomatic and has the interpersonal skills required to overcome conflict among rivals. This chapter covers the nature of power, the ways leaders acquire power and empower others, and the use and control of organizational politics. Chapter 8 continues the discussion of organizational (or office) politics by examining influence tactics.

SOURCES AND TYPES OF POWER

To exercise influence, a leader must have **power,** the potential or ability to influence decisions and control resources. Power is so intertwined with leadership that Dale E. Zand considers it to be one of the three forces of the leadership triad, along with knowledge and trust. Effective leaders use power appropriately and know when and how to be directive and when to delegate. At the same time, they know how to be consultants, providing guidance instead of issuing commands.[2]

Organizational power can be derived from many sources, as shown in Table 7-1. How a person obtains power depends to a large extent on the type of power he or she seeks. Therefore, to understand the mechanics of acquiring power, one must also understand what types of power exist and the sources and origins of these types of power. The seven types or sources of power listed in Table 7-1 are described in the following sections.

TABLE 7-1   Types or Sources of Power
1.   Power granted by the organization (position power)
2.   Power stemming from characteristics of the person (personal power)
3.   Power stemming from ownership
4.   Power stemming from control of resources
5.   Power derived from capitalizing upon opportunity
6.   Power stemming from managing critical problems
7.   Power stemming from being close to power

Position Power

Power is frequently classified according to whether it stems from the organization or the individual.[3] Four such bases of power—legitimate power, reward power, coercive power, and information power—stem from the person's position in the organization.

Legitimate Power.   The lawful right to make a decision and expect compliance is called **legitimate power.**[4] People at the highest levels in the organization have more power than do people below them. However, organizational culture helps establish the limits to anyone's power. Newly appointed executives, for example, are often frustrated with how long it takes to effect major change. A chief financial officer (CFO) recruited to improve the profitability of a telecommunications firm noted: "The company has been downsizing for three years. We have more office space and manufacturing capacity than we need. Yet whenever I introduce the topic of selling off real estate to cut costs, I get a cold reception."

Reward Power.   The authority to give employees rewards for compliance is referred to as **reward power.** If a vice president of operations can directly reward supervisors with cash bonuses for achieving quality targets, this manager will exert considerable power. Of course, leaders can use reward power effectively only when they have meaningful rewards at their disposal.

Coercive Power.   **Coercive power** is the power to punish for noncompliance; it is based on fear. A common coercive tactic is for an executive to demote a subordinate manager if he or she does not comply with the executive's plans for change. Coercive power is limited, in that punishment and fear achieve mixed results as motivators. The leader who relies heavily on coercive power runs the constant threat of being ousted from power.

The continuing emphasis on downsizing, particularly after a corporate acquisition or merger, has given managers an opportunity to use coercive power more extensively. Managers with an inclination toward mistreatment of employees now have a new weapon. According to Harvey Hornstein, downsizing has given many managers broad, blunt, and often unrestrained power to eliminate jobs. Even when jobs are plentiful, being forced to find a new position can be stressful, for it includes the prospect of relocation. More than half the cases of abusive bosses Hornstein uncovered can be attributed to a work environment in which workers are readily dismissed to reduce costs.[5]

Information Power. **Information power** is power stemming from formal control over the information people need to do their work. A sales manager who controls the leads from customer inquiries holds considerable power. As the branch manager of a real estate agency put it: "Ever since the leads were sent directly to me, I get oodles of cooperation from my agents. Before that they would treat me as if I were simply the office manager."

Personal Power

Three sources of power stem from characteristics or behaviors of the power actor: expert power, referent power, and prestige power. All are classified as **personal power,** because they are derived from the person rather than the organization. Expert power and referent power contribute to charisma. Expert power is the ability to influence others through specialized knowledge, skills, or abilities. An example of a leader with substantial expert power is automotive executive Bob Lutz. For many years he had spearheaded new car development at Chrysler Corporation. In 2002, at age 69 he was recruited to General Motors as vice chairman for product development. His mission was to work with designers and engineers to give new GM models sex appeal.[6] Referent power is the ability to influence others through desirable traits and characteristics. Lutz comes up strong here also, being labeled the "preeminent car guy" in the industry, partly because of his charisma.

Another important form of personal power is **prestige power,** the power stemming from one's status and reputation.[7] A manager who has accumulated important business successes acquires prestige power. Integrity is another contributor to prestige power because it enhances a leader's reputation.[8] Executive recruiters identify executives who can readily be placed in senior positions because of their excellent track records (or prestige).

Manager Assessment Quiz 7-1 provides a sampling of the specific behaviors associated with five of the sources of power—three kinds of position power and two kinds of personal power.

Power Stemming from Ownership

Executive leaders accrue power in their capacity as agents acting on behalf of shareholders. The strength of ownership power depends on how closely the leader is linked to shareholders and board members. A leader's ownership power is also associated with how much money he or she has invested in the firm.[9] An executive who is a major shareholder is much less likely to be fired by the board

Manager Assessment Quiz 7-1

Rating a Manager's Power

INSTRUCTIONS   If you currently have a supervisor or can clearly recall one from the past, rate him or her. Circle the appropriate number of your answer, using the following scale: 5 = strongly agree; 4 = agree; 3 = neither agree nor disagree; 2 = disagree; 1 = strongly disagree. (The actual scale presents the items in random order. They are classified here according to the power source for your convenience.)

My manager can (or former manager could) . . .	Strongly Agree				Strongly Disagree

Reward Power

1. increase my pay level.	5	4	3	2	1
2. influence my getting a pay raise.	5	4	3	2	1
3. provide me with specific benefits.	5	4	3	2	1
4. influence my getting a promotion.	5	4	3	2	1

Coercive Power

5. give me undesirable job assignments.	5	4	3	2	1
6. make my work difficult for me.	5	4	3	2	1
7. make things unpleasant here.	5	4	3	2	1
8. make being at work distasteful.	5	4	3	2	1

Legitimate Power

9. make me feel that I have commitments to meet.	5	4	3	2	1
10. make me feel like I should satisfy my job requirements.	5	4	3	2	1
11. give me the feeling that I have responsibilities to fulfill.	5	4	3	2	1
12. make me recognize that I have tasks to accomplish.	5	4	3	2	1

Expert Power

13. give me good technical suggestions.	5	4	3	2	1
14. share with me his or her considerable experience and/or training.	5	4	3	2	1
15. provide me with sound job-related advice.	5	4	3	2	1
16. provide me with needed technical knowledge.	5	4	3	2	1

Referent Power

17.	make me feel valued.	5 4 3 2 1
18.	make me feel that he or she approves of me.	5 4 3 2 1
19.	make me feel personally accepted.	5 4 3 2 1
20.	make me feel important.	5 4 3 2 1

Total score: _____

SCORING AND INTERPRETATION   Add all the circled numbers to calculate your total score. You can make a tentative interpretation of the score as follows:

- 90+   high power
- 70–89   moderate power
- below 70   low power

Also, see if you rated your manager much higher in one of the categories.

SKILL DEVELOPMENT   This skill development rating can help you as a leader because it points to specific behaviors you can use to be perceived as high or low on a type of power. For example, a behavioral specific for establishing referent power is to "make people feel important" (No. 20).

SOURCE: *Adapted from "Development and Application of New Scales to Measure the French and Raven (1959) Bases of Social Power," by Timothy R. Hinkin and Chester A. Schriescheim,* Journal of Applied Psychology, *August 1989, p. 567. Copyright © 1989 by the American Psychological Association. Adapted with permission of American Psychological Association and Timothy R. Hinkin.*

than one without an equity stake. The CEOs of ebusiness firms are typically company founders, who later convert their firm into a publicly held company by selling stock. After the public offering, many of these CEOs own several hundred million dollars worth of stock, making their position quite secure. The New Golden Rule applies: The person who holds the gold, rules.

Power Stemming from Providing Resources

A broad way to view power sources is from the **resource dependence perspective.** According to this perspective, the organization requires a continuing flow of human resources, money, customers and clients, technological inputs, and materials to continue to function. Organizational subunits or individuals who can provide these key resources accrue power.[10]

When leaders start losing their power to control resources, their power declines. A case in point is Donald Trump. When his vast holdings were generating a positive cash flow and his image was one of extraordinary power, he found many willing investors. The name *Trump* on a property escalated its value. As his cash-flow position worsened, however, Trump found it difficult to find investment groups willing to buy his properties at near the asking price. However, by mid-1993, Trump's cash-flow position had improved again and investors showed renewed interest. By 1996 Trump had regained all of his power to control resources, and money from investors flowed freely in his direction. Study more about Trump and his power in one of the case problems at the end of this chapter.

Power Derived from Capitalizing on Opportunity

Power can be derived from being in the right place at the right time and taking the appropriate action. It pays to be "where the action is." For example, the best opportunities in a diversified company lie in one of its growth divisions. A person also needs to have the right resources to capitalize on an opportunity.[11]

Power Stemming from Managing Critical Problems

A simple but compelling theory has been developed to explain why some organizational units are more powerful than others. The **strategic contingency theory** of power suggests that units best able to cope with the firm's critical problems and uncertainties acquire relatively large amounts of power.[12] The theory implies, for example, that when an organization faces substantial lawsuits, the legal department will gain power and influence over organizational decisions.

Another important aspect of the strategic contingency theory concerns the power a subunit acquires by virtue of its centrality. **Centrality** is the extent to which a unit's activities are linked into the system of organizational activities. A unit has high centrality when it is an important and integral part of the work done by another unit. The second unit is therefore dependent on the first subunit. A sales department would have high centrality, whereas an employee credit union would have low centrality.

A study conducted by Herminia Ibarra provides some empirical evidence that holding a position of centrality does influence the power a worker, and therefore his or her subunit, can exert. The research setting was an advertising and public relations agency with ninety-four employees. The firm had recently gone through a period of turbulence and needed to acquire many new clients to replace those that had defected. Centrality was measured in terms of the number of links a given individual had to others in the firm. Although this is not the same measure of centrality as closeness to power, it does indicate the extent to which a person is involved with others in making important decisions. Like formal authority, network centrality indicates a high position in a status hierarchy. Power was measured as bringing new administrative and technical ideas to life.

Among the findings in the study was that being at the center of a network was a strong determinant of individual involvement in administrative innovation. Two examples of such innovations are media training and the creation of a conflict management program. Having a position of centrality, however, did not contribute much to technical innovation (such as a new strategy for generating clients). Bringing forth technical innovations was related as much to informal as to formal power. Being a member of senior management, for example, would give a person the formal authority to create technical innovations.[13]

Power Stemming from Being Close to Power

The closer a person is to power, the greater the power he or she exerts. Likewise, the higher a unit reports in a firm's hierarchy, the more power it possesses. In practice, this means that a leader in charge of a department reporting to the CEO has more power than one in charge of a department reporting to a vice president. Leaders in search of more power typically maneuver toward a higher-reporting position in the organization. Many managers of information systems now report at a higher organizational level than previously. Part of this enhanced power can be attributed to the increasing attention organizations are paying to the Internet as part of their strategy.

BASES OF POWER AND TRANSFORMATIONAL AND TRANSACTIONAL LEADERSHIP

One justification for studying bases of power is that they have direct application to understanding and applying leadership. Leanne E. Atwater and Francis J. Yammarino investigated how the bases of power, both personal and positional, relate to transformational and transactional leadership.[14] Consistent with the definition provided in Chapter 3, transformational leadership is depicted as the influence a leader acquires through being respected and admired by group members. In contrast, transactional leadership is largely based on exchanges between the leader and group members, such as using rewards and punishments to control behavior. Two hundred and eighty employees reporting to 118 supervisors in 45 organizations of many different types provided data for the study. Questionnaires were used to measure bases of power as well as perceptions of transformational and transactional leadership. (The Multifactor Leadership Questionnaire, mentioned in Chapter 3, was used to measure the perceptions of leader behavior.)

Of particular interest here, analysis of the data revealed that personal power, both referent and expert, was related to transformational leadership. Leaders who behave in a transformational manner (being charismatic, inspirational, intellectually stimulating, and considerate of individuals) are perceived to possess referent and expert power. Transformational leadership also showed a positive correlation with reward and legitimate power, yet was unrelated to coercive power. The message is that punitive bosses are rarely perceived as transformational. A less strong finding was that perceptions of power were not clearly linked to transactional leadership.

An important implication of the study derived from regression analysis is that leaders who behave in a transformational manner are likely to be viewed as having a variety of positive bases of power. The data also suggest that transformational leaders are able to influence group members by virtue of the referent power attributed to them. Another implication justifies studying power in relation to leadership: The researchers conclude that power and leader behavior are interrelated.

TACTICS FOR BECOMING AN EMPOWERING LEADER

A leader's power and influence increase when he or she shares power with others. A partial explanation for this paradox is that as team members receive more power, they can accomplish more—they become more productive. And because the manager shares credit for their accomplishments, he or she becomes more powerful. A truly powerful leader makes team members feel powerful and able to accomplish tasks on their own. To empower others is to be seen as an influential person. A similar rationale for empowerment is that in a competitive environment that is increasingly dependent on knowledge, judgment, and information, the most successful organizations will be those that effectively use the talents of all players on the team.[15]

Here we look briefly at the nature of empowerment before describing a number of empowering practices and two cautions about empowerment.

The Nature of Empowerment

In its basic meaning, **empowerment** refers to passing decision-making authority and responsibility from managers to group members. Almost any form of participative management, shared decision making, and delegation can be regarded as empowerment. Gretchen M. Spreitzer conducted research in several work settings to develop a psychological definition of empowerment. Her work provides useful insights for leaders and also builds on the work of other inquiries into the nature of empowerment.[16] Four components of empowerment were identified: meaning, competence, self-determination, and impact. Full-fledged empowerment includes all four dimensions along with a fifth one, internal commitment.

Meaning is the value of a work goal, evaluated in relation to a person's ideals or standards. Work has meaning when there is a fit between the requirements of a work role and a person's beliefs, values, and behaviors. A person who is doing meaningful work is likely to feel empowered. *Competence*, or *self-efficacy*, is an individual's belief in his or her capability to perform a particular task well. The person who feels competent feels that he or she has the capability to meet the performance requirements in a given situation, such as a credit analyst saying, "I've been given the authority to evaluate credit risks up to $10,000 and I know I can do it well."

Self-determination is an individual's feeling of having a choice in initiating and regulating actions. A high-level form of self-determination occurs when a worker feels that he or she can choose which is the best method to solve a particular problem. Self-determination also involves such considerations as choosing the work pace and work site. A highly empowered worker might choose to perform the required work while on a cruise rather than remain in the office. *Impact* is the degree to which the worker can influence strategic, administrative, or operating outcomes on the job. Instead of feeling there is no choice but to follow the company's course, he or she might have a say in the future of the company. A middle manager might say, "Here's an opportunity for recruiting minority employees that we should exploit. And here's my action plan for doing so."

Another dimension of true empowerment is for the group member to develop an *internal commitment* toward work goals. Internal commitment takes place when workers are committed to a particular project, person, or program for individual motives. An example would be a production technician in a lawn mower plant who believes he is helping create a more beautiful world. (At the same time the technician is helping the company reach its goals.)

Empowering Practices

The practices that foster empowerment supplement standard approaches to participative management, such as conferring with team members before reaching a decision. The practices, as outlined in Figure 7-1, are based on direct observations of successful leaders and experimental evidence. Before reading about these practices, do Leadership Self-Assessment Quiz 7-2.

Foster Initiative and Responsibility.   A leader can empower team members simply by fostering greater initiative and responsibility in their assignments. For example, one bank executive transformed what had been a constricted branch manager's job into a branch "president" role. Managers were then evaluated on the basis of deposits because they had control over them. After the transformation, branch managers were allowed to stay with one branch rather than being rotated every three years.[17]

Link Work Activities to the Goals of the Organization.   Empowerment works better when the empowered activities are aligned with the strategic goals of the organization. Empowered workers who have responsibility to carry out activities that support the major goals of the organization will identify more with the company. At the same time, they will develop a feeling of being a partner in the business.[18] Imagine a scenario in which a company auditor is authorized to spend large sums of travel money to accomplish her job. She is given this authority because a strategic goal of top-level management is to become a company admired for its honest business practices. The empowerment is all the more likely to work because the auditor has the authority to carry out activities that make a difference in achieving an important strategic goal.

Provide Ample Information.   An axiom of effective empowerment is that employees should have ample information about everything that affects their work. Especially important is for workers to fully understand the impact of their actions

FIGURE 7–1   **Effective Empowering Practices**

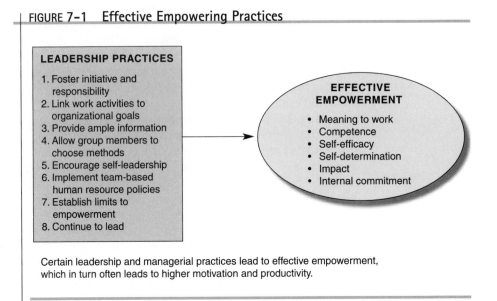

LEADERSHIP PRACTICES

1. Foster initiative and responsibility
2. Link work activities to organizational goals
3. Provide ample information
4. Allow group members to choose methods
5. Encourage self-leadership
6. Implement team-based human resource policies
7. Establish limits to empowerment
8. Continue to lead

EFFECTIVE EMPOWERMENT

- Meaning to work
- Competence
- Self-efficacy
- Self-determination
- Impact
- Internal commitment

Certain leadership and managerial practices lead to effective empowerment, which in turn often leads to higher motivation and productivity.

on the company's costs and profits. Armed with such information, employees are more likely to make decisions that have a positive influence on the bottom line. Consultant Thomas J. McCoy poses these questions about the importance of information for empowerment:

- How can employees know the impact of their actions on the bottom line if they don't have the kinds of financial scorecards that senior management routinely receives to run the business?

- If employees don't have full understanding of how their actions affect the whole operation, how can they act effectively?

When employees have answers to questions of the nature just described, they are more likely to use empowerment to make decisions that contribute to business success.[19] As an example, an empowered sales representative, armed with cost information, is less likely to grant discounts that lose money for the company. The issue of disclosing financial information to employees (or *open-book management*) will be introduced again in Chapter 9 as a method for developing teamwork.

Allow Group Members to Choose Methods.   Under ideal conditions the leader or manager explains to the individual or group what needs to be done (sets a direction) and lets the people involved choose the method. Explaining why the tasks need to be performed is also important. One of the roles of a true professional is to choose the method for accomplishing a task, such as a tax consultant deciding how to prepare the taxes for a business owner. Consultant Norman Bodek explains:

Leadership Self-Assessment Quiz 7-2

Becoming an Empowering Manager

INSTRUCTIONS   To empower employees successfully, the leader has to convey appropriate attitudes and develop effective interpersonal skills. To the best of your ability, indicate which skills and attitudes you now have, and which ones require further development.

Empowering Attitude or Behavior	Can Do Now	Would Need to Develop
1. Believe in team members' ability to be successful	____	____
2. Have patience with people and give them time to learn	____	____
3. Provide team members with direction and structure	____	____
4. Teach team members new skills in small, incremental steps so they can easily learn those skills	____	____
5. Ask team members questions that challenge them to think in new ways	____	____
6. Share information with team members, sometimes just to build rapport	____	____
7. Give team members timely feedback and encourage them throughout the learning process	____	____
8. Offer team members alternative ways of doing things	____	____
9. Exhibit a sense of humor and demonstrate care for workers as people	____	____
10. Focus on team members' results and acknowledge their personal improvement	____	____

SKILL DEVELOPMENT   If, as a leader or manager, you already have most of these attitudes and have engaged in most of these behaviors, you will be good at empowerment. Most of the above attitudes and practices can be developed without transforming your personality.

SOURCE: Supervisory Management *by* Stone, Florence. *Copyright 1991 by* American Management Association (J). *Reproduced with permission of* American Management Association (J) *in the format Textbook via Copyright Clearance Center.*

"What irks people the most is to be told how to do something. Allowing people to determine the most efficient work technique is the essence of empowerment."[20]

Encourage Self-Leadership.   Encouraging team members to lead themselves is the heart of empowerment. When employees practice self-leadership, they feel empowered. At W. L. Gore and Associates, Inc., a manufacturer of insulated material including GORE-TEX®, a popular buzzword is *unmanagement*—no bosses or managers but many leaders. One example of unmanagement takes place during salary reviews. Each associate's (employee's) salary is periodically reviewed by a compensation team drawn from individuals at the associate's work site. Each associate has a sponsor who acts as his or her advocate during the reviews. The sponsor gathers data about the associate's performance by speaking to internal and external customers.

Implement Team-Based Human Resource Policies.   A study of 111 work teams in four organizations found that teams are more likely to feel empowered when the organization implements a variety of team-based human resource policies. Among these policies are basing pay in part on team performance and allowing team members to participate in decisions about the selection, training, discipline, and performance evaluation of other team members. This study focused on empowering *teams,* in contrast to empowering individuals within the team.[21]

Establish Limits to Empowerment.   One of the major situations in which empowerment creates disharmony, dissatisfaction, and dysfunctions is when workers lack a clear perception of the boundaries of empowerment. The general problem is that empowered group members may feel that they can now make decisions unilaterally without conferring with managers, team leaders, or other team members.[22] Limits to empowerment might mean explaining to employees that they have more authority than before, but still they cannot engage in such activities as the following:

- Set their own wages
- Set the wages of top management
- Decide on dividends to shareholders
- Make downsizing decisions
- Hire mostly friends and relatives
- Work less than forty hours for full pay
- Take two-hour lunch breaks
- Devote three hours per day to surfing the Net

As facetious as a few of the above may appear, many employees justify dysfunctional actions by saying, "I'm empowered to do what I want." It is management's responsibility to guide employment activities that support the organization.

Continue to Lead.   Although leaders empower group members, they should still provide guidance, emotional support, and recognition. Consultant Mark Samuel helps companies organize into teams to enhance accountability for results, yet at the same time he emphasizes the leader's role: "Empowerment often becomes an abdication of leadership. In other words, if I empower you, I don't have to guide you. People need guidance. Leadership cannot abdicate the role of providing guidance."[23]

Cultural Differences

All of the empowering practices described above can be influenced by cross-cultural factors. A group member's cultural values might lead to either an easy acceptance of empowerment or reluctance to be empowered. Americans are stereotyped as individualists. Nevertheless, they are so accustomed to working in teams (sports included) that being part of an empowered team would seem natural.

But not all cultures support empowerment. In one study, data from employees of a single firm with operations in the United States, Mexico, Poland, and India were used to test the fit of empowerment and continuous improvement practices with national culture. The company was engaged in light manufacturing, and data were collected from about forty sites. Empowerment was negatively associated with job satisfaction in the Indian plants, but positively associated in the other three samples. The underlying cultural reason is that Indians (at least those working in India) expect the leader or manager to make most of the decisions.[24] Continuous improvement was positively related to satisfaction in all four samples.

Effective Delegation and Empowerment

A major contributor to empowerment is **delegation,** the assignment of formal authority and responsibility for accomplishing a specific task to another person. Delegation is narrower than empowerment because it deals with a specific task, whereas empowerment covers a broad range of activities and a mental set about assuming more responsibility. Delegation, like empowerment, is motivational because it offers group members the opportunity to develop their skills and demonstrate their competence. It is usually discussed more in management studies than in leadership studies. Here we will only briefly discuss guidelines for effective delegation.[25]

In effective delegation, the leader *assigns duties to the right people.* The chances for successful delegation and empowerment improve when the tasks in question are assigned to capable, responsible, and self-motivated group members. Vital tasks should not be assigned to ineffective performers. Insight into the strengths and developmental needs of group members therefore enhances effective delegation. Also, when feasible, *delegate the whole task.* In the spirit of job enrichment, a manager should delegate an entire task to one group member rather than dividing it among several. Doing so gives the group member complete responsibility and enhances his or her motivation, and it also gives the manager more control over results. The leader should *give as much instruction as needed,* depending upon the characteristics of the group member. Some people will require highly detailed instructions, whereas others can operate effectively with general instructions. As explained in relation to empowerment, the most professionally rewarding type of delegation allows the group member to *choose the method* for accomplishing the assignment.

As a leader or manager, *retain some important tasks for yourself.* In general, the manager should handle some high-output or sensitive tasks and any tasks that involve the survival of the unit. However, which tasks the manager should retain always depends on the circumstances. A basic management principle is to *obtain feedback on the delegated task.* A responsible manager does not delegate a complex assignment to a group member, then wait until the assignment is completed before discussing it again. Managers must establish checkpoints and milestones to obtain feedback on progress. A morale-building suggestion is to *delegate both pleasant and unpleasant tasks to group members.* When group members are assigned a mixture of pleasant and unpleasant responsibilities, they are more likely to believe they are being treated fairly. Few group members expect the manager to handle all the undesirable jobs. A related approach is to rotate undesirable tasks among group members. One or two group members should not be "empowered" to handle all the nasty assignments.

A fundamental part of effective delegation is to *step back from the details.* Many managers are poor delegators because they get too involved with technical details. If a manager cannot let go of details, he or she will never be effective at delegation or empowerment. Finally, as in virtually all leadership endeavors, it is important to *evaluate and reward performance.* After the task is completed, the manager should evaluate the outcome. Favorable outcomes should be rewarded, and unfavorable outcomes may either be not rewarded or punished. It is important, however, not to discourage risk taking and initiative by punishing for all mistakes.

Delegation contributes to the practice of leadership because it is an excellent opportunity to coach the person accepting the delegated tasks. The assignment should be challenging enough to stretch the group member to acquire new skills. In the process of skill development, the group member might also benefit from a few constructive suggestions.

Keith McCluskey is the president of a Chevrolet and Auto Nation USA franchise in Cincinnati, Ohio. His company won an award for being the number 1 seller in the world of medium-duty trucks. He offers the following comments about delegation, which support many of the points made here about empowerment and delegation:

> I assign a task or mission to a manager, explain briefly its importance and how it fits into a master plan at the dealership. We set a deadline for completion. It frees my time up to do something more important. When you move the project along to somebody else, his or her confidence grows, and there is a good chance that he or she will do it at least as well and probably better than I would have completed the task. If you move enough of the tasks on, you can think about the vision of the company and growing the revenue.[26]

Before moving on to a study of organizational politics, you are invited to gain some practice in the realities of empowerment by doing Leadership Skill-Building Exercise 7-1. Keep in mind the suggestions about delegation when doing the exercise.

Leadership Skill-Building Exercise 7-1

Conducting an Empowerment Session

A profound cliché floating around organizations is that to empower group members, a leader must do more than say, "Pfft, you're empowered." The description of empowering practices has provided you some useful ideas to get started empowering others if you are already a manager. The role-assuming exercise described here gives you a chance to practice your empowering skills. One person plays the role of a leader, and six other people play the role of group members. You are meeting with your group today to get them started on the road toward empowerment. You will need to engage in dialogue with the group to begin the empowerment process. The empowerment scenarios described next should be staffed by different groups of students:

Information Technology Customer-Service Center. You are in charge of an information technology customer-service center whose primary activity is to respond to telephone inquiries from around the country from customers who are having problems in using the company's software. Visualize the help line of Microsoft or Corel to get an idea of this type of operation. The workers who answer the phone are full-time professionals, many of whom are recent college graduates. A major goal of yours is to empower your workers to do as much as they can to satisfy the demands of the callers. You want your staff to take more personal responsibility for customer problems.

Vision-Care Proprietors. You are the CEO of a nationwide chain of vision-care stores that sell both eyeglasses and contact lenses. You believe strongly that one of the constraining forces in your business is that your store managers, as well as franchise owners, do not take enough responsibility for running their operations. They rely too heavily on the corporate group for guidance and problem resolution. Today you are holding an empowerment meeting with the seven vision-care proprietors in your region. If your approach to empowerment works well, you will expand to other regions. Six other students play the role of store managers and franchise owners who generally believe that the corporate group should take the initiative to lead the stores toward greater prosperity. After all, why be a manager within a corporation or a franchise owner? Without corporate assistance, you might as well open your own vision-care store.

Doing this exercise is useful because it helps you develop the right mental set for a leader who empowers group members. Another advantage is that it sensitizes you to the importance of looking for signs of hesitation and ambivalence when you attempt to empower group members.

FACTORS THAT CONTRIBUTE TO ORGANIZATIONAL POLITICS

As used here, the term **organizational politics** refers to informal approaches to gaining power through means other than merit or luck. Politics are played to achieve power, either directly or indirectly. The power may be achieved in such diverse ways as by being promoted, by receiving a larger budget or other resources, by obtaining more resources for one's work group, or by being exempt from undesirable assignments. The definition of organizational politics presented here is nonevaluative, except that we shall draw a distinction between ethical and unethical political behavior.

The meaning of *organizational politics* continues to shift in a positive, constructive direction. A group of researchers recently concluded: "Political skill is an interpersonal style that combines social awareness with the ability to communicate well."[27] Nevertheless, many writers still regard organizational politics as emphasizing self-interest at the expense of others, engaging in mysterious activities, or "kissing up." Some of our topics do fall under these categories.

Organizational politics is an old subject that is still highly relevant in the Internet age. Teacher and consultant John Elrod was asked, "Isn't the promise of the new economy that we can all just get down to work" (and therefore ignore politics)? He replied that the biggest political mistake is to assume that organizational politics does not exist. "It's often a question of language. When we win on an issue, we call it leadership. When we lose, we call it politics. Practicing politics simply means increasing your options for effective results."[28]

People want power for many different reasons, which is why political behavior is so widespread in organizations. By definition, politics is used to acquire power. A number of individual and organizational factors contribute to political behavior, as outlined in Table 7-2.

Pyramid-Shaped Organization Structure

Organizations have been described as political structures that operate by distributing authority and setting the stage for the exercise of power. The very shape of large organizations is the most fundamental reason why organizational members

TABLE 7-2   Factors Contributing to Political Behavior in Organizations

1. Pyramid-shaped organization structure
2. Subjective standards of performance
3. Environmental uncertainty and turbulence
4. Emotional insecurity
5. Machiavellian tendencies
6. Disagreement over major issues

are motivated toward political behavior. A pyramid concentrates power at the top. Only so much power is therefore available to distribute among the many people who would like more of it. Each successive layer on the organization chart has less power than the layer above. At the very bottom of the organization, workers have virtually no power. Since most organizations today have fewer layers than they previously had, the competition for power has become more intense. Although empowerment may be motivational for many workers, it is unlikely to satisfy the quest to hold a formal position of power.

Subjective Standards of Performance

People often resort to organizational politics because they do not believe that the organization has an objective and fair way of judging their performance and suitability for promotion. Similarly, when managers have no objective way of differentiating effective people from the less effective, they will resort to favoritism. The adage "It's not what you know but who you know" applies to organizations that lack clear-cut standards of performance.

Environmental Uncertainty and Turbulence

When people, or the organizational subunits they represent, operate in an unstable and unpredictable environment, they tend to behave politically. They rely on organizational politics to create a favorable impression because uncertainty makes it difficult to determine what they should really be accomplishing.

The uncertainty, turbulence, and insecurity created by corporate downsizings is a major contributor to office politics. Many people believe intuitively that favoritism plays a major role in deciding who will survive the downsizing. In response to this perception, organizational members attempt to ingratiate themselves with influential people.

Emotional Insecurity

Some people resort to political maneuvers to ingratiate themselves with superiors because they lack confidence in their talents and skills. A pension fund manager who has directed the firm toward investments with an annualized 35 percent return does not have to be overly political because he or she will have confidence in his or her capabilities. A person's choice of political strategy may indicate emotional insecurity. For instance, an insecure person might laugh loudly at every humorous comment the boss makes.

Machiavellian Tendencies

Some people engage in political behavior because they want to manipulate others, sometimes for their own personal advantage. The term *Machiavellianism* traces back to Niccolo Machiavelli (1469–1527), an Italian political philosopher and statesman. His most famous work, *The Prince*, describes how a leader may acquire and maintain power. Machiavelli's ideal prince was an amoral, manipulating tyrant who would restore the Italian city-state of Florence to its former glory. In the modern era, a study by Gerald Biberman showed a positive relationship between Machiavellianism and political behavior, based on questionnaires that measured these tendencies.[29] Leadership Self-Assessment Quiz 7-3 presents an updated version of the political behavior questionnaire used in the study just mentioned.

Disagreement over Major Issues

Many executives attempt to use rational criteria when making major decisions, but rational decision making is constrained by major disagreements over employees' preferences and theories of what the organization should be doing. Unless strategy and goals are shared among key organizational members, political motivation is inevitable in organizational decision making.

An example of disagreement over major issues leading to political behavior took place at a savings bank. Substantial inner turmoil occurred because of power struggles between the consumer loan and home mortgage departments. Each department saw itself as the most important future thrust of the bank. Representatives of both groups often diverted marketing and customer service efforts while they waged their internal power struggle.

POLITICAL TACTICS AND STRATEGIES

To make effective use of organizational politics, leaders must be aware of specific political tactics and strategies. To identify and explain the majority of political tactics would require years of study and observation. Leaders so frequently need support for their programs that they search for innovative types of political behaviors. Furthermore, new tactics continue to emerge as the workplace becomes increasingly competitive. Here we look at a representative group of political tactics and strategies categorized as to whether they are ethical or unethical. (Several of the influence tactics described in Chapter 8, such as ingratiation, might also be considered political behaviors.)

The Leader in Action box (page 214) describes a leader of a small unit of a major organization who applies his political skill to get the right people on his side.

Ethical Political Tactics and Strategies

So far we have discussed organizational politics without pinpointing specific tactics and strategies. This section describes a sampling of ethical political behaviors, divided into three related groups: tactics and strategies aimed at (1) gaining power, (2) building relationships with superiors and coworkers; and (3) avoiding political blunders.

All of these political approaches help the leader gain or retain power. Using them can also help the leader succeed in and manage stressful work environments. As defined by a group of researchers, political skill is a constructive force. It is an interpersonal style that manifests itself in being socially astute and engag-

The Organizational Politics Questionnaire

INSTRUCTIONS   Answer each question "mostly agree" or "mostly disagree," even if it is difficult for you to decide which alternative best describes your opinion.

		Mostly Agree	Mostly Disagree
1.	The boss is always right.	___	___
2.	It is wise to flatter important people.	___	___
3.	If you do somebody a favor, remember to cash in on it later.	___	___
4.	Given the opportunity, I would cultivate friendships with powerful people.	___	___
5.	I would be willing to say nice things about a rival in order to get that person transferred from my department.	___	___
6.	If it would help me get ahead, I would take credit for someone else's work.	___	___
7.	Given the chance, I would offer to help my boss build some shelves for his or her den.	___	___
8.	I laugh heartily at my boss's jokes, even if I do not think they are funny.	___	___
9.	Dressing for success is silly. Wear clothing to work that you find to be the most comfortable.	___	___
10.	Never waste lunchtime by having lunch with somebody who can't help you solve a problem or gain advantage.	___	___
11.	I think using email to zap somebody for his or her mistakes is a good idea (especially if you want to show that person up).	___	___
12.	If somebody higher up in the organization offends you, let that person know about it.	___	___
13.	Honesty is the best policy in practically all cases.	___	___
14.	Power for its own sake is one of life's most precious commodities.	___	___

15. If I had a legitimate gripe against my employer, I would air my views publicly (such as by writing a letter to the editor of a local newspaper or posting my gripe on the Net).   ____   ____

16. I would invite my boss to a party at my home, even if I didn't like him or her.   ____   ____

17. An effective way to impress people is to tell them what they want to hear.   ____   ____

18. Having a high school or skyscraper named after me would be an incredible thrill.   ____   ____

19. Hard work and good performance are usually sufficient for career success.   ____   ____

20. Even if I made only a minor contribution to a project, I would get my name listed as being associated with that project.   ____   ____

21. I would never publicly correct mistakes made by the boss.   ____   ____

22. I would never use my personal contacts to gain a promotion.   ____   ____

23. If you happen to dislike a person who receives a big promotion in your firm, don't bother sending that person a congratulatory note.   ____   ____

24. I would never openly criticize a powerful executive in my organization.   ____   ____

25. I would stay in the office late just to impress my boss.   ____   ____

SCORING AND INTERPRETATION   Give yourself a plus 1 for each answer that agrees with the keyed answer. Each question that receives a score of plus 1 shows a tendency toward playing organizational politics. The scoring key is as follows:

1. Mostly agree	10. Mostly agree	19. Mostly disagree
2. Mostly agree	11. Mostly agree	20. Mostly agree
3. Mostly agree	12. Mostly disagree	21. Mostly agree
4. Mostly agree	13. Mostly disagree	22. Mostly disagree
5. Mostly agree	14. Mostly agree	23. Mostly disagree
6. Mostly agree	15. Mostly disagree	24. Mostly agree
7. Mostly agree	16. Mostly agree	25. Mostly agree
8. Mostly agree	17. Mostly agree	
9. Mostly disagree	18. Mostly agree	

Based on a sample of 750 men and women managers, professionals, administrators, sales representatives, and business owners, the mean score is 10.

- 1–7   below-average tendency to play office politics
- 8–12   average tendency to play office politics
- 13 and above   above-average tendency to play office politics; strong need for power

SKILL DEVELOPMENT   Thinking about your political tendencies in the workplace is important for your career because most successful leaders are moderately political. The ability to use politics effectively and ethically increases with importance in the executive suite. Most top players are effective office politicians. Yet being overly and blatantly political can lead to distrust, thereby damaging your career.

SOURCE: *Reproduced with permission of the publisher from DuBrin, A.J. "Career maturity, organizational rank, and political behavioral tendencies: A correlational analysis of organizational politics and career experience."* Psychological Reports, *1988, 63, 531–537. © Psychological Reports 1988. Also from Andrew J. DuBrin, "Sex Differences in Endorsement of Influence Tactics and Political Behavior Tendencies,"* Journal of Business and Psychology, *Fall 1989, pp. 3–14. Reprinted by permission.*

ing in behaviors that lead to feelings of confidence, trust, and sincerity.[30] For example, a middle manager with political skill might be able to defend her group against an angry CEO looking for a scapegoat.

Strategies Aimed at Gaining Power. All political tactics are aimed at acquiring and maintaining power, even the power to avoid a difficult assignment. Tom Peters points to a fundamental reason that gaining power can justify the effort. He says that although power can often be abused, it can also be used to benefit many people. "And as a career building tool, the slow and steady (and subtle) amassing of power is the surest road to success."[31] Here are seven techniques aimed directly at gaining power.

1. *Develop power contacts.* After powerful people have been identified, alliances with them must be established. Cultivating friendly, cooperative relationships with powerful organizational members and outsiders can make the leader's cause much easier to advance. These contacts can benefit a person by supporting his or her ideas in meetings and other public forums. One way to develop these contacts is to be more social, for example, by throwing parties and inviting powerful people and their guests. Some organizations and some bosses frown on social familiarity, however. And power-holders receive many invitations, so they might not be available.

2. *Control vital information.* Power accrues to those who control vital information, as indicated in the discussion of personal power. Many former government or military officials have found power niches for themselves in industry after leaving the public payroll. Frequently such an individual will be hired as the Washington representative of a firm that does business with the government. The vital information they control is knowledge of whom to contact to

Leader in Action

Chris Newell of Lotus Institute Builds Support for His Brainchild

Chris Newell, 47, is founder and executive director of Lotus Institute, a twenty-member unit of Lotus Development Corp., which develops solutions using Lotus Notes software. The job is fun and interesting, but hardly a position of high power. "We generate new ideas about how software interacts with the culture," he says. "We're the shrinks of the shrinkwrap" (*Fast Company*, April 1998, p. 157).

Last year Newell became convinced that the emerging field of knowledge management represented a big market opportunity for Lotus and its parent company, IBM. So he became a major catalyst behind a series of knowledge-management products that Lotus and IBM began to roll out by the end of the year. Newell didn't have the authority to order such initiatives. But he did know how to play politics.

One of the political tactics Newell used without giving it a label is called *push polling*. You ask questions in ways that build support for the outcome you want. Newell was forever selling his ideas to colleagues even as he was testing out those ideas. "I tried to create an internal groundswell," he says (*Fast Company*, April 1998, p. 160).

Jim Kryzwicki, 36, Lotus's vice president of worldwide customer support and education, says that Newell never wasted an encounter with him—or with anyone else in the organization. "He had his 'elevator speech' ready at all times," Kryzwicki reports. "If he met the president of the company on the elevator, he would have made his point by the time they got off [the elevator]. Chris is continually checking with his people. That gives him very sensitive antennae and it helps him develop broad-based support and understanding" (*Fast Company*, April 1998, p. 160).

How persistent was Newell? "Let me put it this way," Kryzwicki says with a smile. "My wife's the only one with the number to my car phone. But I remember picking it up once and saying, 'Hi, honey.' It turned out to be Chris. He wanted to bounce an idea off me."

Over time, Kryzwicki became a key ally in Newell's campaign. "I would call Jim to test out strategies," Newell says. "But he always gave me more than just information. He became a cheerleader, a champion. He started bringing my ideas to people or into meetings that I couldn't reach" (*Fast Company*, April 1998, p. 160).

QUESTIONS

1. What is Newell's approach?

2. Is Newell a skillful office politician, or just a pest?

3. Lotus Institute is part of the corporate behemoth IBM. Does this fact make the skillful use of politics more important, or less important? What is your reasoning?

SOURCE: *Michael Warshaw, "The Good Guy's (and Gal's) Guide to Office Politics,"* Fast Company, *April 1998, pp. 156–160. See also* www.fastcompany.com/online/14/politics.html.

shorten some of the complicated procedures in getting government contracts approved. The Clinton administration attempted to decrease this blatant use of vital information by establishing a lag time between departure from a government post and assumption of certain types of jobs.

3. *Keep informed.* In addition to controlling vital information, it is politically important to keep informed. Successful leaders develop a pipeline to help

them keep abreast, or ahead, of developments within the firm. For this reason, a politically astute individual befriends the president's assistant. No other source offers the potential for obtaining as much information as the executive administrative assistant.

4. *Control lines of communication.* Related to controlling information is controlling lines of communication, particularly access to key people. Administrative assistants and staff assistants frequently control an executive's calendar. Both insiders and outsiders must curry favor with the conduit in order to see an important executive. Although many people attempt to contact executives directly through email, some executives delegate the responsibility of screening email messages to an assistant. The assistant will also screen telephone calls, thus being selective about who can communicate directly with the executive.

5. *Bring in outside experts.* To help legitimate their positions, executives will often hire a consultant to conduct a study or cast an opinion. Consciously or unconsciously, many consultants are hesitant to "bite the hand that feeds them." A consultant will therefore often support the executive's position. In turn, the executive will use the consultant's findings to prove that he or she is right. This tactic might be considered ethical because the executive believes he or she is obtaining an objective opinion.

6. *Make a quick showing.* A display of dramatic results can help gain acceptance for one's efforts or those of the group.[32] Once a person has impressed management with his or her ability to solve that first problem, that person can look forward to working on problems that will bring greater power. A staff professional might volunteer to spruce up a company web site to make it more appealing ("have a greater eyeball count"). After accomplishing that feat, the person might be invited to join the ecommerce team.

7. *Remember that everyone expects to be paid back.* According to the Law of Reciprocity, everybody in the world expects to be paid back.[33] If you do not find some way to reimburse people for the good deeds they have done for you, your supply of people to perform good deeds will run short. Because many of these good deeds bring you power, such as by supporting your initiative, your power base will soon erode. As a way of paying back the person who supported your initiative, you might mention publicly how the person in question provided you with expert advice on the technical aspects of your proposal.

Strategies and Tactics Aimed at Building Relationships.   Much of organizational politics involves building positive relationships with network members who can be helpful now or later. This network includes superiors, subordinates, other lower-ranking people, coworkers, external customers, and suppliers. The following are several representative strategies and tactics:

1. *Display loyalty.* A loyal worker is valued because organizations prosper more with loyal than with disloyal employees. Blind loyalty—the belief that the organization cannot make a mistake—is not called for; most rational

organizations welcome constructive criticism. An obvious form of loyalty to the organization is longevity. Although job-hopping is more acceptable today than in the past, tenure with the company is still an asset for promotion. Tenure tends to contribute more to promotability in a traditional industry such as automobile manufacturing than in high-technology firms.

2. *Manage your impression.* Impression management includes behaviors directed at enhancing one's image by drawing attention to oneself. Often the attention of others is directed toward superficial aspects of the self, such as clothing and grooming. Yet impression management also deals with deeper aspects of behavior, such as speaking well and presenting one's ideas coherently. Another part of impression management is to tell people about your success or imply that you are an "insider." Email is used extensively today to send messages to others for the purpose of impressing them with one's good deeds. Displaying good business etiquette has received renewed attention as a key part of impression management, with companies sending staff members to etiquette classes to learn how to create favorable impressions on key people. Many management scholars take a dim view of impression management, yet the topic has been carefully researched.[34] Leadership Self-Assessment Quiz 7-4 provides you with an opportunity to relate impression management to yourself.

3. *Ask satisfied customers to contact your boss.* A favorable comment by a customer receives considerable weight because customer satisfaction is a top corporate priority. If a customer says something nice, the comment will carry more weight than one from a coworker or subordinate. The reason is that coworkers and subordinates might praise a person for political reasons. Customers' motivation is assumed to be pure because they have little concern about pleasing suppliers.

4 *Be courteous, pleasant, and positive.* Employment specialist Robert Half said years ago that courteous, pleasant, and positive people are the first to be hired and the last to be fired (assuming they also have other important qualifications).[35] His comments are still valid today, particularly because many people believe that civility has become a rare quality.

5. *Ask advice.* Asking advice on work-related topics builds relationships with other employees. Asking another person for advice—someone whose job does not require giving it—will usually be perceived as a compliment. Asking advice transmits a message of trust in the other person's judgment.

6. *Send thank-you notes to large numbers of people.* One of the most basic political tactics, sending thank-you notes profusely, is simply an application of sound human relations. Many successful people take the time to send handwritten notes to employees and customers to help create a bond with those people. In the words of Tom Peters, "The power of a thank you (note or otherwise) is hard—make that impossible—to beat."[36]

7. *Flatter others sensibly.* Flattery in the form of sincere praise can be an effective relationship builder. By being judicious in your praise, you can lower

Leadership Self-Assessment Quiz 7–4

The Manager Impression Survey

INSTRUCTIONS   Respond to each of the following statements on the following scale: VI = very infrequently; I = infrequently; S = sometimes; F = frequently; VF = very frequently. The VI to VF categories correspond to a 1-to-5 scale. If you do not have a manager currently, think of a previous relationship with a manager, or how you would behave if you were placed in the situation being described.

To what extent do you   **Frequency**

1. Do personal favors for your manager (such as getting   **VI I S F VF**
    him or her coffee or a soft drink)?

2. Offer to do something for your manager that you were   **VI I S F VF**
    not required to do, but are doing as a personal favor?

3. Compliment your immediate manager on his or her   **VI I S F VF**
    dress or appearance?

4. Praise your immediate manager on his or her   **VI I S F VF**
    accomplishments?

5. Take an interest in your manager's personal life?   **VI I S F VF**

6. Try to be polite when interacting with your manager?   **VI I S F VF**

7. Try to be a friendly person when interacting with your   **VI I S F VF**
    manager?

8. Try to act as a "model" employee, such as by never   **VI I S F VF**
    taking longer than the established time for lunch?

9. Work hard when you know the results will be seen   **VI I S F VF**
    by your manager?

10. Let your manager know that you try to do a good   **VI I S F VF**
    job in your work?

Total score: _____

SCORING AND INTERPRETATION   Score each circled response 1, 2, 3, 4, or 5 according to the scale indicated above. Use the following interpretative guide:

- 45–50   You are working diligently at creating a good impression with your manager. You show good political savvy.
- 30–44   You show moderate concern for creating a good impression with your manager. Become more sensitive to the impression you are making on your boss.
- 10–29   You are not making enough effort to create a good impression with your manager. If you want to be recognized, do a more effective job of managing your impression.

Do not underestimate the importance of creating a positive impression on the person who prepares your performance evaluation and recommends your salary increase. He or she is as important to your career as an NBA scout is to a college basketball player wanting to make it to the National Basketball Association.

SOURCE: *Adapted and expanded from Sandy J. Wayne and Robert C. Liden, "Effects of Impression Management on Performance Ratings: A Longitudinal Study,"* Academy of Management Journal, *February 1995, p. 246. Copyright © 1995 Academy of Management. Reproduced with permission of* Academy of Management *in the format Textbook via Copyright Clearance Center.*

the defenses of work associates and make them more receptive to your ideas.[37] A study on how to advance in big business pointed out that a company's top employees tend to be equal in performance. So advancing was based on image (30 percent) and contact time with the manager (50 percent).[38] Flattery can play a big role in both. An effective, general-purpose piece of flattery is to tell another person that you are impressed by something he or she has accomplished.

Strategies Aimed at Avoiding Political Blunders.   A strategy for retaining power is to refrain from making power-eroding blunders. Committing these politically insensitive acts can also prevent one from attaining power. Several leading blunders are described next.

1. *Criticizing the boss in a public forum.* The oldest saw in human relations is to "praise in public and criticize in private." Yet in the passion of the moment, we may still surrender to an irresistible impulse to criticize the boss publicly. In the early days of President Bill Clinton's administration, Senator Richard Shelby (D-Ala.) crossed Clinton publicly by criticizing his economic plan. Clinton promptly yanked federal money from a Huntsville, Alabama, project.

2. *Bypassing the boss.* Protocol is still highly valued in a hierarchical organization. Going around the boss to resolve a problem is therefore hazardous. You might be able to accomplish the bypass, but your career could be damaged and your recourses limited. Except in cases of outrageous misconduct such as blatant sexual harassment or criminal misconduct, your boss's boss will probably side with your boss.

3. *Declining an offer from top management.* Turning down top management, especially more than once, is a political blunder. You thus have to balance sensibly managing your time against the blunder of refusing a request from top management. Today, an increasing number of managers and corporate professionals decline opportunities for promotion when the new job requires geographic relocation. For these people, family and lifestyle preferences are more important than gaining political advantage on the job.

4. *Putting your foot in your mouth* (being needlessly tactless). To avoid hurting your career, it is important to avoid—or at least minimize—being blatantly tactless toward influential people. An example would be telling the CEO that he should delegate speech making to another person because he or she is such a poor speaker. "You don't get to be a senior person if you are repeatedly tactless," advises Hal Reiter, head of a New York recruiting firm.[39] When you feel you are on the verge of being critical, delay your response, and perhaps reword it for later delivery. Use your emotional intelligence! If you are needlessly tactless, compensate the best you can by offering a full apology later.

Unethical Political Tactics and Strategies

Any technique of gaining power can be devious if practiced in the extreme. A person who supports a boss by feeding him or her insider information that could affect the price of company stock is being devious. Some approaches are unequivocally unethical, such as those described next. In the long run they erode a leader's effectiveness by lowering his or her credibility. Devious tactics might even result in lawsuits against the leader, the organization, or both.

Back Stabbing. The ubiquitous back stab requires that you pretend to be nice, but all the while plan someone's demise. A frequent form of back stabbing is to initiate a conversation with a rival about the weaknesses of a common boss, encouraging negative commentary and making careful mental notes of what the person says. When these comments are passed along to the boss, the rival appears disloyal and foolish. Email has become a medium for back stabbing. The sender of the message documents a mistake made by another individual and includes key people on the distribution list. A sample message sent by one manager to a rival began as follows, "Hi, Ted. I'm sorry you couldn't make our important meeting. I guess you had some other important priorities. But we need your input on the following major agenda item we tackled. . . ."

Embrace or Demolish. The ancient strategy of "embrace or demolish" suggests that you remove from the premises rivals who suffered past hurts through your efforts; otherwise the wounded rivals might retaliate at a vulnerable moment. This kind of strategy is common after a hostile takeover; many executives lose their jobs because they opposed the takeover.

A variation of embrace or demolish is to terminate managers from the acquired organization who oppose adapting to the culture of the new firm. When Daimler-Benz AG merged with Chrysler Corporation to form DaimlerChrysler, a culture clash existed despite efforts by top management to smooth out the differences. Chrysler's free-wheeling culture clashed with the more rigid Daimler management system. The German executives exercised more power, and more former Chrysler executives "resigned" than did former Daimler-Benz executives.[40]

Setting a Person Up for Failure.   The object of a setup is to place a person in a position where he or she will either fail outright or look ineffective. For example, an executive whom the CEO dislikes might be given responsibility for a troubled division whose market is rapidly collapsing. The newly assigned division president cannot stop the decline and is then fired for poor performance.

Divide and Rule.   An ancient military and governmental strategy, this tactic is sometimes used in business. The object is to have subordinates fight among themselves, therefore yielding the balance of power to another person. If team members are not aligned with one another, there is an improved chance that they will align with a common superior. One way of getting subordinates to fight with one another is to place them in intense competition for resources. An example would be asking them to prove why their budget is more worthy than the budget requested by rivals.

Playing Territorial Games.   Also referred to as turf wars, **territorial games** involve protecting and hoarding resources that give one power, such as information, relationships, and decision-making authority. Territorial behavior, according to Annette Simmons, is based on a hidden force that limits peoples' desire to give full cooperation. People are biologically programmed to be greedy for whatever they think it takes to survive in the corporate environment.

The purpose of territorial games is to vie for the three kinds of *territory* in the modern corporate survival game: information, relationships, or authority. A relationship is "hoarded" in such ways as not encouraging others to visit a key customer, or blocking a high performer from getting a promotion or transfer.[41] For example, the manager might tell others that his star performer is mediocre to prevent the person from being considered for a valuable transfer possibility. Other examples of territorial games include monopolizing time with clients, scheduling meetings so someone cannot attend, and shutting out coworkers from joining you on an important assignment.

Doing Leadership Skill-Building Exercise 7-2 will give you further practical insights into political behavior. Since the material deals with a sensitive issue, we recommend that you proceed with a positive attitude.

EXERCISING CONTROL OVER DYSFUNCTIONAL POLITICS

Carried to excess, organizational politics can hurt an organization and its members. Too much politicking can result in wasted time and effort, thereby lowering productivity. A recent study of 1,370 employees in four organizations investigated how the perception of political behavior was related to certain outcomes. Among the many findings were the following:

- Perceptions of political behavior taking place in the work group were associated with less commitment to the organization and a stronger turnover intention (planning to leave the firm voluntarily).

Leadership Skill-Building Exercise 7-2

Classroom Politics

Gather in groups of about five students. Each group's task is to identify student political behaviors you have observed in this or other classes. Label the tactics you have observed, and indicate what you think the political actor hoped to achieve by the tactic. Also attempt to indicate what the political behavior achieved. Finally, summarize the leadership implications of what you have observed. If time permits, each team appoints a leader who presents the team's findings to the rest of the class.

The potential contribution of this exercise is that it may help raise your awareness of political behavior around you. Recognizing political behavior can be useful if you want to help prevent unethical and manipulative tactics.

- Perceptions of political behavior taking place throughout the organization were also associated with less commitment to the organization and a stronger turnover intention.[42]

Another study about the impact of organizational politics in the workplace found that conscientiousness could be a moderating factor. Data collected from 234 male and 579 female workers in four organizations indicated that when conscientious workers perceived a high level of political activity they tended to perform better. However, workers who were average or low in conscientiousness tended to perform poorly when they perceived politics to be present. One implication is that if workers are not highly conscientious, they get discouraged and perform poorly if there is too much politicking.[43]

The human consequences of excessive negative and unethical politics can also be substantial. Examples include lowered morale and loss of people who intensely dislike office politics. To avoid these negative consequences, leaders are advised to combat political behavior when it is excessive and dysfunctional.

In a comprehensive strategy to control politics, *organizational leaders must be aware of its causes and techniques.* For example, during a downsizing the CEO can be on the alert for instances of back stabbing and transparent attempts to please him or her. Open communication also can constrain the impact of political behavior. For instance, open communication can let everyone know the basis for allocating resources, thus reducing the amount of politicking. If people know in advance how resources are allocated, the effectiveness of attempting to curry favor with the boss will be reduced. When communication is open, it also makes it more difficult for some people to control information and pass along gossip as a political weapon.

Avoiding favoritism—that is, avoiding giving the best rewards to the group members you like the most—is a potent way of minimizing politics within a

Controlling Office Politics

One student plays the role of a corporate executive visiting one of the key divisions. Six other students play the roles of managers within the division, each of whom wants to impress the boss during their meeting. The corporate executive gets the meeting started by asking the managers in turn to discuss their recent activities and accomplishments. Each division-level manager will attempt to create a very positive impression on the corporate executive. After about fifteen minutes of observing them fawning over him or her, the executive decides to take action against such excessive politicking. Review the information on political tactics and their control before carrying out this role-assuming exercise.

work group. If group members believe that getting the boss to like them is much less important than good job performance in obtaining rewards, they will kiss up to the boss less frequently. In an attempt to minimize favoritism, the manager must reward workers who impress him or her through task-related activities.

Setting good examples at the top of the organization can help reduce the frequency and intensity of organizational politics. When leaders are nonpolitical in their actions, they demonstrate in subtle ways that political behavior is not welcome. It may be helpful for the leader to announce during a staff meeting that devious political behavior is undesirable and unprofessional.

Another way of reducing the extent of political behavior is for *individuals and the organization to share the same goals*, a situation described as *goal congruence*. If political behavior will interfere with the company and individuals achieving their goals, workers with goal congruence are less likely to play office politics excessively. A project leader is less likely to falsely declare that the boss's idea is good just to please the boss if the project leader wants the company to succeed.

L. A. Witt conducted a study with 1,200 workers in five organizations that lends support to the importance of goal congruence in combating politics. Witt concluded that one way to approach the negative impact of organizational politics is for the manager to ensure that group members hold the appropriate goal priorities. In this way they will have a greater sense of control over and understanding of the workplace and thus be less affected by organizational politics.[44]

Politics can sometimes be constrained by a *threat to discuss questionable information in a public forum*. People who practice devious politics usually want to operate secretly and privately. They are willing to drop hints and innuendoes and make direct derogatory comments about someone else, provided they will not be identified as the source. An effective way of stopping the discrediting of others is to offer to discuss the topic publicly.[45] The person attempting to pass on the questionable information will usually back down and make a statement closer to the truth.

Finally, *hiring people with integrity* will help reduce the number of dysfunctional political players. References should be checked carefully with respect to the candidate's integrity and honesty.[46] Say to the reference, "Tell me about _____'s approach to playing politics." Leadership Skill-Building Exercise 7-3 provides an opportunity to practice the subtle art of discouraging excessive political behavior on the job.

SUMMARY

Organizational power is derived from many sources, including position power (legitimate, reward, coercive, and information) and personal power (expert, reference, and prestige). Power also stems from ownership, control of resources, capitalizing upon opportunity, managing critical problems, and being close to power. A study cited here shows that referent power, expert power, and reward power contribute to the leader's being perceived as transformational.

Full-fledged empowerment includes the dimensions of meaning, self-determination, competence, impact, and internal commitment. Actions that can be taken to become an empowering leader include the following: foster initiative and responsibility, link work activities to the goals of the organization, provide ample information, allow group members to choose methods, encourage self-leadership, implement team-based human resource policies, establish limits to empowerment, and continue to lead. Also, take into account cultural differences in how empowerment is accepted.

Delegation is another important part of empowerment. To be effective, delegation should follow certain guidelines, such as assigning tasks to the right people, delegating whole tasks, stepping back from details, and evaluating and rewarding performance. Delegation is an opportunity to coach the person who has accepted the delegated tasks.

To acquire and retain power, a leader must skillfully use organizational politics. The meaning of *politics* continues to shift in a positive, constructive direction. Contributing factors to organizational politics include the pyramidal shape of organizations, subjective performance standards, environmental uncertainty, emotional insecurity, Machiavellianism, and disagreement over major issues.

To make effective use of organizational politics, leaders must be aware of specific political tactics and strategies. Ethical methods can be divided into those aimed directly at gaining power, those aimed at building relationships, and those aimed at avoiding political blunders. Unethical and devious tactics, such as the embrace-or-demolish strategy, constitute another category of political behavior.

Carried to extremes, organizational politics can hurt an organization and its members. Being aware of the causes and types of political behavior can help leaders deal with the problem. Setting good examples of nonpolitical behavior is helpful, as is achieving goal congruence and threatening to publicly expose devious politicking. It is also good to hire people with integrity.

KEY TERMS

Power

Legitimate power

Reward power

Coercive power

Information power

Personal power

Prestige power

Resource dependence perspective

Strategic contingency theory

Centrality

Empowerment

Delegation

Organizational politics

Territorial games

GUIDELINES FOR ACTION AND SKILL DEVELOPMENT

To enhance your interpersonal effectiveness at the outset of joining a firm, it is helpful to size up the political climate. Even if you are new to the firm, it will often be helpful to ask the following seven diagnostic questions during meetings:

1. What method do people use here to offer new ideas?

2. How do staff members offer opposing ideas or disagreement?

3. How much evidence is required and what type of evidence is required to persuade other staff members?

4. What responses does assertive behavior elicit? What facial expressions do you see around the table when someone presents a strong idea? Whose words elicit nods from the meeting leader? Whose words prompt the reaction "Let's move on"?

5. How much personal reference is tolerated?

6. How much display of emotional intensity is tolerated?

7. Who gets heard? Promoted? Passed over?[47]

DISCUSSION QUESTIONS AND ACTIVITIES

1. Why do so many people think that possessing power is a good thing?

2. How can a leader occupy a top-level executive position and still have relatively little power?

3. It is not unusual for a new CEO to receive a signing bonus of around $10 million. Which kind of power or powers do these executives have to command such a large signing bonus?

4. How might you use the Internet to acquire information power?

5. Many business leaders say something to the effect, "We practice empowerment because we don't expect our employees to leave their brains at the door." What are these leaders talking about?

6. Empowerment has been criticized because it leaves no one in particular accountable for results. What is your opinion of this criticism?

7. How does participative leadership contribute to delegation?

8. Why are entrepreneurial leaders often poor delegators?

9. Many people have asked the question "Isn't office politics just for incompetents?" What is your answer to this question?

10. Ask an experienced worker to give you an example of back stabbing that he or she has personally witnessed. Find out what eventually happened to both the stabber and the person stabbed.

Leadership Case Problem A

The Powerful Mr. Trump

The occasion was an interview by a veteran *Fortune* reporter. Donald Trump wasted no time being Donald Trump. "I've brought some things for you," he said, handing the reporter a sheaf of papers as he boarded his private 727. (Trump was on his way to Minnesota, where he was to meet with Governor Jesse Ventura to discuss running for president on the Reform Party Ticket.) These included some glossy brochures and a copy of *New York Construction News*, which had named Trump owner and developer of the year for 1999. "Owner *and* developer of the year," he pointed out, "which is unusual" (*Fortune*, April 3, 2000, p. 189).

At age 53, Trump is possibly the most famous businessman in America. According to the Gallup Organization, fully 98 percent of Americans know who he is. Bill Gates also scores in the high 90s. Roger Stone, Trump's political adviser, says, "I think people say, 'If I won the lottery, that's how I'd want to live.' The plane, the boat, the estate in Florida, the beautiful girls (women supermodels)—our polling showed that people identified with it" (*Fortune*, April 3, 2000, p. 192).

The web site *AskMen.com* offers a similar perspective on Trump. The site explains why the editors like him: "Not like him, we *love* him. He is funny, smart, and unlike seemingly every other billionaire in the world, he lives the privileged life that we can only dream of."

Trump said on the plane, "I was a little surprised *Fortune* hadn't done a cover on me in the last year and a half, because I'm the biggest developer in New York. Now I'm getting story not because I'm the biggest real estate developer but because I'm running for president. There's something about that that I don't really like" (*Fortune*, April 3, 2000, p. 192).

The Trump Empire. The Trump enterprise has complex deals that make it difficult for an outsider to estimate the true worth of Trump's holdings. The Trump organization has 22,000 employees. Exhibit 1 outlines the major Trump holdings. One problem is that Trump puts an exaggerated positive spin on what he owns. When he says he is building a ninety-story skyscraper next to the United Nations, he means a seventy-two-story building that has extra-high ceilings. And when he says his casino company is the "largest employer in the state of New Jersey," he actually means to say it is the eighth largest (*Fortune*, April 3, 2000, p. 194).

Although Trump is prone to self-puffery, he is regarded as an enormously skilled developer. Associates describe an unfailing knack for spotting and ferreting out waste; a memory like a Zip drive; and a grasp of complex zoning laws that he uses to exploit opportunities. Trump is also

EXHIBIT 1   Donald Trump Company Holdings, Organized Geographically

Location	Name of Property	Key Characteristic(s)
Atlantic City	Trump Marina	Gaming revenues, $273 million
	Taj Mahal	Gaming revenues, $525 million
	Trump Plaza	Gaming revenues, $359 million
Palm Beach	Mar-a-Lago	Residence with 33 bathrooms
Manhattan	Trump Place	10 million square feet, over 18 buildings
	General Motors Building	Paid $800 million in 1998
	Trump Tower	757,000 square feet
	Trump World Tower	1.3 million square feet
	Empire State Building	Owns 50% of land underneath
	40 Wall Street	1.1 million square feet
Westchester County, N.Y.	Briar Hill County Club	Closed for repairs
	Seven Springs	Seeking zoning approval
	Indian Hills	Seeking zoning approval
	French Hills	Seeking zoning approval

familiar with technical details of construction, such as the energy efficiency of window glass. He negotiates with subcontractors himself instead of relying on a purchasing department, and he will sometimes use his celebrity status to attain better terms. "He has the ability to relate to the doorman, to the guy who's carrying the iron or steel, and make that guy feel important," says the CEO of a real estate financing firm (*Fortune,* April 3, 2000, p. 194).

In recent years Trump has refrained from putting up large sums of his own money. Instead, he forms a partnership with financial backers that want to tap the power of his name and retain him as sort of a jungle guide. Investors can be readily found because people pay more to live in a Trump building. His condos command an 80 percent premium. Trump's rivals accuse him of being a mere front man for financial interests—a brand slapped on buildings he does not own. Trump denies the charges, saying that he owns at least 50 percent of all the deals he does.

Trump's partners are pleased with his accomplishments. A financier who hired Trump to convert the Mayfair Regent Hotel into condos said: "Bottom line is, the project came in under budget four months ahead of schedule and at prices that were 40 percent above what we had pro forma'd. We didn't have one work stoppage, not one strike not one red city tag. Everything was perfect." Even former New York mayor Ed Koch, a Trump hater if there ever was one, said he is a great builder (*Fortune*, April 3, 2000, p. 196).

Trump Problems. The Trump organization faces difficulty with its casino company, Trump Hotels & Casino Resorts. The company was originally taken public to help Trump stave off bankruptcy in the early 1990s. The strategy worked, and the company was considered a remarkable business turnaround at the time. Today, Trump's 42 percent stake in the company has shriveled from more than $500 million to $53 million. The hotels and casinos generate substantial cash, but much of the money is needed to finance the $1.8 billion high-yield debt that has saddled the company since its inception. Debt servicing eats up $216 million in cash flow.

Another problem is that Trump tends to use the casino company as his personal piggy bank. One year he voted himself a $5 million bonus from the company, the pilots of his personal 727 are on the casino company's payroll, and he borrowed $26 million from the company to pay off a personal loan. Trump denies misusing company funds, saying he would "sue the ass off of FORTUNE" if an article in the magazine disparaged his cash flow (*Fortune*, April 3, 2000, p. 198). A related problem is that some investors shy away from Trump stock because of Donald Trump's flamboyance.

QUESTIONS

1. Which sources of power does Trump use?

2. What steps can Donald Trump take to be perceived more positively by outside observers such as reporters and business professors?

3. If you were Trump's executive coach, what advice would you offer him?

4. How would you describe Trump's interpersonal skills?

SOURCE: *Jerry Useem, "What Does Donald Trump® Really Want?"Fortune, April 3, 2000, pp. 188–200; www.AskMen.com.*

Leadership Case Problem B

Empowerment at Seconds for You

Jenny Parsons was raised in a family of retailers. Her mom and dad owned several different retail stores, including a hardware store, and a home-improvement business. As her parents approached their mid-sixties, they were operating two home-improvement stores that competed directly with national chains such as Home Depot and Lowe's. By that time, Jenny had worked for the family business for five years.

Parsons and her parents decided to revamp their business model. Instead of competing for the same market as traditional home-improvement stores, they would aim at a market one notch lower. The stores were to be named Seconds for You and would feature manufacturer rejects or "seconds," along with inventory manufacturers could not sell at their usual profit margins. The store would also purchase merchandise from other hardware and home-improvement stores that had gone out of business for one reason or another. Representative Seconds for You specials included cinder blocks at 37 cents each, 13 inch black and white television sets for $39, and folding tables for $25.95.

The Parsons family recognized that to operate the two Seconds for You stores profitably, operating costs would have to be reduced substantially. Mom and Dad would become the buyers for the store, at a salary of $15,000 per year each; Jenny would draw a salary of $40,000 and operate the stores. Any new employees would be paid close to the minimum wage, even if it meant hiring workers who had probably been rejected by other retail stores. Among the reject factors could be lack of a high school diploma, limited verbal skills, or an unprofessional appearance.

Dad said to Jenny, "Our planned operating budget sure does cut expenses to the bone, but you are taking on too much responsibility. Each store is about 15,000 square feet, and the merchandise assortment will be enormous. You might need a store manager for each outlet, especially for such matters as approving customer checks."

"Have no fear, Mom and Dad, I have a plan. I'll organize the staff into teams, appoint a few team leaders, and pay them $1.00 more per hour than the other associates. And then, I will *empower* the team leaders and the associates to make managerial decisions. Have you read about empowerment in the business pages?"

Mom replied, "Oh yes, I've read about empowerment, but we're not Wal-Mart or Target. We may not be able to get away with empower-

ing associates who have no interest in retailing as a career."

Jenny responded, "Don't be so sure. Seconds for You might be ready for a modern approach to managing a retail store."

When Jenny met with the store associates to explain the empowerment plan, she encountered a range of reactions. One of the seniors hired primarily to answer customer questions and give advice about home-improvement projects said, "Suits me fine, Jenny. I've been fixing things around the house for forty years, so I think I can handle the responsibility. I won't be needing much help from a boss."

A newly hired 18-year-old cashier said, "Sounds to me like you're asking us to do the work of a supervisor, yet still pay us the minimum wage. I don't think I'm ready to work without supervision." Jenny assured her that the team leader would be available to help, even though the team leader's primary responsibilities were dealing with customers and organizing the merchandise.

Six months after the empowerment program was implemented, Jenny began to wonder if she had made the right decision. The two stores were generally operating smoothly, and Jenny even took off several Sunday afternoons, the busiest day for Seconds for You. Yet several problems did surface. One of the cashiers let three customer checks get past her that bounced. In each case, the cashier had not obtained the three points of identification required for accepting a check. The cashier's plea to Jenny was "It wasn't my fault—each customer had a good story, and they all looked honest. You told me I had the power to accept a check. Besides, you or your parents weren't around to give me any help."

Another problem was inventory shrinkage. Some customers appeared to be loading into their vehicles more merchandise than they paid for, especially with bulk items like lumber, cinder blocks, and topsoil. One of the team leaders explained, "It's tough organizing the merchandise, helping customers, and trying to supervise the loadings all at the same time. I'm supposed to be doing everything at once."

Jenny told the associates, "It looks like we have a couple of holes to plug. But I have too much faith in you to give up on empowerment yet."

QUESTIONS

1. How applicable is empowerment to Seconds for You?

2. How might Jenny Parsons become a more effective empowering leader?

3. What is your evaluation of the business model (basic idea for a business) at Seconds for You?

INTERNET SKILL-BUILDING EXERCISE

Apply the chapter concepts! Visit the Web and complete this Internet skill-building exercise to learn more about current leadership topics and trends.

The Dysfunctional Office and Organizational Politics Scale

Go to www.andersonconsulting.com/doopinto.htm (not to be confused with *Arthur Andersen Consulting*). The test offered there deals with ethics in interpersonal relations, so it might offer you some insights into your interpersonal skills. Navigating through the test requires some adeptness at following directions about using the mouse, but you will be rewarded with a score for the politics test.

Influence Tactics of Leaders

CHAPTER 8

Christina "CJ" Juhasz is a 1990 graduate of the U.S. Military Academy at West Point, New York. Today Juhasz is a director in online ventures at Merrill Lynch. In reflecting on the leadership lessons for business she learned at West Point, Juhasz notes:

> I led a team of incoming plebes during basic training. I thought I had to lead the way I saw others doing it—with stress and shouting like a traditional drill sergeant. Well, my unit performed very badly. And they hated me. That experience shook me up. I realized that leadership isn't rule based. It isn't about stress. It's about inspiration, about setting and communicating a vision. It's about gaining trust. Once you have someone's trust, once you get them [him or her] on the same page, they [he or she] don't [doesn't] want to disappoint you. Then leading becomes very easy.[1]

Christina Juhasz learned early in her career that a leader must use a variety of influence tactics, including inspiration, to achieve important goals. Without effective influence tactics a leader is similar to a soccer player who hasn't learned to kick a soccer ball, or a newscaster who is unable to speak.

Leadership, as oft repeated, is an influence process. To become an effective leader, a person must be aware of the specific tactics leaders use to influence others. Here we discuss a number of specific influence tactics, but other aspects of leadership also concern influence. Being charismatic, as described in Chapter 3, influences many people. Leaders influence others through power and politics, as described in Chapter 7. Furthermore, motivating and coaching skills, as described in Chapter 10, involve influencing others toward worthwhile ends.

The terms *influence* and *power* have understandable, everyday meanings yet present complexities to the scholar. The two terms are sometimes used interchangeably, whereas at other times power is said to create influence and vice versa. In this book, we distinguish between power and influence as follows: **Influence** is the ability to affect the behavior of others in a particular direction,[2] whereas power is the potential or capacity to influence. Keep in mind, however, that recognizing power as the ability to influence others will not interfere with learning how to use influence tactics. Secretary of State Colin Powell says that power is the capacity to influence and inspire.[3]

Leaders are influential only when they exercise power. A leader therefore must acquire power to influence others. Assume that a worker is the informal leader among a group of product developers. The worker exerts a modicum of influence because of his talent, charm, and wit. Move the person into the position of vice president of product development (more formal authority), and his or her influence will multiply.

This chapter presents a simplified model of power and influence, a description and explanation of influence tactics (both ethical and less ethical), and a summary of the research about the relative effectiveness and sequencing of influence tactics.

A MODEL OF POWER AND INFLUENCE

The model shown in Figure 8-1 illustrates that the end results of a leader's influence outcomes are a function of the influence tactics he or she uses. The influence tactics are in turn moderated, or affected by, the leader's traits, the leader's behaviors, and the situation.

Looking at the right side of the model, the three possible outcomes are commitment, compliance, and resistance. **Commitment** is the most successful outcome: The target of the influence attempt is enthusiastic about carrying out the request and makes a full effort. Commitment is particularly important for a complex, difficult task because full concentration and effort are required. If you were influencing a technician to upgrade your operating system software, you would need his or her commitment.

Compliance means that the influence attempt is partially successful: The target person is apathetic (not overjoyed) about carrying out the request and makes only a modest effort. The influence agent has changed the person's behavior but not his or her attitude. A long-distance truck driver might comply with demands that he sleep certain hours between hauls, but he is not enthusiastic about losing road time. Compliance for routine tasks—such as wearing a hard hat on a construction site—is usually good enough.

Resistance is an unsuccessful influence attempt: The target is opposed to carrying out the request and finds ways to either not comply or do a poor job. Resis-

FIGURE 8-1   A Model of Power and Influence

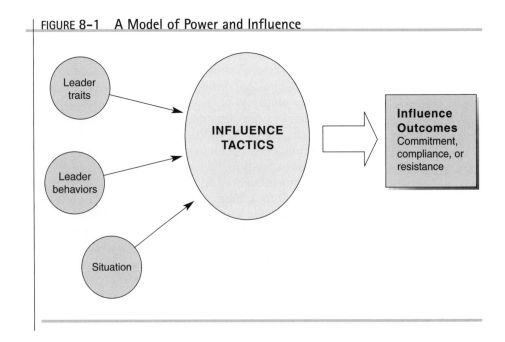

tance includes making excuses for why the task cannot be carried out, procrastination, and outright refusal to do the task.[4]

Going to the left side of the model, the leader's personality traits affect the outcome of influence tactics. For example, an extroverted and warm leader who has personal magnetism can more readily use some influence tactics than a leader who is introverted and cold. For example, he or she can make an inspirational appeal. A highly intelligent leader would be able to influence others because he or she has built a reputation as a subject matter expert.

The leader's behaviors also affect the outcome of influence tactics in a variety of ways, particularly because influence tactics *are* actions or behaviors. For example, setting high standards (refer back to Chapter 4) facilitates making an inspirational appeal. As another example, the leader who provides stable performance is better able to lead by example because he or she is a good role model.

Finally, the situation partly determines which influence tactic will be effective. The organizational culture or subculture is one such key situational factor. For example, in a high-technology environment inspirational appeal, emotional display, and personal magnetism are less likely to be effective than rational persuasion and being a subject matter expert, because high-tech workers are more likely to be impressed by facts than by feeling.

The rest of this chapter identifies and describes influence tactics, including some mention of situational variables. Leader traits and power have been described in previous chapters. Leadership Self-Assessment Quiz 8-1 will give you an opportunity to think about which influence tactics you tend to use.

DESCRIPTION AND EXPLANATION OF INFLUENCE TACTICS

Influence tactics are often viewed from an ethical perspective. Following this perspective, the influence tactics described here are classified into those that are essentially ethical and honest versus those that are essentially manipulative and dishonest.

The categorization presented here is far from absolute. Except for the extremes, most of the tactics could conceivably be placed in either category, depending on how they are used. For example, the tactic "joking and kidding" can be either good spirited or mean spirited. Joking and kidding could therefore be classified as "essentially ethical" or "essentially manipulative."

Essentially Ethical and Honest Tactics

This section describes essentially ethical and honest tactics and strategies for influencing others, as outlined in Table 8-1 (page 236). Used with tact, diplomacy, and good intent, these strategies can facilitate getting others to join you in

Survey of Influence Tactics

INSTRUCTIONS   Indicate how frequently you use the influence tactics listed below. VI = very infrequently or never; I = infrequently; S = sometimes; F = frequently; VF = very frequently. The VI to VF categories correspond to a 1-to-5 scale.

	1 VI	2 I	3 S	4 F	5 VF
1. I am a team player.	___	___	___	___	___
2. I am personally charming.	___	___	___	___	___
3. I make a good personal appearance.	___	___	___	___	___
4. I manipulate the situation.	___	___	___	___	___
5. I manipulate people.	___	___	___	___	___
6. I am assertive (open and forthright in my demands).	___	___	___	___	___
7. I joke with or kid other people.	___	___	___	___	___
8. I exchange favors with the other person.	___	___	___	___	___
9. I promise to reward the person.	___	___	___	___	___
10. I threaten to punish the person.	___	___	___	___	___
11. I get the other person to like me.	___	___	___	___	___
12. I make an appeal to logic or reason.	___	___	___	___	___
13. I form an alliance with the other person.	___	___	___	___	___
14. I threaten to go over the person's head to the boss.	___	___	___	___	___
15. I compliment the other person.	___	___	___	___	___
16. I offer to compromise with the other person.	___	___	___	___	___

SCORING AND INTERPRETATION   The more of the above tactics you use frequently or very frequently, the more influential you probably are. You might also want to compare your scores to normative data. Listed below are the mean scores on each tactic for a group of 523 working adults (292 men and 231 women). The sample was composed of mostly managers and professionals. You will recall that the scale runs from 1 for *very infrequently* to 5 for *very frequently*.

Influence Tactic	Men	Women
1. Team play	4.1	4.2
2. Charm	3.3	3.5
3. Appearance	3.3	3.5
4. Manipulation of situation	3.1	2.7*
5. Manipulation of person	2.6	2.3*
6. Assertiveness	3.9	3.9
7. Joking or kidding	3.7	3.5
8. Exchange of favors	2.9	3.0
9. Promise of reward	2.5	2.2*
10. Threat of punishment	1.8	1.5*
11. Ingratiation	3.2	3.2
12. Logic or reason	4.3	4.1*
13. Alliances	3.3	3.5
14. Threat of appeal	1.5	1.6
15. Compliments	3.6	3.5
16. Compromise	3.4	3.5

SKILL DEVELOPMENT   In comparing your profile to the norms, it could be apparent that you are neglecting to use, or are overusing, one or more influence tactics. For example, being a team player is used "frequently" by men and women. If you are not using team play to influence others, you could be at a competitive disadvantage. Observe also that both men and women make "very infrequent" use of threats of appeal. If you are making threats of appeal very frequently, you could be perceived as using an unacceptable influence tactic.

*Differences between the means are significant at or beyond the 1 percent level of significance.

SOURCE: *Reproduced with permission of the publisher from DuBrin, A. J. "Sex and Gender Differences in Tactics of Influence,"* Psychological Reports, *1991, 68, 635–646.* © *Psychological Reports 1991.*

accomplishing a worthwhile objective. Because these influence tactics vary in complexity, they also vary with respect to how much time is required to develop them.

Leading by Example.   A simple but effective way of influencing group members is by **leading by example,** or acting as a positive role model. The ideal approach is to be a "do as I say and do" manager—that is, one whose actions and words are consistent. Actions and words confirm, support, and often clarify each other.

Bob Nardelli, the CEO of The Home Depot, Inc. (and former GE executive) is an extreme case of leading by example. Out of bed at 5 A.M., he is in the office by 6:15 and usually works until at least 9 P.M. Saturdays and Sundays are typically workdays for him, and he calls in his executives for weekend meetings. "It's not a job," he says. "It's a life."[5] (Nardelli is not overly concerned about work-and-family issues for his management team.)

Using Rational Persuasion.   Rational persuasion is an important tactic for influencing people. It involves using logical arguments and factual evidence to

TABLE 8-1   Essentially Ethical and Honest Influence Tactics

1. Leading by example
2. Using rational persuasion
3. Developing a reputation as a subject matter expert (SME)
4. Exchanging favors and bargaining
5. Getting network members to support your position
6. Legitimating a request
7. Making an inspirational appeal and emotional display
8. Displaying personal magnetism
9. Consulting
10. Forming coalitions
11. Being a team player
12. Practicing hands-on leadership

convince another person that a proposal or request is workable and likely to re-sult in goal attainment.[6] Assertiveness combined with careful research is neces-sary to make rational persuasion an effective tactic. It is likely to be most effective with people who are intelligent and rational. Chief executive officers typically use rational persuasion to convince their boards that an undertaking, such as prod-uct diversification, is mandatory.

A major intervening variable in rational persuasion is the credibility of the in-fluence agent. The obvious link between credibility and persuasiveness is that in-fluence targets are more likely to be influenced by people they believe. A less obvious moderating effect of credibility is that credible people are perceived as having higher social power. Mitchell S. Nesler et al. conducted an experiment with college students in which the credibility and power of a manager were manipu-lated in vignettes. The results indicated that credibility had a direct effect on rat-ings of five bases of power: reward, coercive, expert, referent, and legitimate. When the subjects in the experiment were given evidence that the manager was credible, they tended to give the manager higher ratings than a counterpart who was portrayed in the vignettes as having low credibility.[7]

In short, credibility helps an individual be more persuasive in two ways. First, it makes a person more convincing. Second, credibility contributes to a person's perceived power, and the more power one is perceived to have, the more targets will be influenced.

Bob Nardelli also includes rational persuasion in his tool kit of influence tac-tics. During staff meetings, he hammers away at the logic behind having efficient business processes in place. Nardelli says, "What I'm known for is transferring best practices. That's particularly important in this economic environment, when you have to maximize revenues through existing assets."[8]

Developing a Reputation as a Subject Matter Expert.   Becoming a subject matter expert (SME) on a topic of importance to the organization is an effective strategy for gaining influence. Being an SME can be considered a subset of rational persuasion. A series of interviews conducted by Bernard Keys and Thomas Case support this observation. Managers who possess expert knowledge in a relevant field and who continually build on that knowledge can get others to help them get work accomplished.[9] Many of the leaders described throughout this text use expert knowledge to influence others.

A representative example of the SME influence tactic is Ann Moore, the chairwoman and chief executive of Time Inc., the world's largest publishing company. Her expertise centers on understanding the marketing preferences of women. One of Moore's noteworthy accomplishments was positioning *People* as a woman's magazine. Among her expert decisions was to shift from a Monday delivery to Friday, when more women would see the fresh issue in the grocery store checkout line as they do the weekly shopping.[10]

Exchanging Favors and Bargaining.   Offering to exchange favors if another person will help you achieve a work goal is another standard influence tactic. By making an exchange, you strike a bargain with the other party. The exchange often translates into being willing to reciprocate at a later date. It might also be promising a share of the benefits if the other person helps you accomplish a task. For example, you might promise to place a person's name on a report to top management if that person helps analyze the data and prepare the tables.

A recommended approach to asking for a favor is to give the other person as much time as feasible to accomplish the task, such as by saying, "Could you find ten minutes between now and the end of the month to help me?" Not pressing for immediate assistance will tend to lower resistance to the request. Giving a menu of options for different levels of assistance also helps lower resistance. A manager might ask another manager to borrow a technician for a one-month assignment. A second option might be to request that the technician work ten hours per week on the project.[11] To ensure that the request is perceived as an exchange, explain what reciprocity you have in mind, such as mentioning the coworker's helpfulness to his or her manager.

Getting Network Members to Support Your Position.   Networking is an important strategy for managing a career and becoming an influential person. The ability to establish a network and call on a member of the network when needed helps you exert influence. Other qualified people supporting your position lend credibility to it, as illustrated in the following example:

A plant general manager wanted to convince upper management that running the plant continuously would be profitable for the company. So he contacted two people to support him. The first was a plant manager from another company whose plant runs continuously, and the second was a professor of operations management. The manager in question organized a breakfast meeting with his boss, the vice president of manufacturing, and the two network members to discuss continuous plant operations. The informal discussion of the potential advantages in running three shifts convinced the vice president of manufacturing to give continuous operation a trial.

Legitimating a Request.   To legitimate is to verify that an influence attempt is within your scope of authority. Another aspect of legitimating is showing that your request is consistent with the organizational policies, practices, and expectations of professional people. Making legitimate requests is an effective influence tactic because most workers are willing to comply with regulations. A team leader can thus exert influence with a statement such as this one: "Top management wants a 25 percent reduction in customer complaints by next year. I'm therefore urging everybody to patch up any customer problems he or she can find." According to research conducted by Gary Yukl, behavior intended to establish the legitimacy of a request includes the following:

Providing evidence of prior precedent

Showing consistency with the organizational policies that are involved in the type of request being made

Showing consistency with the duties and responsibilities of the person's position or role expectations

Indicating that the request has been endorsed by higher management or by the person's boss[12]

Legitimating sometimes takes the form of subtle organizational politics. A worker might push for the acceptance of his or her initiative because it conforms to the philosophy or strategy of higher management. At Ford Motor Company, for example, it is well known that Chairman Bill Ford is "green" in the sense of wanting to preserve the external environment. A plant manager might then encourage workers to put all scrap in recycling bins because "It's something 'Bill' would want us to do."

Making an Inspirational Appeal and Emotional Display.   A leader is supposed to inspire others, so it follows that making an inspirational appeal is an important influence tactic. As Jeffrey Pfeffer notes, "Executives and others seeking to exercise influence in organizations often develop skill in displaying, or not displaying, their feelings in a strategic fashion."[13] An inspirational appeal usually involves displaying emotion and appealing to group members' emotions.

For an emotional appeal to be effective, the influence agent must understand the values, motives, and goals of the target. Often this means that the leader must explain how the group efforts will have an impact outside the company. Based on a study, Cynthia G. Emrich concluded:

Business leaders tend to think in terms of bottom-line goals, like boosting revenues or profits. But they need to speak about their goals in terms of how they will make a positive difference in the world. If you can see a goal—if you can touch, feel, and smell it—it seems more doable.[14]

Displaying Personal Magnetism.   Another way of influencing people is closely related to charisma and inspirational appeal. **Personal magnetism** refers to a captivating, inspiring, personality with charm and charismatic-like qualities. The magnetic individual literally draws other people to him or her, and thus can influence others. Personal magnetism encompasses a variety of personality traits and behaviors, and it can be developed along the same lines as charisma. Many of the leaders mentioned throughout this text have high personal magnetism. One of the best examples is Andrea Jung, CEO of Revlon (described in Chapter 3), who has a celebrity allure as she addresses large groups of Avon representatives. Even outside the glitter of being on stage at a company meeting, Jung has a magnetic impact on work associates.

Consulting.   Consulting with others before making a decision is both a leadership style and an influence technique. The influence target becomes more motivated to follow the agent's request because the target is involved in the decision-making process. Consultation is most effective as an influence tactic when the objectives of the person being influenced are consistent with those of the leader.[15]

An example of such goal congruity took place in a major U.S. corporation. The company had decided to shrink its pool of suppliers to form closer partnerships with a smaller number of high-quality vendors. As a way of influencing others to follow this direction, a manufacturing vice president told his staff, "Our strategy is to reduce dealing with so many suppliers to improve quality and reduce costs. Let me know how we should implement this strategy." The vice president's influence attempt met with excellent reception, partially because the staff members also wanted a more streamlined set of vendor relationships.

Forming Coalitions.   At times it is difficult to influence an individual or group by acting alone. A leader will then have to form coalitions, or alliances, with others to create the necessary clout. A **coalition** is a specific arrangement of parties working together to combine their power. Coalition formation works as an influence tactic because, to quote an old adage, "there is power in numbers." Coalitions in business are a numbers game—the more people you can get on your side, the better. However, the more powerful the leader is, the less he or she needs to create a coalition. The Leader in Action insert describes a leader of moderate power who has emphasized creating allies and forming coalitions in order to accomplish meritorious objectives.

Being a Team Player.   Influencing others by being a good team player is an important strategy for getting work accomplished. Refer back to Leadership Self-Assessment Quiz 8-1. Team play, along with logic or reason, was the influence tactic most frequently chosen by men and women. In one study, men and women endorsed team play more frequently than six other tactics (personal charm, manipulation, personal appearance, assertiveness, exchange of favors, and appeal to a higher authority).[16]

We return to Bob Nardelli to illustrate that most leaders use a variety of influence tactics. To adapt to his new position as the chief executive at Home Depot, Nardelli made a deliberate effort to be a team player, including shouting the

Leader in Action

Scott Sleyster at Prudential Builds Allies

After thirteen years at Prudential Insurance Company of America, Scott Sleyster has risen through the ranks to become president of Guaranteed Products, a unit that oversees a range of institutional investments. He got there by "getting things done."

Sleyster prides himself on his partnering skills. He understands how to listen, compromise, and negotiate shrewdly so that both he and his colleagues attain their mutual goals. "In a big organization, you bump off a lot of people in different ways," he says. "You run into these same people again and again, so it's important to work with them to get wins. With each win, you're in a better position to ask more of them in the future."

Sleyster learned early on that technical expertise alone doesn't guarantee success. Armed with an MBA in finance from Northwestern University, he also earned the Chartered Financial Analyst (CFA) designation. But only after climbing the ladder in Prudential's financial businesses did he develop the skill of achieving results through others.

In his current job, Sleyster often serves on teams with other senior executives. He treats these committees as opportunities to help others "optimize their interests." For example, Sleyster participates in a cross-departmental group that sets investment policy and oversees performance for a big pool of assets. He's the highest-ranking member of the team.

"I can go in a hog, declare myself king, and come away with a big win for myself," he says. "But I wasn't invited to join this team so that I could bully them." Sleyster knows that if he overwhelms the group with his demands, they'll rebel and his reputation will sour.

"To get things done, you need to have allies throughout your organization," he says. "If I'm too busy asserting my authority to listen to them, they'll remember me as the guy who railroaded them. They won't forget. When I need them later, they won't be there."

QUESTIONS

1. Which influence tactic(s) does Sleyster use?

2. Which tactic of organizational politics does he use?

3. How ethical are Sleyster's methods of influence?

SOURCE: *"Investment Exec Wins Friends, Influences People,"* Executive Leadership, *August 2000, p. 3.*

---

company cheer; wearing an orange apron whenever he visited a store; saying "sku" as shorthand for stock-keeping unit, not "S.K.U."; and accepting a kiss on the head when he greeted cofounder and chairman Bernard Marcus.[17]

Practicing Hands-on Leadership.   A **hands-on leader** is one who gets directly involved in the details and processes of operations. Such a leader has expertise, is task oriented, and leads by example. By getting directly involved in the group's work activities, the leader influences subordinates to hold certain beliefs and to follow certain procedures and processes. For example, the manager who gets directly involved in fixing customer problems demonstrates to other workers how he or she thinks such problems should be resolved.

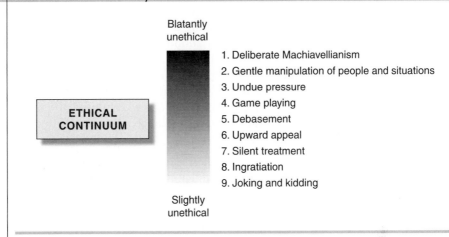

FIGURE 8-2   Essentially Dishonest and Unethical Influence Tactics

Blatantly
unethical

1. Deliberate Machiavellianism
2. Gentle manipulation of people and situations
3. Undue pressure
4. Game playing
5. Debasement
6. Upward appeal
7. Silent treatment
8. Ingratiation
9. Joking and kidding

ETHICAL
CONTINUUM

Slightly
unethical

Jean-René Fourtou is an experienced executive whose most recent assignment is to be chairman of the media giant Vivendi Universal. He has a long track record of managing companies and practices hands-on leadership to help accomplish results. "He's got a real legitimacy as a manager. He's a CEO who gets his hands dirty and goes to see people in the field," says one person familiar with Fourtou's career. "He's the opposite of an investment banker."[18]

Essentially Dishonest and Unethical Tactics

The tactics described in this section are less than forthright and ethical, yet they vary in intensity with respect to dishonesty. Most people would consider the first four strategies presented here as unethical and devious, yet they might regard the last five tactics as still within the bounds of acceptable ethics, even though less than fully candid. The tactics in question are outlined in Figure 8-2.

Deliberate Machiavellianism.   Almost 500 years ago, Niccolo Machiavelli advised that princes must be strong, ruthless, and cynical leaders because people are self-centered and self-serving. People in the workplace who ruthlessly manipulate others have therefore come to be called **Machiavellians.** They tend to initiate actions with others and control the interactions. Machiavellians regularly practice deception, bluffing, and other manipulative tactics.[19]

A current example of deliberate Machiavellianism is the practice of forcing managerial and professional employees into working many extra hours of uncompensated overtime. The employees are told that if they refuse to work extra hours, they will not be considered worthy of promotion or good team players. Even when positions in other companies are readily available, most career-minded people will stay because they want to preserve a good reputation.

Gentle Manipulation of People and Situations.   Some people who attempt to influence others are manipulative, but to a lesser extent than an outright Machiavellian. By making untrue statements or faking certain behaviors, they gain the compliance of another person. For example, a leader might imply that if a colleague supports his position in an intergroup conflict, the person *might* be recommended for promotion. A widely used manipulative approach is the **band-wagon technique,** in which one does something simply because others are doing likewise. An example is a manager who informs the vice president that she wants an enlarged budget for attendance at etailing (Internet retailing) seminars because "all other companies are doing it."

Undue Pressure.   Effective leaders regularly use motivational techniques such as rewards and mild punishments. Yet when rewards become bribes for compliance and threats of punishment become severe, the target person is subjected to undue pressure or coercion. An example of a bribe by a manager might be, "If you can work eighty hours on this project this week, I'll recommend you for the highest pay grade." Several specific behaviors labeled coercive in a research study were as follows:

> I demand that she do it.
>
> I yell at her until she does it.
>
> I criticize her for not doing it.
>
> I curse at her until she does it.
>
> I threaten her with something if she doesn't do it.[20]

Game Playing.   Leaders, as well as others, often play games in order to influence others. A **game** in this context is a repeated series of exchanges between people that seems plausible but has a hidden agenda or purpose. Influence is exerted in a game because the person against whom the game is played is made to feel humble.

    Blemish is an example of a simple game often used by managers to keep team members in line. All that is required is for the leader to find some flaw in every assignment completed by team members. The game-playing boss stays one up with comments such as "You did a great job on that report except in your conclusion. It just didn't seem to fit the body of the report."

    One-time transactions between the influence agent and the influence target sometimes resemble a game. One such tactic is the door-in-the-face technique. The person attempting to exert influence makes a major request that will most likely be rejected. Shortly thereafter comes a more modest request, which was really intended in the first place.[21] In rejecting the first request, the target person may feel guilty and thus be responsive to a future request. For example, a security manager wanted a larger budget for cellular telephones and pagers for her group. At the time the company was carefully controlling expenditures. The security manager approached her manager and requested authorization for new office space for her staff. Her budget request was rejected quickly. She returned two weeks later with a request for an increased cellular telephone and paging system budget to compensate for the denial of new offices. Her request was granted within one week.

Debasement. A subtle manipulative tactic is **debasement,** demeaning or insulting oneself to control the behavior of another person. For example, the security manager just mentioned might say, "I realize our department just contributes to overhead, but we do need more cellular telephones and pagers to get our job done." Specific debasing tactics revealed by research include the following:

> I allow myself to be debased so she'll do it.
>
> I lower myself so she'll do it.
>
> I act humble so she'll do it.[22]

Upward Appeal. In **upward appeal,** the leader exerts influence on a team member by getting a person with more formal authority to do the influencing. An example: "I sent the guy to my boss when he wouldn't listen to me. That fixed him." More than occasional use of upward appeal weakens the leader's stature in the eyes of group members and superiors, thus eroding his or her effectiveness.

Leaders can apply upward appeal in other ways. A leader might attempt to persuade another staff member that his or her request is approved by higher management. The target of the influence event is thus supposed to grant acceptance automatically. Or the leader can request higher management's assistance in gaining another person's compliance with the request. The influence target thus feels pressured.[23]

Silent Treatment. A leader uses the **silent treatment** through saying nothing, sulking, or other forms of passivity until the influence target complies. Research questionnaire items related to sulking are as follows:

> I don't respond to him until he does it.
>
> I ignore him until he does it.
>
> I am silent until he agrees to do it.
>
> I refuse to do something he likes until he does it.[24]

Ingratiation. Getting somebody else to like you can be considered a mildly manipulative influence tactic—particularly if you do not like the other person. Ingratiating tactics identified in a study about influence tactics included the following:

> Made him or her feel important. (For example, "Only you have the brains and talent to do this.")
>
> Acted very humbly toward him or her while making my request.
>
> Praised him or her.
>
> Sympathized with him or her about the added problems that my request caused.
>
> Waited until he or she appeared in a receptive mood before asking.
>
> Asked in a polite way.
>
> Pretended I was letting him or her decide to do what I wanted (acted in a pseudo-democratic manner).[25]

Leaders who ordinarily are the opposite of ingratiating will sometimes go out of their way to be humble and agreeable to fit an important purpose. A case in point is Bill Gates, who is often sarcastic and cutting. When Gates and Microsoft Corp. were being sued by the U.S. Dept. of Justice for possible monopolistic practices, Gates went on a goodwill tour. He scheduled an events-packed trip around San Francisco and Silicon Valley. During his meetings with the public, Gates was modest and at times self-deprecating, even praising the competition. He shook hands, signed autographs, and smiled frequently. Gates was so convincing that a schoolgirl said, "You can tell he's not in it for the money. He wants to make software better."[26]

Leadership Self-Assessment Quiz 8-2 provides you an opportunity to measure your own ingratiating tendencies and to think through further what ingratiating yourself to your boss means in practice. Remember that being liked helps you get promoted, receive more compensation, and avoid being downsized, yet you should avoid being dishonest.

Joking and Kidding.   Good-natured kidding is especially effective when a straightforward statement might be interpreted as harsh criticism. Joking or kidding can thus get the message across and lower the risk that the influence target will be angry with the influence agent. Joking and kidding might be interpreted either as dishonest or as extraordinarily tactful because the criticizer softens the full blow of the criticism. A vice president of manufacturing successfully used joking and kidding to influence his team to improve quality. After examining what he thought were low-quality components for the company's power tools, he commented, "I appreciate your effort, but I'm afraid you misinterpreted my message. I wanted you to produce a component we could use as a positive model of quality. You went out of your way to produce a negative model. Otherwise you did a great job."

In studying the most severe unethical influence (and political) tactics, recognize that the use of these influence approaches can bring about human suffering. For example, bullying and intimidating tactics may not be illegal, but they are unethical. Cruelty in the organization creates many problems. As one observer notes, "Cruelty is blatantly unethical and erodes the organizational character through intellectual, emotional, moral and social vices that reduce the readiness of groups to act ethically (organizational cynicism)."[27] Examples of cruelty include insulting a group member's physical appearance or belittling him or her.

Leadership Skill-Building Exercise 8-1 (page 248) will help you recognize several of the influence tactics described in this chapter. Another tactic, assertiveness, is mentioned in the exercise but was described previously.

RELATIVE EFFECTIVENESS AND SEQUENCING OF INFLUENCE TACTICS

Although we have described influence tactics separately, they must also be understood in relation to one another. Two ways of comparing influence tactics are to

Measure of Ingratiating Behavior in Organizational Settings (MIBOS) ?

Leadership Self-Assessment Quiz 8-2

INSTRUCTIONS   Indicate how frequently you use (or would use) the tactics for pleasing your boss listed below. N = never do it; S = seldom do it; Oc = occasionally do it; Of = often do it; A = almost always do it. The N-to-A categories correspond to a 1-to-5 scale.

		1 N	2 S	3 Oc	4 Of	5 A
1.	Impress upon your supervisor that only he or she can help you in a given situation mainly to make him or her feel good.	___	___	___	___	___
2.	Show your supervisor that you share enthusiasm about his or her new idea even when you may not actually like it.	___	___	___	___	___
3.	Try to let your supervisor know that you have a reputation for being liked.	___	___	___	___	___
4.	Try to make sure that your supervisor is aware of your success.	___	___	___	___	___
5.	Highlight the achievements made under your supervisor's leadership in a meeting he or she does not attend.	___	___	___	___	___
6.	Give frequent smiles to express enthusiasm and interest about something your supervisor is interested in even if you do not like it.	___	___	___	___	___
7.	Express work attitudes that are similar to your supervisor's as a way of letting him or her know that the two of you are alike.	___	___	___	___	___
8.	Tell your supervisor that you can learn a lot from his or her experience.	___	___	___	___	___
9.	Exaggerate your supervisor's admirable qualities to convey the impression that you think highly of him or her.	___	___	___	___	___
10.	Disagree on trivial or unimportant issues but agree on those issues in which he or she expects support from you.	___	___	___	___	___
11.	Try to imitate such work behaviors of your supervisor as working late or occasionally working on weekends.	___	___	___	___	___

12. Look for opportunities to let your supervisor know your virtues and strengths.   ___ ___ ___ ___ ___

13. Ask your supervisor for advice in areas in which he or she thinks he or she is smart to let him or her feel that you admire his or her talent.   ___ ___ ___ ___ ___

14. Try to do things for your supervisor that show your selfless generosity.   ___ ___ ___ ___ ___

15. Look out for opportunities to admire your supervisor.   ___ ___ ___ ___ ___

16. Let your supervisor know the attitudes you share with him or her.   ___ ___ ___ ___ ___

17. Compliment your supervisor on his or her achievement, however it may appeal to you personally.   ___ ___ ___ ___ ___

18. Laugh heartily at your supervisor's jokes even when they are really not funny.   ___ ___ ___ ___ ___

19. Go out of your way to run an errand for your supervisor.   ___ ___ ___ ___ ___

20. Offer to help your supervisor by using your personal contacts.   ___ ___ ___ ___ ___

21. Try to persuasively present your own qualities when attempting to convince your supervisor about your abilities.   ___ ___ ___ ___ ___

22. Volunteer to be of help to your supervisor in matters like locating a good apartment, finding a good insurance agent, etc.   ___ ___ ___ ___ ___

23. Spend time listening to your supervisor's personal problems even if you have no interest in them.   ___ ___ ___ ___ ___

24. Volunteer to help your supervisor in his or her work even if it means extra work for you.   ___ ___ ___ ___ ___

SCORING AND INTERPRETATION   The more of these ingratiating behaviors you use frequently or almost always, the more ingratiating you are. A score of 40 or less suggests that you do not put much effort into pleasing your manager, and you may need to be a little more ingratiating to achieve a good relationship with your supervisor. A score between 41 and 99 suggests a moderate degree of ingratiating behavior. A score of 100 or more suggests that you are too ingratiating and might be perceived as being too political or insincere. So some honesty is called for, providing you are tactful.

Listed below are the mean scores on the 24 items for 148 business students working part time and full time in a wide variety of organizations and jobs. You can compare your score on each item with the mean (or norm) on the frequency scale of 1 to 5, as described above.

Ingratiating Behavior	Mean Score (5 Is Almost Always)
1. Help from supervisor	2.89
2. Share enthusiasm about supervisor's idea	3.34
3. Inform him or her that you are liked	3.51
4. Make supervisor aware of your success	2.77
5. Highlight supervisor's achievements in meeting	3.25
6. Give frequent smiles to express enthusiasm	3.10
7. Express work attitudes similar to supervisor	3.01
8. Say you learn from his or her experience	3.11
9. Exaggerate his or her admirable qualities	3.57
10. Agree on issues where he or she expects support	3.44
11. Imitate working extra hours	3.34
12. Let supervisor know your virtues and strengths	2.58
13. Ask supervisor for advice to show admiration	3.11
14. Show supervisor your selfless generosity	3.16
15. Look for opportunities to admire supervisor	3.36
16. Tell supervisor of shared attitudes	2.80
17. Compliment supervisor's achievement	3.22
18. Laugh at supervisor's jokes even if not funny	3.68
19. Run errand for supervisor	3.07
20. Help supervisor with your personal contacts	3.23
21. Persuasively present your own qualities	2.95
22. Volunteer help for finding apartment, etc.	3.47
23. Listen to supervisor's personal problems	3.11
24. Volunteer to help supervisor in his or her work	2.85

SKILL DEVELOPMENT   Leaders or future leaders should remember that a moderate amount of ingratiating behavior is the norm in relationships with superiors. Ingratiating yourself to people who report to you can also be a useful influence tactic.

SOURCE: *Adapted slightly from Kamalesh Kumar and Michael Beyerlein, "Construction and Validation of an Instrument for Measuring Ingratiatory Behaviors in Organizational Settings,"* Journal of Applied Psychology, *October 1991, p. 623. Copyright © 1991 by the American Psychological Association. Adapted with permission.*

examine their relative effectiveness and to study the order in which they might be used to achieve the best result.

A Study of the Relative Effectiveness of Influence Tactics

Since influence tactics are a major component of leadership, research about their relative effectiveness is worth noting. A study by Gary Yukl and J. Bruce Tracey provides insights about the relative effectiveness of influence tactics.[28] One hundred

Identifying Influence Tactics

Leadership Skill-Building Exercise 8-1

INSTRUCTIONS   After reading each tactic listed here, label it as being mostly an example of one of the following: I = ingratiation; E = exchange of favors; R = rationality; A = assertiveness; U = upward appeal.

Tactic	Code
1. I sympathized with the person about the added problems that my request caused.	____
2. I offered to help if the person would do what I wanted.	____
3. I set a time deadline for the person to do what I asked.	____
4. I obtained the informal support of higher-ups.	____
5. I used logic to convince him or her.	____
6. I made a formal appeal to higher levels to back up my request.	____
7. I had a showdown in which I confronted the person head-on.	____
8. I offered to make a personal sacrifice if the person would do what I wanted (for example, work late or harder).	____
9. I made him or her feel good about me before making my request.	____
10. I explained the reasons for my request.	____

Answers:

1.	I
2.	E
3.	A
4.	U
5.	R
6.	U
7.	A
8.	E
9.	I
10.	R

SKILL DEVELOPMENT   Being able to identify influence tactics is useful because it raises your awareness of how to influence others and which tactics others are using to influence you.

SOURCE: *Based on information in Chester A. Schriescheim and Timothy R. Hinkin, "Influence Tactics Used by Subordinates: A Theoretical and Empirical Analysis and Refinement of the Kipnis, Schmidt, and Wilkinson Subscales,"* Journal of Applied Psychology, *June 1990, p. 246. Copyright © 1990 American Psychological Association. Adapted with permission.*

and twenty managers participated in the study, along with 526 subordinates, 543 peers, and 128 superiors, who also rated the managers' use of influence tactics. The proportion of men and women in the study is unknown because respondents were not asked to reveal demographic information. (Some people prefer to remain anonymous in such studies.) Half the managers worked for manufacturing companies, and half worked for service companies.

The people who worked with the managers completed a questionnaire to identify which of nine influence tactics the managers used. Defined for the participants, the tactics were as follows:

1. Rational persuasion
2. Inspirational appeal
3. Consultation
4. Ingratiation
5. Exchange
6. Personal appeal
7. Coalition
8. Legitimating
9. Pressure

Another question asked how many influence attempts by the agent resulted in complete commitment by the target respondent. The seven response choices were (1) none of them; (2) a few of them; (3) some (less than half); (4) about half of them; (5) more than half of them; (6) most of them; and (7) all of them. Respondents were also asked to rate the overall effectiveness of the manager in carrying out his or her job responsibilities. The item had nine response choices, ranging from the least effective manager I have ever known (1) to the most effective manager I have ever known (9).

The results suggested that the most effective tactics were rational persuasion, inspirational appeal, and consultation. (An effective tactic was one that led to task commitment, and that was used by managers who were perceived to be effective by the various raters.) In contrast, the least effective were pressure, coalition, and appealing to legitimate authority (legitimating). Ingratiation and exchange were moderately effective for influencing team members and peers. The same tactics, however, were not effective for influencing superiors.

A related interpretation of the data from the influence study in question is noteworthy. At least for the American managers sampled, noncoercive tactics that provide a rational and justifiable basis for attitude change are more effective in gaining compliance than are threatening or manipulative attempts.[29]

Inspirational appeal, ingratiation, and pressure were used primarily in a downward direction, that is, toward a lower-ranking person. Personal appeal, exchange, and legitimating were used primarily in a lateral direction. It was also found that coalitions were used most in lateral and upward directions, and that rational persuasion was used most in an upward direction.

The researchers concluded that some tactics are more likely to be successful. Yet they caution that the results do not imply that these tactics will always result in task commitment. The outcome of a specific influence attempt is determined by factors in addition to influence attempts, such as the target's motivation and the organizational culture. Also, any tactic can trigger target resistance if it is not appropriate for the situation or if it is applied unskillfully. Tact, diplomacy, and insight are required for effective application of influence tactics.

Which influence tactic a manager might consider effective, and therefore choose, depends to some extent on how much group members are trusted. When we distrust people, we are likely to attempt to control their actions. Carole V. Wells and David Kipnis conducted a survey about trust involving 275 managers and 267 employees. The managers answered questions about subordinates, and subordinates answered questions about their managers. The two groups, however, were not describing each other. A key finding was that both managers and employees used strong tactics of influence when they distrusted the other party—either a manager or a subordinate. The strong influence tactics studied were appeals to higher authority, assertiveness, coalition building, and sanctions.[30]

The Sequencing of Influence Tactics

Another important consideration in using influence tactics is the sequence or order in which they should be applied. In general, begin with the most positive, or least abrasive, tactic. If you do not gain the advantage you seek, proceed to a stronger tactic. For example, if you want a larger salary increase than that initially assigned you, try rational persuasion. If persuasion does not work, move on to exchange. Use a more abrasive tactic such as upward appeal only as a last resort. The reason is that abrasive tactics trigger revenge and retaliation. Many people who have brought their complaints to an outside agency such as a governmental office have found themselves with a limited future in their organization. Although the appeal is legally justified, it is politically unwise.

The sequencing of tactics can also be considered in terms of cost and risk. A sensible approach is to begin with low-cost, low-risk tactics. If the outcome is important enough to the influence agent, he or she can then proceed to higher-cost and higher-risk influence tactics. An example of a low-cost, low-risk tactic would be joking and kidding. An accounting manager who was disappointed with the budget offered her group might say to her boss, "Does the new budget mean that our group will have to pay for our own floppy disks and green eyeshades?" It would be much more costly in terms of time and potential retaliation to form a coalition with another underbudgeted group to ask for an enlarged budget.

In addition to the sequencing of tactics, the influence agent must also consider the direction of the influence attempt as a contingency factor. In general, the more position power an individual exerts over another, the less the need for being cautious in the use of influence tactics. For example, a vice president can more readily use undue pressure against a supervisor than vice versa. When you have more power, there are likely to be fewer negative consequences from using more powerful tactics.

Applying Influence Tactics

Divide the class into small teams. Each group assigns one leadership influence tactic to each team member. During the next week or so, each team member takes the opportunity to practice the assigned influence tactic in a work or personal setting. Hold a group discussion with the same class teams after the influence attempts have been practiced. Report back the following information: (1) under what circumstances the influence tactic was attempted; (2) how the influence target reacted; and (3) what results, both positive and negative, were achieved.

Practicing influence tactics makes a direct contribution to your leadership effectiveness because leadership centers on influence. If you want to exert leadership as a nonmanager, you will have to be particularly adept at using influence tactics because your formal authority is quite limited.

Leadership Skill-Building Exercise 8-2 provides an opportunity to practice implementing various influence tactics. As with any other skill, influence skills need to be practiced under field conditions.

SUMMARY

To become an effective leader, a person must be aware of specific influence tactics. Influence is the ability to affect the behaviors of others in a particular direction. Power, in contrast, is the potential or capacity to influence. A model presented here indicated that a leader's influence outcomes are a function of the influence tactics he or she uses. The influence tactics are in turn moderated, or affected by, the leader's traits, behaviors, and the situation. The outcomes of influence attempts are commitment, compliance, or resistance, all of which influence end results such as group success or failure.

Influence tactics are often viewed from an ethical perspective. Some tactics are clearly ethical, but others are clearly unethical. Used with tact, diplomacy, and good intent, ethical influence tactics can be quite effective. The essentially ethical tactics described here are leading by example, using rational persuasion, being a subject matter expert, exchanging favors and bargaining, getting network members to support your position, legitimating a request, making an inspirational appeal and emotional display, displaying personal magnetism, consulting, forming coalitions, being a team player, and practicing hands-on leadership.

Essentially dishonest and unethical tactics presented here were divided into two groups: clearly unethical and borderline. The more clearly unethical and devious tactics are deliberate Machiavellianism, gentle manipulation of people and situations, undue pressure, and game playing. The five borderline influence tactics are debasing oneself to gain advantage; upward appeal; silent treatment; ingratiation; and joking and kidding (hardly devious at all).

A study of influence tactics concluded that the most effective were rational persuasion, inspirational appeal, and consultation. The least effective were pressure, coalition, and appealing to legitimate authority. Certain tactics are more effective for exerting influence upward, whereas others are better suited for downward influence. For example, inspirational appeal, ingratiation, and exchange are moderately effective for influencing subordinates and peers. Yet the same tactics are not effective for influencing superiors. When we distrust people we tend to think that stronger influence tactics, such as an appeal to higher authority, will be effective.

Sequencing of influence tactics is another important consideration. In general, begin with the most positive, or least abrasive, tactic. If you do not gain the advantage you seek, proceed to a stronger tactic. Also, begin with low-cost, low-risk tactics.

KEY TERMS

Influence

Commitment

Compliance

Resistance

Leading by example

Personal magnetism

Coalition

Hands-on leader

Machiavellians

Bandwagon technique

Game

Blemish

Debasement

Upward appeal

Silent treatment

GUIDELINES FOR ACTION AND SKILL DEVELOPMENT

A starting point in choosing influence tactics to help you lead others is to select those that fit your ethical code. For example, a person might say, "Being a team player and ingratiation fit my ethics, but I can't use undue pressure."

Another major consideration is to choose the correct combination of influence tactics. You must choose these tactics carefully on the basis of the influence target and your objectives. For example, ingratiation and joking and kidding might not work well with superiors. Quite often it is best to begin with a gentle influence tactic, then strengthen your approach as needed. Keys and Case found that most first influence attempts by managers involved gentle approaches such as requests or logical persuasion. Later attempts included firmer tactics when the influence target was reluctant to comply.[31] (In days of old, this was referred to as tightening the thumbscrews!)

A person must also choose influence tactics to fit the influence objectives. Kipnis and his associates have observed that managers should not rely on a single influence tactic, such as assertiveness, to achieve both organizational and personal objectives. It may be appropriate to insist that one's boss be mindful of cost overruns. It is inappropriate, however, to insist that one be granted time off to golf with network members.[32]

Good communication skills are required to implement influence tactics. As Keys and Case note,

"Managers who choose rational ideas based on the needs of the target, wrap them with a blanket of humor or anecdotes, and cast them in the language of the person to be influenced, are much more likely to see their influence objectives achieved."[33]

DISCUSSION QUESTIONS AND ACTIVITIES

1. Which influence tactic described in this chapter do you think would work the best for you? Why?

2. Which influence tactic do you think would work the most poorly for you? Why?

3. What differences have you observed among the influence tactics used by technically oriented versus people-oriented people?

4. Which of the tactics described in this chapter help explain the widespread use by leaders of person-to-person meetings when they want to accomplish a major objective?

5. How can email be used to implement any of the influence tactics described in this chapter?

6. Identify two exchanges of favor you have seen or can envision on the job.

7. In what way is being a subject matter expert (SME) a source of power as well as an influence tactic?

8. Which of the influence tactics described in this chapter is a charismatic leader the most likely to use? Explain your answer.

9. Which influence tactics have been the most effective in influencing you? Support your answer with an anecdote.

10. Get the opinion of an experienced leader as to the most effective influence tactics. Share your findings with class members.

Leadership Case Problem A

Boeing's Chief Rides the Tiger

The televised plume of smoke from an airplane crash in New York was a familiar but sickening sight for Phil Condit, who was watching during a treadmill workout at a Detroit hotel. "It stopped my day cold," recalls the Boeing Company chairman and CEO, who is so attuned to disaster that he can pick out the words *plane crash* on a radio broadcast across a noisy room (Associated Press). The plane that crashed was an Airbus, not a Boeing.

The Boeing Business. Running the world's largest aircraft manufacturer can be a tense and troubling job these days. The solace for Condit is that the turbulence rocking the commercial jet business since September 2001 would have been far more damaging to his company had he not moved to create a more balanced Boeing—one that is steadily reducing its historic dependence on planes.

"Had we stayed in that mode, September 11 would have been a really dramatic event for us," Condit said in an interview in his corner office atop Boeing's new world headquarters overlooking the Chicago skyline and Lake Michigan beyond (Associated Press).

This was to have been a showcase year for the 60-year-old technocrat and his grand plan, a year for a new, more diversified Boeing, capped by the symbolic shift away from its airplane roots in Seattle. Instead, it turned nightmarish just a week after the Chicago corporate offices opened. Four Boeing planes went down in the terrorist attack, air travel decline precipitously, and Boeing stock sank dramatically. Condit was forced to lay off 30,000 employees. Adding to the misery, in 2001 Boeing lost out to Lockheed Martin for the biggest defense contract ever, the Joint Strike Fighter.

Condit believes that the upheaval has confirmed the wisdom of his bold company makeover. He is convinced that Boeing has made a much more fruitful transition to being a well-balanced aerospace giant than Wall Street gives it credit for. "It's actually been very gratifying to see that the strategies we set were robust," he said (Associated Press).

Condit's Skill as a Manager and Leader. An engineering whiz with early leadership skills, Condit seems to have been programmed for one of the nation's premier aerospace management jobs. Brilliant and ambitious from a young age—he was an Eagle Boy Scout in California and got his pilot's license at 18—he picked up a patent for inventing a new kind of wing in 1965, his very first year at Boeing. Soon he became the lead engineer for the 747, and he later oversaw development of the 777.

Condit is comfortable in engineering meetings, on the factory floor, and in the executive suite. A versatile manager and professional, he has had assignments at Boeing in aircraft design, marketing, sales, and project management. The aspect of Condit's leadership approach that distinguishes him the most from former Boeing CEOs is his strong interest in the company's human resources. He is adamant that Boeing must focus strongly on the contribution people make to the organization. Condit drives an ordinary sports utility vehicle, lunches in the company cafeteria on occasion, and often makes spontaneous visits to the shop floor to talk with workers.

Rising steadily to become chief executive in 1996 and chairman in 1997, Condit made the corporate change-in-course an early hallmark of his tenure. When Boeing acquired McDonnell Douglas, it became the nation's second-largest defense contractor. In 2001, Condit asserted his role as corporate titan when he announced he would select a new headquarters city for the $51 billion company. After selecting Chicago, Condit indulged in pomp and pizzazz, descending from his corporate jet to a red carpet greeting from the mayor. But that wasn't really his style. Business colleagues and friends describe Condit as collegial, ap-proachable, professional, sometimes cautious, private, and even shy.

A former Boeing vice president recalls Condit changing clothes at work three or four times a day—greeting European and Asian customers in coat and tie and switching back to sweater and socks (no shoes) when they left. Those down-to-earth traits have served him well in labor relations, where union officials call him more open and responsive than most CEOs. He has remained popular with the rank-and-file even through tens of thousands of layoffs and sometimes tough labor tactics—partly by delegating firing duties to his second-in-command, Harry Stonecipher.

The affable Condit has built up enough trust to close deals on his own. James Guyette, former chief operating officer of United Airlines, recalls working out a handwritten agreement with Condit in the middle of the night during negotiations for 777s—without lawyers. "If you have a deal with him, you have a deal," says Guyette, now head of Rolls Royce of North America.

Critics have accused Condit of moving too fast away from planes and ceding too much ground to rival Airbus. Boeing engineers went on a crippling strike in 2000. "He had a difficult shift up to become chairman and CEO. The job is more visionary than his earlier posts," says Guyette. "But he has matured in the job. He's had some great successes—the acquistion of Mc-Donnell Douglas, setting up three distinct businesses and allowing them to operate as such, and having the courage to pick up and leave Seattle" (Associated Press).

QUESTIONS

1. Which influence tactics does Condit appear to use?

2. In what ways does Condit appear to be politically skillful? Ethical?

3. What should Condit include in the next vision he creates for Boeing?

4. What is your evaluation of the leadership effectiveness of Phil Condit?

SOURCE: "Boeing's Chief Rides the Tiger," Associated Press, November 22, 2001; Kenneth Labich, "Boeing Finally Hatches a Plan," Fortune, March 1, 1999, pp. 100–106.

Leadership Case Problem B

How Can I Inspire My Team?

Jacques Renfert considered himself fortunate to be chosen as team leader for one of the newly formed work teams in the insurance division of the financial services company where he worked. The purpose of forming teams was to improve customer service. Each team now had the authority to issue insurance policies and settle claims, within limits, for specific geographic regions. Before the division was organized into teams, separate departments existed for sales, administration, underwriting, and claims. Although the company was profitable, it received too many criticisms about poor service. Customers complained that it took too long to settle claims. Company sales representatives contended that the underwriting department took too long to approve and issue policies.

One of Renfert's early initiatives was to call frequent team meetings to discuss how service was going to be improved. He emphasized to the group that the company had moved into the modern era and that teams were empowered to look for ways to improve efficiency. Renfert also emphasized that each team member had more responsibility than under the previous structure. Each team member would be doing some sales administration, some underwriting, and some claims work.

Molly Goldwin, a team member, commented during one of Renfert's meetings: "Just think of it, three jobs in one and being paid just the same as before."

At the same meeting, another team member asked, "What's so special about calling us a team? I had a nice job in the underwriting department before these teams were formed. I enjoyed that work. Now my job is more confusing."

Renfert replied, "The company decided this was the way to go. Trust me, everything will work out fine in the end. Just go along with the team idea for now."

Four months after the work teams were formed, Renfert's boss, Nancy Wong, met with him to discuss progress. Wong told Renfert, "Your team isn't making as much progress as I would like. Policies are not being issued any faster. Customer complaints about slow claims settlements are at the same level as before we converted into teams. The other teams are making more progress. Does your team have a problem?"

"Yes, we have a problem," said Renfert. "Everyone comes to work just as in the days before teams. They do most of their work alone, but they get together when needed. It just seems to be business as usual. So far, the idea of being a high-producing team hasn't caught on."

"Are you being an effective team leader?" asked Wong. "I think I am," said Renfert. "I do everything I'm supposed to. I hold meetings. I take care of the paperwork and email. I try to settle problems. I say thank you when somebody does a good job."

"I'll be back with you in three months to discuss your team's progress. I want to see some improved results in terms of better customer service."

QUESTIONS

1. What can Jacques Renfert do to influence his team to perform better?

2. Which influence tactics (if any) is Renfert using to achieve better results with his team?

3. Based on whatever information you have found in the case, how would you rate Renfert's charisma?

Leadership Skill-Building Exercise 8-3

Inspiring the Team

One student plays the role of Jacques Renfert and calls a meeting meant to inspire the team toward new heights of productivity and customer service. Be dramatic. Use whatever inspirational approaches you think might work. Five other students play the role of a team member, none of whom was expecting an inspirational meeting. If Renfert inspires you, act accordingly. If he fails to inspire you, demonstrate your lack of inspiration.

This role play is important because a major problem many leaders face is how to inspire people and avoid being bland and ordinary. A role play of this nature will help sensitize you to the importance of having some pizzazz as a leader.

INTERNET SKILL-BUILDING EXERCISE

Apply the chapter concepts! Visit the Web and complete this Internet skill-building exercise to learn more about current leadership topics and trends.

How Machiavellian Are You?

Go to www.humanlinks.com/personal/power_orientation.htm, and follow the instructions for taking the Power Orientation Test. Your score will be compared to a national average. Compare your score on this test with the Organizational Politics Questionnaire you took in Chapter 7.

1. Do you think the two tests measure similar tendencies?

2. If the range of your scores on the two tests is quite different, such as high on the Power Orientation Test and low on the Organizational Politics Questionnaire, how do you explain these differences?

3. How does your score on the Power Orientation Test compare with your score on the Leader Integrity Scale from Chapter 6? What do you see as the relationship between ethical behavior and Machiavellianism?

Developing Teamwork

CHAPTER 9

When asked how he viewed teams, Gordon Bethune, CEO and chairman of the board of Continental Airlines, Inc. (www.continental.com), responded, "Running an airline is the biggest team sport there is. We are like a wristwatch—lots of different parts, but the whole has value only when we all work together. It has no value when any part fails. So we are not a cross-functional team, we're a company of multifunctions that has value when we all work cooperatively—pilots, flight attendants, gate agents, airport agents, mechanics, reservation agents. And not to understand that about doing business means you're going to fail. Lots of people failed because they don't get it.

"It's like basic human nature: If you take someone for granted or treat them like they have less value than someone else, they'll go to extraordinary lengths to show you you're wrong. People who try to manage our business and ascribe various values to different functions and treat some with disdain because they are easy to replace might some day find the watch doesn't work—it might be the smallest part that's broken, but the whole watch doesn't work."[1]

As indicated by the comments of the CEO of a company that has gone from being the worst in the industry before his leadership to the best after he arrived, teams and teamwork are a vital part of organizations. Developing teamwork is such an important leadership role that team building is said to differentiate successful from unsuccessful leaders.[2]

A difficulty in understanding teams is that the words *teams* and *teamwork* are often overused and applied loosely. For some people, a team is simply another term for a group. As used here, a **team** is a work group that must rely on collaboration if each member is to experience the optimum success and achievement.[3] **Teamwork** is work done with an understanding and commitment to group goals on the part of all team members. All teams are groups, but not all groups are teams. Jon R. Katzenbach and Douglas K. Smith, on the basis of extensive research in the workplace, make a clear differentiation between teams and groups.[4] A team is characterized by a common commitment, whereas the commitment within a group might not be as strong. A team accomplishes many collective work products, whereas group members sometimes work slightly more independently. Members of a group have a strong leader, whereas a team has shared leadership roles. In a team there is individual and mutual accountability; in contrast, a group emphasizes individual accountability.

Team members produce a collective work product, whereas group members sometimes produce individual work products. A team leader is likely to encourage open-ended discussion and active problem-solving meetings, whereas a group leader is more likely to run an efficient meeting. Also, teams discuss, decide, and do real work together, and a group is more likely to discuss, decide, and delegate.

Although the distinction between a group and a team may be valid, it is difficult to cast aside the practice of using the terms *group* and *team* interchangeably. For example, a customer service team is still a team even if its teamwork is poor.

As background for this chapter, we first examine how team leadership is different from more traditional leadership. We then look briefly at the advantages and disadvantages of working in groups. The central focus of this chapter is a description of specific leader actions that foster teamwork. We also describe outdoor training, a widely used method of teamwork development. In addition, we summarize a leadership theory that provides some insights into how teamwork emerges within a work group.

TEAM LEADERSHIP VERSUS SOLO LEADERSHIP

Various writers have touted the importance of team leadership. Meredith Belbin, for one, contrasts the team leader and the solo leader[5] (see Figure 9-1). Team leaders share power and deemphasize individual glory. They are flexible and adaptable, thus welcoming change. Team leaders function as facilitators who bring out the best in others while still being inspirational. The team leader conforms closely to the consensus and 9,9 (Leadership Grid) styles.

William D. Hitt has observed related characteristics and behaviors of team leaders. In his analysis, team leaders place considerable emphasis on team building and then evaluate their own performance on the basis of how well they have developed the team. Team leaders intuitively recognize that the whole is greater than the sum of the parts. Based on this belief, they look for linkages (members working closely with each other) among team members to help multiply productivity.[6] According to Hitt, team leaders understand that sharing power with group members multiplies their own power. As the team members become stronger, so

FIGURE 9-1   The Solo Leader and the Team Leader

SOLO LEADER	TEAM LEADER
1. Plays unlimited role (interferes)	1. Chooses to limit role (delegates)
2. Strives for conformity	2. Builds on diversity
3. Collects acolytes	3. Seeks talent
4. Directs subordinates	4. Develops colleagues
5. Projects objectives	5. Creates mission

Source: From Meredith Belbin, "Solo Leader/Team Leader: Antithesis in Style and Structure," in Michel Syrett and Clare Hogg, Frontiers of Leadership, *p. 271, copyright © 1992, Blackwell Publishers, Oxford, England. Reprinted by permission of Blackwell Publishers.*

does the leader. A related attitude is that team leaders are not threatened by sharing power. They are therefore willing to surround themselves with capable people in order to multiply the effectiveness of the team.

The solo leader is the traditional leader in a bureaucracy. Basically an autocrat, the solo leader receives much of the credit for the success of his or her firm. Frequently, some of the credit is undeserved. The solo leader may not recognize how dependent he or she is on the team. For example, a manufacturing manager might brag about how under his reign the division became a top-rated supplier to a large customer. The same manager neglects to mention how attaining this high-quality status was really a collective effort.

Advantages and Disadvantages of Group Work and Teamwork

Groups have always been the building blocks of organizations. Yet groups and teams have grown in importance during the past decade as fundamental units of organization structure. In an attempt to adapt to rapidly changing environments, many work organizations have granted teams increased autonomy and flexibility. Cross-functional teams have been formed in many firms to achieve a broader perspective on problem solving and simultaneously to help downplay intergroup rivalries. Teams are also asked to span traditional boundaries by working more closely with groups from other disciplines. Furthermore, teams are often required to work more closely with customers and suppliers.

The increased acceptance of teams suggests that group work offers many advantages. Nevertheless, it is useful to specify several of these advantages and also to examine the potential problems of groups.

Advantages of Group Work and Teamwork

Group work and group decision making offer several advantages over individual effort. If several knowledgeable people are brought into the decision-making process, a number of worthwhile possibilities may be uncovered. It is also possible to achieve synergy, whereby the group's total output exceeds the sum of the various individuals' contribution. For example, it would be a rare person working alone who could build an automobile. Group decision making is also helpful in gaining acceptance and commitment, as described in the context of the normative decision model in Chapter 5.

Group members often evaluate one another's thinking, so the team is likely to avoid major errors. One member might detect a major flaw in a project that might otherwise have slipped by the group. When planning the opening of restaurants in foreign cultures, the Burger King Corporation solicits the opinion of a person from that culture, who becomes a temporary member of the planning team. The intent is to avoid mistakes such as featuring hamburgers in a culture that is opposed to eating animal carcasses.

Top management teams, as well as teams at lower levels in the organization, can often produce results superior to those attributed to individual managers. Milan Moravec notes that a group of top executives becomes a resource that is often richer, more textured and diverse, and more accessible than an individual leader could be.[7] At the executive level, team structures have streamlined management to some extent. Many companies have done away with the job of the chief operating officer, and instead top executives execute strategy themselves. James M. Citrin, a management consultant, explains that in some circumstances the COO is another layer of bureaucracy that separates CEOs from their business.[8] To avoid this problem, top-level management teams often take up the COO role: making spending decisions for various business units, streamlining production, and executing strategy that can change suddenly. In a fluid structure, all executive leaders need an external focus and skill in operations.[9]

Working in groups also enhances many members' job satisfaction. Being a member of a work group makes it possible to satisfy more needs than if one worked alone. Among these needs are needs for affiliation, security, self-esteem, and self-fulfillment. For example, playing a key role in a successful team effort can be fulfilling because of the job challenge and the recognition.

Disadvantages of Group Activity

Group activity has some potential disadvantages for both organizations and individuals. A major problem is that members face pressure to conform to group standards of performance and conduct. Some work groups might ostracize a person who is much more productive than his or her coworkers. Shirking of individual responsibility is another problem frequently noted in groups. Unless work is assigned carefully to each group member, an undermotivated person can often squeeze by without contributing his or her fair share to a group effort.

Social loafing is the psychological term for shirking individual responsibility in a group setting. The social loafer risks being ostracized by the group but may be willing to pay the price rather than work hard. Loafing of this type is sometimes found in groups such as committees and project teams. Many students who have worked on team projects have encountered a social loafer.

A major potential problem with groups and teams is that they can waste considerable time through having too many meetings, lengthy debates, and striving for consensus over obvious issues. A capable person working alone can often accomplish more than a team in a much shorter time. Nordstrom Inc., a department store chain that developed a reputation for excellent customer service, encountered a sales decrease in the late 1990s. Some of their problems were attributed to an extreme form of consensus management among a group of six brothers and cousins who held the title of co-president. Taking so long to develop new marketing and operation strategies resulted in lost momentum.[10]

A well-publicized disadvantage of group decision making is **groupthink,** a deterioration of mental efficiency, reality testing, and moral judgment in the interest of group solidarity. Simply put, groupthink is an extreme form of consensus. The group atmosphere values getting along more than getting things done. The group thinks as a unit, believes it is impervious to outside criticism, and begins to have illusions about its own invincibility. As a consequence, the group loses its own powers of critical analysis.[11]

Groupthink apparently took place among executives at several of the energy and telecommunications firms charged with financial fraud in 2002. As teams of executives discovered that their company was about to sustain substantial losses, they told company employees to hold on to the stock. At the same time, members of the executive team cashed in their stock options at a substantial profit. Furthermore, the executive team at these firms awarded themselves bonuses, such as sharing $100 million, while employee pensions lost about 90 percent of their value. Groupthink was involved because one executive acting alone probably could not be that diabolical—he needed support from the group!

Another concern about teams is that teamwork is an unstable arrangement because team leaders soon revert to exercising most of the authority. As Kenneth Labich observes, "All too often team leaders revert to form and claim the sandbox for themselves, refusing to share authority with the other kids. Everyone else, meanwhile, sets to bickering about peripheral things like who gets credit for what the team produces. Old habits cling to life."[12]

An effective tactic for capitalizing on the advantages of teams while minimizing their disadvantages is to rely on teams only when the task is suited for a team. Alan B. Drexler and Russ Forrester point out that teams can result in wasted effort when people are forced to form and act like a team when a team is not needed. Among the types of work not suited for teams are retail selling, making small loans, and teaching. One key criterion for a group or team approach is the need to collectively produce something, such as a group of people developing a product. Another criterion is interdependence or interlocking of work, such as developing a strategic plan that calls for input from different business functions.[13]

To evaluate how well any work team or group familiar to you is functioning as a team, do Leadership Self-Assessment Quiz 9-1. The quiz will help sensitize you to important dimensions of team effectiveness.

THE LEADER'S ROLE IN THE TEAM-BASED ORGANIZATION

Although an important goal of a team-based organization is for group members to participate in leadership and management activities, leaders still play an important role. Instead of the leader's job disappearing, leaders learn to lead in new

Leadership Self-Assessment Quiz 9–1

The Teamwork Checklist

This checklist serves as an informal guide to diagnosing teamwork. Base your answers on whatever experiences you have in leading a team, at work or outside of work. Indicate whether your team has (or had) the following characteristics:

		Mostly Yes	Mostly No
1.	Definite goals that each member knows and understands	____	____
2.	Clearly established roles and responsibilities	____	____
3.	Members who work together very well without strong egos or personalities creating problems	____	____
4.	Well-documented guidelines for behavior and ground rules	____	____
5.	After a consensus is reached, every team member supporting it	____	____
6.	Team being aware when it has achieved success	____	____
7.	Open communication in an atmosphere of trust	____	____
8.	Continuous learning and training in appropriate skills	____	____
9.	Team members who are flexible, open-minded, and dependable	____	____
10.	Team members who have an "all in it together" attitude	____	____
11.	Higher management's patience and support	____	____
12.	Each member having pride in his or her work	____	____
13.	Rewards tied to individual as well as team results	____	____
14.	Team members who automatically provide backup and support for one another without the team leader's stepping in	____	____

SCORING AND INTERPRETATION   The more statements are answered "mostly yes," the more likely it is that good teamwork is present. The answers will serve as discussion points among team members for improving teamwork and group effectiveness. Negative responses to the statements can be used as suggestions for taking action to improve teamwork in your group.

SOURCE: *Based on material gathered from Mark Kelly,* The Adventures of a Self-Managing Team *(San Diego, Calif.: Pfeiffer & Company, 1991); brochure for "Team Leadership: How to Inspire Commitment, Teamwork & Cooperation," Seminars International, Olathe, Kans., 1996.*

ways. Organizations need leaders who are knowledgeable in the team process and who can help with the interpersonal demands of teams. For example, giving feedback and resolving conflict are important in a team structure. Quite often the leader is a facilitator who works with two or three teams at a time. He or she helps them stay focused when personality and work-style differences create problems. Without effective leadership, teams can get off course, go too far or not far enough, lose sight of their mission, and become blocked by interpersonal conflict. Effective leadership is particularly important early in the history of a group to help it reach its potential. Key roles of a leader in a team-based organization include the following:

- Building trust and inspiring teamwork
- Coaching team members and group members toward higher levels of performance
- Facilitating and supporting the decisions made by the team
- Expanding the team's capabilities
- Creating a team identity
- Anticipating and influencing change
- Inspiring the team toward higher levels of performance
- Enabling and empowering group members to accomplish their work
- Encouraging team members to eliminate low-value work[14]

Several of these roles have already been alluded to in this book, and several others, such as coaching, are described later. All of these roles contribute to effective leadership in general. The enabling role, for example, centers on empowerment. Yet properly motivating team members also enables, or facilitates, work accomplishment. The empowering processes described in Chapter 7 are a major part of enabling. Group members who are empowered are enabled to accomplish their work. The leader behavior and attitudes that foster teamwork, to be described in the next section, might also be interpreted as part of the leader's role in a team-based organization.

LEADER ACTIONS THAT FOSTER TEAMWORK

Sometimes a leader's inspiring personality alone can foster teamwork. Yet inspirational leaders, as well as less charismatic ones, can also encourage teamwork by doing certain things and having certain attitudes. Table 9-1 lists the teamwork-enhancing actions that are described in the following pages. For convenience the actions are divided into two types: those actions leaders can take using their own resources (informal techniques) and those actions that generally require organizational structure or policy (formal techniques).

TABLE 9-1   Leader Actions That Foster Teamwork

Actions Leaders Can Take Using Their Own Resources	Actions Generally Requiring Organization Structure or Policy
1. Defining the team's mission	1. Designing physical structures that facilitate communication
2. Developing a norm of teamwork including emotional intelligence	2. Emphasizing group recognition and rewards
3. Emphasizing pride in being outstanding	3. Initiating ritual and ceremony
4. Holding a powwow	4. Practicing open-book management
5. Serving as a model of teamwork	5. Selecting team-oriented members
6. Using a consensus leadership style	6. Using technology that facilitates teamwork
7. Establishing urgency, demanding performance standards, and providing direction	
8. Encouraging competition with another group	
9. Encouraging the use of jargon	
10. Soliciting feedback on team effectiveness	
11. Minimizing micromanaging	

Most of the actions for improving teamwork are subsets of having effective interpersonal skills. Several examples from the table are numbers 2, 4, and 6 in the left column, and 2 and 5 in the right column.

Actions Leaders Can Take Using Their Own Resources

Defining the Team's Mission.   A starting point in developing teamwork is to specify the team's mission. Commitment to a clear mission has been identified as a key practice of a highly effective team. The mission statement for the group helps answer the question "Why are we doing this?" To answer this question, the mission statement should contain a specific goal, purpose, and philosophical tone. Any goal contained within the mission statement should be congruent with organizational objectives. If a team wants to cut back on its number of suppliers, that should be part of the organization's intent also.[15] Here are two examples of team mission statements:

> To plan and implement new manufacturing approaches to enhance our high-performance image and bolster our competitive edge.

> To enhance our web site development capability so we can provide decision makers throughout the organization with assistance in developing web sites that exceed the state of the art.

The leader can specify the mission when the team is first formed or at any other time. Developing a mission for a long-standing team breathes new life into its activities. Being committed to a mission improves teamwork, as does the process of formulating a mission. The dialogue necessary for developing a clearly articulated mission establishes a climate in which team members can express feelings, ideas, and opinions. Participative leadership is required in developing a mission, as in most other ways of enhancing teamwork.

Developing a Norm of Teamwork Including Emotional Intelligence.

A major strategy of teamwork development is to promote the attitude among group members that working together effectively is an expected standard of conduct. Developing a norm of teamwork is difficult for a leader when a strong culture of individualism exists within a firm. Nokia Inc., the telecommunications firm based in Finland, illustrates the teamwork type of organizational culture. Part of the culture of collegiality can be traced to the Finnish character. It is natural for Nokia employees to work together and iron out differences of opinion.[16]

A belief in cooperation and collaboration rather than competitiveness as a strategy for building teamwork has been referred to as **cooperation theory.** [17] Individuals who are accustomed to competing with one another for recognition, salary increases, and resources must now collaborate. Despite the challenge of making a culture shift, the leader can make progress toward establishing a teamwork norm by doing the following:

- Encourage team members to treat one another as if they were customers, thus encouraging cooperative behavior and politeness.

- Explicitly state the desirability of teamwork on a regular basis both orally and in writing.

- Communicate the norm of teamwork by frequently using words and phrases that support teamwork. Emphasizing the words *team members* or *teammate,* and deemphasizing the words *subordinates* and *employees,* helps communicate the norm of teamwork.

Normative statements about teamwork by influential team members are also useful in reinforcing the norm of teamwork. A team member might take a leadership role by saying to coworkers: "I'm glad this project is a joint effort. I know that's what earns us merit points here."

The leader's role in developing teamwork can also be described as helping the group develop emotional intelligence. The leader contributes to the group's emotional intelligence by creating norms that establish mutual trust among members. It is also important for members to have a sense of group identity as defined in their mission statement. Group efficacy, or feeling competent to complete the group task, also contributes to emotional intelligence. Ensuring that the group has the right skills can enhance such efficacy. The three conditions just mentioned are the foundation of cooperation and collaboration.

The leader can also promote group emotional intelligence by bringing emotions to the surface in both groups and one-on-one meetings. The leader then discusses how these emotions might be affecting the group's work.[18] For example, team members might discuss how they feel about their perceived importance to the organization. One maintenance group expressed the feeling that they felt entirely unappreciated until a key piece of equipment broke down, and this underappreciation was adversely affecting morale. The team leader then helped the group develop an internal public relations campaign about their contribution to productivity.

Another example of dealing with emotions is encouraging group members to speak up when they feel the group is being either unproductive or highly productive. Expressing positive emotion can be an energizer.

Emphasizing Pride in Being Outstanding.   A standard way to build team spirit, if not teamwork, is to help the group realize why it should be proud of its accomplishments. William A. Cohen argues that most groups are particularly good at some task. The leader should help the group identify that task or characteristic and promote it as a key strength. A shipping department, for example, might have the best on-time shipping record in the region. Or a claims-processing unit might have the least overpayments in an insurance company.[19]

To try your hand at being an outstanding team, do Leadership Skill-Building Exercise 9-1.

Holding a Powwow.   An informal approach to laying the groundwork for cooperation among people who will be working together as a team is to hold a *powwow*. Disney Studios began using the term when Walt Disney was asked if he conducted brainstorming sessions. He answered that he preferred to hold a powwow in which people "get together, beat the drum, light a fire, smoke a pipe, and socialize." As practiced at Disney, the powwow is intentionally informal, friendly, and unstructured. It is intended to lay the groundwork for a cooperative working relationship among team members assigned to a new project. Each powwow has three parts. A *skills inventory* gives each group member a chance to describe his or her task-relevant skills, experience, and aptitudes. An *interest inventory* gives group members an opportunity to describe their off-the-job interests. The interests revealed can serve as connectors among group members. During the *data dump*, each group member expresses his or her thoughts and feelings about the project. Other members listen without interrupting the person dumping data. An effective data dump reduces complaining because each member of the group has an opportunity to air any concerns about the project.

Powwows give each group member an opportunity to be heard, thus establishing open communication.[20] As a consequence, the group of people assigned to the project takes an important step toward becoming a team.

Serving as a Model of Teamwork.   A powerful way for a leader to foster teamwork is to be a positive model of team play. And one way to exemplify teamwork is to reveal important information about ideas and attitudes relevant to the group's work. As a result of this behavior, team members may follow suit. A

Shelters for the Homeless

This exercise should take about thirty-five minutes; it can be done inside or outside of class. Organize the class into teams of about six people. Each team takes on the assignment of formulating plans for building temporary shelters for the homeless. The dwellings you plan to build, for example, might be two-room cottages with electricity and indoor plumbing. During the time allotted to the task, formulate plans for going ahead with Shelters for the Homeless. Consider dividing up work by assigning certain roles to each team member. Sketch out tentative answers to the following questions: (1) How will you obtain funding for your venture? (2) Which homeless people will you help? (3) Where will your shelters be? (4) Who will do the actual construction?

After your plan is completed, evaluate the quality of the teamwork that took place within the group. Search the chapter for techniques you might have used to improve it.

The same kind of teamwork skills you use in this exercise can be readily applied to most teamwork assignments on the job. Note carefully that although some types of teams call for members to be generalists, dividing up the tasks is still a basic principle of collective effort.

leader's self-disclosure fosters teamwork because it leads to shared perceptions and concerns.[21]

Interacting extensively with team members serves as a model of teamwork because it illustrates the mechanism by which team development takes place—frequent informal communication. While interacting with team members, the team leader can emphasize that he or she is a team member. For example, he or she might say, "Remember the deadline. We must all have the proposal in the mail by Thursday." A less team-member-oriented statement would be, "Remember the deadline. I need the proposals in the mail by Thursday."[22]

Using a Consensus Leadership Style. Teamwork is enhanced when a leader practices consensus decision making. Contributing input to important decisions helps group members feel that they are valuable team members. Consensus decision making also leads to an exchange of ideas within the group, with group members supporting and refining each other's suggestions. As a result, the feeling of working jointly on problems is enhanced. Generation X managers (those who were born in 1965 or later) are likely to practice consensus leadership. Part of the reason is that so many of these people have taken leadership courses! Bonnie Stedt, who holds the job title of senior relationship leader and executive vice president for American Express in New York City, makes this analysis of Gen X managers:

> I look at them as a very promising generation. They bring so much to the work force especially as managers. Xers tend to be flexible, good at collaboration and consensus building and mature beyond their years. They are also capable of

multitasking. Gen X managers are very team oriented, and they absolutely want everyone on the team to get credit.[23]

Another way of framing the consensus leadership style is saying that it reflects a belief in shared governance and partnerships instead of patriarchal caretaking.[24] The team, rather than hierarchical departments, becomes the focus of organizational activity. As with the other tactics and techniques for enhancing teamwork, people have to participate in a cultural shift to fully accept shared governance.

Striving for consensus does not mean that all conflict is squelched to make people agree. Disagreements over issues are healthy, and team members are more likely to be committed to the consensus decision if their voice has been heard. An example of a conflict over an issue would be the marketing team of an automotive company debating whether dealer discounts really improve sales in the long run.

Establishing Urgency, Demanding Performance Standards, and Providing Direction. Team members need to believe that the team has urgent, constructive purposes. Team members also want to have a list of explicit expectations. The more urgent and relevant the rationale, the more likely it is that the team will achieve its potential. A customer service team was told that further growth for the corporation would be impossible without major improvements in providing service to customers. Energized by this information, the team met the challenge.

To help establish urgency, it is helpful for the leader to challenge the group regularly. Teamwork is enhanced when the leader feeds the team valid facts and information that motivate team members to work together to modify the status quo. New information prompts the team to redefine and enrich its understanding of the challenge it is facing. As a result, the team is likely to focus on a common purpose, set clearer goals, and work together more smoothly.[25] Feeding the group relevant facts and information is also valuable because it helps combat groupthink.

Encouraging Competition with Another Group. One of the best-known methods of encouraging teamwork is rallying the support of the group against a real or imagined threat from the outside. Beating the competition makes more sense when the competition is outside your organization. When the enemy is within, the team spirit within may become detrimental to the overall organization, and we-they problems may arise.

When encouraging competition with another group, the leader should encourage rivalry, not intense competition that might lead to unethical business practices. One factor contributing to the success of the Saturn automobile is the rivalry created with competitive brands. One of the marketing executives asked his staff several times, "How much longer are you going to take the insult that Americans can't make a world-class car in the low-price range? The Japanese are great automakers, but I know you people from Tennessee can be just as good." Observe that the executive encouraged rivalry with a formidable opponent but did not bash the competition.

Team in Action

A Technical Group at Microsoft Corporation

Microsoft organization members, headed by the charismatic Bill Gates, are known for their cohesiveness and team spirit. Part of the organizational culture is to learn and use *Microspeak*, as sampled in the following representative comments made by a software development team within the firm.

Person A: He's very bandwidth.
Person B: Bill sent me some wicked flame mail.
Person C: Your idea has no granularity.
Person D: She's hardcore about spreadsheets.
Person E: He went nonlinear on me.
Person F: That's the most random thing I've ever heard.

TRANSLATION

Bandwidth: a measure of a person's intelligence, much like IQ.
Flame mail: hypercritical, emotional, and inflammatory electronic mail, often containing vulgarisms.
Granularity: fineness of detail.
Hardcore: serious about work.
Nonlinear: out of control, angry.
Random: illogical.

SOURCE: *"Microsoft: Bill Gates' Baby Is on Top of the World. Can It Stay There?" Reprinted from February 24, 1992 issue of* BusinessWeek *by special permission, copyright © 1992 by The McGraw-Hill Companies, Inc.*

Encouraging the Use of Jargon. An analysis by Lee G. Bolman and Terrence E. Deal suggests that the symbolic and ritualistic framework of a group contributes heavily to teamwork. An important part of this framework is a specialized language that fosters cohesion and commitment. In essence, this specialized language is in-group jargon. The jargon creates a bond among team members and sets the group apart from outsiders. It also reinforces unique values and beliefs, thus contributing to corporate culture. Jargon also allows team members to communicate easily, with few misunderstandings.[26]

The accompanying Team in Action box illustrates the colorful, jargon-laden speech of an organization known for its teamwork among highly intelligent individuals.

Soliciting Feedback on Team Effectiveness. Yet another approach to building teamwork is for the team to receive feedback on how well it is performing. Performance standards are set at the outset, following other suggestions here for building teamwork. Then the group establishes a team critique procedure, including self-evaluation by the team and evaluation by those who use the team's output, such as other units and customers. Once a month, about one hour is set aside for the team to evaluate its progress and compare it to the performance standards.[27]

When the feedback is positive, the team may experience a spurt of energy to keep working together well. Negative feedback, so long as it is not hostile, might bring the team together to develop action plans for improvement. The head of a maintenance team in a nuclear power plant told his team, "The ratings I have here tell us our performance in making repairs on time is next to last in the corporation. Will you join me in the challenge to improve?" His challenge was greeted with cheers of approval.

Minimizing Micromanagement.   A strategic perspective on encouraging teamwork is for the leader to minimize **micromanagement,** the close monitoring of most aspects of group member activities. To be a good team leader, the manager must give group members ample opportunity to manage their own activities. Avoiding micromanagement is a core ingredient of employee empowerment because empowered workers are given considerable latitude to manage their own activities. Research has shown that leaders of self-managing teams encourage self-reinforcement, self-goal setting, self-criticism, self-observation/evaluation, self-expectation, and rehearsal (mental review of upcoming events).[28]

United Auto Workers president Ronald A. Gettlefinger is an example of how a hands-on manager can often slip into the micromanagement mode. Gettlefinger values firsthand knowledge rather than filtered summaries. Part of his role is to be actively involved in union-management negotiations. But Gettlefinger is accused of being a micromanager because he has been known to pore over group members' telephone bills looking for personal phone calls.[29]

Leadership Self-Assessment Quiz 9-2 provides some assistance in helping you avoid becoming a micromanager. This skill is important because in most leadership situations, being perceived as a micromanager is a liability.

Actions Generally Requiring Organization Structure or Policy

Designing Physical Structures That Facilitate Communication.   Group cohesiveness, and therefore teamwork, is enhanced when team members are located close together and can interact frequently and easily. In contrast, people who spend most of their time in private offices or cubicles are less likely to interact. Frequent interaction often leads to camaraderie and a feeling of belongingness. A useful tactic for achieving physical proximity is to establish a shared physical facility, such as a conference room, research library, or beverage lounge. This area should be decorated differently from other areas in the building and a few amenities should be added, such as a coffeepot, microwave oven, and refrigerator. Team members can then use this area for refreshments and group interaction.

Recognizing the contribution of a shared physical facility to promoting teamwork, many organizations today have incorporated more open working space into the workplace, often eliminating private offices.

For many people, this lack of privacy in the modern office creates dissatisfaction. However, so far no information has been published about the productivity loss and morale problems stemming from limited opportunity for quiet reflection on the job.

Overcoming Micromanagement

Whether or not you are currently a manager, this brief self-quiz and accompanying suggestions provides some useful insights about avoiding micromanagement. Keeping micromanagement tendencies under control is important because the team is likely to feel more empowered, and your most capable team members will feel less like quitting. Furthermore, holding on to unimportant tasks cuts dramatically into your productivity and that of your staff. Is micromanagement impeding your progress?

INSTRUCTIONS   Ask yourself these four questions and circle the appropriate answer:

1. I sign off on all projects, from large to small.	YES	NO
2. Most decisions end up in my lap.	YES	NO
3. I feel overwhelmed by administrative tasks.	YES	NO
4. Staff turnover is high and morale is low.	YES	NO

INTERPRETATION   If you answered "Yes" two or more times, you need to learn how to modify your "death grip" management style.

SKILL DEVELOPMENT   The following three steps can help you feel more comfortable delegating and also encourage employee growth.

1. **Establish a trust level for each staffer.** For example, Helen has excellent judgment, so give her project authority. On the other hand, even though Tim is an excellent worker, you need to supervise him closely.

2. **Make sure staffers understand your instructions.** Ask them to repeat assignments verbally and confirm complex tasks with a follow-up email message.

3. **Open multiple avenues of communication.** Establish check-in, interim, and deadline dates. Follow up faithfully. Tell employees that your door is always open, but give them a good sense of how much authority they have and when they should consult you.

Ask staffers, "How's it going?" occasionally. Then let them get on with their work.

SOURCE: *Adapted from "Power Productivity: Stop Micromanaging and Spur Productivity,"* Manager's Edge, *July 2002, p. 6. Adapted from* The Organized Executive, *Briefings Publishing Group, (800) 722-9221.*

Emphasizing Group Recognition and Rewards. Giving rewards for group accomplishment reinforces teamwork because people receive rewards for what they have achieved collaboratively. The recognition accompanying the reward should emphasize the team's value to the organization rather than that of the individual. Recognition promotes team identity by enabling the team to take pride in its contributions and progress. The following are examples of team recognition:

- A display wall for team activities such as certificates of accomplishment, schedules, and miscellaneous announcements
- Team logos on items such as identifying T-shirts, athletic caps, mugs, jackets, key rings, and business cards
- Celebrations to mark milestones such as first-time activities, cost savings, and safety records
- Equipment painted in team colors
- Athletic team events such as softball, volleyball, and bowling
- Team-of-the-Month award, with gifts from the organization to team members or to the entire team

An extensive study of high-performing work teams concluded that financial rewards for teams should take the following form: pay for skills, team performance pay, gainsharing, and profit sharing. The last two of these practices require the organization to modify traditional reward systems that reinforce individual accomplishment. A caution is that many employees may view switching to a team-based pay plan that places much of their pay at risk as a scary proposition.[30] Another study showed that team rewards are associated with superior team self-management. Reward systems that were evenly split between individual rewards and group rewards were much less effective.[31]

Initiating Ritual and Ceremony. Another way to enhance teamwork is to initiate ritual and ceremony.[32] Ritual and ceremony afford opportunities for reinforcing values, revitalizing spirit, and bonding workers to one another and to the team. An example would be holding a team dinner whenever the group achieves a major milestone, such as making a winning bid on a major contract. Another formal ritual is to send a team on a retreat to further develop their mission and goals and to build camaraderie. When the team is working and socializing closely together during the retreat—even one long day—teamwork is reinforced.

Practicing Open-Book Management. An increasingly popular method of getting the company working together as a team is to share information about company finances and strategy with large numbers of employees. In **open-book management** every employee is trained, empowered, and motivated to understand and pursue the company's business goals. In this way the employees become business partners and perceive themselves to be members of the same team. In a full form of open-book management, workers share strategic and financial information as well as responsibility. The company also shares risks and rewards based on results, so workers are likely to pull together as a team so that the company can succeed.[33] The idea is to have a well-informed, partner-oriented, high-performance company. Part of keeping workers well informed is for company leaders to host roundtable discussions about company financial information. Another approach is to regularly disseminate over email information about the company's financial progress.[34]

Selecting Team-Oriented Members. A heavy-impact method of building teamwork is to select team members who are interested in and capable of teamwork. A starting point is self-selection. It is best for the team leader to choose workers who ask to be members of a team. A person's record of past team activity can also help one determine whether a person is an effective team player. Many managers believe that individuals who participate in team sports now, or in the past, are likely to be good team players on the job. Many female executives contend that the sports they played while growing up helped prepare them for the team aspects of corporate life. In one study, 81 percent of the 401 businesswomen surveyed agreed that sports helped them function better on a team. In addition, 69 percent said that sports promoted the leadership skills that contributed to professional success.[35]

Using Technology That Enhances Teamwork. Workers can collaborate better when they use information technology that fosters collaboration, often referred to as *groupware*. For example, the straightforward act of exchanging frequent email messages and instant messages can facilitate cooperation. Electronic brainstorming is another example of groupware. An important new development is web sites where workers can collaborate to save time and money on activities as varied as product design and mergers. Companies can now make products more cheaply and quickly by using the Web to synchronize the various aspects of design with suppliers. For example, using a system of collaborative software at General Motors Corporation factories, management has cut the time it takes to complete a vehicle mock-up from twelve weeks to two weeks.[36]

The link to teamwork is that members of different groups work more smoothly as a team with members outside the group. This is somewhat different from the emphasis in this chapter on teamwork *within* the group.

The accompanying Leader in Action insert describes a small-company CEO who uses several of the techniques already described to build teamwork in his company.

Outdoor Training and Team Development

Cognitive information about strategies and tactics for improving teamwork is potentially valuable. The person reading such information can selectively apply the concepts, observe the consequences, and then fine-tune his or her approach.

Leader in Action

Marque, Inc. CEO Scott Jessup Boosts Productivity Through Teamwork

Scott Jessup, CEO of Marque, Inc., Goshen, Indiana, fears the notion that the CEO has to be the smartest guy in the plant. "If that's the case I think we're all in trouble," reflects Jessup. "I truly believe I'd rather have ten smart people tackle a problem. I could [couldn't] care less who comes up with a solution. I would rather that than have ten people staring at me hoping like hell I make the right decision."

Business is good for Marque, which manufactures 150 medical-emergency-squad trucks a year. The forty-five-employee company is growing at about 20 percent a year. CEO Jessup, by his own admission not the smartest guy in the plant, was nevertheless smart enough to know that if the company wanted to expand its market share, it needed to reach new levels of productivity.

To raise the productivity bar at Marque, Jessup decided to form a cross-functional team that would spot bottleneck production problems throughout the plant; he then gave the team authority, within parameters, to resolve the constraints.

"A lot of bottleneck problems they have identified are not major business-altering issues. It's these constant, nagging, little issues that everybody has to confront every day," Jessup explains.

For example, plant workers were using an old forklift that was operating only 70 percent of the time because parts were wearing out and it needed constant maintenance. The bottleneck team determined it would be more cost effective to buy a new forklift that wouldn't need so much maintenance and that would be available 100 percent of the time.

Marque's cross-functional team consists of employees from production, quality assurance, and fabrication, along with a multiskilled employee and a consultant who help facilitate the team's development. Jessup decided against being a team member. He keeps track of the team's progress by reading the team's meeting minutes and by talking with team members.

"When a CEO wanders into a team meeting, an entirely different dynamic takes place, and everybody sits back and waits for the CEO to put forth these pearls of wisdom," he says. "I think at times I stifle our best thinking."

QUESTIONS

1. In what way is Scott Jessup practicing empowerment?

2. Which style of leadership is Jessup using?

3. In what way is Jessup "tapping the collective brainpower" of his employees?

SOURCE: *Peter Strozniak, "Teams at Work,"* IndustryWeek.com, *September 18, 2000.*

Another approach to developing teamwork is to participate in experiential activities, several of which are presented throughout this text.

One popular experiential approach to building teamwork and leadership skills is having outdoor training, also referred to as offsite training. Wilderness training is closely associated with outdoor training, except that the setting is likely to be much rougher—perhaps in the frozen tundra of northernmost Minnesota. Some forms of outdoor training take place in city parks.

Both outdoor and wilderness training are forms of learning by doing. Participants are supposed to acquire leadership and teamwork skills by confronting physical challenges and exceeding their self-imposed limitations. The goals of outdoor training are reasonably consistent across different training groups. The Big Rock Creek Camp, which offers team building and leadership training, specifies these representative goals:

- Discover your strengths and weaknesses.
- Test your limits (they're far broader than you imagine).
- Work together as a team.
- Have fun.
- Face the essence of who you are and what you are made of.
- Have the opportunity to break through barriers within yourself.
- Have the opportunity to break through barriers between yourself and others.

Features of Outdoor and Offsite Training Programs

Program participants are placed in a demanding outdoor environment. They have to rely on skills they did not realize they had, and on one another, to complete the program. The emphasis is on building not only teamwork but also self-confidence for leadership. Sometimes lectures on leadership, self-confidence, and teamwork precede the activity. The list of what constitutes a team-building activity continues to grow and now includes tightrope walking, adventure racing, treasure hunts (such as finding a store mannequin with red hair), and cooking.

What transpires in outdoor training can also be gleaned from the training instructors receive. The corporate program for Australian Outdoor Training & Tours includes courses in survival, navigation, vehicle handling, canoeing, roping, caving, parachuting, communications, and first aid."[37] At *Entrepreneur* (the magazine), the following took place:

> Some of the editorial and art staff . . . participated in a team-building workshop run by the Center for Strategic Leadership at Irvine Valley College in Irvine, California. The event included maneuvering a wooden A-frame across a field (to teach teamwork); cramming seven people on three squares of carpet remnants while moving toward a finish line (to teach closeness, presumably); and grabbing hands to form a human knot, then untangling ourselves (to teach creative problem solving).[38]

Outward Bound is the best known and largest outdoor training program. The program offers more than 500 courses in wilderness areas in twenty states and provinces. The courses typically run from three days to four weeks. Worldwide, Outward Bound runs about forty-eight schools on five continents.

The Outward Bound Professional Development Program is geared to organizational leaders because it emphasizes teamwork, leadership, and risk taking. The wilderness is the classroom, and the instructors draw analogies between each outdoor activity and the workplace. Among the courses offered are dogsledding, skiing and winter camping, desert backpacking, canoe expeditioning, sailing, sea kayaking, alpine mountaineering, mountain backpacking and horsetrailing, and cycling.

The Trust Fall

Perhaps the most widely used team-building activity is the trust fall, which may be familiar to many readers. Nevertheless, each application of this exercise is likely to produce new and informative results. The class organizes itself into teams. In each team, each willing member stands on a chair and falls backwards into the arms of teammates. A less frightening alternative to falling off a chair is to simply fall backwards standing up. Those team members who for whatever physical or mental reason would prefer not to fall back into others or participate in catching others are unconditionally excluded. However, they can serve as observers. After the trust falls have been completed, a team leader gathers answers to the following questions, and then shares the answers with the rest of the class.

1. How does this exercise develop teamwork?

2. How does this exercise develop leadership skills?

3. What did the participants learn about themselves?

Rope activities are typical of outdoor training. Participants are attached to a secure pulley with ropes; then they climb up a ladder and jump off to another spot. Sometimes the rope is extended between two trees. Another activity is a "trust fall," in which each person takes a turn standing on a platform and falling backwards into the arms of coworkers. The trust fall can also be done on ground level.[39] To examine a trust fall firsthand, do Leadership Skill-Building Exercise 9-2. A similar activity used in offsite training is presented in Leadership Skill-Building Exercise 9-3.

Outdoor training enhances teamwork by helping participants examine the process of getting things done through working with people. Participants practice their communication skills in exercises such as rappeling down a cliff by issuing precise instructions to one another about how to scale the cliff safely. At the same time, they have to learn to trust one another more because survival appears to depend on trust.

Evaluation of Outdoor Training for Team Development

Many outdoor trainers and participants believe strongly that they derived substantial personal benefits from outdoor training. Among the most important are greater self-confidence, appreciating hidden strengths, and learning to work better with people. Strong proponents of outdoor training believe that those who do not appreciate the training simply do not understand it. Many training directors also have positive attitudes toward outdoor training. They believe that a work

Trust Me

Part of trusting team members is to trust them with your physical safety. The trust builder described next has been incorporated into many team-building programs. Proceed as follows:

Step 1: Each group member takes a turn being blindfolded, perhaps using a bandanna.

Step 2: The remaining team members arrange between five and eight chairs into a formation of their choosing. Use a different formation for each blindfolded member.

Step 3: At the appropriate signal from a team member, the blindfolded person starts to walk. The rest of the team gives instructions that will enable the blindfolded person to get past the formation of chairs without a collision.

Step 4: At the end of the blindfolded person's experience, he or she immediately answers the following questions: (a) How did you feel when blindfolded in this exercise? (b) Explain why you either trusted or did not trust your team members. (c) What did you need from your team members while you were blindfolded?

Step 5: After each person has taken a turn, discuss in your team (a) the impact of this exercise on the development of trust in teams and (b) what you learned about teamwork from the exercise.

team that experiences outdoor training will work more cooperatively back at the office.

Many people have legitimate reservations about outdoor training, however. Although outdoor trainers claim that almost no accidents occur, a threat to health and life does exist. (To help minimize casualties, participants usually need medical clearance.) Another concern is that the teamwork learned in outdoor training does not spill over into the job environment. As Jay Conger explains, the workplace is a different environment from the wilderness. And real workplace teams tend to gain and lose their members rapidly as teammates are transferred, promoted, terminated, or quit. This mobility often negates all the team-building efforts that take place during the wilderness experience. Another problem is that when teams return to work, they often revert to noncollaborative behavior.[40]

An insightful perspective on the pros and cons of outdoor training comes from the *Entrepreneur* work group mentioned earlier.

The verdict? Mixed. Some participants had fun. "It was a field trip," was a common phrase. Others, those not keen on their personal space being invaded, left feeling unhappy rather than inspired. Did we return to the office a better team? Not really. The lessons about every person being integral to the larger mission and the need for flexibility rang true but, um, we sort of already knew that.

Still, we probably could have gotten more out of the session if time constraints hadn't kept us from attending the pre- and post-training meetings typically held. The pre-training meetings would have identified areas we needed to work on: the post-training meeting would have helped us translate what we accomplished to the office.[41]

One way to facilitate the transfer of training from outdoors to the office is to hold debriefing and follow-up sessions. Debriefing takes place at the end of outdoor training. The participants review what they learned and discuss how they will apply their lessons to the job. Follow-up sessions can then be held periodically to describe progress in applying the insights learned during outdoor training.

The Leader-Member Exchange Model and Teamwork

Research and theory about the development of teamwork lag far behind research and theory about many other aspects of leadership. Nevertheless, the leader-member exchange model, developed by George Graen and associates, helps explain why one subgroup in a unit is part of a cohesive team and another group is excluded.[42] The **leader-member exchange model (LMX)** proposes that leaders develop unique working relationships with group members. One subset of employees, the in-group, is given additional rewards, responsibility, and trust in exchange for their loyalty and performance. The in-group becomes part of a smoothly functioning team headed by the formal leader. In contrast, the out-group employees are treated in accordance with a more formal understanding of leader-group member relations. Out-group members are less likely to experience good teamwork.

Figure 9-2 depicts the major concept of the leader-exchange model. Here we look at several aspects of LMX as it relates most closely to teamwork. Leader-member exchange has also been researched in relationship to many other aspects of workplace behavior.

Different-Quality Relationships

Graen and his associates argue that leaders do not typically use the same leadership style in dealing with all group members. Instead, they treat each member somewhat differently. According to the model, the linkages (relationships) that exist between the leader and each individual team member probably differ in quality. In theory, the differences lie on a continuum of low quality to high quality. With group members on the top half of the continuum, the leader has a good relationship; with those on the lower half of the continuum, the leader has a poor relationship. Each of these pairs of relationships, or dyads, must be judged in terms of whether a group member is "in" or "out" with the leader. Leaders and members liking each other is a major contributor to the quality of their relationship, as documented by a study conducted in the marketing division of an electric company.[43]

Members of the in-group are invited to participate in important decision making, are given added responsibility, and are privy to interesting gossip. Members of the out-group are managed according to the requirements of their employment contract. They receive little warmth, inspiration, or encouragement. Robert Vecchio explains that an in-group member is elevated to the unofficial role of trusted assistant.[44] An out-group member is treated much like a hired hand. In-group members tend to achieve a higher level of performance, commitment, and satisfaction than do out-group members. Furthermore, they are less likely to quit. A recent study found strong support for the proposition that when the quality of the leader-member exchange is high, group members are more strongly committed to company goals.[45] In turn, this commitment leads to stronger teamwork because the workers pull together to pursue goals.

The in-group versus out-group status also includes an element of reciprocity or exchange. The leader grants more favors to the in-group member, who in turn works harder to please the leader. Two studies provide more specific information about the consequences of a positive exchange between a supervisor and group

FIGURE 9–2   The Leader–Member Exchange Model

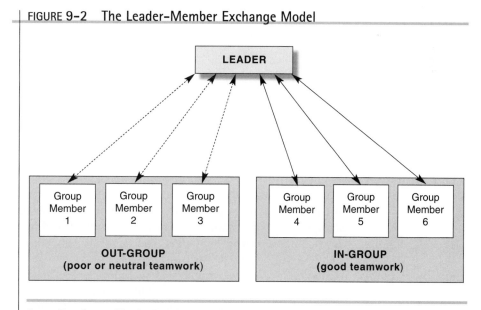

Source: From Gregory Moorhead and Ricky W. Griffin, Organizational Behavior: Managing People and Organizations, 4/e, p. 314. Copyright © 1995 by Houghton Mifflin Company. Reprinted by permission of Houghton Mifflin Company.

members. In a hospital setting, positive exchanges involved group members engaging in increased good citizenship behavior and also in-group role behaviors such as putting extra effort into performing duties.[46] As a result, the leader would feel justified in granting the in-group members more resources, such as a larger salary increase or a larger budget.

In a study conducted in diverse industrial settings, it was also found that high-quality exchanges between supervisors and employees contribute to employees' engaging in extra-role behavior, or being cooperative in ways that were not expected of them. Helping behaviors were measured by supervisors rating their employees on altruism. An example would be for an accountant to help a sales representative prepare a sales forecast. The researchers concluded that through the development of high-quality relationships with group members, supervisors are able to motivate the group members and enable them to engage in helping behaviors that benefit them as well as their coworkers.[47]

Being part of the in-group can facilitate a member's future promotional opportunities. Unfortunately, choices about who becomes an in-group or out-group member are sometimes based on factors unrelated to job performance. Leaders sometimes form bonds with group members who play golf with them, who belong to the same ethnic, religious, or racial group, or who are the same sex.

One contribution of positive leader-member exchanges is that they facilitate good safety performance, which is an important aspect of teamwork in many work environments. Sixty-four group leaders in a manufacturing plant participated in a study. A major finding of the study was that positive leader-member exchanges were associated with more communication about safety. The enhanced communication led to more commitment to safety, which in turn led to fewer accidents on the job.[48]

First Impressions

The leader's first impression of a group member's competency plays an important role in placing the group member into the in-group or the out-group. Another key linking factor is whether the leader and team member have positive or negative chemistry. We can assume that group members who make effective use of influence and political tactics increase their chances of becoming members of the in-group.

A field study seems to confirm that first impressions make a difference. The researchers gathered ratings of six aspects of the manager–group member dyad. One measure was the group members' perceived similarity with the leader. For example, "My supervisor and I are alike in a number of ways." A second measure was feelings about the manager, such as "I like my supervisor very much as a friend." A third rating dealt directly with the member's view of the leader-member exchange (LMX). An example is "I can count on my supervisor to 'bail me out,' even at his or her expense, when I really need it."

A fourth rating measured the leader expectation of the member, such as "I think my new employee will be an excellent employee." A fifth rating measured leader liking of the member, such as "I like my subordinate very much as a person." A sixth rating was the leader's view of the LMX, including a rating of the statement, "I would be willing to 'bail out' my subordinate, even at my own expense, if he or she really needed it."

Results showed that the initial leader expectations of members and member expectations of the leader were good predictors of the leader-member exchanges at two weeks and at six weeks. Member expectations of the leader also accurately predicted member assessments of the quality of the leader-member exchange at six months. An important interpretation of these results is that the leader-member exchange is formed in the first several days of the relationship.[49] As the adage states, "You have only one chance to make a first impression."

In summary, the leader-member exchange model provides a partial explanation of teamwork development. Members of the in-group work smoothly together and with the leader because they feel privileged. Being a member of the out-group may not diminish teamwork, but it certainly does not make a positive contribution.

SUMMARY

Leaders are required to build teamwork because it is needed for such key activities as group problem solving and achieving high quality. Teamwork is an understanding of and commitment to group goals on the part of all group members. Team leaders share power, deemphasize individual glory, and understand that power sharing increases their own power. The solo style of leader is the traditional autocratic leader in a bureaucracy.

Group work and group decision making offer several advantages, including the possibility of synergy and of catching major errors. Team structures can sometimes streamline the management of the firm. Working in groups often enhances job satisfaction, and many personal needs can be satisfied. Group activity also has some potential disadvantages, including pressures toward conformity, social loafing, wasting of time, and groupthink.

Leaders still play an important role in a team-based organization, such as being expert in the team process, being facilitators, building trust and inspiring teamwork, and enabling and empowering group members to accomplish their work. The enabling role centers on empowerment.

A wide range of leader actions foster teamwork. Measures leaders can take using their own resources include (1) defining the team's mission; (2) developing a norm of teamwork including emotional intelligence; (3) emphasizing pride in being outstanding; (4) holding a powwow; (5) serving as a model of teamwork; (6) using a consensus leadership style; (7) establishing urgent, demanding performance standards, and giving direction; (8) encouraging competition with another group; (9) encouraging use of jargon; (10) soliciting feedback on team effectiveness; and (11) minimizing micromanagement.

Techniques to foster teamwork that require relying on organizational structure or policy include the following: (1) designing physical structures that facilitate communication; (2) emphasizing group recognition and rewards; (3) initiating ritual and ceremony; (4) practicing open-book management; (5) selecting team-oriented members; and (6) using technology that facilitates teamwork.

In outdoor (or offsite) training, a popular experiential approach to building teamwork and leadership skills, building self-confidence is the focus. Outdoor training enhances teamwork by helping participants examine the process of getting things done collaboratively. The Outward Bound Professional Development Program is particularly geared toward organization leaders. Opinion about the effectiveness of outdoor training for developing teamwork and leadership skills is mixed. Concern has been expressed that the skills learned in the field do not carry over to the workplace.

The leader-exchange model helps explain why one subgroup in a work unit is part of a cohesive team and another unit is excluded. According to the model, leaders develop unique working relationships with subordinates. As a result, in-groups and out-groups are created. Members of the in-group tend to perform better, have higher satisfaction, and exhibit more teamwork. The leader's first impression of a group member's competency plays an important role in placing that person into the in-group or the out-group.

KEY TERMS

Team

Teamwork

Social loafing

Groupthink

Cooperation theory

Micromanagement

Open-book management

Leader-member exchange model (LMX)

GUIDELINES FOR ACTION AND SKILL DEVELOPMENT

Improving teamwork through the design of offices is receiving considerable attention. Professional Training Associates explains how to customize your (you being the leader/manager) space to promote teamwork:

1. **Create common areas.** Have ample space, accessible from throughout your office, for the team to meet both formally and informally. Leave your team-meeting tools—flipcharts, white-boards—in place even when the team is not meeting.

2. **Put yourself in the center.** Instead of reserving the back office, try to put yourself in the middle. You can be close to day-to-day action and more accessible to your team.

3. **Set up multipurpose rooms.** The back office can be used as a well-equipped workroom or library whenever team members—individually or in groups—feel they would be more productive away from their desks.

4. **Insert "activity generators."** Lively activity depends on having "generators" to draw traffic and bring people together. In your office, this could be the coffeepot, the mailboxes, or the reception desk. Turn these areas into places for team members to gather and interact comfortably and productively.[50]

DISCUSSION QUESTIONS AND ACTIVITIES

1. What would be the potential disadvantages of selecting a team leader who is highly charismatic and visionary?

2. Identify several *collective work products* from any group in which you have worked.

3. Identify and describe any team you have been a member of, or know about otherwise, that has a strong norm of teamwork.

4. Is there a role for independent-thinking, decisive, and creative leaders in a team-based organization? Explain.

5. What forces for and against being a good team player are embedded in American culture?

6. You have probably been told many times to minimize jargon in speech and writing in order to enhance communication, yet this chapter advocated using jargon to encourage teamwork. How do you reconcile the difference between the two pieces of advice?

7. How might open-book management be helpful in reducing dishonest and unethical financial reporting by business executives?

8. What is your opinion of the value of experience in team sports for becoming a good team player in the workplace?

9. What should be done about the team members who refuse to participate in team-building activities they perceive to be physically dangerous?

10. How can political skill help a person avoid being adversely affected by the leader-member exchange model?

Leadership Case Problem A

Radius Cooks up Teamwork

What are the ingredients of a great restaurant? Superb cuisine, a special ambience, a chef with presence. Radius, which opened in December 1998, has those ingredients in abundance. Its modern French fare has won raves from food critics. A restaurant reviewer rated Radius a 10, and said: "This is the place to go for a very special event. It's quite pricey, but well worth the money" (*Boston.citysearch.com*, p. 1). The average meal price is over $41 (2002 dollars), not including drinks. Its location, in a bank building in Boston's Financial District, is quite distinctive.

"We chose the name partly because of the architecture of the space," explains Christopher Myers, 41, co-owner and wine director. Co-owner Michael Schlow is committed to teamwork. As he says, "This restaurant is about creating something bigger than any of us could accomplish alone" (*Fast Company*, January–February, 2000, p. 54).

Radius wants to rank among the top twenty-five restaurants in the country. And it follows ten commandments to achieve that goal. "Achieving greatness is hard enough," says the tenth. "Sustaining greatness is the mark of true excellence" (*Fast Company*, p. 54).

Greatness at Radius starts with great teamwork, and great teamwork starts in the kitchen. The Radius kitchen is made up of stations: the meat station, the fish station, the garde-manger station, the pastry station. (A *garde-manger* is the French term for an armoire or chest of drawers where food is stored.) In other words, the team at the meat station not only cooks the meat but also butchers it and seasons it—a sharp departure from the task specialization approach followed at most restaurants.

Different also is the setup of the "career ladder" inside the kitchen. At most places, cooks start out at the garde-manger station and work their way up to preparing meat and fish. At Radius, cooks work at one station for six weeks and then rotate to another. "We asked how we can make the Radius experience fun, exciting, and educational?" says Schlow (*Fast Company*, p. 54).

Radius also developed a series of meetings in which both the spirit and the practice of teamwork get reinforced. One weekly meeting focuses on frontline service. The sous-chef and the pastry chefs meet with the back waiters and the food runners (the waiter's support staff) to review dishes and procedures. Because servers at Radius announce each course, they need to know what is on each plate, how to put it down in front of a guest, and how to pronounce it.

A daily meeting (the kitchen-staff session) focuses on behind-the-scenes operations. About thirty staffers gather around Schlow to discuss plans for the evening. He reminds them about his obsession with using as much of every ingredient as possible. "Can we make a sauce with the extra crème fraîche?" he asks. "What about that extra port?" (*Fast Company*, p. 56).

Then there's the daily service meeting. Led by Myers and general manager Esti Benson, 29, it includes all of the waitstaff, the floor managers, and the hosts and hostesses. About forty people gather around a large, rotunda-like lounge located in the restaurant's lower level. Benson begins by going over the night's reservations, who the customers are—their names, what they do, if they've been to Radius before. Then all eyes shift

to a plate of food. Benson calls on a server to describe the dish. She follows with a series of highly detailed questions. "What are the red beads around the plate?" she asks. "Spicy tomato oil," the server answers (*Fast Company*, p. 54).

Schlow runs the kitchen like a cooking school because he believes that most young cooks leave one restaurant for another so they can learn more. Everyone in the kitchen is given the ongoing assignment to keep up with the latest trends in the restaurant business. There is also the daily food fact. Each day, a member of the kitchen staff is responsible for researching a morsel of information about food. He or she presents that fact to the service staff at the daily meeting. Staff members are given exams that take about thirty minutes to complete and that cover a broad range of topics about the restaurant, its cuisines, and its staff.

"The tests are a way for me to monitor who's not getting enough instruction," says Myers. "That way, while people are learning, I'm also learning about them" (*Fast Company*, p. 54).

Radius has developed a loyal following—and a growing reputation among the industry's rising stars. One such star is Jap Caputo, a 26-year-old line cook who is a recent graduate of the Culinary Institute of America. "The first time I walked into Radius, the whole atmosphere was beautiful," he says. "You could tell that people really believed in what they were doing. I knew this was the place for me" (*Fast Company*, p. 54).

QUESTIONS

1. What actions is chef Michael Schlow taking to develop teamwork at Radius?

2. In what way does the continuous learning activity at Radius contribute to teamwork?

3. In what way are the co-owners of Radius showing a balanced concern for task and people?

4. Is this any way to run a deluxe restaurant?

SOURCE: *Adapted slightly from Gina Imperato, "Their Specialty? Teamwork,"* Fast Company, *January/February 2000, pp. 54-56;* http://boston.citysearch.com/profile/4721543/.

Leadership Case Problem B

Showboat Brent

Mary Tarkington, CEO of one of the major dot-com retailers, became concerned that too many employees at the company were stressed out and physically unhealthy. Tarkington said, "I have walked through our distribution center at many different times of the day and night, and I see the same troublesome scene. The place is littered with soft-drink cans and fast-food wrappers. Loads of our workers have stomachs bulging out of their pants. You always see a few workers huddled outside the building smoking. The unhealthiness around the company is also reflected in high absenteeism rates and health insurance costs that are continually rising.

"I want to see a big improvement in the health of our employees. It makes sense from the standpoint of being a socially responsible company, and from the standpoint of becoming more profitable. With this in mind, I am appointing a project team to study how we can best design and implement a company wellness program. Each member of the team will work about five hours per week on the project. I want to receive a full report in forty-five days, and I expect to see progress reports along the way."

Five people were appointed to the wellness task force: Ankit, a programmer; Jennifer, a web site designer; Brent, a systems analyst; Derek, a logistics technician; and Kristine, a human resource specialist. During the first meeting, the group appointed Kristine as the Wellness Task Force head because of her professional specialty. Ankit, Jennifer, and Derek offered Kristine their congratulations and wished her the best. Brent offered a comment with a slightly different tone: "I can see why the group chose you to head our task force. I voted for you also, but I think we should be starting with a blank tablet. We are making no assumptions that anybody's ideas carry more professional weight than anybody else's ideas."

The next time the group met, each member reported some preliminary findings about wellness programs they had researched. Ankit summarized a magazine article on the topic; Jennifer reported on a friend's experience with his company wellness program; Derek presented some data on how wellness programs can boost productivity and morale; Kristine reported on www.workforce.com, a human resources web site that carries information about wellness programs. Each spent about six minutes on the presentation.

Brent then walked up to the front of the conference room, and engaged his laptop computer. He then began a twenty-five minute PowerPoint presentation about what he thought the committee should be doing, along with industry data about wellness programs. At the end of Brent's presentation Kristine commented with a quizzical look, "Thanks Brent, but I thought we agreed to around a five-minute presentation this first time around."

Brent replied, "Good point Kristine, yet I'm only doing what I considered best for getting our mission accomplished."

Ten days later, CEO Tarkington visited the task force to discuss its progress. Kristine, as the task force head, began the progress report. She pointed out that the group had gathered substantial information about corporate wellness programs. Kristine also noted that so far establishing one at the company looked feasible and worthwhile. She also noted that the group was beginning to assemble data about the physical requirements for having a wellness program, and the cost of implementation.

With a frown Brent said, "Not so fast Kristine. Since we last met, I have taken another look at the productivity figures about wellness centers. People who run wellness programs apparently supplied these figures, so the information could be tainted. I say that we are rushing too fast to reach a decision. Let's get some objective data before making a recommendation to the company."

Kristine groaned as she looked at Mary Tarkington and the task force members. She whispered to Jennifer to her right, "There goes Brent, showboating again."

QUESTIONS

1. What steps should Mary Tarkington take to develop better teamwork among the members of her task force?

2. What actions, if any, should the other task force members take to make Brent a better team player?

3. What kind of power is Brent attempting to establish for himself?

INTERNET SKILL-BUILDING EXERCISE

Learning More About Outdoor Training

Apply the chapter concepts! Visit the Web and complete this Internet skill-building exercise to learn more about current leadership topics and trends.

Go to www.Teambuilding.com (the Team Building Supersite), click onto *Building High Performance Teams*, and then go to the new video introduction. A talking head will surface on the screen. Listen to what he has to say. In addition, see the "Articles" section to read something about team building. In the process of listening to the video and reading one or two articles, identify four advantages that team building is supposed to bring to an organization. How do these advantages compare to those mentioned in the text?

Motivation and Coaching Skills

CHAPTER 10

Over two decades ago, as CEO of PepsiCo, Inc., Andy Pearson was named one of the ten toughest bosses in America, based on his ability to inflict pain. Now at Tricon Global Restaurants, Inc., Pearson has found a new way to lead—one that's based on personal humility and employee recognition. (Tricon operates KFC, Pizza Hut, and Taco Bell.)

At Tricon, 75-year-old Pearson has seen employees weep in gratitude in reaction to nothing more than a few simple words of praise. Where before he might have dismissed that kind of display as sentimentality, he now recognizes emotion for what it is: the secret to a company's competitive edge.

When Pearson came to Tricon to help lead the company, he absorbed what he saw in chairman and CEO David Novak's method. Almost overnight, Pearson saw how the human heart drives a com-pany's success one person at a time. He also saw how this kind of success cannot be imposed from the top but must be *kindled* through attention, awareness, recognition, and reward.

The logic was clear: If the need for recognition and approval is a fundamental human drive, then the willingness to give it is not a sign of weakness. Pearson says, "Great leaders find a balance between getting results and how they get them. A lot of people make the mistake of thinking that getting results is all there is to the job. They go after results without building a team or without building an organization that has the capacity to change. Your real job is to get results *and* to do it in a way that makes your organization a great place to work—a place where people enjoy coming to work, instead of just taking orders and hitting this month's numbers."[1]

The comments from the well-recognized Andy Pearson underscore the importance of a leader motivating employees and helping them grow. Effective leaders are outstanding motivators and coaches. They influence others in many of the ways previously described. In addition, they often use specific motivational and coaching skills. These techniques are important because not all leaders can influence others through formal authority or charisma and inspirational leadership alone. Face-to-face, day-by-day motivational skills are also important. Good coaching is a related essential feature of management because motivating workers is an important part of coaching them.

In this chapter we approach motivation and coaching skills from various perspectives. We examine first how leaders make effective use of expectancy theory, behavior modification, recognition, and goal setting to motivate group members. Second, we describe coaching as a leadership philosophy, followed by a descrip-

EXPECTANCY THEORY AND MOTIVATIONAL SKILLS

tion of specific coaching skills and the role of the executive coach.

Expectancy theory is a good starting point in learning how leaders can apply systematic explanations of motivation, for two major reasons. First, the theory is comprehensive because it incorporates and integrates features of other motivation theories, including goal theory and behavior modification. Second, it offers the leader many guidelines for triggering and sustaining constructive effort from group members.

The **expectancy theory** of motivation is based on the premise that the amount of effort people expend depends on how much reward they expect to get in return. In addition to being broad, the theory deals with cognition and process. Expectancy theory is cognitive because it emphasizes the thoughts, judgments, and desires of the person being motivated. It is a process theory because it attempts to explain how motivation takes place.

The theory is really a group of theories based on a rational, economic view of people.[2] Expectancy theory as applied to work has recently been recast as a theory called *motivation management.* In any given situation, people want to maximize gain and minimize loss. The theory assumes that people choose among alternatives by selecting the one they think they have the best chance of attaining. Furthermore, they choose the alternative that appears to have the biggest personal payoff. Given a choice, people will select the assignment that they think they can handle the best and that will benefit them the most.

Basic Components of Expectancy Theory

Expectancy theory contains three basic components: valence, instrumentality, and expectancy. Because of these three components, the theory is often referred to as VIE theory. Figure 10-1 presents a basic version of expectancy theory. All three elements must be present for motivation to take place. To be motivated, people must value the reward, think they can perform, and have reasonable assurance that performance will lead to a reward.

FIGURE 10-1   The Expectancy Theory of Motivation

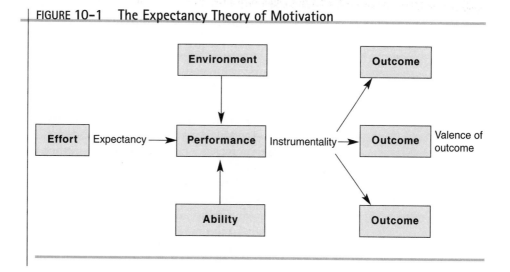

Valence.   The worth or attractiveness of an outcome is referred to as **valence.** As shown in Figure 10-1, each work situation has multiple outcomes. An **outcome** is anything that might stem from performance, such as a reward. Each outcome has a valence of its own. And each outcome can lead to other outcomes or consequences, referred to as *second-level outcomes.* A person who receives an outstanding performance appraisal (a first-level outcome) becomes eligible for a promotion (a second-level outcome). Second-level outcomes also have valences. The sum of all the valences must be positive if the person is to work hard. However, if the sum of all the valences is negative, the person might work hard to avoid the outcome.

Valences range from −100 to +100 in the version of expectancy theory presented here. (The usual method of placing valences on a −1.00 to +1.00 scale does not do justice to the true differences in preferences.) A valence of +100 means that a person intensely desires an outcome. A valence of −100 means that a person is strongly motivated to avoid an outcome such as being fired or declaring bankruptcy. A valence of zero signifies indifference to an outcome and is therefore of no use as a motivator.

Instrumentality.   An individual's assessment of the probability that performance will lead to certain outcomes is referred to as **instrumentality.** (An instrumentality is also referred to as a *performance-to-outcome expectancy* because it relates to the outcome people expect from performing in a certain way.) When people engage in a particular behavior, they do so with the intention of achieving a desired outcome or reward. Instrumentalities range from 0 to 1.0, where 0 is no chance of receiving the desired reward, and 1.0 is a belief that the reward is certain to follow. For example, an hourly worker might say, "I know for sure that if I work overtime, I will receive overtime pay."

Expectancy.   An individual's assessment of the probability that effort will lead to correct performance of the task is referred to as **expectancy.** (The same concept is also referred to as *effort-to-performance expectancy.*) An important question people ask themselves before putting forth effort to accomplish a task is "If I put in all this work, will I really get the job done properly?" Expectancies range from 0 to 1.0, where 0 is no expectation of performing the tasks correctly, and 1.0 signifies absolute faith in being able to perform the task properly. Expectancies thus influence whether a person will even strive to earn a reward. Self-confident people have higher expectancies than do less self-confident people. Being well trained increases a person's subjective hunch that he or she can perform the task.

The importance of having high expectancies for motivation meshes well with a new thrust in work motivation that emphasizes the contribution of **self-efficacy,** the confidence in your ability to carry out a specific task. If you have high self-efficacy about the task, your motivation will be high. Low self-efficacy leads to low motivation. Some people are poorly motivated to skydive because they doubt they will be able to pull the ripcord while free-falling at 120 mph. A more technical definition and explanation will help you appreciate the contribution of self-efficacy to motivation:

> Self-efficacy refers to an individual's convictions (or confidence) about his or her abilities to mobilize the motivation, cognitive resources, and course of action needed to successfully execute a specific task within a given context.[3]

In short, if you are confident about your task-related skills, you will get your act together to do the task. This is one reason why you should give people the skills and confidence they need to put forth effort.

A seeming contradiction in expectancy theory requires explanation. Some people will engage in behaviors with low expectancies, such as trying to invent a successful new product or become the CEO of a major corporation. The compensating factor is the large valences attached to the second-level outcomes associated with these accomplishments. The payoffs from introducing a successful new product or becoming a CEO are so great that people are willing to take a long shot.

A Brief Look at the Evidence.   The application of expectancy theory, especially the VIE version, to work motivation has been the subject of research for over thirty years. Two researchers performed a meta-analysis of seventy-seven studies of how well various aspects of expectancy theory were related to workplace criteria such as performance and effort. Although the results were not consistent, the general conclusion reached was that the three components of expectancy theory are positively related to workplace criteria. For example, job performance showed a positive correlation with valence, instrumentality, expectancy, and the total VIE model. The total VIE model typically refers to a multiplication of the values for valence, instrumentality, and expectancy. Another finding was that effort expended on the job was positively correlated with valence, instrumentality, expectancy, the VIE model, and performance.[4] The last correlation helps verify the justification for leaders and managers being concerned about motivating employees: People who try harder perform better!

Leadership Skills and Behaviors Associated with Expectancy Theory

Expectancy theory has many implications for leaders and managers with respect to motivating others.[5] Some of these implications would also stem from other motivational theories, and they fit good management practice in general. As you read each implication, reflect on how you might apply the skill or behavior during a leadership assignment.

1. *Determine what levels and kinds of performance are needed to achieve organizational goals.* Motivating others proceeds best when workers have a clear understanding of what needs to be accomplished. At the same time, the leader should make sure that the desired levels of performance are possible. For example, sales quotas might be set too high because the market is already saturated with a particular product or service.

2. *Make the performance level attainable by the individuals being motivated.* If the group members believe that they are being asked to perform extraordinarily difficult tasks, most of them will suffer from low motivation. A task must generally be perceived as attainable to be motivational.

3. *Train and encourage people.* Leaders should give group members the necessary training and encouragement to be confident they can perform the required task. (We will return to the encouragement aspect of leadership in the discussion of coaching.) Some group members who appear to be poorly motivated simply lack the right skills and self-confidence.

4. *Make explicit the link between rewards and performance.* Group members should be reassured that if they perform the job up to standard, they will receive the promised reward.

5. *Make sure the rewards are large enough.* Some rewards fail to motivate people because although they are the right kind, they are not in the right amount. The promise of a large salary increase might be motivational, but a 1 percent increase will probably have little motivational thrust for most workers.

6. *Analyze what factors work in opposition to the effectiveness of the reward.* Conflicts between the leader's package of rewards and other influences in the work group may require the leader to modify the reward. For example, if the work group favors the status quo, a large reward may be required to encourage innovative thinking.

7. *Explain the meaning and implications of second-level outcomes.* It is helpful for employees to understand the value of certain outcomes, such as receiving a favorable performance appraisal. (For example, it could lead to a salary increase, assignment to a high-status task force, or promotion.)

8. *Understand individual differences in valences.* To motivate group members effectively, leaders must recognize individual differences or preferences for rewards. An attempt should be made to offer workers rewards to which they attach a high valence. One employee might value a high-adventure assignment; another might attach a high valence to a routine, tranquil assignment. Cross-cultural differences in valences may also occur. For example, many (but not all) Asian workers prefer not to be singled out for recognition in front of the group. According to their cultural values, receiving recognition in front of the group is insensitive and embarrassing. Leadership Skill-Building Exercise 10-1 deals further with the challenge of estimating valences.

Despite the utility of expectancy theory, leaders need to supplement it with other approaches to motivating group members. Three very applied approaches to motivation—goal theory, behavior modification, and giving recognition—are presented next.

Estimating Valences for Applying Expectancy Theory

INSTRUCTIONS   A major challenge in applying expectancy theory is estimating what valence attaches to possible outcomes. A leader or manager also has to be aware of the potential rewards or punishment in a given work situation. Listed below are a group of rewards and punishments, along with a space for rating the reward or punishment on a scale of −100 to +100. Work with about six teammates, with each person rating all the rewards and punishments.

Potential Outcome	Rating (−100 to +100)
1. Promotion to vice president	____
2. One-step promotion	____
3. Above-average performance rating	____
4. Top-category performance rating	____
5. $6,000 performance bonus	____
6. $2,000 performance bonus	____
7. $75 gift certificate	____
8. Employee-of-the-month plaque	____
9. Note of appreciation placed in file	____
10. Luncheon with boss at good restaurant	____
11. Lunch with boss in company cafeteria	____
12. Challenging new assignment	____
13. Allowed to accumulate frequent flyer miles for own use	____
14. Allowed to purchase software of choice	____
15. Assigned new equipment for own use	____
16. Private corner office with great view	____
17. Assigned a full-time administrative assistant	____
18. Documentation of poor performance	____
19. Being fired	____
20. Being fired and put on industry "bad-list"	____

21. Demoted one step   ____

22. Demoted to entry-level position   ____

23. Being ridiculed in front of others   ____

24. Being suspended without pay   ____

25. Being transferred to undesirable location   ____

After completing the ratings, discuss the following issues:

1. Which rewards and punishments received the most varied ratings?

2. Which rewards and punishments received similar ratings?

Another analytical approach would be to compute the means and standard deviations of the valences for each outcome. Each class member could then compare his or her own valence ratings with the class norm. To add to the database, each student might bring back two sets of ratings from employed people outside of class.

To apply this technique to the job, modify the above form to fit the outcomes available in your situation. Explain to team members that you are attempting to do a better job of rewarding and disciplining, and that you need their input. The ratings made by team members might provide fruitful discussion for a staff meeting.

GOAL THEORY

Goal setting is a basic process that is directly or indirectly part of all major theories of work motivation. Goal setting is accepted widely by leaders and managers as a means to improve and sustain performance. A vision, for example, is really an exalted goal. The core finding of goal-setting theory is that individuals who are provided with specific hard goals perform better than those who are given easy, nonspecific, "do your best" goals or no goals. At the same time, however, the individuals must have sufficient ability, accept the goals, and receive feedback related to the task.[6] Our overview of goal theory elaborates on this basic finding.

The premise underlying goal theory is that behavior is regulated by values and goals. A **goal** is what a person is trying to accomplish. Our values create within us a desire to behave in a way that is consistent with them. For example, if a leader values honesty, she will establish a goal of hiring only honest employees. The leader would therefore have to make extensive use of reference checks and honesty testing. Edwin A. Locke and Gary P. Latham have incorporated hundreds of studies about goals into a theory of goal setting and task performance.[7] Figure 10-2 summarizes some of the more consistent findings, and the information that follows describes them. A leader should keep these points in mind when motivating people through goal setting.

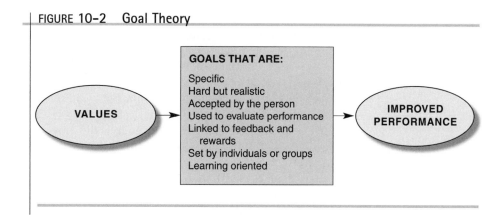

FIGURE 10-2   Goal Theory

To begin, remember that *specific goals lead to higher performance than do generalized goals.* Telling someone to "do your best" is a generalized goal. A specific goal would be "Increase the number of new hires to our management training program to fifteen for this summer." Another key point is that *performance generally improves in direct proportion to goal difficulty.* The harder one's goal, the more one accomplishes. An important exception is that when goals are too difficult, they may lower performance. Difficulty in reaching the goal leads to frustration, which in turn leads to lowered performance (as explained in relation to expectancy theory).

The finding about effective goals being realistic has an important exception for the accomplishment of high-level complex tasks. Effective leaders often inspire constituents by setting outrageous (or audacious) goals, or visions. Nicholas Lore writes that you can set reasonable, attainable goals for yourself and your staff. However, reasonable goals rarely inspire; instead, they lead to dull, comfortable lives. Here are two suggestions for developing powerful goals:

- Create a big, comprehensive goal. What would be an ideal accomplishment for your group?

- Break the goal down into smaller steps, such as hiring two top-notch workers for the group. Treat each step (or subgoal) as a project designed to get you to your destination.[8]

For goals to improve performance, the group member must accept them. If a group member rejects a goal, he or she will not incorporate it into planning. This is why it is often helpful to discuss goals with group members, rather than impose goals on them. New research, however, suggests that the importance of goal commitment may be overrated. A meta-analysis of mostly laboratory studies about the effect of goal commitment on performance concluded that commitment had a small impact on performance. Goals appeared to improve performance whether or not people participating in the studies felt committed to the goal.[9] Despite these recent findings, many managers and leaders think employee commitment to goals is important.

Participating in goal setting has no major effect on the level of job performance except when it improves goal acceptance. Yet the leader should recognize that participation is valuable because it can lead to higher satisfaction with the goal-setting process. *Goals are more effective when they are used to evaluate perform-ance.* When workers know that their performance will be evaluated in terms of how well they attain their goals, the impact of goals increases.

Keep in mind the key principle that *goals should be linked to feedback and re-wards.* Rewarding people for reaching goals is the most widely accepted principle of management. Another goal-setting principle is that *group goal setting is as im-portant as individual goal setting.* Having employees work as teams with a spe-cific team goal, rather than as individuals with only individual goals, increases productivity. Furthermore, a combination of compatible group and individual goals is more effective than either individual or group goals alone.

A final goal-setting principle is that a *learning goal orientation* improves per-formance more than a *performance goal orientation.* A person with a learning goal orientation wants to develop competence by acquiring new skills and mas-tering new situations. In contrast, the person with a performance goal orientation wants to demonstrate and validate his or her competence by seeking favorable judgments and avoiding negative judgments. In support of the distinction being made, a study with medical supply sales representatives found that a learning goal orientation had a positive relationship with sales performance. In contrast, a performance goal orientation was unrelated to sales performance.[10]

Despite their contribution to performance, goals are not, technically speaking, motivational in themselves. Rather, the discrepancies created by what individuals do and what they aspire to creates self-dissatisfaction. This dissatisfaction, in turn, creates a desire to reduce the discrepancy between the real and the ideal.[11] When a person has a desire to attain something, the person is in a state of arousal. The tension created by not having already achieved a goal spurs the person to reach the goal. As a leader, you can sometimes create this tension by suggesting possibilities that group members might strive for.

Goal setting is widely practiced by leaders and managers, but they typically do not give careful consideration to goal-setting theory. Leadership Skill-Building Ex-ercise 10-2 gives you an opportunity to apply what you have learned about goal setting.

BEHAVIOR MODIFICATION AND MOTIVATIONAL SKILLS

Behavior modification, a well-known system of motivation, is an attempt to change behavior by manipulating rewards and punishment. Behavior modifica-tion stems directly from reinforcement theory. Since many readers are already fa-miliar with reinforcement theory and behavior modification (often shortened to "behavior mod"), we will limit our discussion to a brief summary of the basics of behavior modification, and focus instead on its leadership applications.

The Application of Goal Theory

Working in a group of about five to six people, visualize your group as a task force whose mission is to make and implement suggestions for reducing water consumption in your company, a manufacturer of camping equipment. Water is a major company expense, and there is a distinct possibility that the county in which you are located will soon be rationing water. One of the group members plays the role of the task force leader. The leader must help the group establish goals that are likely to be motivational, following the principles of goal theory. The goal of today's meeting is to establish four goals that are likely to lead to high performance. After each team has established its goals, present them to other class members. Students listening to the goals of the other groups should be willing to offer whatever constructive feedback comes to mind.

Practice in setting effective goals is useful because leaders and managers are frequently expected to set goals. When the goal follows at least some of the major findings of goal theory, there is a greater likelihood that productivity will increase.

An underlying principle of behavior modification is the law of effect: Behavior that leads to a positive consequence for the individual tends to be repeated. In contrast, behavior that leads to a negative consequence tends not to be repeated. Leaders typically emphasize linking behavior with positive consequences, such as expressing enthusiasm for a job well done.

Behavior Modification Strategies

The techniques of behavior modification apply to both learning and motivation; they can be divided into four strategies. *Positive reinforcement*, which rewards the right response, increases the probability that the behavior will be repeated. The phrase *increases the probability* means that positive reinforcement improves learning and motivation but is not 100 percent effective. The phrase *the right response* is also noteworthy. When positive reinforcement is used properly, a reward is contingent upon the person doing something right. If the company achieves a high-quality award, the company president might recognize the accomplishment by giving a bonus to all. Authorizing a bonus for no particular reason might be pleasant, but it is not positive reinforcement.

Avoidance motivation (or *negative reinforcement*) is rewarding people by taking away an uncomfortable consequence of their behavior. It is the withdrawal or avoidance of a disliked consequence. A leader offers avoidance motivation when he or she says, "We have performed so well that the wage freeze will now be lifted." Removal of the undesirable consequence of a wage freeze was contingent upon performance above expectation. Be careful not to confuse negative reinforcement with punishment. Negative reinforcement is the opposite of punishment: It involves rewarding someone by removing a punishment or an uncomfortable situation.

Punishment is the presentation of an undesirable consequence, or the removal of a desirable consequence, because of unacceptable behavior. A leader or manager can punish a group member by demoting him or her for an ethical violation such as lying to a customer. Or the group member can be punished by losing the opportunity to attend an executive development program.

Extinction is decreasing the frequency of undesirable behavior by removing the desirable consequence of such behavior. Company leaders might use extinction by ceasing to pay employees for making frivolous cost-saving suggestions. Extinction is sometimes used to eliminate annoying behavior. Assume that a group member persists in telling ethnic jokes. The leader and the rest of the group can agree to ignore the jokes and thus extinguish the joke telling.

A guiding principle for motivating workers through behavior modification is that you *get what you reinforce*. If the leader or manager wants workers to perform in certain ways, such as answering customer inquiries over the Internet within twenty-four hours, that particular behavior must be reinforced. Reinforcing other behaviors, such as handling many inquiries, will not lead to the performance improvement sought. In a behavior modification program in a bank, supervisors gave feedback and recognition in front of coworkers to tellers who performed certain customer service behaviors. These included using the customer's name, providing a statement balance, and making eye contact. Customer satisfaction as measured by a survey increased after these customer service behaviors were reinforced.[12]

Rules for the Use of Behavior Modification

Behavior modification in organizations, often called OB Mod, frequently takes the form of a companywide program administered by the human resources department. Our focus here is on leaders' day-by-day application of behavior mod, with an emphasis on positive reinforcement. The coaching role of a leader exemplifies the application of positive reinforcement. Although using rewards and punishments to motivate people seems straightforward, behavior modification requires a systematic approach. The rules presented here are specified from the standpoint of a leader or manager trying to motivate an individual or a group.[13]

Rule 1: Target the desired behavior. An effective program of behavior modification begins with specifying the desired behavior—that which will be rewarded. The target or critical behaviors chosen are those that have a significant impact on performance, such as asking to take an order, conducting performance appraisals on time, or troubleshooting a customer problem. According to Fred Luthans, the critical behaviors are the 5 to 10 percent of behaviors that may account for as much as 70 or 80 percent of the performance in the area in question.[14]

Rule 2: Choose an appropriate reward or punishment. An appropriate reward or punishment is one that is (1) effective in motivating a given group member or group and (2) feasible from the company standpoint. If one reward does not work, try another. Feasible rewards include money, recognition, challenging new assignments, and status symbols such as a private work area. Stock options are widely used to motivate executives, and sometimes workers at all levels. Companies such as Starbucks Corporation, Cisco Systems, First Tennessee Bank, and General Mills offer stock options for all employees. The expectation is that each recipient of a stock option will work hard to improve company performance so that the stock price will rise and he or she will benefit personally.

Most of the rewards mentioned so far are extrinsic. However, intrinsic rewards can also be part of behavior modification. A person who performs well might be offered the opportunity to engage in more work that is exciting or fun, such as being a company representative at a trade show.

When positive motivators do not work, it may be necessary to use negative motivators (punishment). It is generally best to use the mildest form of punishment that will motivate the person or group. For example, if a group member reads a newspaper during the day, the person might simply be told to put away the newspaper. Motivation enters the picture because the time not spent on reading the newspaper can now be invested in company work. If the mildest form of punishment does not work, a more severe negative motivator is selected. Written documentation placed in the person's personnel file is a more severe punishment than a mere mention of the problem.

Rule 3: Supply ample feedback. Behavior modification cannot work without frequent feedback to individuals and groups. Feedback can take the form of simply telling people when they have done something right or wrong. Brief paper or electronic messages are another form of feedback. Be aware, however, that many employees resent seeing a message with negative feedback flashed across their video display terminals.

Rule 4: Do not give everyone the same-sized reward. Average performance is encouraged when all forms of accomplishment receive the same reward. Say one group member makes substantial progress in providing input for a strategic plan. He or she should receive more recognition (or other reward) than a group member who makes only a minor contribution to solving the problem.

Rule 5: Find some constructive behavior to reinforce. This rule stems from **behavior shaping,** rewarding any response in the right direction and then rewarding only the closest approximation. Using this approach, the desired behavior is finally attained. Behavior shaping is useful to the manager because the technique recognizes that you have to begin somewhere in teaching a worker a new skill or motivating a worker to make a big change. For example, if you were attempting to motivate a group member to make exciting computer graphics (such as PowerPoint), you would congratulate the first step forward from preparing a mundane overhead transparency. You would then become more selective about what type of presentation received a reward.

Rule 6: Schedule rewards intermittently. Rewards for good performance should not be given on every occasion. *Intermittent* rewards sustain desired behavior longer, and also slow the process of behavior fading away when it is not rewarded. If a person is rewarded for every instance of good performance, he or she is likely to keep up the level of performance until the reward comes, then slack off. Another problem is that a reward that is given continuously may lose its impact. A practical value of intermittent reinforcement is that it saves time. Few leaders have enough time to dispense rewards for every good deed forthcoming from team members.

Rule 7: Ensure that rewards and punishments follow the behavior closely in time. For maximum effectiveness, people should be rewarded shortly after doing something right, and punished shortly after doing something wrong. A built-in feedback system, such as a computer program working or not working, capitalizes on this principle. Many effective leaders get in touch with people quickly to congratulate them on an outstanding accomplishment.

Rule 8: Change the reward periodically. Rewards do not retain their effectiveness indefinitely. Team members lose interest in striving for a reward they have received many times in the past. This is particularly true of a repetitive statement such as "Nice job" or "Congratulations." Plaques for outstanding performance also lose their motivational appeal after a group receives many of them. It is helpful for the leader or manager to formulate a list of feasible rewards and try different ones from time to time.

Rule 9: Make the rewards visible and the punishments known. Another important characteristic of an effective reward is the extent to which it is visible, or noticeable to other employees. When other workers notice the reward, its impact multiplies because other people observe what kind of behavior is rewarded.[15] Assume that you are told about a coworker having received an exciting assignment because of high performance. You might strive to accomplish the same level of performance. Most people are aware that public punishments are poor human relations. Yet when coworkers become aware of what behaviors are punished, they receive an important message. A good example took place in a security systems office when a new member of the team distributed a series of sexually offensive jokes by email to coworkers. The man was immediately put on probation, and coworkers received a message about what constitutes unacceptable behavior.

Research indicates that behavior modification leads to important outcomes such as productivity improvement. For example, an experiment was conducted in the operations division of a company that processes and mails credit card bills for several hundred financial institutions, ecommerce customers included. The four groups in the study were those receiving (1) routine pay for performance, (2) monetary incentives based on behavior mod, (3) social recognition, such as public compliments, and (4) performance feedback. Monetary rewards based on the principles of behavior modification outperformed routine pay for performance, with a performance increase of 37 percent versus 11 percent. Monetary incentives also had stronger effects on performance than social recognition and performance feedback.[16] Evidence like this is reassuring to the leader or manager who intends to apply behavior modification in the workplace.

USING RECOGNITION TO MOTIVATE OTHERS

You will recall that the food company executive described at the outset of the chapter emphasized motivation through recognition. Motivating others by giving them recognition and praise can be considered a direct application of positive reinforcement. Nevertheless, recognition is such a potentially powerful motivator that it merits separate attention. Also, recognition programs to reward and motivate employees are a standard practice in business and nonprofit firms. An example would be rewarding high-performing employees with a crystal vase (company logo inscribed) or designating them "employee of the month."

Recognition is a strong motivator because craving recognition is a normal human need. At the same time, recognition is effective because most workers feel they do not receive enough recognition. Several studies conducted over a fifty-year time span have indicated that employees welcome praise for a job well done as much as they welcome a regular paycheck. This finding should not be interpreted to mean that praise is an adequate substitute for salary. Employees tend to regard compensation as an entitlement, whereas recognition is perceived as a gift.[17] Workers, including your coworkers, want to know that their output is useful to somebody.

To appeal to the recognition need of others, identify a meritorious behavior and then recognize that behavior with an oral, written, or material reward. The rules for the use of behavior modification are directly applicable. Two specific examples of using recognition to sustain desired behavior (a key aspect of motivation) follow.

- As the team leader, you receive a glowing letter from a customer about how Kent, one of your team members, solved the customer's problem. You have the letter laminated and present it as a gift to Kent. (The behavior you are reinforcing is good customer service.)

- One member of your department, Jason, is a mechanical engineer. While at a department lunch taking place during National Engineers Week, you stand up and say, "I want to toast Jason in celebration of National Engineers Week. I certainly wouldn't want to be sitting in this office building today if a mechanical engineer hadn't assisted in its construction." (Here the only behavior you are reinforcing is the goodwill of Jason, so your motivational approach is general, not specific.)

An outstanding advantage of recognition, including praise, as a motivator is that it is no cost or low cost, yet powerful. Recognition thus has an enormous return on investment in comparison to a cash bonus. A challenge in using recognition effectively is that not everyone responds well to the same form of recognition. A good example is that highly technical people tend not to like general praise like "Great job" or "Awesome, baby." Instead, they prefer a laid-back, factual statement of how their output made a contribution.

In addition to incorporating recognition into the process of leadership, leaders and managers also rely on formal recognition programs (as mentioned above). Kenneth Hain states that an effective recognition award possesses at least one of the following qualities:[18]

- *It has symbolic meaning.* Hugh McColl, CEO of Bank of America, awards his performing employees crystal replicas of hand grenades. McColl is a former Marine who believes in a take-no-prisoners style of management. (Would you suspect that employees perceive McColl as having a militaristic leadership style?)

- *It inspires pride of ownership.* Sales consultants who attain prescribed goals at Mary Kay Cosmetics are permitted to purchase specific outfits for their wardrobes. Once a consultant becomes a director, for example, she is invited to attend Mary Kay's management conference. While there the sales consultant is fitted for a director's suit. (Kay is deceased but the tradition continues.)

- *It helps to reinforce the philosophy or identity of the giver.* A company that practiced the quality standard Six Sigma (3.4 errors in one million opportunities) might give recognition awards that were inscribed with a mention of the firm having products of outstanding quality.

Before moving on to the section about coaching, you are invited to take Leadership Self-Assessment Quiz 10-1, which deals with motivation. Also, read the Leader in Action profile (page 307) about a successful leader who uses motivational techniques.

COACHING AS A LEADERSHIP PHILOSOPHY

Effective leaders are good coaches. The coaching demands are much less rigorous for leaders who have little face-to-face contact with organization members, such as financial deal makers, CEOs, and chairpersons of the board. Nevertheless, there is a coaching component at all levels of leadership. CEO Bill Ford (of Ford Motor Company) says, "I see myself as a coach, and my job is to set the direction of the company, to make sure we have the right players and eliminate the politicking."[19] Do you think Ford took the same leadership course as you?

The quality of the relationship between the coach and the person or persons coached distinguishes coaching from other forms of leader-member interactions. The person being coached trusts the leader's judgment and experience and will listen to advice and suggestions. Similarly, the coach believes in the capacity of the group member to profit from his or her advice. The coach is a trusted superior, and the person being coached is a trusted subordinate. Several of the points made here about coaching as a philosophy of management present more details about the quality of the relationship between the coach and the team member. It is also possible, however, to receive coaching from a coworker.

Leadership Self-Assessment Quiz 10-1

My Approach to Motivating Others

INSTRUCTIONS   Describe how often you act or think in the way indicated by the following statements when you are attempting to motivate another person. Scale: very infrequently (VI); infrequently (I); sometimes (S); frequently (F); very frequently (VF).

		VI	I	S	F	VF
1.	I ask the other person what he or she is hoping to achieve in the situation.	1	2	3	4	5
2.	I attempt to figure out if the person has the ability to do what I need done.	1	2	3	4	5
3.	When another person is heel-dragging, it usually means he or she is lazy.	5	4	3	2	1
4.	I explain exactly what I want to the person I'm trying to motivate.	1	2	3	4	5
5.	I like to give the other person a reward up front so he or she will be motivated.	5	4	3	2	1
6.	I give lots of feedback when another person is performing a task for me.	1	2	3	4	5
7.	I like to belittle another person enough so that he or she will be intimidated into doing what I need done.	5	4	3	2	1
8.	I make sure that the other person feels fairly treated.	1	2	3	4	5
9.	I figure that if I smile nicely, I can get the other person to work as hard as I need.	5	4	3	2	1
10.	I attempt to get what I need done by instilling fear in the other person.	5	4	3	2	1
11.	I specify exactly what needs to be accomplished.	1	2	3	4	5
12.	I generously praise people who help me get my work accomplished.	1	2	3	4	5
13.	A job well done is its own reward. I therefore keep praise to a minimum.	5	4	3	2	1
14.	I make sure to let people know how well they have done in meeting my expectations on a task.	1	2	3	4	5
15.	To be fair, I attempt to reward people similarly no matter how well they have performed.	5	4	3	2	1

16.	When somebody doing work for me performs well, I recognize his or her accomplishments promptly.	1 2 3 4 5
17.	Before giving somebody a reward, I attempt to find out what would appeal to that person.	1 2 3 4 5
18.	I make it a policy not to thank somebody for doing a job they are paid to do.	5 4 3 2 1
19.	If people do not know how to perform a task, motivation will suffer.	1 2 3 4 5
20.	If properly laid out, many jobs can be self-rewarding.	1 2 3 4 5

Total Score _____

SCORING AND INTERPRETATION   Add the circled numbers to obtain your total score.

- ■ 90–100   You have advanced knowledge and skill with respect to motivating others in a work environment. Continue to build on the solid base you have established.
- ■ 50–89   You have average knowledge and skill with respect to motivating others. With additional study and experience, you will probably develop advanced motivational skills.
- ■ 20–49   To effectively motivate others in a work environment, you will need to greatly expand your knowledge of motivation theory and techniques.

SOURCE: *The general idea for this quiz comes from David Whetton and Kim Cameron,* Developing Management Skills, *5th ed. (Upper Saddle River, N.J.: Prentice Hall, 2002), pp. 302–303.*

Coaching is a way of enabling others to act and build on their strengths. To coach is to care enough about people to invest time in building personal relationships with them.[20] The organization also benefits from coaching because of the elevated productivity of many of the workers who are coached.[21]

Key Characteristics of Coaching

Roger D. Evered and James C. Selman regard coaching as a paradigm shift from traditional management, which focuses heavily on control, order, and compliance. Coaching, in contrast, focuses on uncovering actions that enable people to contribute more fully and productively. Furthermore, people feel less alienated than when working under the control model.[22] Coaching is also seen as a partnership for achieving results. At the same time, it represents a commitment to collaborating in accomplishing new possibilities rather than holding on to old structures. Figure 10-3 (page 309) depicts coaching as a philosophy of management.

Leader in Action

The Motivational Ken Chenault of AmEx

Back in his college days, Ken Chenault argued that African Americans could best rise to power by working within the establishment instead of attacking it from the outside. Today he is chairman and CEO of American Express Company, the owner of one of the world's premier consumer brands. Chenault is also a member of the board of directors of IBM Corporation.

After graduating from Bowdoin College, Chenault earned a degree from Harvard Law School. A member of a law firm for several years, he later worked as a management consultant before joining AmEx. He rose rapidly at the consulting firm and was regarded as a person with the potential to become a corporate CEO, partly because of his strategic thinking and his ability to work with and motivate others.

Chenault makes an impressive physical appearance; he is also quietly charismatic, is eventempered, and has exceptional drive. His admirers lavish him with praise. The chairman of the leading advertising agency for AmEx offers this description: "Ken radiates such a depth of belief that people would do anything for him" (*BusinessWeek*, December 21, p. 61).

Chenault has a quiet warmth that puts people at ease and makes them want to be on his team. At the same time he is a tough-minded risk taker who demands results. A former competitor for the top job at AmEx said of Chenault: "He's impossible to dislike, even when you're competing for the top job. If you work around him, you feel like you'd do anything for the guy" (*Fortune*, January 22, 2001, p. 62).

Chenault worked his way up through the giant credit and travel unit (TRS), which generates most of American Express's revenue and profits. He was instrumental in reviving and reinventing TRS, which was suffering from widespread complacency.

Work associates regard Chenault as hard driving and pragmatic. Yet at the same time he is able to engage the emotions of his colleagues as well as their intellects. Another former AmEx executive said, "Ken has the hearts and minds of the people at the TRS company" (*BusinessWeek*, December 21, p. 63). A survey of work associates indicates that Chenault lacks the rough edges and impatience that usually accompany highly ambitious people. None of the people interviewed could recall his losing his temper or even raising his voice. He takes the time to make small talk with secretaries when he telephones their bosses. Chenault has taken the initiative to mentor dozens of high-potential AmEx managers. He has also contributed to making layoff decisions during difficult times for the company.

Chenault is a methodical decision maker who collects input from others, encourages candor, and leaves his door open to direct reports. A veteran AmEx executive said, "With Ken, there is no game-playing, no politics whatsoever" (*BusinessWeek*, December 21, p. 63). When involved in a marketing strategy debate with other executives, "Ken would stand up for what he believed in, present his argument effectively—and forcefully when necessary," says former AmEx CEO James Robinson. "But it was always done in a professional way rather than in a stubborn way. He wasn't political; he was just someone you listened to" (*Fortune*, January 22, 2001, p. 64). Yet despite his even temper, Chenault has fired managers he thought lacked the skills he needed for his organization. While AmEx was going through substantial changes to stop the slide in American Express card use, he fired most of a group of managers who resisted the changes.

An important part of Chenault's managerial approach is to interact directly with rank-and-file employees. He regularly conducts a monthly "meet the CEO" session over lunch, and he says that he has picked up some of his best ideas this way. An example is a promotion that enabled

Platinum card members to purchase two business-class airline tickets for the price of one.

In Chenault's opinion, the role of the leader is to define reality and give hope. He prefers to occupy the role of team leader, rather than that of boss. He says that it is critical to share the credit. He openly acknowledges staff members who have contributed useful ideas, often mentioning them in meetings.

Chenault is a strong self-motivator as well as a motivator of others. "My father used to tell me that whatever happens, there is one thing I can control, and that's the quality of my performance," he says. "Regardless of the attitude of others, personal fortitude could overcome the odds" (*Emerge*).

September 11, 2001 presented new challenges for Chenault as he and 3,000 other employees were driven from the American Express Tower across the street from the World Trade Center. Eleven AmEx employees died in the neighboring towers. Chenault shifted operations to a cramped and windowless office in Jersey City only ten months after being appointed as CEO. During his first ten months as CEO, Chenault faced another crisis: he had to announce to the public that the firm was forced to write off a total of over $1 billion on some high-yield junk bonds in the Minneapolis money-management operation. The cutback on business and personal travel in the months following September 11 created even more pressures on AmEx.

Chenault told the 3,000 employees evacuated from company headquarters: "The values of this brand are real, far more real than the bricks and mortar of our headquarters building. The tower does not represent American Express. You represent American Express. All the people of American Express are what this company is about" (*BusinessWeek*, October 29, 2001, p. 70).

Chenault assembled 5,000 American Express employees at the Paramount Theatre in New York on September 20 for an emotionally charged town-hall meeting. He told employees that he had been filled with such despair, sadness, and anger that he had seen a counselor. Twice, he rushed to spontaneously embrace grief-stricken employees. Chenault said he would donate $1 million of the company's profits to the families of the eleven AmEx employees who died during the attack. "I represent the best company and the best people in the world," he concluded. "In fact, you are my strength, and I love you" (*BusinessWeek*, October 29, 2001, p. 66). An AmEx board member said of Chenault, "The manner in which he took command, the comfort and the direction he gave to what was obviously an audience in shock . . . was of a caliber one rarely sees" (*BusinessWeek*, October 29, 2001, p. 66).

Six weeks after the World Trade Center attacks, Chenault said, "I don't feel like we're a dispirited group. We are going to emerge a stronger and better company" (*BusinessWeek*, October 29, 2001, p. 70).

QUESTIONS

1. What indicators do you find that Kenneth Chenault is a motivational leader?

2. What methods does Chenault use to motivate employees?

3. When Chenault informed employees that he sought counseling for his grief, what effect might this have had on his leadership image?

4. How would you like working for Ken Chenault?

SOURCE: *Based on facts reported in Anthony Bianco, "The Rise of a Star,"* BusinessWeek, *December 21, 1998, pp. 60–68; Ernest Holsendolph, "Beating the Odds in the Fortune 500: New Black CEOs,"* Emerge *(July–August 1999),* www.msbet.com/content/live/2770.asap; *Carrie Shook, "Leader, Not Boss,"* Forbes Magazine, *December 1, 1997; John A. Byrne and Heather Timmons, "Tough Times for a New CEO,"* BusinessWeek, *October 29, 2001, pp. 63–70; Nelson D. Schwartz, "What's in the Cards for Amex?"* Fortune, *January 22, 2001, pp. 58–70; "Black History Month 2002,"* www.cnn.com/SPECIALS/ black.history/stories/08.chenault/.

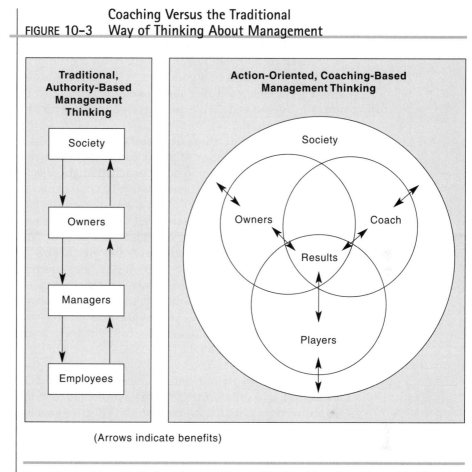

FIGURE 10-3 Coaching Versus the Traditional Way of Thinking About Management

Traditional, Authority-Based Management Thinking

Society

Owners

Managers

Employees

Action-Oriented, Coaching-Based Management Thinking

Society

Owners

Coach

Results

Players

(Arrows indicate benefits)

Source: Reprinted from Organizational Dynamics, *Autumn 1989, Copyright © 1989 with permission from Elsevier Science.*

When coaching is elevated to a philosophy of leadership, it becomes more complex than a handy technique leaders and managers use to rev up and sustain performance. Evered and Selman have observed a number of characteristics of coaching that contribute to its close relationships with leadership.

Coaching is a comprehensive and distinctive way of being linked to others in the organization. Mentoring is one example of this unique relationship. Protégés are inspired to greater achievement partially because of the quality of their relationship with their mentors. More will be said about mentoring in Chapter 15, which covers leadership development.

Coaching in the workplace might ordinarily be explained as the "art of management." Because of the uniqueness of a coaching relationship, the person being coached is better motivated to accomplish goals for the good of the organization.

Coaching is a dyad—that is, like leader/group member, or director/actor, it cannot exist without at least two participants. The interaction of the two personalities influences the coaching outcome. Some leaders, for example, can successfully coach certain people but not others. An executive vice president of finance was highly regarded as a good coach. Yet a newly appointed special assistant asked to be transferred after she worked for him for several months. The explanation she offered was, "My working relationship with Marty (the executive vice president) is just flat."

Coaching requires a high degree of interpersonal risk and trust on the part of both people in the relationship. The coach might give the person being coached wrong advice. Or the person being coached might reject the coach's encouragement. Think of the risk involved when a basketball player asks the coach for advice on how to correct a shot that is not working well. As a result of the coaching, the player might shoot more poorly, to the embarrassment of both. Similarly, an organizational leader might coach a team member in a direction that backfires—for example, that results in even fewer sales than before.

A key advantage of coaching is that it generates new possibilities for action and facilitates breakthroughs in performance. A vice president might say to a lower-ranking manager, "Have you thought of getting your people more involved in setting objectives? If you did, you might find greater commitment and follow-through." The middle manager begins to involve managers more in setting objectives, and performance increases. Coaching in this situation has achieved substantial results.

Despite all the exalted statements made about coaching as a philosophy of leadership, it is still useful to specify a few concrete contributions of coaching. One advantage is higher motivation. An effective coach keeps up the spirit and administers praise and recognition frequently. Good coaching also leads to personal development. Group members are encouraged to cross-train and serve as backups for each other. Good coaching also improves group performance. The effective coach makes team members aware of one another's skills and how these skills can contribute to attaining the group's goals.

Fallacies About Coaching

Another approach to understanding the coaching function of leadership is to examine certain common misperceptions about coaching. Several of these false stereotypes, as explained by Ian Cunningham and Linda Honold, are presented next.[23] One false belief is that *coaching only applies in one-to-one work*. In reality, the team or other group can also be coached. As a team leader, you might make a suggestion to the group, such as "Why are you rushing through such an important issue?"

A major misperception is that *coaching is mostly about providing new knowledge and skills*. The truth is that people often need more help with underlying habits than with knowledge and skills. A good example is coaching another person about work habits and time management. You can provide the individual with loads of useful knowledge and techniques. However, if the person is a procrastinator, he or she must reduce procrastination before time management skills will help.

Another stereotype deals with an important ethical issue: *If coaches go beyond giving instruction in knowledge and skills, they are in danger of getting into psychotherapy.* The counterargument is that coaches should simply follow the model of effective parents. This involves listening to the other person, attempting to understand his or her real concerns, and offering support and encouragement. Another stereotype particularly resistant to extinction is that *coaches need to be expert in something in order to coach.* To use a sports analogy, a good coach doesn't have to be or have been an outstanding athlete. An important role for the coach is to ask pertinent questions and listen. Questioning and listening can help the other person set realistic learning goals.

An understandable stereotype is that *coaching has to be done face-to-face.* The face-to-face approach facilitates coaching. Nevertheless, telephone and email are useful alternatives when time and distance create barriers. A worker on a field trip, for example, might send his manager an email message asking, "The customer says that if I make a mistake with this installation, he'll never do business with us again. Any suggestions?"

COACHING SKILLS AND TECHNIQUES

Leaders and managers have varied aptitudes for coaching. One way to acquire coaching skill is to study basic principles and suggestions, and then practice them. Another way is to attend a training program for coaching that involves modeling (learning by imitation) and role playing. Here we examine a number of suggestions for coaching. If implemented with skill, the suggestions will improve the chances that coaching will lead to improved performance.

1. *Communicate clear expectations to group members.* For people to perform well and to continue to learn and grow, they need a clear perception of what is expected of them. The expectations of a position become the standards by which performance will be judged, thus serving as a base point for coaching. If a team member is supposed to contribute three new ideas for improvement of operations per month, coaching is justified when an average of only one idea per month is forthcoming. It is not unusual for group members and managers to have only 50 percent overlap in their perceptions of the group member's job responsibilities.[24]

2. *Build relationships.* Effective coaches build personal relationships with team members and work to improve their interpersonal skills.[25] Having established rapport with team members facilitates entering into a coaching relationship with them. The suggestions below about active listening and giving emotional support are part of relationship building.

3. *Give feedback on areas that require specific improvement.* To coach a group member toward higher levels of performance, the leader pinpoints what specific behavior, attitude, or skills require improvement. An effective coach might say, "I read the product-expansion proposal you submitted. It's okay, but it falls short of your usual level of creativity. Our competitors are already carrying each product you mentioned. Have you thought about . . . ?" Another important factor in giving specific feedback is to avoid generalities and exaggerations such as "You never come up with a good product idea" or "You are the most unimaginative product-development specialist I have ever known." To give good feedback, the leader or manager has to observe performance and behavior directly and frequently, such as by watching a supervisor dealing with a safety problem.

4. *Listen actively.* Listening is an essential ingredient in any coaching session. An active listener tries to grasp both facts and feelings. Observing the group member's nonverbal communication is another part of active listening. The leader must also be patient and not poised for a rebuttal of any difference of opinion between him or her and the group member. Beginning each coaching session with a question helps set the stage for active listening. The question will also spark the employee's thinking and frame the discussion. For example, "How might we use the new computer system to help our staff generate more sales?"[26]

   Part of being a good listener is encouraging the person being coached to talk about his or her performance. Asking open-ended questions facilitates a flow of conversation. For example, ask: "How did you feel about the way you handled conflict with the marketing group yesterday?" A close-ended question covering the same issue would be "Do you think you could have done a better job of handling conflict with the marketing group yesterday?"

5. *Help remove obstacles.* To perform at anywhere near top capacity, individuals may need help in removing obstacles such as a maze of rules and regulations and rigid budgeting. An important role for the leader of an organizational unit is thus to be a "barrier buster." A leader or manager is often in a better position than a group member to gain approval from a higher-level manager, find money from another budget line, expedite a purchase order, or authorize hiring a temporary worker to provide assistance. Yet William D. Hitt cautions that deciding when to intervene requires considerable judgment on the manager's part. His advice to managers is: "Don't take your people's 'monkeys' when the monkeys should clearly rest with them."[27]

6. *Give emotional support.* By being helpful and constructive, the leader provides much-needed emotional support to the group member who is not performing at his or her best. A coaching session should not be an interrogation. An effective way of giving emotional support is to use positive rather than negative motivators. For example, the leader might say, "I liked some things you did yesterday, yet I have a few suggestions that might

bring you closer to peak performance." Another facet of giving emotional support is for the leader or manager to be a *toxic-handler,* a person who shoulders the sadness, frustration, bitterness, anger, and despair of group members so they can work productively.[28] Being available as a sympathetic and empathic listener is a major part of being a toxic-handler, and coming forth with creative solutions to vexing problems is also helpful.

Displaying empathy is an effective way to give emotional support. Indicate with words that you understand the challenge the group member faces with a statement such as "I understand that working with a reduced staff has placed you under heavy time pressures." The genuine concern you show will help establish the rapport useful in working out the problem together.[29]

7. *Reflect content or meaning.* An effective way of reflecting meaning is to rephrase and summarize concisely what the group member is saying. A substandard performer might say, "The reason I've fallen so far behind is that our company has turned into a bureaucratic nightmare. We're being hit right and left with forms to fill out for customer satisfaction. I have fifty email messages that I haven't read yet." You might respond, "You're falling so far behind because you have so many forms and messages that require attention." The group member might then respond with something like "That's exactly what I mean. I'm glad you understand my problem." (Notice that the leader is also giving the group member an opportunity to express the feelings behind his or her problem.)

8. *Give some gentle advice and guidance.* Too much advice giving interferes with two-way communication, yet some advice can elevate performance. The manager should assist the group member in answering the question "What can I do about this problem?"[30] Advice in the form of a question or suppositional statement is often effective. One example is, "Could the root of your problem be insufficient planning?" A direct statement—such as "The root of your problem is obviously insufficient planning"—often makes people resentful and defensive. By responding to a question, the person being coached is likely to feel more involved in making improvements.

Part of giving gentle guidance for improvement is to use the word *could* instead of *should.* To say "You should do this" implies that the person is currently doing something wrong, which can trigger defensiveness. Saying "You could do this" leaves the person with a choice; he or she can accept or reject your input and weigh the consequences.[31] (You *could* accept this advice to become a better coach!)

9. *Allow for modeling of desired performance and behavior.* An effective coaching technique is to show the group member by example what constitutes the desired behavior. Assume that a manager has been making statements to customers that stretch the truth, such as falsely saying that the product met a zero-defects standard. In coaching him, the manager's boss might allow the manager to observe how she handles a similar situation with a customer. The manager's boss might telephone a customer and say,

"You have been inquiring about whether we have adopted a zero-defects standard for our laser printers. Right now we are doing our best to produce error-free products. Yet, so far we do not have a formal zero-defects program. We stand by our printers and will fix any defect at no cost to you."

10. *Gain a commitment to change.* Unless the leader receives a commitment from the team member to carry through with the proposed solution to a problem, the team member may not attain higher performance. An experienced manager develops an intuitive feel for when employees are serious about performance improvement. Two clues that commitment to change is lacking are (1) overagreeing about the need for change, and (2) agreeing to change without display of emotion.

11. *Applaud good results.* Effective coaches on the playing field and in the workplace are cheerleaders. They give encouragement and positive reinforcement by applauding good results. Some effective coaches shout in joy when an individual or team achieves outstanding results; others clap their hands in applause.

Leadership Self-Assessment Quiz 10-2 will help you think through the development you need to be an effective coach. If you are already an effective coach, look for ways to improve. Leadership Skill-Building Exercise 10-3 gives you a chance to practice coaching.

EXECUTIVE COACHING AND LEADERSHIP EFFECTIVENESS

A form of coaching currently in vogue is for managers to consult professional coaches to help them be more effective leaders and to guide them in their careers. An **executive coach** (or **business coach**) is an outside or inside specialist who advises a person about personal improvement and behavioral change. Executive coaches provide such a variety of services that they have been described as a combination of "a counselor, adviser, mentor, cheerleader, and best friend."[32] In the past, management psychologists were typically hired as outside coaches to help managers become more effective leaders. Today, people from a wide variety of backgrounds become business coaches. Executive coaches help managers become more effective leaders by helping them in ways such as the following:

- Counseling the leader about weaknesses that could interfere with effectiveness, such as being too hostile and impatient.
- Helping the leader understand and process feedback from 360-degree surveys.
- Serving as a sounding board when the leader faces a complex decision about strategy, operations, or human resource issues.
- Making specific suggestions about self-promotion and image enhancement, including suggestions about appearance and mannerisms.

Characteristics of an Effective Coach

INSTRUCTIONS Below is a list of traits, attitudes, and behaviors characteristic of effective coaches. Place a checkmark next to each trait, attitude, or behavior that you need to develop along those lines (for example, whether you need to become more patient). On a separate sheet of paper, design an action plan for improvement for each trait, attitude, or behavior that you need to develop. An example of an action plan for improving patience might be "I'll ask people to tell me when I appear too impatient. I'll also try to develop self-control about my impatience."

Trait, Attitude, or Behavior

1. Empathy (putting self in other person's shoes) ____
2. Listening skill ____
3. Insight into people ____
4. Diplomacy and tact ____
5. Patience toward people ____
6. Concern for welfare of people ____
7. Low hostility toward people ____
8. Self-confidence and emotional security ____
9. Noncompetitiveness with group members ____
10. Enthusiasm for people ____
11. Satisfaction in helping others grow ____
12. Interest in development of group members ____
13. High expectations for each group member ____
14. Ability to give authentic feedback ____
15. Interest in people's potential ____
16. Honesty and integrity (or trustworthiness) ____
17. Friendliness ____

SOURCE: *Items 1–10 adapted with permission from Andrew J. DuBrin,* Participant Guide to Module 10: Development of Subordinates, *p. 11. Copyright © 1985. Items 11–15 gathered from information in William D. Hitt,* The Leader-Manager: Guidelines for Action *(Columbus, Ohio: Battelle Press, 1988), pp. 183–186.*

Coaching for Improved Performance

Jennifer is a financial consultant (stockbroker) at a branch office of an established financial services firm. Her manager Derek is concerned that Jennifer is 25 percent below quota in sales of a new Internet mutual fund offered by the company. Derek schedules a late-afternoon meeting in his office to attempt to help Jennifer make quota. He has told Jennifer, "I want to talk about your sales performance on the new Net fund, and see if I can be helpful." Jennifer is concerned that the meeting might be a discipline session in disguise. One person assumes the role of Derek, the other of Jennifer. Derek, of course, will attempt to implement recommended coaching techniques. Other class members will watch, and then provide constructive feedback.

This exercise is a key skill builder because so much of face-to-face leadership involves working out performance problems with group members. If every employee were an outstanding, independent performer, we would have less need for managers and leaders.

- Helping the leader achieve a better balance between work and family life, thereby having more focused energy for the leadership role.
- Helping the leader uncover personal assets and strengths he or she may not have known existed. (An example would be discovering that the leader has untapped creativity and imagination.)
- Serving as a trusted confidante to discuss issues the leader might feel uncomfortable talking about with others. An example would be talking about feeling insecure in his or her position.
- Pointing out a blind spot in the leader's decision making, such as neglecting part of the human consequences of a decision.
- Giving advice about career management, such as developing a career path.

Note that the coach works as an adviser about behavior but does not explicitly help the leader with functional details of the job, such as how to develop a new product strategy or design an organization.

Executive coaches are often hired by the leader/manager's employer. However, many managers and professional people hire their own coach, much as they might hire a personal trainer. Typically the coach spends about one hour per week with the client. Many coaches rely on the telephone and email to conduct much of their coaching. For example, the leader might send an email message to the coach asking advice about how to handle an upcoming meeting. The coach would respond within twenty-four hours.

A refinement of individual coaching is for the coach to work with both the individual and his or her work associates. The coach will solicit feedback from the group members, as well as involve them in helping the manager improve. For example, the coach might tell team members to assert their rights when the manager throws a temper tantrum or makes unreasonable demands. The coach might also work with the superiors or peers of the person being coached. Coach Marshall Goldsmith says, "My success rate as a coach has improved dramatically as I've realized that people's getting better is not a function of me; it's a function of the person and the people around the person."[33]

Executive coaching may frequently accomplish several of the ends specified in the above list. A study of executives and coaches found that such coaching was perceived as adding value. The managers involved acquired new skills, abilities, and perspectives that often resulted in improved performance, such as making better use of staff. Beneficial behavior changes also took place, such as becoming more patient and being more comfortable in dealing with group members' personal issues.[34]

Company evidence about the contribution of business coaching is sometimes impressive. A huge global services company offered coaching to 127 senior managers, and then observed the results. The coached executives scored higher than a contrast group of executives on a long list of measures, including "results obtained," "builds relationships," and "applies integrative thinking."[35]

Executive coaching, however, has some potential drawbacks for the leader. A major problem is that a coach may give advice that backfires because he or she does not understand the particular work setting. A coach told a manager in an information technology firm that she should become more decisive in her decision making and less dependent on consensus. The advice backfired because the culture of the firm emphasized consensus decision making.

An ethical problem is that many coaches delve into personal and emotional issues that should be reserved for mental health professionals. Psychotherapist Steven Berglas contends that executive coaches can make a bad situation worse when they ignore psychological problems they do not understand.[36] The leader who is performing poorly because of a deep-rooted problem such as hostility toward others is given superficial advice about "making nice." Another potential ethical problem is that the leader/manager may become too dependent on the coach, checking with him or her before making any consequential decision.

SUMMARY

Effective leaders are outstanding motivators and coaches, and the role of the modern leader and manager emphasizes coaching. The expectancy theory of motivation is useful for developing motivational skills because it is comprehensive, building on other explanations of motivation.

Expectancy theory has three major components: valence, instrumentality, and expectancy. Valence is the worth or attractiveness of an outcome. Each work situation has multiple outcomes, and each outcome has a valence of its own. Valences range from -100 to $+100$ in the version of expectancy theory presented here. Zero valences reflect indifference and therefore are not motivational. Very high valences help explain why some people will persist in efforts despite a low probability of payoff. Instrumentality is the individual's assessment of the probability that performance will lead to certain outcomes. (An outcome is anything that might stem from performance, such as a reward.) Expectancy is an individual's assessment of the probability that effort will lead to performing the task correctly.

Expectancy theory has implications and provides guidelines for leaders, including the following: (1) determine necessary performance levels; (2) make the performance level attainable; (3) train and encourage people; (4) make explicit the link between rewards and performance; (5) make sure the rewards are large enough; (6) analyze factors that oppose the effectiveness of the reward; (7) explain the meaning and implications of second-level outcomes; and (8) understand individual differences in valences.

Goal setting is a basic process that is directly or indirectly part of all major theories of motivation. Goal theory includes the following ideas: Specific and difficult goals result in high performance (yet outrageous goals can inspire); goals must be accepted by group members; goals are more effective when they are linked to feedback and rewards; the combination of individual and group goals is very effective; and a learning goal orientation is effective.

Behavior modification is a widely used motivational strategy. Its key principle is the law of effect: Behavior that leads to a positive effect tends to be repeated, and the opposite is also true. The basic behavior modification strategies are positive reinforcement, avoidance motivation, punishment, and extinction. A guiding principle is that you get what you reinforce.

Rules for the effective use of behavior modification include the following: (1) target the desired behavior; (2) choose an appropriate reward or punishment; (3) supply ample feedback; (4) do not give everyone the same-size reward; (5) find some constructive behavior to reinforce; (6) schedule rewards intermittently; (7) give rewards and punishments soon after the behavior; (8) change the reward periodically; and (9) make the rewards visible and the punishments known.

Motivating others by giving them recognition and praise can be considered a direct application of positive reinforcement. Recognition programs to reward and motivate employees are standard practice. Recognition is a strong motivator because it is a normal human need to crave recognition, and workers do not feel they receive enough recognition. To appeal to the recognition need, identify a meritorious behavior and then recognize that behavior with an oral, written, or material reward. Formal recognition programs are also useful.

A major purpose of coaching is to achieve enthusiasm and high performance in a team setting. Coaching can also be regarded as a paradigm shift from traditional management, which focuses heavily on control, order, and compliance. Coaching is a partnership for achieving results. Several characteristics of coaching contribute to its close relationship with leadership. Coaching is a comprehensive and distinctive way of being linked to others in the organization. Coaching is also a two-way process, suggesting that being a great coach requires having a talented team. Coaching requires a high degree of interpersonal risk and trust on the part of both sides in the relationship.

The coaching function can also be understood by recognizing several common misperceptions: Coaching applies only to one-on-one work; coaching is mostly about providing new knowledge and skills; coaching easily falls into psychotherapy; coaches need to be experts in what they are coaching; and coaching has to be done face-to-face.

Suggestions for improving coaching are as follows: (1) communicate clear expectations, (2) build relationships, (3) give feedback on areas that require specific improvement, (4) listen actively, (5) help remove obstacles, (6) give emotional support including empathy, (7) reflect content or meaning, (8) give gentle advice and guidance, (9) allow for modeling of desired performance and behavior, (10) gain a commitment to change, (11) applaud good results.

Managers frequently consult personal executive or business coaches to help them be more effective leaders. Such coaches provide a variety of services, including counseling about weaknesses, helping achieve balance in life, helping the leader uncover hidden assets, and giving career advice. Studies show that executive coaching is effective, yet there are potential problems: executive coaches can give bad advice, the coach may be unqualified to deal with mental health issues, and the leader may become too dependent on the coach.

KEY TERMS

Expectancy theory

Valence

Outcome

Instrumentality

Expectancy

Self-efficacy

Goal

Behavior modification

Behavior shaping

Executive (or business) coach

GUIDELINES FOR ACTION AND SKILL DEVELOPMENT

Given that recognition can be such a relatively low-cost, yet highly effective, motivator, the leader/manager should keep in mind available forms of recognition. In addition to considering those in the following list, use your imagination to think of other forms of recognition. For the recognition technique to work well, it should have high valence for the person or group under consideration.

- Compliments
- Encouragement for job well done
- Comradeship with boss
- Access to confidential information
- Pat on back or handshake

- Public expression of appreciation
- Meeting of appreciation with executive
- Team uniforms, hats, tee shirts, or mugs
- Note of thanks to individual, handwritten or email
- Flattering letter from customer distributed over email.
- Employee-of-month award
- Wall plaque indicating accomplishment
- Special commendation placed in employee file
- Gift from company recognition program, such as watch, clock, or pin

DISCUSSION QUESTIONS AND ACTIVITIES

1. Andrew Pearson, one of the two top executives at Tricon (described in the chapter opener) was 76 at the time of the story. Yet the clientele of KFC, Pizza Hut, and Taco Bell tend to be young. Explain whether you think Pearson's age is an asset or a liability for the position.

2. Identify several outcomes you expect from occupying a leadership position. What valences do you attach to them?

3. How can the influence exerted by a charismatic leader tie in with expectancy theory?

4. Explain how valence, instrumentality, and expectancy could relate to job performance.

5. What is a potential second-level outcome a person could gain from receiving an A grade in the course for which you are reading this text? From receiving an F grade?

6. What does goal theory tell managers that they probably don't already know about using goals to motivate people?

7. Which forms of recognition are likely to be the most effective in motivating professional-level workers?

8. In what ways is coaching related to hands-on leadership?

9. How might a leader use coaching to help increase ethical behavior among group members?

10. Ask a manager or coach to describe the amount of coaching he or she does on the job. Be prepared to bring your findings back to class.

Leadership Case Problem A

Rewards and Recognition at Tel-Service

Tel-Service is a fast-growing customer service and fulfillment firm based in New Jersey. The company's core business is responding to customer questions, complaints, and comments that arrive via 800 telephone numbers. Companies such as Sony, Tetley, and PR Newswire outsource much of their customer service activities to Tel-Service. Any time a customer of the client companies calls the 800 number listed on the packaging and literature, they are actually reaching Tel-Service.

At Tel-Service headquarters, 300 employees respond to customer phone calls. In order to maintain high levels of both direct customer and end-customer satisfaction, Tel-Service employees are closely monitored. Workers are evaluated on the basis of criteria such as courteousness, thoroughness, and calls answered per hour. A particular challenge is meeting performance standards when dealing with very annoyed customers.

Up until one year ago, employee turnover at Tel-Service was unacceptably high. Employees stayed at the job for an average of only eight months. Considering that each new employee received two months of training, the eight-month average stay was particularly troublesome to management. Nathan Samuels, the director of operations at Tel-Service, knew that the high turnover had to be reduced. An increasing amount of money was invested in training staff, and less skilled customer service representatives (CSRs) were responding to customer inquiries. If the CSRs were doing a poor job, customers might complain, and Tel-Service could lose a client. Samuels recognized that skilled CSRs were critical to the success of the firm.

Samuels decided that the first step in fixing the high turnover problem was to determine what was wrong in the first place. He decided to interview a sample of CSRs. Samuels thought that a good perspective on the problem could be reached by interviewing experienced employees and those less experienced. The sample consisted of those who had been working for the company for three years, and others who were barely out of training.

The interview questions focused mostly on the working atmosphere. Among the questions were "What do you enjoy about your work?" and "What could make your work time better?" Interviewees were encouraged to be frank, and it was made clear that there would be no repercussions from making negative comments. Samuels observed several themes from the interviews:

- The more experienced employees remained because they needed the job. Most of these employees were not thrilled with the work, but they stayed with it to pay for necessities. Samuels reasoned that the motivation of this group of employees was not high enough to result in superior performance.
- The new employees were excited about the work but nervous about the horror stories told by their peers.
- CSRs felt overworked and underappreciated by the rude and degrading customers they dealt with daily.

On the basis of these interview findings, Samuels believed he had a good grasp of the problems facing the CSRs. After reading a few leadership trade journals, he decided that a reward and recognition program might be enough to motivate the reps and make them feel appreciated. Some sort of reward could be given to those employees that maintained a superior level of customer service. The reward would serve a dual function. First, it would motivate the CSRs to work harder to achieve their reward. Second, it would help the CSRs feel better appreciated by management to help compensate for the lack of appreciation by customers.

The plan was to hold an office party during the presentation of rewards. In this way, other employees in addition to the winner would receive something of value. After receiving approval from the CEO, Samuels decided that every three months one employee would win a vacation to Disney World. Tel-Service would pay for the accommodations and airfare.

Samuels and the CEO thought that a reward of this magnitude would be very motivational.

The CSRs were elated when they heard about the new program. Average performance based on the standards in use jumped 39 percent, including the number of telephone calls handled per hour. For the next three months not a single CSR left without giving notice. Several clients sent letters or email messages explaining how satisfied their customers were with the telephone support. During this same period, two large new accounts joined Tel-Service through recommendations from other firms.

When the first three months were completed, it was time to reward the winner and throw the party. Since not all representatives could leave the phones at the same time, coffee and cake were placed at a central location where the reps could serve themselves at breaks. During lunch hour, when the largest number of reps were off the phone, the winner was announced—Kristine Santora. Although the competition was fierce, all employees were very proud of Santora. Samuels made sure to remind them that the next contest began immediately, and that everyone else had a chance to win. The fervor and motivation that had been created in the previous three months were now fueled with new life.

After giving the reward of the Disney trip three times, Samuels phased down the program and replaced it with smaller, more personalized rewards like watches and sporting equipment. The office parties to celebrate the rewards were retained.

One year after the start of the program, CSR turnover at Tel-Service is approximately 15 percent, and the representatives appear happier in their jobs. Said Samuels, "I doubt we would have ever gotten the customer service rep problem under control without having implemented the reward and recognition program."

QUESTIONS

1. Identify the motivational techniques used by Samuels to enhance performance of the customer service reps.

2. What can Samuels do to keep the customer service staff motivated in the future?

3. Use expectancy theory to analyze why the reward and recognition program is working.

SOURCE: *Case researched by Brian Romanko, Rochester Institute of Technology, November 2000.*

Leadership Case Problem B

The Reality Coach

Steve Randall was concerned that his managerial career had hit a plateau regarding his impact on others and his career progress. Pondering what to do, he decided to get an appointment with Lorie LeBrun, an executive coach he heard being interviewed on a local talk show. After an initial interview, Randall signed a one-year contract with LeBrun. She would meet with him personally once a month. The two would also exchange a maximum of three email messages per week related to job problems and career concerns. Following are selected excerpts from face-to-face meetings and email exchanges:

Steve: After listening to you on the talk show, I came away with the impression that you can make a person a better leader. That's why I came to see you. If I were a heavy-impact leader, I would be more successful.

Lorie: What is a "heavy-impact leader"?

Steve: What I'm getting at is a leader who impresses people, who is seen as a powerhouse, who gets others to bend over backwards for him.

Lorie: Hold on, Steve. I don't like what I'm hearing. It sounds like you want to win friends and influence people, but what about doing well for the company? What about helping people achieve goals that are important to them?

Steve: Whose side are you on, Lorie? Are you representing me? Or are you are representing my company?

Lorie: I'm trying to represent the truth. I want you to grow, and you can't grow unless you get some honest feedback. It sounds like you are more of a glory seeker than a results-focused manager.

Steve: Maybe there is a grain of truth in what you say. But if I didn't have a problem looking and acting like a leader, I wouldn't be here.

Lorie: I hear you Steve, but I have an assignment for you. For the next five times you interact with your group, focus more on them, and less on yourself. Act like a servant leader. You serve the group. Help them achieve what they want. Then see what happens. I think you are too self-centered right now.

Steve (one month later): I did pay more attention to what the group wanted to accomplish. My team said they were afraid that we would lose funding for next year. So I am working on getting a straight answer from higher management about where the group is headed. As a result, the group seems a little bit more positive toward me.

Lorie: Hats off to you, Steve. It sounds like you are making progress as a true leader.

Steve: The progress is really quite modest. I still need to make a big impact on key people. Toward that end, I'm thinking of going for Botox treatments. This way I could get rid of most of the wrinkles in my face. It would give me a more youthful, positive appearance.

Lorie: Right, Steve. You would have a frozen face like a fading Hollywood star who made one trip too many to the plastic surgeon. You're not getting the point, Steve. In terms of leadership, it's what is inside that counts. Is Bill Gates a glamour boy? Was Jack Welch (the legendary GE chief) a beautiful physical specimen? I don't think so!

Steve: I get your point, and I will give it some consideration. There is something else on my mind I want to discuss with you. My boss has turned out to be a backstabbing jerk, so I'm thinking about complaining about him to his boss.

Lorie: Those are pretty harsh words. In what way is your boss a "backstabbing jerk"?

Steve: He befriends me when he is with me, but he appears to be bad-mouthing me to the managers in the company. Two different reliable sources gave me that feedback.

Lorie: Grow up, Steve. Fight your own battles. Are you an adult person? Or are you a mouse? Get a face-to-face appointment with your boss, and share the vicious feedback with him. A true leader must confront problems head on.

Steve: I'll give what you said some thought, and I will email you with the results.

QUESTIONS

1. What do you think of Lorie LeBrun's coaching techniques?

2. How literally should Steve Randall accept LeBrun's advice?

3. What would you advise Randall about the Botox treatments?

INTERNET SKILL–BUILDING EXERCISE

Dream Job Coaching

Apply the chapter concepts! Visit the Web and complete this Internet skill-building exercise to learn more about current leadership topics and trends.

Visit **www.dreamjobcoaching.com** and find answers to the following questions:

1. According to the Internal Coach Federation, what does coaching entail?

2. How does Dream Job Coaching help you find an ideal position?

3. How could the principles of Dream Job Coaching help you be a more effective coach?

Creativity, Innovation, and Leadership

CHAPTER 11

Since *iWon.com*'s founding several years ago, the company has become one of the fastest-growing web sites. The site attracts viewers by acting like a lottery in which large amounts of money are given away, such as $10,000 a day and $1 million every month. However, the web portal retains viewers by offering services. The NPD Group, a market research firm, discovered that *iWon.com*'s portal and search engine were ranked number 1 or number 2 in 20 of the 21 attributes that determine satisfaction.

Bill Daugherty and Jonas Steinman, the co-founders of *iWon.com*, became friends as classmates at Harvard Business School. Before they joined forces to form the web portal, both had significant corporate experience. "Bill and I can't program our VCRs, so we wanted to be sure our viewers didn't have to try to figure out how to personalize things," said Steinman.

The two men came up with the idea for a web portal over lunch one day. The problem was that web portals were all offering essentially the same services: search, email, news, and other features. Steinman said that the marketing campaign he most admired was McDonald's Monopoly, in which the odds increased with each return trip from a customer. So the cash giveaway idea was born. "We're one of the stickiest sites on the Internet," says Steinman. On the Web, being "sticky" is a major success factor. It refers to the number of times consumers return to a site and the length of each visit.

The partners note that in an Internet-based business, innovation and execution are a financial imperative. "You have to be very flexible to succeed in the Internet world, and we've structured the organization to be very open and adaptable, constantly reinventing processes to keep ahead," says Steinman. "We've also been good at fostering creativity and innovation so we have something that is ahead of the market. Some people probably think we're impatient to the point of being crazy."[1]

The success of the two Internet entrepreneurs illustrates an important link between creativity and leadership. By thinking creatively (such as developing a web site with the chance for the visitor to win serious money), a person can form a new enterprise that can keep many people engaged in productive activity. However, the creative idea has to be executed properly for innovation to take place. Although the terms *creativity* and *innovation* are often used interchangeably, **innovation** refers to the creation of new ideas and *their implementation*.[2]

Creative thinking enables leaders to contribute novel insights that can open up new opportunities or alternatives for the group or the organization.[3] The role of a creative leader is to bring into existence ideas and things that did not exist previously or that existed in a different form. Leaders are not bound by current solutions to problems. Instead, they create images of other possibilities. Leaders often move a firm into an additional business or start a new department that offers another service.

This chapter emphasizes creativity development for the leader. It also explains the nature of creativity and creative people and examines the leader's role in establishing an atmosphere conducive to creativity among group members, along with leadership practices conducive to innovation.

STEPS IN THE CREATIVE PROCESS

An important part of becoming more creative involves understanding the stages involved in **creativity,** which is generally defined as the production of novel and useful ideas. An attempt has been made to understand creativity more specifically as it pertains to the workplace. As defined by Richard Woodman, John Sawyer, and Ricky Griffin, **organizational creativity** is the "creation of a valuable, useful new product, service, idea, procedure, or process by individuals working together in a complex social system."[4]

An old but well-accepted model of creativity can be applied to organizations. This model divides creative thinking into five stages,[5] as shown in Figure 11-1. Step 1 is *opportunity or problem recognition:* A person discovers that a new opportunity exists or a problem needs resolution. Thirty-five years ago an entrepreneurial leader, Robert Cowan, recognized a new opportunity and asked, "Why do business meetings have to be conducted in person? Why can't they connect through television images?"[6]

Step 2 is *immersion.* The individual concentrates on the problem and becomes immersed in it. He or she will recall and collect information that seems relevant, dreaming up alternatives without refining or evaluating them. Cowan grabbed every fact he could about teleconferencing. At one point he helped NASA and the University of Alaska produce the first videoconference by satellite. Cowan synthesized all his information into a book about teleconferencing.

Step 3 is *incubation.* The person keeps the assembled information in mind for a while. He or she does not appear to be working on the problem actively; however, the subconscious mind is still engaged. While the information is simmering, it is being arranged into meaningful new patterns. Cowan did not actively pursue his business videoconferencing idea for several years.

FIGURE 11-1   Steps in the Creative Process

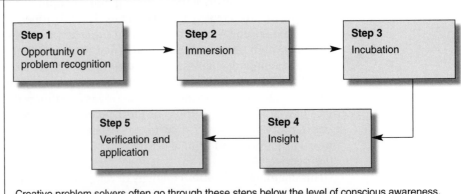

Creative problem solvers often go through these steps below the level of conscious awareness. Yet being aware of these steps (such as immersing yourself in knowledge) when faced with a challenging problem will often increase the probability of finding a creative solution.

Step 4 is *insight.* The problem-conquering solution flashes into the person's mind at an unexpected time, such as on the verge of sleep, during a shower, or while running. Insight is also called the *Aha! experience:* All of a sudden something clicks. At one point Cowan suddenly thought of forming a teleconferencing business to exploit the potential of his idea.

Step 5 is *verification and application.* The individual sets out to prove that the creative solution has merit. Verification procedures include gathering supporting evidence, using logical persuasion, and experimenting with new ideas. Application requires tenacity because most novel ideas are first rejected as being impractical. When banks refused to finance Cowan's startup business, Cowan and his wife raised $45,000 from friends and obtained a second mortgage on their house. Cowan did start his business, but he faced financial trouble. With his company on the verge of folding, Charles Schwab, the brokerage firm, hired Cowan's company to connect its 100 branch offices.

Note that the end product of Cowan's creative thinking was a business possibility rather than an invention. Nevertheless, businesspeople typically follow the same five steps of creative thought that inventors do. Even though creativity usually follows the same steps, it is not a mechanical process that can be turned on and off. Much of creativity is intricately woven into a person's intellect and personality. Furthermore, creativity varies among individuals, and creative people themselves have peaks and valleys in their creativity.[7]

CHARACTERISTICS OF CREATIVE LEADERS

Creative leaders, like creative workers of all type, are different in many ways from their less creative counterparts. They are devoted to their fields and enjoy intellectual stimulation, and they challenge the status quo, which leads them to seek improvements. The cofounders of *iWon.com* challenged the status quo with respect to web portals, and so started a new service that became a rapid success. Above all, creative people are mentally flexible and can see past the traditional ways of looking at problems.

As described next, the specific characteristics of creative people, including creative leaders, can be grouped into four areas: knowledge, intellectual abilities, personality, and passion for the task and the experience of flow.[8] These characteristics are highlighted in Figure 11-2. In addition, we present a theory of creativity that helps explain how these characteristics lead to creative output. Before studying this information, compare your thinking to that of a creative person by doing Leadership Self-Assessment Quiz 11-1 (page 329).

Knowledge

Creative problem solving requires a broad background of information, including facts and observations. Knowledge provides the building blocks for generating and combining ideas. Most creative leaders are knowledgeable, and their knowledge

FIGURE 11-2   Characteristics of Creative Leaders

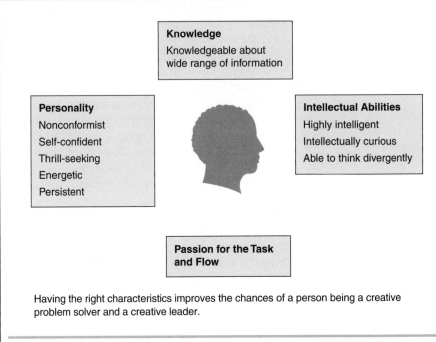

Knowledge
Knowledgeable about
wide range of information

Personality
Nonconformist
Self-confident
Thrill-seeking
Energetic
Persistent

Intellectual Abilities
Highly intelligent
Intellectually curious
Able to think divergently

**Passion for the Task
and Flow**

Having the right characteristics improves the chances of a person being a creative
problem solver and a creative leader.

contributes to their charisma. A well-known case in point is Steven P. Jobs, the chief
executive of Apple Computer, Inc. (and also Pixar Animation Studios). He contributes design and marketing decisions to most of Apple's key products, and he
played a major role in the development of the popular iMac computer. A contributor to Jobs's creativity is his in-depth technical knowledge of computer hardware
and software. As with most creative people, Jobs has had his share of failed innovations, including the cube-shaped Mac. However, a few failures along the way rarely
discourage a creative person.

Intellectual Abilities

Intellectual abilities comprise such abilities as general intelligence and abstract reasoning. Creative problem solvers, particularly in business, tend to be bright but are
not at the absolute top end of the brilliance scale. Extraordinarily high intelligence
is not required in order to be creative, yet creative people are facile at generating
creative solutions to problems in a short period of time. A paradox, however, is that
one sometimes has to be highly intelligent to be hired for a position requiring creative work. Microsoft Corporation for example, hires only people whom the hiring
manager evaluates as being outstandingly intelligent. The company uses standard
measures of intelligence such as mental ability tests, grades in school, and past accomplishments. In addition, the company has developed its own set of interview

The Creative Personality Test

Leadership Self-Assessment Quiz 11-1

INSTRUCTIONS   Describe each of the following statements as "mostly true" or "mostly false."

	Mostly True	Mostly False
1. It is generally a waste of time to read magazine articles, Internet articles, and books outside my immediate field of interest.	____	____
2. I frequently have the urge to suggest ways of improving products and services I use.	____	____
3. Reading fiction and visiting art museums are time wasters.	____	____
4. I am a person of very strong convictions. What is right is right; what is wrong is wrong.	____	____
5. I enjoy it when my boss hands me vague instructions.	____	____
6. Making order out of chaos is actually fun.	____	____
7. Only under extraordinary circumstances would I deviate from my To Do list (or other ways in which I plan my day).	____	____
8. Taking a different route to work is fun, even if it takes longer.	____	____
9. Rules and regulations should not be taken too seriously. Most rules can be broken under unusual circumstances.	____	____
10. Playing with a new idea is fun even if it doesn't benefit me in the end.	____	____
11. Some of my best ideas have come from building on the ideas of others.	____	____
12. In writing, I try to avoid the use of unusual words and word combinations.	____	____
13. I frequently jot down improvements in the job I would like to make in the future.	____	____
14. I prefer to stay with technology devices I know well rather than frequently updating my equipment or software.	____	____
15. I prefer writing personal notes or poems to loved ones rather than relying on greeting cards.	____	____

16. At one time or another in my life I have enjoyed doing puzzles. _____ _____

17. If your thinking is clear, you will find the one best solution to a problem. _____ _____

18. It is best to interact with coworkers who think much like you. _____ _____

19. Detective work would have some appeal to me. _____ _____

20. Tight controls over people and money are necessary to run a successful organization. _____ _____

SCORING AND INTERPRETATION   Give yourself a +1 for each answer in the creative direction for each statement, indicated as follows:

1. Mostly false	8. Mostly true	15. Mostly true
2. Mostly true	9. Mostly true	16. Mostly true
3. Mostly false	10. Mostly true	17. Mostly false
4. Mostly false	11. Mostly true	18. Mostly false
5. Mostly true	12. Mostly false	19. Mostly true
6. Mostly true	13. Mostly true	20. Mostly false
7. Mostly false	14. Mostly false	Total ____

Extremely high or low scores are the most meaningful. A score of 15 or more suggests that your personality and attitudes are similar to those of creative people, including creative leaders. A score of 8 or less suggests that you are more of an intellectual conformist at present. Don't be discouraged. Most people can develop in the direction of becoming more creative.

How does your score compare to your self-evaluation of your creativity? We suggest you also obtain feedback on your creativity from somebody familiar with your thinking and your work.

questions that its managers think measure intelligence, such as "Why are manholes and manhole covers round instead of square?" In defense of Microsoft's screening procedures, the ability to creatively develop software is closely associated with high raw intelligence.

Creative people also maintain a youthful curiosity throughout their lives, and the curiosity is not centered just on their own field of expertise. Instead, their range of interests encompasses many areas of knowledge, and they are enthusiastic about puzzling problems. Creative people are often open and responsive to others' feelings and emotions.

Creative people show an identifiable intellectual style, being able to think divergently. They are able to expand the number of alternatives to a problem, thus moving away from a single solution. Yet the creative thinker also knows when it is time to narrow the number of useful solutions. For example, the divergent thinker might think of twenty-seven ways to reduce costs. Yet at some point he or she will have to move toward choosing the best of several cost-cutting approaches.

Personality

The noncognitive aspects of a person heavily influence creative problem solving. Creative people tend to have a positive self-image without being blindly self-confident. Because they are self-confident, they are able to cope with criticism of their ideas, and they can tolerate the isolation necessary for developing ideas. Talking to others is a good way to get ideas, yet at some point the creative problem solver has to work alone and concentrate.

Creative people are frequently nonconformists and do not need strong approval from the group. Nonconformity can also mean being a maverick. Richard E. Cheverton observes: "The maverick is really the person who is the focus of creativity in a company, but a lot of people perceive them as jerks because they like to stir the pot. But these are just people driven to accomplish things anonymously. They just want to get things done, and they don't care about office politics or organizational charts. They like to spread the credit around."[9] A maverick personality who is not granted the freedom to develop new ideas is likely to join another firm or start a business.

Many creative problem solvers are thrill seekers who find that developing imaginative solutions to problems is a source of thrills. Creative people are also persistent, which is especially important for the verification and application stage of creative thinking. Selling a creative idea to the right people requires considerable follow-up. Finally, creative people enjoy dealing with ambiguity and chaos. Less creative people become quickly frustrated when task descriptions are unclear and disorder exists.

Passion for the Task and the Experience of Flow

A dominant characteristic of creative people that is closely related to personality is a passion for the work. You may recall that passion for the work, or a high degree of intrinsic motivation, is also part of emotional intelligence. More than twenty years of research in industry conducted by Teresa M. Amabile and her associates led to the *intrinsic motivation principle of creativity:* People will be at their creative best when they feel motivated primarily by the interest, satisfaction, and challenge of the work itself—and not by external pressures.[10] Some of this research about intrinsic motivation is based on work with physical scientists, but the same principle is also true of businesspeople.

Passion for the task and high intrinsic motivation contribute in turn to a total absorption in the work and intense concentration, or the **experience of flow.** It is an experience so engrossing and enjoyable that the task becomes worth doing for its own sake regardless of the external consequences.[11] Perhaps you have had this experience when completely absorbed in a hobby or being at your best in a sport or dance. (Flow also means *being in the zone.*) The highly creative leader, such as a business owner developing a plan for worldwide distribution of a product, will often achieve the experience of flow.

Steve Jobs exemplifies passion for the task and the flow experience. Jobs becomes totally absorbed in intimate details of the design and introduction of a new model computer, as well as details about the cartoon characters who appear in full-length movies made by computers. During a product launch for new models of the iMac computer, Jobs shouted directions to stagehands about using lights to display the model to best advantage.[12]

To fully understand the contribution of personal characteristics to creativity, we should return to the basic formula of human behavior presented in Chapter 1: $B = f(P \times E)$. (Behavior is a function of a person interacting with the environment.) In this context, certain personal characteristics may facilitate a leader's being creative, but the right environment is necessary to trigger creative behavior. Greg R. Oldham and Anne Cummings conducted a study with 171 employees from two manufacturing facilities. Creativity was measured by patent disclosures, contributions to an employee suggestion program, and supervisory ratings. It was found that the participants who produced the most creative work had creativity-relevant characteristics such as self-confidence and tolerance of ambiguity. It was also important, however, for employees to work on complex, challenging jobs and to be supervised in a supportive, noncontrolling fashion.[13] The combination of the right personal characteristics with the right environmental conditions yielded the most creative output.

The Componential Theory of Individual Creativity

The *componential theory of individual creativity* developed by Amabile integrates some of the information presented so far about the contribution of personal characteristics to creativity. According to this theory, creativity takes place when three components join together: expertise, creative thinking skill, and task motivation.[14] *Expertise* refers to the necessary knowledge to put facts together (the knowledge required for creativity already explained). *Creative thinking skill* refers to the ability to imaginatively approach problems. If you know how to keep digging for alternatives and to avoid getting stuck in the status quo, your chances of being creative multiply. The exercises to be presented in this chapter foster this type of mental flexibility. Finally, *task motivation* refers to persevering, or sticking with a problem to a conclusion, which is essential for finding creative solutions. A few rest breaks to gain a fresh perspective may be helpful, but the creative person keeps coming back until a solution emerges. Quite often an executive will keep sorting through different compensation plans before settling on one that will motivate the team.

The combined forces of the three factors lead to individual creativity as follows: expertise $\times$ creative-thinking skill $\times$ task motivation = creativity. Because there are substantial individual differences for each factor, such as wide variation in domain-relevant expertise, not all leaders are equally creative.

OVERCOMING TRADITIONAL THINKING AS A CREATIVITY STRATEGY

A unifying theme runs through all forms of creativity training and suggestions for creativity improvement: Creative problem solving requires an ability to overcome traditional thinking. The concept of *traditional thinking* is relative, but it generally refers to a standard and frequent way of finding a solution to a problem. A traditional solution to a problem is thus a modal or most frequent solution. For example, traditional thinking suggests that to increase revenue, a retail store should conduct a sale. Creative thinking would point toward other solutions. As an example, a retail store might increase sales by delivering goods for a small fee, or providing for online shopping (of the store's products) in the store.

The creative person looks at problems in a new light and transcends conventional thinking about them. A historically significant example is Henry Ford, who was known for his creative problem-solving ability. A meat-packing executive invited Ford to visit his Chicago plant and observe how employees processed beef. The automotive executive noticed that at one end of the plant whole carcasses of steers were placed on a giant conveyor belt. As the meat traveled through the plant, workers carved it into various cuts until the carcass was consumed. A flash of whimsical insight hit Ford: If the process were reversed, all the pieces would become a whole steer again. Ford asked himself, "Why can't an automobile be built that way?" He took his creative idea back to the Ford Motor Company in Detroit and constructed the world's first manufacturing assembly line.[15]

The central task in becoming creative is to break down rigid thinking that blocks new ideas. At the same time, the problem solver must unlearn the conventional approach.[16] Henry Ford unlearned the custom approach to building autos so he could use an assembly line. (In the current era, people who have unlearned the assembly-line approach and switched to customization are considered to be creative!) A conventional-thinking leader or manager might accept the long-standing policy that spending more than $5,000 requires three levels of approval. A creative leader might ask, "Why do we need three levels of approval for spending $5,000? If we trust people enough to make them managers, why can't they have budget authorization to spend at least $10,000?"

Overcoming traditional thinking is so important to creative thinking that the process has been characterized in several different ways. Listed next are five concepts of creative thinking. These concepts have much in common and can be considered variations of the same theme. Distinguishing among them is not nearly as important as recognizing that they all carry the same message: Creative thinking requires nontraditional thinking.

1. *A creative person thinks outside the box.* A *box* in this sense is a category that confines and restricts thinking. Because you are confined to a box, you do not see opportunities outside the box. For example, if an insurance executive thinks that health insurance is only for people, he or she might miss out on the growing market for domestic animal (the politically correct term for *pet*) health insurance. Inside the accompanying box insert, you will find several business examples of thinking outside the box.

2. *People who are not creative suffer from "hardening of the categories."* A low-creativity individual thinks categorically: "Only men can drive bulldozers"; "Only women can work in child care centers as caregivers"; "Passenger vehicles can only be sold by having potential customers visit a dealer showroom or outdoor lot."

Current Business Examples of Thinking Outside the Box

- Conventional wisdom says that ATM monitors are used only to display bank-statement-related information. Not Bank of America—they started a program of selling advertising space on ATMs, such as a Connie Chung promotion for CNN. Larry Goodman, president of CNN ad sales, said about the promotion: "It was innovative and hadn't been done before; it was a place to have some exclusivity" (*The Wall Street Journal*, July 25, 2002, p. B8).

- Cell telephones were once considered simple communication devices. Bill Gates of Microsoft then thought of converting the cell phone into a mini PC. In alliance with Intel Corporation, the two companies license their blueprint of the inner workings of a cell phone to manufacturers. Wireless companies can decide on the external design of the handset and how much of the Microsoft software it will contain.

- Conventional wisdom is that you have to take your laptop computer with you to transport files you will be using on your business trip, such as graphic slides, data files, and photos. (A problem is that some portable computers do not have a floppy disk drive.) Outside-the-box thinkers at several computer manufacturers have developed a key chain memory device, such as DiskOnKey. When you get to your destination, you plug your three-inch-long portable memory device into a USB port on a computer and download your data, graphics, or even music.

- Who says companies have to sign long-term, fixed-price contracts to use hardware and software that is dedicated only to that customer? IBM Corporation introduced a service that will allow customers to run their own software applications on mainframes in IBM's data centers and pay rates based mostly on the amount of computing power they use. The pay-for-use model follows the logic of paying for utilities.

- Everybody knows that the best way to promote athletic shoes is to pay megabucks to professional basketball superstars. Nike, however, has departed from conventional wisdom by attempting to create heroes out of no-names. As part of a new marketing strategy, Nike and several other sneaker makers have hired "street ballers" to be their pitchpersons. For beginners, Nike hired Luis Dasilva (aka "Trickz") for around $50,000. He shows off his playground moves on television commercials. He never played professional basketball, was an average high school player, and was working as a clerk in an Athlete's Foot store. In the ad, Trickz wears a flimsy pair of orange hot pants and an Afro wig, and slides the ball up and down his arms to a funk beat.

SOURCE: *Sally Beatty, "Bank of America Puts Ads in ATMs,"* The Wall Street Journal, *July 25, 2002, p. B8; Chris Taylor, "Turning Your Phone into a Mini-PC,"* Time, *March 4, 2002, p. 48; William M. Bulkeley, "New IBM Service Will Test Vision of Computing Power as Utility,"* The Wall Street Journal, *July 1, 2001, p. B4; Maureen Tkacik, "Hoop Dreams: In Search of Stars. Shoe Makers Turn to the Playground,"* The Wall Street Journal, *July 3, 2002, p.1.*

3. *To be creative, one must develop new paradigms.* A paradigm is a model or framework. An example of a quality-inhibiting paradigm is that suppliers should be treated shabbily because they need the company more than the company needs them. In reality, creative companies form partnerships of mutual respect with suppliers. Developing a new paradigm can also benefit an organization by giving a business a new twist, thus leading to a new source of revenues. eBay established a new paradigm for a retailer because it functions as a broker, thereby eliminating the expense of inventory, handling, and shipping.

4. *Creativity requires overcoming traditional mental sets.* A **traditional mental set** is a conventional way of looking at things and placing them in familiar categories. Overcoming traditional wisdom refers to the same idea. One traditional mental set is that the only way for people to obtain the death benefit on their life insurance policy is to die. Several years ago an investor initiated the concept of *viatical settlement,* in which a person with a terminal illness sells his or her policy to an investor for about 80 percent of the policy value. When the person dies, the investor receives the death benefit from the insurance company. The sooner the person dies, the better the return on the investment (for the person who buys the policy from the ailing or aging person). Viatical settlements grew out of the AIDS epidemic, as many young people with no dependents and meager savings were faced with overwhelming medical bills. Today the concept has been extended to cancer patients and nursing home residents who prefer to cash in life insurance policies rather than cash in other assets. In the present form of viatical settlements, sellers and buyers are matched by a "living benefits" broker.

5. *Creative people engage in lateral thinking in addition to vertical thinking.* **Vertical thinking** is an analytical, logical process that results in few answers. The vertical, or critical, thinker is looking for the one best solution to a problem, much like solving an equation. In contrast, **lateral thinking** spreads out to find many different solutions to a problem. The vertical-thinking leader attempts to find the best possible return on investment strictly in financial terms. The lateral-, or creative-thinking, leader might say, "A financial return on investment is desirable. But let's not restrict our thinking. Customer loyalty, quality, being a good corporate citizen, and job satisfaction are also important returns on investment."

As illustrated in Figure 11-3, the essential element in lateral thinking is to find multiple solutions to a problem. A good example of such lateral thinking in solving both a scientific and business problem took place in the communications industry. A problem with many communications satellites is that the satellite is so far away. Also, buildings and terrain block many of the signals from tower-based systems. Angel Technologies Corporation has developed an aircraft that serves as a satellite. A metropolitan region could receive twenty-four-hour service from a fleet of three planes, each flown by two-person crews on eight-hour shifts. The aircraft would fly 50,000 feet high, with a fixed pattern providing coverage to an area seventy-five miles in diameter. The aircraft was designed by Burt Ratan and

FIGURE 11-3   Vertical and Lateral Thinking

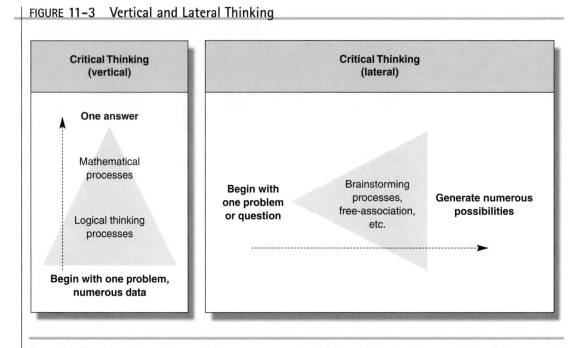

Source: From Becoming a Master Manager: A Competency Framework, by Robert E. Quinn, Sue R. Faerman, Michael P. Thompson, and Michael R. McGrath, Copyright © 1990 John Wiley & Sons, Inc. This material is used by permission of John Wiley & Sons, Inc.

bears a resemblance to his famed Voyager, the first airplane to make a non-stop flight around the globe without refueling.[17] (The lateral thinking here is that the Angel Technologies president was looking for additional ways to offer satellite service.)

The accompanying Leader in Action profile describes a leader who found an excellent business opportunity by taking a fresh look at the process of providing an important service to the airline industry.

ORGANIZATIONAL METHODS TO ENHANCE CREATIVITY

To enhance creative problem solving, the majority of organizations regularly engage in brainstorming. Many others also maintain suggestion programs to solicit creative ideas from employees. In recent years the size of the awards has decreased, yet some workers still receive cash awards for creative ideas approved by the suggestion committee. Many companies now believe that making creative suggestions is a regular part of a team member's position. Here we focus on new developments in brainstorming and other creativity-enhancing methods. Programs of this nature are applied to actual problems, while at the same time they

Leader in Action

Seth Hall Flies High with Refurbished Airplane Parts

Seth Hall is a happy man. In three short years, the 28-year-old president has made Source One Spares Inc., based in Houston, Texas, a global phenomenon. Source One provides after-market component support to virtually every major commercial airline in the world. The company maintains a comprehensive inventory of overhauled airplane parts and components for Boeing, McDonnell Douglas, and Airbus aircraft.

With a 100,000-square-foot facility located at Houston's George Bush Intercontinental Airport and with offices in Dallas, Hong Kong, London, Los Angeles, and Tulsa, Oklahoma, the company shows no sign of slowing. Source One specializes in just-in-time delivery of refurbished aircraft parts and components, including flight controls and landing gears. The company has over 10,000 refurbished components in stock.

While attending college, Hall worked for a small company that repaired airplane parts. Right away he noticed that it took anywhere from thirty to ninety days to repair a part. "If you're an airplane operator, you can't wait that long for your part—you have to have a spare," Hall says (*Entrepreneur*, June 2000, p. 80). So, while in graduate school at Southern Methodist University in Dallas, Hall devised a plan for putting overhauled parts on a shelf and then exchanging them when another part comes in.

"If American Airlines needs a part right away, we send our overhauled component to them and they send us their damaged component, which we repair. We end up with an overhauled part back in our inventory, and they pay us an exchange fee, plus the price for fixing the part," Hall says (*Entrepreneur*). This way, Hall constantly turns over inventory and turns profits.

Thanks to the successful business plan, Source One Spares now has the world's largest exchange pool of overhauled flight controls and airframe components. And because Source One services all Boeing, McDonnell Douglas, and Airbus aircraft models, all the major airlines benefit from the service.

Hall attributes his international success to a top-notch marketing campaign and his sixty-five employees. "It's neat to see them out in the warehouse . . . or staying late to make that call," he says. "They just chip right in and do whatever it takes to get things done" (*Entrepreneur*).

Hall is quoted on the company web site as follows: "Source One Spares has thrived in one of the most competitive industries in the marketplace. The principles upon which the organization was founded, world-class service, superior technology, and dedicated teamwork, are key in every successful business. Based on the commitment, hard work, and determination of everyone on our team, I'm confident we will continue to grow and be a part of the Houston 100 for years to come" (*www.sourceonespares.com/press/100201.htm*).

QUESTIONS

1. What does Seth Hall illustrate about creative thinking and innovation?

2. What type of creative problem solving should Seth Hall tackle next?

3. Do you think the Source One Spares business model could be expanded to the repair of auto and truck parts and components?

SOURCE: *P. Kelly Smith, "Flight Club,"* Entrepreneur, *June 2000, p. 80; www.sourceonespares.com/press/10020/.htm; www.sourceonespares.com.*

provide an opportunity to improve creative thinking, along with a new brainstorming game.

The leader has a dual role in implementing creative problem-solving techniques: He or she facilitates group interaction and also provides a fair share of creative output. The six creativity-enhancing, problem-solving techniques described here are (1) collecting fresh ideas systematically; (2) brainstorming; (3) using the pet-peeve technique; (4) using the forced-association technique; (5) equipping a kitchen for the mind; and (6) engaging in playful physical activities.

Systematically Collecting Fresh Ideas

Creativity is often referred to as a numbers game, because the more ideas you try, the greater the probability of finding one that works. Creativity professor Robert Sutton notes, "The truth is, creativity isn't about wild talent as much as it's about productivity. To find a few ideas that work, you need to try a lot that don't."[18]

A notable way of collecting fresh ideas is for employees to furnish them to a company database so that when somebody needs a fresh idea it can be accessed through a company search engine. Google, the search-engine company, uses an internal web site to collect and retrieve ideas. Many of the ideas are used to improve the company's enormously popular search engine. Google's idea search begins with a company-use-only web page. Using a program called Sparrow, Google employees can readily create a page of ideas. This enables company leaders (such as a product manager) to cast a net across the company's 300 employees. Using this method, every Google staff member invests a fraction of the workday on research and development.[19]

To facilitate having fresh ideas, the leader or manager can establish idea quotas, such as by asking staff members to bring one new idea to each meeting. Although the vast majority of these ideas may not lead to innovation, a few good ones will emerge. Thomas Edison, the man whose name is almost synonymous with creativity, set idea quotas for his workers. He established a personal quota of a minor invention every ten days and a major one every six months, which helped him achieve 1,093 patents during his career.[20] One reason idea quotas work is that they are a goal. Another is that an environmental need (in this case, the idea quota) is an excellent creativity stimulant.

Brainstorming

The best-known method for creativity improvement is brainstorming, which most of you have already done. As a refresher, do Leadership Skill-Building Exercise 11-1, which presents rules and guidelines for brainstorming. Because the vast majority of employers use brainstorming, it is helpful to have some advanced knowledge of the topic other than that it is simply shouting out ideas.

A key aspect of brainstorming is that all ideas can be steppingstones and triggers for new and more useful ideas. Any idea might lead to other associations and connections. Thus, during the idea-generating part of brainstorming, potential solutions are not criticized or evaluated in any way, so that spontaneity is encour-

Leadership Skill-Building Exercise 11–1

Brainstorming and www.GetRich.com

INSTRUCTIONS   First study the rules for brainstorming to refresh your memory. Then do the brainstorming exercise.

1. The ideal group size is five to seven people.

2. The expression of ideas should be spontaneous. All suggestions are welcome, even if they seem outlandish or outrageous.

3. Quantity and variety are important. The greater the number of ideas, the greater the likelihood of a breakthrough idea.

4. Group members should encourage combination and improvement of ideas. This process is called piggybacking or hitchhiking.

5. One person serves as the secretary and records ideas, writing them on a chalkboard or flip chart, or inputting them into a computer.

6. In many instances, a moderator can help keep the session on track by preventing one or two members from dominating the session. If the moderator takes notes, a secretary is not needed.

7. The session should not be overstructured; rules should not be followed too rigidly. Brainstorming is a spontaneous process.

8. Allowing for natural light in the brainstorming room can be helpful for idea generation. A regular supply of snacks and beverages can also contribute to a relaxed feeling that encourages flexible thinking.[21]

Organize into groups to play www.GetRich.com. Assume the role of a small group of friends who want to launch an Internet business. Develop an appropriate Net address, such as www.surfing.com for a company that sells surfing equipment. You must also explain the nature of the business, not necessarily restricting yourself to the same business model as many others have used. Think in terms of a business that might be successful enough to eventually sell stock to the public—an initial public offering (IPO). This is why the exercise is called "www.GetRich.com." The brainstorming team leader will then present the team's solution to the rest of the class.

aged. The idea for an antitheft device for automobiles, The Club, is reported to have stemmed from brainstorming. One marketing person suggested that cars should have a portable steering wheel that the driver could remove after the car is parked. Somebody else suggested that the steering wheel be made inoperative, which led to the idea of an ultra-strong bar to lock the steering wheel in place. The Club and its imitators have become highly successful products; a version of The Club has been developed for securing doors.

Brainstorming continues to evolve as a method of creative problem solving. A recent variation is the *6-3-5 method*. Six people take five minutes to write down three ideas each on a sheet of paper or large index card. After five minutes, the participants pass their papers or cards clockwise and add their own ideas to the new sheet. Continue passing along and writing down ideas until the sheets or cards get back to the people who originated them. Next, hold a group discussion of the merits of the various ideas.[22] During the discussion, it is likely that some members will modify their ideas or think of new ones because they will be stimulated by the list of eighteen ideas. Often, however, the list will contain many duplicate or similar ideas.

Brainstorming can be conducted through email as well as through group discussion. In brainstorming by email, group members simultaneously enter their suggestions into a computer. The ideas are distributed to the monitors of other members. Or ideas can be sent back at different times to a facilitator who passes the contributions along to other members. In either approach, although group members do not talk to each other, they are still able to build on each other's ideas and combine ideas. Electronic brainstorming researcher Keng L. Siau suggests that brainstorming via email can increase both the quantity and quality of ideas. When participants do not face each other directly, they can concentrate on the creativity task at hand and less on the interpersonal aspects of interaction.[23]

Brainstorming, much like other creative problem-solving techniques, works best in an organizational culture that fosters innovation. It is an integral part of the famous design firm IDEO. The company's employees believe passionately in innovation. As a result they are able to argue about alternative solutions to problems yet still unite to produce an effective design.[24]

Using the Pet-Peeve Technique

An important part of quality leadership is for organizational units to find ways to continuously improve their service to external and internal customers. The **pet-peeve technique** is a method of brainstorming in which a group identifies all the possible complaints others might have about the group's organizational unit.[25] Through brainstorming, group members develop a list of complaints from any people who interact with their group. Sources of complaints include inside customers, outside customers, competitors, and suppliers.

Group members can prepare for the meeting by soliciting feedback on themselves from the various target groups. In keeping with the informal, breezy style of the pet-peeve group, feedback should be gathered informally. Rather than approach target groups with a survey, members might tell others about the upcoming pet-peeve session and then ask, "What complaints can you contribute?"

During the no-holds-barred brainstorming session, group members throw in some imaginary and some humorous complaints. Humorous complaints are especially important, for humor requires creative thinking. After all complaints have been aired, the group can process the information during a later session, when they can draw up action plans to remedy the most serious problems.

A pet-peeve session in the human resources department of a small electronic appliances manufacturer generated the following complaints:

"A lot of people wonder what we are doing. They think we just fill out forms and create work for ourselves."

"Some line managers think our job is to find good reasons why they shouldn't hire their best job candidates."

"A lot of employees think we're the corporate ax carriers. We tell line management whom to fire and whose job to eliminate."

"They call us the happiness people. They think our purpose is to keep everybody happy and create a big happy family."

"Job candidates from the outside think our job is to shred résumés. They think we throw away 90 percent of the résumés that arrive at the company."

As a result of these penetrating, albeit exaggerated, self-criticisms, the human resources department developed an effective action plan. The department leader arranged brief meetings with units throughout the organization to discuss the department's role and to answer questions.

Leadership Skill-Building Exercise 11-2 presents an opportunity to practice the pet-peeve technique.

Using the Forced–Association Technique

A widely used method of releasing creativity is the **forced-association technique,** in which individuals or groups solve a problem by making associations between the properties of two objects. An individual (working alone or in a group) selects a word at random from a dictionary. Next, the person (or group) lists all the properties and attributes of this word.

Leadership Skill-Building Exercise 11–2

The Pet–Peeve Technique

Review the description of the pet-peeve technique given in the text. Break into groups of about five contributors each. Each group assumes the role of an organizational unit. (Pick one that is familiar to the group, either through direct contact or through secondhand knowledge. For example, you might assume the role of the auditing group of an accounting firm, the financial aid office at your school, or the service department of an automobile dealer.) Generate a number of real and imagined criticisms of your group. Take the two most serious criticisms and develop an action plan to move your group to a higher plane.

Assume you randomly chose the word *pickle*. Among its attributes are "tasty," "green," "oblong," and "moderately priced." You then force-fit these properties and attributes to the problem you are facing. If you were trying to improve sunglasses, for example, making them "green" and "moderately priced" could be useful. The forced association is supposed to help solve the problem. A link is found between the properties of the random object and the properties of the problem object. An additional, supposedly true, example will help clarify this abstract process. A pharmaceutical company was investigating new ways of delivering medicine. In a forced-association session, someone picked *time bomb* from the dictionary. One of the key properties to emerge from the session was "slow release," which ultimately led to the development of "time capsules," medicine capsules that deliver medicine to the body over a period of time instead of all at once.[26]

The pet-peeve technique is potentially valuable for a leader because it can help the group improve its work processes. Because it has a good-spirited touch, it is not likely to be perceived as threatening.

Equipping a Kitchen for the Mind

According to Mike Vance, the former dean of Disney University (the training program for The Walt Disney Company), every business needs a *kitchen for the mind*, a space designed to nurture creativity. The supplies can be ordinary items such as a chalkboard, flip charts, a coffeepot, a refrigerator, a pencil sharpener, and a personal computer with graphics software. Creativity rooms are also sometimes supplied with children's toys, such as dart guns, Frisbees, nerf balls, and stuffed animals. The purpose of the toys is to help people loosen up intellectually and emotionally, thus stimulating creative thinking. Many large corporations, including General Electric and Motorola, have established creative kitchens, often supplying them with VCRs and multimedia computers.

More important than the equipment within the kitchen for the mind is the existence of a communal meeting place where people can get together to think creatively. Vance contends that even when people's resources are limited, they can still use their ingenuity to produce creative ideas.[27]

Engaging in Playful Physical Activities

Another creativity training technique is to engage participants in playful physical activities that are intended to rejuvenate the spirit and encourage uninhibited thinking. Among these activities are tossing nerf balls, riding children's tricycles, and climbing a jungle gym. After these activities are completed, the participants tackle a creative task. Part of the rationale for playful physical activities is that they help develop a youthful creative outlook and lower inhibitions. Furthermore, the humor involved in these activities helps spark creativity.

Mattel, Inc., the toy maker, has launched Project Platypus, a program designed to get employees to think outside the box so they can better invent new toys. Employees are asked to give up their regular jobs for three months and move to nearby open-plan offices whose various properties, such as desks on wheels, enhance collaboration. Throwing stuffed bunnies at each other and dropping an egg from a fourteen-foot ladder, are some of the activities included in the program. (The egg activity is also a contest to invent a method to prevent the egg from cracking.) To stimulate fresh thinking, fifteen to twenty employees from different disciplines, such as engineering, design, marketing, and copywriting, participate in each session. The director of the program, Adrienne Fontanella, says Platypus helps employees think in an imaginative way and understand the sociology and psychology that underlie children's play patterns. As in brainstorming, employees learn to improve on the ideas of each other and not be negative. Project Platypus is therefore close in concept to a kitchen for the mind, but it adds physical activities. The first team effort produced Ello, a construction and activity toy brand for girls.[28]

SELF-HELP TECHNIQUES TO ENHANCE CREATIVE PROBLEM SOLVING

Leaders and others who want to solve problems more creatively can find hundreds of methods at their disposal, all of them aiming to increase mental flexibility. A representative group of seven strategies and specific techniques for enhancing creative problem solving are presented below and outlined in Table 11-1. These strategies and techniques support and supplement the organizational programs described previously. An underlying contribution of these techniques is that they facilitate intuitive thinking. Intuition is not a mechanical process that can be learned directly, yet a person can develop the mental flexibility that enhances intuition.

Practicing Creativity-Enhancing Exercises

An established way to sharpen creative thinking is to regularly engage in activities that encourage flexible thinking. If you enjoy photography, put yourself on assignment to take a photograph illustrating a theme. You might, for example,

---

TABLE 11-1 Self-Help Techniques for Creativity Improvement

1. Practicing creativity-enhancing exercises

2. Staying alert to opportunities

3. Using multiple senses when seeking solutions

4. Maintaining an enthusiastic attitude

5. Speaking to lead users

6. Maintaining and using an idea notebook or computer file

7. Playing the roles of explorer, artist, judge, and lawyer

take photographs illustrating the proper use of your company's product. Puzzles of all types are useful in stretching your imagination; many creative people regularly do crossword puzzles. Another mind stretcher is to force yourself to write jokes around a given theme. Can you create a joke about the creativity of a leader?

Learning a second language, including sign language, can facilitate creativity because you are forced to shift mental sets. For example, your second language may require you to remember the gender of every noun and to match the spelling of each adjective to the gender and number (singular versus plural) of the noun.

Leadership Skill-Building Exercise 11-3 gives you an opportunity to practice creative thinking. Doing exercises of this nature enhances creative problem solving.

Staying Alert to Opportunities

The ability to spot opportunities that other people overlook characterizes creative leaders. Opportunity seeking is associated with entrepreneurial leadership because the entrepreneur might build an organization around an unmet consumer need. You will recall how the founder of Source One Spares was alert to a business opportunity to deliver spare parts just in time to airline companies. The idea behind the international chain of Starbucks coffee shops began when Howard Schultz, the director of a four-store retail operation called Starbucks Coffee, Tea, and Spice, was attending a housewares convention in Milan, Italy. Schultz noticed the coffee-bar phenomenon. Milan alone had 1,500 of them, all serving trendy beverages such as espresso. Believing that coffee bars would also prosper in the United States, Schultz convinced Starbucks to open one. Schultz left the company to form his own small chain of coffee bars, then bought out Starbucks's two founding partners and merged Starbucks with his firm.[29] (What unmet consumer need did Schultz identify?)

Using Multiple Senses When Seeking Solutions

Another way of becoming more mentally flexible—and therefore more creative—is to use multiple senses when searching for alternative solutions to a problem. Think in terms of the five basic senses—sight, sound, taste, touch, and smell—and any combination of the five. If possible, add the kinesthetic sense, which allows us to be aware of the movement and position of different parts of the body. Mike Vance and Diane Deacon, who recommend the tactic, think it is particularly appropriate for products or services that will be experienced broadly, such as a restaurant or retail store.[30]

To use the multiple-sense technique, visualize how a solution to your problem might look, sound, taste, feel, and smell, and how the body might be positioned while experiencing the solution. Suppose your assignment is to develop a theme and a motif for a booth to showcase your company's new product, an electric-powered home tractor, at a trade show. To gain attention for your tractor, seek answers to such questions as:

- What should the display look like?
- What sounds should the display emit?

Word Hints to Creativity

INSTRUCTIONS   Find a fourth word that is related to the other three words in each row. *Example:*

poke   go   molasses   ____

The answer is *slow:* slow-poke, go slow, and slow as molasses. Now try these words:

1.	surprise	line	birthday	____
2.	base	snow	dance	____
3.	rat	blue	cottage	____
4.	nap	litter	call	____
5.	golf	foot	country	____
6.	house	weary	ape	____
7.	tiger	plate	news	____
8.	painting	bowl	nail	____
9.	jump	sea	priest	____
10.	maple	beet	loaf	____
11.	oak	show	plan	____
12.	light	village	golf	____
13.	merry	out	up	____
14.	jelly	green	kidney	____
15.	bulb	house	lamp	____

SCORING AND INTERPRETATION   Answers appear on page 514. If you were able to think of the "correct" word, or another plausible one, for ten or more of these words, your score compares favorably to that of creative individuals. More important than the score is the fact that you acquired some practice in making remote associations— a characteristic talent of creative people.

SOURCE: *Updated and adapted from "Ideas: Test Your Creativity," by Eugene Raudsepp,* Nation's Business *(June 1965), p. 80.*

- Should you give out food at the display to give the prospective dealers a taste sensation?
- What kind of feel should be built into the display?
- Should you accentuate the smell of new equipment and of freshly cut grass?
- Should you encourage dealers to sit on the tractor so they achieve the same kinesthetic sensation their customers might experience when riding the tractor?

By the time you have answered all of these questions, you may have arrived at a catchy theme. Even without a theme, you may have at least thought of an appropriate display for your electric-powered tractor.

Maintaining an Enthusiastic Attitude

The managerial leader faces a major hurdle in becoming a creative problem solver. He or she must resolve the conflict between being judicial and being imaginative. In many work situations, being judicial (or judgmental) is necessary. Situations calling for judicial thinking include reviewing proposed expenditures and inspecting products for quality or safety defects. Imaginative thinking is involved when searching for creative alternatives. Alex F. Osburn, a former advertising executive and the originator of brainstorming, notes how judgment and imagination are often in conflict:

> The fact that moods won't mix largely explains why the judicial and the creative tend to clash. The right mood for judicial thinking is largely negative. "What's wrong with this?. . . . No this won't work." Such reflexes are right and proper when trying to judge.
>
> In contrast, our creative thinking calls for a positive attitude. We have to be hopeful. We need enthusiasm. We have to encourage ourselves to the point of self-confidence. We have to beware of perfectionism lest it be abortive.[31]

The action step is therefore to project oneself into a positive frame of mind when attempting to be creative. The same principle applies when attempting to be creative about a judicial task. For instance, a leader might be faced with the task of looking for creative ways to cut costs. The manager would then have to think positively about thinking negatively!

Speaking to Lead Users

Part of a leader's role is to furnish breakthrough ideas. An advanced tactic to obtain such an idea is to speak to lead users of your product or service. A **lead user** is an organization or individual who is well ahead of market trends. Because lead users' needs are so far beyond those of the typical user of the product or service, they create innovations that often contribute to commercially valuable advancements.[32] For example, an innovation team at 3M was searching for breakthrough product ideas in pattern recognition. The team consulted with specialists in the military who had worked for a long time with pattern recognition methods based on their need to answer questions such as "Is that a rock lying under that tree, or is it the tip of a ballistic missile?" These lead users had developed ways to enhance the resolution of images by adapting pattern recognition software. After studying this military use, 3M developed a new pattern recognition product that became commercially successful.

Lead users constantly improve products to match them with new opportunities. Leading-edge users have produced inventions such as the electron microscope, CAD-CAM engineering systems, and a host of consumer products. Another application of the leading-edge technique is to look for someone who does what you do but has a larger stake.[33] If you want to make durable tires, for instance, investigate what types of tires airplane manufacturers use. The reason is that airplane manufacturers have a considerable stake in tires that don't pop under heavy pressure.

Maintaining and Using an Idea Notebook or Computer File

It is difficult to capitalize on creative ideas unless you keep a careful record of them. A creative idea trusted to memory may be forgotten in the press of every-day business. An important suggestion kept on your daily planner may become obscured. Creative ideas can lead to breakthroughs for your group and your career, so they deserve the dignity of a separate notebook or computer file. A cautious or forgetful person is advised to keep two copies of the idea book or computer file: one at home and one in the office.

Playing the Roles of Explorer, Artist, Judge, and Lawyer

Another creativity-improvement method incorporates many of the preceding methods. Say you want to enhance your creativity on the job. This method calls for you to adopt four roles in your thinking.[34] First, be an *explorer.* Speak to people in different fields and get ideas that can bring about innovations for your group. For example, if you manage a telecommunications group, speak to salespeople and manufacturing specialists.

Second, be an *artist* by stretching your imagination. Strive to spend about 5 percent of your day asking what-if questions. For example, the leader of a telecommunications group might ask, "What if some new research suggests that the extensive use of telecommunications devices is associated with high rates of cancer?" Also remember to challenge the commonly perceived rules in your field. A bank manager, for example, asked why customers needed their cancelled checks returned each month. The questioning led to a new bank practice: returning cancelled checks only if the customer pays an additional fee.

Third, know when to be a *judge.* After developing some imaginative ideas, at some point you have to evaluate them. Do not be so critical that you discourage your own imaginative thinking. Be critical enough, however, so that you don't try to implement weak ideas. A managing partner in an established law firm formulated a plan for opening two storefront branches that would offer legal services to the public at low prices. The branches would advertise on radio, on television, and in newspapers. After thinking through her plan for several weeks, however, she dropped the idea. She decided that the storefront branches would most likely divert clients away from the parent firm, rather than create a new market.

Fourth, achieve results with your creative thinking by playing the role of *lawyer.* Negotiate and find ways to implement your ideas within your field or place of work. The explorer, artist, and judge stages of creative thought might take only a short time to develop a creative idea. Yet you may spend months or even years getting your breakthrough idea implemented. For example, many tax-preparation firms now loan clients instant refunds in the amount of their anticipated tax refunds. It took a manager in a large tax-preparation firm a long time to convince top management of the merits of the idea.

Establishing a Climate for Creative Thinking

Leaders need to develop creative ideas of their own to improve productivity, quality, and satisfaction. Establishing a climate conducive to creative problem solving is another requirement of effective leadership. A foundation step in fostering organizational creativity is to establish a vision and mission that include creativity, such as "We will become the most innovative provider of automobile undercare (mufflers, brakes, etc.) products and services in North America" [Monro Muffler Brake]. Vision statements and mission statements set the pace, but they must be supported by the right climate and extensive use of the techniques described throughout this chapter.

Information about establishing a climate for creativity can be divided into leadership and managerial practices for enhancing creativity, and methods for managing creative workers. To sensitize you to this vast amount of information, do Leadership Diagnostic Activity 11-1. The instrument gives you an opportunity to ponder many of the management and leadership practices that encourage or discourage creative problem solving.

Leadership Practices for Enhancing Creativity

Six leadership and managerial practices are particularly helpful in fostering creative thinking, as revealed by the work of Amabile and her associates, as well as by other researchers and observers.[35]

1. *Intellectual challenge.* Matching people with the right assignments enhances creativity because it supports expertise and intrinsic motivation. The amount of stretch is consistent with goal theory; too little challenge leads to boredom, but too much challenge leads to feelings of being overwhelmed and loss of control. The leader or manager must understand his or her group members well to offer them the right amount of challenge.

   Time pressures can contribute to intellectual challenge because you have to think faster to meet a creativity deadline. The evidence about the impact of time pressures on creativity is mixed. When survival is at stake, such as when a firm is headed toward bankruptcy or dealing with a disaster, time pressures can stimulate creative thinking. High time-pressure days without a clear, urgent focus usually dampen creativity. In general, because complex cognitive processing takes time, leaders should avoid extreme time pressure.

2. *Freedom to choose the method.* Workers tend to be more creative when they are granted the freedom to choose which method is best for attaining a work goal (as described in our study of delegation in Chapter 7). Stable goals are important because it is difficult to work creatively toward a moving target.

3. *Ample supply of the right resources.* Time and money are the most important resources for enhancing creativity. Deciding how much time and money to give to a team or project is a tough judgment call that can either support or stifle creativity. Under some circumstances setting a time deadline will trigger creative thinking because it represents a favorable challenge. An

Assessing the Climate for Innovation

INSTRUCTIONS Respond "mostly yes" or "mostly no" as to how well each of the following characteristics fits an organization familiar to you. If you are currently not familiar with an outside organization, respond to these statements in regard to your school.

	Mostly Yes	Mostly No
1. Creativity is encouraged here.	____	____
2. Our ability to function creatively is respected by the leadership.	____	____
3. Around here, people are allowed to try to solve the same problems in different ways.	____	____
4. The main function of members of this organization is to follow orders that come down through channels.	____	____
5. Around here, a person can get into a lot of trouble by being different.	____	____
6. This organization can be described as flexible and continually adapting to change.	____	____
7. A person can't do things that are too different around here without provoking anger.	____	____
8. The best way to get along in this organization is to think the way the rest of the group does.	____	____
9. People around here are expected to deal with problems in the same way.	____	____
10. This organization is open and responsive to change.	____	____
11. The people in charge around here usually get credit for others' ideas.	____	____
12. In this organization, we tend to stick to tried and true ways.	____	____
13. This place seems to be more concerned with the status quo than with change.	____	____
14. Assistance in developing new ideas is readily available.	____	____
15. There are adequate resources devoted to innovation in this organization.	____	____

16. There is adequate time available to pursue creative ideas here.   _____ _____

17. Lack of funding to pursue creative ideas is a problem in this organization.   _____ _____

18. Personnel shortages inhibit innovation in this organization.   _____ _____

19. This organization gives me free time to pursue creative ideas during the workday.   _____ _____

20. The reward system here encourages innovation.   _____ _____

21. This organization publicly recognizes those who are innovative.   _____ _____

22. The reward system here benefits mainly those who don't rock the boat.   _____ _____

SCORING AND INTERPRETATION   The score in the direction of a climate for innovation is "mostly yes" for statements 1, 2, 3, 6, 10, 14, 15, 16, 19, 20, and 21, and "mostly no" for statements 4, 5, 7, 8, 9, 11, 12, 13, 17, 18, and 22. A score of 16 or higher suggests a climate well suited for innovation, 9 to 15 is about average, and 8 or below suggests a climate that inhibits innovation.

SOURCE: *From Susanne G. Scott and Reginald Bruce, "Determinants of Innovative Behavior: A Path Model of Individual Innovation in the Workplace,"* Academy of Management Journal, *by Hitt, Michael A., June 1994, p. 593. Copyright 1994 Academy of Management. Reproduced with permission of* Acad of Mgmt *in the format Textbook via Copyright Clearance Center.*

example would be hurrying to be first to market with a new product. False deadlines or impossibly tight ones can create distrust and burnout. To be creative, groups also need to be adequately funded.

4. *Effective design of work groups.* Work groups are the most likely to be creative when they are mutually supportive and when they have a diversity of backgrounds and perspectives. Blends of gender, race, and ethnicity are recognized today as contributing to creative thought, similar to cross-functional teams with their mix of perspectives from different disciplines. The various points of view often combine to achieve creative solutions to problems. Homogeneous teams argue less, but they are often less creative. Putting together a team with the right chemistry—just the right level of diversity and supportiveness—requires experience and intuition on the leader's part.

5. *Supervisory encouragement.* The most influential step a leader can take to bring about creative problem solving is to develop a permissive atmosphere that encourages people to think freely. Praising creative work is important because, for most people to sustain their passion, they must feel that their work

matters to the organization. Creative ideas should be evaluated quickly rather than put through a painfully slow review process. (Although Amabile does not emphasize external rewards such as money for enhancing creativity, many workers perceive bonuses and salary increases to be very encouraging.)

6. *Organizational support.* The entire organization as well as the immediate manager should support creative effort if creativity is to be enhanced on a large scale. The companywide reward system should support creativity, including recognition and financial incentives. Organizational leaders should encourage information sharing and collaboration, which lead to the development of the expertise so necessary for creativity and to more opportunities for intrinsic motivation. Executives who combat excessive politics can help creative people focus on work instead of fighting political battles. In a highly political environment, a worker would be hesitant to suggest a creative idea that was a political blunder, such as replacing a product particularly liked by the CEO.

The above list covers important leadership and management initiatives for creating an environment conducive to creativity, yet several other points also merit attention. *Loose-tight leadership* enhances creativity. *Looseness* refers to granting space for new ideas and exploration, whereas the tight approach means finally making a choice among the alternatives. When The Gillette Company was exploring various alternatives for a breakthrough razor, many potentially useful ideas surfaced. The management group in charge said "let's go for it" when the idea to add flexible blades to the Trac II razor was presented (it became the Sensor razor).[36] Innovation is also enhanced when workers throughout the organization are able to pursue absurd ideas without penalty for being wrong or for having wasted some resources. An axiom of creativity is that many ideas typically have to be tried before a commercially successful one emerges.

A recent insight into encouraging a creative climate is for leaders to have favorable exchanges with group members, as defined by LMX theory (see Chapter 9). A study with 191 research and development specialists found a positive relationship between LMX ratings and creativity of workers as measured by supervisory ratings.[37] When group members have positive relationships with their manager, they may have a more relaxed mental attitude that allows the imagination to flow. A useful strategy for enhancing creativity throughout the organization is to emphasize the importance of working with a sense of heightened awareness, of being alert to new possibilities. For example, the discoverer of 3M's Scotchgard® fabric protector fought a long and complicated battle to find an audience for her unintended discovery.[38] Although this example may appear negative, it illustrates that even a creative company like 3M may miss the value of an unexpected breakthrough.

Methods of Managing Creative Workers

Closely related to establishing organizational conditions favoring creativity is choosing effective methods for managing creative workers. The suggestions that follow supplement effective leadership and management practices in general.[39]

1. *Give creative people tools and resources that allow their work to stand out.* Creative workers have a high degree of self-motivation, and therefore want to achieve high-quality output. To achieve such high quality, they usually need adequate resources, such as state-of-the-art equipment and an ample travel budget for such purposes as conducting research.

2. *Give creative people flexibility and a minimum amount of structure.* Many creative workers regard heavy structure as the death knell of creativity. "Structure" for these workers means rules and regulations, many layers of approval, strict dress codes, fixed office hours, rigid assignments, and fill-in-the-blank paperwork. (Typically, the leader/manager will have to achieve a workable compromise in this area that stays within the framework of organizational policy. Regular office hours, for example, are a must for team assignments.)

3. *Employ creative people to manage and evaluate creative workers.* Managers of creative workers should have some creative ability of their own so that they can understand creativity and be credible as leaders. Understanding the creative process is important for evaluating the creative contribution of others. What constitutes creative output is somewhat subjective, but the output can be tied to objective criteria. At Hallmark Cards, Inc., for example, creativity is measured by such factors as how well the creative work sold and how well it performed in a consumer preference test. In general, a manager's intuition about the potential contribution of a creative idea or product still weighs heavily in the evaluation.

ADDITIONAL LEADERSHIP PRACTICES THAT ENHANCE INNOVATION

Creativity in organizations leads to innovations in products, services, and processes (such as a billing system or quality improvement). All leadership and management practices that enhance creative problem solving therefore also enhance innovation. Here we describe four additional leadership initiatives that enhance innovation.

1. *Continually pursue innovation.* A major characteristic of the Most Admired Companies, as compiled by the Hay Group consultancy for *Fortune*, is constant innovation. Translated into practice, this means that company leaders stay alert to innovative possibilities. Innovation is important because a new technology can make an industry obsolete or place it in grave danger. What will happen to petroleum refineries when (and if) the fuel cell takes hold? One of the many reasons that General Electric Company is at the top of the Most Admired List so frequently is that it has an innovative global strategy. GE leadership has transplanted its corporate culture successfully into many Asian countries, and now Asia is GE's fastest-growing market.[40]

2. *Take risks and encourage risk taking.* "No risk, no reward" is a rule of life that applies equally well to the leadership of innovation. Keith Hammonds admonishes business executives that even in a slow-growth economy, companies cannot win big in the marketplace by doing things just a teeny bit better than the competition. It is necessary to gamble intelligently, shrewdly, and selectively even during a period of insecurity and instability. A notable example of a risk taker is Dave Lyon, the chief designer at the Buick Brand Center. To minimize risk, Buick once relied on focus groups when designing a new car. Lyon stepped out of the mold and took a risk on a dramatic redesign of the LeSabre, one of the company's most conservative models.[41]

3. *Acquire innovative companies.* The innovation process takes a long time as it proceeds from a creative idea, through initial experimentation, to feasibility determination, and then to final application.[42] To shorten the process and reduce the risk of a failed innovation, many companies acquire smaller companies that have the innovation they seek. Cisco Systems, Inc., spearheaded by chief executive John Chambers, was for many years a model of innovation through acquisition. During an eight-year period Cisco gobbled up more than seventy companies, mostly because each one offered a technology Cisco needed for its product mix. For example, it would buy a company that produced a specialty router. Largely because of the slide in its stock price, which made buying other companies more difficult, by 2002 Cisco was shifting more toward in-house innovation.[43]

4. *Avoid innovation for its own sake.* Leaders also have to exercise good judgment: Innovation just because it is innovation is not always valuable. Many gadgets are scientific marvels, yet they have limited market appeal. A possible example is the pop-up advertisements that cover your email when you are composing or reading a message. Most people treat these windows as if they were mosquitoes, and the uninvited windows have not proven to be an effective form of advertising. Most companies have loads of interesting ideas floating to the surface, but very few will even translate into a profitable product or service. The information presented earlier about playing the role of a judge in creativity is particularly relevant here. Jennifer Brown, the executive vice president of ebusiness at Fidelity Investments, says, "We have more good ideas than we can handle. We have so many good ideas here—truly innovative ideas—that sometimes our people get a little frustrated that we can't act on most of them."[44]

SUMMARY

A creative leader brings forth ideas or things that did not exist previously, or that existed in a different form. The creative process has been divided into five steps: opportunity or problem recognition; immersion (the individual becomes immersed in the idea); incubation (the idea simmers); insight (a solution surfaces); and verification and application (the person supports and implements the idea).

Distinguishing characteristics of creative people fall into five areas: knowledge, intellectual abilities, personality, and passion for the task and the experience of flow. Creative people possess extensive knowledge, good intellectual skills, intellectual curiosity, and a wide range of interests. Personality attributes of creative people include a positive self-image, tolerance for isolation, nonconformity, and the ability to tolerate ambiguity and chaos. Passion for the work and flow are related to intense intrinsic motivation. Creative people also enjoy interacting with others. The right personal characteristics must interact with the right environment to produce creative problem solving. The componential theory of creativity focuses on the expertise, creative-thinking skills, and task motivation of creative people.

A major strategy for becoming creative is to overcome traditional thinking, or a traditional mental set. Also, it is necessary to break down rigid thinking that blocks new ideas. A related idea is that creative people engage in lateral thinking in addition to vertical thinking. Lateral thinking seeks many different answers to problems, whereas vertical thinking looks for the one best answer.

Creative thinking can be enhanced by collecting fresh ideas systematically, and brainstorming. A spinoff of brainstorming is the pet-peeve technique, in which a group of people think of all the possible complaints others might have about their unit. Another technique to facilitate creative thinking is to force associations between the properties of two objects. Some organizations also equip a kitchen for the mind, or a space designed for creativity. Playful physical activities can also stimulate creativity.

Self-help techniques to enhance creative problem solving include (1) practicing creativity-enhancing exercises, (2) staying alert to opportunities, (3) using multiple senses, (4) maintaining enthusiasm, (5) speaking to lead users (customers who make advanced use of the product), (6) maintaining and using an idea notebook or computer file, and (7) playing the roles of explorer, artist, judge, and lawyer.

Establishing a climate conducive to creative problem solving is another requirement of effective leadership. A foundation step is to establish a vision statement and mission that include creativity. Specifically, leaders should (1) provide intellectual challenge, (2) allow freedom to choose the method, (3) supply the right resources, (4) design work groups effectively, (5) have supervisors encourage creative workers, and (6) give organizational support for creativity. It is also important to provide loose-tight leadership, and to allow people to pursue absurd ideas without penalty. Positive leader-member exchanges also foster creativity, as does emphasizing the importance of heightened awareness throughout the organization.

Special attention should be paid to managing creative workers. One should provide excellent tools and resources, give creative people flexibility, and employ creative managers.

Four additional leadership initiatives that enhance innovation are the following: continually pursue innovation; take risks; acquire innovative companies; and avoid innovation for its own sake.

KEY TERMS

Innovation

Creativity

Organizational creativity

Experience of flow

Traditional mental set

Vertical thinking

Lateral thinking

Pet-peeve technique

Forced-association technique

Lead user

 GUIDELINES FOR ACTION AND SKILL DEVELOPMENT

To encourage creative problem solving among team members, the leader should avoid certain creativity dampeners and inhibitors, as implied in this chapter. Ten more of these creativity blockers are as follows:

1. Expressing attitudes that preserve the status quo by using such clichés as "Don't rock the boat"; "Don't make waves"; and "If it ain't broke, don't fix it."

2. Policing team members by every device imaginable.

3. Saying yes to new ideas but not doing anything about them.

4. Being the exclusive spokesperson for everything in the area of responsibility.

5. Putting every idea through formal channels.

6. Responding to most suggestions for change with a pained look and saying, "But that will cost *money*."

7. Promoting the "not-invented-here" syndrome (if the manager did not invent it, the manager will not consider it).

8. Being suspicious of any idea from below, because it's new and because it's from below.

9. Treating problems as signs of incompetence and failure.

10. Being free and open with criticism but stingy with praise.[45]

DISCUSSION QUESTIONS AND ACTIVITIES

1. Give an example of creativity in business that does *not* relate to the development or marketing of a product or service.

2. At the height of its prosperity, many business strategy experts acclaimed Enron Corporation as a model of an innovative organization. What cautions about innovation does the preceding statement suggest?

3. How might you use information about the five stages of creative thought to become a more creative problem solver?

4. Find an example in print or on the Internet of creative problem solving by a leader. Be prepared to share your findings with classmates.

5. In many companies, it is expected for managerial and professional workers to wear

formal business attire to work (such as suits and high heels). What effect do you think this dress code has on creativity?

6. In what way does your present program of study contribute to your ability to solve problems creatively?

7. The opinion has often been expressed that too much emphasis on teamwork inhibits creativity. What do you think of this argument?

8. What is the underlying process by which creativity-building exercises, such as the forced-association technique, are supposed to increase creativity?

9. How might a manager physically lay out an office to improve the chances that creative problem solving will take place?

10. Speak to the most creative person you know in any field, and find out if he or she uses any specific creativity-enhancing technique. Be prepared to bring your findings back to class.

Leadership Case Problem A

Will Innovation Survive at 3M?

At 3M, stories are an important part of the culture. Every employee knows about the 3M scientist who spilled chemicals on her tennis shoe—and came up with Scotchgard. Everyone knows about the researcher who wanted a better way to mark the pages of his hymnal—and invented the Post-it Note. Collectively these stories help explain the greatness of 3M. Lately, however, a new story has been unfolding. This one involves no heroic innovators, just terms like *cost controls*, *Six Sigma*, and *sourcing effectiveness*, not exactly the stuff of company lore. But it does indicate how 3M is changing under CEO James McNerney, the first outside leader in the company's 100-year history.

Since he arrived from General Electric in December 2000, McNerney has given 3M's freewheeling culture a dose of GE's management science. He has slashed costs, rationalized purchasing, introduced a companywide process-improvement program, and challenged 3M to amp up its growth. Furthermore, McNerney has brought more centralized direction to a company that has always favored laissez-faire experimentation and doodling.

Fears of management's heavy hand have deep roots in 3M mythology. Since its inception as the Minnesota Mining and Manufacturing Company, the company has followed a simple formula for growth: Hire good scientists, give them ample resources, and get out of their way. The company remains a model of decentralization and small government, with dozens of product laboratories scattered across forty autonomous business units. Researchers can spend 15 percent of their time on any project of their choosing. If management denies them funding, they can apply for a Genesis Grant, awarded by fellow scientists, or pitch their idea elsewhere in the company. Nothing is considered too small or too zany. One-third of 3M's $16 billion in revenues comes from products that didn't exist four years ago.

However, recently 3M has produced mediocre growth of earnings per share. An analyst at Edward Jones says, "3M was not poorly run, but I think to a certain extent it was starting to get fat and happy. It was the ideal situation for Jim McNerney to come to" (*Fortune*, August 12, 2002, p. 128).

Diplomatic and affable, McNerney, 52, looked like a dream candidate for 3M. Besides having degrees from Yale and Harvard Business School, he had worked in a variety of business units at GE. In his most recent assignment, he had revived a sagging commercial jet engine project. He also had two years of overseas experience running GE's Asian operations. "It was as close to a perfect fit as one could find," says a 3M board member (*Fortune*, p. 128).

In some ways, the company McNerney joined resembled the one he had left: it was diversified, industrial, and roughly a century old. Yet for the most part the two companies contrasted sharply. GE gave its managers a toolbox; 3M functioned more like a sandbox. GE was organized into eleven giant business units; 3M had 50,000 niche products scattered across a bewildering organizational chart. Most important, GE's corporate headquarters drove earnings growth across the whole organization; 3M's corporate group placed less emphasis on financial growth standards.

McNerney's Changes and Initiatives.   Some early moves by McNerney were not well received, such as his announcement of the layoff of 6,500 of 3M's 75,000 workers (*Fortune*, August 12, 2002). Yet after his first twenty months on the job, other initiatives have been well received. 3M scientists particularly like the data-driven nature of Six Sigma. "More people told me to change things than told me not to change things," says McNerney. "I think the story here is rejuvenation of a talented group of people rather than replacement of a mediocre group of people" (*Fortune*, p. 130).

One of McNerney's most urgent problems was overhead: Costs had grown at twice the rate of sales in recent years. Efforts to contain costs saved a quick $500 million in 2001, and centralized purchasing saved another $100 million. 3M is also moving more manufacturing to lower-wage sites overseas. A longer-term priority was leadership development. McNerney opened a leadership development institute modeled after GE's famous Crotonville Center. He also blew up 3M's seniority-based pay structure, forcing managers to grade every employee on a curve and to promote emerging stars faster.

McNerney's plan to acquire other companies has engendered controversy. He wants to use acquisitions to increase sales by 10 percent a year, nearly double the rate of the past decade. 3M has the money to purchase other companies, but it has limited experience integrating them. Some insiders feel the task could distract management from the core task of innovating. As McNerney strengthens the corporate center, he also wants it to play a more active role in allocating resources. Cash from mature businesses, like adhesives and abrasives, will be diverted to growth businesses like pharmaceuticals. McNerney has eliminated the 3M requirement that each division get 30 percent of sales from products introduced in the past four years. To make that number, some managers were resorting to rather dubious "innovations" such as pink Post-it Notes.

Acceleration is the name McNerney has chosen for one of his major initiatives. At any given time, 3M has about 1,500 products in the development pipeline. He thinks that is too many. His idea is to funnel more R&D spending—such as $100 million or more per year—toward the ideas with the biggest market potential while culling the weaker ones earlier. "I've got to make it culturally okay to say no," he says. "A no means you can get back onto something that has a greater chance of success" (*Fortune*, p. 132). In addition to specifying where research and development dollars are spent, McNerney and his team are establishing uniform performance standards across 3M. In the past, individual business heads had free rein. An executive with thirty-three years of tenure at the company says, "The most important thing about 3M—the single most important thing—is you get to do things your own way" (*BusinessWeek*, p. 51). This is now changing.

McNerney believes strongly that 3M must find new avenues for growth. Part of his reasoning is that the brand could support a company perhaps five times as big, and a global infrastructure to match. (He admits to exaggeration here.)

McNerney's Analysis of 3M Concerns. Some 3M watchers are concerned about McNerney's changes because it is difficult to tell which of today's tiny projects will become tomorrow's homeruns. No one predicted that Scotchgard or the Post-it Note would earn millions. They began as little experiments—solutions to a problem that people didn't know they had—on the 3M principle that "no market, no end product is so small as to be scorned" (*Fortune*, p. 132). Yet McNerney insists he simply wants to stop people from spending so much money before they know if they have a product of potential value. For example, it is important to speak to a marketing representative about the market potential of a product idea early in the product-development cycle.

In slowing down spending on product development, McNerney knows he's going up against decades of 3M stories in which naysaying management is always the villain. He says that the mythology at 3M is: "Against all odds, I ended up with Post-it Notes. Mythology supports a lot of important and good behavior. But when it becomes apocryphal, it becomes dysfunctional. You want to get people onto a more reality-based way of looking at the world" (*Fortune*, p. 132).

McNerney has praised the 3M culture at every turn, making it clear that he wants to give employees tools, not orders. "This is a fundamentally strong company. The inventiveness of the people here is in contrast with any other place I've seen. Everybody wakes up in the morning trying to figure out how to grow. They really do" (*Fortune*, p. 130). He also says he understands the balancing act facing him: "My job is to add scale in a fast-moving entrepreneurial environment. If I end up killing that entrepreneurial spirit, I will have failed" (*BusinessWeek*, p. 51).

QUESTIONS

1. To what extent might McNerney's leadership and management approach damage the culture of innovation that has been characteristic of 3M?

2. How well does McNerney appear to be managing the delicate balance between the company's center and its periphery—between efficiency and innovation?

3. The observation was made in the case that "GE gave its managers a toolbox; 3M functioned more like a sandbox." How does this statement relate to creativity and innovation?

SOURCE: *Jerry Useem, "Can McNerney Reinvent GE?"* Fortune, *August 12, 2002, pp. 127–132; Michael Arndt, "3M: A Lab for Growth?"* BusinessWeek, *January 21, 2002, pp. 50–51; "Q&A with 3M's James McNerney,"* *www.businessweek.com/magazine/content/02_03/ b3766086.htm.*

Leadership Case Problem B

The Food Company Skunk Works

Melrose Foods is a large food manufacturer and processor consisting of twenty-one divisions. Many of these divisions are smaller companies that have been purchased in recent years. The executive office, headed by Gardner Appleby, recently decided to establish a research and development group with responsibility to develop new food products. Appleby explained it in these words to the corporate staff and division heads:

"The time has arrived for Melrose to copy the high-tech approach to R&D. Effective July 1 of this year, we are building our own skunk works. The executive office has chosen Manuel Seda for this key assignment. As you recall, Manuel was a dynamically successful entrepreneur who established Tangy Tacos. Starting in his mother's kitchen, he built up a national distribution for his product in three years. We bought Tangy Tacos for its growth and profitability. But even more important, we bought the talent of Manuel Seda.

"Tangy Tacos will be headed by Wanda Morales while Manuel is on indefinite assignment as manager of our skunk works. Manuel will begin with six competent employees. He and his group can have all the budget they need, so long as it looks like they are on the path to developing successful products."

At this point in Appleby's presentation, Garth Laidlaw, division head of Tiger Pet Foods, waved his hand. "We need clarification, Gardner. You mention that the skunk works will be funded as long as it looks like they are about to develop successful products. Developing a successful new food product is a risky business. About 90 percent of new product ideas never make it to the marketplace. And about half of the 10 percent that do arrive on the market fail within one year."

"I'm aware of those dismal statistics," said Appleby. "But without a push on new product development, Melrose Foods is doomed to stagnation and mediocrity. Members of the management team, let us all move forward toward a successful skunk works. And let us all wish Manuel the best of luck."

Three months after the skunk works was established, Seda received a visit from Appleby. After a brief tour of the facility, Appleby said to Seda: "Manuel, I do get the impression that there is a lot of activity going on here, but it does not seem to be focused activity. Could you give me an update?"

"Gardner, it's premature to expect results. We have been set aside so that we can think at our own pace. This is not a crash program. Don't forget, I had been working in the food business for three years before I thought of the idea for Tangy Tacos."

"It's true, we are not expecting immediate results from the skunk works, but you are a pretty well funded group. Could you please give me a hint of any new product idea you have developed so far?"

Seda answered: "Actually we are pretty excited about one new idea. It's a form of instant fish called 'Sudden Seafood.' Today's busy and health-conscious professional will love it. You add boiling water to pulverized seafood, and you get a mashed-potato-like substance that is actually tasty seafood. We would certainly be the first on the market."

"Revolting," responded Appleby. "I would definitely turn thumbs down on Melrose investing money to market instant fish. Maybe you should interest our Tiger Pet Foods division in that idea. It could be used when traveling with cats."

Three months later, Appleby revisited Seda at the skunk works. The president said, "I'm just doing an informal check again. What new product idea is the skunk works toying with these days?"

"I think we have a real winner on the drawing board," said Manuel. "The country is sick of wimpy soft drinks that have no real flavor, no gusto, and give no boost to the psyche. We have been experimenting with a raspberry-flavored soft drink that has four times the caffeine and three times the sugar of anything on the market. It's tentative name is 'Razzle Razzberry.' It's destined to be a winner."

"Hold on, Manuel. You're running counter culture. The country is moving away from heavy soft drinks and you're suggesting a product that's practically a narcotic. It sounds like our skunk works might be getting carried away."

"Gardner, it's too bad you don't like this promising idea. Maybe I could meet with you and other members of the executive office to discuss the mission of the company skunk works. I don't feel things are going right."

"It sounds to me like you're getting a little touchy," said Appleby.

QUESTIONS

1. How effective is Appleby's leadership approach for enhancing innovation at Melrose Foods?

2. What suggestions can you offer Appleby for getting a better return on investment from the company skunk works?

3. What do you think of Seda's request to review the mission of the skunk works with the executive office?

4. What is your hunch about the potential success of Sudden Seafood and Razzle Razzberry?

INTERNET SKILL-BUILDING EXERCISE

Creativity in Business

Apply the chapter concepts! Visit the Web and complete this Internet skill-building exercise to learn more about current leadership topics and trends.

Here is an opportunity to interact with the work of creativity guru Michael Ray of Stanford University. Visit www.michael-ray.com/creativity.shtml. Look over the site, then go to "take our survey." The survey gives you the opportunity to examine your creative process and the type of work that brings meaning to your life. Your questionnaire will be scored, and you will be provided with comparative results from work done at Stanford. After you have completed the experience, reflect on these questions:

1. What did you learn about your creative process?

2. How does the feedback about your creativity that you acquired on this site compare to the feedback you received from the exercises in this chapter?

Communication and Conflict Resolution Skills

CHAPTER 12

Michael Daly's staff told him he needed to hire another dining room helper to pour coffee at breakfast. But Daly, 38, the chief executive officer of a small chain of upscale retirement rental residences, wasn't buying it. Why hire someone else when the nursing aides could pitch in and serve? "I'm the CEO. I've got a big ego. I didn't believe it," he said.

That is until Daly, President of Sterling Glen Communities, ditched his suit and cell phone for a day on the job, following a work schedule set by the staff at Chancellor Park, a Philadelphia retirement home.

So far he has done his "Walking in Your Shoes" program at two other of the company's nine facilities. When Daly reports for duty at 7 A.M., he has no idea what will be in store. "They want me to have the most difficult day they can," he said. Typically he works in the kitchen, handles a stint on the reception desks, empties trash, makes repairs, and cleans apartments. "They give me the dirtiest room, and I don't know how to clean a room," he said.

Daly said the work gives him a grass-roots knowledge of the facility, particularly when he manages to penetrate layers of middle management. His favorite spot for picking up knowledge is folding laundry with the housekeeping staff. Daly said it takes the crew about half an hour to loosen up enough to give him the lowdown.

At Chancellor Park, Daly's day started in the dining room, and that was when he saw how frantic it was. "I realized the aides were barely able to keep with the shower schedule. They couldn't pour coffee," he said. "We'll have to do something."

William Brown, executive director of Chancellor Park, said he would like Daly to authorize an additional maintenance worker. The last maintenance worker got so backed up that he left a big stack of work orders when he quit. Brown assigned Daly to complete four repair jobs in one hour and twenty minutes. It took Daly an hour longer, and he did not get everything done.

Daly visited Edith Creskoff, 94, who wanted a television moved into her apartment. "You're pretty efficient for a president," she said. Then it was on to Ron Polenz, a man in his 60s, who needed the hinges on his refrigerator door switched so he could open it from his wheelchair. "I had no idea they were reversible," Daly said. "I have to order 166 refrigerators, and now that I know, I'll make sure I order reversible ones."

Polenz watched Daly struggle to turn the refrigerator on its side as Daly muttered under his breath about not having the right tools for the job. "You're seeing my first bead of sweat of the day," Daly said.

"I thought you were hot stuff already with that tool kit," Polenz joked before delivering his opinion of Daly's "Walking in Your Shoes" program. "The man's the CEO, and he comes down and sees for himself rather than wait for somebody to report to somebody else," said Polenz. "The more I think about it, the more I like the idea."[1]

The "Walking in Your Shoes" program implemented by the retirement community CEO illustrates how an effective leader invests time and effort to develop empathy for his or her workers. The empathy, in turn, serves as a way of communicating supportively.

Effective communication between leaders and other workers is characteristic of highly regarded and very successful companies. Effective managers and leaders listen to employees, and open communications contribute to leadership effectiveness. Another key issue about communication is that effective communication skills contribute to inspirational leadership. Chapter 3 described how charismatic leaders are masterful oral communicators. This chapter expands on this theme and also covers the contribution of nonverbal, written, and supportive communication. Furthermore, it describes how the ability to overcome cross-cultural communication barriers enhances leadership effectiveness. Finally, the chapter presents conflict resolution skills, because leaders spend a substantial amount of time resolving conflicts.

EVIDENCE ABOUT COMMUNICATION AND LEADERSHIP

Research evidence supports the conventional wisdom that effective leaders are also effective communicators. Based on his synthesis of studies, Bernard M. Bass found substantial evidence of a positive relationship between competence in communicating and satisfactory leadership and management performance. An interview study of two hundred successful organizational leaders indicated that they had similar communication patterns. The leaders expanded their thinking regularly by actively soliciting new ideas and feedback from others. Furthermore, they continuously sought fresh information. They possessed the persuasive skills necessary to convince others of the quality of their ideas.[2]

Research has also been conducted on the contribution of nonverbal behavior to leadership effectiveness. One study suggested that when nonverbal messages contradict verbal messages, the listener tends to place more reliance on the nonverbal messages. A manager who talks about wanting to empower employees but looks bored during the discussion will be regarded as insincere and manipulative. To be effective, the leader must synchronize verbal and nonverbal behavior.[3]

Technology has had a meaningful impact on leaders' communication and coordination. By relying on information technology, leaders and managers can be in frequent contact with group members without being physically present. Managers can also be part of a **virtual office** in which employees work together as if they were part of a single office despite being physically separated. Although frequent contact with company employees, customers, and suppliers enhances coordination, the manager can exercise leadership by inspiring, motivating, and persuading people more readily with this technology than by telephone and in-person contacts alone. Many leaders regularly send email messages to motivate and inspire their constituents—locally, regionally, and internationally. The alternative is for the manager to communicate primarily when back at the office. A high-tech leader is never away from the office—even if he or she would like to be!

Despite these findings, many companies are not communicating their mission, vision, and values as well as they might. An American Management Association survey of more than 10,000 U.S. manufacturing and service firms uncovered significant problems in the basis for effective communication at many firms.[4] One such finding was that a majority of managers and supervisors from different business functions were perceived to lack a high level of understanding of the company's mission, vision, and values. Furthermore, less than a third of the respondents agreed that their firm regularly sought feedback to make sure that messages were perceived as intended. A vice president at Monsanto Company expressed the problem in these terms: "We all think we're communicating more and better with each other because we now have email, voice mail, and various other technologies. But I don't believe that's necessarily been the case at all."[5]

To focus your thinking on your communication effectiveness, complete Leadership Self-Assessment Quiz 12-1.

INSPIRATIONAL AND POWERFUL COMMUNICATION

Information about communicating persuasively and effectively is extensive. Here we focus on suggestions for creating the high-impact communication that contributes to effective leadership. Both formal and informal leaders must be persuasive and dynamic communicators. Effective communication often helps informal leaders be selected for formal leadership positions. In this section, suggestions for becoming an inspirational and emotion-provoking communicator are divided into the following two categories: (1) speaking and writing, and (2) nonverbal communication. We also discuss six basic principles of persuasion.

Speaking and Writing

Most of you are already familiar with the basics of effective spoken and written communication. Yet the basics—such as writing and speaking clearly, maintaining eye contact, and not mumbling—are only starting points. The majority of effective leaders have an extra snap or panache in their communication style. The same energy and excitement is reflected in both speaking and writing. James M. Kouzes and Barry Z. Posner underscore the importance of colorful language in communicating a vision (one of the leader's most important functions) in these words:

> Language is among the most powerful methods for expressing a vision. Successful leaders use metaphors and figures of speech; they give examples, tell stories, and relate anecdotes; they draw word pictures; and they offer quotations and recite slogans.[6]

Group members and other constituents have more exposure to the spoken word of leaders. Nevertheless, with the increased use of email and printed memos, the written word exerts considerable influence. Suggestions for dynamic and persuasive oral and written communication are presented below and outlined in Table 12-1 (page 366).

Leadership Self-Assessment Quiz 12-1

A Self-Portrait of My Communication Effectiveness

INSTRUCTIONS The statements below relate to various aspects of communication effectiveness. Indicate whether each of the statements is mostly true or mostly false, even if the most accurate answer would depend somewhat on the situation. Asking another person who is familiar with your communication behavior to help you answer the questions may improve the accuracy of your answers.

		True	False
1.	When I begin to speak in a group, most people stop talking, turn toward me, and listen.	___	___
2.	I receive compliments on the quality of my writing.	___	___
3.	The reaction to the outgoing message on my answering machine has been favorable.	___	___
4.	I welcome the opportunity to speak in front of a group.	___	___
5.	I have published something, including a letter to the editor, an article for the school newspaper, or a comment in a company newsletter.	___	___
6.	I have my own web site.	___	___
7.	The vast majority of my written projects in school have received a grade of B or A.	___	___
8.	People generally laugh when I tell a joke or make what I think is a witty comment.	___	___
9.	I stay informed by reading newspapers, watching news on television, or logging on to news information.	___	___
10.	I have heard such terms as "enthusiastic," "animated," "colorful," or "dynamic" applied to me.	___	___

Total: ___

SCORING AND INTERPRETATION If eight or more of the above statements are true in relation to you, it is most likely that you are an effective communicator. If three or fewer statements are true, you may need substantial improvement in your communication skills. Keep in mind also that scores on the quiz you just took are probably highly correlated with charisma.

SKILL DEVELOPMENT   The behaviors indicated by the ten statements in the self-assessment quiz are significant for leaders because much of a leader's impact is determined by his or her communication style. Even though effective leaders vary considerably in their communication style, they usually create a positive impact. Observe some current business leaders on CNBC news or a similar channel to develop a feel for the communication style of successful business leaders.

Be Credible.   Attempts at persuasion, including inspirational speaking and writing, begin with the credibility of the message sender. It has long been recognized that source credibility is a powerful element in the persuasive process. If the speaker is perceived as highly credible, the attempt at persuasive communication is more likely to be successful.[7] The perception of credibility is influenced by many factors, including those covered in this entire section. Being trustworthy heavily influences being perceived as credible. A leader with a reputation for lying will have a difficult time convincing people about the merits of a new initiative such as downsizing. Being perceived as intelligent and knowledgeable is another major factor contributing to credibility.

Use the Persuade Package of Influence Tactics.   One approach to being persuasive is to rely on research findings about which combination of influence tactics is likely to be effective across many situations. The **persuade package** is a small, standard set of influence tactics that leads the target to behave in a particu-

---

TABLE 12-1   Suggestions for Inspirational Speaking and Writing

A. A Variety of Inspirational Tactics

1. Be credible.
2. Use the persuade package of influence tactics.
3. Gear your message to the listener.
4. Sell group members on the benefits of your suggestions.
5. Use heavy-impact and emotion-provoking words.
6. Use anecdotes to communicate meaning.
7. Back up conclusions with data (to a point).
8. Minimize language errors, junk words, and vocalized pauses.
9. Write crisp, clear memos, letters, and reports, including a front-loaded message.

B. The Power-Oriented Linguistic Style

Included here are a variety of factors such as downplaying uncertainty, emphasizing direct rather than indirect talk, and choosing an effective communication frame.

lar way. The package is really a mental framework about influencing others that directs the encoding, storage, and retrieval of information. Using a persuade package gives the influence agent a preference order for influence tactics.

Herman Aguinis and several associates conducted a study with college students in which the students were asked to rate the degree to which they believed the source would use each of four tactics in three situations. The four tactics were ingratiation, assertiveness, rationality, and exchange. The three situations were a landscaping company, a public relations department, and a manufacturing plant in which a supervisor wanted a subordinate to perform a task. Data analysis revealed that for all three situations, the preference order for use of influence tactics (the persuade package) was the same: ingratiation → rationality → assertiveness → exchange.[8] In other words, butter up, be logical, use moderate force, and then strike a bargain.

Gear Your Message to the Listener.
An axiom of persuasive communication is that a speaker must adapt the message to the listener's interests and motivations. The company president visiting a manufacturing plant will receive careful attention—and build support—when he says that jobs will not be outsourced to another country. The same company president will receive the support of stockholders when he emphasizes how cost reductions will boost earnings per share and enlarge dividends.

A review of the evidence concludes that the average intelligence level of the group is a key contingency factor in designing a persuasive message. People with high intelligence tend to be more influenced by messages based on strong, logical arguments. Bright people are also more likely to reject messages based on flawed logic.[9]

Sell Group Members on the Benefits of Your Suggestions.
A leader is constrained by the willingness of group members to take action on the leader's suggestions and initiatives. As a consequence, the leader must explain to group members how they can benefit from what he or she proposes. From the standpoint of expectancy theory, the leader attempts to increase the instrumentality for receivers of the message. Jürgen Schrempp, the chairman of DaimlerChrysler, persuaded his executives to go along with a reorganization that would create three divisions: Chrysler brands, Mercedes-Benz, and a commercial truck division. The benefits Schrempp promised were increased profitability and potentially higher salaries and bonuses because of better-focused divisions. Equally important, he suggested that the division heads would have more autonomy under the new structure.

Selling group members is quite often done more effectively when the persuader takes the time to build consensus. Instead of inspiring the group in a flash, the leader wins the people over gradually. Persuasion guru (note the appeal to credibility) Jay Conger writes that successful persuasion often requires ongoing effort, following this pattern: (1) At the first meeting, you convince a few teammates to consider your initiative carefully. (2) At the second meeting, you win several teammates over to your viewpoint after having modified your original position slightly. (3) The following week, events outside your control weaken your efforts or strengthen them. (4) Successive meetings and discussions finally bring all the team members to consensus. Along the way, you keep adjusting your position to satisfy diverse demands.[10] One caution is that this deliberate method of persuasion through consensus is poorly suited to crises and other urgent situations.

Use Heavy-Impact and Emotion-Provoking Words.

Certain words used in the proper context give power and force to your speech. Used comfortably, naturally, and sincerely, these words will project the image of a self-confident person with leadership ability or potential. A mortgage officer at a bank made the following progress report to her manager:

> It's important that I fill you in on my recent activities. This bank's strategic plan is to get into the next generation of financial marketing. I've bought into the strategy, and it's working. Instead of simply selling commercial mortgages, I'm heavily into relationship banking. I've been building long-term symbiotic relations with some very big potential clients.
>
> So far, the short-term results I've achieved have been modest. But the long-term results could be mind boggling. We may soon become the dominant supplier of financial services to a key player in commercial real estate.

The mortgage officer framed her accomplishments and progress in buzzwords of interest to top management. She talked about supporting the corporate strategy, relationship banking, outstanding long-term results, and her company becoming a dominant supplier. Using powerful and upbeat language of this type enhances her leadership image. Yet if she had taken the embellishment too far, she might have shown herself to be deceptive and devious.

Closely related to heavy-impact language is the use of emotion-provoking words. An expert persuasive tactic is to sprinkle your speech with emotion-provoking—and therefore inspiring—words. Emotion-provoking words bring forth images of exciting events. Examples of emotion-provoking and powerful words include "*outclassing* the competition," "*bonding* with customers," "*surpassing* previous profits," "*capturing* customer loyalty," and "*rebounding* from a downturn." It also helps to use words and phrases that connote power. Those now in vogue include *learning organization*, *virtual organization*, and *transparent organization*.

Use Anecdotes to Communicate Meaning.

Anecdotes are a powerful part of a leader's kit of persuasive and influence tactics, as already mentioned in this chapter and in Chapter 3 about charismatic leadership. A carefully chosen anecdote is also useful in persuading group members about the importance of organizational values. So long as the anecdote is not repeated too frequently, it can communicate an important message.

Teresa Lever-Pollary is the CEO of Nighttime Pediatric Clinics Inc. in Midvale, Utah. She noticed that as the company grew to four clinics and seventy employees, it was losing touch with the values that helped make it such a successful provider of after-hours pediatric care. Lever-Pollary collected more than eighty stories from her employees and printed them in a book that she distributes to stakeholders. One of her favorite anecdotes was a nurse's recollection of the manner in which a pediatrician lured an ant from inside a child's ear using a morsel of cake frosting. The ant crawled out, and the doctor gently released it outdoors. The story precisely illustrates Nighttime's focus on carefully and professionally caring for small living organisms.[11]

Back Up Conclusions with Data.   You will be more persuasive if you support your spoken and written presentations with solid data. One approach to obtaining data is to collect them yourself—for example, by conducting an email survey of your customers or group members. The sales manager of an office supply company wanted to begin a delivery service for his many small customers, such as dental and real-estate offices. He sent email messages to a generous sampling of these accounts and found they would be willing to pay a premium price if delivery were included. The sales manager used these data to support his argument, thus convincing the company owner to approve the plan. He thus exercised leadership in providing a new service.

Published sources also provide convincing data for arguments. Supporting data for hundreds of arguments can be found in the business pages of newspapers, in business magazines and newspapers, and on the Internet. The *Statistical Abstract of the United States*, published annually, is an inexpensive yet trusted reference for thousands of arguments.

Relying too much on research has a potential disadvantage, though. Being too dependent on data could suggest that you have little faith in your intuition. For example, you might convey a weak impression if, when asked your opinion, you respond, "I can't answer until I collect some data." Leaders are generally decisive. An important issue, then, is for the leader to find the right balance between relying on data versus using intuition alone when communicating an important point.

Minimize Language Errors, Junk Words, and Vocalized Pauses.   Using colorful, powerful words enhances the perception that you are self-confident and have leadership qualities. Also, minimize the use of words and phrases that dilute the impact of your speech, such as "like," "you know," "you know what I mean," "he goes," (to mean he says), and "uhhhhhhh." Such junk words and vocalized pauses convey the impression of low self-confidence—especially in a professional setting—and detract from a sharp communication image.

An effective way to decrease the use of these extraneous words is to tape-record or video-record your side of a phone conversation and then play it back. Many people aren't aware that they use extraneous words until they hear recordings of their speech.

A good leader should be sure always to write and speak with grammatic precision to give the impression of being articulate and well-informed, thereby enhancing his or her leadership stature. Here are two examples of common language errors: "Just between you and I" is wrong; "just between you and me" is correct. *Irregardless* is a nonword; *regardless* is correct.

Another very common error is using the plural pronoun *they* to refer to a singular antecedent. For example, "The systems analyst said that *they* cannot help us" is incorrect. "The systems analyst said *she* cannot help us" is correct. Using *they* to refer to a singular antecedent has become so common in the English language that many people no longer make the distinction between singular and plural. Some of these errors are subtle and are made so frequently that many people don't realize they're wrong—but again, avoiding grammatical errors may enhance a person's leadership stature.[12]

When in doubt about a potential language error, consult a large dictionary. An authoritative guide for the leader (and anyone else) who chooses to use English accurately is *The Elements of Style* by William Strunk and E. B. White.[13]

Write Crisp, Clear Memos and Reports, Including a Front-Loaded Message.

According to Michael Mercer, high achievers write more effective reports than do their less highly achieving counterparts. Mercer examined the business writing (memos, letters and reports) of both high achievers and low achievers. He observed that high achievers' writing was distinctive in that it had more active verbs than passive verbs, more subheadings and subtitles, and shorter paragraphs.[14]

Writing, in addition to speaking, is more persuasive when key ideas are placed at the beginning of a conversation, email message, paragraph, or sentence.[15] Front-loaded messages are particularly important for leaders because people expect leaders to be forceful communicators. A front-loaded and powerful message might be "Cost reduction must be our immediate priority," which emphasizes that cost reduction is the major subject. It is clearly much more to the point than, for example, "All of us must reduce costs immediately."

One way to make sure messages are front loaded is to use the active voice, making sure the subject of the sentence is doing the acting, not being acted upon. Compare the active (and front-loaded) message "Loyal workers should not take vacations during a company crisis" to the passive (non-front-loaded) message "Vacations should not be taken by loyal company workers during a crisis."

Use a Power-Oriented Linguistic Style.

A major part of being persuasive involves choosing the right **linguistic style,** a person's characteristic speaking pattern. According to Deborah Tannen, linguistic style involves such aspects as amount of directness, pacing and pausing, word choice, and the use of such communication devices as jokes, figures of speech, anecdotes, questions, and apologies.[16] A linguistic style is complex because it includes the culturally learned signals by which people communicate what they mean, along with how they interpret what others say and how they evaluate others. The complexity of linguistic style makes it difficult to offer specific prescriptions for using one that is power oriented. Many of the elements of a power-oriented linguistic style are included in other suggestions made in this section of the chapter. Nevertheless, here are several components of a linguistic style that would give power and authority to the message sender in many situations, as observed by Deborah Tannen and other language specialists.[17]

- Downplay uncertainty. If you are not confident of your opinion or prediction, make a positive statement anyway, such as saying, "I know this new system will cure our inventory problems."

- Use the pronoun *I* to receive more credit for your ideas. (Of course, this could backfire in a team-based organization.)

- Minimize the number of questions you ask that imply that you lack information on a topic, such as, "What do you mean by an IPO?"

- Apologize infrequently, and particularly minimize saying, "I'm sorry."

- Offer negative feedback directly, rather than softening the feedback by first giving praise and then moving to the areas of criticism.

- Accept verbal opposition to your ideas as a business ritual rather than becoming upset when your ideas are challenged.

- Emphasize direct rather than indirect talk, such as saying, "I need your report by noon tomorrow," rather than, "I'm wondering if your report will be available by noon tomorrow."

- Weed out wimpy words. Speak up without qualifying or giving other indices of uncertainty. It is better to give dates for the completion of a project rather than say "Soon" or "It shouldn't be a problem." Instead, make a statement like "I will have my portion of the strategic plan shortly before Thanksgiving. I need to collect input from my team and sift through the information."

- Know exactly what you want. Your chances of selling an idea increase to the extent that you have clarified the idea in your own mind. The clearer and more committed you are at the outset of a session, the stronger you are as a persuader and the more powerful your language becomes.

- Speak at length, set the agenda for a conversation, make jokes, and laugh. Be ready to offer solutions to problems, as well as suggesting a program or plan. All of these points are more likely to create a sense of confidence in listeners.

- Strive to be bold in your statements. As a rule of thumb, be bold about ideas, but tentative about people. If you say something like "I have a plan that I think will solve these problems," you are presenting an idea, not attacking a person.

- Frame your comments in a way that increases your listener's receptivity. The *frame* is built around the best context for responding to the needs of others. An example would be to use the frame "let's dig a little deeper" when the other people present know something is wrong but pinpointing the problem is elusive. Your purpose is to enlist the help of others in finding the underlying nature of the problem.

Despite these suggestions for having a power-oriented linguistic style, Tannen cautions that there is no one best way to communicate. How you project your power and authority is often dependent upon the people involved, the organizational culture, the relative rank of the speakers, and other situational factors. The power-oriented linguistic style should be interpreted as a general guideline.

The Six Basic Principles of Persuasion

One way to be persuasive is to capitalize on scientific evidence about how to persuade people. Robert B. Ciadini has synthesized knowledge from experimental and social psychology about methods for getting people to concede, comply, or change. These principles can also be framed as influence principles, but with a focus on persuasion.[18] The six principles described next have accompanying tactics that can be used to supplement the other approaches to persuasion described in this chapter.

1. *Liking: People like those who like them.* As a leader, you have a better chance of persuading and influencing group members who like you. Emphasizing similarities between you and the other person and offering praise are the two most reliable techniques for getting another person to like you. The leader should therefore emphasize similarities, such as common interests with group members. Praising others is a powerful influence technique and can be used effectively even when the leader finds something relatively small to compliment. Genuine praise is the most effective.

2. *Reciprocity: People repay in kind.* Managers can often influence group members to behave in a particular way by displaying the behavior first. The leader might therefore serve as a model of trust, good ethics, or strong commitment to company goals. In short, give what you want to receive.

3. *Social proof: People follow the lead of similar others.* Persuasion can have high impact when it comes from peers. If you as the leader want to influence a group to convert to a new procedure, such as virtually eliminating paper records in the office, ask a believer to speak up in a meeting or send his or her statement of support via email. (But don't send around paper documents.)

4. *Consistency: People align with their clear commitments.* People need to feel committed to what you want them to do. After people take a stand or go on record in favor of a position, they prefer to stay with that commitment. Suppose you are the team leader and you want team members to become more active in the community as a way of creating a favorable image for the firm. If the team members talk about their plans to get involved and also put their plans in writing, they are more likely to follow through. If the people involved read their action plans to each other, the commitment will be even stronger.

5. *Authority: People defer to experts.* As explained in our study of expert power and credibility, people really do defer to experts. The action plan here is to make constituents aware of your expertise to enhance the probability that your plan will persuade them. A leader might mention certification in the technical area that is the subject of influence. For example, a leader attempting to persuade team members to use statistical data to improve quality might mention that he or she is certified in the quality process Six Sigma.

6. *Scarcity: People want more of what they can have less of.* An application of this principle is that the leader can persuade group members to act in a particular direction if the members believe that the resource at issue is

shrinking rapidly. They might be influenced to enroll in a course in diversity training, for example, if they are told that the course may not be offered again for a long time. Another way to apply this principle is to persuade group members by using information not readily available to others. The leader might say, "I have some preliminary sales data. If we can increase our sales by just 10 percent in the last month of this quarter, we might be the highest performing unit in the company."

The developer of these principles explains that they should be applied in combination to multiply their impact. For example, while establishing your expertise you might simultaneously praise people for their accomplishments. It is also important to be ethical, such as by not fabricating data to influence others.[19]

Nonverbal Communication

Effective leaders are masterful nonverbal as well as verbal communicators. Nonverbal communication is important because leadership involves emotion, which words alone cannot communicate convincingly. A major component of the emotional impact of a message is communicated nonverbally—perhaps up to 90 percent.[20] The classic study behind this observation has been misinterpreted to mean that 90 percent of communication is nonverbal. If this were true, facts, figures, and logic would make a minor contribution to communication, and acting skill would be much more important for getting across one's point of view.

A self-confident leader not only speaks and writes with assurance but also projects confidence through body position, gestures, and manner of speech. Not everybody interprets the same body language and other nonverbal signals in the same way, but some aspects of nonverbal behavior project a self-confident, leadership image in many situations.[21]

- Using an erect posture when walking, standing, or sitting. Slouching and slumping are almost universally interpreted as an indicator of low self-confidence.

- Standing up straight during a confrontation. Cowering is interpreted as a sign of low self-confidence and poor leadership qualities.

- Patting other people on the back, nodding slightly while patting.

- Standing with toes pointing outward rather than inward. Outward-pointing toes are usually perceived as indicators of superior status, whereas inward-pointing toes are perceived to indicate inferiority.

- Speaking at a moderate pace, with a loud, confident tone. People lacking in self-confidence tend to speak too rapidly or very slowly.

- Smiling frequently in a relaxed, natural-appearing manner.

- Maintaining eye contact with those around you.

- Gesturing in a relaxed, nonmechanical way, including pointing toward others in a way that welcomes rather than accuses, such as using a gesture to indicate, "You're right," or "It's your turn to comment."

A general approach to using nonverbal behavior that projects confidence is to have a goal of appearing self-confident and powerful. This type of autosuggestion makes many of the behaviors seem automatic. For example, if you say, "I am going to display leadership qualities in this meeting," you will have taken an important step toward appearing confident.

Your external image also plays an important role in communicating messages to others. People pay more respect and grant more privileges to those they perceive as being well dressed and neatly groomed. Even on dress-down days, the majority of effective leaders will choose clothing that gives them an edge over others. Appearance includes more than the choice of clothing. Self-confidence is projected by such small items as the following:

- Neatly pressed and sparkling clean clothing
- Freshly polished shoes
- Impeccable fingernails
- Clean jewelry in mint condition
- Well-maintained hair
- Good-looking teeth with a white or antique-white color

Of course, what constitutes a powerful and self-confident external image is often influenced by the organizational culture. At a software development company, for example, powerful people might dress more casually than at an investment banking firm. Your verbal behavior and the forms of nonverbal behavior previously discussed contribute more to your leadership image than your clothing, providing you dress acceptably.

A subtle mode of nonverbal communication is the use of time. Guarding time as a precious resource will help you project an image of self-confidence and leadership. A statement such as "I can devote fifteen minutes to your problem this Thursday at 4 P.M." connotes confidence and being in control. (Too many of these statements, however, might make a person appear unapproachable and inconsiderate.) Other ways of projecting power through the use of time include such behaviors as being prompt for meetings, and starting and stopping meetings on time. It may also be helpful to make references to dates one year into the future and beyond, such as, "By 2005 we should have a 25 percent market share."

Nonverbal communication has many other applications in addition to helping a person project a leadership image. For example, leader/managers who direct airport security operations have found new respect for the importance of body language as an indicator of security risks. Since the terrorist attacks, the Federal Bureau of Investigation has been teaching nonverbal behavior analysis to all new recruits. Suspicious nonverbal behavior among passengers includes darting eyes, hand tremors, and swollen carotid arteries (in the neck). Individuals who exhibit such behavior are then interrogated.[22]

Now that you have refreshed your thoughts on effective verbal and nonverbal communication, do Leadership Skill-Building Exercise 12-1.

Feedback on Verbal and Nonverbal Behavior

Ten volunteers have one week to prepare a three-minute presentation on a course-related subject of their choice. The topics of these presentations could be as far-reaching as "The Importance of the North American Free Trade Agreement" or "My Goals and Dreams." The class members who observe the presentations prepare feedback slips on 3 × 5 cards, describing how well the speakers communicated powerfully and inspirationally. One card per speaker is usually sufficient. Notations should be made for both verbal and nonverbal feedback.

Emphasis should be placed on positive feedback and constructive suggestions. Students pass the feedback cards along to the speakers. The cards can be anonymous to encourage frankness, but they should not be mean-spirited.

Persuading and inspiring others is one of the main vehicles for practicing leadership. Knowing how others perceive you helps you polish and refine your impact.

SUPPORTIVE COMMUNICATION

Communicating powerfully and inspirationally facilitates influencing and inspiring people, but a more mellow type of communication is needed to implement the people-oriented aspects of a leader's role. A leader who uses supportive communication nurtures group members and brings out their best. Instead of dazzling them with a power presence, the leader is low-key and interested in the other person's agenda. **Supportive communication** is a communication style that delivers the message accurately and that supports or enhances the relationship between the two parties. The process has eight principles or characteristics, which have emerged from the work of many researchers.[23] They are described below and outlined in Table 12-2.

1. *Supportive communication is problem oriented, not person oriented.* Effective leaders and managers focus more on the problem than on the person when communicating with group members. Most people are more receptive to a discussion of what can be done to change a work method than to a discussion of what can be done to change them. Many people might readily agree that more alternative solutions to a problem are needed. Fewer people are willing to accept the message "You need to be more creative."

    A helpful adjunct to problem-oriented communication is for the leader or manager to encourage the other person to participate in a solution to the

TABLE 12-2   Principles and Characteristics of Supportive Communication
1. Problem oriented, not person oriented
2. Descriptive, not evaluative
3. Based on congruence, not incongruence
4. Focused on validating, rather than invalidating, people
5. Specific, not global
6. Conjunctive, not disjunctive
7. Owned, not disowned
8. Requires listening as well as sending messages

problem. In the example at hand, the leader might say, "Perhaps you can find a method that will generate more alternative solutions to the problem."

2. *Supportive communication is descriptive, not evaluative.* A closely related principle is that when a person's worth is being evaluated, he or she often becomes defensive. If a leader says to a group member, "You are a low-quality performer," the person will probably become defensive. The descriptive form of communication—for example, "I found errors in your last two reports that created problems"—allows the person to separate the errors from himself or herself. A supervisor's "I message" ("I found errors") is less accusatory than a "you message" ("You are a low-quality performer").

3. *Supportive communication is based on congruence, not incongruence.* A superior form of communication is **congruence,** the matching of verbal and nonverbal communication to what the sender is thinking and feeling. A leader is more credible when his or her nonverbal signals mesh with his or her spoken words. A chief executive officer might say to his staff, "I'm no longer concerned about the firm having to declare bankruptcy. Sales have improved substantially, and our costs are way down." If at the same time, the CEO is fidgeting and has a sickly, upset appearance, the message will not be convincing. In this case the leader's message doesn't fit; it is incongruent. If the CEO delivers the same message with a smile and a relaxed manner, his credibility will increase.

4. *Supportive communication validates rather than invalidates people.* Validating communication accepts the presence, uniqueness, and importance of the other person. Whether or not the person's ideas are totally accepted, he or she is acknowledged. During a meeting, the manager of internal auditing said to a recently hired auditor, "Your suggestion of bonus pay for au-

ditors when they have to stay away from home more than two weekends has some merit. We can't act on your suggestion now, but please bring it up again in a future meeting." The young auditor felt encouraged to make other suggestions in the future. An invalidating communication would have been for the manager to flat out ignore the auditor, or to make a snide comment such as "Your naiveté is showing. Nobody with much business experience would make such a bad suggestion."

5. *Supportive communication is specific, not global.* As described in Chapter 10, most people benefit more from specific than from global, or general, feedback. To illustrate, the statement "We have terrible customer service" is too general to be very useful. A more useful statement would be "Our customer satisfaction ratings are down 25 percent from previous years": It is more specific and provides an improvement target.

6. *Supportive communication is conjunctive, not disjunctive.* **Conjunctive communication** is linked logically to previous messages, thus enhancing communication. **Disjunctive communication** is not linked to the preceding messages, resulting in impaired communication. Conjunctive communication makes it easier for group members and other constituents to follow the leader's thoughts. David A. Whetton and Kim S. Cameron explain that communication can be disjunctive in three ways: (1) People might have unequal opportunity to speak because of interruptions and simultaneous speaking; (2) lengthy pauses are disjunctive because listeners lose the speaker's train of thought; and (3) communication is perceived as disjunctive when one person controls the topics. Many leaders, as well as group members, fail to relate their comments to the topics introduced by others.[24]

7. *Supportive communication is owned, not disowned.* Effective communicators take responsibility for what they say and do not attribute the authority behind their ideas to another person. The effective leader might say, "I want everybody to work eight extra hours per week during this crisis." The less effective leader might say, "The company wants everybody to work overtime." Other ways of disowning communication include using statements such as "they say," or "everybody thinks." Using the word *I* indicates that you strongly believe what you are saying.

8. *Supportive communication requires listening as well as sending messages.* Truly supportive communication requires active listening (as described in the discussion of coaching). The relationship between two parties cannot be enhanced unless each listens to the other. Furthermore, leaders cannot identify problems unless they listen carefully to group members. Listening is a fundamental management and leadership skill. It also provides the opportunity for dialogue, in which people understand each other better by taking turns having their point of view understood. The accompanying

Leader in Action

Public Relations CEO Chris Komisarjevsky Listens for Success

In business, you cannot tell people what to do, according to Komisarjevsky, the CEO of Burson-Marsteller, a public relations firm with 2,000 employees worldwide. After five years in the U.S. army, including being a helicopter pilot, he earned an MBA and then joined Hill and Knowlton, a leading public relations firm. After many years of rising through the ranks there, Komisarjevsky left to join his current firm in 1995.

Above all, Komisarjevsky attributes his success to listening skills. He says he strives to shove aside distractions and give speakers his full attention, even when he's dying to get a word in. To show that he cares about what others say, Komisarjevsky asks lots of questions and then waits patiently. If people need a few extra seconds to ponder their answers, he indulges them. He says he resists the urge to rush them by jumping in with his own opinion or answering his own question.

His listening was tested last year when he sought opinions from various managers before committing to several major acquisitions. "The toughest thing was keeping quiet when I had a point of view about a deal," he admits. "But I had to listen to people who would ultimately make the deal work. They need to be involved early, giving me input, without my interrupting them or imposing my views."

When analyzing the financial aspects of a deal, for example, Komisarjevsky avoided loaded questions such as "I like these numbers. What do you think?" Instead, he maintained a neutral but inquisitive tone and subtly asked, "Do you think these numbers will work?"

Another key to Komisarjevsky's listening involves his expectations. He says he tries to keep an open mind when others speak, rather than making snap judgments or letting his biases interfere with their message. "I operate on the understanding that people are smart," he says. "That helps me listen to them fairly and concentrate more easily."

QUESTIONS

1. In what ways does Chris Komisarjevsky practice supportive communication?

2. To what extent might Komisarjevsky's communication style make him appear indecisive to group members?

SOURCE: *"The Secrets of My Success: Public Relations CEO Leads by Listening,"* Executive Leadership, *September 2000, p. 3.*

Leader in Action insert illustrates how careful listening can enhance a business leader's effectiveness.

Supportive communication requires considerable practice and must be integrated into one's leadership style to be implemented successfully. The coaching style of the leader finds supportive communication to be a natural way of relating to others. Leadership Skill-Building Exercise 12-2 gives you an opportunity to try out supportive communication.

Supportive Communication

Six or seven students gather for a team meeting to discuss an important operational problem, such as finding new ways to reduce the cycle time required to complete their tasks, or deciding how to convince top management to expand the team budget. One person plays the role of the team leader. All the group members take turns at making both useful and apparently not-useful suggestions. The team leader, along with team members, will use supportive communication whenever ideas surface. Students not directly involved in the group role play will take note of the supportive (or nonsupportive) communication they observe so that they can provide feedback later. If class time allows, another team of six or seven students can repeat the group role play.

One of many reasons that practicing supportive communication is useful is that it creates an atmosphere in which group members are more likely to contribute productive ideas. People typically shy away from making suggestions under conditions of nonsupportive communication because they fear being criticized for foolish ideas.

OVERCOMING CROSS-CULTURAL COMMUNICATION BARRIERS

Another communication challenge facing leaders and managers is to overcome communication barriers created by dealing with people from different cultures and subcultures. In today's workplace, leaders communicate with people from other countries and with a more diverse group of people in their own country. The latter is particularly true in culturally diverse countries such as the United States and Canada. Because of this workplace diversity, leaders who can manage a multicultural and cross-cultural work force are in strong demand. Here we describe the role of attributions in helping to overcome cross-cultural communication barriers, and give some guidelines for overcoming them. Before reading this material, take Leadership Self-Assessment Quiz 12-2 to help you think through your cross-cultural skills and attitudes.

Attributions and Cross-Cultural Communication

A major underlying factor in overcoming cross-cultural communication barriers is to understand **attributions,** the judgments we make about the behavior and attitudes of others. Three factors affect the attributions or judgments we make.[25] (The judgments in attributions typically deal with interpretations of causation.) *Perception* refers to the various ways in which people interpret things in the

Cross–Cultural Skills and Attitudes

INSTRUCTIONS   Listed below are various skills and attitudes that various employers and cross-cultural experts think are important for relating effectively to coworkers in a culturally diverse environment. Indicate whether or not each statement applies to you.

		Applies to Me Now	Not There Yet
1.	I have spent some time in another country.	___	___
2.	At least one of my friends is deaf, blind, or uses a wheelchair.	___	___
3.	Currency from other countries is as real as the currency from my own country.	___	___
4.	I can read in a language other than my own.	___	___
5.	I can speak in a language other than my own.	___	___
6.	I can write in a language other than my own.	___	___
7.	I can understand people speaking in a language other than my own.	___	___
8.	I use my second language regularly.	___	___
9.	My friends include people of races different than my own.	___	___
10.	My friends include people of different ages.	___	___
11.	I feel (or would feel) comfortable having a friend with a sexual orientation different from mine.	___	___
12.	My attitude is that although another culture may be very different from mine, that culture is equally good.	___	___
13.	I would be willing to (or already do) hang art from different countries in my home.	___	___
14.	I would accept (or have already accepted) a work assignment of more than several months in another country.	___	___
15.	I have a passport.	___	___

SCORING AND INTERPRETATION   If you answered "Applies to Me Now" to ten or more of the above questions, you most likely function well in a multicultural work environment. If you answered "Not There Yet" to ten or more of the above questions, you need to develop more cross-cultural awareness and skills to work effectively in a multicultural work environment. You will notice that being bilingual gives you at least five points on this quiz.

SOURCE: *Several ideas for statements on this quiz are derived from Ruthann Dirks and Janet Buzzard, "What CEOs Expect of Employees Hired for International Work,"* Business Education Forum, *April 1997, pp. 3–7; Gunnar Beeth, "Multicultural Managers Wanted,"* Management Review, *May 1997, pp. 17–21.*

outside world and how they react on the basis of these interpretations. For example, when visiting another city, you might see a large number of people on the street asking for money. During a business meeting in that city, one interpretation of this event that you might share is "I guess you have a problem with a lot of lazy people in your city." Another interpretation of the same event might be "My impression is that your city could benefit from economic expansion. A lot of people are still looking for work." When we are unfamiliar with another culture, it is more difficult to make accurate perceptions.

Stereotyping is evaluating an individual on the basis of our perception of the group or class to which he or she belongs. Although *stereotype* has a negative connotation, positive stereotypes can be useful in dealing with people from another culture. Suppose you stereotype Italians as being creative, artistic, and strongly interested in product design. On a business trip to Italy, you make many references to the design aspects of your product. So doing will foster communication with that group of Italians. Negative stereotypes, of course, can create substantial cross-cultural communication problems. A businesswoman from London visited a New York City affiliate during the winter. As she and three colleagues from the New York office entered a restaurant for dinner, the woman insisted on taking her overcoat to the table. She told the group, "I have been told that when visiting New York, you shouldn't let anything valuable out of your sight." Rapport between this woman and the group quickly deteriorated.

A third key attribution factor is *ethnocentrism*, the assumption that the ways of one's culture are the best ways of doing things. Displaying ethnocentrism can lead to complete communication breakdowns, such as an American's expressing pity for his work associates in Ireland because they are unable to watch NFL teams on Sunday.

Guidelines for Overcoming and Preventing Communication Barriers

In addition to being aware of the role of attributions, the leader attempting to communicate with members of a different culture should also follow certain guidelines. Implementing these guidelines will help overcome and prevent many communication problems.

1. *Be sensitive to the fact that cross-cultural communication barriers exist.* Awareness of these potential barriers is the first step in dealing with them. When dealing with a person of a different cultural background, solicit feedback to minimize cross-cultural barriers to communication. For example, investigate which types of praise or other rewards might be ineffective for a particular cultural group. In many instances, Asians newly arrived in the United States feel uncomfortable being praised in front of others, because in Asian cultures group performance is valued more than individual performance.

   Being alert to cultural differences in values, attitudes, and etiquette will help you communicate more effectively with people from different cultures. Observe carefully the cultural mistakes listed in Table 12-3.

2. *Challenge your cultural assumptions.* Much like the attributions mentioned previously, the assumptions we make about cultural groups can create communication barriers. The assumption you make about another group may not necessarily be incorrect, but stopping to challenge the assumptions may facilitate communication. An American leader, for example, might assume that the norms of independence and autonomy are valued by all groups in the workplace. Trudy Milburn notes that even the concept of equality can be phrased to alienate cultural groups. A sentence from the Johnson & Johnson mission statement reads, "Everyone must be considered as an individual." However, the word *individual* does not have positive connotations for all groups. Among many Latino cultural groups, the term *individual* is derogatory because it may connote the separation of one person from the rest of the community.[26]

3. *Show respect for all workers.* The same behavior that promotes good cross-cultural relations in general helps overcome communication barriers. A widely used comment that implies disrespect is to say to a person from another culture, "You have a funny accent." Should you be transposed to that person's culture, you too might have a "funny accent." The attitude of highest respect is to communicate your belief that although another person's culture is different from yours, it is not inferior to your culture. Showing respect for another culture can be more important than being bilingual in overcoming communication barriers.[27]

4. *Use straightforward language, and speak slowly and clearly.* When working with people who do not speak your language fluently, speak in an easy-to-understand manner. Minimize the use of idioms and analogies specific to your language. A systems analyst from New Delhi, India, left a performance review with her manager confused. The manager said, "I will be giving you more important assignments because I notice some good chemistry between us." The woman did not understand that *good chemistry* means *rapport*, and she did not ask for clarification because she did not want to appear uninformed.

   Speaking slowly is also important because even people who read and write a second language at an expert level may have difficulty catching

TABLE 12–3   **Cultural Mistakes to Avoid with Selected Cultural Groups**

Europe

Great Britain	■ Asking personal questions. The British protect their privacy.
	■ Thinking that a businessperson from England is unenthusiastic when he or she says, "Not bad at all." English people understate positive emotion.
	■ Gossiping about royalty.
France	■ Expecting to complete work during the French two-hour lunch.
	■ Attempting to conduct significant business during August—*les vacances* (vacation time).
	■ Greeting a French person for the first time and not using a title such as *sir* or *madam* (or *monsieur, madame,* or *mademoiselle*).
Italy	■ Eating too much pasta, as it is not the main course.
	■ Handing out business cards freely. Italians use them infrequently.
Spain	■ Expecting punctuality. Your appointments will usually arrive 20–30 minutes late.
	■ Make the American sign for "okay" with your thumb and forefinger. In Spain (and many other countries) this is vulgar.
Scandinavia (Denmark, Sweden, Norway)	■ Being overly rank-conscious in these countries. Scandinavians pay relatively little attention to a person's place in the hierarchy.

Asia

All Asian countries	■ Pressuring an Asian job applicant or employee to brag about his or her accomplishments. Asians feel self-conscious when boasting about individual accomplishments and prefer to let the record speak for itself. In addition, they prefer to talk about group rather than individual accomplishment.
Japan	■ Shaking hands or hugging Japanese (as well as other Asians) in public. Japanese consider the practices offensive.
	■ Not interpreting "We'll consider it" as a no when spoken by a Japanese businessperson. Japanese negotiators mean no when they say, "We'll consider it."
	■ Not giving small gifts to Japanese when conducting business. Japanese are offended by not receiving these gifts.
	■ Giving your business card to a Japanese businessperson more than once. Japanese prefer to give and receive business cards only once.
China	■ Using black borders on stationery and business cards because black is associated with death.
	■ Giving small gifts to Chinese when conducting business. Chinese are offended by these gifts.
	■ Making cold calls on Chinese business executives. An appropriate introduction is required for a first-time meeting with a Chinese official.
Korea	■ Saying "no." Koreans feel it is important to have visitors leave with good feelings.
India	■ Telling Indians you prefer not to eat with your hands. If the Indians are not using cutlery when eating, they expect you to do likewise.

(continued)

TABLE 12-3 Cultural Mistakes to Avoid with Selected Cultural Groups *(cont'd.)*

Mexico and Latin America	
Mexico	■ Flying into a Mexican city in the morning and expecting to close a deal by lunch. Mexicans build business relationships slowly.
Brazil	■ Attempting to impress Brazilians by speaking a few words of Spanish. Portuguese is the official language of Brazil.
Most Latin American countries	■ Wearing elegant and expensive jewelry during a business meeting. Most Latin Americans think American people should appear more conservative during a business meeting.

Note: A cultural mistake for Americans to avoid when conducting business in most countries outside the United States and Canada is to insist on getting down to business too quickly. North Americans in small towns also like to build a relationship before getting down to business.

some nuances of conversation. Facing the person from another culture directly also improves communication because your facial expressions and lips contribute to comprehension. And remember, there is no need to speak much louder.

5. *When the situation is appropriate, speak in the language of the people from another culture.* Americans who can speak another language are at a competitive advantage when dealing with businesspeople who speak that language. The language skill, however, must be more advanced than speaking a few basic words and phrases. A new twist in knowing another language has surged recently: As more deaf people have been integrated into the work force, knowing American Sign Language can be a real advantage to a leader when some of his or her constituents are deaf.

6. *Observe cross-cultural differences in etiquette.* Violating rules of etiquette without explanation can erect immediate communication barriers. A major rule of business etiquette in most countries is that the participants conducting serious business together should first share a meal. So if you are invited to a banquet that takes place the night before discussions about a major business deal, regard the banquet as a major opportunity to build a relationship. To avoid the banquet is a serious faux pas.

7. *Do not be diverted by style, accent, grammar, or personal appearance.* Although these superficial factors are all related to business success, they are difficult to interpret when judging a person from another culture. It is therefore better to judge the merits of the statement or behavior. A highly intelligent worker from another culture may still be learning English and thus make basic mistakes. He or she might also not yet have developed a sensitivity to dress style in your culture.

8. *Avoid racial or ethnic identification except when it is essential to communication.* Using a person's race or ethnicity as an adjective or other descrip-

tor often suggests a negative stereotype.[28] For example, suppose a leader says, "I am proud of André. He is a very responsible African-American customer service rep." One possible interpretation of this statement is that most African-American customer service reps are not so responsible. Or, a leader might say, "We are happy to have Martha on our team. She is an easy-to-get-along-with British lady." A possible implication is that British women are usually not too easy to work with.

9. *Be sensitive to differences in nonverbal communication.* A person from another culture may misinterpret nonverbal signals. To use positive reinforcement, some managers will give a sideways hug to an employee or will touch the employee's arm. People from some cultures resent touching from workmates and will be offended. Koreans in particular dislike being touched or touching others in a work setting. A more common cross-cultural communication error is for an American to symbolize OK by making a circle with the thumb and first finger. In some other cultures, including those of Spain and India, the "OK circle" symbolizes a vulgarity.

10. *Be attentive to individual differences in appearance.* A major cross-cultural insult is to confuse the identity of people because they are members of the same race or ethnic group. An older economics professor reared in China and teaching in the United States had difficulty communicating with students because he was unable to learn their names. The professor's defense was "So many of these Americans look alike to me." Recent research suggests that people have difficulty seeing individual differences among people of another race because they code race first, such as thinking, "He has the nose of an African American." However, people can learn to search for more distinguishing features, such as a dimple or eye color.[29]

A general way to understand cross-cultural differences in nonverbal communication is to recognize that some cultures emphasize nonverbal communication more than others. People from high-context cultures are more sensitive to the surrounding circumstances or context of an event. As a result, they make extensive use of nonverbal communication. Among these high-context cultures are those of Asians, Latinos, and African Americans. People from low-context cultures pay less attention to the context of an event and therefore make less use of nonverbal communication. Among these low-context cultures are those of northern Europeans and Swiss. Anglo-Americans are from a medium-context culture.[30] Many new members of the work force are from high-context cultures. Leaders from medium-context cultures must therefore learn to be extra responsive to nonverbal communication.

In dealing with people from a high-context culture, recognize that the people need to know how to place you in context in order to understand you better. People from a high-context culture will want to know something about your background and the company you represent. Without that knowledge, it may be difficult to establish good communication.[31]

THE LEADER'S ROLE IN RESOLVING CONFLICT AND NEGOTIATING

Leaders and managers spend considerable time resolving conflicts and negotiating. A frequent estimate is that they devote about 20 percent of their time to dealing with conflict. For example, according to Accountemps, managers spend roughly nine workweeks a year resolving employee personality clashes.[32] Conflict arises frequently among top executives, and it can have enormous consequences for the organization. If this conflict is ignored, the result can be an enterprise that competes more passionately with itself that with the competition.[33] An example of self-competition would be two divisions competing for resources.

An extensive description of conflict resolution is more appropriate for the study of managerial skills than for the study of leadership skills because it has more to do with establishing equilibrium than with helping the firm or organizational unit reach new heights. Here we focus on a basic framework for understanding conflict resolution styles, and we offer a few suggestions for negotiating and bargaining.

Conflict Management Styles

As shown in Figure 12-1, Kenneth Thomas identified five major styles of conflict management: competitive, accommodative, sharing, collaborative, and avoidant. Each style is based on a combination of satisfying one's own concerns (assertiveness) and satisfying the concerns of others (cooperativeness).[34]

Competitive Style.   The competitive style is a desire to win one's own concerns at the expense of the other party, or to dominate. A person with a competitive orientation is likely to engage in win-lose power struggles.

Accommodative Style.   The accommodative style favors appeasement, or satisfying the other's concerns without taking care of one's own. People with this orientation may be generous or self-sacrificing just to maintain a relationship. An irate customer might be accommodated with a full refund, "just to shut him (or her) up." The intent of such accommodation might also be to retain the customer's loyalty.

Sharing Style.   The sharing style is halfway between domination and appeasement. Sharers prefer moderate but incomplete satisfaction for both parties, which results in a compromise. The term *splitting the difference* reflects this orientation, which is commonly used in such activities as purchasing a house or car.

Collaborative Style.   In contrast to the other styles, the collaborative style reflects a desire to fully satisfy the desires of both parties. It is based on the underlying philosophy of the **win-win approach to conflict resolution,** the belief that after conflict has been resolved, both sides should gain something of value. The user of win-win approaches is genuinely concerned about arriving at a settlement

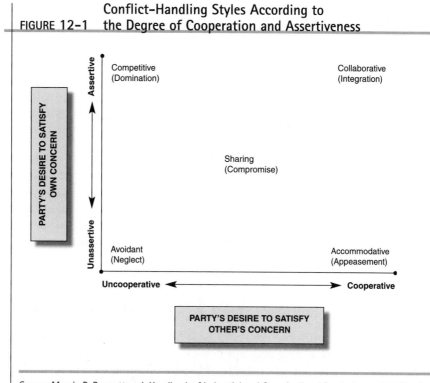

FIGURE 12-1   **Conflict-Handling Styles According to the Degree of Cooperation and Assertiveness**

Source: Marvin D. Dunnette, ed., Handbook of Industrial and Organizational Psychology, *p. 900 (Rand McNally). Copyright © 1976, Marvin D. Dunnette. Used by permission of Marvin D. Dunnette.*

that meets the needs of both parties, or at least does not badly damage the welfare of the other side. When collaborative approaches to resolving conflict are used, the relationships among the parties are built on and improved.

The collaborative style of conflict management has many variations, one of which is to agree with the person criticizing you. According to Dianna Booher, when you agree with a critic, you show that you seek a solution, not a way to demonstrate that you are right. If you agree with the substance of the criticism, you show that you are aware of the situation and ready to do what is best to solve the problem.[35]

To illustrate, if a group member criticizes you for having been too harsh in your evaluation of him or her, you might say: "I agree that my evaluation was harsh, but I was harsh for a purpose. I want to be candid with you, so you will be motivated to make what I think are necessary improvements." Your agreement is likely to spark further discussion about how the group member can improve. The collaborative style is the approach an effective leader is most likely to use because the outcome leads to increased productivity and satisfaction.

Avoidant Style.   The avoider combines lack of cooperation and unassertiveness. He or she is indifferent to the concerns of either party. The person may actually be withdrawing from the conflict or be relying upon fate. An example of an avoider is a manager who stays out of a conflict between two team members, leaving them to resolve their own differences.

People engaged in conflict resolution typically combine several of the five resolution styles to accomplish their purpose. For example, a generally effective approach to resolving conflict is to be competitive with regard to a cost that is important to oneself but unimportant to the opponent, and at the same time use accommodation for a cost that is unimportant to oneself but important to the opponent.[36]

Which mode or modes of conflict handling to use depends upon a number of variables, as presented in detail in Table 12-4. The major contingency factors are the importance of the conflict issue and the relative power of the opposing parties. An issue may be so important to a leader, such as preventing his or her organization unit from being outsourced, that domination may be the most effective mode. At other times a leader may use the accommodating mode when the opposing side has much more power, and he or she may want to save domination for a more important issue in the future.

Negotiating and Bargaining

Conflicts can be considered situations calling for negotiating and bargaining, or conferring with another person in order to resolve a problem. When you are trying to negotiate a fair salary for yourself, you are simultaneously trying to resolve a conflict. At first the demands of the two parties may seem incompatible, but through negotiation a salary may emerge that satisfies both parties. Two general approaches to negotiation are *distributive bargaining* and *integrative bargaining*. In distributive bargaining, the two sides operate under zero-sum conditions. What one wins is at the expense of the other, and the purpose of bargaining is to distribute the resources. This is the common-sense approach to negotiation. Integrative bargaining reflects the collaborative mode of managing conflict because it assumes that win-win solutions can be found. Table 12-5 on page 390 outlines the differences between distributive and integrative bargaining. Following are several negotiation techniques leaders may need to have at their disposal.[37]

Begin with a Plausible Demand or Offer.   Most people believe that compromise and allowing room for negotiation includes beginning with an extreme demand or offer. The theory is that the final compromise will be closer to the true demand or offer than if the negotiation were opened more realistically. But a plausible demand is better because it reflects good-faith bargaining. Also, if a third party has to resolve the conflict, a plausible demand or offer will receive more sympathy than an implausible one.

Focus on Interests, Not Position.   Rather than clinging to specific negotiating points, one should keep overall interests in mind and try to satisfy them. Remember that the true object of negotiation is to satisfy the underlying interests of both sides.

TABLE 12-4 Appropriate Situations for Using the Five Modes of Conflict Resolution

Conflict-Handling Mode	Appropriate Situation
Competing	1. When quick decisive action is vital, such as in an emergency
	2. On important issues when unpopular actions need implementing, such as cost cutting, enforcing unpopular rules, or discipline
	3. On issues vital to organization welfare when you know you are right
	4. Against people who take advantage of noncompetitive behavior
Collaborating	1. To find an integrative solution when both sets of concerns are too important to be compromised
	2. When your objective is to learn
	3. To merge insights from people with different perspectives
	4. To gain commitment by incorporating concerns into a consensus
	5. To work through feelings that have interfered with a relationship
Compromising	1. When goals are important but not worth the effort or potential disruption of more assertive modes
	2. When opponents with equal power are committed to mutually exclusive goals
	3. To achieve temporary settlements of complex issues
	4. To arrive at expedient solutions under time pressure
	5. As a backup when collaboration or competition is unsuccessful
Avoiding	1. When an issue is trivial or more important issues are pressing
	2. When you perceive no chance of satisfying your concern
	3. When the potential disruption outweighs the benefits of a resolution
	4. To let people cool down and regain perspective
	5. When gathering information supersedes making an immediate decision
	6. When others can resolve the conflict more effectively
Accommodating	1. When you find you are wrong—to allow a better position to be heard, to learn, and to show your reasonableness
	2. When issues are more important to others than to yourself—to satisfy others and maintain cooperation
	3. To build social credits for later issues
	4. To minimize the loss when you are outmatched and losing
	5. When harmony and stability are especially important
	6. To allow group members to develop by learning from mistakes

Source: Slightly adapted from Kenneth W. Thomas, "Toward Multidimensional Values in Teaching: The Example of Conflict Behaviors," Academy of Management Review by Klimoski, Richard J., April 1977, p. 487. Copyright 1977 Academy of Management. Reproduced with permission of Acad of Mgmt in the format Textbook via Copyright Clearance Center.

TABLE 12-5   Distributive Versus Integrative Bargaining

	Distributive Bargaining	**Integrative Bargaining**
Resources to be distributed	Fixed amount	Variable amount
Primary motivations of parties	To gain at the expense of the other side (I win, you lose)	To maximize gains for both sides (I win, you win)
Primary interests	180 degrees apart	Convergent or congruent
Focus of relationships	Short-term	Long-term

Here is how the strategy works: Your manager asks you to submit a proposal for increasing sales volume. You see it as an important opportunity to link up with another distributor. When you submit your ideas, you learn that management wants to venture further into ecommerce, not to expand the dealer network. Instead of insisting on linking with another dealer, be flexible. Ask to be included in the decision making for additional involvement in ecommerce. You will increase your sales volume (your true interest), and you may enjoy such secondary benefits as having helped the company develop a stronger ecommerce presence.

Search for the Value in Differences Between the Two Sides.   Negotiation researcher and practitioner James K. Sebenius explains that according to conventional wisdom we negotiate to overcome the differences dividing the two sides. So we hope to find win-win agreements by searching for common ground. However, many sources of value in negotiation arise from differences among the parties. The differences may suggest useful ideas for breaking a deadlock and reaching a constructive agreement. Framed differently, the differences might suggest what solution will work for both sides. Here is an example:

> A small technology company and its investors were stuck in a difficult negotiation with a large acquiring company insistent on paying much less than the asking price. Exploring the differences, it turned out that the acquirer was actually willing to pay the higher price but was concerned about elevating price expectations for further companies it might purchase in the same sector. The solution was for the two sides to agree on a moderate, well-publicized purchase price. The deal contained complex contingencies that almost guaranteed a much higher price later.[38]

(So, in the end, searching for values in differences functions like win-win.)

Be Sensitive to International Differences in Negotiating Style.   A challenge facing the multicultural leader is how to negotiate successfully with people from other cultures. Frank L. Acuff notes that Americans often have a no-nonsense approach to negotiation. Key attitudes underlying the American approach to negotiation include:

"Tell it like it is."

"What's the bottom line?"

"Let's get it out."

A problem with this type of frankness and seeming impatience is that people from other cultures may interpret such remarks as rudeness. The adverse interpretation, in turn, may lead to a failed negotiation. Acuff gives a case example: "It is unlikely in Mexico or Japan that the other side is going to answer yes or no to any question. You will have to discern answers to questions through the context of what is being said rather than from the more obvious direct cues that U.S. negotiators use."[39] By sizing up what constitutes an effective negotiating style, the negotiator stands a reasonable chance of achieving a collaborative solution.

Another example of how culture can influence negotiation comes from an experiment comparing the negotiation behaviors of Japanese and U.S. managers. Comparisons were made between how managers negotiate with people from their own culture versus another culture. A major finding was that U.S. and Japanese negotiators relied on different negotiation tactics when negotiating intraculturally (same culture). U.S. negotiators exchanged information directly and avoided using influence tactics when negotiating both within their own culture and with Japanese negotiators. Japanese negotiators exchanged information indirectly and used influence tactics when negotiating within their own culture. (In the experiment, direct information exchange included information on priorities, comparisons and contrasts between the parties, and direct reactions to offers and proposals. Indirect information exchange consisted of offers and counteroffers.) Yet, when negotiating with Americans the Japanese were more likely to adapt their negotiating behaviors to the American approach. Another finding was that the Japanese negotiators were more likely to find integrative solutions to differences when working intraculturally.[40] A possible lesson is that it is easier to negotiate with people from your own culture, so the leader/manager has to work extra hard when negotiating interculturally.

When asked to describe the essence of good negotiating in a few sentences, master negotiator Roger Fisher replied, "Be firm and friendly. Hard on the problem, soft on the people. Find out what the other side views as important and negotiate on that. Let the other side make the deal better from its point of view, at the same time that you gain what you are looking for."[41]

Negotiating and bargaining, as with any other leadership and management skill, require conceptual knowledge and practice. Leadership Skill-Building Exercise 12-3 gives you an opportunity to practice collaboration, the most integrative form of negotiating and bargaining. Practice in finding options for mutual gains is helpful for the leader because negotiating is a high-impact part of his or her job.

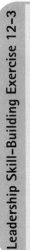

Leadership Skill-Building Exercise 12-3

Integrative Bargaining

The class is organized into groups of six, with each group being divided into two negotiating teams of three each. The members of the negotiating teams would like to find an integrative (win-win) solution to the issue separating the two sides. The team members are free to invent their own pressing issue, or choose one from among the following:

- Management wants to control costs by not giving cost-of-living adjustments in the upcoming year. The employee group believes that a cost-of-living adjustment is absolutely necessary for its welfare.

- The marketing team claims it could sell 250,000 units of a toaster wide enough to toast bagels if the toasters could be produced at $10 per unit. The manufacturing group says it would not be feasible to get the manufacturing cost below $15 per unit.

- Blockbuster Video would like to build in a new location that is adjacent to a historic district in one of the oldest cities in North America. The members of the town planning board would like the tax revenue and jobs that the Blockbuster store would bring, but they do not want a Blockbuster store adjacent to the historic district.

After the teams have arrived at their solutions through high-level negotiating techniques, the creative solutions can be shared with teammates.

SUMMARY

Systematic observation and empirical research support the idea that effective leaders are also effective communicators. There is substantial evidence of a positive relationship between competence in communication and leadership performance. However, a survey has revealed that top business executives may not be doing a good job of communicating the company's mission, vision, and values. Nonverbal skills are also important for leadership effectiveness.

Inspirational and powerful communication helps leaders carry out their roles. Suggestions for inspirational and powerful speaking and writing include the following: (1) be credible; (2) use the persuade package of influence tactics; (3) gear your message to your listener; (4) sell group members on the benefits of your suggestions; (5) use heavy-impact and emotion-provoking words; (6) use anecdotes to communicate meaning; (7) back up conclusions with data; (8) minimize language errors, junk words, and vocalized pauses; and (9) write crisp, clear memos, letters, and reports, including a front-loaded message.

A power-oriented linguistic style is another way to communicate with inspiration and power. The style includes a variety of factors, such as downplaying uncertainty, emphasizing direct rather than indirect talks, and choosing an effective communication frame. Leaders can also improve their communication skills by following the six principles of persuasion: liking, reciprocity, social proof, consistency, authority, and scarcity.

Skill can also be developed in using nonverbal communication that connotes power, being in control, forcefulness, and self-confidence. Among the suggestions are to stand erect; speak at a moderate pace with a loud, clear tone; and smile frequently in a relaxed manner. A person's external image also plays an important part in communicating messages to others. People pay more respect and grant more privileges to those they perceive as being well dressed and neatly groomed.

Supportive communication enhances communication between two people and therefore contributes to leadership effectiveness. The process has identifiable principles and characteristics. Supportive communication is (1) problem oriented, not person oriented; (2) descriptive, not evaluative; (3) based on congruence, not incongruence; (4) focused on validating, rather than invalidating, people; (5) specific, not global; (6) conjunctive, not disjunctive; (7) owned, not disowned; and (8) characterized by intense listening, including dialogue.

Overcoming communication barriers created by dealing with people from different cultures is another leadership and management challenge. A major factor in overcoming cross-cultural barriers is to understand attributions—the judgments we make about the behaviors and attitudes of others. Three key factors in forming attributions are perception, stereotyping, and ethnocentrism. Guidelines for overcoming cross-cultural barriers include the following: (1) be sensitive to the existence of cross-cultural communication barriers; (2) challenge your cultural assumptions; (3) show respect for all workers; (4) use straightforward language, and speak slowly and clearly; (5) when appropriate, speak in the language of the people from another culture; (6) observe cross-cultural differences in etiquette; (7) do not be diverted by style, accent, grammar, or personal appearance; (8) avoid racial or ethnic identification except when it is essential to communication; (9) be sensitive to differences in nonverbal communication; and (10) be attentive to individual differences in appearance.

A general way to understand cross-cultural differences in nonverbal communication is to recognize that some cultures emphasize nonverbal communication more than others. People from high-context cultures are more sensitive to the surrounding circumstances or context of an event.

Leaders and managers spend considerable time managing conflict. Five major styles of conflict management are as follows: competitive, accommodative, sharing, collaborative (win-win), and avoidant. Each style is based on a combination of satisfying one's own concerns (assertiveness) and satisfying the concerns of others (cooperativeness). When resolving conflict, people typically combine several of the five resolution styles to accomplish their purpose, such as combining dominating and accommodating. Which modes of conflict handling to use depends upon a number of variables, as presented in detail in Table 12-4.

Conflicts can be considered situations calling for negotiating and bargaining. Distributive bargaining and integrative bargaining are two general approaches to negotiation. In distributive bargaining, the two sides operate under zero-sum conditions. Integrative bargaining reflects the collaborative mode of managing conflict because it assumes that win-win solutions can be found. Specific negotiating techniques include the following: (1) begin with a plausible demand or offer; (2) focus on interests, not positions; (3) search for the value in differences between the two sides; and (4) be sensitive to international differences in negotiating style.

KEY TERMS

Virtual office

Persuade package

Linguistic style

Supportive communication

Congruence

Conjunctive communication

Disjunctive communication

Attributions

Win-win approach to conflict
resolution

GUIDELINES FOR ACTION AND SKILL DEVELOPMENT

Gay Lumsden and Donald Lumsden recommend a specific communications improvement program that can supplement the suggestions already made in this chapter.

1. **Seek congruity with your messages.** The information and feelings you communicate should be consistent with the verbal and nonverbal messages you use to send them.

2. **Ask for feedback from family, friends, coworkers, and managers.** Ask people who are familiar with your communication style about the congruence between your verbal and nonverbal messages.

3. **Observe others' responses.** Watch for positive, negative, and comprehending responses from others. Question how well your messages are received.

4. **Observe a videotape of yourself.** Obtain a videotape of yourself in daily conversation or making a presentation. Scrutinize your strengths and areas for development. Look for ways to appear more powerful and inspiring. Be particularly alert to voice quality, junk words, and weak expressions.

5. **Decide what to change.** Identify specific verbal and nonverbal behaviors you think you should change to enhance your communication effectiveness. Follow up by practicing the new or modified behaviors.[42]

DISCUSSION QUESTIONS AND ACTIVITIES

1. Now that you have studied this chapter, what are you going to do differently to improve your communication effectiveness as a leader?

2. Find an example of a powerful written or spoken message by a leader. Bring the information back to class to share with others.

3. What would be an effective *communication frame* for telling group members that they will be expected to work about seventy hours per week for the next five weeks?

4. Identify a leader who you think has a power-oriented linguistic style. How did you arrive at your conclusion?

5. Why is persuasion considered one of the leader's essential tools?

6. Given that people really do defer to experts, how might the leader establish his or her expertise?

7. Give three examples of positive ethnic stereotypes.

8. What concrete steps can a leader take to demonstrate that he or she respects a group member from another culture?

9. In recent years, shareholders have verbally attacked CEOs for receiving so much compensation from the company. How should these CEOs approach resolving this type of conflict?

10. Give two examples in which it would probably be effective for a leader to use the accommodative style of conflict handling.

Leadership Case Problem A

Infighting and Intrigue at Yahoo!

Several years ago, when America Online, Inc. was about to buy Time Warner, Inc., the world began to change for Yahoo! Inc. CEO Timothy A. Koogle, President Jeffrey Mallett, and cofounder Jerry Yang held a council of war in a conference room at company headquarters. Should Yahoo! stick to its knitting and remain an independent assembler of news and entertainment supplied by others? Or should it purchase an old-media company of its own?

Koogle favored staying the course, saying that Yahoo! had a better chance of lining up quality content if it teamed with all comers instead of buying one big media company. Mallett was on the fence. After four hours of discussion, the group reached consensus about Yahoo! concentrating on the Net. Soon thereafter both Yahoo!'s revenue and stock price plunged, and about 10 percent of its work force was laid off. Longtime leader Koogle was pushed out.

Terry S. Semel, the former co-CEO of Warner Bros., replaced Koogle. Semel was a close friend of Yang. Two of his major initial tasks were to increase ad revenues and to look for new sources of revenue, such as increasing premium subscription services. Semel believed that his experience running a media company would be a strong asset to Yahoo! One of his biggest tasks

was rebuilding what some observers regarded as a dysfunctional management team. Koogle had emerged into the role of chief visionary, distancing himself from operational problems. Mallett, who had been running daily operations, was angling for the CEO job. An operations specialist, he was growing frustrated with Koogle's consensus-style management. Tension mounted between Mallett and Koogle. In this situation, Jerry Yang, cofounder and board member, emerged stronger than ever. While Yahoo!'s professional managers Koogle and Mallett were blamed for Yahoo!'s slipups, Yang's image as goodwill ambassador shielded him from criticism.

Key Yahoo! Mistakes. Interviews with Yahoo! current and former executives and well-placed outside sources revealed key company mistakes. Yahoo! had had a second chance to make a key acquisition when it began negotiating to buy eBay Inc. in March 2000. Koogle wanted the deal, but Mallett was concerned about having eBay CEO Margaret Whitman on Yahoo!'s executive team. Whitman wanted to report directly to Koogle, while Mallett insisted that she report through him. Koogle and Mallett also differed on the strategic importance of the deal. An eBay board member said, "Tim could see the wisdom of challenging the Yahoo! culture through a deal with eBay. Others were more threatened" (*BusinessWeek*, May 21, 2001, p. 117).

With the deal looming, Mallett went on the offensive. He appealed to cofounders Yang and David Filo, trying to convince them that the eBay culture would be a poor fit for Yahoo! Soon both founders were in his camp. Filo sent an email to Koogle urging him to back away from the deal. "The whole thing got very dysfunctional. They were clashing," says a source close to the negotiations (*BusinessWeek*, p. 117). With Koogle outnumbered, the potential deal unraveled. "This was Yahoo!'s most fundamental problem. It was always management by persuasion, not management by dictation," said a former Yahoo! manager.

If the eBay deal had gone through, Yahoo! would have been able to share in the auction site's continued prosperity despite the downturn in the Internet industry. Also, Yahoo! would have been less dependent on advertising revenues.

Many Yahoo! observers were concerned that the company made no special effort to make traditional advertisers see the value of creating a presence online. It was accustomed to getting the rates it asked for, cutting a deal, and then moving on. Mallett once said, "We ran Yahoo! to optimize market share. I make no apologies for that. If there was a company that didn't get it [the relevance of Internet advertising], we moved on very quickly" (*BusinessWeek*, p. 118).

In October 2000, Yahoo! took its first serious look in the mirror. At a retreat in California's Yosemite National Park for Yahoo!'s top brass and managers, Mallett took the stage and prodded the several hundred attendees to change the way they did business. Yahoo! needed to treat its advertisers and business partners better. A former exec who attended the retreat said, "It was just what everyone needed to hear." However, many of the managers didn't take the message seriously. "The business development people all had smirks on their faces," recalls the executive (*BusinessWeek*, p. 118).

Later a stock analyst's report tore into Yahoo!, prompting the Yahoo! board to attempt reforms. However, executive meetings continued to plod along with Koogle's consensus-style decision making. Mallett believed that he could fix Yahoo! if only Koogle would get more involved.

A source close to Yahoo! said a contributor to the company's problems was Koogle's inability to say no to projects. "The manifestation of Koogle's inability to say no is how Yahoo! ended up in every imaginable business and spread itself too thin," the source said. "He couldn't say no to anyone who came to him with the next idea for a property or service—even though Yahoo! should have been run in a more focused way" (*CNET.com*, May 1, 2002, p. 2).

By January 2001, the board was focused on leadership. Ad sales were dropping rapidly, and turnover among its international executives was frighteningly high, with six key departures. Two former international managers say that heavy-handed control from Yahoo! headquarters had left some overseas executives irked. So Koogle accepted the board's decision for him to step down as CEO, but he remained as chairman. He felt that his lack of media experience had hurt the company. The search for a replacement CEO began, and Semel surfaced as the leading candidate. Even though Mallett was bitterly disappointed about being passed over, Semel charmed him. Semel agreed to join Yahoo! only if Koogle would give up the chairmanship, allowing Semel to be both chairman and CEO.

The Recovery. About one year after Semel began his rebuilding efforts, analysts regarded Yahoo!'s turnaround efforts as an unfinished case study in dot-com comebacks. During his first year, Semel helped Yahoo! offset its heavy dependence on display advertising revenues. The firm is gradually drawing more revenue from alternate businesses such as classified job listings and premium services.

QUESTIONS

1. Why was Koogle's consensus style of leadership criticized so strongly?

2. What might the Yahoo! group have done differently to resolve their conflicts about purchasing a media company?

3. What suggestions can you offer Yahoo! to increase its revenues (and thereby end a lot of squabbling about fixing the business)?

SOURCE: *Adapted and abridged from Ben Elgin, "Inside Yahoo!"* BusinessWeek, *May 21, 2001, pp. 114–123;* Jim Hu, "Semel Rises to Yahoo Challenge," CNET.com, *May 1, 2002.*

Leadership Case Problem B

Can He Be the Real Bill Gates?

It wasn't surprising that conference attendees at the Linux-World trade show stopped to stare. They were probably wondering if they were gazing at the world's richest man. Only the person they were staring at was not Bill Gates. Oracle Corporation had hired a Bill Gates look-alike to hand out fliers promoting its CEO Larry Ellison's keynote speech at the San Francisco trade show. The bespectacled impersonator of the Microsoft chairman (or chief software architect) was reminding people not to miss his software rival's talk. (Readers may recall that Larry Ellison had previously hired a detective to sort through Microsoft dumpsters looking for negative information about Microsoft leaders.)

Olaf Ruehl, or "Bill," is a 20-something look-alike who offers his impersonation services part time. While he primarily dons his Gates persona, he also does general appearances for other "nerd"-type characters.

At least a dozen people commented on the irony of seeing "Bill Gates" at a Linux show this week, even though Microsoft actually does have a small booth there. Linux is the free software based on a shared computer code that is consid-

ered an alternative to Microsoft's Windows operating system franchise.

QUESTIONS

1. What messages is Oracle sending about itself by hiring the impersonator to encourage conference attendees to attend Larry Ellison's talk?

2. How would you rate the persuasive effectiveness of this method of encouraging people to listen to Ellison's talk?

3. In what way does the incident about the Bill Gates impersonator illustrate conflict between Oracle and Microsoft?

4. What would you advise Bill Gates to do, if anything, about the Oracle stunt of hiring the impersonator?

SOURCE: *Adapted from Ann Grimes, "Who Is That Geek?"* The Wall Street Journal, *August 15, 2002, p. B4 (in "Digits/Gambits & Gadgets in the World of Technology").* Wall Street Journal, Central Edition (Staff Produced Copy Only) *by* Wall Street Journal. *Copyright 2002 by* Dow Jones & Co. Inc. *Reproduced with permission of* Dow Jones & Co. Inc. *in the format Textbook via Copyright Clearance Center.*

INTERNET SKILL-BUILDING EXERCISE

What Is Your Influence Quotient?

Apply the chapter concepts! Visit the Web and complete this Internet skill-building exercise to learn more about current leadership topics and trends.

Visit www.influenceatwork.com and take the NQ test that measures knowledge of a certain type of influence tactic. After taking the test, compare the type of influence tactics measured by the test with the influence tactics (a) mentioned in this chapter about communications and conflict, and (b) the leadership influence tactics described in Chapter 8. In a few words, how might the type to influence attempts described in the test help you be a more effective leader?

Strategic Leadership and Knowledge Management

CHAPTER 13

Most Fridays at Google, the search-engine company, Marissa Mayer and about 50 engineers and other employees sit down to do a search of their own. Product manager Mayer scribbles rapidly as the engineers race to explain and defend the new ideas that they've posted to an internal web site. By the end of the hour-long meeting, a handful of new ideas are fleshed out enough to take to the next level of development.

To stay on top of competitor search engines, Google needed a stream of new ideas. "We always had great ideas, but we didn't have a good way of expressing them or capturing them," says Craig Silverstein, Google's director of technology. Mayer's proposal: Search for ideas in the same way that the Google search engine combs the Web.

Google's idea search starts with an internal web page that takes minutes to set up. Using a program called Sparrow, even Google employees without Internet savvy (there are a few) can create a page of ideas. That enables the company to cast its net across its 300-plus employees. "We never say, 'This group should innovate, and the rest should do their jobs,'" says Jonathan Rosenberg, vice president of product management. "Everyone spends a fraction of their day on R&D."

Mayer combs the site daily, searching for relevant ideas. She digs out the ones that generate the most comments and that seem the most doable. Relevance isn't necessarily measured by how much money an idea makes; it's more about making Google searches *better.*

In the Friday meetings, Mayer insists on speed. The sessions are kept to one hour, and individual presenters never get more than 10 minutes. But everyone knows that the conversation won't end when the meeting does. Promising ideas are quickly outlined on the intranet site. Usually, the person who came up with the idea is put in charge of turning it into a feature. Two recent ideas include a news-search feature that debuted in 2002 and a pilot project that keeps track of persistent searches on the Web.[1]

The famous search engine company just mentioned was implementing a program of knowledge management in order to make better use of the knowledge stored in the brains of its professional staff. Knowledge management is one important aspect of business strategy because the approach helps the firm achieve its goals. A key leadership role is to form a **strategy,** an integrated, overall concept of how the firm will achieve its objectives.[2] (Note that this is but one representative meaning and definition of strategy.)

In this chapter we approach strategic leadership by emphasizing the leader's role rather than by focusing on strategy and strategic planning in great detail. Our approach is to first examine the nature of strategic leadership and to describe a frequently used tool for development strategy, SWOT analysis. We then describe the strategies most frequently used by leaders to bring about success. Following that is a description of a leader's contribution to a current thrust in strategy, knowledge management and developing a learning organization.

THE NATURE OF STRATEGIC LEADERSHIP

Strategic leadership deals with the major purposes of an organization or an organizational unit, and thus differs more in level than in kind from leadership in general. We study strategic leadership separately because in practice it is the province of top-level executives. The term *strategic leadership* is sometimes considered synonymous with transformational leadership. For our purposes here, **strategic leadership** is the process of providing the direction and inspiration necessary to create, provide direction to, or sustain an organization. The founder of Starbucks Corporation provided strategic leadership because he developed a concept for an organization, grew the organization, and inspired large numbers of people to help him achieve his purpose.

Another perspective on strategic leadership is that it is the type of leadership necessary to effectively carry out strategic management. **Strategic management** refers to the process of ensuring a competitive fit between the organization and its environment. Strategic leadership is thus a complex of personal characteristics, thinking patterns, and effective management, all centering on the ability to think strategically. Do Leadership Self-Assessment Quiz 13-1 to explore your present orientation toward thinking strategically.

Our approach to understanding the nature of strategic leadership will be to describe certain associated characteristics, behaviors, and practices, as outlined in Figure 13-1 on page 403. The information about charismatic and transformational leadership presented in Chapter 3 is also relevant here.

High–Level Cognitive Activity of the Leader

Thinking strategically requires high-level cognitive skills, such as the ability to think conceptually, to absorb and make sense of multiple trends, and to condense all this information into a straightforward plan of action. The ability to process information and understand its consequences for the organization in its interaction with the environment is often referred to as *systems thinking*. In one analysis of the cognitive requirements of leadership, the work of management is divided into a system of seven levels within organizations. At each level there are qualitatively different task demands and skill requirements as one moves across higher and lower strata. A contributing factor is that the longer the time span incorporated into a manager's job, the greater the demands on intellectual ability.[3] A CEO, who might work with a twenty-five-year perspective, would therefore need to have greater problem-solving ability than a first-level supervisor, who typically has a one-week perspective.

According to the systems approach under consideration, the decisions required of first-level supervisors are less cognitively demanding than those typically encountered by executive decision makers. As one moves up the hierarchy, more problem-solving ability and imagination are required to effectively handle the task environment. To engage in strategic management and leadership, a person must therefore have conceptual prowess. An organization will be successful

Are You a Strategic Thinker?

INSTRUCTIONS   Indicate your strength of agreement with each of the following statements: SD = strongly disagree; D = disagree; N = neutral; A = agree; SA = strongly agree.

		SD D N A SA
1.	Every action I take on my job should somehow add value for our customers, our clients, or the public.	1 2 3 4 5
2.	Let top management ponder the future; I have my own job to get done.	5 4 3 2 1
3.	Strategic thinking is fluff. Somebody down the organization has to get the job done.	5 4 3 2 1
4.	A company cannot become great without an exciting vision.	1 2 3 4 5
5.	What I do on the job each day can affect the performance of the company many years into the future.	1 2 3 4 5
6.	It's rather pointless to develop skills or acquire knowledge that cannot help you on the job within the next month.	5 4 3 2 1
7.	Strategic planning should be carried out in a separate department rather than involve people throughout the organization.	5 4 3 2 1
8.	It makes good sense for top management to frequently ask themselves the question "What business are we really in?"	1 2 3 4 5
9.	If a company does an outstanding job of satisfying its customers, there is very little need to worry about changing its mix of goods or services.	5 4 3 2 1
10.	Organizational visions remind me of pipe dreams and hallucinations.	5 4 3 2 1

SCORING AND INTERPRETATION   Find your total score by summing the point values for each question. A score of 42 to 50 suggests that you already think strategically, which should help you provide strategic leadership to others. Scores of 20 to 41 suggest a somewhat neutral, detached attitude toward thinking strategically. Scores of 10 to 19 suggest thinking that emphasizes the here and now and the short term. People scoring in this category are not yet ready to provide strategic leadership to group members.

when the cognitive abilities of its leaders are a good fit with the nature of the work. This is one of many reasons why tests of problem-solving ability correlate positively with success in managerial work.[4]

Creative problem solving is also important because the strategic leader has to develop alternative courses of action for shaping the organization. Furthermore, asking what-if questions requires imagination. The founders of several small PC companies several years ago asked, "What if we didn't charge for PCs?" By giving away the PCs and then requiring the purchaser to sign a contract for Internet service, the companies were able to find a niche in a crowded industry. The Internet service provider fees, along with advertising revenues earned by the Internet service, kept the free-PC companies afloat.

FIGURE 13-1   Components of Strategic Leadership

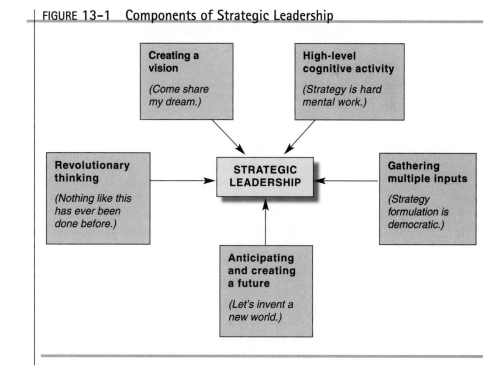

Gathering Multiple Inputs to Formulate Strategy

Strategic leaders are often thought of as mystics who work independently and conjure up great schemes for the future. In reality, many strategic leaders arrive at their ideas for the organization's future by consulting with a wide range of interested parties, in a process similar to conducting research to create a vision. Strategy theorist Gary Hamel advises executives to make the strategy-creation process more democratic. He reasons that imagination is scarcer than resources. As a consequence, "We have to involve hundreds, if not thousands, of new voices in the strategy process if we want to increase the odds of seeing the future."[5]

An example of using multiple inputs to formulate a successful business strategy took place with Cadillac, a few years before the auto's 100th anniversary. For a long time, the Cadillac was known as the older set's left-lane land yacht. At a cost of $4 billion, General Motors Corporation overhauled its flagship Cadillac Division, adding products that appealed to a younger market. The key vehicles in Cadillac's comeback were the Escalade and EXT sport utility vehicles, and the CTS sedan. In 2002, despite a down year for the auto business, the demand for the Escalade and the CTS was exceeding supply.[6] Many of the ideas for revamping the Cadillac line came from company leaders, but many also came from GM employees, dealers, customers, purchasers of competitive vehicles, and service station technicians.

Anticipating and Creating a Future

A major component of leadership is *direction setting*, which involves anticipating and sometimes creating a future for the enterprise or organizational unit. To set a direction is also to tell the organization what it should be doing. To set a productive direction for the future, the leader must accurately forecast or anticipate that future. Insight into tomorrow can take many forms, such as a leader's making accurate forecasts about consumer preferences, customer demands, and the skill mix needed to operate tomorrow's organization. A truly visionary leader anticipates a future that many people do not think will come to pass. A classic example is that in the early days of xerography, market research indicated that most people polled saw no need for a product to replace carbon paper. (If you are unfamiliar with the term, find somebody over 45 to explain the meaning of *carbon paper*.) As another example, leaders at both FedEx Corporation and United Parcel Service anticipated a surge in worldwide demand for time-guaranteed delivery, thus setting the stage for an industry that has reached $40 billion a year. The rapid growth of etailing and ecommerce has created another surge in demand for package delivery.

Creating the future is a more forceful approach than anticipating the future. The leader, assisted by widespread participation of team members, creates conditions that do not already exist. He or she must ask questions about the shape of the industry in five to ten years and decide how to ensure that the industry evolves in a way that is highly advantageous to the company. Furthermore, the leader must recognize the skills and capabilities that must be acquired now if the company is to occupy the industry high ground in the future. Another relevant issue is how the company can organize to capitalize upon opportunities that may not fit neatly within the current boundaries of organizational units.

Creating the future has also been conceptualized as reinventing an industry. Entrepreneurial leaders frequently engage in such activity. C. K. Prahalad explains that the shoe industry is a good example of reinvention. Nike and Reebok have fundamentally reinvented their industry, and consequently are fast-growing businesses in a mature industry. One factor is that they have changed the price-performance relationship in the industry. (Have you priced high-end basketball shoes recently?) Both companies have introduced very high technology, new materials, large-scale advertising, and global brands. None of these factors was so pronounced previously in the shoe industry.[7]

Nike and Reebok also illustrate that an industry may have to be reinvented more than once. By the late 1990s demand for expensive athletic shoes had declined substantially, as many young people began to rebel from high-style athletic wear. Instead, they reverted to *brown shoes*, a more ordinary type of footwear. High-fashion name-brand sport clothing also took a hit, as many young people wore less fashionable clothing. While searching for another reinvention, both Nike and Reebok moved more heavily into selling soccer-related gear both in the United States and abroad.

Revolutionary Thinking

Using even stronger terms than *reinventing the future*, Gary Hamel characterizes strategy as being revolutionary.[8] According to Hamel, corporations are reaching the limits of incrementalism. Incremental improvements include squeezing costs, introducing a new product a few weeks earlier, enhancing quality a notch, and capturing another point of market share. These continual improvements enhance an organization's efficiency and are therefore vital to a firm's success, but they are not strategic breakthroughs or radical innovations.[9]

To be an industry leader, a company's leaders must think in revolutionary terms. Revolutionary companies, such as the Charles Schwab & Co., Inc., Dell Computer Corporation, and Swatch, create the rules for others to follow. According to Hamel, any strategy that does not seriously challenge the status quo should not even be considered a strategy. What passes for strategy in most companies is often sterile and unimaginative.

An effective leader thinks in revolutionary terms, partly by ferreting out revolutionary ideas that are harbored somewhere within the firm. What constitutes a *revolutionary* idea, however, is subjective. Is selling customers computers by telephone, and later by Internet (Dell Computer), really revolutionary? Furthermore, contract firms essentially manufacture Dell computers. Selling all sorts of other merchandise by telephone and the Internet predated selling computers the same way. One could argue that the combination of mass customization, highly efficient machine assembly, and selling direct was revolutionary. Eminent strategist Michael Porter agrees somewhat with the revolutionary aspect of business strategy by insisting that a key component of strategy is deliberately choosing to be different.[10]

Although the idea that strategy focuses on revolution and differences is widely accepted, many leaders still successfully use a business strategy of imitating a product or service of proven value. The strategy of *imitation* will be described later. In China a business strategy of copying successful products is part of the national business culture. Furthermore, the preferred strategy for many small business owners is to produce "knock-off" brands.

Creating a Vision

We have already mentioned vision in several places, including the description in Chapter 3 of the vision component of charismatic leadership. Here we examine the concept of vision in more depth, because visions are an integral part of strategic leadership. Although the term *vision* in relation to leadership has achieved common-use status, it is really a multifaceted concept. Laurie Larwood and her associates conducted a study in which 331 chief executives in one national sample and three regional samples were asked about the content and structure of their organizational visions.[11] The executives came from firms that were in a variety of industries and that ranged in size from $1 million to $1 billion in sales per year.

The chief executives were asked to write a brief, one-sentence statement of their organizational vision. Participants in the study were also asked to analyze the statements by applying twenty-six descriptors from a list the researchers provided. Each descriptor was rated on a 1-to-5 scale from "very little" to "very much." Among the terms used to describe the vision were "action-oriented," "responsive to competition," "product of leadership," "strategic," "directs effort," and "risky." Factor analysis reduced the twenty-six descriptors to seven identifiable factors:

1. Involving far-reaching strategic planning
2. Involving sharing with others
3. Involving innovative realism
4. General
5. Detailed
6. Including risk taking
7. Profit-oriented

The visions based on these factors extended from six months to more than twenty years with an average of sixty-four months. The current visions (those in use at the time of the study) were retained between three months and twenty years, with an average of seventy-four months. Another important aspect of the study was to relate this analysis of visions to previous research. The factor results were thought to provide good support for what is known about visions. Of major importance, the concept of a vision as involving far-reaching strategic planning (factor 1) and the ability and willingness to share with others (factor 2) was supported. Innovative realism (factor 3) includes items considered important to visionary and charismatic leadership.

Another conclusion from the study is also relevant for strategic leadership: Executives with a triple emphasis on long-term strategy, wide communication and acceptance of their visions, and operational realism or style are the most likely to be successful in creating change within their organizations. One reason for this conclusion is that this group of executives scored highest on a question about perceived firm change.[12]

The components of a vision just described are important, but the final vision statement is relatively short. James R. Lucas, a specialist in vision formulation, writes that a carefully considered and articulated vision helps us know who we are and who we are not. The vision also points to what we do successfully and what we don't, which activities we should take on and which activities we should avoid.[13] (A few more specifics about developing a vision statement are presented in the Guidelines for Action and Skill Development section of this chapter.)

A current vision statement of Amazon.com fits many of the criteria of a strong vision statement, including pointing to what the organization can do well: "Our job is to accelerate access to things that inspire, educate, and entertain." (With this vision as a guide, the company now sells and distributes a wide range of products and services over the Internet.) Founder Jeff Bezos believes that constantly articulating the vision of what is to be achieved is one of the keys to the success of his firm. He explains that even if you have the best people, if they are not all moving toward the same vision, the company will not work well.[14] (The term *current vision statement* just mentioned refers to the fact that organizations change their visions periodically.)

At times a simple statement of intention can be an inspirational vision. The leader points the firm in a new direction that will stretch the capabilities of individuals and the capacity of the firm and be socially responsible at the same time. Hewlett-Packard Company CEO Carly Fiorina presented such a vision several years ago. Fiorina has developed a massive program to sell products to the poor of the Third World. The program is called World e-inclusion. "Smart people are not confined to the developed world," she says. "Any company that doesn't figure out a way to get connected with these people will not tap huge potential."[15]

The early focus of World e-inclusion is to sell tools that will make small farms more efficient. To launch the program, HP and its partners sold, leased, or donated $1 billion in products and services to governments, development agencies, and nonprofit organizations in such countries as Bangladesh and Senegal. Also, HP is creating basic low-power or solar-powered devices that will connect to the Net without wires or by satellite.

Conducting a SWOT Analysis

The emphasis in this chapter is on the leadership aspects of strategy. It is important, however, to review a method widely used for strategic planning. **Strategic planning** encompasses those activities that lead to the statement of goals and objectives and the choice of strategy. Under ideal circumstances, a firm arrives at its strategy after completing strategic planning. In practice, many executive leaders choose a strategy prior to strategic planning. Once the firm has the strategy, such as forming strategic alliances, a plan is developed to implement it.

Quite often strategic planning takes the form of a **SWOT analysis,** a method of considering **s**trengths, **w**eaknesses, **o**pportunities, and **t**hreats in a given situation. A SWOT analysis represents an effort to examine the interaction between the particular characteristics of your organization or organizational unit and the external environment, or marketplace, in which you compete.[16] The framework, or technique, is useful in identifying a niche the company has not already exploited. Given that SWOT has a straightforward appeal, it has become a popular framework for strategic planning. The four components of SWOT are described next.

Strengths

What are the good points about a particular alternative? What are your advantages? What do you do well? What is there really wonderful about this company or organizational unit? Use your own judgment and intuition, and also ask knowledgeable people. As a business owner, you may have a favorable geographic location that makes you more accessible to customers than your competitor. The name of your firm may begin with an "A," thereby giving you an edge when potential customers finger through the Yellow Pages. (Have you ever noticed an entry like "AAAA Automotive Body Repair"?) Another strength is that you may have invested in state-of-the art equipment that only recently became available.

Weaknesses

Consider the risks of pursuing a particular course of action, such as subcontracting work to a low-wage country (outsourcing). What could be improved? What is done badly? What should be avoided? Examine weaknesses from internal and external perspectives. Do outsiders perceive weaknesses that you do not see? (You may have to ask several outsiders to help you identify these weaknesses.) Are there products, services, or work processes your competitors perform better? You are advised to be realistic now and face any unpleasant truths as soon as possible. Again, use your judgment and ask knowledgeable people.

As a manager or business owner, you may have problems managing your inventory, or you may have employees who are not up to the task of implementing a new plan or venture. Identify those areas in which your competitors pose a threat. For example, companies that offer the consumer several channels for buying, the so-called *click-and-mortar* companies, have become a competitive threat.

Opportunities

Think of the opportunities that await you if you choose a promising strategic alternative, such as creating a culturally diverse customer base. Use your imagination and visualize the possibilities. Look for interesting trends. Useful opportunities can derive from such events as the following:

- Changes in technology and markets on both a broad and narrow scale
- Changes in government policy related to your field
- Changes in social patterns, population profiles, life styles, and so forth.

Threats

There's a downside to every alternative, so think ahead to allow for contingency planning. Ask people who may have tried in the past what you are attempting now. Answer questions such as:

- What obstacles do you face?
- What is your competition doing?
- Are the required specifications for your job, products, or services changing?
- Is changing technology changing your ability to compete successfully?
- Do you have bad debt or cash-flow problems?

An example of a threat facing many business firms today is the prospect of being pushed into obsolescence by ecommerce or etailing. Consultant Oren Harari advises that one question may surpass all others in a digital economy: "What do I need you for?"[17] The point is that many services, such as acting as an intermediary in arranging mortgages for house and condominium purchases, can now be done over the Internet. An existing firm that arranges such loans may no longer be necessary for borrowers who can shop online nationwide for the same services.

Despite a careful analysis of threats, don't be dissuaded by the naysayers, heel-draggers, and pessimists. To quote Nike, "Just do it."

Carrying out a SWOT analysis will often be illuminating, both in terms of pointing out what needs to be done and in putting problems into perspective. Although much more complex schemes have been developed for strategic planning, they all include some analysis of strengths, weaknesses, and opportunities.[18] Leadership Skill-Building Exercise 13-1 gives you an opportunity to conduct a SWOT analysis.

A SAMPLING OF BUSINESS STRATEGIES FORMULATED BY LEADERS

We have been focusing on the process by which leaders and managers make strategic decisions. Also of interest to leaders and potential leaders is the content of such decisions, with an emphasis on the actual business strategies. Business strategies are often classified according to their focus of impact: corporate level, business level, or functional level. Corporate-level strategy asks, "What business are we in?" Business-level strategy asks, "How do we compete?" And functional-

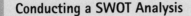

Conducting a SWOT Analysis

Now that you have studied the essentials of conducting a SWOT analysis, gather in small groups to conduct one. Develop a scenario for a SWOT analysis, such as the group starting a chain of coffee shops, pet-care service centers, or treatment centers for online addictions. Or, conduct a SWOT analysis for reorganizing a company that is hierarchical to make it team based. Since you will probably have mostly hypothetical data to work with, you will have to rely heavily on your imagination. Group leaders might share the results of the SWOT analysis with the rest of the class.

Conducting a SWOT analysis is intrinsically motivating, yet it is also important because it reinforces the skill of thinking strategically about a given course of action.

level strategy asks, "How do we support the business-level strategy?" As you will see, some of the business strategies listed next might cut across more than one of these three levels. You may recognize the first three of these strategies as the generic strategies espoused by the well-recognized business strategist Michael Porter.[19]

1. *Differentiation.* A differentiation strategy attempts to offer a product or service that is perceived by the customer as being different from available alternatives. The organization may use advertising, distinctive features, exceptional service, or new technology to gain this perception of uniqueness. The stunning appearance of Apple's iMac personal computers is part of the company's differentiation strategy. The extraordinary success of Swatch watches was based on a strategy of producing a watch that had a dramatically different face at a competitive price. What differentiates one of your favorite products?

2. *Cost leadership.* A basic strategy is to produce a product or service at a low cost in order to lower the selling price and gain market share. At the end of the chapter you will read a case about Samsung Electronics, a Korean electronics firm whose initial success was based on producing low-cost electronic gadgets. After gaining market share, the company shifted strategy to become a supplier of upscale goods. Wal-Mart is a master at cost leadership because the company's massive buying power enables it to receive huge price concessions from suppliers. The company's super-efficient methods of inventory control also facilitate cost leadership. Kmart attempted to compete against Wal-Mart on price and failed miserably, adding to Kmart's financial troubles.[20]

3. *Focus.* In a focus strategy, the organization concentrates on a specific regional market or buyer group. To gain market share, the company will use either a differentiation or a cost leadership approach in a targeted market. Targeting poor people is an example of a focus strategy that can work surprisingly well. The Casas Bahia chain of retail stores in Brazil has about $1.5 billion dollars in annual sales of furniture, household goods, and appliances. About 90 percent of sales are on credit to poor people who visit the store to make their installment purchases. The visits, in turn, lead to more store purchases. The stripped-down stores are located in some of the poorest urban neighborhoods. Customers have an average monthly income of $190, below the national average of $290. Owner Samuel Klein says, "The poorer the customer, the more punctual his payments. The poor know they need to guard their reputations or they jeopardize buying on credit."[21] Interest payments by poor customers, of course, enhance the profitability for Casas Bahia, leading to mixed reactions about the firm's social responsibility.

   The accompanying Leader in Action insert describes the application of a focus (or niche) strategy in a growing field.

4. *High quality.* A basic business strategy is to offer goods or services of higher quality than the competition. Leaders today continue to emphasize quality, even if there is less explicit emphasis today on **total quality management.** The term refers to a management system for improving performance throughout the firm by maximizing customer satisfaction and making continuous improvements based on extensive employee involvement. One reason that quality is classified as a strategy is that it contributes to competitive advantage in cost and differentiation. Ford Motor Company has long used a quality strategy with excellent results. In recent years, when Ford bought Jaguar Motors, it quickly fixed the luxury vehicle's quality problems, such as a faulty electronic system. As a result, the Jaguar brand was revitalized.

   Because many customers now expect high quality, a quality strategy must be supplemented with other points of differentiation, such as supplying customized features and services that customers desire. A couple of European companies make highly efficient, stainless-steel coffee-grinding machines that emit no noise or odor as they produce coffee. U.S. customers balked because, although they wanted efficient machines, they also wanted aromatic, noisy machines that would grind out a pungent product to help create a coffee-bar ambiance.[22]

5. *Imitation.* If you cannot be imaginative, why not imitate the best? The entire PC clone industry is based on an imitation strategy that has two key components: strategic followership and learning by watching. The company waits for the right time to introduce a lower-priced competitor. Benchmarking is a form of learning by watching.[23]

6. *Strategic alliances.* An increasingly popular business strategy is to form alliances, or share resources, with other companies to exploit a market

opportunity. A strategic alliance is also known as a virtual corporation. A large-scale strategic alliance took place when Motorola, Inc. was looking to cut costs yet remain on the cutting edge of technology. The company joined three other international manufacturers in a $1.4 billion alliance to develop chip-making technologies in France. The other firms in the alliance are from Switzerland, Holland, and Taiwan. Such high-tech alliances have become more common as the high-tech industry struggles with needed yet expensive innovation.[24]

7. *Growth through acquisition.* A standard strategy for growth is for one company to purchase others. Growth in size is important, but companies may also purchase other companies to acquire a new technology or to complete a product line. Buying a new technology is often less expensive than investing huge sums in R&D that might not yield a marketable product. Cisco Systems achieved much of its growth by purchasing smaller companies, and much of GE's growth over the years can be attributed to acquiring other companies.

8. *High speed and first-mover strategy.* High-speed managers focus on speed in all of their business activities, including product development, sales response, and customer service. Knowing that "time is money," they choose time as a competitive resource. It is important to get products to market quickly because the competition might get there first or might deliver a product or service more rapidly. Getting to market first is also referred to as the *first-mover strategy.* Starbucks was the first national chain of coffee bars. The many storefronts served as marketing devices to acquire more customers. Founder Howard Schultz built Starbucks into a global Goliath after first purchasing a small chain from its founders.[25]

   A contributing factor to Dell Computer's success has always been how rapidly Dell can deliver a custom computer to your office or home after receiving an order—sometimes within four days. But watch out for the negative side effects of high speed. Pizza delivery specialists have often been involved in automobile accidents while attempting to rush their way through traffic to make tight delivery schedules!

9. *Global diversification.* A widely practiced business strategy, especially with products, is to diversify globally in order to expand business. Even several restaurant chains, such as McDonald's and Pizza Hut, employ a diversification strategy. Global diversification is such a widely accepted strategy that the burden of proof would be on a business leader who shunned globalization.

10. *Sticking to core competencies.* Many firms of all sizes believe they will prosper if they confine their efforts to the activities they perform best—their core competencies. Many firms that expanded through diversification later trimmed back operations to activities on which they had built their reputation.

    PepsiCo is an example of a major company that implemented the strategy of returning to its core competence. In the late 1990s the company

Leader in Action

CEO Michael Catalano Finds a Niche for ASG Behind Bars

Governments are increasingly eager to off-load the costly task of providing health services to inmates. A strong player in this market is America Service Group, Inc. (ASG). Its corporate lineage dates to 1978, when Jacqueline Moore, a nurse fed up with the quality of prison care, founded Prison Health Services, Inc. She has since left to be a consultant on the health care of prisoners, and CEO Michael Catalano, a former general counsel in the health care field, now runs the company. Under his guidance, ASG has been running strong, with revenues jumping an average annual 51 percent in three recent years.

ASG recently landed some high-profile contracts, including a three-year $300 million to care for 13,000 prisoners at New York's Rikers Island. "If they execute the Rikers contract well, it could generate a tremendous amount of new business from governments who are still on the fence about outsourcing," predicts a money manager heavily invested in ASG (*BusinessWeek*, June 11, 2001, p. 112).

While private prison management remains controversial, government officials are slowly acknowledging that health care is so specialized that it may indeed best be left to outsiders. Governments are driven to outsource not just for the liability risks—prisoners and their families are quick to sue for malpractice—but for costs. Economies of scale allow ASG to negotiate greater discounts from suppliers. As a result, ASG promises savings as much as 27 percent below what states and municipalities would spend on the same services.

Catalano likes to brag that the service is not just cheaper, but better. In Indiana, Robert Ohlemiller, deputy commissioner of the Corrections Department, says that ASG so improved care for its 21,400 inmates that the state recently received its first-ever accreditation from the National Commission on Correctional Health Care. The Corrections Department also saved $26 million in three years.

In some states, ASG has faced criticisms that it stints on care to make its profits. In Maine, Cumberland County Sheriff Mark K. Dion cited a "tidal wave of inmate grievances" about inadequate medications and dental care at a Portland jail. Dion says that ASG nurses were pulling 24-hour shifts. Some inmate suits allege that substandard care led to deaths. Catalano says that patient deaths are not out of line with those at traditional hospitals.

The niche that ASG serves appears to be a growth market, with the prison population projected to grow at a 6 percent annual rate. By 2002, one in every thirty-two adults in the United States was behind bars or on probation, according to a federal government report. This translates into a record 6.6 million people in the nation's correctional system. Catalano is confident that ASG has room for growth. "There's a big market for clinical staffing, and that's a core competency of ours," he says (*BusinessWeek*, p. 112). ASG may make a jailbreak, but for now, prison suits it just fine.

QUESTIONS

1. What suggestions might you offer ASG for capitalizing further on the niche it has established, such as related markets to enter?

2. Which business strategies are mentioned or alluded to in the above case history?

3. What might be an appropriate vision for ASG?

SOURCE: *Dean Foust, "This Company Likes It in Jail,"* BusinessWeek, *June 11, 2001, p. 112; "6.6 Million in Jail or on Probation," Associated Press, August 26, 2002.*

exited the restaurant business by divesting itself of Pizza Hut, Taco Bell, and Kentucky Fried Chicken. In addition, it spun off its huge bottling operation into an independent company. As a result, PepsiCo focused on its Pepsi-Cola, Frito-Lay, and Tropicana operations. The proceeds from the restaurant sales and the spinoff gave PepsiCo more money to compete better with Coca-Cola in fountain soda sales.[26]

11. *Brand leadership.* As obvious as it may appear, succeeding through developing the reputation of your brand name can be considered a business strategy. The opposite strategy is to build components for others, to build products that others market under their names, or to be a commodity like cinder blocks. The Starbucks brand leadership strategy was to create a premium-priced brand where previously there existed only a cheaper commodity-priced product. Chairman Howard Schultz cites Coca-Cola, along with other brand masters like Gap, Disney, Nike, and Kodak, as companies he wants to emulate.[27] Jeffrey Bezos of Amazon has implemented a relentless brand leadership strategy to the point that his company has become almost synonymous with etailing. The ultimate goal of the brand leadership strategy is to make Amazon the best-known destination for purchasing anything that might be for sale on the Internet.

12. *Conducting business on the Internet.* Developing a presence on the Net has emerged as a strategy for survival and growth in recent years for both retailers and industrial companies. Because the Internet profoundly influences many aspects of customer relations and operations, the leader must choose a specific strategy that relates to conducting business on the Internet. In recent years it has been discovered that all Internet players are not equal: one person trading oil with an iMac from a loft apartment cannot compete successfully with Exxon. The matching Internet strategy is to capitalize on advantages of scale. Big established companies are discovering that their advantages of scale, their established brands, their loyal customer base, and their long-standing supplier relationships are as valuable online as offline.[28]

Philip Evans and Thomas S. Wurster believe that a second generation of ecommerce is emerging, one that will be determined more by true strategy than by experimentation. The struggle for competitive advantage will be waged along three dimensions: reach, richness, and affiliation. *Reach* deals with how many customers a business can connect with, and how many products the customers are offered. Barnes & Noble (bn.com), for example, offers the customer a choice of millions of books, videos, and CDs. *Richness* is the depth and detail of information that the business firm can provide the customer, such as in a description of the features of an electronic appliance or a ski boot. *Affiliation* refers to whose interests the business represents. Traditionally the business represented its own side, but now some firms make money by representing the consumer, such as by enabling the consumer to find the lowest price for a particular product or service.[29] Priceline.com is an example of this strategy for purchasing travel tickets, hotel rooms, and other services.

13. *Peoplepalooza (competitive advantage through hiring talented people.)* A powerful strategy for gaining competitive advantage is to build the organization with talented, well-motivated people at every level. According to the authors who coined the term *peoplepalooza*, to build great companies the most urgent need is to find and keep great people.[30] Talented people may need some leadership direction, but they will think of new products and services and develop effective work processes. Larry Bossidy and Ram Charan, the authors of *The Discipline of Getting Things Done*, believe that a top-notch process for assessing and developing employees is more important than devising a strategy or streamlining operations.[31] (Here, we are saying that focusing on talented people *is* a strategy.) The leader can contribute to this people-focus strategy by recruiting, selecting, and developing talented people.

All of the impressive strategies just described have limited impact unless they are implemented properly, meaning that effective management must support strategic leadership. In Chapter 4, we mentioned that visions must be followed up with execution. A study of several dozen CEO failures found that the majority of them could be attributed to poor execution—not getting things done, not being decisive, or not following through on commitments.[32]

KNOWLEDGE MANAGEMENT AND THE LEARNING ORGANIZATION

Another thrust of leaders is to help their organizations better adapt to the environment by assisting workers and the organization to become better learners. To accomplish this feat, the leader manages knowledge and cultivates a learning organization. **Knowledge management (KM)** is the systematic sharing of information to achieve such goals as innovation, nonduplication of effort, and competitive advantage. When knowledge is managed effectively, information is shared as needed, whether it be printed, stored electronically, or resting in the brains of workers. Managing knowledge well helps an organization learn. A **learning organization** is one that is skilled at creating, acquiring, and transferring knowledge, and at modifying behavior to reflect new knowledge and insights.[33]

Knowledge management and the learning organization are discussed in separate sections here, although the two ideas are tightly intertwined. To develop a sensitivity toward some of the key ideas in knowledge management and the learning organization, take Leadership Self-Assessment Quiz 13-2.

Knowledge Management

As implied in its definition, knowledge management, or KM, deals with a cultural focus on knowledge sharing. Managing knowledge is an important leadership role because so few organizations make systematic use of the collective wisdom of

?

Do You Work for a Learning Organization?

INSTRUCTIONS   Indicate for each of the following statements whether it is mostly true or mostly false in relation to your current, or most recent, place of work. Indicate a question mark when the statement is either not applicable or you are not in a position to judge.

	Mostly True	?	Mostly False
1. Company employees often visit other locations or departments to share new information or skills they have learned.	___	___	___
2. Our company frequently repeats mistakes.	___	___	___
3. We get most of our market share by competing on price.	___	___	___
4. Loads of people in our organization are aware of and believe in our vision.	___	___	___
5. Top management assumes that the vast majority of employees are experts at what they do.	___	___	___
6. Almost all of our learning takes place individually rather than in groups or teams.	___	___	___
7. In our company, after you have mastered your job you do not have to bother with additional learning such as training programs or self-study.	___	___	___
8. Our firm shies away from inviting outsiders into our company to discuss our business because few outsiders could understand our uniqueness.	___	___	___
9. If it weren't for a few key individuals in our company, we would be in big trouble.	___	___	___
10. Our new product launches go smoothly and quickly.	___	___	___
11. Our company creates a lot of opportunities for employees to get together and share information, such as conferences and meetings.	___	___	___
12. We are effective at pricing the service we provide to customers.	___	___	___
13. Very few of our employees have any idea about company sales and profits.	___	___	___

14. I often hear employees asking questions about why the company has taken certain major actions.   ___ ___ ___

15. The company maintains a current database about the knowledge and skills of almost all our employees.   ___ ___ ___

16. Having specialized knowledge brings you some status in our company.   ___ ___ ___

17. It would be stretching the truth to say that many of our employees are passionate about what our organization is attempting to accomplish.   ___ ___ ___

18. Our performance appraisal system makes a big contribution to helping employees learn and improve.   ___ ___ ___

19. Following established rules and procedures is important in our company, so creativity and imagination are not encouraged.   ___ ___ ___

20. Most of our employees believe that if you do your own job well, you don't have to worry about what goes on in the rest of the organization.   ___ ___ ___

21. We get loads of useful new ideas from our customers.   ___ ___ ___

22. I have frequently heard our managers talk about how what goes on in the outside world has an impact on our company.   ___ ___ ___

23. We treat customer suggestions with a good deal of skepticism.   ___ ___ ___

24. During breaks you sometimes hear employees discussing the meaning and implication of the work they are doing.   ___ ___ ___

25. Employees at every level tend to rely on facts when making important decisions.   ___ ___ ___

26. If a process or procedure works well in our company, we are hesitant to experiment with other approaches to a problem.   ___ ___ ___

27. Our company treats mistakes as a valuable learning experience about what not to do in the future.   ___ ___ ___

28. Our company rarely copies ideas from the successful practices of other companies.   ___ ___ ___

29. Each time we face a significant problem, our company seems to start all over to find a solution.

30. It's a waste of time to be reading about a learning   ___   ___   ___
organization, when my real interest is in learning
how to prevent problems.

Total score: ___

SCORING AND INTERPRETATION   (A) Record the number of "mostly true" answers
you gave to the following questions: 1, 4, 5, 10, 11, 12, 14, 15, 16, 18, 21, 22, 24, 25, 27.
(B) Record the number of "mostly false" answers you gave to the following questions:
2, 3, 6, 7, 8, 9, 13, 17, 19, 20, 23, 26, 28, 29, 30. (C) Add the numbers for **A** and **B.** (D) Add
half of your (?) responses to **A,** and half to **B.**

- 25 or   You are most likely a member of a learning organization. This
  higher   tendency is so pronounced that it should contribute heavily to your
               company's success.
- 13–24   Your company has an average tendency toward being a learning or-
               ganization, suggesting an average degree of success in profiting from
               mistakes and changing in response to a changing environment.

SOURCE: *From* Looking Around Corners, *Copyright © 1999 by Andrew J. DuBrin.
Reprinted by permission of Chandler House Press.*

employees. As illustrated in Figure 13-2, most knowledge in the organization resides in the brains of employees or in documents not readily accessible to others.
This limited accessibility of knowledge is still true despite the widespread use of
company databases.

Xerox Corporation is a pioneer in knowledge management, both in applying
KM to its own company and in providing equipment and services that enable
their customers to manage knowledge more effectively.[34] The strategy is to create
value by capturing and leveraging knowledge. Xerox leaders recognize that in the
past the company failed to exploit numerous advanced technologies it had developed, such as the mouse and pull-down menus that were later commercialized by
Apple.

Encouraging and developing systems for knowledge sharing is a key part of
knowledge management. In companies where power is acquired by hoarding and
controlling knowledge, learning cannot take place effectively. Xerox developed a
practical system of knowledge sharing for internal purposes. Several years ago the
company developed Eureka, an intranet communication system linked with a
corporate database that helps service reps (field repair technicians) share tips. To
date, more than 5,000 suggestions for making tough repairs have been entered by
Xerox technicians. The tips can be accessed through the laptop computers carried
by service reps throughout the world.

Getting employees to bother with documenting their knowledge is a management challenge. Xerox found that if credit was offered for service rep input to the
system, the participation rate became substantial. In other areas of the company,
Xerox found that understanding the human elements of knowledge sharing was

FIGURE 13-2 Where Corporate Knowledge Lives

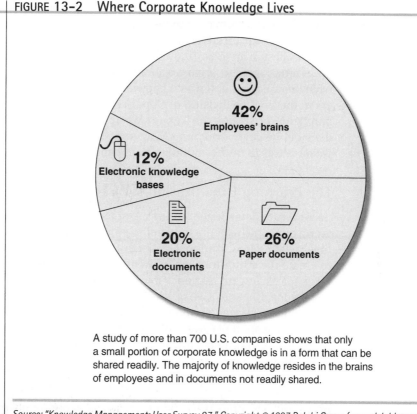

A study of more than 700 U.S. companies shows that only a small portion of corporate knowledge is in a form that can be shared readily. The majority of knowledge resides in the brains of employees and in documents not readily shared.

Source: "Knowledge Management: User Survey 97," Copyright © 1997 Delphi Group (www.delphigroup.com), p. 14, as adapted and published in Michael Hickins, "Xerox Shares Its Knowledge," Management Review, September 1999, p. 42.

as important as the information technology. It was found that laboratory scientists were willing to use a common knowledge-exchange platform under these conditions—no training needed to use it, no maintenance, and no bureaucracy. Xerox management also found that scientists were willing to share some information, but not all. (Despite the merits of knowledge sharing, some people like to hold on to their best ideas until they can receive full credit.)

A recent advance in knowledge management is to deliver information just in time, or at the point in which it is most needed. The idea is to "bake" specialized knowledge into the jobs of workers with advanced skills. For example, Partners HealthCare System, Inc. embeds knowledge into the technology that physicians use so that retrieving the knowledge is no longer a separate activity. When a staff physician orders medicine or a lab test, the order-entry system automatically checks his or her decision against a huge clinical database as well as the patient's own medical record. Just-in-time delivery of knowledge is also useful in business. Customer service representatives at Hewlett-Packard and Dell work with computer systems that give them immediate access to information to help them respond to customer problems.[35] In this way, the representative does not have to have reams of information in his or her head.

Whatever advanced technology is used to implement knowledge management, it works best in an organization culture that values knowledge and encourages its dissemination. The organizational subculture shapes our assumptions about what knowledge is and which knowledge is worth managing.[36] Professional workers in the finance division of Gap Inc. might think that watching MTV on company time, or surfing the Net, is a waste of company time. In the merchandising division, however, watching MTV and surfing the Net might be perceived as a valuable way of understanding present and future clothing trends.

The Learning Organization

According to Peter Senge, a learning organization can be looked upon simply as a group of people working together to enhance their capacities to create the results they value.[37] Organizational leadership, however, must usually take the initiative to create the conditions whereby such enhancement of capacities, or learning, takes place. Toward this end, many firms have created a position labeled chief knowledge officer (CKO), or its equivalent. The major justification for creating a knowledge manager position is that in many companies human skills, intuition, and wisdom are replacing capital as the most precious resource. Chief knowledge officers seek to disperse those assets throughout the firm and convert them into innovations.[38] They are in charge of systematically collecting information and connecting people with others who might have valuable information.

A major challenge in creating a learning organization is that the concept covers so much ground and is perceived in many different ways by researchers and executives. Here we identify major leadership initiatives that enhance a learning organization. Understanding them will help you grasp the concept of what a leader might do to enhance organizational learning.[39] To begin with, a top-level leader should *create a strategic intent to learn*. Organizational learning then becomes a vehicle for gaining competitive advantage. *Creating a shared vision* enhances learning as organization members develop a common purpose and commitment to having the organization keep learning. If workers at all levels believe that the company is headed toward greatness, they will be motivated to learn to help deliver greatness.

Systems thinking is almost synonymous with organizational learning. The leader helps organization members regard the organization as a system in which everybody's work affects the activities of everybody else. Systems thinking also means keeping the big picture foremost in everybody's mind and being keenly aware of the external environment. In addition to the big picture of systems thinking, the leader must encourage the little picture of *personal mastery of the job*. As team members gain personal mastery of their jobs, they contribute to *team learning*, which is also an essential part of a learning organization. Team learning centers on collective problem solving, in which members freely share information and opinions to facilitate problem solving. Team learning is widely practiced today, with Hewlett-Packard being an outstanding example. Even such tasks as finding new ways to enhance the delivery of products are subject to team learning, as encouraged by team leaders.

Action learning, or learning while working on real problems, is a fundamental part of a learning organization. Participants in action learning are asked to work in teams to attack a significant organizational problem, such as decreasing the cycle time on a project. In the process of resolving an actual work problem, the participants acquire and use new skills, tools, or concepts. As the project progresses, new skills are applied later while working with the problem. For example, if the team learned how to eliminate duplication of effort in one aspect of the work process, it would look to eliminate duplication at other points in the cycle. Motorola is one company that systematically uses action learning. Teams of twenty to twenty-five senior managers from various parts of the company work on significant problems as defined by executives to whom the managers report. Quite often the starting point in problem solving is to enhance product quality.

Learning from failure contributes immensely to a learning organization. A company that diversified into an area unsuccessfully might analyze why it failed and then not repeat the same mistake. *Encouraging continuous experimentation* is another important practice for crafting a learning strategy. The leader encourages workers to learn from competitors, customers, suppliers, and other units within the organization. For example, a division of Johnson & Johnson developed a profitable line of specialty contact lenses (Accuvue) based on a suggestion from an employee who worked in an entirely different division. The path to a profitable product was rocky, yet J&J leadership was willing to experiment for a long-range gain.

A final perspective on the learning organization is that the leader must encourage organizational members to think creatively—to imagine possibilities that do not already exist. Instead of merely adapting to the environment, the organization engages in the type of breakthrough thinking described in our previous discussions of creativity and strategic leadership. Organizations cannot rely on CKOs alone to manage knowledge. The entire knowledge process must be embedded in the position of line manager.[40]

SUMMARY

Strategic leadership deals with the major purposes of an organization or organizational unit, and provides the direction and inspiration necessary to create, provide direction to, or sustain an organization. As described here, strategic leadership has five important components: (1) the high-level cognitive activity by the leader; (2) gathering multiple inputs to formulate strategy; (3) anticipating and creating a future; (4) revolutionary thinking; and (5) creating a vision.

Creating a vision is an integral part of strategic leadership. One study found that visions contain seven identifiable factors: vision formulation, implementation, innovative realism, general, detailed, risk taking, and profit orientation. The visions based on these factors extended from six months to more than twenty years, with an average of sixty-four months. After formulating a vision, the leader should be involved in its communication and implementation.

A carefully considered and articulated vision helps us know who we are and who we are not. The vision also points to what we do successfully and what we don't, which activities we should take on and which to avoid.

Strategic planning quite often takes the form of a SWOT analysis, taking into account strengths, weaknesses, opportunities, and threats in a given situation. A SWOT analysis examines the interaction between the organization and the environment.

Strategic leaders use many different types of business strategies, including the following: (1) differentiation, (2) cost leadership, (3) focus, (4) high quality, (5) imitation, (6) strategic alliances, (7) growth through acquisition, (8) high speed and first-mover strategy, (9) global diversification, (10) sticking to core competencies, (11) brand leadership, (12) conducting business on the Internet, and (13) peoplepalooza—gaining competitive advantage through hiring talented people.

Another strategic thrust of leaders is to help their organizations adapt to the environment by assisting workers and the organization to become better learners. To accomplish this feat, the leader manages knowledge and cultivates a learning organization. Knowledge management focuses on the systematic sharing of information. Major leadership initiatives for creating a learning organization include creating a strategic intent to learn, creating a shared vision, encouraging systems thinking, encouraging personal mastery of the job, and team learning. Action learning, or learning while working on real problems, learning from failures, and encouraging creative thinking are also part of the learning organization.

KEY TERMS

Strategy

Strategic leadership

Strategic management

Strategic planning

SWOT analysis

Total quality management

Knowledge management (KM)

Learning organization

✔ GUIDELINES FOR ACTION AND SKILL DEVELOPMENT

According to planning consultant Mark Graham Brown, to make sure that all workers understand the company's vision of where it wants to go, the vision statement should have certain key characteristics:[41]

1. **Brief.** The statement should be short enough so employees can recall it with ease. Several years ago Starbucks maintained the vision "2,000 stores by 2000."

2. **Verifiable.** A verifiable vision is one that ten people could agree that an organization has achieved. By the year 2003, Starbucks had attained approximately 5,900 stores (coffee shops).

3. **Focused.** Vision statements often contain too many ideas. It is better to focus on a major goal such as the vision of Ford Motor Company: "Employee involvement is our way of life." (Notice that this vision is about human resource management, not about a product or brand.)

4. **Understandable.** A major purpose of the vision statement is that employees will know where the organization wants to go and how

to help it get there. Being understandable is therefore a key quality of the vision statement. Terms such as "world-class" and "leading-edge" might be subject to wide interpretation. The following component of the H&R Block vision statement would be understandable by most company employees: "Quality products, excellent service, reasonable fees."

5. **Inspirational.** To inspire, a vision statement should make employees feel good about working for the organization and should focus them on measurable business goals. The Starbucks vision statement about 2,000 stores helped employees feel good about being part of company growth; it also spelled out an easy-to-measure goal.

DISCUSSION QUESTIONS AND ACTIVITIES

1. Why is *strategic leadership* thought to have the same meaning as *transformational leadership*?

2. In what way can a business strategy motivate employees?

3. How could you adapt a business strategy to guide you in your own career as a leader?

4. Many top-level managers say that they want lower-ranking managers to think strategically. How can a middle manager or a first-level manager "think strategically"?

5. What sources of information should a leader use to find helpful input for formulating strategy?

6. Working by yourself or with several team members, provide a recent example of revolutionary thinking by a company.

7. The average age of Cadillac owners, across the various models, was about 63 until the Escalade (a luxury SUV) was introduced into the market. The Cadillac Escalade had an immediate appeal to affluent rappers, professional athletes, and a variety of other young, wealthy entertainers. What is the business strategy lesson here?

8. In what way might doing a good job of knowledge management give a company a competitive advantage?

9. How might an organization that provides extensive training and development programs to employees still not be classified as a *learning organization*?

10. What steps might a leader take to help group members become *systems thinkers*?

Leadership Case Problem A

Samsung Sings a Different Tune

Samsung Electronics of South Korea manufactures and sells high-tech consumer products like cell phones that are voice activated, that surf the Internet, and that play MP3 tunes. Like many Samsung devices, the phone combines cutting-edge technology with award-winning design at premium prices. Yet three years ago the company was known as a mass marketer of cheap TVs and VCRs—the kind you bought at a shipping pallet at a discount store if you couldn't afford an upscale brand. On the industrial products side, Samsung had become the world's largest maker of memory chips.

For much of the past three decades, Samsung and South Korea's other massive conglomerates, known as *chaebols*, were looked down upon abroad as low-end makers of refrigerators, VCRs, and sedans. Samsung ran the risk of becoming a faceless supplier of computer monitors and semiconductors to more powerful multinationals. Even that niche was under threat from low-cost producers springing up in China. So leadership at the Samsung Electronics unit agreed on a key strategic move.

The Changing Image of Samsung. Since 1997 Samsung has begun rubbing shoulders with the market leaders in high-end cell phones, DVD players, elegant flat plasma TVs, and a wide range of other consumer products. These electronic devices are sometimes less expensive than those of Japanese and Finnish competitors, but not inferior in quality.

Samsung is among a small group of Korean companies that have emerged from the Asian financial crisis in the late 1990s as focused and lean competitors on the world stage. Samsung is approaching global recognition and has a $450 million annual advertising budget to promote its brand. "They successfully shifted from semicon-ductors to branded products like mobile phones, came in as a sponsor of the Sydney Olympic Games, and have been running heavy advertising in the U.S.," says Jan Lindemann, Interbrand's global director for brand valuation (*BusinessWeek online*, August 6, 2001, p. 1).

All this favorable attention to Samsung products has prompted Eric Kim, 46, Samsung's savvy Korean-American executive vice president for marketing, to assert that he hopes to surpass Sony Corporation in brand recognition by 2005. At Samsung Electronics, many executives express a near obsession with outperforming Sony. Oh Dong Jin, president of Samsung Electronics in America, says: "Sony is now only strong in audio and video, like DVDs and TVs. We are much stronger now in other fields such as mobile phones and flat-panel screens" (*The Wall Street Journal*, June 13, 2002, p. A6).

According to the consultancy Interbrand, Samsung has the second most recognizable consumer electronics brand in the world. A researcher for the Japanese investment bank, Nomura Securities, says Samsung is "no longer making poor equivalents of Sony products. It is making things people want" (*Time*, March 25, 2002, p. 49).

Furthermore, during a period when most of the world's high-technology companies were still shutting plants and trimming research and development to cope with the global economic slump, Samsung was extending its reach. Bolstered by the resurgent Korean economy, Samsung Electronics' worldwide revenues are running over $25 billion per year. The company is growing fast and is the best performer in the family-controlled conglomerate that spawned it, the Samsung Group.

In addition to developing its own brand, Samsung remains an important supplier of components for other companies. In 1997, Kim helped put together a deal to provide Sprint Corporation with 1.8 million mobile-phone handsets that were delivered in eighteen months—one-half the contracted time. Sprint executives now say Samsung Electronics is their biggest supplier of mobile-phone handsets. Rival Sony is also an important customer, buying semiconductors and displays from the Korean company. Sony chairman Nobuyuki Idei says he sees Samsung more as a supplier than a threat. "We still believe that Samsung is basically a components company," he says. "We feel that keeping good relations is a benefit for both companies" (*The Wall Street Journal*).

Kim Takes Action.   Much of this success is attributable to Eric Kim. After being recruited to Samsung as executive vice president for marketing, the former Lotus Development executive overhauled Samsung Electronics' marketing arm. He consolidated fifty-five advertising agencies into one to create a global brand image for the company. Progress was swift. "Just 24 months ago, Samsung was seen as a third-tier company, but now it's broken into the top level," says Ray Brown, vice president for general merchandising, electronics, at Sears, Roebuck and Co. (*The Wall Street Journal*).

Kim started developing relationships with American's top retail chains. Up through 1999, Samsung products had virtually no space on U.S. store shelves. At many electronic retailers, store associates still claim that Samsung has very little brand recognition. Kim explains that his company has exploited an opening created by new digital technology. Consumers are now more open to consider different brands. "That

transition, and our strategy to move upmarket very aggressively, are the main reasons why our brand improved rapidly," Kim says (*Business-Week online*, p. 2).

But that is changing. The consumer electronics chain Best Buy has become a major distributor of Samsung products. CompUSA is another strong partner. Samsung dropped Wal-Mart, perceiving the mammoth retailer as incompatible with its upscale image. "During the 1980s and '90s, the Japanese and Europeans dominated the electronics industry," Kim said at a New York City meeting. "But now we believe Samsung can dominate any market, including the U.S." (*The Wall Street Journal*).

QUESTIONS

1. Identify at least three business (or marketing) strategies Samsung uses now or used in the past.

2. What suggestions can you offer Kim and other Samsung leaders so they can become even more successful in building the Samsung brand?

3. What is your opinion of Eric Kim as a strategic leader?

SOURCE: *Frank Gibney, Jr., "Samsung Moves Upmarket,"Time, March 25, 2002, pp. 49–51; Jay Solomon, "Seoul Survivors: Back from the Brink, Korea Inc. Wants a Little Respect,"The Wall Street Journal, June 13, 2002, pp. A1, A6; Moon Ihlwan, "Samsung: No Longer Unsung,"BusinessWeek online, August 6, 2001.*

Leadership Case Problem B

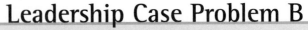

The Reluctant Information Sharers

Blueberry Capital Management specializes in managing the portfolios of individuals and small businesses with a net worth of at least $2 million. Almost all the clients are people with advanced knowledge of investments themselves. Because investors have so many options, including investing through online investment firms, a major challenge to the business is attracting new clients. Blueberry earns a large share of its profits by receiving a commission on the profits it generates for clients.

An important part of the Blueberry investment strategy is to seek investments for clients it usually cannot find through traditional sources, such as financial service companies. For example, some client money is invested in business startups, giving clients the opportunity to become venture capitalists.

Mike Basilio, the founder of the firm, has been concerned lately that his company develops ideas inefficiently. He said to Lindsay Taylor, the executive vice president at Blueberry, "I keep hearing the same discussions over and over about how to attract new clients or solve a client investment problem. The financial consultants keep sifting through the alternatives that others have done before. People don't capitalize on all the good problem solving that has taken place in the past. We go through the same agonizing process of dealing with similar problems."

Taylor replied, "Are you suggesting, Mike, that we should offer canned solutions to clients so we could save lots of time?"

"Not at all," responded Mike. "We could at least save some time and offer similar types of assistance to clients that we offered to other clients in the past. I'll give you a good example. Allan Whitcomb was recently working with a restaurant owner. The client wanted to invest in a high-risk, high-yield instrument. So Allan spent a week researching interest possibilities for his client. He finally discovered a way to invest in wine futures (betting on the future price of rare wines) that appealed to his client.

"If Allan could have picked up some ideas inhouse, he could have found some good ideas a lot more quickly. Also, if he had spent less time, the client might have been willing to invest a larger sum up front. Instead, the client invested some of his money into a hedge fund."

Looking perplexed, Lindsay said, "But how would Allan have known about who had tackled a similar client problem in the past?"

Mike jumped in, "Lindsay, you have pinpointed the problem. We have done a poor job of systematically pooling all that great information in our heads. Not only do we reinvent the wheel, we reinvent the idea that a wheel would be useful.

"I'm proposing that we find a way of sharing knowledge that will pay big dividends for the firm. The major consulting firms have developed pretty effective systems of knowledge management and knowledge sharing in recent years.

"I'm not implying that we hire somebody to be our chief knowledge officer or that we invest $500,000 in sophisticated software. I just want us to do a better job of sharing ideas with each other."

"I've got an idea," said Lindsay. "Let's schedule a combination dinner and focus group for the professional staff. The subject will be why we weren't doing a better job of information sharing." Among the comments that emerged from the dinner/focus group were the following:

Gerry: I would like to share more of my experiences with the other financial consultants. I'm concerned, though, about the good of the firm. Suppose I give some of my best ideas to another consultant, and then he or she leaves the firm? My good ideas are fed right to the competition.

Barbara: Unlike Gerry, I have no hesitancy in sharing ideas. The problem is the time involved. We were encouraged at one time to do a writeup of how we solved unusual client problems. The task proved to be busywork. We had to follow a complicated format. Maybe we should use a briefer method of recording good ideas.

Samantha: I'm not opposed to sharing ideas, but it makes me a little self-conscious. To ask someone else for ideas suggests that I'm not so creative myself. Take that restaurant owner account. If it were my account, I would have been a little self-conscious admitting that I didn't have any creative ideas of my own for the client.

Kurt: So long as we are all being brutally honest here, let me get to the heart of the problem. We're creative types. Our careers are dependent on having good ideas and investment strategies. Once you share an idea with another exec, the idea becomes public knowledge. It loses its originality. So if you use that idea again, you are no longer creative because other consultants are using it.

Amber: Kurt has a point. Teamwork is nice but you still have to look out for *numero uno.* Sure I have warm, fuzzy feelings toward top management and the other consultants. Yet I'm still evaluated by Blueberry management in terms of my originality, including ways to find new clients and finding high-yield investments.

Mike Basilio said to the group, "Lindsay and I both thank you for being so candid. I see a few glimmers of hope in terms of knowledge sharing in our firm. But this is just the start of a continuing dialogue. We have a long way to go to manage knowledge well at Blueberry Capital."

Lindsay nodded in agreement.

QUESTIONS

1. What suggestions can you offer Mike Basilio and Lindsay Taylor to improve knowledge sharing at Blueberry Capital?

2. How valid are the points made by the financial consultants for not doing a better job sharing information?

3. What cultural changes might be needed at Blueberry to improve knowledge sharing?

INTERNET SKILL–BUILDING EXERCISE

Professional Assistance in Implementing Knowledge Management

Apply the chapter concepts! Visit the Web and complete this Internet skill-building exercise to learn more about current leadership topics and trends.

Visit www.knowledgebase.net to learn about Knowledge Base, a group of engineers, scientists, and entrepreneurs whose aim is to help their clients and partners achieve corporate objectives by unlocking and leveraging the power of intelligent knowledge management. Take the PowerPoint tour (www.knowledgebase.net/tour/tour1.html). After your tour is complete, answer these questions: (1) What are the goals of Knowledge Base? (2) What is your opinion of the value of the service offered by the company?

International and Culturally Diverse Aspects of Leadership

CHAPTER 14

Several years ago, leadership at computer workstation manufacturer Silicon Graphics, Inc. faced some stark choices, and the executive group agonized over which businesses to shutter and which employees to lay off. Ultimately, 1,000 workers—10 percent of the work force—lost their jobs. But as one team at SGI headquarters in Mountain View, California, scrutinized the bottom line, another kept close tabs on a different metric, the color line. By monitoring layoffs to ensure that no one group of employees was disproportionately hit, SGI maintained the overall ethnic, gender, and age makeup of its work force. (The company ranks number 7 on *Fortune*'s fourth annual list of the best companies for minority employees.)

The active interest that SGI leadership takes in maintaining cultural and demographic diversity in the work force points to the importance of diversity issues for the modern leader. At the same time the leader must be culturally sensitive. Working in another country—dealing with cultural groups different from one's own—is becoming a requirement for many senior-level management positions.

SGI's commitment to diversity is not unique. However, the fact that it upheld the commitment during a downturn in business conditions indicates how seriously corporate leadership now takes diversity.[1] Corporate success, profit, and growth depend increasingly on the management of a diverse work force.[2]

For example, the average age of the American worker is increasing, and white males now constitute less than 50 percent of the work force. An increasing number of new entrants are women and people of color. The diversity umbrella in the work force encompasses such groups as men, women, people of color, white people, able-bodied people, the physically disabled, gay males, lesbians, the old, the young, married people with children, unmarried people with children, and single parents. These groups want their leaders and coworkers to treat them with respect, dignity, fairness, and sensitivity. Because the focus on diversity is including so many people in an opportunity to participate fully in the organization, the word *inclusion* is often used to replace *diversity*.

Not only is the work force becoming more diverse, but business has become increasingly global. Small and medium-size firms, as well as corporate giants, are increasingly dependent on trade with other countries. An estimated 10 to 15 percent of jobs in the United States depend on imports or exports. Furthermore, most manufactured goods contain components from more than one country.

Our approach to cultural diversity both within and across countries emphasizes the leadership perspective. Key topics include the ethical and competitive advantage of managing for diversity, how cultural factors influence leadership practices, and how cultural sensitivity and global leadership skills contribute to leadership effectiveness. This chapter also describes initiatives that enhance the acceptance of cultural diversity and shows how to achieve cultural diversity among organizational leaders. The underlying theme is that effective leadership of diverse people requires a sensitivity to and enjoyment of cultural differences.

THE ADVANTAGES OF MANAGING FOR DIVERSITY

The ethical and social responsibility goals of leaders and their organizations include providing adequately for members of the diverse work force. Ethics is involved because treating people fairly is considered morally right from the *deontological* view of ethics. The deontological approach is based on universal principles such as honesty, fairness, justice, and respect for persons and property. Leaders who ascribe to this view of ethics would therefore feel compelled to use merit as a basis for making human resource decisions.

A firm that embraces diversity is also behaving in a socially responsible manner. A leader, for example, who chose to hire five environmentally disadvantaged, unemployed people would be acting in a socially responsible manner. Hiring these people would transfer responsibility for their economic welfare from the state or private charity to the employer. (Some would argue that unless hiring these people is cost-effective, the company is neglecting its responsibility to shareholders.)

The many spheres of activity that managing for diversity encompasses are shown in Figure 14-1. According to research and opinion, managing for diversity also brings the firm a competitive advantage. Here we review evidence and opinion about that competitive advantage.[3]

1. *Reduction of turnover and absenteeism costs.* As organizations become more diverse, the cost of managing diversity poorly increases. Turnover and absenteeism decrease when minority groups perceive themselves as receiving fair treatment. More effective management of diversity may increase the job satisfaction of diverse groups, thus decreasing turnover and absenteeism and their associated costs. The major initiatives in managing diversity well at Allstate Corporation have substantially reduced turnover among Latinos and African Americans, both in corporate headquarters and in field locations.

2. *Managing diversity well offers a marketing advantage.* A representational work force facilitates selling products and services. A key factor is that a multicultural group of decision makers may be at an advantage in reaching a multicultural market. At least one member of the multicultural group may be able to focus a marketing strategy to demonstrate an appreciation of the targeted audience. Pepsi-Cola North America recently developed a beverage specifically designed for the Latino community, Dole Aguas Frescas, a line of noncarbonated, caffeine-free juice. The idea came from Latino input within Pepsi-Cola. Tested in the Chicago area, the brand is supported by outdoor advertising, in-store merchandising, and sampling. "Latinos have been making this type of product in their home for years," said Chris Jogis, senior marketing manager of new products for the company.[4]

   Another marketing advantage is that many people from culturally diverse groups prefer to buy from a company with a good reputation for managing diversity. Allstate Insurance Company is well known for its diversity

FIGURE 14-1   Spheres of Activity in the Management of Cultural Diversity

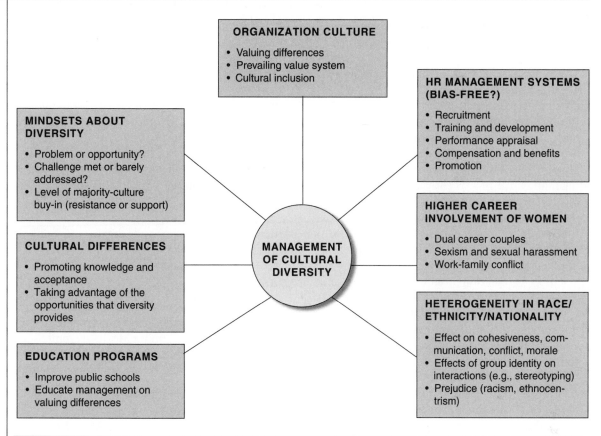

ORGANIZATION CULTURE

- Valuing differences
- Prevailing value system
- Cultural inclusion

HR MANAGEMENT SYSTEMS (BIAS-FREE?)

- Recruitment
- Training and development
- Performance appraisal
- Compensation and benefits
- Promotion

MINDSETS ABOUT DIVERSITY

- Problem or opportunity?
- Challenge met or barely addressed?
- Level of majority-culture buy-in (resistance or support)

CULTURAL DIFFERENCES

- Promoting knowledge and acceptance
- Taking advantage of the opportunities that diversity provides

EDUCATION PROGRAMS

- Improve public schools
- Educate management on valuing differences

MANAGEMENT OF CULTURAL DIVERSITY

HIGHER CAREER INVOLVEMENT OF WOMEN

- Dual career couples
- Sexism and sexual harassment
- Work-family conflict

HETEROGENEITY IN RACE/ ETHNICITY/NATIONALITY

- Effect on cohesiveness, communication, conflict, morale
- Effects of group identity on interactions (e.g., stereotyping)
- Prejudice (racism, ethnocentrism)

Source: Taylor H. Cox and Stacy Blake, "Managing for Cultural Diversity: Implications for Organizational Competitiveness," Academy of Management Executive, August 1991, p. 46. Academy of Management Executive by Newsom, Walter B. Copyright 1991 by Academy of Management. Reproduced with permission of Acad of Mgmt in the format Textbook via Copyright Clearance Center.

initiatives, and the company has become the nation's leading insurer of African Americans and Latinos. The large number of agents and customer service representatives from these two groups facilitates attracting and retaining a high percentage of African Americans and Latinos as customers. The accompanying Leader in Action insert illustrates how companies are using cultural knowledge to help target an ethnic group.

3. *Companies with a favorable record in managing diversity are at a distinct advantage in recruiting and retaining talented people.* Those companies with a favorable reputation for welcoming diversity attract the strongest job candidates among women and racial and ethnic minorities. Also, a company that does not welcome a diverse work force shrinks its supply of potential candidates.

Leader in Action

Carrie Tolstedt at Wells Fargo Targets Mexican Americans

The Wells Fargo Bank branch in the Los Angeles suburb of South Gate looks like it belongs in Mexico—a white exterior has been repainted in the reddish brown hues of a pueblo, and the lobby displays Mexican artwork. The remodeling is one of the ways in which bankers are trying to appeal to the nation's Hispanics, a rapidly growing market that has recently attracted special attention from the financial services industry. "Once you see an emerging opportunity like this, you have to ask yourself what you need to do better," said Carrie Tolstedt, who oversees Wells Fargo's retail operations in California.

Banks are creating programs to make it easier for Mexican immigrants to open accounts, spending more money on Hispanic ads, and overhauling branches in communities like South Gate, where more than 80 percent of the 96,000 residents are Hispanic. The remodeled branch is "like a security blanket for our customers. It's much more comfortable for them to come in here now," said Iliana Concepcion, a personal banking officer whose desk sits in front of a painting by Mexican artist Diego Rivera.

In the first year after the renovations, the number of South Gate households with an account at the office increased by 6 percent, Tolstedt said. Before the remodeling, the growth rate was 1 percent. The up-tick in business means longer lines at the branch, but the customers waiting up to thirty minutes to see a teller on a Friday afternoon didn't seem to mind. "They seem to want to help you more," said Patricia Nava, a customer.

If bankers hope to succeed in the Hispanic market, they probably will have to prepare for crowded lobbies and offer more personal services, because much of Latino culture revolves around face-to-face contact, said Andrew Erlich, a minority marketing consultant in Woodland Hills, California. The preference for more human interaction contradicts the industry's increasing emphasis on automating services through computers and telephones. But as so many upscale customers shift money into mutual funds and brokerage accounts, revenue-hungry bankers are more willing to accommodate Hispanics, particularly those who don't have U.S. bank accounts.

QUESTIONS

1. Aside from this one positive case history, from a marketing standpoint how effective do you think it is to apply a Mexican architectural style to a bank in a Mexican American neighborhood?

2. To what extent will many Mexican Americans feel that Wells Fargo management is patronizing them because of the Mexican architecture? (The input of Mexican Americans will be particularly valuable here.)

3. How should banks deal with the issue that many Latinos prefer person-to-person banking rather than a reliance on information technology?

SOURCE: *"Big Banks Target Hispanic Market," Associated Press, May 26, 2002.*

4. *Managing diversity well unlocks the potential for excellence.* By providing workers from all groups the tools, resources, and opportunities to succeed, the companies that hire culturally diverse workers are more likely to display their full talents. A man raised in China earned an MBA from an American institute. After carefully searching for companies with an envi-

able record of managing diversity, he landed a position as a financial analyst with PepsiCo. After one year, his manager complimented his ability to generate ideas, and asked why he tried so hard. The analyst said, "In this company, there is nothing to hold me back so long as I am a star performer."

5. *Heterogeneity in the work force may offer the company a creativity advantage, plus improved problem solving and decision making.* Creative solutions to problems are more likely to be reached when a diverse group attacks a problem. Joanna Miller, a managing director at an executive search firm, notes: "The most sophisticated employers realize that when it comes to solving problems and challenges, a diverse work group brings a variety of perspectives, backgrounds, and experiences, which can lead to creative and innovative outcomes."[5] Managing diversity well also has the potential to improve problem solving and decision making. Decision quality appears to be best when the group is neither excessively homogeneous nor overly heterogeneous. With a culturally diverse group present, there is less likelihood of groupthink.

Diversity offers both a substantial advantage for organizations and a formidable challenge. Some research suggests that a diverse group is likely to consider a greater range of perspectives and to generate more high-quality solutions than a homogeneous group. Yet the greater the amount of diversity within an organizational subunit, the less cohesive the group. The result may be dissatisfaction and turnover. According to Frances J. Milliken and Luis L. Martins, diversity thus appears to be a double-edge sword: It increases both the opportunity for creativity and the likelihood that group members will be dissatisfied and fail to identify with the group.[6]

However, research at one of the world's largest employers substantiates many of the points already mentioned about the advantages of a culturally diverse work force. The goal of the Diversity Development Program of the United States Postal Service is to build an inclusive work force to serve its diverse customer base. The department in charge of the program conducted a study to determine the return on investment (ROI) from employing a diverse work force within diverse communities. Work force inclusiveness was measured in terms of the percentages of underrepresentation of ten different ethnic groups in comparison to the local civilian labor force. For example, if 15 percent of the local work force were Native American and only 8 percent of the local Postal Service employees were Native American, this group would be underrepresented by 7 percent. All eighty-five postal districts were included in the study. Work force inclusiveness (the opposite of underrepresentation) was positively correlated with more favorable levels of performance. The following criteria were used:

- Customer ratings of overall satisfaction
- Customer ratings of courteous and friendly service from clerks
- Customer ratings of the ability of clerks to explain products and services
- Employee ratings regarding not feeling excluded from the work unit

- Employee ratings regarding concern over being a victim of workplace violence
- Employee ratings regarding freedom from sexual harassment
- Employee ratings regarding the Postal Service as a place to work
- Corporate productivity rate

On the basis of these results, the researchers concluded that diversity initiatives provide a worthwhile ROI to the Postal Service. Also, when an organization embraces the communities it serves and its work force is representative of those communities, customer and employee satisfaction increase, as well as organizational productivity.[7] An important situational factor here is that the U.S. government has always been a leader in hiring a diverse work force. Employees therefore expect to be part of a culturally and demographically diverse environment.

To raise your level of awareness about how to capitalize on the potential advantages of diversity, do Leadership Skill-Building Exercise 14-1, which illustrates that diversity skills are another important subset of interpersonal skills associated with leadership. To capitalize upon diversity, the leader/manager must be able to work well with workers from different cultural groups.

CULTURAL FACTORS INFLUENCING LEADERSHIP PRACTICE

A **multicultural leader** is a leader with the skills and attitudes to relate effectively to and motivate people across race, gender, age, social attitudes, and lifestyles. To influence, motivate, and inspire culturally diverse people, the leader must be aware of overt and subtle cultural differences. Such culturally based differences are generalizations, but they function as starting points in the leader's attempt to lead a person from another culture. For example, many Asians are self-conscious about being praised in front of the group because they feel that individual attention clashes with their desire to maintain group harmony. A manager might refrain from praising an Asian group member before the group until he or she understands that group member's preferences. The manager is likely to find that many Asians welcome praise in front of peers, especially when working outside their homeland.

Here we examine three topics that help a leader learn how to manage in a culturally diverse workplace: (1) understanding key dimensions of differences in cultural values; (2) the influence of cultural values on leadership style; and (3) applying a motivational theory across cultural groups.

Key Dimensions of Differences in Cultural Values

One way to understand how national cultures differ is to examine their values. Here we examine seven different values and the ways in which selected nationali-

Leadership Skill-Building Exercise 14–1

Capitalizing on Diversity

The class organizes into small groups of about six students each who assume the roles of the top management team of a medium-size manufacturing or service company. Being socially aware, ethical, and modern in its thinking, your company already has a highly diverse work force. Yet somehow, your company isn't any more profitable than the competition. As the company leaders (yourself a diverse group), today you will work on the problem of how to better capitalize on the cultural diversity within your company. Working for about fifteen minutes, develop a few concrete ideas to enable your company to capitalize upon diversity. After the problem solving has been completed, the team leaders might present their ideas to the other groups.

ties relate to them. Geert Hofstede identified the first five value dimensions in research spanning eighteen years and involving over 160,000 people from over sixty countries.[8] The qualitative research of Arvind V. Phatak identified two other values.[9] The eighth value is newly formulated. A summary of these values is described next and is also outlined in Figure 14-2.

1. *Individualism/collectivism.* At one end of the continuum is **individualism,** a mental set in which people see themselves first as individuals and believe their own interests and values take priority. **Collectivism,** at the other end of the continuum, is a feeling that the group and society should receive top priority. Members of a society that value individualism are more concerned with their careers than with the good of the firm. Members of a society who value collectivism, on the other hand, are typically more concerned with the organization than with themselves. Individualistic cultures include the United States, Canada, and Great Britain; collectivistic cultures include Japan, Hong Kong, Mexico, and Greece.

2. *Power distance.* The extent to which employees accept the idea that members of an organization have different levels of power is referred to as **power distance.** In a high-power-distance culture, the boss makes many decisions simply because he or she is boss, and group members readily comply. In a low-power-distance culture, employees do not readily recognize a power hierarchy. They accept directions only when they think the boss is right or when they feel threatened. High-power-distance cultures include France, Spain, Japan, and Mexico. Low-power-distance cultures include the United States, Israel, Germany, and Ireland.

3. *Uncertainty avoidance.* People who accept the unknown and tolerate risk and unconventional behavior are said to have low **uncertainty avoidance.**

FIGURE 14–2   **Dimensions of Individual Values**

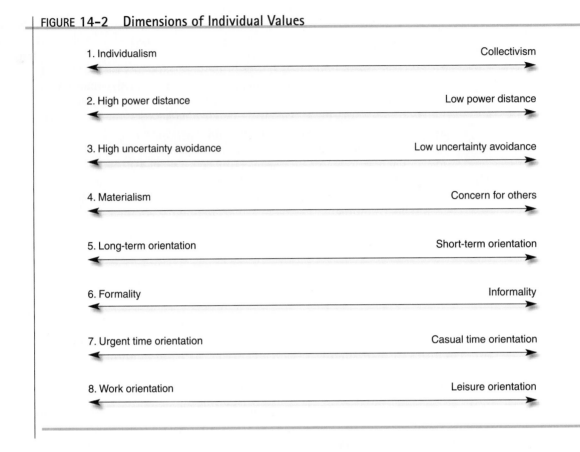

1. Individualism ←——————————————————————————→ Collectivism

2. High power distance ←——————————————————————————→ Low power distance

3. High uncertainty avoidance ←——————————————————————————→ Low uncertainty avoidance

4. Materialism ←——————————————————————————→ Concern for others

5. Long-term orientation ←——————————————————————————→ Short-term orientation

6. Formality ←——————————————————————————→ Informality

7. Urgent time orientation ←——————————————————————————→ Casual time orientation

8. Work orientation ←——————————————————————————→ Leisure orientation

In other words, these people are not afraid to face the unknown. A society ranked high in uncertainty avoidance contains a majority of people who want predictable and certain futures. Low-uncertainty-avoidance cultures include the United States, Canada, and Australia. At the other end of the continuum, workers in Israel, Japan, Italy, and Argentina value certainty and predictability more highly.

4. *Materialism/concern for others.* In this context, **materialism** refers to an emphasis on assertiveness and the acquisition of money and material objects, and a deemphasis on caring for others. At the other end of the continuum is **concern for others,** which refers to an emphasis on personal relationships, caring for others, and a high quality of life. (Hofstede uses the terms *masculinity/femininity* to describe this dimension of cultural values.) Materialistic countries include the United States, Japan, and Italy, whereas "concern for others" cultures include Sweden and Denmark.

5. *Long-term orientation/short-term orientation.* Workers from a culture with a **long-term orientation** maintain a long-range perspective, and thus are thrifty and do not demand quick returns on their investments. A **short-**

term orientation is characterized by a demand for immediate results and a propensity not to save. Pacific Rim countries are noted for their long-term orientation. In contrast, the cultures of the United States and Canada are characterized by a more short-term orientation.

6. *Formality/informality.* A country that values **formality** attaches considerable importance to tradition, ceremony, social rules, and rank. In contrast, **informality** refers to a casual attitude toward tradition, ceremony, social rules, and rank. Workers in Latin American countries highly value formality, such as lavish public receptions and processions. American and Canadian workers are much more informal.

7. *Urgent time orientation/casual time orientation.* Long- and short-term orientations focus mostly on planning and investment. Another time-related value dimension is how much importance a person attaches to time. People with an **urgent time orientation** perceive time as a scarce resource and tend to be impatient. People with a **casual time orientation** view time as an unlimited and unending resource and tend to be patient. Americans are noted for their urgent time orientation. They frequently impose deadlines and are eager to "get down to business." Asians and Middle Easterners, in contrast, are patient negotiators. In fact, businesspersons in the Middle East are known to allow a business meeting to run over while another visitor waits outside the office.

8. *Work orientation/leisure orientation.* A major cultural value difference is the number of hours per week people expect to invest in work versus leisure or other nonwork activities. American corporate professionals typically work about fifty-five hours per week, take forty-five-minute lunch breaks, and go on two weeks of vacation. Japanese workers share similar values with respect to amount of work per week. European professionals, in contrast, are more likely to work forty hours per week, take two-hour lunch breaks, and go on six weeks of vacation. European countries have steadily reduced the workweek in recent years, while lengthening vacations. The average German worker invests about 1,400 hours a year in work, a 17 percent decrease from 1980. Europeans, particularly Swedes, also are likely to take much more sick leave than workers from other countries. To compensate for the leisure orientation of European workers, many European companies are outsourcing jobs outside of Europe. French car manufacturer PSA Peugeot Citroën, for example, more than doubled the size of its work force outside France, to 68,000, during the last decade. Countries with stronger work orientations, such as Slovakia, Brazil, and South Africa, are absorbing European manufacturing jobs.[10]

How might a manager use information about differences in values to become a more effective leader? A starting point would be to recognize that a person's national values might influence his or her behavior. Assume that a leader wants to influence a person with a low-power-distance orientation to strive for peak performance. The "low-power" person will not spring into action just because the boss makes the suggestion. Instead, the leader needs to patiently explain the personal payoffs of achieving peak performance. Another example is a leader who wants to improve quality and therefore hires people who value collectivism. A backup tactic would be to counsel people who value individualism on the merits of collective action. Leadership Self-Assessment Quiz 14-1 will help you think about how values can moderate (or influence) work performance.

Cultural Values and Leadership Style

The values embedded in a culture influence the behavior of leaders and managers as well as the behavior of other workers. As Hofstede explains, relationships between people in a society are affected by the values programmed in the minds of these people. Because management deals heavily with interpersonal relationships, management and leadership are affected by cultural values. Management and leadership processes may vary from culture to culture, but, being value-based, these processes show strong continuity in each society.[11]

One example of the influence of values on management and leadership style is the behavior of French managers. France has always been a class society, somewhat like the caste society of India. Within a typical manufacturing plant, different classes meet. Managers and professionals are labeled the *cadres;* first-level supervisors are called the *maîtrise;* and lower-level workers are the *non-cadres.* Within each of these classes, there are further status distinctions such as higher and lower cadres. French managers who have attended the major business schools (*Grand Écoles*) have the highest status of all. The implication for leadership style is that French managers, particularly in major corporations, are part of an elite class, and they behave in a superior, authoritarian manner. A stereotype of this style of manager would expect obedience and high respect from group members.

Another example of a distinctive leadership style related to culture is the stereotype of the German manager. German managers were studied as part of the GLOBE (Global Leadership and Organizational Behavior Effectiveness) project. Data were collected on culture and leadership from 457 middle managers in the telecommunications, food processing, and finance industries. A strong performance orientation was found to be the most pronounced German cultural value. German middle managers thus tend to avoid uncertainty, are assertive, and are not terribly considerate of others. The managers typically show little compassion, and their interpersonal relations are straightforward and stern.[12] This strong performance orientation must be packed into a short workweek!

Specific research has been conducted about differences in leadership and management style across cultures. Roland Calori and Bruno Dufour conducted one such investigation by interviewing fifty-two top executives from some of Western Europe's best-known firms.[13] In spite of differences across Europe, it was found that European firms share some common management philosophies and practices. Four common characteristics were noted among managers and leaders in prominent European firms.

Charting Your Cultural Value Profile

INSTRUCTIONS   For each of the eight value dimensions, circle the number that most accurately fits your standing on the dimension. For example, if you perceive yourself to be "highly concerned for others," circle the 7 on the fourth dimension.

1. Individualism   Collectivism

| 1 | 2 | 3 | 4 | 5 | 6 | 7 |

2. High Power Distance   Low Power Distance

| 1 | 2 | 3 | 4 | 5 | 6 | 7 |

3. High Uncertainty Avoidance   Low Uncertainty Avoidance

| 1 | 2 | 3 | 4 | 5 | 6 | 7 |

4. Materialism   Concern for Others

| 1 | 2 | 3 | 4 | 5 | 6 | 7 |

5. Long-Term Orientation   Short-Term Orientation

| 1 | 2 | 3 | 4 | 5 | 6 | 7 |

6. Formality   Informality

| 1 | 2 | 3 | 4 | 5 | 6 | 7 |

7. Urgent Time Orientation   Casual Time Orientation

| 1 | 2 | 3 | 4 | 5 | 6 | 7 |

8. Work Orientation   Leisure Orientation

| 1 | 2 | 3 | 4 | 5 | 6 | 7 |

SCORING AND INTERPRETATION   After circling one number for each dimension, use a felt-tip pen to connect the circles; this gives you a *profile of cultural values*. Do not be concerned if your marker cuts through the names of the dimensions. Compare your profile to others in class. Should time allow, develop a class profile by computing the class average for each of the eight dimensions and then connecting the points. If the sample size is large enough, compare the cultural value profiles of Westerners and Easterners.

One possible link to leadership development is to hypothesize which type of profile would be the most responsive and which would be the least responsive to your leadership.

1. *A greater orientation toward people.* Compared to their U.S. and Japanese counterparts, European managers are more likely to believe that they share a common inclination to foster the fulfillment of people. (German managers appear to be the exception.) As the European business leaders see it, in the United States profits dominate everything, and people are considered a resource that you can take or leave. In Japan, evidence is surfacing of mental and physical harassment of employees in an attempt to force them to resign as their employers face stiffer competition.

2. *A higher level of internal negotiation.* European managers invest considerable time negotiating inside the firm—between different levels of management, between management and the workers, with trade unions, and between headquarters and divisions or subsidiaries. U.S. executives tend to be more top-down in making major decisions, while Japanese managers typically strive for consensus management.

3. *Greater skill in managing international diversity.* Based on the interviews, the researchers concluded that European managers have an ability to recognize diversity. They respect and appreciate diversity, and have developed skill in managing it to advantage. (Of course, this edge is disappearing as Americans take courses in leadership!) European managers generally respect the host country and are less imperialistic than the Americans and Japanese, who have a tendency to export their way of thinking.

4. *Ability to manage between extremes.* Management philosophies and styles in the United States and Japan are often characterized as lying at the extremes on certain dimensions, such as the short-term perspective of Americans versus the long-term perspective of Japanese. If a European style of management exists, it is halfway between the extremes of the U.S. and Japanese styles on various leadership dimensions, such as extent of concern for human resources.

Identifying typical European styles of management and leadership may be helpful in relating to European managers and group members. If a group of European workers are accustomed to considerable negotiation, they will expect such behavior from a North American manager on assignment in Europe. Nevertheless, cultural stereotypes are limited because they do not take into account differences within a culture. For example, American managers who practice empowerment are strongly oriented toward a negotiating style. Another consideration is that as leadership and management knowledge continues to be disseminated widely, effective managers from different geographic regions may develop similar styles. One of the executives in the study under consideration put it this way: "The real difference will be between the best companies (wherever they come from), between the best management practices and mediocre management practices. Management in the world and in Europe will be homogeneous at its best."[14]

Applying a Motivational Theory Across Cultural Groups

A practical way of understanding how cultural factors influence leadership is to illustrate how motivation theory might be applied to different cultural groups. Expectancy theory, which provides specific guidelines to leaders and managers, can be used to illustrate cross-cultural motivation. Doing so will illustrate the principle that some aspects of motivation theory apply across cultures, whereas other aspects must be modified. Two aspects of expectancy theory are especially important for understanding cross-cultural differences in motivation: perception of individual control over the environment, and appropriateness of rewards.

Environmental Control.   As analyzed by Nancy J. Adler, expectancy theories depend on the extent to which workers believe they have control over the outcome of their efforts, and how much faith they have in leaders to deliver rewards.[15] The assumption that workers believe they have control over their own fate may be culturally dependent. In countries where individualism dominates, employees may believe more strongly that they can influence performance and outcomes. In collectivist societies, such as Taiwan and Japan, the ties between the individual and the organization have a moral component. In the United States and similar cultures, many people believe that "where there is a will, there is a way."

Adler argues that the reasons that people in individualistic societies become committed to organizations are quite different from those of people in collectivist societies. An employee in an individualistic culture (such as the United States, Canada, or Germany) is more likely to ask, "What's in it for me?" before responding to a motivational thrust. Employees with collectivistic values commit themselves to the organization more because of ties with managers and coworkers than because of intrinsic job factors or individual incentives.

Despite the cultural generalization, the leader must be alert to individual and subcultural differences. Many Japanese workers are becoming less loyal to their employers and thus more self-centered and eager for individual recognition. Workers from rural areas in the United States are much more collectivist than their counterparts from large cities. One of the many reasons Saturn Motors located its plant in Tennessee is the presence of a more harmonious and loyal work force.

Appropriateness of Rewards.   Expectancy theories are universal because the motivator must search for rewards that have valence for individual employees. Leaders themselves must analyze the type and level of rewards that have the highest valence for individuals. The appropriateness of rewards is most strongly tied to individual differences, yet cultural differences are also important. The challenge is to find which rewards are effective in the particular culture.

A study was conducted in a cotton mill in the Russian Republic of the former Soviet Union. One aspect of the study offered intrinsic rewards in the form of American goods to ninety-nine weavers from different shifts. Praise and recognition were also used as rewards. Receiving the goods as well as recognition and praise were contingent upon increases in the amount of top-grade fabric they produced. The rewards resulted in increased production. Another motivational technique, employee participation, contributed to performance decline.[16] The study relates to valence because many people believe that participation in decision making is a reward for virtually all workers. But among these Russian weavers, participative management was perceived to have negative valence. Perhaps participating in decision making was too foreign to their work culture to be acceptable.

Many American managers have mistakenly assumed that a reward with a high valence among American workers will also have a high valence among workers from other cultures. In one situation, raising the salary of a particular group of Mexican workers motivated them to work fewer rather than more hours. A spokesperson for the Mexican workers said, "We can now make enough money to live and enjoy life in less time than previously. Now, we do not have to work so many hours."[17]

CULTURAL SENSITIVITY AND GLOBAL LEADERSHIP SKILLS

Some managers are more effective at leading diverse groups than others. The traits and behaviors described in Chapters 2, 3, and 4 would equip a person to lead diverse groups. In addition, cultural sensitivity and certain specific global leadership skills are essential for inspiring people from cultures other than one's own. Although they reinforce each other, here we describe cultural sensitivity and global leadership skills separately.

Cultural Sensitivity

Leaders, as well as others, attempting to influence a person from a foreign country must be alert to possible cultural differences. Thus, the leader must be willing to acquire knowledge about local customs and learn to speak the native language at least passably. A cross-cultural leader must be patient, adaptable, flexible, and willing to listen and learn. All these characteristics are part of **cultural sensitivity,** an awareness of and a willingness to investigate the reasons why people of another culture act as they do. A person with cultural sensitivity will recognize certain nuances in customs that will help build better relationships with people in his or her adopted cultures. Refer back to Table 12-3 for a sampling of appropriate and less appropriate behaviors in a variety of countries. (These are suggestions, not absolute rules.)

Cultural sensitivity is also important because it helps a person become a **multicultural worker.** Such an individual is convinced that all cultures are equally good and enjoys learning about other cultures. Multicultural workers and leaders are usually people who have been exposed to more than one culture in childhood. (Refer back to Leadership Self-Assessment Quiz 12-2, about cross-cultural relations.) Being multicultural leads to being accepted by a person from another culture. According to Gunnar Beeth, a *multilingual* salesperson can explain the advantages of a product in other languages, but it takes a *multicultural* salesperson to motivate foreigners to buy.[18]

Sensitivity is the most important characteristic for leading people from other cultures because cultural stereotypes rarely provide entirely reliable guides for dealing with others. An American manager, for example, might expect Asian group members to accept his or her directives immediately because Asians are known to defer to authority. Nevertheless, an individual Asian might need considerable convincing before accepting authority. The link to leadership here is that cultural sensitivity helps one become a multicultural leader.

Problems of cultural misunderstanding that leaders should be aware of cluster in five areas.[19] *Language* differences create problems because U.S. workers (most of whom are monolingual) can become frustrated by coworkers' accents and limited English skills. Non-English speakers may feel that they do not fit well into the team. Differences in *religion* are the source of many misunderstandings. In many cultures, religion dominates life in ways that Americans find difficult to comprehend. *Work habits* vary enough across cultures to create friction and frustration. Employees in some cultures are unwilling to spend personal time on work. Problems can also stem from office rituals. An international manager noted, "Here in the UAE (United Arab Emirates), everyone has to shake hands and have tea or coffee first thing in the morning—which wastes a lot of time according to American standards."[20]

Women's roles may differ considerably from those in the United States. Women in many countries may not have the same independence or access to education and higher-level jobs as American women. Workers from various countries may therefore have difficulty accepting the authority of an American manager who is female. *Personal appearance and behavior* vary considerably across cultures. Grooming, office attire, eating habits, and nonverbal communication may deviate significantly from the U.S. standards. Many workers around the world may perceive American workers as overfriendly, aggressive, or rude.

Cultural sensitivity is enhanced by diversity training (or valuing differences training), and also by simply listening carefully and observing. A key principle is to be flexible when dealing with people from other cultures. An excellent example is the attitude of Zhang Xin Sheng, the mayor of Suzho, China, whose strategic goal is to make Westerners feel comfortable in his city. Zhang says in fluent English, "It's not necessary to use chopsticks. A knife and fork are okay."[21]

Global Leadership Skills

Global leadership skills are so important that they improve a company's reputation and contribute to a sustainable competitive advantage. (Global leadership skills are those especially important in dealing with workers from different companies.)[22] Excellent global leaders have a leadership style that generates superior corporate performance in terms of four criteria: (1) profitability and productivity, (2) continuity and efficiency, (3) commitment and morale, and (4) adaptability and innovation. *Behavioral complexity* is the term given to this ability to attain all four criteria of organizational performance. Excellent global leaders are able to understand complex issues from the four perspectives just mentioned and to achieve the right balance. For example, when a company is facing a mature market, it might be necessary to invest more effort into temporarily achieving innovation than into achieving high profits.

The Coca-Cola executive team under the leadership of the late Roberto Goizueta is a good example. The team exhibited behavioral complexity by enhancing the brand name and global reputation of Coca-Cola, and it ultimately contributed to its sustainable competitive advantage—even through occasional hard times.

Global leadership skills also include *stewardship*, because excellent global leaders act as responsible stewards of human and natural resources. By being responsible they promote simultaneously economic, social, biological, and ecological development; they act with social responsibility.

The global leader must tap into a deep, universal layer of human motivation to build loyalty, trust, and teamwork in different cultures. Universal needs are found among people in all cultures; for example, both Dominican Republicans and Inuit want to be part of a group. To get at universal needs (such as the desire for affiliation and exploration), the global leader must satisfy three metavalues: community, pleasure, and meaning.

1. *Community.* The leaders of successful multinational firms nurture good citizenship behavior, or the desire to serve the common good. In these organizations, teamwork is highly valued and workers are more concerned with the common good than their individual concerns.

2. *Pleasure.* In successful global organizations, fun or intrinsic motivation is an important energizer. Enjoying work by engaging in new activities is an essential part of the organizational culture. The fun, in turn, facilitates productivity and creativity.

3. *Meaning.* Meaningful work is another universal motivator. As one CEO said, "People will work for money but die for a cause." Employees prefer to feel that they are contributing something to society through their efforts.[23]

What is a global leader supposed to do to satisfy these three key metavalues? In general, he or she would have to engage in the type of leadership practices and behaviors described throughout this text. A more specific action plan would be to use team-development tactics, including empowerment, to promote a sense of community. Pleasure and meaning would derive from job enrichment, with its emphasis on challenging, interesting work.

A study was conducted of success factors in international management positions. Two traits were specifically related to success in conducting international business: sensitivity to cultural differences, and being culturally adventurous.[24] Cultural sensitivity has already been described. The adventurous aspect refers to a willingness to take chances and experiment with a new culture. A Mexican American from Phoenix, Arizona, who volunteered for a six-month assignment in Johannesburg, South Africa, would be culturally adventurous.

A confusing skill issue for many international workers is the importance of having a good command of a second language. Part of the confusion comes from the fact that English has become the standard language of business, technology, engineering, and science. For example, when Europeans from different countries assemble at a business conference, they communicate in English. However, when you are trying to influence a person from another culture, you are more influential if you can speak, read, and write well in his or her language. On the Internet, consumers are four times more likely to purchase from a web site written in their preferred language.[25] A command of a second language also enhances personal charisma.

LEADERSHIP INITIATIVES FOR ACHIEVING CULTURAL DIVERSITY

For organizations to value diversity, top management must be committed to it. The commitment is clearest when it is embedded in organizational strategy. A true diversity strategy should encourage all employees to contribute their unique talents, skills, and expertise to the organization's operations, independent of race, gender, ethnic background, and any other definable difference. In addition, leaders should take the initiative to ensure that dozens of activities are implemented to support the diversity strategy. Figure 14-3 lists the most frequent issues (such as race) around which diversity efforts are directed in large firms. Table 14-1 lists the five leadership initiatives for encouraging diversity that are discussed in the following text.

Hold Managers Accountable for Achieving Diversity

A high-impact diversity initiative is for top-level organizational leaders to hold managers accountable for diversity results at all levels. If managers are held accountable for behavior and business changes in the diversity arena, an organizational culture supportive of diversity will begin to develop. Accountability for diversity results when achieving diversity objectives is included in performance appraisals and when compensation is linked in part to achieving diversity results.[26]

Allstate Corporation exemplifies a firm that has worked hard to hold managers accountable for achieving cultural diversity within the firm. One of the methods used to gauge leadership effectiveness in managing diversity is an employee feedback survey. All 53,000 employees of Allstate are surveyed twice a year through a quarterly leadership measurement system (QLMS). Conducted online, the survey includes measures of satisfaction with both leadership and diversity accomplishment. (Table 14-2 presents the diversity index.) An Allstate human resource specialist has noted that satisfaction with diversity and company leadership are positively correlated.[27]

The Coca-Cola Company, which once faced lawsuits for racial discrimination, has become a diversity leader. One of the leadership initiatives to move the company forward was to tie 25 percent of each manager's compensation to how well he or she achieved specific diversity goals.[28]

Establish Minority Recruitment, Retention, and Mentoring Programs

An essential initiative for building a diverse work force is to recruit and retain members of the targeted minority group. Because recruiting talented members of

FIGURE 14-3   Diversity Initiatives at Major Business Firms

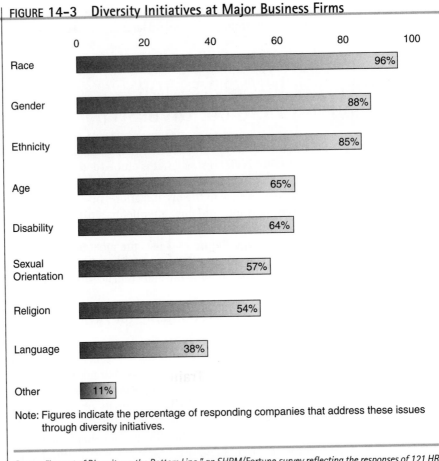

Note: Figures indicate the percentage of responding companies that address these issues through diversity initiatives.

Source: "Impact of Diversity on the Bottom Line," an SHRM/Fortune survey reflecting the responses of 121 HR professionals from 1,000 companies on Fortune magazine's list of the "100 Top Companies to Work For." Presented in Lin Grensing-Pophal, "Reaching for Diversity," HR Magazine, May 2002, p. 56. Human Resource Magazine by Lin Grensing-Pophal. Copyright 2002 by Society for Human Resource Mgmt. Reproduced with permission of Soc for Human Resource Mgmt, Alexandria, VA in the format Textbook via Copyright Clearance Center.

minority groups and women is competitive, careful human resources planning is required. Intel Corporation, for example, hired a consulting firm to compile a closely guarded list of the ten colleges and universities with the highest minority enrollments in circuitry design.[29]

Efforts at recruiting a culturally diverse work force must be supported by a leadership and management approach that leads to high retention. To increase retention rates, diversity consultants advise employers to strengthen cultural training programs, recognize employees' hidden skills and talents, and give diversity committees clout with top management.[30] Retaining employees is also a function of good leadership and management in general, such as offering workers challenging work, clear-cut goals, feedback, and valuable rewards for goal attainment.

TABLE 14–1   Leadership Initiatives for Achieving Cultural Diversity
1. Hold managers accountable for achieving diversity.
2. Establish minority recruitment, retention, and mentoring programs.
3. Conduct diversity training.
4. Encourage the development of employee networks.
5. Avoid group characteristics when hiring for person-organization fit.

Mentoring is a key initiative for retaining minority-group members, as well as for facilitating their advancement. In a survey of successful minority executives, 48 percent of the respondents said they had a role model who guided them toward early career goals. The role model or mentor was primarily of the same ethnic, racial, or cultural origin as the respondent. A specific finding was that successful minorities with supportive managers and coworkers have faster compensation growth and progress more rapidly in their firms. A sponsor of the survey said, "Minority executives believe that mentors are very helpful in advocating for upward mobility and teaching them how to navigate through the corporation."[31] More will be said about mentoring in Chapter 15 in relation to leadership development.

Conduct Diversity Training

Diversity training has become a widely used, though controversial, method for enhancing diversity within organizations. The purpose of **diversity training** is to bring about workplace harmony by teaching people how to get along better with diverse work associates. Quite often the program is aimed at minimizing open expressions of racism and sexism. All forms of diversity training center on

TABLE 14–2   The Diversity Index at Allstate
The diversity index at Allstate asks the following questions on employee surveys:
1. To what extent does our company deliver quality service to customers regardless of their ethnic background, etc.?
2. To what extent are you treated with respect and dignity at work?
3. To what extent does your immediate manager/team leader seek out and utilize diverse backgrounds and perspectives?
4. How often do you observe insensitive behavior at work, e.g., inappropriate comments or jokes?
5. To what extent do you work in an environment of trust?

Source: From Allstate Insurance Co. (www.allstate.com).

increasing people's awareness of and empathy for people who are different from themselves in some important way.

Training sessions in valuing differences focus on the ways in which men and women, or people of different races, reflect different values, attitudes, and cultural backgrounds. These sessions can vary from several hours to several days or longer. Sometimes the program is confrontational, sometimes not. As described by diversity consultant R. Roosevelt Thomas, Jr., the objectives of this training include one or more of the following:[32]

- Fostering awareness and acceptance of individual differences
- Helping participants understand their own feelings and attitudes about people who are "different"
- Exploring how differences might be tapped as assets in the workplace
- Enhancing work relations between people who are different from one another

An essential part of relating more effectively to diverse groups is to empathize with their point of view. To help training participants develop empathy, representatives of various groups explain their feelings related to workplace issues. Leadership Skill-Building Exercise 14-2 gives you the opportunity to engage in an effective diversity training exercise. A useful way of framing diversity training is to say that it represents a subset of interpersonal skills: relating effectively to coworkers who are different from you in some meaningful way adds to your interpersonal effectiveness.

Leadership Skill-Building Exercise 14-2

The Diversity Circle

Some diversity trainers use the *diversity circle* exercise to help workers appreciate diversity and overcome misperceptions. The exercise adapts well for classroom use. Form a group of about ten students. Arrange your chairs into a circle, and put one additional chair in the center of the circle. A "diverse" group member volunteers to sit in the center chair and become the first "awareness subject." Because most people are diverse in some way, most people are eligible to occupy the center chair.

The person in the center tells the others how he or she has felt about being diverse or different and how people have reacted to his or her diversity. For example, an Inuit described how fellow workers were hesitant to ask him out for a beer, worrying whether he could handle alcohol.

An equally effective alternative to the procedure just described is for each class member to come up in front of the class to describe a significant way in which he or she is different. After each class member has presented, a discussion might be held of observations and interpretations.

What lessons did you learn about interpersonal relations from this exercise that will help you be a more effective leader?

A frequently mentioned concern about diversity training is that it reinforces stereotypes about groups. Participants are informed about group differences, such as cultural values, and tactics might be suggested for coping with these differences—such as using more body language when relating to Latinos. A human resources specialist offers this whimsical example of stereotype reinforcement:[33]

> You gather your employees for training. You break up into groups of all women and all men for a problem-solving exercise. The goal is generally something completely unimportant—say, marketing a fictional product. After the groups present their plans, the diversity trainer notes how differently the two teams worked. The women's team is invariably "collaborative," "intuitive" and "creative." The men's team, conversely, is "competitive," "logical" and "linear." See how differently men and women work? Respect that.

Leaders of diversity training exercises are cautioned to guard against encouraging participants to be too confrontational and expressing too much hostility. Companies have found that when employees are too blunt during these sessions, it may be difficult to patch up interpersonal relations in the work group later on. Sometimes the diversity trainer encourages the group to engage in outrageous behavior, such as women sexually harassing men so the men "know what it feels like." Key themes of negative reactions to diversity training are charges of "political correctness" and "white-male bashing."

Based on a review of relevant studies and theory, Patricia L. Nemetz and Sandra L. Christensen concluded that diversity training is most likely to lead to behavioral and attitudinal change under three conditions: (1) participants have not yet committed to strong views of their own based on long-standing paradigms; (2) a conflicting informal influence (such as peer pressure) is not present; and (3) the organizational culture supports a well-defined ideal of multiculturalism.[34]

Encourage the Development of Employee Networks

Another leadership initiative toward recognizing cultural differences is to permit and encourage employees to form **employee network groups.** The network group is composed of employees throughout the company who affiliate on the basis of a group characteristic such as race, ethnicity, sex, sexual orientation, or physical ability status. Group members typically have similar interests and look to the groups as a way of sharing information about succeeding in the organization. Although some human resources specialists are concerned that network groups can lead to divisiveness, others believe they play a positive role. At 3M, employee network groups serve as advisers to business units. For example, the company's network group for employees with disabilities is often consulted by 3M product development groups. Company network groups also help their organizations recruit through such means as providing links to minority-group members in the community.[35]

Dan Sapper, a divisional quality leader at Eastman Kodak Company, illustrates the potential contribution of an employee network group to an employee's well-being. Sapper felt relatively isolated when he began employment at Kodak. To widen his contacts within the company, he became a charter member of Kodak's group for gay and lesbian employees. Sapper now chairs the group's board and says he wants to keep his leadership role to help employees who "might be in my shoes in the future." These are employees who "may be thinking of 'coming out'" or employees who "left something of themselves at the gate when they entered work."[36]

Avoid Group Characteristics When Hiring for Person-Organization Fit

An important consideration in employee recruitment and hiring is to find a good *person-organization fit*, the compatibility of the individual and the organization. The compatibility often centers on the extent to which a person's major work-related values and personality traits fit major elements of the organization culture. Following this idea, a person who is adventuresome and prone to risk taking would achieve highest performance and satisfaction where adventuresome behavior and risk taking are valued. Conversely, a methodical and conservative individual should join a slow-moving bureaucracy.

Many business firms today are investing time and effort into recruiting and hiring employees who show a good person-organization fit. A selection strategy of this type can lead to a cohesive and strong organizational culture. The danger, however, is that when employers focus too sharply on cultural fit in the hiring process, they might inadvertently discriminate against protected classes of workers. Specifically, the hiring manager might focus on superficial aspects of conformity to culture, such as physical appearance and which schools the candidates attended. Selecting candidates who look alike and act alike conflicts with a diversity strategy. Elaine Fox, a labor and employment attorney, cautions that "one of the biggest problems that can occur when hiring based on culture is if the culture you're comfortable with doesn't open the way for women and minorities."[37]

Leaders can take the initiative to guard against this problem. The way to circumvent it is to avoid using group characteristics (such as race, sex, ethnicity, or physical status) in assessing person-organization fit. The alternative is to focus on traits and behaviors, such as intelligence or ability to be a team player. Leaders at Microsoft emphasize hiring intelligent people only because bright people fit their culture best. Being intelligent is an individual difference rather than a group characteristic.

DEVELOPING THE MULTICULTURAL ORGANIZATION

The leadership initiatives just reviewed strongly contribute to valuing diversity. An even more comprehensive strategy is to establish a **multicultural organization.** Such a firm values cultural diversity and is willing to encourage and even capitalize on such diversity. Developing a multicultural organization helps achieve the benefits of valuing diversity described previously. In addition, the multicultural organization helps avoid problems stemming from diversity, such as increased turnover, interpersonal conflict, and communication breakdowns.

According to Taylor Cox, the multicultural organization has six key characteristics, all requiring effective leadership to achieve.[38] A seventh characteristic, having a culturally diverse group of leaders, also merits consideration.[39] These characteristics are shown in Figure 14-4 and summarized next.

1. *Creating pluralism.* In a pluralistic organization, both minority- and majority-group members are influential in creating behavioral norms, values, and policies. Diversity training is a major technique for achieving pluralism. Another useful technique is to encourage employees to be conversant in a second language spoken by many coworkers, customers, or both.

2. *Achieving leadership diversity.* To achieve a multicultural organization, firms must also practice **leadership diversity,** the presence of a culturally heterogeneous group of leaders. Many global firms have already achieved leadership diversity with respect to ethnicity. Sex is another key area for leadership diversity, with many organizations today having women in top

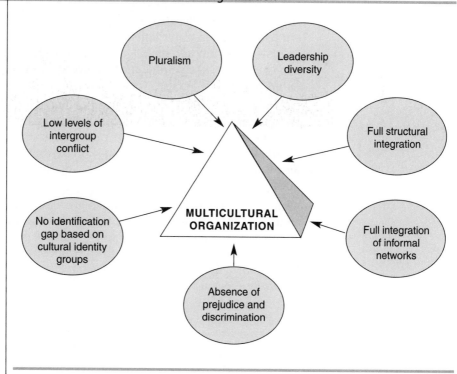

FIGURE 14-4   The Multicultural Organization

executive positions. An organization with true leadership diversity also has a heterogeneous group of leaders in such positions as supervisors, middle managers, and team leaders.

3. *Creating full structural integration.* The objective of full structural integration is a zero correlation between culture-group identity and job status—that is, no one should be assigned to a specific job just because of his or her ethnicity or gender. One approach to achieving full structural integration is to upgrade the education of minority-group members where needed. Affirmative action programs and career development programs also help achieve integration. The firm's performance appraisal and reward systems should reinforce the importance of effectively managing for diversity.

4. *Creating full integration of informal networks.* Minorities are often excluded from informal networks, making it difficult for them to achieve career advancement. Several things can help integrate informal networks: company-sponsored mentoring programs that target minorities; company-sponsored social events that minorities are encouraged to attend; and the creation of employee networks within an organization, provided they do not foster a "minority-versus-majority" attitude. Xerox Corp.'s Hispanic Professional Association is a positive example of a minority association within a company.

5. *Creating a bias-free organization.* Bias and prejudice create discrimination, so organizational efforts to reduce bias help prevent discrimination. Northern Telecom, for example, offers a sixteen-hour program designed to help employees identify and modify cultural biases and prejudices. Some companies create task forces that monitor organizational policy and practices for evidence of unfairness.

6. *Organizational identification.* In a multicultural organization, there is a zero correlation between the cultural identity group and levels of organizational identification. This would mean, for example, that Asians would identify as strongly with the organization as would white males. All the techniques mentioned in the other five steps help foster such strong identification.

7. *Minimizing intergroup conflict.* To achieve a multicultural organization, conflict must be at healthy levels. Taylor Cox believes that the most effective approach to minimizing conflict among cultural groups is to collect and share data about sensitive issues. Corning Incorporated, for example, collected data to help white males understand that diversity programs had not adversely affected their promotion rates.

SUMMARY

The modern leader must be multicultural because corporate success, profit, and growth depend increasingly on the management of a diverse work force. The ethical and social responsibility goals of leaders and their organizations include providing adequately for the members of the diverse work force.

Managing for diversity brings a competitive advantage to the firm in several ways. Turnover and absenteeism costs may be lower because minorities are more satisfied. Marketing can be improved because a representational work force facilitates selling products and services, and a good reputation for diversity management may attract customers. Companies with a favorable record in managing diversity are at an advantage in recruiting and retaining talented minority-group members. Managing diversity also helps unlock the potential for excellence among employees who might otherwise be overlooked. A heterogeneous work force may also offer an advantage in creativity and problem solving. Research at the United States Postal Service documents the many advantages of diversity.

To influence, motivate, and inspire culturally diverse people, the leader must be aware of overt and subtle cultural differences. Differences in cultural values help explain differences among people. Eight of these values are as follows: degree of individualism or collectivism; power distance (how much the power hierarchy is accepted); uncertainty avoidance; materialism versus concern for others; long-term versus short-term orientation; degree of formality; time orientation; and work orientation.

Cultural values influence leadership style as well as the behavior of other workers. For example, French managers believe in a class system. Another way to understand how culture influences leadership is to compare leadership styles across cultural groups. One study identified four common characteristics among managers, with European managers in general taking an intermediate position between U.S. and Japanese managers. The European managers were found to have a greater orientation toward people, to negotiate more within the company, to have greater skill in managing international diversity, and to be capable of managing between extremes of certain dimensions.

Understanding differences between cultural groups is important for applying motivational techniques. For example, when applying expectancy theory, recognize that cultures differ in how much control they perceive themselves to have over the environment. Also, appropriate rewards (those with high valence) have to be selected for each cultural group.

Cultural sensitivity is essential for inspiring people from different cultures. Part of this sensitivity is the leader's willingness to acquire knowledge about local customs and to learn to speak the native language. A person with cultural sensitivity will recognize certain nuances in customs that help him or her build better relationships with people from different cultures. Cultural misunderstandings tend to cluster in five key areas: language differences, religious differences, work habits, women's roles, and personal appearance and behavior.

Global leadership skills help improve a company's reputation and contribute to a sustainable competitive advantage. Behavioral complexity helps a leader attain high organizational performance. Stewardship is also important. To tap into universal needs, global leaders should satisfy three meta-values: community, pleasure, and meaning.

Top management commitment to valuing diversity is clearest when valuing diversity is embedded in organizational strategy. Specific leadership initiatives for valuing diversity can be divided into five categories: (1) hold managers accountable for diversity; (2) establish minority recruitment, retention, and mentoring programs;

(3) conduct diversity training; (4) encourage the development of employee networks; and (5) avoid group characteristics when hiring for person-organization fit.

A comprehensive strategy for valuing diversity is to establish a multicultural organization. Such a firm values cultural diversity and is willing to en-courage such diversity. A multicultural organization has seven key characteristics: pluralism; leadership diversity; full structural integration; full integration of informal networks; absence of prejudice and discrimination; no identification gap based on cultural identity groups; and low levels of intergroup conflict.

KEY TERMS

Multicultural leader

Individualism

Collectivism

Power distance

Uncertainty avoidance

Materialism

Concern for others

Long-term orientation

Short-term orientation

Formality

Informality

Urgent time orientation

Casual time orientation

Cultural sensitivity

Multicultural worker

Diversity training

Employee network groups

Multicultural organization

Leadership diversity

 ## GUIDELINES FOR ACTION AND SKILL DEVELOPMENT

When asked for concrete advice for managers who want to do an effective job at diversity management, the human resource manager of a multicultural firm said: "Any manager starting a Diversity Program should be ready to walk the talk before embarking or the effort will backfire. The walk should be seen in communication, compensation, recruiting, committee membership, promotions, advertising, and family and work/life initiatives. Also, setting up a strong support system within the social structure of the organization is critical to success."

The researchers who interviewed the manager add that using diversity solely as a public relations tool will not bring forth lasting organizational change aimed at achieving more inclusion.[40]

DISCUSSION QUESTIONS AND ACTIVITIES

1. Given that the U.S. work force is becoming increasingly Latino (or Hispanic), should managers all be required to speak and read Spanish?

2. How does the concept of diversity in organizations relate to *political correctness?*

3. An old refrain goes, "Why can't the cowboys and Indians just be friends?" Translate this line from a song into a diversity lesson for modern business leaders.

4. What actions might a leader take to demonstrate that his or her interest in diversity goes beyond rhetoric?

5. How does a culturally heterogeneous staff contribute to the leader's ability to make effective decisions?

6. In your own words, what is a *multicultural* leader?

7. Assume that an outstanding sales representative works for a company that considers it unethical to bribe officials to make a sale. The sales representative is about to close a major deal in a country where bribing is standard practice. Her commission will be $60,000 for a signed contract. What should the representative do if an official demands a $4,000 *gift* before closing the deal?

8. With so much business being conducted over the Internet, including email, why is it important to understand cross-cultural differences in values?

9. Suppose you are a team leader and one of your team members has a strong work ethic, based on his or her cultural values. Is it fair to assign this member much more work just because he or she is willing to work longer and harder than the other team members?

10. Find an article, book, or Internet reference, or interview a business leader to help answer the question "How can I prepare myself to become a multicultural leader?"

Leadership Case Problem A

Carlos Gutiérrez Intends to Make Kellogg Company Special Again

Note to the student: Information from Chapters 13 and 14 will be helpful in answering the case questions.

Four months into his president and CEO position at Kellogg Company, articulate and immaculately dressed Carlos M. Gutiérrez knew that he was not the most popular man in town. Battle Creek, Michigan is a community where the smell of cereal fills the air, and generations of families have worked for the company that W. K. Kellogg founded almost 100 years ago. Despite this tradition, the cereal maker announced in 1999 that it was closing most of its aging, hometown plant. The move cost about 550 jobs in a city of nearly 54,000. Reducing the plant size, however, saves the financially troubled company about $35 to $45 million per year.

Gutiérrez says he's doing what's best for Kellogg's long-term survival. But some have accused the company of putting profits ahead of the family values that the company has historically championed. The criticism hurt Gutiérrez, a career Kellogg worker who joined the company twenty-seven years ago. Visiting a local grocery store, he half joked that he hopes no one would recognize him. "I care very much about this company and community," Gutiérrez says. "These are painful but necessary decisions to make" (Associated Press, September 20, 1999).

Despite some local early criticism, Gutiérrez is a hero among Hispanics who follow business closely. "He is a role model for our Hispanic community," said Anna Escobedo Cabral, president and CEO of the Hispanic Association on Corporate Responsibility (HACR) (*Hispanic-Magazine.com*, March 2002). Gutiérrez is one of only fourteen Hispanics currently in the position of chairman, vice chairman, president, and/or CEO of a *Fortune* 1000 company, according to HACR.

Correcting Mistakes. The company has been hurt by competition from less expensive private-label cereals, as well as by demographic changes. Fewer Americans are eating cereal in the morning, preferring foods like bagels that can be eaten on the run. In the past decade, Kellogg's global market share in cereal has declined from 44 percent to 38 percent. Its sales and earnings were relatively flat for four years. And Gutiérrez doesn't hesitate to name Kellogg's own mistakes: uninspired advertising and an insular corporate culture that discouraged people from speaking about problems. Gutiérrez, the youngest CEO in the company's history, believes he is prepared to overcome the problems.

"I think what the board wanted to see was leadership from someone who can really put the institution first," he says. "They know I love this institution . . . but they also know I've demonstrated a willingness to change" (Associated Press).

Confronting change came early in life to Gutiérrez. The son of a Cuban pineapple planta-tion owner, he was six when Fidel Castro came to power and his family fled to Florida. The family started over, but never regained the influence and wealth it had in Cuba. Gutiérrez recalls his father telling him, "Success is about results. Anything else is a bit fluffy" (Associated Press). The advice would become Gutiérrez's mantra.

Gutiérrez went to work for Kellogg in 1975 as a sales representative in Mexico City. Since then, he has been supervisor of Latin American marketing services, general manager of Kellogg de Mexico, president and CEO of Kellogg Canada Inc., and president of Kellogg Asia-Pacific. He went to Michigan as an executive vice president of business development and, in June 1998, was named president and chief operating officer, and then chief executive officer ten months later.

Gutiérrez studied business administration at the Monterrey Institute of Technology in Quere-taro, Mexico. He says his Spanish-speaking skill and awareness of different cultures have come in handy in a company that distributes products in 160 countries. And while he is proud of his Cuban roots, he says he'd rather be known for his accomplishments than as "The Hispanic CEO."

Retired Kellogg CEO Bill LaMothe strongly endorses Gutiérrez. He says, "His whole career has been one of many successes in almost any situation we threw him into. He's a tremendously hard worker" (Associated Press).

Product Focus. Kellogg's backbone has been cereal. But Gutiérrez envisions a future for Kellogg as a "healthy snack" company, with convenience foods like Rice Krispie Treats squares and Nutri-Grain Twist bars making up half the company's sales by 2005. Analysts like the double-digit growth Kellogg is seeking in its convenience foods but caution against moving too quickly into unfamiliar territory—a concern that Gutiérrez appears to share. Gutiérrez's strategy is to reawaken dormant cereal sales while spending heavily to pump up new snack foods at a rapid pace, tailoring them to specific consumers around the globe.

With cereals, Gutiérrez is trying a bunch of marketing tricks. The company is selling iron-fortified Corn Flakes in Mexico and adding freeze-dried strawberries and raspberries to Special K Plus in France. "We have to reinvent cereal," Gutiérrez says (*www.global.forbes.com*).

To help improve the company outlook, Gutiérrez has cut costs, shuffled management, offered customers more discount coupons, and pressured Kellogg's scientists to develop new products. Recognizing that the initial recovery steps he took were not substantial enough, Gutiérrez did something more radical. He invested $4.4 billion to buy Keebler Foods, maker of Cheez-its and a variety of crackers and cookies. In a single act, the cereal veteran transformed Kellogg into a $10 billion snack-foods company. Kellogg now derives just 40 percent of its sales from breakfast cereals, down from 75 percent before the acquisition. The purchase of Keebler also helped quiet critics who think Kellogg is averse to taking risks.

Additional Changes.   Even before Gutiérrez became CEO, Kellogg was changing. The company had cut 500 white-collar jobs in its North American divisions as part of a reorganization while raising cereal prices by nearly 3 percent. Gutiérrez also made his own changes by picking outsiders to lead the company's North American and Asian-Pacific divisions. In addition, Gutiérrez decided to close the South Plant, the largest part of the company's historic Battle Creek factory. Some people believe this was a financially sound decision that no one else had the guts to make.

Gutiérrez says Kellogg must make profitable innovation its priority and points to the W. K. Kellogg Institute, a $75 million research facility built in 1997, to try to bring down some of the walls between food scientists and marketers. About one dozen new Kellogg products are released each year.

Gutiérrez has also initiated a program of one-on-one exchanges with important customers. This program helped resolve a dispute with Wal-Mart during which the retail giant had removed some Kellogg products from its stores because of supply problems.

Minority Suppliers.   Ensuring that Kellogg makes adequate use of minority-owned suppliers is a major Gutiérrez diversity initiative. Baldwin Richardson Foods Co. in small town Macedon, New York, makes the fruit filling for all of Kellogg Co.'s Nutri-Grain cereal bars. The contract, worth about $14 million annually, led to a 14,000-square-foot addition to the Baldwin Richardson plant and the hiring of twenty additional employees. Kellogg chose the Macedon firm after conducting a nationwide search for a company with the right fit. Baldwin Richardson, one of the largest African American–owned food companies in the United States, is now the largest minority supplier for Kellogg. "This event is symbolic of our commitment to increasing our relations with minority suppliers," Gutiérrez said (*Democrat and Chronicle*). He added that this strategy reflects the company's cultural values.

QUESTIONS

1. How will Gutiérrez's cross-cultural background assist him in achieving the growth goals established for Kellogg?

2. How can Kellogg use cultural diversity within the organization to help with product innovation?

3. Identify the business strategies that Gutiérrez is using to improve the future of the Kellogg Company.

4. What other business strategies do you recommend that might help Gutiérrez improve the future of the Kellogg Company?

5. Is Kellogg discriminating against majority suppliers in its attempt to build good relations with minority suppliers?

SOURCE: *"Making Kellogg Co. Special Again,"* Associated Press, September 20, 1999; Terrill Yue Jones, *"Thinking Outside the (Cereal) Box,"* www.global.

forbes.com/forbes/99/0614/0212026a.htm; *"Thinking Out of the Cereal Box,"* BusinessWeek, *January 15, 2001, pp. 54–55; Paloma Dalls, "Thinking Out of the Box: With Courage and Competence, Carlos Gutiérrez Guides Kellogg's,"* HispanicMagazine.com, *March 2002; Mary Chao, "Kellogg Boosts Macedon: Contract for Minority-Owned Foods Company Creates 20 Jobs,"* Rochester, New York, Democrat and Chronicle, *June 20, 2002;* www.Kelloggs.com.

Leadership Case Problem B

Ralph Lauren Seeks Racial Harmony

Fashion magnate Ralph Lauren says he first became aware of racial tension within his company after an incident in 1997 at a Long Island sportswear boutique. A regional manager with Polo Ralph Lauren Corporation dropped by the new Polo Sport store in anticipation of an inspection by an important visitor: Jerome Lauren, Ralph's older brother and the executive overseeing Polo menswear. The Roosevelt Field Mall where the boutique was located attracts a middle-class, racially integrated clientele. But apparently the regional manager was afraid that the store's ambiance was too "urban." He ordered two black and two Latino sales associates off the floor and back into the stock room so they wouldn't be visible to Mr. Lauren, according to Polo ex-officials. The sales associates followed orders, but they later hired a lawyer and threatened to sue Polo for discrimination. The company reached confidential settlements.

Ralph Lauren says he learned about the incident several weeks after it happened and "was just sick" about it. The regional manager, Greg Ladley, was ordered to undergo racial-relations training but wasn't fired. A company spokesman says that Ladley's recollection is that some sales associates working on inventory were asked to move to the stock room because they weren't "dressed appropriately."

After the episode, Ralph Lauren told subordinates, "We have to correct this. Let's make a change." But executives who worked at Polo at the time say their boss didn't make clear what changes he wanted.

Air of Exclusiveness. Polo, like some of its rivals, presents a multiracial face to the world, with black models in some of its ads and a following of young black consumers wearing its familiar logo of a horseman wielding a polo mallet. Yet internally, big fashion houses tend to exude an exclusiveness that is uninviting to many nonwhites. Few blacks or Latinos have penetrated the upper ranks of major clothes manufacturers and retailers.

In response to complaints that have flared up at Polo over the last five years, Lauren has met with lawyers, hired lieutenants to overhaul company personnel practices, and embraced diversity training. But he says he has left the details to others, since he is usually preoccupied with design work at his headquarters studio. "For me it has always been about the clothes," he says.

Polo is the standard-bearer for American fashion's fantasy of life-as-country-club. In much of its advertising and retailing, the company sells clothes, home furnishings, and cosmetics with images of old-money privilege: English country mansions, and prep school reunions and summers on Nantucket. British accents, even among American employees, aren't rare.

This aura of Anglo-Saxon elitism is the elaborate creation of Polo's founder, Ralph Lauren, 62 years old, who remade himself as he rose from modest roots in the Bronx to become the chairman and CEO of a fashion powerhouse. As teenagers in the late 1950s, he and his brother, Jerome, 67, Americanized their last name from the Russian *Lifshitz*. Polo retail supervisors routinely tell salespeople to think Hollywood. "Ralph is the director," the instruction goes, "and you are the actors, and we are here to make a movie." But some black and Latino employees say the movie seems to lack parts for them.

In August 2001, the Equal Employment Opportunity Commission (EEOC) cleared the way for a private discrimination suit by a pair of ex-Polo employees. The agency's letter of determination said that "testimony from several witnesses suggests that [Polo] managers sought to maintain a 'blond-hair-and-blue-eyes' image of employees, who often advanced the image over more qualified and experienced minority employees." Mitchell Kosh, Polo's senior vice president for human resources, says the agency "never asked us to do anything specific." The EEOC was impressed by "the programs and diversity initiatives we had put in place," he adds. Some argue that it isn't unusual for discrimination claims to crop up from time to time in a company the size of Polo, which has 10,000 employees worldwide.

Color-Blind? Lauren says he is color-blind when it comes to hiring talent. He frequently points out the wide visibility he has given Tyson Beckford, the striking, shaven-headed, black fashion model who has appeared in Polo ads since 1994. "Tyson is not just in jeans," Lauren says. "We put him in a pinstripe suit, in our best Purple Label brand. Tyson is in the annual report, in our advertisements on TV."

However, Polo declines to provide the de facto makeup of its work force or executive ranks. At least 3 black or Latino executives hold the rank of vice president, or higher, out of a total of more than 100. In 2001, Polo appointed the firm's minority director to its ten-member board: Joyce Brown, president of the Fashion Institute of Technology in New York.

Lauren says Polo "is a leader to do the right things to bring in the people who are the best in the industry." Some of his subordinates complain, however, that it is difficult to find black and Latino applicants with the credentials for design jobs coming out of the New York fashion schools where Polo usually recruits.

A Polo staffer recommended in 1998 that Lauren meet Lacey Moore, a 20-year-old African American from Brooklyn who had taken some college-level communications courses and had aspirations to be in the music business. Since high school, Moore had worn Polo Oxford shirts and knit tops with flashy gold chains and a hip-hop attitude: precisely the sort of hybrid image Lauren hoped would draw younger customers: "Lacey is edgy—he gets it," Mr. Lauren recalls thinking, snapping his fingers for effect. He hired the young man as a design assistant.

The new recruit's rap-influenced personal style and lingo confounded his coworkers. Moore felt isolated. He says he understood that in any competitive workplace "there are people who don't like you." But in Polo's cliquish and overwhelmingly white Madison Avenue headquarters, he says coworkers made it clear he wasn't welcome. "I kept getting this bad vibe," he says. He quit in 2000.

Shocked, Lauren telephoned Moore at home. "Lacey, I want you to come back," he recalls saying. After listening to Moore's complaints, Lauren says he made it clear to the young man's white coworkers, "I want you all to work this out." A couple of weeks later, Moore returned, but warily.

Advice and Pressure.   Polo has received advice and pressure on the race issue from a variety of outside counselors and advocates. A civil rights authority advised Lauren that achieving a truly diverse work force requires hiring more than a few black employees. A black activist minister met with Polo officials and helped some minority workers reach confidential settlements with the company.

Roger Farah was hired into the company as chief operating officer in 1999. Soon Farah introduced Polo's first formal policies for job postings and employee reviews, as well as a toll-free hot line for employee complaints. Two human resource managers were hired; one is Paul Campbell, an African American with experience in handling racial issues. Campbell soon became a company vice president. Lauren also hired diversity expert Roosevelt Thomas to conduct a series of two-day race relation seminars. A message communicated in these seminars, as well as by Lauren, is that to get along in the office, you don't have to like another person—or even abandon negative stereotypes of a person's ethnic group. But you have to be tolerant.

Today Moore (the young design assistant) says his colleagues seem friendlier. Campbell, the human resources vice president, has given Moore reassurance. "You feel there is someone looking out for you," says the young assistant, who helps prepare for fashion shows and consults on clothing design.

Lauren says he is paying more attention to what he sees at work. For example, he recalls that at a company Christmas party in 2000 he was surprised that a group of blacks and Latinos had congregated in a separate room. "Why is this happening?" he wondered. "What's not welcoming to those employees?" Lauren says he didn't approach his workers to ask them, however, and is still wondering about the answers to those questions.

QUESTIONS

1. To what extent is Ralph Lauren on the right track to developing a multicultural organization?

2. What further advice can you offer Lauren to achieve fuller workplace diversity at Polo?

3. Is the Christmas party incident a symptom of an organizational problem? Or were the black and Latino employees just behaving as they chose?

4. Does Ralph Lauren "get it" as a leader with respect to cultural diversity in the workplace?

SOURCE: *Adapted from Teri Agins, "Color Line: A Fashion House with an Elite Aura Wrestles with Race,"* The Wall Street Journal, *August 19, 2002, pp. A1, A9.*

INTERNET SKILL–BUILDING EXERCISE

Test Yourself for Hidden Bias

Apply the chapter concepts! Visit the Web and complete this Internet skill-building exercise to learn more about current leadership topics and trends.

In order to be an effective multicultural leader and to promote diversity, it is helpful to be aware of your own biases. Visit **www.tolerance.org/hidden_bias**, a web project of the Southern Poverty Law Center. The site gives you an opportunity to test yourself for hidden bias. Created by psychologists at Yale University and the University of Washington, this collection of Implicit Association Tests claims to measure unconscious bias in the following eleven areas: Native Americans; sexual orientation; six types of racial bias (Arab Muslims, weapons, black/white children, black/white adults, skin tone, Asian Americans); age bias, gender bias; body image bias. After reflecting on the results of these tests, what ideas did you gather that might help you be less biased in your dealings with other people in the workplace?

Leadership Development, Succession, and Followership

CHAPTER 15

Bayer Corporation has a pyramidal approach to developing leadership. At the base is an orientation program for every leader in the company. On the next layer is a partnership with the University of Notre Dame to teach management skills to staff members. At the top is a three-week session aimed at improving executives' interpersonal leadership styles.

"We all have a good handle on the technical aspects of being a good manager," says Barbara Stelluto, manager of executive education and leadership for Bayer Corporation. "But times like this of turmoil and change require not only that you have good management skills but also that you're able to bring the best out in other people . . . and actually have people take a stake in the organization and be responsible for making it a success."

The three-week session, held at the Center for Creative Leadership (CCL) in Greensboro, North Carolina, is restricted to about 250 managers at or near the vice-presidential level and above. It is spread out in single weeks over the course of six months. Leaders are expected to apply what they've learned to an actual project in the workplace. Their superiors are encouraged to support the new behaviors and help measure results, Stelluto says.

"What we do is ask them to pick two things that their new skills have impacted, and try to put dollars and percentages on the changes, if possible. But we'll also take anecdotal conformation of how they've changed; we're tickled to have even that."[1]

The leadership development program at Bayer illustrates several current representative approaches to developing leaders. Outside experts, such as Notre Dame management professors and CCL professional staff members, conduct development programs for Bayer managers. Also, as part of the development process, the new knowledge is applied to the job and an attempt is made to evaluate the outcomes of the program.

Programs to develop leadership are provided today to all levels of management, and sometimes also to staff professionals, because so many people are expected to exert leadership.[2] Aside from whatever value development programs have in enhancing leadership effectiveness, an organization's commitment to leadership development helps attract talented employees. William A. Cohen says, "Even those who leave the company spread the word after moving on."[3]

The previous chapters in this book, like the Bayer program, have been aimed at enhancing leadership effectiveness. Each chapter has included information and activities designed to develop leaders. This chapter describes the processes organizations use to develop present and future leaders. (It also describes how self-development can enhance leadership effectiveness.) Such activities and processes are typically referred to as leadership development, or management development.

In addition to describing various approaches to leadership development, this chapter also describes two related topics: succession and followership. Leadership succession is included here because an important part of leadership development is being groomed for promotion. We include a description of the qualities of effective group members (followers) because these people are the leaders of the future. The text concludes with a glimpse of the next generation of leaders.

DEVELOPMENT THROUGH SELF-AWARENESS AND SELF-DISCIPLINE

Leadership development is often perceived in terms of education and training, job experience, and coaching. Nevertheless, self-help also contributes heavily to developing leadership capabilities. Self-help takes many forms, including working on one's own to improve communication skills, to develop charisma, and to model effective leaders. Two major components of leadership self-development are self-awareness and self-discipline.

Leadership Development Through Self-Awareness

An important mechanism underlying self-development is **self-awareness,** insightfully processing feedback about oneself to improve personal effectiveness. For example, a managerial leader might observe that three key group members left her group over a six-month time span. The leader might defensively dismiss this fact with an analysis such as, "I guess we just don't pay well enough to keep good people." Her first analysis might be correct. With a self-awareness orientation, however, the leader would dig deeper for the reasons behind the turnover. She might ask herself, "Is there something in my leadership approach that creates turnover problems?" She might ask for exit-interview data to sharpen her perceptions about her leadership approach.

Chris Argyris has coined the terms *single-loop learning* and *double-loop learning* to differentiate between levels of self-awareness.[4] **Single-loop learning** occurs when learners seek minimum feedback that might substantially confront their basic ideas or actions. As in the example of the high-turnover leader, single-loop learners engage in defensive thinking and tend not to act on the clues they receive. Argyris offers the example of a thermostat that automatically turns on the heat whenever the room temperature drops below 68 degrees Fahrenheit (20 degrees Celsius).

Double-loop learning is an in-depth type of learning that occurs when people use feedback to confront the validity of the goal or the values implicit in the situation. The leader mentioned above was engaged in double-loop learning when she questioned the efficacy of her leadership approach. To achieve double-loop learning, one must minimize defensive thinking. Argyris explains that a double-loop learning thermostat would ask, "Why am I set at 68 degrees?" The thermostat would then ask whether another temperature might more economically achieve the goal of heating the room. Figure 15-1 illustrates the difference between single-loop and double-loop learning.

An important contribution of double-loop learning is that it enables the leader to learn and profit from setbacks. Interpreting the reason that a setback occurred may help the leader to do better the next time. Faced with a group in crisis, a leader might establish a vision of better days ahead for group members. The leader observes that the vision leads to no observable changes in performance

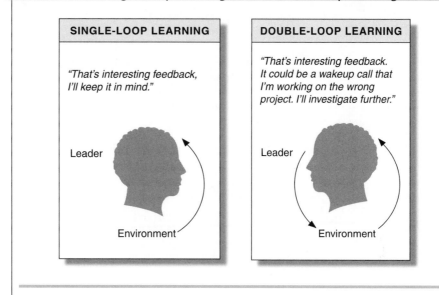

FIGURE 15-1   Single-Loop Learning Versus Double-Loop Learning

and behavior. Perhaps the group was not ready for a vision. In a comparable situation in the future, the leader might hold back on formulating a vision until the group is headed out of the crisis.

Leadership Development Through Self-Discipline

As with other types of personal development, leadership development requires considerable self-discipline. In the present context, **self-discipline** is mobilizing one's effort and energy to stay focused on attaining an important goal. Self-discipline is required for most forms of leadership development. Assume, for example, that a leader is convinced that active listening is an important leadership behavior. The leader reads about active listening and also attends a workshop on the subject. After the reading and workshop are completed, the leader will need to concentrate diligently in order to remember to listen actively. Self-discipline is particularly necessary because the pressures of everyday activities often divert a person's attention from personal development.

Self-discipline plays an important role in the continuous monitoring of one's behavior to ensure that needed self-development occurs. After one identifies a developmental need, it is necessary to periodically review whether one is making the necessary improvements. Assume that a person recognizes the developmental need to become a more colorful communicator as a way of enhancing charisma. The person would need self-discipline to make the conscious effort to communicate more colorfully when placed in an appropriate situation. Leadership Self-Assessment Quiz 15-1 contains an interpersonal skills checklist that will help you identify your own developmental needs related to interpersonal relationships.

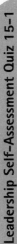

The Interpersonal Skills Checklist

INSTRUCTIONS   Below are a number of specific aspects of behavior that suggest that a person needs to improve his or her interpersonal skills related to leadership and influence. Check each statement that is generally true for you. You can add to the reliability of this exercise by asking one or two other people who know you well to rate you. Then compare your self-analysis with their analysis of you.

Developmental Needs and Areas for Improvement

1. I'm too shy and reserved. _____
2. I bully and intimidate others too frequently. _____
3. I tell others what they want to hear rather than emphasizing the truth. _____
4. I have trouble expressing my feelings. _____
5. I make negative comments about group members too readily. _____
6. Very few people pay attention to the ideas I contribute during a meeting. _____
7. My personality isn't colorful enough. _____
8. People find me boring. _____
9. I pay too little attention to the meaning behind what team members and coworkers are saying. _____
10. It is very difficult for me to criticize others. _____
11. I'm too serious most of the time. _____
12. I avoid controversy in dealing with others. _____
13. I don't get my point across well. _____
14. It's difficult for me to make small talk with others. _____
15. I boast too much about my accomplishments. _____
16. I strive too much for individual recognition instead of looking to credit the team. _____
17. Self-confidence is my weak point. _____
18. My spoken messages are too bland. _____
19. My written messages are too bland. _____

20. I relate poorly to people from cultures different from my own.   _____

21. I read people poorly.   _____

22. _____   _____

(Fill in your own statement.)

Now that you (and perhaps one or two others) have identified specific behaviors that may require change, draw up an action plan. Describe briefly a plan of attack for bringing about the change you hope to achieve for each statement that is checked. Ideas might come from personal development books or from human relations and leadership development workshops. After formulating an action plan, you will need self-discipline for its successful implementation. For example, if you checked, "People find me boring," you might want to expand your fund of knowledge by extensive reading and by talking to dynamic people. You will then need the self-discipline to continue your quest for ideas and to incorporate some of these ideas into your conversation.

Another approach to this exercise is for each student to choose one developmental need, combined with an action plan, that he or she is willing to share with others. Next, students present their developmental need and action plan to the rest of the class. After all students have presented, a class discussion is held about whatever observations and generalizations students have reached.

DEVELOPMENT THROUGH EDUCATION, EXPERIENCE, AND MENTORING

Much of leadership development takes place through means other than self-awareness and self-discipline or leadership development programs. Leadership is such a comprehensive process that almost any life activity can help people prepare for a leadership role. The president and owner of a large residential and commercial heating and cooling company made these comments:

> One of my best preparations for running a company came from my early days as a waiter. I learned how to handle difficult people and how to accept compliments. I also learned how to persuade people to make choices on the menu that gave them pleasure and increased the restaurant's profits. Those lessons are all important in running a $45 million business.

Three important life and work experiences that contribute to leadership development are education, experience as a leader, and mentoring. Let's look at the link between each of these three factors and leadership.

Education

Education generally refers to acquiring knowledge without concern about its immediate application. If a potential leader studies mathematics, the logical reasoning acquired might someday help him or her solve a complex problem facing the organization. As a result, the leader's stature is enhanced. Formal education is positively correlated with achieving managerial and leadership positions. Furthermore, there is a positive relationship between amount of formal education and level of leadership position attained.

Bernard M. Bass has concluded that educational credentials, demonstrated by degrees in engineering, law, or business administration, provide avenues to success in business leadership.[5] The correlation between education and leadership status, however, may not reflect causation. Many people get the opportunity to hold a business leadership position *only if* they have achieved a specified level of education. A more important issue than the statistical association between leadership and formal education is *how* education contributes to leadership effectiveness.

Most high-level leaders are intelligent, well-informed people who gather knowledge throughout their career. The knowledge that accrues from formal education and self-study provides them with information for innovative problem solving. Being intellectually alert also contributes to exerting influence through logical persuasion.

Experience

On-the-job experience is an obvious contributor to leadership effectiveness. Without experience, knowledge cannot readily be converted into skills. For example, you will need experience to put into practice the appropriate influence tactics you studied in Chapter 8. Leadership experience also helps build skills and insights that a person may not have formally studied.

Challenging Experiences.   Based on the research of Morgan W. McCall, the best experiences for leadership development are those that realistically challenge the manager. Creating an environment for development requires that an organization first rid itself of the belief in survival of the fittest. The goal of leadership development is to provide meaningful development opportunities, not to push managers to the point where they are most likely to fail.[6] An example of a stretch experience for many managers would be to be placed in charge of an organizational unit with low productivity and morale. The manager would need to apply many leadership skills to improve the situation. Table 15-1 lists a number of powerful learning experiences for developing leadership and managerial skills.

An important part of capitalizing on challenging experiences is for the leader/manager to be given leeway in choosing how to resolve the problem. An interview study of 80,000 managers in more than 400 companies concluded that the best way to develop talent is to define the right outcomes and then encourage each person to find his or her own route toward those outcomes.[7] A team leader, for example, might be told, "Increase productivity by 10 percent, while at the same time decreasing costs by 10 percent." The team leader would have the developmental opportunity of finding a solution to this challenge.

Sources of Experience. The two major developmental factors in any work situation are work associates and the task itself.[8] Work associates can help a person develop in myriad ways. An immediate superior can be a positive or negative model of effective leadership. You might observe how your boss skillfully confronts a quality problem during a staff meeting. You observe carefully and plan to use a similar technique when it becomes necessary for you to confront a problem

---

TABLE 15-1 Powerful Learning Experiences for Developing Leadership Skills

Research with managers has revealed fifteen types of powerful learning experiences that contribute to one's development as a leader and manager.

1. *Unfamiliar responsibilities.* Handling responsibilities that are new, quite different, or much broader than previous ones.

2. *Proving yourself.* The feeling of pressure to show others that one can get the job done.

3. *Developing new directions.* The responsibility for starting something new, implementing a reorganization, or responding to rapid changes in the business environment.

4. *Inherited problems.* Fixing problems created by a former manager or being handed the responsibility for problem employees.

5. *Downsizing decisions.* Making decisions about shutting down operations or reducing staff.

6. *Dealing with problem employees.* The group members lack adequate experience, are incompetent, or are resistant.

7. *Facing high stakes.* Being faced with tight deadlines, pressure from senior management, high visibility, and responsibility for success and failure.

8. *Managing business complexity.* Having a job with large scope, responsibilities for multiple functions, groups, products, customers, or markets.

9. *Role overload.* The size of the job requires a large investment of time and energy.

10. *Handling external pressure.* Being forced to deal with external factors that affect the business, such as negotiating with unions or government agencies, or coping with serious community problems.

11. *Having to exert influence without authority.* To accomplish the job it is necessary to influence peers, higher management, external parties, or other key people over whom one has no formal control.

12. *Adverse business conditions.* The business unit faces a drop in revenues or a drastic budget cut.

13. *Lack of top management support.* Senior management is reluctant to provide direction, support, or resources for the manager's major work activities, or for a new project.

14. *Lack of personal support.* The manager is excluded from key networks and receives little encouragement from others about the work activities.

15. *Difficult boss.* A personality clash with the boss is evident, or he or she is incompetent.

Source: Adapted from C. McCauley, M. Ruderman, P. Ohlott and J. Morrow, "Assessing the Development Components of Managerial Jobs," Journal of Applied Psychology 79, 4(1994), 544–560. Copyright © 1994 by the American Psychological Association. Adapted with permission.

with a group. In contrast, assume that your boss's confrontational approach back-fires and the group becomes defensive and recalcitrant. You have learned how *not* to confront. Members of upper management, peers, and reporting staff can also help a worker profit from experience. For example, by trial and error the worker might learn which type of praise is best for influencing others.

Work-related tasks can also contribute to leadership development because part of a leader's role is to be an effective and innovative problem solver. The tasks that do most to foster development are those that are more complex and ambiguous than a person has faced previously. Starting a new activity for a firm, such as establishing a dealer network, exemplifies a developmental experience.

Another way of obtaining experience helpful for development is to learn from the wisdom of leaders who have been through challenges. Often this type of experience sharing comes through mentoring, discussed below. The CEO Academy, part of a club for chief executives, represents a formal approach to experience sharing. One of the academy's activities is a one-day immersion course administered by a group of longtime chief executives and a few corporate critics and business professors. The academy originated as a way for recently appointed CEOs to learn the perils of life in the executive suite and for experienced executives to discuss the challenges of being a CEO before a receptive audience. So what type of advice do these CEOs receive for the $10,000 fee for the one-day seminar? Dennis Kozlowski, the former CEO of superconglomerate Tyco International Ltd., told the group that once a deal closes, "you have a very short window to create change, so speed is of the essence."[9] (Unrelated to his ability to manage acquisitions, Kozlowski was forced out of office in 2002 because he was charged with income tax evasion and stealing millions of dollars from the company.)

Broad Experience.   Many aspects of leadership are situational. A sound approach to improving leadership effectiveness is therefore to gain managerial experience in different settings. An aspirant to executive leadership is well advised to gain management experience in at least two different organizational functions, such as marketing and operations. Daphna F. Raskas and Donald C. Hambrick use the term *multifunctional managerial development* to refer to the process of achieving broad experience. **Multifunctional managerial development** is an organization's intentional efforts to enhance the effectiveness of managers by giving them experience in multiple functions within the organization.[10]

As shown in Figure 15-2, the most modest level of commitment to multifunctional management development would be for managers merely to study other functions. Studying other functions, however, is quite useful because it provides a person with the necessary background to profit from experience. Participation in multifunctional task forces indicates more commitment to the acquisition of breadth.

The highest level of commitment is complete mobility across functions. Hewlett-Packard represents this approach through its *career maze* program. For example, an employee may begin in product design, and then move on to assignments in marketing, manufacturing, customer service, purchasing, human re-

---

FIGURE 15-2 Continuum of Practical Options for Multifunctional Managerial Development

High commitment

- Complete mobility across functions, i.e., "career maze"

- Temporary (six-month to two-year) assignments outside the person's "home function"

- Brief, orientational rotation through functions

- Exposure to other functions on task forces project teams

- Classroom education about other functions

Low commitment

Source: "Continuum of Practical Options for Multifunctional Managerial Development." Reprinted from Organizational Dynamics, *Autumn 1992, Copyright © 1992, with permission from Elsevier Science.*

---

sources, and so forth. Employees judged to have leadership potential are the most likely to be offered the career maze.

Achieving broad experience fits well with the current emphasis on growth through learning new skills rather than a preoccupation with vertical mobility. A successful manufacturing company studied by Michael Beer, Russell Eisenstadt, and Bert Spector gives its most promising managers lateral transfers, including experience in the human resources department. The company also uses its most innovative manufacturing facilities as "hothouses" for developing managers. The innovative units become leadership development centers for the company.[11]

The accompanying Leader in Action profile describes a highly placed leader who has benefited from multifunctional management development.

Pivotal Life Experiences. Another perspective on how experience contributes to leadership effectiveness is that certain pivotal events—often occurring early in life—help people recognize a capacity to make things happen and gain the support of others. These transformational experiences vary from being mentored to climbing a mountain or losing an election. The pivotal experience might be an event or a relationship, sad or joyous, but it is always a powerful process of learning and adaptation. A case in point is Jack Kahl, the founder and former CEO of the company that makes the Duck® brand of duct tape. He remarks that he learned his most crucial leadership experience from his mother when he was seven years old. Kahl's father had fallen ill with tuberculosis, and his mother informed her children that they would have to work as a team to hold the family together financially and emotionally. Kahl started a newspaper route, quickly learning the importance of doing the job well and pleasing customers.[12]

Leader in Action

Linda Sanford of IBM, Cross-Developed Leadership Star

Linda Sanford began her career at IBM Corp. in a job and position that no longer exist. Sanford's task twenty-eight years ago was to develop simulation models to predict how much pounding IBM Selectric typewriters could take. Years later, the rising star took on a job of much broader scale: to help resurrect the company's mainframe computer division, which was once at the height of technology and a money-maker that could not be rivaled by the competition.

Today, 50 year old Sanford is one of the top four highest-ranking female executives at IBM, and the highest-ranking technical woman. She is Senior Vice President of Enterprise on Demand Transformation. Sanford is responsible for the internal business transformation of IBM to an on-demand business. The goal of e-business on demand is to allow customers to pay for computing power only as they use it, following the model of a utility company. E-business on demand has the potential of reducing the information technology costs of companies by fifty percent.

Several years ago, Sanford held the position of general manager of global industries. This business unit deals with IBM's large customers, who generate about 70 percent of the company's revenues. She then was appointed the Senior Vice President and Group Executive of IBM Storage Systems Group, the unit that develops the company's Enterprise Storage Server.

Sanford's blend of warmth and humor, along with her technological and marketing savvy, have brought her fans within IBM as well as from outside the company. Fellow IBM executives say she has a knack for getting the job done while making few enemies. Analysts say she's very good at dividing her focus among the key qualities that make for good business, including product development and sales growth.

Sanford graduated from St. John's University where she majored in mathematics, and she received a graduate degree from Rensselaer Polytechnic Institute in operations research. IBM recruited Sanford while she was in school, and she joined the company in August 1975. Sanford recalled, with a smile, standing out on her first day on the job. She had come from New York, where miniskirts had been the major fashion but had since been replaced by longer skirts. In Lexington, Kentucky, miniskirts were still the trend. "I walked into the cafeteria, and everyone looked at me because I was the only one in a long skirt," she remembers (*Gannet News Service*).

Sanford spent a year in Lexington, then ten years in Boulder, Colorado, where one of the products she worked on was IBM's first color inkjet printer. She began to rise up the corporate ladder and was selected as one of several assistants to John F. Akers, IBM's chief executive at the time. Because of her potential, Sanford was invited to participate in a variety of IBM-sponsored management and leadership development programs. When Sanford joined the mainframe division in 1995, midrange computers—smaller, cheaper, and more versatile—had suddenly emerged, and IBM's mainframe business was under siege. Sanford, however, knew that mainframes were still essential to business firms, so she set out to fix them.

Sanford lead a group who performed a revolutionary overhaul of mainframes, which resulted in smaller, sleeker models that helped bring back the demand for them. (E-commerce and the Internet are two other factors that have revitalized this demand.) As chief of Global Services, Sanford held IBM's top sales job, but she had never been part of the sales force. Her expertise still lies in development.

SOURCE: *Phil Waga, "Savvy IBM Star Leading Force of 17,000," Gannett News Service, November 14, 1999; Nicola Godfrey, "Key Player,"Working Woman, December/January 2000, pp. 32-34; Spencer E. Ante, "The New Blue,"BusinessWeek, March 17, 2003, pp. 80-88; "Women Who Inspire Us: Linda Sanford,"* www. girlgeeks.org/innergeek/inspiringwomen/Sanford. shtml, *accessed March 20, 2003.*

QUESTIONS

1. How does Sanford's case history illustrate multifunctional management development?

2. Explain whether Sanford appears to be on the road to becoming a CEO of a technology company?

3. In what way does Sanford demonstrate both hard skills and soft skills?

Mentoring

Another experience-based way to develop leadership capability is to be coached by an experienced, knowledgeable leader. Quite often this person is a **mentor,** a more experienced person who develops a protégé's abilities through tutoring, coaching, guidance, and emotional support. The mentor, a trusted counselor and guide, is typically a person's manager. However, a mentor can also be a staff professional or coworker. An emotional tie exists between the protégé (or mentee) and the mentor.

Informal Versus Formal Mentoring.   Mentoring is traditionally thought of as an informal relationship based on compatibility or spark between two personalities. In reality it is widespread practice for employers to formally assign a mentor to a new employee to help him or her adjust well to the organization and to succeed. Belle Rose Ragins and John L. Cotton conducted a study comparing the effectiveness of informal versus formal mentoring programs for men and women.[13] Three occupations were studied: engineering (male dominated); social work (female dominated); and journalism (gender integrated). Formal mentoring programs were used in all three of these occupations.

Protégés with informal mentors received greater benefits than protégés with formal mentors. Informal mentors were also perceived as more effective. The protégés with informal mentors reported that their mentors provided more career development and psychological and social support than protégés with formal mentors. Protégés with informal mentors also reported higher incomes. A possible explanation for these findings is that people who are able to attract their own mentor are more career-driven and have the type of interpersonal skills that help one earn a higher income. Three key human resource elements are associated with a successful mentoring program. First, the human resource department in conjunction with senior management needs to set the goals of the program and base its design on those goals. Second, the program administrators must carefully pair the mentors and protégés, set realistic expectations for both parties, and follow up with the pairs to insure that the arrangement is satisfactory. Third, top management must be committed to the program.[14] An example of a realistic goal for a given protégé might be to develop better interpersonal and strategic leadership skills.

A recently popular approach to mentoring is **shadowing,** or directly observing the work activities of the mentor by following the person around for a stated period of time, such as one day per month. The protégé might be invited to strategy meetings, visits with key customers, discussions with union leaders, and the like. The protégé makes observations about how the mentor handles situations, and a debriefing session might be held to discuss how and why certain tactics were used.

Impact on Leadership.   Mentors enhance the career of protégés in many ways, such as by recommending them for promotion and helping them establish valuable contacts. A survey of large companies found that 96 percent of executives credited mentoring as an important developmental method, and 75 percent said mentoring played a key role in their career success.[15] Mentoring is also mentioned frequently as an effective method of helping minorities advance. "For women and people of color, mentoring provides them access to leadership and power that they'd normally be shut out of," says mentoring specialist Belle Rose Ragins.[16] Of interest here is how (the process by which) a mentor can help you become a better leader. The mentor can serve as a model of effective (or sometimes ineffective) leadership.

A high level of mentor involvement is to coach the apprentice on how he or she handles certain leadership assignments. The mentor is usually not physically present when the protégé is practicing leadership. A substitute is for the protégé to recap a leadership situation and ask for a critique. Wendy Lopez, who is the data processing manager for a payroll services firm, recounts a mentoring session with her boss about a leadership incident:

> I explained to Max [her mentor and the vice president of administration] that I had some trouble motivating my supervisors to pitch in with weekend work. We had received a surge of new clients because many firms had decided to downsize their own payroll departments. Our group was having trouble adjusting to the new workload. Instead of operations running smoothly, things were a little spastic. Although I tried to explain the importance of getting out the work, the supervisors were still dragging their heels a little.
>
> Max reviewed the incident with me. He told me that I might have helped the supervisors take a broader view of what this new business meant to the firm. Max felt I didn't communicate clearly enough how the future of our firm was at stake. He also suggested that I should have been more specific about how pitching in during an emergency would benefit the supervisors financially.
>
> With Max's coaching behind me, I did a much better job of enlisting cooperation the next time an emergency surfaced.

To help you capitalize on experience as a source of leadership development, do Leadership Skill-Building Exercise 15-1.

Maintaining a Personal Leadership Journal

A potentially important aid in your development as a leader is to maintain a journal or diary of your leadership experiences. Make a journal entry within twenty-four hours after you carried out a significant leadership action, or failed to do so when the opportunity arose. You will therefore have entries dealing with leadership opportunities both capitalized upon and missed. An example: "A few of my neighbors were complaining about exhaust fumes from a restaurant blowing directly into our apartments. I volunteered to take up the problem with the restaurant manager and the town board." Or, in contrast: "A few of my neighbors . . . apartments. I thought to myself that someone else should take care of the problem. My time is too valuable."

Also include in your journal such entries as feedback you receive on your leadership ability, leadership traits you appear to be developing, key leadership concepts you learn about, and leadership books and articles you intend to read. You might also want to record observations about significant acts of leadership or leadership blunders that you have observed in others, either firsthand or through the media.

Review your journal monthly, and make note of any progress you think you have made in developing your leadership skills. Also consider preparing a graph of your leadership skill development. The vertical axis can represent skill level on a 1-to-100 scale, and the horizontal axis might be divided into time intervals, such as calendar quarters.

LEADERSHIP DEVELOPMENT PROGRAMS

A time-honored strategy for developing prospective, new, and practicing leaders is to enroll prospective leaders in leadership development programs. These programs typically focus on such topics as personal growth, leadership style, strategy formulation, influence, motivation, and persuasive communication. Outdoor and wilderness training, as described in Chapter 9, is one important type of leadership training. Many management development programs are also aimed at leadership development. The difference, however, is that management development programs offer courses that cover hundreds of topics within the functions of planning, organizing, controlling, and leading. Table 15-2 lists a sample of leadership development programs.

A term in vogue to cover company activities geared toward leadership and management development, as well as other forms of high-level training, is *corporate university*. As noted by HRevents™, corporate universities come in many forms. They range from training departments with a new sign on the door to massive organizations that strategically propel their corporate parent[17] (such as the

A Sampling of Leadership Development Programs
TABLE 15-2   Offered by Universities and Training and Development Firms
The Executive Program (four-week program for senior executives involved in the strategic management of their firms)
Executive Effectiveness Course
Strategic Business Leadership: Creating and Delivering Value
Business Ethics for the Professional Manager
The Disney Approach to Leadership Excellence
Leading Change and Innovation
Leadership Training for Managers
Leadership, Women
Implementing Successful Organizational Change
Managing People for Maximum Performance
The Essentials of Executive Decision Making
Enhancing Executive Influence
Outdoor Training

Note: Organizations offering such seminars and courses are the Wharton School of the University of Pennsylvania, Cornell University School of Industrial and Labor Relations, University of Michigan Business School, University of Chicago Graduate School of Business, Center for Creative Leadership, Center for Management Research, American Management Association, Dale Carnegie Training, and the Disney Institute.

GE facility in Crotonville, New York). Corporate universities use internal specialists as well as outside experts to conduct the training and development sessions.

Key Characteristics of a Leadership Development Program

Developing and training leaders is far more complex than merely sending aspiring leaders to a one-week seminar. The leadership development program has to be appropriately sponsored, carefully designed, and professionally executed. Presented next are the key things that a successful leadership development program should do.[18]

1. *Begin by carefully selecting participants for the program.* An axiom of training is that intelligent and well-motivated trainees profit the most from training. The situation is the same with leadership development. The program will produce more favorable outcomes if the participants have strong leadership traits such as intelligence, motivation, and charisma.

2. *Involve executives and secure their sponsorship.* For a leadership development program to receive high priority, top executives must set the program's tone and objectives. They should also sponsor implementation, as is done with the four-week executive program at General Electric.

3. *Gear the development program to participants' level of management.* Managers at different levels should receive different types of leadership development and training. General managers might have a workshop on vision setting and organizational change, whereas motivation and coaching might be better for middle managers and first-level managers.

4. *Address current and future organizational needs.* A company heavily engaged in globalization would provide training on global leadership skills, such as developing the multicultural organization and adapting to rapid change.

5. *Use an appropriate model or theory.* Leadership skills are often instilled better when they are taught in a solid conceptual framework. Several of the models or theories presented in this text are often used in leadership development, including the situational leadership model and the normative decision model.

6. *Give ongoing reinforcement and emotional support.* After a leadership or management development seminar or program is launched, some follow-up is advised to help reinforce the new learning. Follow-up formats include luncheon meetings, telephone conferences, and email exchanges. Network groups can provide emotional support for continuing the new learning and for discussing challenges facing the leader/manager. For example, a participant might follow up with other members from the development program as to how well they are thinking strategically on a regular basis.

7. *Support individual improvement with diagnostic tools.* Many leadership development programs include self-evaluation using assessment instruments like the ones presented throughout this text. In addition to self-evaluation, other people who know the participant also complete the forms. (You will recall the description of 360-degree feedback in Chapter 4.)

8. *Ensure practical and relevant content.* Many leadership development programs present participants with problems closely related to those found on the job. A widespread practice in such programs is for an instructor to coordinate with an employer representative so the participants work on a company-relevant problem.

9. *Emphasize interpersonal relationships and teamwork.* Many leadership development programs emphasize team building and outdoor training because leaders at every level must have good interpersonal and teamwork skills.

10. *Conclude with individual action plans.* In a high-quality leadership program, attendees must develop personalized action plans for improvement (such as those requested in Leadership Skill-Building Exercise 15-1). At Motorola, participants prepare a self-letter describing personal changes to which they are willing to commit.

Types of Leadership Development Programs

In practice, the various programs for developing leaders often overlap. For ease of comprehension, we divide these programs into six categories: feedback-intensive programs, and those based on skills, conceptual knowledge, personal growth, socialization, and action learning.

Feedback–Intensive Programs.   As implied at many places in this text, an important vehicle for developing as a leader is to obtain feedback on various aspects of your behavior. A **feedback-intensive development program** helps leaders develop by seeing more clearly their patterns of behaviors, the reasons for such behaviors, and the impact of these behaviors and attitudes on their effectiveness. Such a program also helps leaders or potential leaders find more constructive ways of achieving their goals.

Feedback-intensive programs combine and balance three key elements of a developmental experience: assessment, challenge, and support. The program typically takes place in a classroom or conference room. At the Center for Creative Leadership, the program lasts six days. Assessment and feedback are almost constant, immersing participants in rich data about themselves and how they interact with others.[19] The amount and intensity of the feedback create intense challenges. Among them are the need to look inward, the discomfort of being observed and rated while engaging in such tasks as group problem solving, and encounters with new ideas. An example of uncomfortable feedback is being told that you are a poor delegator because you basically distrust most people.

To help participants cope with these challenges, the program provides intensive support from both the program staff and other participants. When the program goes well, a good team spirit develops among participants. Support continues after the program with follow-up letters by the staff and continued contact with program participants.

Feedback in the program comes from many sources, including interviews with the participant's boss, personality tests, leadership tests, and videotapings. Ratings by others, including 360-degree surveys, are included. The feedback is supposed to result in increased self-awareness. Combined with an explanation of the findings, the feedback often results in behavior change. For example, the person cited above may become more trustful of others and consequently a better delegator. Helping participants understand why they engage in certain behaviors contributes to the behavior change.

Skill-Based Programs.   Skill training in leadership development involves acquiring abilities and techniques that can be converted into action. Acquiring knowledge precedes acquiring skills, but in skill-based training the emphasis is on learning how to apply knowledge. A typical example would be for a manager to develop coaching skills so he or she can be a more effective face-to-face leader. Skills training, in short, involves a considerable element of "how to."

Five different methods are often used in skill-based leadership training: lecture, case study, role play, behavioral role modeling, and simulations. Since the first three methods are quite familiar, only the last two are described here. *Behavioral role modeling* is an extension of role playing and is based on social learning theory. You first observe a model of appropriate behavior, and then you role-play the behavior and gather feedback. A person might observe a video of a trainer giving positive reinforcement, then role-play giving positive reinforcement. Finally, the classroom trainer and the other participants would offer feedback on performance.

Simulations give participants the opportunity to work on a problem that simulates a real organization. In a typical simulation participants receive a hard copy or computerized packet of information about a fictitious company. The participants are given details such as the organization chart, the company's financial status, descriptions of the various departments, and key problems facing the organization and/or organizational units. Participants then play the roles of company leaders and devise solutions to the problems. During the debriefing, participants receive feedback on the content of their solutions to problems and the methods they used. The group might be told, for example, "Your decision to form a strategic alliance was pretty good, but I would have liked to have seen more group decision making."

Conceptual Knowledge Programs. A standard university approach to leadership development is to equip people with a conceptual understanding of leadership. The concepts are typically supplemented by experiential activities such as role playing and cases. Nonuniversity learning firms such as the American Management Association and the Brookings Institution also offer conceptually based leadership development programs. Conceptual knowledge is very important because it alerts the leader to information that will make a difference in leadership. For example, if a person studies how a leader brings about transformations, he or she can put these ideas into practice. Table 15-2 presents examples of the types of conceptual knowledge contained in leadership development programs.

Personal Growth Programs. Leadership development programs that focus on personal growth assume that leaders are deeply in touch with their personal dreams and talents and that they will act to fulfill them. Therefore, if people can get in touch with their inner desires and fulfill them, they will become leaders. A tacit assumption in personal-growth training programs is that leadership is almost a calling.

The Institute for Women's Leadership exemplifies a private firm that offers a program of leadership development through personal growth. (The program is also available to men.) The director, Rayona Sharpnack, guides participants through a process of unlearning what they assume to be true about what they can (or cannot) accomplish. Sharpnack emphasizes that for most people leadership is what people need to know or do, whereas her approach is learning *who you need to be*. It is the being part of leadership that facilitates breakthroughs in what people do and learn. The emphasis is on learning to perceive events differently, such as coming to believe that one can bring about key changes in the firm. Changing perception is also like double-loop learning because you might challenge the validity of what you are doing. A leader might ask, "Is giving out $750 watches to employees an effective form of recognition? Or maybe a word of appreciation here and there would be more effective?"

A financial vice present who attended a Women's Leadership seminar later commented, "You walk in with a challenge, some mountain that you don't think you can climb. When you walk out, you've built a *higher* mountain that you know you *can* climb."[20]

Socialization Programs.   From the company standpoint, an essential type of leadership development program emphasizes socializing—becoming acclimated to and accepting the company vision and values. Senior executives make presentations in these programs because they serve as role models who thoroughly understand the vision and values participants are expected to perpetuate.[21] Many of the other types of programs presented so far also include a segment on socialization, particularly in the kick-off session. Quite frequently the chief executive makes a presentation of the company's vision and values. An embarrassing problem in recent years is that many of these role models (such as Jack Welch, the legendary chief executive of GE) have later been accused of receiving questionable forms of compensation from the company or of approving unsavory accounting practices.

Action Learning Programs.   A directly practical approach to leadership development is for leaders and potential leaders to work together in groups to solve organizational problems outside of their usual sphere of influence. You will recall that action learning is part of the learning organization, as described in Chapter 13. Much of the development relates to problem solving and creativity, yet collaborating with a new set of people from your firm can also enhance interpersonal skills.

A final point about leadership development is that the process continues to evolve. According to executive development specialist Robert M. Fulmer, the kind of learning that results in competitive advantage will not be limited by time, space, or matter (such as notebooks and physical facilities). Leadership developers will often visit company sites, and some learning will take place through distance learning and virtual classrooms. Development programs can be delivered anytime, anyplace. The new paradigm will be focused on learning that is action-oriented, meaning that the emphasis is on immediate application. Learning has also become a lifelong process, whereby global partners work collectively to produce a positive, profitable future for all.[22]

EVALUATION OF LEADERSHIP DEVELOPMENT EFFORTS

A comprehensive approach to leadership development would include a rigorous evaluation of the consequences of having participated in a developmental experience. Executives and human resource professionals would ask such tough questions as the following:

Do people who receive mentoring actually become more effective leaders?

Do leaders who attend outdoor training become better team leaders than (1) those who do not attend the training, or (2) those whose "team development" consists of playing softball with the office gang?

Does the Advanced Management Program at Harvard improve the decision-making skills of participants?

The evaluation of training and development programs is a comprehensive topic that includes such considerations as the design of experiments and the development of accurate outcome measures.[23] Here we examine the traditional approach to evaluating training and development outcomes and an approach that is better adapted to leadership development.

The Traditional Approach to Evaluation

The traditional approach to the evaluation of leadership training and development programs would first specify the program objectives. After training was completed, measurements would be made of the extent to which those objectives were met. Two sets of outcomes are especially relevant. First, an assessment is made of the extent to which the participants acquired new skills during the program. For example, did the seminar participants acquire new skills in giving supportive feedback? Second, an assessment is made of whether the organization has become more effective as a result of this new skill acquisition. Did the bottom line improve because of the new skills? For example, has supportive feedback by leaders resulted in higher quality and profits?

Human resource specialists will often ask participants if the development program helped them perform their jobs better and how. Unit heads should be asked if the training program helped them achieve their units' business goals.[24] Development specialists at the Boeing Leadership Center take such an objective approach to program evaluation. Data indicate that workers who report to the managers who have participated in programs at the center consistently give them higher ratings in employee satisfaction than they give managers who have not attended. Also, when answering the question "I am given a real opportunity to improve my skills at Boeing," leadership center alumni scored an 85 percent response in comparison to the 69 percent scored by managers who did not attend.[25]

A more rigorous approach to the evaluation of leadership training and development would include an experiment, as shown in Table 15-3. The experimental group would consist of the participants in the development program. Before-and-after measures of skills would be taken to determine if improvements took place. Outcome measures from the experimental group would then be compared to those from two control or contrast groups. All three groups would be composed of people similar in education, intelligence, job level, job experience, and so forth. People in one control group would receive no special development. Members of the second control group would receive a different kind of development. Instead of training in giving supportive feedback, they might be trained in business

TABLE 15-3   Evaluating Leadership Development Through the Experimental Method

	Pretraining Measures	Training	Posttraining Measures
Experimental group	Yes	Supportive feedback	Yes
Control group I	Yes	None	Yes
Control group II	Yes	Business communications	Yes

communications. The purpose of the second control (or contrast) group is to determine if training in supportive feedback has an edge over simply sending people to any sensible training program.

Evaluation Through Domains of Impact

The traditional method of evaluation is best suited to evaluating structured, definable skills, such as running software or performing a breakeven analysis. Leadership training and development, however, involves much broader, less structured behaviors, such as inspiring others and identifying problems. Another problem is that few organizations would be willing to randomly assign managers to expensive and time-consuming leadership development programs.

Following the position presented so far, a useful method of measuring the outcome of leadership development is to differentiate types of learning and to measure them separately.[26] Areas of possible changes are referred to as **domains of impact.** Figure 15-3 presents five such domains of impact. Knowledge acquisition, self-awareness building, skill development, and behavior change have already been described in this chapter. *Perspective change* is similar to increasing personal awareness because it is a change in attitude rather than an observable behavior. A leader with an improved perspective focuses more attention on gathering insights about people and the environment. An example of a change in perspective would be to suddenly realize that an effective leader does not necessarily have to please everybody. Another important perspective would be to recognize that individual differences must be taken into account in managing others. After attending a feedback-intensive program, a manager said:

> The program got me to thinking that people are different—and that they are motivated differently, their priorities are different—and to start looking for it. When I came back, I started analyzing the people who were working directly for me, and than I started managing differently—not just one big blanket "Here it is folks."[27]

Understanding the domains of impact of a leadership development program may help evaluate the essence of such a program. Nevertheless, some executives who authorize payment for the program may want to know how improvement in the domains of impact leads to improved productivity and profits.

FIGURE 15-3   Model of Domains of Impact

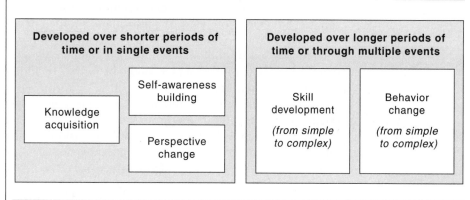

Source: From "Assessing the Impact of Development Experiences," by Cynthia D. McCauley, Russ S. Moxley, and Ellen Van Velsor, Handbook of Leadership Development, Copyright © 1998 Jossey-Bass. Reprinted by permission of Jossey-Bass, Inc., a subsidiary of John Wiley & Sons, Inc.

LEADERSHIP SUCCESSION

In a well-managed organization, replacements for executives who quit, retire, or are dismissed are chosen through **leadership succession,** an orderly process of identifying and grooming people to replace managers. Succession planning is linked to leadership development in two important ways. First, being groomed as a successor is part of leadership development. Second, the process of choosing and fostering a successor is part of a manager's own development.

Our approach to understanding the leadership aspects of succession focuses on four topics: (1) how the board chooses a new chief officer; (2) succession planning at GE; (3) the emotional aspects of leadership succession; and (4) developing a pool of successors.

How the Board Chooses a Successor

A major responsibility of the board of directors is to select a successor to the chief executive, typically a CEO. The general approach is to follow standard principles of human resource selection, such as thoroughly screening candidates, including speaking to several people who have worked with the individual. Conducting a background investigation to uncover any possible scandalous or illegal behavior is also important. When the successor is an outsider, boards consistently use executive search firms (also known as *headhunters*) to locate one or several candidates. For example, both Hewlett-Packard and Xerox Corporation used an executive search firm to hire their current highest-ranking executive. Even when the board has an outside candidate in mind, a search firm might be hired to act as an intermediary.

George D. Kennedy, a person with experience on many boards, provides a few specifics of a representative approach to selecting an internal candidate for the top executive position. First, the information from a development program for successors must be carefully reviewed, including documentation of performance. Second, the board should have direct and regular contact with all the promising candidates. Some of the contact should be formal, including the candidate making regular presentations at board meetings. Informal connections are also important. Board members should invest the time to develop a feel for the personal chemistry of the candidates through such means as casual conversations over dinner and lunch.[28] (Because some of the decision making about succession is based on subjective judgments, it is imperative for CEO candidates to be skilled at organizational politics and influence tactics.)

Succession Planning at General Electric

General Electric Company is often noted for its progressive and thorough management techniques. Its system for identifying and developing talent is considered exemplary. Much of this activity is linked closely to succession planning. Board members are closely involved in an ongoing evaluation of the company's 130 highest-ranking managers. Twice a year, directors scrutinize about 15 of these people. The information they use comes from lengthy interviews with the managers, their managers, former associates, and group members. Directors investigate the managers' strengths and weaknesses, make suggestions for leadership development, and discuss future assignments. Should the day arrive when a manager must be chosen to replace a higher-level manager, the board will be prepared to make an independent decision rather than giving automatic approval to an insider's recommendations.[29]

Key advantages of the GE system for identifying successors are that it is based on multiple opinions and that it tracks longitudinal performance. Yet the system may still be replete with political biases. The board members, for example, are not exempt from giving high ratings to the people they like the best or to people who have personal characteristics similar to theirs.

The Emotional Aspects of Leadership Succession

Leadership succession should not be regarded as a detached, objective management process. Even financially independent executives are likely to experience an emotional loss when they are replaced, such as yearning for the power and position they once possessed. Leadership succession in family-owned firms is a highly emotional process for many reasons. Family members may fight over who is best qualified to take the helm, or the owner and founder may not feel that any family member is qualified. An intensely emotional situation exists when the owner would like a family member to succeed him or her, yet no family member is willing. The business may therefore have to be sold or simply abandoned; in any case, its identity will be lost.

The emotional aspects of leadership succession are also evident when a business founder is replaced by another leader, whether or not the enterprise is a family business. Jane Plitt, a business consultant, has noted that a founder's leaving can be "one of the highest traumas that can be experienced by a company. When it is done successfully, it is really a major accomplishment."[30] After the sale of his or her company, the business founder often stays on in some capacity, such as a consultant or chairperson. Watching the new owner manage the business can be uncomfortable for the founder. The issue transcends concerns about delegation. The entrepreneurial leader is typically emotionally involved in the firm he or she has founded and finds it difficult to look on while somebody else operates the firm.

Developing a Pool of Successors

Research conducted by Development Dimensions International indicates that a massive shortage of business leaders is becoming a major problem. Early retirements and downsizings have depleted the deep pool of middle managers who would ordinarily be successors. The recommended solution to the shortage is to stock pools of candidates with high leadership potential. Developing a pool of successors goes beyond succession planning, which usually involves identifying one or two candidates for a specific job. The steps involved in developing a pool of successors (or succession management) are as follows:[31]

- Evaluate the extent of an organization's pending leadership shortage.
- Identify needed executive competencies based on the firm's future business needs, values, and strategies.
- Identify high-potential individuals for possible inclusion in the pool, and assess these individuals to identify strengths and developmental needs to determine who will stay in the high-potential pool.
- Establish an individually tailored developmental program for each high-potential candidate that includes leadership development programs, job rotation, special assignments, and mentoring.
- Select and place people into senior jobs based on their performance, experience, and potential.
- Continuously monitor the program and give it top management support.

Developing a pool of candidates, therefore, combines evaluating potential with giving high-potential individuals the right type of developmental experiences. To the extent that these procedures are implemented, a leadership shortage in a given firm is less likely to take place.

Another approach to developing a pool of successors is the **leadership pipeline,** a model of leadership development that tightly links leadership development with management responsibilities at each level of the organization. The pipeline model has been used successfully at GE for many years, partly because it supports the company's approach to leadership succession.[32] The pipeline model has six levels, each having its unique management challenges: (1) managing individual contributors, (2) managing managers, (3) being a functional manager,

(4) being a business manager, (5) being a group manager, and (6) being an enterprise manager. The model applies primarily to a large, hierarchical organization but can be adapted to fewer levels.

The leadership pipeline feeds succession because managers are prepared to be leaders at the next level. Each level requires the manager to develop skills, invest time in the most appropriate activities, and adjust values to perform successfully. For example, coaching is an important skill at level 1, and strategic planning at level 6. When moving from managing individual contributors to managing managers, leaders must learn to value a different type of work and have fewer quantitative measures to evaluate the results of their direct reports.

FOLLOWERSHIP: BEING AN EFFECTIVE GROUP MEMBER

To be an effective leader, one needs good followers. Leaders cannot exist without followers.[33] As we mentioned at the outset of this book, the word *followers* suffers from political incorrectness, yet it is a neutral term as used by leadership researchers. Most of the topics in our study of leadership so far have been aimed at inspiring, motivating, and influencing group members to want to achieve organizational goals. It is also valuable, however, to focus on two key aspects of being an effective group member: the personal characteristics of productive followers and the importance of collaboration between leaders and followers.

Essential Qualities of Effective Followers

As observed by Robert E. Kelley, effective followers share four essential qualities:[34]

1. *Self-management.* The key to being a good follower is to think for oneself and to work well without close supervision. Effective group members see themselves as being as capable as their leaders.

2. *Commitment.* Effective followers are committed to something beyond themselves, be it a cause, product, department, organization, idea, or value. To a committed group member, the leader facilitates making progress toward achieving a goal.

3. *Competence and focus.* Effective followers build their competence and focus their efforts for maximum impact. Competence centers around mastering skills that will be useful to the organization. Less effective group members rarely take the initiative to engage in training and development.

4. *Courage.* Effective followers establish themselves as independent, critical thinkers and will fight for what they believe is right. A good follower, for example, might challenge the company's policy of taking ninety days to make good on accounts payable, or recruiting key people almost exclusively from people with demographic characteristics similar to those of top management.

The above list is illustrative, since almost any positive human quality would contribute directly or indirectly to being an effective group member or follower. Another way of framing the qualities of effective followers is that such followers display the personal characteristics and qualities of leaders. Although leaders cannot be expected to change the personalities of group members, they can take steps to encourage the above qualities. Interventions such as coaching, empowerment, supportive communication, and frequent feedback would support effective followership. Leadership Skill-Building Exercise 15-2 will give you more insight into the multidimensional nature of effective group membership.

Collaboration Between Leaders and Followers

A key role for followers is to collaborate with leaders in achieving organizational goals, as implied by the study of teamwork. As described by leadership guru Warren Bennis, the postbureaucratic organization requires a new kind of alliance between leaders and the led. When high-level leaders do not make all the decisions but solicit input from knowledgeable group members, leaders and followers work together more closely. In the words of Bennis:[35]

> Today's organizations are evolving into federations of networks, clusters, cross-functional teams, temporary systems, ad hoc task forces, lattices, modules, matrices—almost anything but pyramids with their obsolete TOPdown leadership. The new leader will encourage healthy dissent and values those followers courageous enough to say no.

A related point here is that the new leader and the led are close allies. Great leaders are made by great groups, placing a burden on every organizational member to contribute energy and talent to help leaders carry out their roles successfully.

Leadership Skill-Building Exercise 15-3 may give you a few good insights into the type of leader you are becoming.

WHO WILL BE THE NEW TOP BUSINESS LEADERS?

In the last several years, the often-neglected middle managers have come back in style as being major contributors to the success of business firms. Part of the reason is that middle managers are often perceived as having more credibility and goodwill than members of the executive suite.

The middle managers most likely to advance into top jobs are likely to have financial know-how and an ability to communicate with a range of constituents—in addition to many of the traits, attitudes, and behaviors emphasized in earlier chapters in this book. Another asset for middle managers is that they often have more frequent contact with customers, suppliers, and workers than do high-level executives, so they have a chance to show the all-important leadership trait of integrity.[36]

The Followership Evaluation Form

If you are the leader of a relatively stable group, use the following set of standards as material for group discussion. Get the group members' opinions on the validity of these statements as indicators of being an effective group member or follower. A group member who exhibits most of the behaviors in the "outstanding" and "excellent" categories and does not exhibit those in the "needs improvement" category will have strong leadership potential.

Outstanding

a. Is a loyal, effective team player with a contagious, positive attitude

b. Is ready and willing to accept and act on tasks, even on short notice or under pressure

c. Spurs the team to remain positive in confusing or changing situations

d. Readily volunteers in a way that makes a difference

e. Offers supportive suggestions that the chain of command adopts

f. Facilitates team progress

g. Adopts unpopular higher headquarters decision as own

h. Regards peers well and is well regarded by peers

i. Acts for the good of the team

Excellent

a. Is an effective team player

b. Accepts and acts on assigned tasks

c. Volunteers in useful ways

d. Remains positive when the situation is confused or changing

e. Offers suggestions, but supports the chain of command

f. Helps the team make progress

g. Properly executes unpopular headquarters decisions

h. Gets along with peers

i. Gets own share of work done

j. Acts for the good of the team

Needs Improvement

a. Does not contribute much to team morale or effectiveness

b. Is reluctant or unwilling to accept assigned tasks

c. Does not volunteer or does so ineffectively or superficially

d. Is visibly upset by confusing or changing situations; tends to aggravate the situation

e. Does not offer helpful suggestions or argues with the chain of command, thereby hindering team progress

f. Fails to execute higher headquarters decisions properly and/or openly complains about or blames the higher headquarters

g. Has trouble getting along with some peers

h. Needs help from others to get own share of work done

i. Acts primarily for reasons of personal gain

j. Expects more of others when in charge than is willing to produce when others are in charge

SOURCE: *Adapted from material in Cadet Command Regulation 145-3, "Army Reserve Officers' Training Corps: Precommissioning Training and Leadership Development," U.S. Army Cadet Command, Fort Monroe, Va., March 1996. Reprinted by permission.*

Leadership Skill-Building Exercise 15-3

Building for the Future

Our final skill-building exercise, the use of a feedback circle, encompasses many aspects of leadership covered in this and the previous fourteen chapters. Ten members of the class arrange their chairs in a circle. One person is selected as the feedback "target," and the other nine people take turns giving him or her supportive feedback. Assume it is "Ralph's" turn. Each person in the circle gives Ralph two pieces of feedback: (a) his best leadership attribute, and (b) how he needs to develop for the future. The feedback should take about thirty seconds per feedback giver. After receiving input from all the circle members, Ralph is free to comment. It is then the next person's turn to be the feedback target.

Class members who are not in the circle observe the dynamics of what is happening and report their observations after the circle finishes. With diligence, the whole process will take about ninety minutes. If time permits, a new feedback circle can form. Alternatively, the class can break into several circles that operate simultaneously, or run just one circle with ten volunteers.

Roger Ailes, who helped Ronald Reagan rise from governor to president to legend, believes that the class of 2006 will redefine power for the next ten years. Ailes believes that people with dynamic personalities will rise to the top. These leaders will make institutions even flatter, simpler, and faster moving, but they will not hunger for the perks of leadership. Furthermore, because people are looking for strong institutions, these leaders will bring back institutional trust.[37]

SUMMARY

Leadership and management development are widely practiced in a variety of organizations and take many forms, including self-development. Self-awareness involves the insightful processing of feedback about oneself to improve personal effectiveness. Single-loop learning occurs when learners seek minimum feedback that may substantially confront their basic ideas or actions. Double-loop learning occurs when people use feedback to confront the validity of the goal or values implicit in the situation; it enables the leader to learn and profit from failure.

Leadership development requires considerable self-discipline. For example, self-discipline is needed to monitor one's behavior to ensure that the necessary self-development takes place.

Education, leadership experience, and mentoring are all major contributors to leadership development. Most high-level leaders are intelligent, well-informed people who gather knowledge throughout their career. The best experiences for leadership development are those that realistically challenge the manager. An important part of capitalizing on challenging experiences is for the leader/manager to be given leeway in how to resolve the problem. Two important aspects of leadership experience are work associates and the task itself (such as a complex and ambiguous assignment). Learning from the wisdom of leaders who faced challenges is another source of experience. Broad experience is important for leadership development, as suggested by multifunctional managerial development.

Another experience-based way to develop leadership capability is to receive mentoring. Although usually an informal relationship, mentoring can also be assigned. A study showed that informal mentors typically were more helpful to a person's career than formal mentors, and informal mentoring is also associated with higher income. The human resource department often coordinates a formal mentoring program. Shadowing is a form of mentoring. Mentors enhance the career of protégés in many ways, such as by recommending them for promotion and helping them establish valuable contacts. Also, the mentor can serve as a model for effective (or ineffective) leadership.

A comprehensive leadership development program includes certain key features: carefully selecting participants; gaining executive involvement and sponsorship; gearing the program to different levels of management; addressing current and future organization needs; using an appropriate model or theory; giving ongoing reinforcement and emotional support; using diagnostic tools; ensuring practical and relevant content; emphasizing interpersonal relations and teamwork; and concluding with individual action plans.

Feedback-intensive development programs help leaders develop by seeing more clearly their patterns of behavior, the reasons for such behaviors, and the impact of these behaviors and attitudes on their effectiveness. Skill training in leadership development involves acquiring abilities and techniques that can be converted into action. Such training involves a considerable element of "how to." Five methods of skill-based training are lecture, case study, role play, behavior role modeling, and simulations. During simulations, participants play the role of company leaders and devise solutions to problems. Feedback on performance is provided.

A standard university approach to leadership development is to equip people with a conceptual understanding of leadership. The concepts can be applied to leadership situations. Personal growth experiences for leadership development assume that leaders are deeply in touch with their personal dreams and talents and will act to fulfill them. Another emphasis in these programs is learning who you need to be. From the company standpoint, an essential type of leadership development is socializing the company vision and values. Action learning is a directly practical approach to leadership development and may be directed at areas outside the participant's expertise.

The traditional approach to the evaluation of leadership development programs includes specifying objectives and then measuring whether they were met. Measures of organizational outcomes, such as increased profits, might also be made. A more rigorous approach to evaluation would be based on an experimental design. An alternative approach to evaluation is to examine the domains of impact (ranges of possible effects) a program might have. Among these domains are knowledge acquisition, self-awareness building, skill development, behavior change, and perspective change (such as gathering insights about people and the environment).

Leadership succession is linked to leadership development because being groomed as a successor is part of a leader's development. Boards of directors use standard selection methods in choosing a CEO. In addition, they look for both formal and informal contact with insiders. When recruiting an outsider, organizations often employ executive search firms. General Electric is an example of rigorous succession planning. Leadership succession is highly emotional for the leader who is being replaced, especially when a founder sells a business. The succession problem in a family business often leads to conflict among family members. One way to cope with potential shortages of leaders is to identify a pool of high-potential individuals and provide them with developmental experiences. The leadership pipeline, a model of leadership development, feeds succession because managers are prepared to be leaders at the next level.

To be an effective leader, one needs good followers with characteristics such as self-management; commitment; competence and focus; and courage. A key role for followers is to collaborate with leaders in achieving organizational goals. The postbureaucratic organization requires a new kind of alliance between leaders and the led.

Middle managers are again being perceived as major contributors to the success of business firms, and many of them will be the next top business leaders. It is predicted that financial know-how, good communication skills, and a dynamic personality will help leaders rise to the top.

KEY TERMS

Self-awareness

Single-loop learning

Double-loop learning

Self-discipline

Multifunctional managerial development

Mentor

Shadowing

Feedback-intensive development program

Domains of impact

Leadership succession

Leadership pipeline

GUIDELINES FOR ACTION AND SKILL DEVELOPMENT

An important method for enhancing both the acceptance and the effectiveness of leadership development is *needs analysis*, the diagnosis of needs for development. A needs analysis is based on the idea that there are individual differences among leaders and future leaders. For example, Jennifer might have excellent conceptual knowledge about leadership, but limited team experience. She might be a good candidate for outdoor training. Jack might be an excellent team leader with limited conceptual knowledge. He might be a good candidate for a leadership development program concentrating on formal knowledge about leadership. Sources of data for assessing leadership developmental needs include the following:

1. Self-perceptions of developmental needs, including the results of many of the diagnostic instruments presented in this text

2. Perceptions by superiors, subordinates, and peers of the person's developmental needs, including 360-degree survey results

3. Psychological evaluation of developmental needs

4. A statement of organizational needs for development, such as the importance of leaders who can deal effectively with diversity (within company, with customers, and globally)

Multiple sources of data are useful because of possible errors in perception, biases, and favoritism.

DISCUSSION QUESTIONS AND ACTIVITIES

1. Many business executives believe that playing team sports helps a person develop as a leader. Based on your knowledge of leadership development, where do you stand on this issue?

2. How can a person increase self-awareness?

3. Give an example from your own life in which you engaged in double-loop learning, or in which you *should* have engaged in such learning.

4. Suppose you aspired to become a senior executive in a large company. How would working as an office supervisor, production supervisor, or manager in a fast-food restaurant help you achieve your goal?

5. Assume that you were responsible for selecting a leadership development program for your organization. What questions would you ask a potential provider of these services?

6. How will you know if the course for which you are reading this book will have helped you in your development as a leader or manager?

7. What are the advantages and disadvantages of having an outsider succeed the top executive in an organization?

8. What can you as a parent, future parent, or close relative do to help a child under ten years old become a leader later in life?

9. Why are many CEOs who are planning to retire reluctant to identify a replacement a year or two in advance?

10. Ask an experienced leader what he or she thinks is the most effective method of developing leadership skills. Bring your findings back to class.

Leadership Case Problem A

Len Riggio, Barnes & Noble's Baron of Books

No details escape the careful eye of Leonard S. Riggio, chief executive of Barnes & Noble, Inc., as he tours the chain's newest store in Atlanta, Georgia. He proudly points to features he supported, including cathedral ceilings designed to bring a feeling of grandeur to book buying, and hand-painted signs that give a soft decor. Riggio has transformed the book industry, and he has loved doing it. While drinking espresso, he joyfully describes the changes, from deep discounts to Sunday hours and public restrooms, he imposed on a reluctant industry. Riggio says, "The bookstore business was an elitist, stand-offish institution. I liberated them from that" (*BusinessWeek*, June 29, 1998, p. 109).

Barnes & Noble, Inc. is the parent company of Barnes & Noble, B. Dalton, and Doubleday bookstores. The company also runs Game-Stop, the largest operator of stores that sell video game and entertainment software; Barnes & Noble.com (www.bn.com), Barnes & Noble College Bookstores, and MBS Textbook Exchange. In all, the companies controlled by Riggio operate more than 2,400 retail stores and employ more than 80,000 people.

Riggio is credited with making bookstores fun by turning them into public meeting places, where people gather as much for the entertainment value as for the huge selection of books. A retailing professor at Texas A&M University said Riggio was the first retailer to understand that the store is a stage and that retailing is theater. Riggio enjoys being controversial and has had many conflicts with publishers and other retailers about his policies, such as deep discounts on books.

Both Riggio's abrasive style and his business strategies have created controversy. Some peo-

ple are concerned that a massive consolidation of the book industry could restrict freedom of speech and thought. "The reason the Constitution guarantees freedom of speech and not freedom to purchase rubber bands is that the health of the culture depends on the availability and diversity of ideas, not the availability of rubber bands. Leonard Riggio wields immense power over the long-term health of our culture," says Todd Gitlin, a professor of culture at New York University (*BusinessWeek*, pp. 109–110).

The Exceptional Entrepreneur. Riggio receives high praise as an entrepreneur. The former head of the B. Dalton division describes him as a genius. An advertising executive who works with Riggio describes him as a brilliant son of a [mother dog]. A money manager who thinks Barnes & Noble stock is undervalued also believes Riggio is undervalued: "This guy Len, he's really something. This guy knows how to make money. The problem is, he doesn't look like an investment banker, so he doesn't get credit. He's way underappreciated" (*Fortune*, June 21, 1999, p. 94). An executive at publisher Random House thinks that Riggio should be accepted as a visionary and embraced. Some publishers even consult with Barnes & Noble employees in order to better understand consumer preferences in books.

A simple decision by the powerful chain to buy or not buy, to display or not display, can create success or failure for a new book—particularly one by a little-known author. Many people in the literary world are concerned about this reality; they regard Riggio as a number-crunching businessman who would sacrifice literary merit to earn a profit.

Riggio believes strongly that his business is not predatory and that he is not harming culture. While touring the Atlanta store, he commented, "I have come here to look around to remind myself that we're giving the world a gift. It gives me goose bumps to remember what we're doing" (*BusinessWeek*, p. 110). Many small-book publishers and less-well-recognized authors agree that Barnes & Noble has created new opportunities for them.

A business reporter who interviewed Riggio found him to be a surprising mix of liberal idealism and market-driven expedience. Although a symbol of Big Business, he perceives himself to be an entrepreneurial champion. Although he has been accused of stifling free speech, even his adversaries applaud his defiance of an April 1998 subpoena from special prosecutor Kenneth Starr, who demanded the book-buying records of Monica Lewinsky.

Personal Life and Personality.   Riggio is married, has three children and grandchildren, and lives with his wife in a huge apartment in Manhattan. He spends most weekends at a lavish estate in Bridgehampton, N.Y. Riggio's dinner guests often include blue-collar friends from his youth. A friend notes that Riggio avoids celebrities and prefers to hang out with pals from the old neighborhood. Riggio grew up in an Italian neighborhood in Brooklyn, and his father was a successful prizefighter before he retired to become a cab driver. Riggio dislikes comparing his personal style to that of his father. He emphasizes that his father taught him that being a quick thinker is as important as having a knockout punch. Riggio's forty-seven-year-old brother is the company vice chairman, charged with leading and managing the online business. Another brother owns a part interest in a freight company that hauls books for Barnes & Noble.

Riggio is often prickly and foul-mouthed, but he is also funny, philosophical, and a major donor to the Democratic Party and the arts. Riggio angrily denies that he is a hothead. He says the accusation was started by a publishing executive who wanted to cut the Barnes & Noble discount by 2 percent. "I asked him whether he wanted to take the door or the window" says Riggio with passion (*BusinessWeek*, p. 111). Riggio believes that the competitiveness he learned at Brooklyn Tech High School, particularly in playing basketball, shaped his future. He has been listed in Forbes's 400 Richest Americans and America's Most Powerful People.

The History of His Business.   While an engineering night student at New York University, Riggio worked days at the college bookstore. He was as much influenced by running a business as by books themselves. He says, "If I got a job at a hardware store, I would have been Home Depot today" (*BusinessWeek*, p. 111). Soon he started his own bookstore with a $5,000 loan. In 1971 he borrowed $1.2 million to buy Barnes & Noble, an ailing, century-old bookstore in lower Manhattan. Shortly thereafter, Riggio was offering huge discounts on new books and selling some older books by the pound.

When a retail-store executive threatened to drive him out of business, Riggio responded with expletives of his own. Despite the warnings, Riggio continued to expand. In 1986 he bought B. Dalton Bookseller and became the nation's biggest book retailer. In 1990 Riggio acquired Bookstop, a Texas-based chain of twenty-four superstores. A year later the Barnes & Noble superstore installations began. The stores were open on Sundays and had a climate-controlled village square atmosphere, with cappuccino for sale, comfortable armchairs, and even cooking demonstrations. Riggio successfully implemented his plan of developing a store that would draw customers from every economic and ethnic segment.

As Barnes & Noble has continued to expand, the firm has grabbed considerable market share from independent booksellers. Riggio says he has competed strenuously but fairly. He explains also that because he built an empire for himself starting with nothing, he does not shed a tear for the little guy.

The Amazon.com Problem.   Riggio and his team acknowledge that Amazon.com continues to gain its own large share of the retail book business, as well as of other merchandise sold at Barnes & Noble. So far bn.com has not caught up with Amazon.com, yet overall Barnes & Noble still has about 15 percent of the U.S. book market, compared to 2 percent for Amazon.com. Suzanne Zak, the head of a money management firm, believes that Riggio will find a way to deal with the competition. "Len Riggio is a lunatic—and I mean that in a good way: He's pathologically competitive. The trouble is, the guys at Amazon are too," she said (*Fortune*, p. 86). Barnes & Noble, like many other retailers, is being forced into being successful as a traditional bricks-and-mortar retailer and successful as an online retailer also. An analyst said that Barnes & Noble is obtaining market share, not by expanding the market for books, but by cannibalizing sales from other outlets (and former outlets).

Riggio believes this is no time to panic, and that he will emerge successful by doing new entrepreneurial things. The Barnes & Noble commitment to books while Amazon expands into selling almost anything may give Riggio's firm a competitive advantage. A Barnes & Noble executive said, "I think if we are focused on being the best at what we do, we will earn a larger market share" (*Fortune*, p. 86). Also, Barnes & Noble will continue to expand the sales of other things that appeal to book lovers, such as Godiva chocolates and reading glasses. Digital books are now sold through bn.com.

The Future.   Riggio believes that the revolution he created has only started. He hopes to add 500 supersize Barnes & Noble stores over the next decade. He also hopes that his online venture, www.bn.com, will create a powerful promotional channel that will generate interest in books and his bookstores, in addition to selling books and other merchandise. He is also planning a large magazine store and a cavernous art store that will sell many forms of art from posters to original paintings. With forthcoming software developments, Riggio foresees a day when customers could tap into millions of titles and be able to print out any part of these works on the spot.

QUESTIONS

1. Identify several of Len Riggio's developmental needs.

2. If you were Len Riggio's executive coach, what would you advise him?

3. Identify at least two business strategies that Riggio has already used.

4. Recommend a business strategy to help Barnes & Noble be even more successful.

5. Is there a particular leadership development program you would recommend for Riggio?

SOURCES: *Nina Munk, "Title Fight,"* Fortune, *June 21, 1999, pp. 84–94; I. Jeanne Dugan, "The Baron of Books,"* BusinessWeek, *June 29, 1998, pp. 108–117; www. bn.com; "Leonard Riggio: Chairman of the Board at Barnes & Noble, Inc.," www.forbes.com/finance, September 7, 2002; "Leonard Riggio, Founder and Chairman, Barnes & Noble, Inc.," www.barnesandnobleinc. com/company/management/co_plriggio.html; "Len Riggio, Chairman and former CEO, Barnes & Noble," www.roadtripnation.com/public/10/45.*

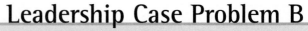

Leadership Case Problem B

"Help! I'm the New Boss."

You are the new boss, a couple of years younger than your colleagues. Shortly after your honeymoon ends, you invite a group member to your office and nicely suggest that she change her approach to improve her efficiency, bring herself in line with department changes, etc., etc. She listens. Sits back. Unblinking, she says, "Thanks, but no thanks. I'll keep doing things my way. Will that be all?"

What do you do? Go ballistic? Calmly explain to her that she will make the changes or be fired? When it happened to me, I didn't quite know how to react. I was a first-time boss, a 26-year-old free agent turned manager. No one had taught me how to react to outright disregard for my newfound authority. So finally I shrugged. I sort of mumbled, "Okay, um, I understand how you feel, and, you know, we'll talk about it another time."

As one might expect, my career as a manager at the company effectively ended that day. Word of my meekness spread, as good gossip always does. I would go on to make every mistake imaginable, to the chagrin of most of the staff. I made Coach from *Cheers* (a television show) look masterful. My boss, who had hoped I would find my inner bossness on my own, eventually cut back the number of people who reported to me. It was a tough, but, yes, merciful call.

There is some solace in realizing now that I was not simply a young and clueless manager but one of many young and clueless managers.

QUESTIONS

1. What type of leadership development program do you recommend for the person who wrote this case history?

2. What specific traits and behaviors does the boss in question need to work on?

3. How would you deal with the situation of a group member who refuses to act on your suggestions for improved performance?

SOURCE: *Dimitry Elias Léger, "Help! I'm the New Boss,"* Fortune, *May 29, 2000, p. 281.*

INTERNET SKILL-BUILDING EXERCISE

Apply the chapter concepts! Visit the Web and complete this Internet skill-building exercise to learn more about current leadership topics and trends.

A Scientific Approach to Succession Planning

Visit **www.successionwizard.com**, a human resources consultancy located in the United Kingdom. Go to the "animated tutorials" to see a demonstration of how the Succession Wizard works. You will have a choice of six different tutorials to view. Begin with "1. Introduction," which gives a quick demonstration of the key program features. The tutorial will take you through an elaborate series of charts and dialogue boxes that help executives and human resource specialists engage in succession planning. Imagine that you are a senior executive of a company that wants to engage in serious succession planning.

1. What do you think of the potential value of the Succession Wizard?

2. Do you think it will be possible for your firm to do succession planning with such precision?

3. Why would any medium-size or large firm *not* use such a system?

Chapter 1

1. Adapted from Bill Carter, "He's Cool. He Keeps MTV Sizzling. And, Oh Yes, He's 56," *New York Times,* June 16, 2002, Section 3, pages 1, 13. Copyright© 2002 by The New York Times Co. Reprinted with permission.

2. W. Kan Kim and Renee A. Maubourgne, "Parables of Leadership", *Harvard Business Review,* July–August 1992, p. 123.

3. Derived from a literature review in Bernard M. Bass, *Bass & Stogdill's Handbook of Leadership: Theory, Research, and Managerial Applications* (New York: The Free Press, 1990), pp. 11–18.

4. Jeffrey Zaslow, "Joe Montana: Leadership, Says the Legendary Quarterback of Four Super Bowls, Means 'Being Willing to Take the Blame,'" *USA Weekend,* January 30–February 1, 1998, p. 15.

5. Keith M. Hammonds, "Leaders for the Long Haul," *Fast Company,* July 2001, p. 56.

6. Amy Barrett and Louis Lavelle, "It's Getting Lonely at the Top. Too Lonely," *BusinessWeek,* November 13, 2000, p. 60.

7. Peter Block, *Stewardship: Choosing Service over Self-Interest* (San Francisco: Berrett-Koehler Publishers, 1993), pp. 27–32.

8. Ibid., pp. 29–31.

9. James H. Davis, F. David Schoorman, and Lex Donaldson, "Toward a Stewardship Theory of Management," *Academy of Management Review,* January 1997, p. 20.

10. John P. Kotter, *A Force for Change: How Leadership Differs from Management* (New York: The Free Press, 1990); Bill Leonard, "From Management to Leadership," *HR Magazine,* January 1999, pp. 34–38; Edwin A. Locke and Associates, *The Essence of Leadership: The Four Keys to Leading Successfully* (New York: Lexington/Macmillan, 1991), p. 4.

11. "Qwest CEO Quits; Wall Street Cheers," Associated Press, June 18, 2002.

12. David A. Waldman, Gabriel G. Ramirez, Robert J. House, and Phanish Puranam, "Does Leadership Matter? CEO Leadership Attributes and Profitability Under Conditions of Perceived Environmental Uncertainty," *Academy of Management Journal,* February 2001, pp. 134–143.

13. Stephanie Anderson, "Can an Outsider Fix J. C. Penney?" *BusinessWeek,* February 12, 2001, pp. 56–58; www.jcpenney.com.

14. Michael Maccoby, "Leadership Needs of the 1980s," *Current Issues in Higher Education,* vol. 2, 1979, pp. 17–23.

15. Gary A. Yukl, *Leadership in Organizations,* 3rd ed. (Upper Saddle River, N.J.: Prentice-Hall, 1994), pp. 384–387.

16. Jon P. Howell, David E. Bowen, Peter W. Dorfman, Steven Kerr, and Philip Podaskoff, "Substitutes for Leadership: Effective Alternatives to Ineffective Leadership," *Organizational Dynamics,* Summer 1990, p. 23.

17. Bass, *Bass & Stogdill's Handbook,* p. 686.

18. Shelly D. Dionne, Francis J. Yammarino, Leanne E. Atwater, and Lawrence R. James, "Neutralizing Substitutes for Leadership Theory: Leadership Effects and Common-Source Bias," *Journal of Applied Psychology,* June 2002, pp. 454–464.

19. Jeffrey Pfeffer, "The Ambiguity of Leadership," *Academy of Management Review,* April 1977, pp. 104–112.

20. Jerry Useem, "Conquering Vertical Limits," *Fortune,* February 19, 2001, p. 94.

21. Thomas H. Hout, "Are Managers Obsolete?" *Harvard Business Review,* March–April 1999, pp. 161–162. (Books in Review.)

22. Updated and expanded from Henry Mintzberg, *The Nature of Managerial Work* (New York: Harper & Row, 1973); and Kenneth Graham, Jr., and William M. Mihal, *The CMD Managerial Job Analysis Inventory* (Rochester, N. Y.: Rochester Institute of Technology, Center for Management Development, 1987), pp. 132–133.

23. Christopher A. Bartlett and Sumantra Ghosal, "Changing the Role of Top Management Beyond Systems to People," *Harvard Business Review*, May–June 1995, pp.132–133.

24. Ronald A. Heifetz and Marty Linsky, "A Survival Guide for Leaders," *Harvard Business Review*, June 2002, pp. 65–74.

25. Thomas A. Stewart, "The Nine Dilemmas Leaders Face," *Fortune*, March 18, 1996, pp. 112–113.

26. Two examples are Martin M. Chemers, *An Integrative Theory of Leadership* (Mahwah, N. J.: Lawrence Erlbaum Associates, 1997), pp. 151–173; and Francis J. Yammarino, Fred Dansereau, and Christina J. Kennedy, "A Multiple-Level Multidimensional Approach to Leadership: Viewing Leadership Through an Elephant's Eye," *Organizational Dynamics*, Winter 2001, pp. 149–162.

27. Paul Hersey, Kenneth Blanchard, and Dewey E. Johnson, *Managing Organizational Behavior: Utilizing Human Resources* (Upper Saddle River, N. J.: Prentice Hall, 1997), pp. 418–420.

28. Stephen P. Robbins, *Managing Today!* (Upper Saddle River, N.J.: Prentice Hall, 1997), pp. 418–420.

29. Cited in "What Leadership Skills Do Executives Seek?" *Manager's Edge*, November 1998, p. 106.

30. Dana G. McDonald-Mann, "Skill-Based Training," in Cynthia D. McCauley, Russ S. Moxley, and Ellen Van Velsor, eds., *The Center for Creative Leadership: Handbook of Leadership Development* (San Francisco: Jossey-Bass Publishers, 1998), p. 106.

Chapter 2

1. "Required Eating Makes This Job Fun," Associated Press, June 3, 2002. Reprinted with permission of the Associated Press.

2. Shelley A. Kirkpatrick and Edwin A. Locke, "Leadership: Do Traits Matter?" *Academy of Management Executive*, May 1991, pp. 48–60; Daniel Goleman, "What Makes a Leader?" *Harvard Business Review*, November–December 1998, pp. 92–102.

3. Stephen G. Harrison, "Leadership and Hope Go Hand in Hand," *Executive Leadership*, June 2002, p. 8.

4. Jim Collins, "Level 5 Leadership: The Triumph of Humility and Fierce Resolve," *Harvard Business Review*, January 2001, p. 70.

5. See Gareth R. Jones and Jennifer M. George, "The Experience and Evolution of Trust: Implications for Cooperation and Teamwork," *Academy of Management Review*, July 1998, pp. 531–546; Jenny C. McCune, "That Elusive Thing Called Trust," *Management Review*, August 1998, pp. 10–16.

6. Roy J. Lewicki, Daniel McAllister, and Robert J. Bies, "Trust and Distrust: New Relationships and Realities," *Academy of Management Review*, July 1998, p. 439.

7. Robert Glaser, "Paving the Road to Trust," *HRfocus*, January 1997, p. 5; Thomas A. Stewart, "Whom Can You Trust? It's Not So Easy to Tell," *Fortune*, June 12, 2000, p. 334.

8. Kurt T. Dirks and Donal L. Ferrin, "Trust in Leadership: Meta-Analytic Findings and Implications for Research and Practice," *Journal of Applied Psychology*, August 2002, pp. 611–628.

9. "Use Assertiveness, Not Aggressiveness," *Working Smart*, November 1998, p. 2.

10. Edwin A. Locke and Associates, *The Essence of Leadership: The Four Keys to Leading Successfully* (New York: Lexington/Macmillan, 1992), p. 55.

11. "The Hot Seat: Leadership in the 90s Is a Different Ball Game," *Executive Strategies*, September 1992, p. 1.

12. Sandra McElwaine, "A Different Kind of War: A Blunt Interview with the Army's First Three-Star General," *USA Weekend*, October 3–5, 1997, p. 6.

13. Quoted in "Leadership Concepts," *Executive Strategies*, July 9, 1991, p. 1.

14. Chris Piotrwoski and Terry R. Armstrong, "The CEO: Analysis of the CNN Telecast 'Pinnacle,'" *Psychological Reports*, vol. 65, 1989, pp. 435–438.

15. " 'The Company Is Not the Stock': Amazon's Jeff Bezos Sees a Pro Forma Profit This Year," *BusinessWeek*, April 30, 2001, p. 96.

16. "Randy Komisar: Virtual CEO," *Success*, December–January 2001, p. 29.

17. Daniel Goleman, "What Makes a Leader?" *Harvard Business Review*, November–December 1998, p. 94. For more research supporting the same conclusion, see Jennifer Laabs, "Emotional Intelligence at Work," *Workforce*, July 1999, pp. 68–71.

18. Daniel Goleman, Richard Boyatzis, and Annie McKee, "Primal Leadership: The Hidden Driver of Great Performance," *Harvard Business Review*, December 2001, pp. 42–51.

19. Ram Charan and Jerry Useem, "Why Companies Fail," *Fortune*, May 27, 2002, p. 42.

20. Goleman, Boyatzis, and McKee, "Primal Leadership," pp. 42–51.

21. Avis L., Johnson, Fred Luthans, and Harry W. Hennessey, "The Role of Locus of Control in Leader

Influence Behavior," *Personnel Psychology,* Spring 1984, p. 70.

22. David C. McClelland and Richard Boyatzis, "Leadership Motive Pattern and Long-Term Success in Management," *Journal of Applied Psychology,* December 1982, p. 727.

23. Locke and Associates, *The Essence of Leadership,* p. 22.

24. Adapted from Jerry Useem, "What Does Donald Trump® Really Want?" *Fortune,* April 3, 2000, p. 189.

25. Locke and Associates, *The Essence of Leadership,* p. 22.

26. John B. Miner, Normal R. Smith, and Jeffrey S. Bracker, "Role of Entrepreneurial Task Motivation in the Growth of Technologically Innovative Firms," *Journal of Applied Psychology,* August 1989, p. 554.

27. Gerald Secor Couzens, "Pat Croce," *Success,* September 1998, p. 50.

28. Cited in Julie Cohen Mason, "Leading the Way to the 21st Century," *Management Review,* October 1992, p. 19.

29. Richard Mullins, "Ex-IBM Exec Is New CFO at Xerox," Rochester, New York, *Democrat and Chronicle,* May 29, 2002, p. 10D.

30. Charles M. Farkas and Suzy Wetlaufler, "The Ways Chief Executive Officers Lead," *Harvard Business Review,* May–June 1996, p. 112.

31. From Jeffrey E. Garten, *The Mind of the C.E.O.* (Cambridge, Mass.: Perseus Publishing, 2001). Quoted in "Random Wisdom," *Executive Leadership,* April 4, 2002, p. 1.

32. Manfred F. R. Kets De Vries, "The Leadership Mystique," *Academy of Management Executive,* August 1994, p. 74.

33. David Tyler, "Twin Visionaries," Rochester, New York, *Democrat and Chronicle,* February 3, 2002, pp. 1E, 6E.

34. Goleman, "What Makes a Leader?" p. 97.

35. Scott Gummer, "CEO DNA," *Fortune,* November 26, 2001, pp. 259–264.

36. Kirkpatrick and Locke, "Leadership: Do Traits Matter?" p. 59.

37. Frances Hesselbein, Marshall Goldsmith, and Richard Beckhard, eds., *The Leader of the Future* (San Francisco: Jossey Bass, 1996).

38. Gary A. Yukl, *Leadership in Organizations,* 5th ed. (Upper Saddle River, N. J.: Prentice Hall, 2002), pp. 201–202; Martin M. Chemers, *An Integrative Theory of Leadership* (Mahwah, N. J.: Lawrence Erlbaum Associates, 1997), p. 20.

Chapter 3

1. Nanette Byrnes, "Avon: The New Calling," *BusinessWeek,* September 18, 2000, pp. 137–138.Text adapted and reprinted from Sept. 18, 2000 issue of Business Week, by special permission, Copyright © 2000 by The McGraw Companies, Inc.

2. Jay A. Conger and Rabindra N. Kanungo, *Charismatic Leadership in Organizations* (Thousand Oaks, CA: Sage, 1998).

3. Juan-Carlos Pastor, James R. Meindl, and Margarit C. Mayo, "A Network Effects Model of Charisma Attributions," *Academy of Management Journal,* April 2002, pp. 410–420.

4. Cited in Jay A. Conger, *The Charismatic Leader: Beyond the Mystique of Exceptional Leadership* (San Francisco: Jossey-Bass, 1989).

5. William L. Gardner and Bruce J. Avolio, "The Charismatic Relationship: A Dramaturgical Perspective," *Academy of Management Review,* January 1998, pp. 32–58.

6. Eugene Schmuckler, book review in *Personnel Psychology,* Winter 1989, p. 881.

7. Robert J. House, "A 1976 Theory of Charismatic Leadership," in *Leadership: The Cutting Edge* (Carbondale: Southern Illinois University Press, 1977), pp. 189–207; Martin M. Chemers, *An Integrative Theory of Leadership* (Mahwah, N.J.: Lawrence Erlbaum, 1997), pp. 80–82.

8. Jane A. Halpert, "The Dimensionality of Charisma," *Journal of Business Psychology,* Summer 1990, p. 401.

9. Jeffrey D. Kudisch et al., "Expert Power, Referent Power, and Charisma: Toward the Resolution of a Theoretical Debate," *Journal of Business and Psychology,* Winter 1995, pp. 177–195.

10. Conger, Kanungo, and Associates, *Charismatic Leadership* (San Francisco: Jossey Bass, 1988); Bernard M. Bass, *Bass & Stogdill's Handbook of Leadership: Theory, Research, and Managerial Applications,* 3rd ed. (New York: The Free Press, 1990), pp. 185–186.

11. Jane M. Howell and Bruce Avolio, "The Ethics of Charismatic Leadership: Submission or Liberation?" *Academy of Management Executive,* May 1992, pp. 43–52; Patricia Sellers, "What Exactly Is Charisma?" *Fortune,* January 15, 1996, pp. 72–75; David A. Waldman and Francis J. Yammarino, "CEO Charismatic Leadership: Levels-of-Management and Levels-of-Analysis Effects," *Academy of Management Review,* April 1999, pp. 266–285.

12. Alex Taylor III, "Schrempp Shifts Gears," *Fortune,* March 13, 2002, p. 98.

13. Michael Krantz, "AOL, You've Got Netscape," *Time*, December 7, 1998, p. 60.

14. Howell and Avolio, "The Ethics of Charismatic Leadership," p. 46.

15. Noel Tichy and Christopher DeRose, "Roger Enrico's Master Class," *Fortune*, November 27, 1995, p. 406.

16. Jay A. Conger, "Inspiring Others: The Language of Leadership," *Academy of Management Executive*, February 1991, p. 39.

17. Ibid.

18. "Management by Anecdote," *Success*, December 1992, p. 35.

19. Ibid.

20. Dennis A. Romig, *Side by Side Leadership: Achieving Outstanding Results Together* (Marietta, Ga.: Bard Press, 2001), p. 157.

21. Gerald Secour Couzens, "Pat Croce," *Success*, September 1998, p. 50.

22. Karl Taro Greenfield, "Ralph's Rough Ride," *Time*, March 15, 1999, p. 50.

23. Bernard M. Bass, "Does the Transactional-Transformational Leadership Paradigm Transcend National Boundaries?" *American Psychologist*, February 1997, p. 130.

24. Linda Tischler, "The Road to Recovery," *Fast Company*, July 2002, pp. 76–78.

25. John J. Hater and Bernard M. Bass, "Superiors' Evaluations and Subordinates' Perceptions of Transformational and Transactional Leadership," *Journal of Applied Psychology*, November 1988, p. 65; Noel M. Tichy and Mary Anne Devanna, *The Transformational Leader* (New York: Wiley, 1990).

26. Peter Koestenbaum, *Leadership: The Inner Side of Greatness* (San Francisco: Jossey-Bass, 1991).

27. Alan J. Dubinsky, Francis J. Yammarino, and Marvin A. Jolson, "An Examination of Linkages Between Personal Characteristics and Dimensions of Transformational Leadership," *Journal of Business and Psychology*, Spring 1995, p. 316.

28. Carlos Ghosn, "First Person: Saving the Business Without Losing the Company," *Harvard Business Review*, January 2002, p. 40.

29. Literature reviewed in Sally A. Carless, Alexander J. Wearing, and Leon Mann, "A Short Measure of Transformational Leadership," *Journal of Business and Psychology*, Spring 2000, pp. 389–405.

30. Timothy A. Judge and Joyce E. Bono, "Five-Factor Model of Personality and Transformational Leadership," *Journal of Applied Psychology*, October 2000, pp. 751–765.

31. Robert E. Ployhart, Being-Chong Lim, and Kim-Yin Chan, "Exploring Relations Between Typical and Maximum Performance Ratings and the Five Factor Model of Personality," *Personnel Psychology*, Winter 2001, pp. 809–843.

32. Jane M. Howell and Bruce J. Avolio, "Transformational Leadership, Transactional Leadership, Locus of Control, and Support for Innovation: Key Predictors of Consolidated-Business-Unit Performance," *Academy of Management Journal*, August 1998, pp. 387–409.

33. Boas Shamir, Eliav Zakay, Esther Breinin, and Micha Poppa, "Correlates of Charismatic Leadership Behavior in Military Units: Subordinates' Attitudes, Unit Characteristics, and Superiors' Appraisal of Leadership Performance," *Academy of Management Journal*, August 1998, pp. 387–409.

34. Warren G. Bennis and Burt Nanus, *Leaders: Strategies for Taking Charge* (New York: Harper & Row, 1985), p. 223.

35. Robert C. Tucker, "The Theory of Charismatic Leadership," *Daedalus*, Summer 1968, pp. 731–756.

36. Howell and Avolio, "The Ethics of Charismatic Leadership," pp. 52–53.

37. Roger Dawson, *Secrets of Power Persuasion: Everything You'll Need to Get Anything You'll Ever Want* (Upper Saddle River, N.J.: Prentice-Hall, 1992), pp. 179–194.

Chapter 4

1. Adapted from Mark Gimein, "Sam Walton Made Us a Promise," *Fortune*, March 18, 2002, p. 122.

2. Ralph M. Stogdill and Alvin E. Coons, eds., *Leader Behavior: Its Description and Measurement* (Columbus: The Ohio State University Bureau of Business Research, 1957); Carroll L. Shartle, *Executive Performance and Leadership* (Upper Saddle River, N.J.: Prentice Hall, 1956).

3. Margaret Littman, "Best Bosses Tell All," *Working Woman*, October 2000, p. 50.

4. Darnell Little, "A Knight Who Is Not Errant," *BusinessWeek*, July 24, 2000, p. 80.

5. Thomas J. Peters and Robert H. Waterman, Jr., *In Search of Excellence: Lessons from America's Companies* (New York: Harper & Row, 1982).

6. Desa Philadelphia, "Q&A: Larry Bossidy on Execution." *Time*, **Global Business,** July 2002, p. B5. See also Larry Bossidy and Ram Charan, *Execution: The Discipline of Getting Things Done* (New York: Crown Business, 2002).

7. Shawn Tully, "Rebuilding Wall Street," *Fortune*, October 1, 2001, pp. 95–96.

8. Ronald A. Heifetz and Donald R. Laurie, "The Work of Leadership," *Harvard Business Review,* January–February 1997, pp. 124–134.

9. "A CEO on the Go: Randy Komisar on the Art of Snap Leadership," *Executive Strategies,* July 2000, p. 3.

10. John P. Kotter, "What Leaders Really Do," *Harvard Business Review,* May–June 1990, pp. 105–106.

11. David S. Brown, "Manager's New Job Is Concert Building," *HR Magazine,* September 1990, p. 42.

12. Henry Mintzberg, "Covert Leadership: Notes on Managing Professionals," *Harvard Business Review,* November–December 1998, pp. 140–147.

13. Jay A. Conger, *Learning to Lead: The Art of Transforming Managers into Leaders* (San Francisco: Jossey-Bass, 1992), p. 131.

14. "What Would Jack Welch Do Next?" *Worth,* November 2001. Cited in "Leadership Is Back," *Executive Leadership,* January 2002, p. 1.

15. Kotter, "What Leaders Really Do," p. 107.

16. Gerald Secour Couzens, *Success,* November 1998, p. 55.

17. Don Dinkmeyer and Dan Eckstein, *Leadership by Encouragement* (Delray Beach, Fla.: St. Lucie Press, 1995).

18. "Covey Proposes Principle-Based Leadership," *Management Review,* September 1995, p. 21.

19. Michael Warshaw, "Guts and Glory," *Success,* March 1997, p. 31.

20. Robert K. Greenleaf, *The Power of Servant Leadership* (San Francisco: Berrett-Koehler Publishers Inc., 1998).

21. Based on Greenleaf, *Servant Leadership: A Journey into the Nature of Legitimate Power and Greatness* (Mahwah, N.J.: Paulist Press, 1997); Michael Useem, "The Leadership Lessons of Mt. Everest," *Harvard Business Review,* October 2001, pp. 53–54; and "Blueprint for a Servant Leader," *Working Smart,* March 2000, p. 7. Studies reviewed in Jai Ghorpade, "Managing Six Paradoxes of 360-Degree Feedback," *Academy of Management Executive,* February 2000, pp. 140–150.

22. Robert Hoffman, "Ten Reasons Why You Should Use 360-Degree Feedback," *HR Magazine,* April 1995, p. 84.

23. D. Douglas Huet-Cox, Tjai M. Nielsen, and Eric Sundstrom, "Get the Most from 360-Degree Feedback: Put It on the Internet," *HR Magazine,* May 1999, pp. 92–103.

24. Jai Ghorpade, "Managing Six Paradoxes of 360-Degree Feedback," *Academy of Management Executive,* February 2000, p. 141.

25. Bruce Pfau and Ira Kay, "Does 360-Degree Feedback Negatively Affect Company Performance?" *HR Magazine,* June 2002, pp. 58–59.

26. Joan F. Brett and Leanne E. Atwater, "360° Feedback: Accuracy, Reactions, and Perceptions of Usefulness," *Journal of Applied Psychology,* October 2001, pp. 930–942.

27 Research by Michael Useem, reported in Bill Breen, "Trickle-Up Leadership," *Fast Company,* November 2001, p. 70.

28. Brent Schlender, "All You Need Is Love, $50 Billion and Killer Software Code-Named Longhorn," *Fortune,* July 8, 2002. p. 59.

29. Robert R. Blake and Anne Adams McCarse, *Leadership Dilemmas and Solutions* (Houston, Tex.: Gulf Publishing, 1991).

30. Bruce M. Fisher and Jack E. Edwards, "Consideration and Initiating Structure and Their Relationship with Leader Effectiveness: A Meta-Analysis," *Academy of Management Best Papers Proceedings,* 1988, p. 204.

31. Gayle Sato Stodder, "Goodbye Mom & Pop: The Neighborhood's Not Big Enough for Today's Entrepreneur. Only the World Will Do," *Entrepreneur,* May 1999, pp. 145–151; Michael Warshaw, "The Mind-Style of the Entrepreneur," *Success,* April 1993, pp. 28–33.

32. Jay Greene, "The Man Behind All Those E-Ads," *BusinessWeek,* June 26, 2000, pp. 76–77.

33. Fred Vogelstein, "Can Schwab Get Its Mojo Back?" *Fortune,* September 17, 2001, pp. 93–98.

34. Stodder, "Goodbye, Mom & Pop," p. 151.

35. John Greenwald, "Slice, Dice and Devour," *Time,* October 26, 1998, p. 65.

36. Judy Rosener, "Ways Women Lead," *Harvard Business Review,* November–December 1990, pp. 119–125.

37. Cited in "Debate: Ways Men and Women Lead," *Harvard Business Review,* January–February 1991, p. 151.

38. Debra Phillips, "The Gender Gap," *Entrepreneur,* May 1995, pp. 110, 111.

39. Rochelle Sharpe, "As Leaders, Women Rule," *BusinessWeek,* November 20, 2000, pp. 75–84.

40. Michele Conlin, "She's Gotta Have 'It'," *BusinessWeek,* July 22, 2002, p. 88.

41. Research reported in Michael Schrage, "Why Can't a Woman Be More Like a Man?" *Fortune,* August 16, 1999, p. 184.

42. Much of the research on this topic is summarized in Mary Crawford, *Talking Difference: On Gender and Language* (London: Sage Publications, 1995).

43. Jan Grant, "Women Managers: What Can They Offer Organizations?" *Organizational Dynamics,* Winter 1988.

44. Bernard M. Bass, *Bass & Stogdill's Handbook of Leadership: Theory, Research and Managerial Applications,* 3rd ed. (New York: The Free Press, 1990), p. 112.

45. Quoted in Phillips, "The Gender Gap," p. 112.

46. Daniel Goleman, "Leadership That Gets Results," *Harvard Business Review,* March–April 2000, pp. 78–90.

47. Felix Brodbeck, Michael Frese, and Mansour Havidan, "Leadership Made in Germany: Low on Compassion, High on Performance," *Academy of Management Executive,* February 2002, pp. 16–30.

48. Ralph M. Stogdill, "Historical Trends in Leadership Theory and Research," *Journal of Contemporary Business,* Autumn 1974, p. 7.

49. "Directive Management or Not?" *Working Smart,* December 1992, p. 3.

Chapter 5

1. Erin Strout, "Dealing with Disaster: Preparation Is Key When Tragedy Strikes," *Working Woman,* February 2001, p. 71.

2. Donald M. Moretti, Carol L. Morken, and Jeanne M. Borkowski, "Profiles of the American CEO: Comparing *Inc.* and *Fortune* Executives," *Journal of Business and Psychology,* Winter 2001, pp. 193–205.

3. For a synthesis of contingency theory by one of its developers, see Martin M. Chemers, *An Integrative Theory of Leadership* (Mahwah, N.J.: Lawrence Erlbaum Associates, 1997), pp. 28–38. See also Fred E. Fiedler, Martin M. Chemers, and Linda Mahar, *Improving Leadership Effectiveness: The Leader-Match Concept,* 2nd ed. (New York: Wiley, 1994).

4. Robert J. House, "A Path-Goal Theory of Leader Effectiveness," *Administrative Science Quarterly,* September 1971, pp. 321–328; Robert T. Keller, "A Test of the Path-Goal Theory with Need for Clarity as a Moderator in Research and Development Organizations," *Journal of Applied Psychology,* April 1989, pp. 208–212; Robert J. House and Terence R. Mitchell, "Path-Goal Theory of Leadership," *Journal of Contemporary Business,* Autumn 1974, pp. 81–97.

5. House and Mitchell, "Path-Goal Theory," p. 84; Bernard M. Bass, *Bass & Stogdill's Handbook of Leadership: Theory, Research, & Managerial Applications,* 3rd ed. (New York: The Free Press, 1990), p. 633.

6. Chemers, *An Integrative Theory of Leadership,* p. 48.

7. Paul Hersey, Kenneth H. Blanchard, and Dewey E. Johnson, *Management of Organizational Behavior: Utilizing Human Resources,* 7th ed. (Upper Saddle River, N.J.: Prentice Hall, 1996), pp. 188–223.

8. Bass, *Bass & Stogdill's Handbook,* p. 493.

9. Victor H. Vroom, "Leadership and the Decision-Making Process," *Organizational Dynamics,* Spring 2000, pp. 82–93.

10. Richard H. G. Field and Robert J. House, "A Test of the Vroom-Yetton Model Using Manager and Subordinate Reports," *Journal of Applied Psychology,* June 1990, pp. 362–366.

11. Susan Caminiti, "Turnaround Titan," *Working Woman,* December–January 1999, p. 57.

12. Fred E. Fiedler and Joseph E. Garcia, *New Approaches to Effective Leadership: Cognitive Resources and Organizational Performance* (New York: Wiley, 1987); Robert P. Vecchio, "Theoretical and Empirical Examination of Cognitive Resource Theory," *Journal of Applied Psychology,* April 1990, p. 141; Chemers, *An Integrative Theory of Leadership,* pp. 38–40.

13. Vecchio, "Theoretical and Empirical Examination of Cognitive Resource Theory," pp. 141–147; Vecchio, "Cognitive Resource Theory: Issues for Specifying a Test of the Theory," *Journal of Applied Psychology,* June 1992, p. 66.

14. Charles M. Farkas and Suzy Wetlaufer, "The Ways Chief Executive Officers Lead," *Harvard Business Review,* May–June 1996, pp. 110–122; Charles M. Farkas and Philippe DeBacker, *Maximum Leadership: The World's Leading CEOs Share Their Five Strategies for Success* (New York: Henry Holt, 1996).

15. Farkas and Wetlaufer, "The Ways Chief Executive Officers Lead," p. 116.

16. "How Situational Leadership Fits Today's Organizations," *Supervisory Management,* February 1996, p. 3.

17. Research cited in Gary Yukl, *Leadership in Organizations,* 5th ed. (Upper Saddle River, N.J.: Prentice Hall, 2002), p. 344.

18. James E. Dutton et al., "Leading in Times of Trauma," *Harvard Business Review,* January 2002, p. 56.

19. Charles Fishman, "Crisis and Confidence at Ground Zero," *Fast Company,* December 2001, pp. 108–113.

20. Suzanne Koudsi, "How to Cope with Tragedy," *Fortune,* October 1, 2001, p. 34.

21. Chester Dawson, "What Japan's CEOs Can Learn from Bridgestone," *BusinessWeek,* January 29, 2001, p. 50.

22. Barbara Baker Clark, "Leadership During a Crisis," *Executive Leadership,* December 2001, p. 8.

23. Michael E. McGill and John W. Slocum, Jr., "A Little Leadership Please?" *Organizational Dynamics,* Winter 1998, p. 48.

Suggested path for Leadership Skill-Building Exercise 5-2: Analysis for time-driven decision: H H H L H H L CONSULT GROUP.

Chapter 6

1. Excerpted from Maureen McDonald, "Businesswoman's Dream Brings Coats to School," from the *Detroit News,* June 14, 2002. Copyright © 2002 the Detroit News. Reprinted with permission from the Detroit News.

2. James G. Clawson, *Level Three Leadership: Getting Below the Surface,* 2nd ed. (Upper Saddle River, N.J.: Prentice-Hall, 2002), p. 54.

3. Thomas E. Becker, "Integrity in Organizations: Beyond Honesty and Conscientiousness," *Academy of Management Review,* January 1998, pp. 154–161.

4. Robert Simons, Henry Mintzberg, and Kunal Basu, "Memo to CEOs Re Five Half-Truths of Business," *Fast Company,* June 2002, p. 118.

5. Peter G. Northouse, *Leadership: Theory and Practice,* 2nd ed. (Thousand Oaks, Calif: Sage, 2001), p. 263.

6. Clawson, *Level Three Leadership,* p. 57.

7. Joseph L. Badaracco, Jr., "We Don't Need Another Hero," *Harvard Business Review,* September 2001, pp. 120–126.

8. "Fed Chief Points to Cautious Recovery," Gannett News Service, July 17, 2002.

9. Research synthesized in Richard L. Daft, *Leadership: Theory and Practice* (Fort Worth, Tex.: The Dryden Press, 1999), pp. 369–370.

10. James L. Bowditch and Anthony F. Buono, *A Primer on Organizational Behavior,* 5th ed. (New York: Wiley, 2001), p. 4.

11. Kris Maher, "Wanted: Ethical Employer," *Wall Street Journal,* July 9, 2002, p. B1.

12. Keith A. Lavine and Elina S. Moore, "Corporate Consciousness: Defining the Paradigm," *Journal of Business and Psychology,* Summer 1996, pp. 401–413.

13. Robert Levering and Milton Moskowitz, "The 100 Best Companies to Work for: The Best in the Worst of Time," *Fortune,* February 4, 2002, p. 72.

14. Brenda L. Flannery and Douglas R. May, "Environmental Ethical Decision Making in the U. S. Metal Finishing Industry," *Academy of Management Journal,* August 2000, pp. 642–662.

15. Susan Berfield, "Selling Furniture and Tolerance," *BusinessWeek,* October 22, 2001, p. 68.

16. Karl Taro Greenfield, "A New Way of Giving," *Time,* July 24, 2000, pp. 48–51; Anamaria Wilson, "Better Reading for $100 Million," *Time,* January 31, 2000. p. 55.

17. John A. Byrne, "The New Face of Philanthropy," *BusinessWeek,* December 2, 2002, p. 84.

18. Adam Cohen, "Peeping Larry," *Time,* July 10, 2000, p. 94.

19. Dayton Fandray, "The Ethical Company," *Workforce,* December 2000, p. 76.

20. Michael Duffy, "What Did They Know . . . When Did They Know It?" *Time,* January 28, 2002, pp. 19–20.

21. Study reported in www.business-ethics.org, and cited in Deb Koen, "Ethical Conduct Is Good for Business," Rochester, New York, *Democrat and Chronicle,* June 16, 2002, p. 4E.

22. Sandra A. Waddock and Samuel B. Graves, "The Corporate Social Performance–Financial Performance Link," *Strategic Management Journal,* Spring 1997, pp. 303–319.

23. Daniel J. Brass, Kenneth D. Butterfield, and Bruce C. Skaggs, "Relationships and Unethical Behavior: A Social Network Perspective," *Academy of Management Review,* January 1998, pp. 14–31.

Chapter 7

1. Adapted from "The Top 24 Managers, Noël Forgeard," *BusinessWeek,* January 8, 2001, p. 76. Reprinted from January 8, 2001 issue of *BusinessWeek* by special permission, copyright © 2001 by The McGraw-Hill Companies, Inc.

2. Dale E. Zand, *The Leadership Triad: Knowledge, Trust, and Power* (New York: Oxford University Press, 1997), p. 4.

3. John R. French and Bertram Raven, "The Basis of Social Power," in Dorwin Cartwright, ed., *Studies in Social Power* (Ann Arbor, Mich.: Institute for Social Research, 1969); Timothy R. Hinkin and Chester A. Schriescheim, "Power and Influence: The View from Below," *Personnel,* May 1988, pp. 47–50.

4. Zand, *The Leadership Triad,* p. 138.

5. Cited in Marshall Loeb, "The Bad Boss Gets a New Life," *Fortune,* May 27, 1996, p. 138.

6. Frank Gibney, Jr., "Vroooom at the Top," *Time,* January 14, 2002, p. 42.

7. Sydney Finkelstein, "Power in Top Management Teams: Dimensions, Measurement, and Validation," *Academy of Management Journal,* August 1992, p. 510.

8. Michael Warshaw, "The Good Guy's (and Gal's) Guide to Office Politics," *Fast Company,* April 1998,

p. 158. See also, www.fastcompany.com/online/14/politics.html.

9. Finkelstein, "Power in Top Management Teams," p. 510.

10. Jeffrey Pfeffer, *Managing with Power: Power and Influence in Organizations* (Boston: Harvard Business School Press, 1992), pp. 100–101.

11. Morgan McCall, Jr. *Power, Influence, and Authority: The Hazards of Carrying a Sword* (Greensboro, N.C.: Center for Creative Leadership, 1978), p. 5.

12. C. R. Hinings, D. J. Hickson, C. A. Lee, R. E. Schenck, and J. W. Pennings, "Strategic Contingencies Theory of Intraorganizational Power," *Administrative Science Quarterly*, 1971, pp. 216–229.

13. Hermina Iberra, "Network Centrality, Power, and Innovation Involvement: Determinants of Technical and Administrative Roles," *Academy of Management Journal*, June 1993, pp. 471–501.

14. Leanne E. Atwater and Francis J. Yammarino, "Bases of Power in Relation to Leader Behavior: A Field Investigation," *Journal of Business and Psychology*, Fall 1996, pp. 3–22.

15. Gregory G. Dess and Joseph Picken, "Changing Roles: Leadership in the 21st Century," *Organizational Dynamics*, Winter 2000, p. 22.

16. Gretchen M. Spreitzer, "Psychological Empowerment in the Workplace: Dimensions, Measurement, and Validation," *Academy of Management Journal*, October 1995, pp. 1442–1465.

17. Jay A. Conger, "Leadership: The Art of Empowering Others," *Academy of Management Executive*, August 1995, pp. 21–31.

18. Barbara Ettorre, "The Empowerment Gap: Hype vs. Reality," *HRfocus*, July 1997, p. 5.

19. Ibid.

20. Quoted in Phillip M. Perry, "Seven Errors to Avoid When Empowering Your Staff," *Success Workshop* (a supplement to *Manager's Edge*), March 1999, p. 3.

21. Bradley L. Kirkman and Benson Rosen, "Beyond Self-Management: Antecedents and Consequences of Team Empowerment," *Academy of Management Journal*, February 1999, p. 59.

22. Kyle Dover, "Avoiding Empowerment Traps," *Management Review*, January 1999, p. 52.

23. Dimitry Elias Léger, "Tell Me Your Problem, and I'll Tell You Mine," *Fortune*, October 16, 2000, p. 408.

24. Christopher Robert et al., "Empowerment and Continuous Improvement in the United States, Mexico, Poland, and India: Predicting Fit on the Basis of the Dimensions of Power Distance and Individualism," *Journal of Applied Psychology*, October 2000, pp. 751–765.

25. Several of the ideas in this section are based on David A. Whetton and Kim S. Cameron, *Developing Management Skills*, 5th ed. (Upper Saddle River, N.J.: Prentice Hall, 2002), pp. 425–431; Odette Pollar, "Delegation of Duties Is the Key to Growth in the Workplace," *The Pryor Report*, July 1998, p. 10; "Tom Sawyer at Work: The Art of Delegation," www.employer-employee.com; "Management by Delegation," *Manager's Intelligence Report*, sample issue, distributed 2002.

26. Quoted in John Eckberg, "Learning How to Delegate," Gannett News Service, January 11, 1999.

27. Gerald R. Ferris et al., "Political Skill at Work," *Organizational Dynamics*, Spring 2000, p. 25.

28. Polly Labarre, "The New Face of Office Politics," *Fast Company*, October 1999, p. 80.

29. Gerald Biberman, "Personality Characteristics and Work Attitudes of Persons with High, Moderate, and Low Political Tendencies," *Psychological Reports*, vol. 57, 1985, p. 1309.

30. Pamela L. Perrewé et al., "Political Skill: An Antidote for Workplace Stressors," *Academy of Management Executive*, August 2000, p. 115.

31. Tom Peters, "Power," *Success*, November 1994, p. 34.

32. William H. Newman, *Administrative Action: The Techniques of Organization and Management* (Upper Saddle River, N.J.: Prentice-Hall, 1963), p. 90.

33. Warshaw, "The Good Guy's (and Gal's) Guide," p. 160.

34. A good example is Sandy J. Wayne and Robert C. Liden, "Effects of Impression Management on Performance Ratings," *Academy of Management Journal*, February 1995, pp. 232–260.

35. "Career 'Insurance' Protects DP Professionals from Setbacks: Encourages Growth," *Data Management*, June 1986, p. 33.

36. Peters, "Power," p. 34.

37. "When Flattery Pays," *Executive Strategies*, March 1998, p. 1.

38. Research reported in Laura Lippman, "The Age of Obsequiousness: Flattering Your Way up the Corporate Ladder," Baltimore, Maryland, *The Sun*, October 24, 1994.

39. Joann S. Lublin, "'Did I Just Say That?! How You Can Recover from Foot-in-Mouth," *The Wall Street Journal*, June 18, 2002, p. B1.

40. "German Grip Tightens at Daimler/Chrysler," Associated Press, September 25, 1998.

41. Annette Simmons, *Territorial Games: Understanding and Ending Turf Wars at Work* (New York: AMACOM, 1998).

42. John M. Maslyn and Donald B. Fedor, "Perceptions of Politics: Does Measuring Foci Matter?" *Journal of Applied Psychology,* August 1998, p. 650.

43. Wayne A. Hochwarter, L. A. Witt, and K. Michele Kacmar, "Perceptions of Organizational Politics as a Moderator of the Relationship Between Conscientiousness and Job Performance," *Journal of Applied Psychology,* June 2000, pp. 472–478.

44. L. A. Witt, "Enhancing Organizational Goal Congruence: A Solution to Organizational Politics," *Journal of Applied Psychology,* August 1998, pp. 666–674.

45. Robert P. Vecchio, *Organizational Behavior,* 4th ed. (Fort Worth, Tex.: The Dryden Press, 2000), p. 136.

46. "Throw Politics Out of Your Office," *Fred Pryor's Manager's Edge* (Alexandria, Va.: Briefings Publishing Group, July 2001), p. 8.

47. Adapted from Sarah Myers McGinty, *Power Talk: Using Language to Build Authority* (New York: Warner Books, 2001), as cited in "6 Ways to Judge Internal Dynamics," *Executive Leadership,* August 2001, p. 7.

Chapter 8

1. Keith H. Hammonds, "Grassroots Leadership: U. S. Military Academy," *Fast Company,* June 2001, p. 114.

2. Allan R. Cohen, Stephen L. Fink, Herman Gadon, and Robin D. Willits, *Effective Behavior in Organizations: Cases, Concepts, and Student Experiences,* 5th ed. (Homewood, Ill.: Irwin, 1992), p. 139.

3. Colin Powell, "A Leadership Primer," PowerPoint presentation for Department of the Army, United States of America, undated.

4. Gary Yukl, *Leadership in Organizations,* 5th ed. (Upper Saddle River, N.J.: Prentice Hall, 2002), p. 143.

5. Patricia Sellers, "Something to Prove," *Fortune,* June 24, 2002, p. 94.

6. Gary Yukl and J. Bruce Tracey, "Consequences of Influence Tactics Used with Subordinates, Peers, and the Boss," *Journal of Applied Psychology,* August 1992, p. 526.

7. Mitchell S. Nesler, Herman Aguinis, Brian M. Quigley, and James T. Tedeschi, "The Effect of Credibility on Perceived Power," *Journal of Applied Social Psychology,* vol. 23, no. 17, 1993, pp. 1407–1425.

8. Patricia Sellers, "Exit the Builder, Enter the Repairman," *Fortune,* March 19, 2001, p. 87.

9. Bernard Keys and Thomas Case, "How to Become an Influential Manager," *Academy of Management Executive,* November 1990, p. 44.

10. Corie Brown, "Time Inc.'s Woman of the Fiscal Year," *Los Angeles Times* (www.latimes.com), July 20, 2002.

11. "You Scratch My Back . . . Tips on Winning Your Colleague's Cooperation," *Working Smart,* October 1999, p. 1.

12. Gary Yukl, *Skills for Managers and Leaders: Texts, Cases, and Exercises* (Upper Saddle River, N.J.: Prentice-Hall, 1990), pp. 58–62.

13. Jeffrey Pfeffer, *Managing with Power: Power and Influence in Organizations* (Boston: Harvard Business School Press, 1992), p. 224.

14. Cited in: "Choose Words That Inspire," *Executive Leadership,* March 2001, p. 2.

15. Yukl, *Skills for Managers,* p. 65.

16. Andrew J. DuBrin, "Sex Differences in the Endorsement of Influence Tactics and Political Behavior Tendencies," *Journal of Business and Psychology,* Fall 1989, p. 10.

17. Aixa M. Pascual, "Tidying Up at Home Depot," *BusinessWeek,* November 26, 2001, p. 102.

18. John Carreyrou and Vanessa Fuhrmans, "Vivendi Names CEO with Skills Messier Lacked," *Wall Street Journal,* July 5, 2002, p. A9.

19. Bernhard M. Bass, *Bass & Stogdill's Handbook of Leadership: Theory, Research, and Managerial Applications,* 3rd ed. (New York: The Free Press, 1990), p. 134.

20. David M. Buss, Mary Gomes, Dolly S. Higgins, and Karen Lauterbach, "Tactics of Manipulation," *Journal of Personality and Social Psychology,* December 1987, p. 1222.

21. Chad T. Lewis, Joseph E. Garcia, and Sarah M. Jobs, *Managerial Skills in Organizations* (Boston: Allyn & Bacon, 1990), p. 234.

22. Buss et al., "Tactics of Manipulation," p. 1222.

23. Gary Yukl and Cecilia M. Falbe, "Influence Tactics and Objectives in Upward, Downward, and Lateral Influence Attempts," *Journal of Applied Psychology,* April 1990, p. 133.

24. Buss et al., "Tactics of Manipulation," p. 1222.

25. David Kipnis and Stuart Schmidt, "Intraorganizational Influence Tactics: Explorations in Getting One's Way," *Journal of Applied Psychology,* August 1980, p. 445.

26. Amy Cortese, "I'm Humble, I'm Respectful," *BusinessWeek,* February 9, 1998, p. 40.

27. Comment contributed anonymously to author by a professor of organizational behavior, September 1996.

28. Yukl and Tracey, "Consequences of Influence Tactics," pp. 525–535.

29. Martin M. Chemers, *An Integrative Theory of Leadership* (Mahwah, N.J.: Lawrence Erlbaum Associates, 1997), p. 76.

30. Carole V. Wells and David Kipnis, "Trust, Dependency, and Control in the Contemporary Organization," *Journal of Business and Psychology*, Summer 2001, pp. 593–603.

31. Keys and Case, "How to Become an Influential Manager," p. 46.

32. David Kipnis and Stuart M. Schmidt, "Upward Influence Styles: Relationships with Performance Evaluation, Salary, and Stress," *Administrative Science Quarterly*, 1988, pp. 528–542.

33. Keys and Case, "How to Become an Influential Manager," p. 48.

Chapter 9

1. Excerpted from Sheila M. Puffer, "Continental Airlines' CEO Gordon Bethune on Teams and New Product Development," *Academy of Management Executive*, by Newsom, Walter B. Copyright © 1999 by *Academy of Management. Reproduced with permission of Academy of Management* in the format textbook via Copyright Clearance Center. August 1999, p. 28.

2. Edwin A. Locke and Associates, *The Essence of Leadership: The Four Keys to Leading Successfully* (New York: Lexington/Macmillan, 1991), p. 94.

3. W. Dyer, *Team Building: Issues and Alternatives* (Reading, Mass.: Addison-Wesley, 1977), as cited in Lynn R. Offerman and Rebecca K. Spiros, "The Science and Practice of Team Development: Improving the Link," *Academy of Management Journal*, April 2001, p. 380.

4. Jon R. Katzenbach and Douglas K. Smith, "The Discipline of Teams," *Harvard Business Review*, March–April 1993, p. 112.

5. Meredith Belbin, "Solo Leader/Team Leader: Antithesis in Style and Structure," in Michel Syrett and Clare Hogg, eds., *Frontiers of Leadership* (Oxford, England: Blackwell Publishers, 1992), p. 271.

6. William D. Hitt, *The Leader-Manager: Guidelines for Action* (Columbus, Ohio: Battelle Press, 1988), pp. 68–69.

7. Cited in Ellen Hart, "Top Teams," *Management Review*, February 1996, p. 90.

8. Diane Brady, "An Executive Whose Time Has Gone," *BusinessWeek*, August 28, 2000, p. 125.

9. Ibid.

10. Seanna Browder, "Great Service Wasn't Enough," *BusinessWeek*, April 19, 1999, p. 127.

11. Irving L. Janus, *Victims of Groupthink: A Psychological Study of Foreign Policy Decisions and Fiascoes* (Boston: Houghton Mifflin, 1972); Glen Whyte, "Groupthink Reconsidered," *Academy of Management Review*, January 1989, pp. 40–56.

12. Kenneth Labich, "Elite Teams," *Fortune*, February 19, 1996, p. 90.

13. Alan B. Drexler and Russ Forrester, "Teamwork—Not Necessarily the Answer," *HR Magazine*, January 1998, pp. 55–58.

14. Shari Caudron, "Teamwork Takes Work," *Personnel Journal*, February 1994, p. 45; Andrew J. DuBrin, *The Reengineering Survival Guide: Managing and Succeeding in the Changing Workplace* (Mason, Ohio: Thomson Executive Press, 1996), pp. 129–144.

15. Ruth Wageman, "Critical Success Factors for Creating Superb Self-Managing Teams," *Organizational Dynamics*, Summer 1997, p. 57.

16. Stephen Baker, "Nokia: Can CEO Ollila Keep the Cellular Superstar Flying High?" *BusinessWeek*, August 10, 1998, p. 56.

17. Dean Tjosvold and Mary M. Tjosvold, *The Emerging Leader: Ways to a Stronger Team* (New York: Lexington Books, 1993).

18. Vanessa Urch Druskat and Steven B. Wolff, "Building the Emotional Intelligence of Groups," *Harvard Business Review*, March 2001, pp. 80–90.

19. William A. Cohen, *The Art of the Leader* (Upper Saddle River, N.J.: Prentice Hall, 1990).

20. Mike Vance and Diane Deacon, *Think Outside the Box* (Franklin Lakes, N.J.: Career Press, 1995).

21. Paul S. George, "Teamwork Without Tears," *Personnel Journal*, November 1987, p. 129.

22. Clive Goodworth, "Some Thoughts on Creating a Team," in Syrett and Hogg, *Frontiers of Leadership*, p. 472.

23. Quoted in Nancy Hatch Woodward, "The Coming of the X Managers," *HR Magazine*, March 1999, pp. 75, 76.

24. Susan Sonnesyn Brooks, "Managing a Horizontal Revolution," *HR Magazine*, June 1995, p. 56.

25. Katzenbach and Smith, "The Discipline of Teams," pp. 118–119.

26. Lee G. Bolman and Terrence E. Deal, "What Makes a Team Work?" *Organizational Dynamics*, Autumn 1992, p. 6.

27. Anthony R. Montebello, "How to Jump the 5 Barriers to Good Teamwork," a supplement to the *Pryor Report Management Newsletter*, 1995.

28. Charles C. Manz and Henry P. Sims, Jr., "Leading Workers to Lead Themselves: The External Leadership of Self-Managing Work Teams," *Administrative Science Quarterly*, March 1987, p. 118.

29. Joann Muller, "Next Up: A No-Nonsense Hoosier," *BusinessWeek,* June 10, 2002, p. 80.

30. Dale E. Yeatts and Cloyd Hyten, *High Performing Self-Managed Work Teams: A Comparison of Theory and Practice* (Thousand Oaks, Calif.: Sage, 1998).

31. Wageman, "Critical Success Factors," p. 56.

32. Bolman and Deal, "What Makes a Team Work?" pp. 41–42.

33. Thomas J. McCoy, *Creating an "Open Book" Organization . . . Where Employees Think and Act like Business Partners* (New York: AMACOM, 1999); John Case, "HR Learns How to Open the Books," *HR Magazine,* May 1998, pp. 71–76.

34. "Open the Books to Educate Your Team: Motivate Your Employees with Bottom-Line Figures," *Working Smart,* May 1999, p. 7.

35. Study cited in "Poll Says Sports Helps Women's Career Paths," Rochester, New York *Democrat and Chronicle,* March 3, 2002, p. 1E.

36. Faith Keenan and Spencer E. Ante, "The New Teamwork," *BusinessWeek e.biz,* February 18, 2002, pp. EB 12–EB 16.

37. "Australian Outdoor Training & Tours: Corporate Training," www.aott.net/corporate.htm.

38. Adapted slightly from Nichole L. Torres, "Go, Team!" *Entrepreneur,* July 2002, p. 22.

39. Jennifer J. Laabs, "Team Training Goes Outdoors," *Personnel Journal,* June 1991, p. 59.

40. Jay A. Conger, *Learning to Lead: The Art of Transforming Managers into Leaders* (San Francisco: Jossey-Bass, 1992), p. 159.

41. Torres, "Go, Team!" p. 22.

42. George Graen and J. E. Cashman, "A Role Making Model of Leadership in Formal Organizations: A Developmental Approach," in J. G. Hunt and L. L. Larson, eds., *Leadership Frontiers* (Kent, Ohio: Kent State University Press, 1975), pp. 143–165; Robert P. Vecchio, "Leader-Member Exchange, Objective Performance, Employment Duration, and Supervisor Ratings: Testing for Moderation and Mediation," *Journal of Business and Psychology,* Spring 1998, p. 328.

43. Elaine M. Engle and Robert G. Lord, "Implicit Theories, Self-Schemas, and Leader-Member Exchange," *Academy of Management Journal,* August 1997, pp. 988–1010.

44. Robert P. Vecchio, "Are You IN or OUT with Your Boss?" *Business Horizons,* 1987, pp. 76-78. See also, Charlotte R. Gerstner and David W. Day, "Meta-Analytic Review of Leader-Member Exchange Theory: Correlates and Construct Issues," *Journal of Applied Psychology,* December 1997, pp. 827–844.

45. Howard J. Klein and Jay S. Kim, "A Field Study of the Influences of Situational Constraints, Leader-Member Exchange, and Goal Commitment on Performance," *Academy of Management Journal,* February 1998, pp. 88–95.

46. Randall P. Settoon, Nathan Bennett, and Robert C. Liden, "Social Exchange in Organizations: Perceived Organizational Support, Leader-Member Exchange, and Employee Reciprocity," *Journal of Applied Psychology,* June 1995, pp. 219–227.

47. Pamela Tierney and Talya N. Bauer, "A Longitudinal Assessment of LMX on Extra-Role Behavior," *Academy of Management Best Papers Proceedings,* 1996, pp. 298–302.

48. David A. Hofman and Frederick P. Morgeson, "Safety-Related Behavior as a Social Exchange: The Role of Perceived Organizational Support and Leader-Member Exchange," *Journal of Applied Psychology,* April 1999, pp. 286–296.

49. Robert C. Liden, Sandy J. Wayne, and Deal Stilwell, "A Longitudinal Study on the Early Development of Leader-Member Exchanges," *Journal of Applied Psychology,* August 1993, pp. 662–674.

50. "Promote Teamwork by Rearranging the Office," *people@work,* sample issue, 1999, published by Texas Professional Training Associates, Inc.

Chapter 10

1. Adapted from David Dorsey, "Andy Pearson Finds Love," *Fast Company,* August 2001, pp. 78, 80, 84.

2. Thad Green, *Motivation Management: Fueling Performance by Discovering What People Believe About Themselves and Their Organizations* (Palo Alto, Calif.: Davies-Black Publishing, 2000). An original version of expectancy theory applied to work motivation is Victor H. Vroom, *Work and Motivation* (New York: Wiley, 1964).

3. Alexander D. Stajkovic and Fred Luthans, "Social Cognitive Theory and Self-Efficacy: Going Beyond Traditional Motivational and Behavioral Approaches," *Organizational Dynamics,* Spring 1998, p. 66.

4. Wendelien Van Eerde and Henk Thierry, "Vroom's Expectancy Models and Work-Related Criteria: A Meta-Analysis," *Journal of Applied Psychology,* October 1996, pp. 548–556.

5. David A. Nadler and Edward E. Lawler III, "Motivation: A Diagnostic Approach," in Richard Hackman, Edward E. Lawler III, and Lyman W. Porter, eds., *Perspectives on Behavior in Organizations,* 2nd ed. (New York: McGraw-Hill, 1983), pp. 67–78; James A. F. Stoner and R. Edward Freeman, *Management,* 4th ed. (Upper Saddle River, N. J.: Prentice Hall, 1989), p. 448.

6. Uwe Kleinbeck, Hans-Henning Quast, Henk Thierry, and Hartmut Häcker, eds., *Work Motivation* (Hillsdale, N. J.: Lawrence Erlbaum Associates, 1990).

7. Edwin A. Locke and Gary P. Latham, *A Theory of Goal Setting and Task Performance* (Upper Saddle River, N. J: Prentice Hall, 1990).

8. Cited in "Set Outrageous Goals," *Executive Leadership*, June 2001, p. 7.

9. John J. Donovan and David J. Radosevich, "The Moderating Role of Goal Commitment on the Goal Difficulty-Performance Relationship: A Meta-Analytic Review and Critical Reanalysis," *Journal of Applied Psychology*, April 1998, pp. 308–315.

10. Don VandeWalle, Steven P. Brown, William L. Cron, and John W. Slocum, Jr., "The Influence of Goal Orientation and Self-Regulation Tactics on Sales Performance: A Longitudinal Field Test," *Journal of Applied Psychology*, April 1999, pp. 249–259.

11. P. Christopher Earley and Terri Lituchy, "Delineating Goal and Efficacy Effects: A Test of Three Models," *Journal of Applied Psychology*, February 1991, p. 83.

12. Fred Luthans and Alexander D. Stajkovic, "Reinforce for Performance: The Need to Go Beyond Pay and Even Rewards," *Academy of Management Executive*, May 1999, pp. 49, 56.

13. An update on some of the behavior modification rules is presented in ibid., pp. 49–57.

14. Fred Luthans, *Organizational Behavior*, 6th ed. (New York: McGraw-Hill, 1992), p. 237.

15. Steven Kerr, *Ultimate Rewards: What Really Motivates People to Achieve* (Boston: Harvard Business School Publishing, 1997).

16. Alexander D. Stajkovic and Fred Luthans, "Differential Effects of Incentive Motivators on Work Performance," *Academy of Management Journal*, June 2001, pp. 580-590.

17. Jennifer Laabs, "Satisfy Them with More Than Money," *Workforce*, November 1998, p. 43.

18. Kenneth Hain, *Incentive*, June 1999, as cited in "Reward + Performance Measurement = Success," *Executive Leadership*, January 2001, p. 2.

19. Frank Gibney Jr., "Is He Built Ford Tough?" *Time*, November 12, 2001, p. 83.

20. William D. Hitt, *The Leader-Manager: Guidelines for Action* (Columbus, Ohio: Battelle Press, 1988), pp. 186–187.

21. David B. Peterson and Mary Dee Hicks, *Leader as Coach: Strategies for Coaching and Developing Others* (Minneapolis, Minn.: Personnel Decisions, Inc., 1996).

22. Roger D. Evered and James C. Selman, "Coaching and the Art of Management," *Organizational Dynamics*, Autumn 1989, p. 15.

23. Ian Cunningham and Linda Honold, "Everyone Can Be a Coach," *HR Magazine*, June 1998, pp. 63–66.

24. Hitt, *The Leader-Manager*, pp. 186–187.

25. "Coaching—One Solution to a Tight Training Budget," *HRfocus*, August 2002, p. 7.

26. "Coach Your Employees to Success with This Plan," *Manager's Edge*, May 2000, p. 1.

27. Hitt, *The Leader-Manager*, pp. 187–188.

28. Peter Frost and Sandra Robinson, "The Toxic Handler: Organizational Hero and Casualty," *Harvard Business Review*, July–August 1999, pp. 96–106.

29. "Ease into Coaching with This Advice," *Manager's Edge*, October 2000, p. 3.

30. Richard J. Walsh, "Ten Basic Counseling Skills," *Supervisory Management*, November 1990, p. 6.

31. "Fast Tips for Savvy Managers," *Executive Strategies*, April 1998, p. 1.

32. Amy Joyce, "Career Watch: Business Coach," *Washington Post* syndicated story, September 14, 1998.

33. Interview by Bob Rosner, "'Team Players' Expect Real Choices," *Workforce*, May 2001, p. 63.

34. Douglas T. Hall, Karen L. Otazo, and George P. Hollenbeck, "Behind Closed Doors: What Really Happens in Executive Coaching," *Organizational Dynamics*, Winter 1999, pp. 48–49.

35. Annie Fisher, "Readers Weigh In on Coaches, Crazy Colleagues," *Fortune*, July 23, 2001, p. 272.

36. Steve Berglas, "The Very Real Dangers of Executive Coaching," *Harvard Business Review*, June 2002, pp. 86–92.

Chapter 11

1. Adapted from Scott Smith and Paul Gallagher, "How iWon Won the Web," *Success*, November 2000, pp. 28–33.

2. Edward R. Roberts, "Managing Invention and Innovation," *Research Technology Management*, January–February 1998, pp. 1–19.

3. Cynthia D. McCauley, Russ S. Moxley, and Ellen Van Velsor, *The Center for Creative Leadership Handbook of Leadership Development* (San Francisco: Jossey-Bass, 1998), p. 20.

4. Richard W. Woodman, John E. Sawyer, and Ricky W. Griffin, "Toward a Theory of Organizational Creativity," *Academy of Management Review*, April 1993, p. 293.

5. G. Wallas, *The Art of Thought* (New York: Harcourt Brace, 1926).

6. Anna Esaki-Smith and Michael Warshaw, "Renegades 1993: Creating the Future," *Success,* January–February 1993, p. 36.

7. Teresa M. Amabile, "The Social Psychology of Creativity: A Componential Conceptualization," *Journal of Personality and Social Psychology,* August 1993, pp. 357–376.

8. John A. Gover, Royce Ronning, and Cecil R. Reynolds, eds., *Handbook of Creativity* (New York: Plenum Press, 1989); Teresa M. Amabile, "How to Kill Creativity," *Harvard Business Review,* September–October 1998, pp. 78–79.

9. Cited in Anita Bruzzeset, "Seek Out Creative Free Spirit," Gannett News Service, October 31, 2000.

10. Amabile, "How to Kill Creativity," p. 79.

11. Mihaly Csikszentmihalyi, "If We Are So Rich, Why Aren't We Happy?" *American Psychologist,* October 1999, p. 824.

12. Michael Krantz, "Steve's Two Jobs," *Time,* October 18, 1999, pp. 62–68.

13. Greg R. Oldham and Anne Cummings, "Employee Creativity: Personal and Contextual Factors at Work," *Academy of Management Journal,* June 1996, pp. 607–634.

14. Amabile, "How to Kill Creativity," pp. 78–79; Amabile, *Creativity in Context* (Boulder, CO: Westview Press, 1996).

15. "Putting Creativity into Action," *Success Workshop,* supplement to *The Pryor Report,* April 1996, p. 1.

16. McCauley, Moxley, and Van Velsor, *The Center for Creative Leadership Handbook of Leadership Development,* p. 111.

17. "Jets May Serve as Satellites," Associated Press, September 24, 1998.

18. Quoted in Polly LaBarre, "Weird Ideas That Work," *Fast Company,* January 2002, p. 70.

19. Fara Warner, "How Google Searches Itself," *Fast Company,* July 2002, pp. 50, 52.

20. Richard Lally, "How to Produce More Creative Ideas," *Getting Results,* November 1996, p. 6.

21. "Future Edisons of America: Turn Your Employees Into Inventors," *Working Smart,* June 2000, p. 2.

22. "Brainstorm Better Ideas with the 6-3-5 Method," *Manager's Intelligence Report,* undated sample distributed in September 1996.

23. Keng L. Siau, "Electronic Brainstorming," *Innovative Leader,* April 1997, p. 3.

24. Michael Schrage, "Playing Around with Brainstorming," *Harvard Business Review,* March 2001, pp.

149–154. [Review of Tom Kelley with Jonathan Littman, *The Art of Innovation: Lessons in Creativity from IDEO, America's Leading Design Firm*] (New York: Doubleday/Currency, 2001).

25. Anne Sagen, "Creativity Tools: Versatile Problem Solvers That Can Double as Fun and Games, *Supervisory Management,* October 1991, pp. 1–2.

26. Edward Glassman, "Creative Problem Solving: New Techniques," *Supervisory Management,* March 1989, p. 16.

27. Cited in Robert McGarvey, "Turn It On: Creativity Is Crucial to Your Business' Success," *Entrepreneur,* 1996, p. 156.

28. Lisa Bannon, "Think Tank in Toyland," *The Wall Street Journal,* June 6, 2002, p. B1.

29. Scott S. Smith, "Grounds for Success," *Entrepreneur,* May 1998, p. 120.

30. Mike Vance and Diane Deacon, *Think Out of the Box* (Franklin Lakes, N.J.: Career Press, 1995).

31. Alex F. Osburn, quoted in "Breakthrough Ideas," *Success,* October 1990, p. 50.

32. Eric von Hipple, Stefan Thomke, and Mary Sonnack, "Creating Breakthroughs at 3M," *Harvard Business Review,* September–October 1999, pp. 49, 183.

33. "Breakthrough Ideas," *Success,* October 1990, p. 38.

34. "Be a Creative Problem Solver," *Executive Strategies,* June 6, 1989, pp. 1–2.

35. Amabile, "How to Kill Creativity," pp. 80-81; Teresa M. Amabile, Constance N. Hadley, and Steven J. Kramer, "Creativity Under the Gun," *Harvard Business Review,* August 2002, pp. 52–61; Annie Finnigan, "Different Strokes," *Working Woman,* April 2001, pp. 42–48; G. Pascal Zachary, "Mighty Is the Mongrel," *Fast Company,* July 2000, pp. 270–274.

36. Robert McGarvey, "Idea Inc.," *Entrepreneur,* March 1998, pp. 127, 129.

37. Pamela Tierney, Steven M. Farmer, and George B. Graen, "An Examination of Leadership and Employee Creativity: The Relevance of Traits and Relationships," *Personnel Psychology,* Autumn 1999, pp. 591–620.

38. Alan G. Robinson and Sam Stern, *Corporate Creativity: How Innovation and Improvement Actually Happen* (San Francisco: Berrett-Koehler Publishers, 1997).

39. Shari Caudron, "Strategies for Managing Creative Workers," *Personnel Journal,* December 1994, pp. 104–113.

40. Jim Rohwer, "GE Digs into Asia," *Fortune,* October 2, 2000, p. 165.

41. Keith H. Hammonds, "No Risk, No Reward," *Fast Company,* April 2002, pp. 81–93.
42. John R. Schermerhorn, Jr., James G. Hunt, and Richard N. Osburn, *Organizational Behavior,* 7th ed. (New York: Wiley, 2000), p. 403; Gareth Morgan, *Creative Organization Theory: A Resource-Book* (Newbury Park, Calif.: Sage, 1990); Rosabeth Moss Kanter, *The Change Masters* (New York: Simon & Schuster, 1983).
43. Ben Elgin, "A Do-It-Yourself Plan at Cisco," *BusinessWeek,* September 10, 2001, p. 52.
44. Michael Schrage, "Getting Beyond the Innovation Fetish," *Fortune,* November 13, 2000, p. 232.
45. Morgan, *Creative Organization Theory;* Kanter, *The Change Masters.*

Solutions to Leadership Skill-Building Exercise 11–3, Word Hints to Creativity

1. party	5. club	9. high	13. make
2. ball	6. dog	10. sugar	14. bean
3. cheese	7. paper	11. floor	15. light
4. cat	8. finger	12. green	

Chapter 12

1. "CEO Demotes Himself for a Day," Knight Ridder, September 23, 2002. Copyright © 2002 Knight Ridder/Tribune Media Services, Reprinted with permission
2. Bernard M. Bass, *Bass & Stogdill's Handbook of Leadership: Theory, Research, & Managerial Applications,* 3rd ed. (New York: The Free Press, 1990), p. 111.
3. M. Remland, "Leadership Impressions and Nonverbal Communication in a Superior-Subordinate Interaction," *Journal of Business Communications,* vol. 18, no. 3, 1981, pp. 17–29.
4. Peter Lowry and Byron Reimus, "Ready, Aim, Communicate!" *Management Review,* July 1996, pp. 40–43.
5. Ibid., p. 40.
6. James M. Kouzes and Barry Z. Posner, *The Leadership Challenge: How to Get Extraordinary Things Done in Organizations* (San Francisco: Jossey-Bass, 1987), p. 118.
7. Roberta H. Krapels and Vanessa D. Arnold, "Speaker Credibility in Persuasive Work Situations," *Business Education Forum,* December 1997, pp. 24–25.
8. Herman Aguinis, Mitchell S. Nesler, Meguimi Hosada, and James T. Tedeschi, "The Use of Influence Tactics in Persuasion," *Journal of Social Psychology,* vol. 134, no. 4, 1994, pp. 429–438.
9. Stephen P. Robbins and Phillip L. Hunsaker, *Training in Interpersonal Skills: Tips for Managing People at Work* (Upper Saddle River, N.J.: Prentice Hall, 1996), p. 115.
10. Jay Conger, "The Six Myths of Persuasion," *Executive Leadership,* October 2000, p. 8.
11. Mark Hendricks, "Wag Your Tale," *Entrepreneur,* February 2001, pp. 78–81.
12. Several of these examples are from "Avoid These Top Ten Language Errors," *Working Smart,* October 1991, p. 8.
13. William Strunk, Jr., and E. B. White, *The Elements of Style,* 4th ed., with a foreword by Roger Angell (Boston: Allyn and Bacon, 1999).
14. Michael W. Mercer, "How to Make a Fantastic Impression," *HR Magazine,* March 1993, p. 49.
15. Sherry Sweetham, "How to Organize Your Thoughts for Better Communication," *Personnel,* March 1986, p. 39.
16. Deborah Tannen, "The Power of Talk: Who Gets Heard and Why?" *Harvard Business Review,* September–October 1995, pp. 138–148.
17. Tannen, "The Power of Talk," pp. 138–148; "How You Speak Shows Where You Rank," *Fortune,* February 2, 1998, p. 156; "Frame Your Persuasive Appeal," *Executive Strategies,* September 1998, p. 7; "Weed Out Wimpy Words: Speak Up Without Backpedaling, Qualifying," *Working Smart,* March 2000, p. 2.
18. Robert B. Ciadini, "Harnessing the Science of Persuasion," *Harvard Business Review,* October 2001, pp. 72–79.
19. Ibid., p. 79.
20. Albert Mehrabian and M. Wiener, "Decoding Inconsistent Communications," *Journal of Personality and Social Psychology,* vol. 6, 1947, pp.109–114.
21. Several of the suggestions here are from *Body Language for Business Success* (New York: National Institute for Business Management, 1989), pp. 2–29; and "Attention All Monotonous Speakers," *Working Smart,* March 1998, p. 1.
22. Ann Davis, Joseph Pereira, and William M. Bulkeley, "Silent Signals: Security Concerns Bring New Focus on Body Language," *The Wall Street Journal,* August 15, 2002, p. 1.
23. The literature is reviewed in David A. Whetton and Kim S. Cameron, *Developing Management Skills,* 5th ed. (Upper Saddle River, N.J.: Prentice Hall, 2002), pp. 223–233.
24. Ibid., p. 230.
25. Paul Hersey, Kenneth H. Blanchard, and Dewey E. Johnson, *Management of Organizational Behavior: Utilizing Human Resources* (Upper Saddle River, N.J.: Prentice Hall, 1996), pp. 354–355.

26. Trudy Milburn, "Bridging Cultural Gaps," *Management Review,* January 1997, pp. 26–29.

27. Gunnar Beeth, "Multicultural Managers Wanted," *Management Review,* May 1997, p. 17.

28. "Cross Cultural Communication: An Essential Dimension of Effective Education," *Northwest Regional Educational Library: CNORSE—www.nwrel.org/cnorse.*

29. Siri Carpenter, "Why Do 'They All Look Alike'?" *Monitor on Psychology,* December 2000, p. 44.

30. Jim Kennedy and Anna Everest, "Put Diversity in Context," *Personnel Journal,* September 1991, pp. 50–52.

31. Lowell H. Lamberton and Leslie Minor, *Human Relations: Strategies for Success* (Chicago: Irwin/Mirror Press, 1995), p. 124.

32. Cited in "Best Tips," *Working Smart,* July 1996, p. 1.

33. Howard M. Guttman, "Conflict at the Top," *Management Review,* November 1999, p. 50.

34. Kenneth Thomas, "Conflict and Conflict Management," in Marvin D. Dunnette, ed., *Handbook of Industrial and Organizational Psychology* (Chicago: Rand McNally, 1976), pp. 900–922.

35. Cited in "Replace Criticism with Agreement," *Manager's Edge,* May 1999, p. 50.

36. Elizabeth A. Mannix, Leigh L. Thompson, and Max H. Bazerman, "Negotiation in Small Groups," *Journal of Applied Psychology,* June 1989, pp. 508–517.

37. For a comprehensive look at current thinking about negotiation and bargaining in the workplace, see G. Richard Shell, *Bargaining for Advantage: Negotiation Strategies for Reasonable People* (New York: Viking, 1999).

38. James K. Sebenius, "Six Habits of Merely Effective Negotiators," *Harvard Business Review,* April 2001, pp. 91–92.

39. Frank Acuff, *The World Class Negotiator: An Indispensable Guide for Anyone Doing Business with Those from a Foreign Culture* (New York: AMACOM, 1992).

40. Wendi L. Adair, Tetsushi Okumura, and Jeanne M. Brett, "Negotiation Behavior When Cultures Collide: The United States and Japan," *Journal of Applied Psychology,* June 2001, pp. 371–385.

41. "Roger Fisher: Master Negotiator and Best-Selling Author," *In Their Own Words,* National Institute of Business Management Special Report 250, 1997, p. 7.

42. Adapted from Gay Lumsden and Donald Lumsden, *Communicating in Groups and Teams: Sharing Leadership* (Belmont, Calif.: Wadsworth, 1993), p. 233.

Chapter 13

1. Fara Warner, "How Google Searches Itself," *Fast Company,* July 2002, pp. 50–52.

2. Donald C. Hambrick and James W. Fredrickson, "Are You Sure You Have a Strategy?" *Academy of Management Executive,* November 2001, p. 48.

3. Robert L. Phillips and James G. Hunt, eds., *Strategic Leadership: A Multiorganizational-Level Perspective* (Westport, Conn.: Quorum Books, 1992).

4. Bruce J. Avolio and David A. Waldman, "An Examination of Age and Cognitive Test Performance Across Job Complexity and Occupational Types," *Journal of Applied Psychology,* February 1990, pp. 43–50.

5. Quoted in John A. Byrne, "Three of the Busiest New Strategists," *BusinessWeek,* August 26, 1996, p. 50.

6. Ed Garsten, "100 Years Old, Caddy Turns Heads Again," *Detroit News,* August 22, 2002.

7. "A Strategy Session with C. K. Prahalad," *Management Review,* April 1995, pp. 50–51.

8. Gary Hamel, "Strategy as Revolution," *Harvard Business Review,* July–August 1996, pp. 69–82; Hamel, *Leading the Revolution* (New York: Penguin/Putnam, 2002).

9. Gary Hamel, "Revolution vs. Evolution: You Need Both," *Harvard Business Review,* May 2001, p. 150.

10. Keith H. Hammonds, "Michael Porter's Big Ideas," *Fast Company,* March 2001, p. 153.

11. Laurie Larwood, Cecilia M. Falbe, Mark P. Kriger, and Paul Miesing, "Structure and Meaning of Organizational Vision," *Academy of Management Journal,* June 1995, pp. 740–769 "Looking for Profits in Poverty," *Fortune,* February 5, 2001, p.169.

12. Hamel, "Strategy as Revolution," p. 72.

13. James R. Lucas, "Anatomy of a Vision Statement," *Management Review,* February 1998, p. 26.

14. Lesley Hazelton, "Jeff Bezos," *Success,* July 1998, p. 58.

15. David Kirkpatrick, "Great Leap Forward: Looking for Profits in Poverty," *Fortune,* February 5, 2001, p. 175.

16. Several ideas for this version of SWOT are from "SWOT Analysis," *Business Owner's Tool Kit,* November 8, 1999, *www.toolkit.cch.com/text/p02_4341.asp;* "SWOT Analsyis—Strengths, Weaknesses, Opportunities, Threats," *www.mondtools.com/swot.html.*

17. Oren Harari, "Obsolete.com?" *Management Review,* October 1999, p. 31.

18. A representative example of a complex strategic planning scheme is Joseph C. Picken and Gregory G. Dess, "Right Strategy—Wrong Problem," *Organizational Dynamics,* Summer 1998, pp. 35–49.

19. Michael Porter, *Competitive Strategy* (New York: The Free Press, 1980), pp. 36–46.
20. Joann Muller, "Kmart's Last Chance," *BusinessWeek*, March 11, 2002, p. 69.
21. Miriam Jordan, "Down Market: A Retailer in Brazil Has Become Rich Courting the Poor," *The Wall Street Journal*, June 11, 2002, p. 1.
22. Oren Harari, "Beyond Zero Defects," *Management Review*, October 1999, p. 34.
23. Michele Kremen, "Imitation Versus Innovation: Lessons to Be Learned from the Japanese," *Organizational Dynamics*, Winter 1993, pp. 30–45.
24. Jane Larson, "Motorola Joins New Chipmaking Tech Alliance," *Arizona Republic*, April 13, 2002, p. 1.
25. Dina ElBoghdady, "The Starbucks Strategy? Locations, Locations, Locations," *Washington Post*, August 25, 2002, pp. H1, H4.
26. Frank Gibney, Jr., "Pepsi Gets Back in the Game," *Time*, April 26, 1999, pp. 44–46.
27. Nelson D. Schwartz, "Still Perking After All These Years," *Fortune*, May 24, 1999, p. 208.
28. Paul C. Judge, "Internet Strategies That Work," *Fast Company*, March 2001, p. 170.
29. Philip Evans and Thomas S. Wurster, "Getting Real About Virtual Commerce," *Harvard Business Review*, November–December 1999, p. 87.
30. Bill Breen and Anna Muoio, "Peoplepalooza," *Fast Company*, January 2001, pp. 80–81.
31. Larry Bossidy and Ram Charan, *The Discipline of Getting Things Done* (New York: Crown Business, 2002).
32. Ram Charan and Geoffrey Colvin, "Why CEOs Fail," *Fortune*, June 21, 1999, p. 70. See also Bossidy and Charan, *The Discipline of Getting Things Done.*
33. David A. Garvin, "Building a Learning Organization," *Harvard Business Review*, July–August 1993, p. 80.
34. Michael Hickins, "Xerox Shares Its Knowledge," *Management Review*, September 1999, pp. 40–45.
35. Thomas H. Davenport and John Glaser, "Just-in-Time Delivery Comes to Knowledge Management," *Harvard Business Review*, July 2002, pp. 107–111.
36. David W. De Long and Liam Fahey, "Diagnosing Cultural Barriers to Knowledge Management," *Academy of Management Executive*, November 2000, pp. 115–117.
37. Robert M. Fulmer and J. Bernard Keys, "A Conversation with Peter Senge: New Developments in Organizational Learning," *Organizational Dynamics*, Autumn 1998, p. 35.
38. Neil Gross, "Mining a Company's Mother Lode of Talent," *BusinessWeek*, August 28, 2000, p. 137.
39. Robert M. Fulmer and Philip Gibbs, "The Second Generation Learning Organizations: New Tools for Sustainable Competitive Advantage," *Organizational Dynamics*, Autumn 1998, pp. 7–20; Peter M. Senge, *The Fifth Discipline* (NewYork: Doubleday, 1990); Daniel R. Tobin, *The Knowledge-Enabled Organization* (New York: AMACOM, 1998).
40. Gross, "Mining a Company's Mother Lode," p. 137.
41. Cited in "Making Vision Statements 'Visionary'," *Manager's Edge*, December 1998, p. 1.

Chapter 14

1. Adapted from Jeremy Kahn, "Diversity Trumps the Downturn," *Fortune*, July 9, 2001, pp. 114–115.
2. Louisa Wah, "Diversity at Allstate: A Competitive Weapon," *Management Review*, July–August 1999, p. 24.
3. Ibid., p. 24; Jeremy Kahn, "Diversity Trumps the Downturn," *Fortune*, July 9, 2001, pp. 114–116; Sharon Davis, "Minority Execs Want an Even Break," *Workforce*, April 2000, p. 50; Daren Fonda, "Selling in Tongues," *Time*, November 26, 2001, pp. B12–B15; Jim Kirk, "PepsiCo Wants Hispanics to Feel at Home," *Chicago Tribune* online edition, June 20, 2002; Elena Gaona, "PR Firms Are Making a Pitch for Latino Market," *Los Angeles Times* syndicated story, June 10, 2002.
4. Kirk, "PepsiCo Wants Hispanics to Feel at Home."
5. Davis, "Minority Execs Want an Even Break," p. 50.
6. Frances J. Milliken and Luis L. Martins, "Searching for Common Threads: Understanding the Multiple Effects of Diversity in Organizational Groups," *Academy of Management Review*, April 1996, p. 403.
7. Study reported in brochure for Diversity Summit 2002, IQPC, 150 Clove Road, P.O. Box 401, Little Falls, NJ 07424-0401.
8. Geert Hofstede, *Culture's Consequences: International Differences in Work-Related Values* (Beverly Hills, Calif.: Sage, 1980); updated and expanded in Geert Hofstede, "The Universal and the Specific in 21st-Century Global Management," *Organizational Dynamics*, Summer 1999, pp. 39–41.
9. Arvind V. Phatak, *International Dimensions of Management* (Boston: Kent, 1983), pp. 22–26.
10. Facts are from Christopher Broads, "Clocking Out: Short Work Hours Undercut Europe in Economic Drive," *The Wall Street Journal*, August 8, 2002, pp. A1, A6; Karl Ritter, "Swedes See Surge in Sick Leave," Associated Press, September 1, 2002.
11. Hofstede, "The Universal and the Specific," pp. 35–37.

12. Felix C. Brodbeck, Michael Frese, and Mansour Javidan, "Leadership Made in Germany: Low on Compassion, High on Performance," *Academy of Management Executive*, February 2002, pp. 16–30.

13. Roland Calori and Bruno Dufour, "Management European Style," *Academy of Management Executive*, August 1995, pp. 61–71.

14. Ibid., p. 70.

15. Our analysis of expectancy theory across cultures is based on Nancy J. Adler, *International Dimensions of Organizational Behavior*, 2nd ed. (Mason, Ohio: South-Western College Publishing, 1991), pp. 157–160.

16. Dianne H. B. Welsh, Fred Luthans, and Steven M. Somner, "Managing Russian Factory Workers: The Impact of U.S.-Based Behavioral and Participative Techniques," *Academy of Management Journal*, February 1993, pp. 58–79.

17. Adler, *International Dimensions of Organizational Behavior*, p. 159.

18. Gunnar Beeth, "Multicultural Managers Wanted," *Management Review*, May 1997, p. 17.

19. Carla Johnson, "Cultural Sensitivity Adds Up to Good Business Sense," *HR Magazine*, pp. 83–85.

20. Ibid., p. 84.

21. Louis Kraar, "Need a Friend in Asia? Try the Singapore Connection," *Fortune*, March 4, 1996, p. 180.

22. Joseph A. Petrick, Robert F. Scherer, James D. Bodzinski, John F. Quinn, and M. Fall Ainina, "Global Leadership Skills and Reputational Capital: Intangible Resources for Sustainable Competitive Advantage," *Academy of Management Executive*, February 1999, pp. 58–69.

23. Manfred F. R. Ket De Vries and Elizabeth Florent-Treacy, "Global Leadership from A to Z: Creating High Commitment Organizations," *Organizational Dynamics*, Spring 2002, pp. 295–309.

24. Gretchen M. Spreitzer, Morgan W. McCall, Jr., and Joan D. Mahoney, "Early Identification of International Executive Potential," *Journal of Applied Psychology*, February 1997, pp. 6–29.

25. Daren Fonda, "Selling in Tongues," *Time*, November 26, 2001, pp. B12–B15.

26. Patricia Digh, "The Next Challenge: Holding People Accountable," *HR Magazine*, October 1998, pp. 63–69.

27. Louisa Wah, "Diversity at Allstate," *Management Review*, July–August 1999, p. 28.

28. Dean Foust, "Coke: Say Good-Bye to the Gold Ol' Boy Culture," *BusinessWeek*, May 29, 2000, p. 58.

29. Marc Adams, "Building a Rainbow One Stripe at a Time," *HR Magazine*, August 1998, p. 73.

30. Ibid., pp. 73–74.

31. Jerry Langdon, "Minority Executives Benefit from Mentors," Gannett News Service, December 7, 1998. See also Letty C. Hardy, "Mentoring: A Long-Term Approach to Diversity," *HRfocus*, July 1998, p. S11.

32. R. Roosevelt Thomas, Jr., *Beyond Race and Gender: Unleashing the Power of Your Total Workforce by Managing Diversity* (New York: AMACOM, 1991), p. 25.

33. Gillian Flynn, "The Harsh Reality of Diversity Programs," *Workforce*, December 1998, p. 28.

34. Patricia L. Nemetz and Sandra L. Christensen, "The Challenge of Cultural Diversity: Harnessing a Diversity of Views to Understand Multiculturalism," *Academy of Management Review*, April 1996, p. 455.

35. Patricia Digh, "Well-Managed Employee Networks Add Business Value," *HR Magazine*, August 1997, pp. 67–72.

36. Lin Grensing-Pophal, "Reaching for Diversity," *HR Magazine*, May 2002, p. 54.

37. Quoted in Lin Grensing-Pophal, "Hiring to Fit Your Corporate Culture," *HR Magazine*, August 1999, p. 52.

38. Taylor Cox, Jr. "The Multicultural Organization," *Academy of Management Executive*, May 1991, p. 34.

39. Ann M. Morrison, *The New Leaders: Guidelines for Leadership Diversity in America* (San Francisco: Jossey-Bass, 1992).

40. Jacqueline A. Gilbert and John M. Ivancevich, "Valuing Diversity: A Tale of Two Organizations," *Academy of Management Executive*, February 2000, pp. 103–104.

Chapter 15

1. Adapted from Dale Buss, "When Managing Isn't Enough: Nine Ways to Develop the Leaders You Need," *Workforce*, December 2001, p. 46.

2. Jay A. Conger and Beth Benjamin, *Building Leaders: How Successful Companies Develop the Next Generation* (San Francisco: Jossey-Bass, 1999).

3. Catherine Fredman with Paul Rogers, "Nine Things CEOs Need to Know About Leadership," *Chief Executive*, June 2002, as cited in "To Become a Leader, Learn to Develop Leaders," *Executive Leadership*, September 2002, p. 7.

4. Chris Argyris, "Teaching Smart People How to Learn," *Harvard Business Review*, May–June 1991, pp. 99–109.

5. Bernard M. Bass, *Bass & Stogdill's Handbook of Leadership: Theory, Research, and Managerial Applications*, 3rd ed. (New York: The Free Press, 1990), p. 173.

6. Morgan W. McCall, Jr., *High Flyers: Developing the Next Generation of Leaders* (Boston: Harvard Business School Press, 1998); Cynthia D. McCauley, Russ S. Moxley, and Ellen Van Velsor, *Handbook of Leadership Development* (San Francisco: Jossey-Bass, 1998), pp. 132–133.

7. Marcus Buckingham and Curt Coffman, "How Great Managers Develop Top People," *Workforce*, June 1999, p. 103; Buckingham and Coffman, *First Break the Rules: What the World's Greatest Managers Do Differently* (New York: Simon & Schuster, 1999).

8. Richard L. Hughes, Robert C. Ginnett, and Gordon J. Curphy, *Leadership: Enhancing the Lessons of Experience* (Burr Ridge, Ill.: Irwin, 1993), pp. 33–36.

9. William G. Symonds, "Basic Training for CEOs," *BusinessWeek*, June 11, 2001, pp. 103–104.

10. Daphna F. Raskas and Donald C. Hambrick, "Multifunctional Managerial Development: A Framework for Evaluating the Options," *Organizational Dynamics*, Autumn 1992, p. 5.

11. Michael Beer, Russell Eisenstadt, and Bert Spector, *The Critical Path to Corporate Renewal* (Boston: Harvard Business School Press, 1995).

12. Carol Hymowitz, "Effective Leaders Say One Pivotal Experience Sealed Their Careers," *Wall Street Journal*, August 27, 2002, p. B1; Warren Bennis and Robert Thomas, *Geeks and Geezers* (Boston: Harvard Business School Press, 2002).

13. Belle Rose Ragins and John L. Cotton, "Mentor Functions and Outcomes: A Comparison of Men and Women in Formal and Informal Mentoring Relationships," *Journal of Applied Psychology*, August 1999, pp. 529–550.

14. Andrea C. Poe, "Establishing Positive Mentoring Relationships," *HR Magazine*, February 2002, p. 64.

15. Shimon-Craig Van Collie, "Moving Up Through Mentoring," *Workforce*, March 1998, p. 36.

16. Poe, "Establishing Positive Mentoring Relationships," p. 65.

17. Flyer for *Corporate University Week 2002*, presented by HRevents™, p. 4.

18. Marshall Whitmire and Philip R. Nienstedt, "Lead Leaders into the '90s," *Personnel Journal*, May 1991, pp. 80–85; Shari Caudron, "Building Better Bosses," *Workforce*, May 2000, pp. 32–39; Dale Buss, "When Managing Isn't Enough," *Workforce*, December 2001, pp. 44–48.

19. Victoria A. Guthrie and Lily Kelly-Radford, "Feedback Intensive Programs," in Cynthia D. McCauley, Russ S. Moxley, and Ellen Van Velsor, eds., *Handbook of Leadership Development* (San Francisco: Jossey-Bass, 1998), pp. 66–105.

20. Cheryl Dahle, "Natural Leader," *Fast Company*, December 2000, p. 270.

21. Jay A. Conger and Beth Benjamin, *Building Leaders: How Successful Companies Develop the Next Generation* (San Francisco: Jossey-Bass, 1999), p. 79.

22. Robert M. Fulmer, "The Evolving Paradigm of Leadership Development," *Organizational Dynamics*, Spring 1997, p. 70.

23. Dale S. Rose and Karen E. Fiore, "Practical Considerations and Alternative Research Methods for Evaluating HR Programs," *Journal of Business and Psychology*, Winter 1999, pp. 235–240.

24. Bruce Pfau and Ira Kay, "Playing the Training Game and Losing," *HR Magazine*, August 2002, p. 53.

25. Caroline Louise Cole, "Boeing U," *Workforce*, October 2000, p. 68.

26. Ellen Van Velsor, "Assessing the Impact of Development Experiences," in McCauley, Moxley, and Van Velsor, *Handbook of Leadership Development*, pp. 264–268.

27. Ibid., p. 267.

28. Jay W. Lorsch and Rakesh Khurana, "Changing Leaders: The Board's Role in CEO Succession," *Harvard Business Review*, May–June 1999, p. 100.

29. Linda Grant, "GE: The Envelope, Please," *Fortune*, June 26, 1995, pp. 89–90.

30. Cited in Mark Helm, "Giving Up the Helm: Tackling Transition When Founders Step Aside," Rochester, New York, *Democrat and Chronicle*, December 1996, pp. 1D, 6D; Jeff Wuorio, "The Succession Crisis," *Success*, December 1998, pp. 74–81.

31. William C. Byham, "Grooming Next-Millennium Leaders," *HR Magazine*, February 1999, pp. 46–50.

32. Ram Charan, Steve Drotter, and Jim Noel, *The Leadership Pipeline: How to Build the Leadership Powered Company* (San Francisco: Jossey-Bass, 2001).

33. Robert Goffee and Gareth Jones, "Followership: It's Personal Too," *Harvard Business Review*, December 2001, p. 148.

34. Robert E. Kelley, "In Praise of Followers," *Harvard Business Review*, November–December 1988, pp. 142–148.

35. Warren Bennis, "The End of Leadership: Exemplary Leadership Is Impossible Without Full Inclusion, Initiatives, and Cooperation of Followers," *Organizational Dynamics*, Summer 1999, pp. 76–78.

36. Carol Hymowitz, "In the Lead: Middle Managers Find Their Skills, Integrity Now Carry More Weight," *The Wall Street Journal*, July 30, 2002, p. B1.

37. Harriet Rubin, "Power," *Fast Company*, September 2002, p. 72.

Note: The number in brackets following each term refers to the chapter in which the term first appears.

Achievement motivation Finding joy in accomplishment for its own sake. [2]

Assertiveness Forthrightness in expressing demands, opinions, feelings, and attitudes. [2]

Attributions The judgments we make about the behavior and attitudes of others. [12]

Attribution theory The process of attributing causality to events. [1]

Autocratic leader A person in charge who retains most of the authority for himself or herself. [4]

Bandwagon technique A manipulative approach emphasizing that "everybody else is doing it." [8]

Behavior modification An attempt to change behavior by manipulating rewards and punishment. [10]

Behavior shaping Rewarding any response in the right direction and then rewarding only the closest approximation. [10]

Blemish A simple game in which the manager always finds a flaw in a group member's work. [8]

Casual time orientation The view that time is an unlimited and unending resource, leading toward extreme patience. [14]

Centrality The extent to which a unit's activities are linked into the system of organized activities. [7]

Charisma A special quality of leaders whose purposes, powers, and extraordinary determination differentiate them from others. [3]

Coalition A specific arrangement of parties working together to combine their power. [8]

Coercive power The power to punish for noncompliance; power based on fear. [7]

Cognitive factors Problem-solving and intellectual skills. [2]

Cognitive resource theory An explanation of leadership emphasizing that stress plays a key role in determining how a leader's intelligence is related to group performance. [5]

Collectivisim A belief that the group and society should receive top priority. [14]

Commitment The most successful outcome of a leader's influence tactic: The person makes a full effort. [8]

Compliance Partial success of an influence attempt by a leader: The person makes a modest effort. [8]

Concern for others In Hofstede's research, an emphasis on personal relationships, concern for others, and a high quality of life. (Also known as **femininity.**) [14]

Concert building A conception of the leader's role that involves both aligning and mobilizing. [4]

Congruence The matching of verbal and nonverbal communication to what the sender is thinking and feeling. [12]

Conjunctive communication Communication that is linked logically to previous messages, thus enhancing communication. [12]

Consensus leader The person in charge who encourages group discussion about an issue and then makes a decision that reflects general agreement and will be supported by group members. [4]

Consideration of others Creating an environment of emotional support, warmth, friendliness, and trust. [4]

Consultative leader A person in charge who confers with group members before making a decision. [4]

Contingency approach to leadership The contention that leaders are most effective when they make their behavior contingent upon situational forces, including group member characteristics. [5]

Cooperation theory A belief in cooperation and collaboration rather than competitiveness as a strategy for building teamwork. [9]

Crisis leadership   The process of leading group members through a sudden and largely unanticipated, intensely negative and emotionally draining circumstance. [5]

Creativity   The production of novel and useful ideas. [11]

Cultural sensitivity   An awareness of and a willingness to investigate the reasons why people of another culture act as they do. [14]

Debasement   The act of demeaning or insulting oneself to control the behavior of another person. [8]

Delegation   The assignment of formal authority and responsibility for accomplishing a specific task to another person. [7]

Democratic leader   A person in charge who confers final authority on the group. [4]

Disjunctive communication   Communication that is not linked to the preceding messages, resulting in impaired communication. [12]

Diversity training   A learning experience designed to bring about workplace harmony by teaching people how to get along better with diverse work associates. [14]

Domains of impact   Areas of possible change in leadership development programs. [15]

Double-loop learning   An in-depth style of learning that occurs when people use feedback to confront the validity of the goal or the values implicit in the situation. [15]

Drive   A propensity to put forth high energy into achieving goals, and persistence in applying that energy. [2]

Effective leader   One whose actions facilitate group members' attainment of productivity, quality, and satisfaction. [4]

Emotional intelligence   Qualities such as understanding one's feelings, empathy for others, and the regulation of emotions to enhance living. [2]

Emotional stability   The ability to control emotions to the point that one's emotional responses are appropriate to the occasion. [2]

Employee network group   A group of employees throughout the company who affiliate on the basis of a group characteristic such as race, ethnicity, sex, sexual orientation, or physical ability status. [14]

Empowerment   Passing decision-making authority and responsibility from managers to group members. [7]

Ethics   The study of moral obligations, or separating right from wrong. [6]

Executive coach (or **business coach**)   An outside or inside specialist who advises a person about personal improvement and behavioral change. [10]

Expectancy   An individual's assessment of the probability that effort will lead to correct performance of the task. [10]

Expectancy theory   A theory of motivation based on the premise that the amount of effort people expend depends on how much reward they can expect in return. [10]

Experience of flow   An experience so engrossing and enjoyable that the task becomes worth doing for its own sake regardless of the external consequences. [11]

Expert power   The ability to influence others because of one's specialized knowledge, skills, or abilities. [3]

Expertise approach   A belief that the leader's most important responsibility is providing an area of expertise that will be a source of competitive advantage. [2]

Farsightedness   The ability to understand the long-range implications of actions and policies. [2]

Feedback-intensive development program   A learning experience that helps leaders develop by seeing more clearly their patterns of behaviors, the reasons for such behaviors, and the impact of these behaviors and attitudes on their effectiveness. [15]

Flexibility   The ability to adjust to different situations. [2]

Forced-association technique   A method of releasing creativity in which individuals or groups solve a problem by making associations between the properties of two objects. [11]

Formality   The attachment of considerable importance to tradition, ceremony, social rules, and rank. [14]

Game   A repeated series of exchanges between people that seems plausible but has a hidden agenda or purpose. [8]

Goal   What a person is trying to accomplish. [10]

Groupthink   A deterioration of mental efficiency, reality testing, and moral judgment in the interest of group solidarity. [9]

Hands-on leader   A leader who gets directly involved in the details and process of operations. [8]

High tolerance for frustration   The ability to cope with a hindrance to goal attainment. [2]

Individualism   A mental set in which people see themselves first as individuals and believe their own interests and values take priority. [14]

Influence   The ability to affect the behavior of others in a particular direction. [8]

Informality   A casual attitude toward tradition, ceremony, social rules, and rank. [14]

Information power   Power stemming from formal control over the information people need to do their work. [7]

Initiating structure   Organizing and defining relationships in the group by activities such as assigning specific tasks, specifying procedures to be followed, scheduling work, and clarifying expectations of team members. [4]

Innovation   The process of creating new ideas and putting them into action. [11]

Insight   A depth of understanding that requires considerable intuition and common sense. [2]

Instrumentality   An individual's assessment of the probability that performance will lead to certain outcomes. [10]

Integrity   Loyalty to rational principles, thereby practicing what one preaches, regardless of emotional or social pressure. [6]

Internal locus of control   The belief that one is the primary cause of events happening to oneself. [2]

Knowledge management (KM)   The systematic sharing of information to achieve goals such as innovation, nonduplication of effort, and competitive advantage. [13]

Lateral thinking   A thinking process that spreads out to find many different solutions to a problem. [11]

Leader-member exchange model (LMX)   An explanation of leadership proposing that leaders develop unique working relationships with group members. [9]

Leadership   The ability to inspire confidence and support among the people who are needed to achieve organizational goals. [1]

Leadership diversity   The presence of a culturally heterogeneous cadre of leaders. [14]

Leadership effectiveness   Attaining desirable outcomes such as productivity, quality, and satisfaction in a given situation. [1]

Leadership Grid®   A framework for specifying the concern for the production and people dimensions of leadership simultaneously. [4]

Leadership pipeline   A model of leadership development that tightly links leadership development with management responsibilities at each level of the organization. [15]

Leadership polarity   The disparity in views of leaders: They are revered or vastly unpopular, but people rarely feel neutral. [3]

Leadership style   The relatively consistent pattern of behavior that characterizes a leader. [4]

Leadership succession   An orderly process of identifying and grooming people to replace executives. [15]

Leading by example   Influencing others by acting as a positive role model. [8]

Lead user   An organization or individual that is well ahead of market trends. [11]

Learning organization   An organization that is skilled at creating, acquiring, and transferring knowledge, and at modifying behavior to reflect new knowledge and insights. [13]

Legitimate power   The lawful right to make a decision and expect compliance. [7]

Linguistic style   A person's characteristic speaking pattern. [12]

Long-term orientation   A long-range perspective by workers, who thus are thrifty and do not demand quick returns on investments. [14]

Machiavellians   People in the workplace who ruthlessly manipulate others. [8]

Management by anecdote   The technique of inspiring and instructing group members by telling fascinating stories. [3]

Materialism   In Hofstede's research, an emphasis on assertiveness and the acquisition of money and material objects, and a deemphasis on caring for others. [14]

Mentor   A more experienced person who develops a protégé's abilities through tutoring, coaching, guidance, and emotional support. [15]

Micromanagement   The close monitoring of most aspects of group member activities by the manager or leader. [9]

Morals   An individual's determination of what is right or wrong influenced by his or her values. [6]

Multicultural leader   A leader with the skills and attitudes to relate effectively to and motivate people across race, gender, age, social attitudes, and lifestyles. [14]

Multicultural organization   A firm that values cultural diversity and is willing to encourage and even capitalize on such diversity. [14]

Multicultural worker   A worker who is convinced that all cultures are equally good and enjoys learning about other cultures. [14]

Multifunctional managerial development   An organization's intentional efforts to enhance the effectiveness of managers by giving them experience in multiple functions within the organization. [15]

Normative decision model   A view of leadership as a decision-making process in which the leader examines certain factors within the situation to determine which decision-making style will be the most effective. [5]

Open-book management   An approach to management in which every employee is trained, empowered, and motivated to understand and pursue the company's business goals. [9]

Organizational creativity   The creation of novel and useful ideas and products that pertain to the workplace. [11]

Organizational politics   Informal approaches to gaining power through means other than merit or luck. [7]

Outcome   Anything that might stem from performance, such as a reward. [10]

Participative leader   A person in charge who shares decision making with group members. [4]

Partnership   A relationship between leaders and group members in which power is approximately balanced. [1]

Path-goal theory   An explanation of leadership effectiveness that specifies what the leader must do to achieve high productivity and morale in a given situation. [5]

Personal magnetism   A captivating, inspiring personality with charm and charismatic-like qualities. [8]

Personal power   Power derived from the person rather than from the organization. [7]

Personalized charismatic   One who exercises few restraints on the use of power, in order to best serve his or her own interests. [3]

Persuade package   A small, standard set of influence tactics that leads the target to behave in a particular way. [12]

Pet-peeve technique   A method of brainstorming in which a group identifies all the possible complaints others might have about the group's organizational unit. [11]

Power   The potential or ability to influence decisions and control resources. [7]

Power distance   The extent to which employees accept the idea that the members of an organization have different levels of power. [14]

Prestige power   The power stemming from one's status and reputation. [7]

Pygmalion effect   The situation that occurs when a managerial leader believes that a group member will succeed, and communicates this belief without realizing it. [4]

Readiness   In situational leadership, the extent to which a group member has the ability and willingness to accomplish a specific task. [5]

Referent power   The ability to influence others that stems from the leader's desirable traits and characteristics. [3]

Relationship behavior   The extent to which the leader engages in two-way or multiway communication. [5]

Resistance   The state that occurs when an influence attempt by a leader is unsuccessful: The target is opposed to carrying out the request. [8]

Resource dependence perspective   The view that an organization requires a continuing flow of human resources, money, customers and clients, technological inputs, and materials to continue to function. [7]

Reward power   The authority to give employees rewards for compliance. [7]

Self-awareness   Insightfully processing feedback about oneself to improve personal effectiveness. [15]

Self-discipline   The ability to mobilize one's efforts to stay focused on attaining an important goal. [15]

Self-efficacy   The confidence in your ability to carry out a specific task. [10]

Servant leader   One who serves constituents by working on their behalf to help them achieve their goals, not the leader's own goals. [4]

Shadowing   An approach to mentoring in which the trainee follows the mentor around for a stated period of time. [15]

Short-term orientation   A focus by workers on immediate results, and a propensity not to save. [14]

Silent treatment   A means of influence characterized by saying nothing, sulking, or engaging in other forms of passivity. [8]

Single-loop learning   A situation in which learners seek minimum feedback that might substantially confront their basic ideas or actions. [15]

Situational leadership model   A model that explains how to match leadership style to the readiness of the group members. [5]

Socialized charismatic   A leader who restrains the use of power in order to benefit others. [3]

Social loafing   Shirking individual responsibility in a group setting. [9]

Social responsibility   The idea that organizations have an obligation to groups in society other than owners or stockholders and beyond that prescribed by law or union contract. [6]

Stewardship theory   An explanation of leadership that depicts group members (or followers) as being pro-organizational, collectivists, and trustworthy. [1]

Strategic contingency theory   An explanation of sources of power suggesting that units best able to cope with the firm's critical problems and uncertainties acquire relatively large amounts of power. [7]

Strategic leadership   The process of providing the direction and inspiration necessary to create, provide direction to, or sustain an organization. [13]

Strategic management   The process of ensuring a competitive fit between the organization and its environment. [13]

Strategic planning   Those activities that lead to the statement of goals and objectives and the choice of strategies to achieve them. [13]

Strategy   An integrated, overall concept of how the firm will achieve its objectives. [13]

Substitutes for leadership   Factors in the work environment that provide guidance and incentives to perform, making the leader's role almost superfluous. [1]

Supportive communication   A communication style that delivers the message accurately and that supports or enhances the relationship between the two parties. [12]

SWOT analysis   A method of considering strengths, weaknesses, opportunities, and threats in a given situation. [13]

Task behavior   The extent to which the leader spells out the duties and responsibilities of an individual or group. [5]

Team   A work group that must rely on collaboration if each member is to experience the optimum success and achievement. [9]

Teamwork   Work done with an understanding and commitment to group goals on the part of all team members. [9]

Territorial games   Also referred to as turf wars, political tactics that involve protecting and hoarding resources that give one power, such as information, relationships, and decision-making authority. [7]

360-degree feedback   A formal evaluation of superiors based on input from people who work for and with them, sometimes including customers and suppliers. [4]

Total quality management (TQM)   A management system for improving performance throughout the firm by maximizing customer satisfaction and making continuous improvements based on extensive employee involvement. [13]

Tough question   One that makes a person or group stop and think about why they are doing or not doing something. [4]

Traditional mental set   A conventional way of looking at things and placing them in familiar categories. [11]

Transformational leader   A leader who brings about positive, major changes in an organization. [3]

Trust   A person's confidence in another individual's intentions and motives and in the sincerity of that individual's word. [2]

Uncertainty avoidance   A dislike of—and evasion of—the unknown. [14]

Universal theory of leadership   The belief that certain personal characteristics and skills contribute to leadership effectiveness in many situations. [2]

Upward appeal   A means of influence in which the leader enlists a person with more formal authority to do the influencing. [8]

Urgent time organization   A view of time as a scarce resource, leading to impatience. [14]

Valence   The worth or attractiveness of an outcome. [10]

Vertical thinking   An analytical, logical process that results in few answers. [11]

Virtual office   A situation in which employees work together as if they were part of a single office despite being physically separated. [12]

Virtuous cycle   The idea that corporate social performance and corporate financial performance feed and reinforce each other. [6]

Vision   The ability to imagine different and better conditions and the ways to achieve them. [3]

Whistleblower   An employee who discloses organizational wrongdoing to parties who can take action. [6]

Will to lead   A determination to accomplish important goals for the good of others. [2]

Win-win approach to conflict resolution   The belief that after conflict has been resolved, both sides should gain something of value. [12]

Work ethic   A firm belief in the dignity of work. [2]